THE HISTORICAL DICTIONARY OF WORLD POLITICAL GEOGRAPHY

AN ENCYCLOPAEDIC GUIDE TO
THE HISTORY OF NATIONS

CARLOS RAMIREZ-FARIA

THE HISTORICAL DICTIONARY OF WORLD POLITICAL GEOGRAPHY

AN ENCYCLOPAEDIC GUIDE TO THE HISTORY OF NATIONS

CARLOS RAMIREZ-FARIA

palgrave

First published 2001 by
PALGRAVE
Houndmills, Basingstoke, Hampshire RG21 6XS and
175 Fifth Avenue, New York, N.Y. 10010
Companies and representatives throughout the world

PALGRAVE is the new global academic imprint of
St. Martin's Press LLC Scholarly and Reference Division and
Palgrave Publishers Ltd (formerly Macmillan Press Ltd).

Outside North America
ISBN 0–333–78177–5

In North America
1–56159–254–4

This book is printed on paper suitable for recycling and made from fully managed and sustained forest sources.

British Library Cataloguing in Publication Data:
Ramirez-Faria, Carlos, 1936–
    The historical dictionary of world political geography
    1. Political geography – Dictionaries
    2. World history – Dictionaries
    I. Title
    320.1'2

Typeset by Wearset, Boldon, Tyne and Wear

10   9   8   7   6   5   4   3   2   1
10   09   08   07   06   05   04   03   02   01

Printed and bound in Great Britain by Antony Rowe Ltd, Chippenham, Wiltshire

CONTENTS

INTRODUCTION

This work is a practical guide, in dictionary form, to the history of the world. Its purpose is to facilitate the reading and understanding of history and to show how the present is the result of a complex world-historical process. It assumes that history is not chaotic. This is not to insinuate ultimate purpose or 'meaning' – 'ultimate' in this context being no more at best than the world we know today – but it does presuppose that the process of history is explainable as opposed to arbitrary.

Before there were territorial states the world was mostly in flux. Populations were on the move and there were no political bounds on the land. There must have been tribal territoriality, localized and 'portable'. What the birth of civilizations marks is the culmination of a series of gradual achievements that were possible when in certain areas of the planet the flux ceased, sedentary societies were formed, and eventually states were created.

Although states originally arose from the cessation of the flux – and the further back in time we go the more flux we find – the flux in history is known from its co-existence with states and tended itself to engender states of variable duration, mostly realms with circumstantial names, doomed to instability and extinction, although this is not to deny or even belittle their impact on world history.

The extinct and the extant

The overall concept that informs this work is that everything in history is begotten by something and tends to beget something else. There is one obvious way in which the present can never be like the past again. The world-historical process created two basic categories: the extinct and the extant. The distance between them can be merely nominal, as when Congo became Zaire and Congo again or Burma Myanmar (capital Yangon instead of Rangoon). Most often they are separated by the chasm between having been in existence and no longer existing. Nevertheless, if we can relate the past and the present despite the radical changes from the past in today's political geography, then another of the purposes of this work is to bridge the seemingly unbridgeable between what once was and is no longer and what exists now. Without the links between the past and the present that this work documents, the reading of history can seem like a litany of exotic names without meaningful content. This work defines and illustrates the changing configuration over the ages of the political geography of the world by listing every significant sovereign entity in history (and many minor ones), even when only a change of names is involved, and by indicating the areas of today's political geography that were occupied by extinct empires and states. In a sense, it is an inventory of the 'tags' that have been stuck onto most of the globe since the beginning of civilization.

The flux and how to manage it

How do we deal with the flux in a work like this? The problem is that non-sedentary folk are frequently known only indirectly. Which nomads and semi-nomads to include and which to exclude? A simple distinction between nomads and semi-nomads – setting aside the complex and sometimes subtle distinction between pastoralists and cultivators – is that nomads roamed over wider expanses than semi-nomads, who seem like peoples in search of a territorial home. The rule of thumb here is that the flux is included whenever some parts of it detached themselves and entered world history through contact, usually unfriendly, with the area of delimited sovereignties. From such contacts, empires and states of sorts emerged, usually to disappear in time. They do not correspond to any extant national sovereignty. This makes naming them problematical. The same issue arises with the spread of ISLAM and the establishment of Islamic states.

The solution to these nomenclature problems is to go by the names of the groups or dynasties that sponsored or created such states. When the collective reference is to groups, e.g., KIRGHIZ, SHAYBANIDS *et al.*, and not specifically to a dynasty, the implication is that rulership was exercised by the ruling class of the group. This can also be true of entries such as the ALMORAVIDS and ALMOHADS which were dynasties more in the sense of collective or shared leadership than of successive kingship.

The Dictionary

The main part of this work is the dictionary. The entries refer to sovereign states and to peoples that engendered or were instrumental in the creation of sovereign states. Sovereignty is implicitly continuous control, at the very least relative, of a territory. Certain entries, such as PALESTINE or the SPANISH NETHERLANDS, are included not as sovereign states, but as political entities that were important in the formation of states. This applies also to the entries on COLONIAL EMPIRES. The basic guideline for all entries is the territorial formation of states. All entries contain references to origins and successor states. The time frame is the start of civilizations in the Near East to the present, even when, within those limits, the only evidence for an entry is archaeological. For the sake of clarity, there are deliberately duplicative entries, such as BYZANTINE EMPIRE and BYZANTINE ITALY, but for the sake of simplicity HABSBURG EMPIRE subsumes pre-World War I Austria and the Austro-Hungarian or Dual Monarchy, just as ROME embraces the entire history of the Roman Empire in the west. All unconventional designations, such as PERIOD OF DISUNITY (AFTER T'ANG/TANG) obey considerations of either clarity or simplicity, but they also have strictly historical grounds. Parenthetical references next to the entries are to durations and locations. Chinese provinces and cities have been transliterated in Pinyin. The dynasties and most names are in Wade-Giles with Pinyin in brackets.

Of centralized states, historiographical myths, and statelets

History is replete with real or presumed 'statelets'. If we were to chronicle each one of them, this work would not fit in one book. Still, no project this ambitious can be thought of as realized unless it confronts the issue of statelets and how to accommodate them in the world-historical process.

Statelets can be defined by contrast with modern centralized states. We are not referring to tiny modern states, such as MONACO or VATICAN CITY, nor to the countless principalities, duchies, etc. of IMPERIAL ITALY or the HOLY ROMAN EMPIRE. The statelets we have in mind have little history and few or no sequels. We know of them through the reports of external observers either of their own or of other cultures. European empire-builders were great reporters of statelets. The memoirs of Arab travellers such as Ibn Khaldun are also mines of information on statelets. However, nothing beats Chinese chronicles for the multiplicity and thoroughness of their references to the political neighbours of the Middle Kingdom regardless of their insignificance.

Though fragile and relatively ephemeral as a group, statelets originated in wider cultural frameworks. They were particularly abundant in areas such as western Turkestan (the steppes of central Asia were more the breeding ground of equally fragile and ephemeral empires), the Near East (the Sumerian statelets were one of the fonts of civilization), and especially the coastlines of Africa, Asia, and even ancient America. It is tempting to conclude that statelets are a non-European phenomenon. But where does that leave Ancient GREECE?

The historiographical solution to the statelets of western Europe after the fall of the Roman Empire is the creation of semi-fictive categories such as Merovingian France or Visigothic Spain or Ostrogothic Italy. Were any of these 'entities' ever more than agglomerations of autonomous fragments barely linked by ethnic, linguistic, or religious affinities? Are we merely perpetuating such 'fictions', as well as their homologues in Asia, in a work that deals mainly in relatively large political formations? However, if we take the European historical categories cited above to mean 'predominant political influence', then we can accept them at their face value; and, even though we do not even attempt to enumerate the multiple subdivisions within their orbits, at least we have firm grounds for claiming that statelets have not been neglected in this work.

Provinces and Regions

To facilitate the reading of some entries in the dictionary proper, this work includes a section on 'Provinces and Regions'. The entries in this part correspond principally to cross-references which are not in the Dictionary itself.

The simplest definition of a province is a territory that is part of a sovereign state. But what mainly characterizes a province is having a history of its own occupying a special chapter in the history of the state to which it belongs. Provinces also frequently have dialects or even languages of their own. They are political subdivisions of nations with certain national traits.

The distinction between provinces and regions is sometimes evanescent. The only reasonable and concrete touchstone is that regions lack political definition. This means that they are 'informal' and difficult to delimit. It can also mean that they overlap boundaries. Regions may be proto-provinces or even proto-states. In our time the term is frequently used to designate administrative entities which may correspond to former provinces, but which generally embrace various political subdivisions.

The General Index

There is a distinction to be made between 'entries' and 'mentions'. A 'General Index' contains, in addition to all the entries in the 'Dictionary' and in 'Provinces and Regions', all significant mentions not included as entries in either of those parts. It is meant as a handy guide to the entire work. References in the 'General Index' are to the entries in the 'Dictionary' and in 'Provinces and Regions'. And at the end there is a 'Basic Glossary of Names for States and Rulers', which should orient the reader among the many ways that humanity across ages and cultures has found to establish distinctions between types of governances and between rulers and the rest of the mortals.

Chronologies

To establish unifying threads through different entries that deal with the same country or region, schematic chronologies have been included in the appropriate pages. These chronologies establish the sequences of predominant political influences for selected particularly complex areas. For each century or centuries within each chronology the political influences are usually stacked up according to their durations. Most references in them are to entries in the 'Dictionary'.

Facts and probabilities

Propositions about history are either factual or probabilistic. In all historical works, and particularly in reference works of this sort, factual errors are inevitable but corrigible. Probabilistic statements are another matter. These involve, at the most elementary level, the spelling of names, and at more complex levels, choices between different probable alternatives about any area of the knowledge of the past. Here all we can say is that we have tried to come as close as possible to prevalent scholarship.

DICTIONARY

References to nations and provinces are in the 'Dictionary' or in 'Provinces and Regions'.

Important cross-references are capitalized in both the 'Dictionary' and 'Provinces and Regions'.

References in italics are mostly to entries in 'Provinces and Regions'.

All entries and mentions in the 'Dictionary' and in 'Provinces and Regions' are listed alphabetically in the 'General Index'.

PREDOMINANT WORLD POLITICAL INFLUENCES AND THEIR DURATIONS

3000–1750 BC

Sumer
Egypt
China
Minoan Civilization
Indus River Valley Civilization

1749–600 BC

Egypt
Babylonia
Assyria
China
Anatolia
Levant
Greeks
Mayan Civilization
Mesoamerican Civilizations

599–1 BC

China
Greece
Mayan Civilization
Mesoamerican Civilizations
Etruria
Persia
India
Rome

AD 1–AD 500

China
Mayan Civilization
Mesoamerican Civilizations
Persia
Northern India
Rome

Central Asian Hordes
Germanic Peoples
Constantinople

501–900

China
Mayan Civilization
Mesoamerican Civilizations
Persia
Central Asian Hordes
Germanic Peoples
Constantinople
Islam
Córdoba
Carolingian Empire
Norsemen

901–1300

China
Mayan Civilization
Mesoamerican Civilizations
Persia
Central Asian Hordes
Constantinople
Córdoba
Southern India
Afghanistan
Turks
Mongol Empire
Western Europe
Holy Roman Empire
Egypt
Maghreb
Inca Empire
Aztec Empire

1301–1500
China
Constantinople
Afghanistan
Mongol Empires
Western Europe
Holy Roman Empire
Egypt
Inca Empire
Aztec Empire
Northern India
Ottoman Empire
Samarkand
Habsburg Empire
Lithuania/Poland
Iberia

1501–1600
China
Persia/Afghanistan
Mughal India
Ottoman Empire
Habsburg Empire
Poland
Iberia
England
France
Russia

1601–1700
China
Mughal India
Ottoman Empire
Habsburg Empire
Spain
England
France
Russia
Netherlands
Sweden

1701–1800
China
Ottoman Empire
Habsburg Empire
Spain
Great Britain
France
Russia
Prussia

1801–1870
Ottoman Empire
Habsburg Empire
Great Britain
France
Russia
Prussia
United States
Italy

1871–1918
Habsburg Empire
Great Britain
France
Russia
Germany
United States
Italy
Japan

1919–1940
Great Britain
France
USSR
Germany
United States
Italy
Japan

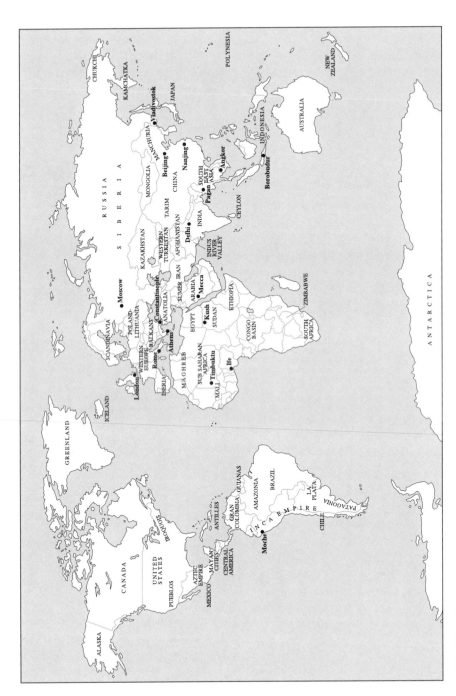

Map 1 The World

A

Abbasid Caliphate (8th–13th cents.; *Middle East*)
The Abbasids, an Arab clan descended from Abbas, an uncle of the Prophet
Muhammad, overthrew the Umayyad caliphate in 749–750 (ISLAM). The
Caliph Al Masur moved the capital of Islam from Damascus to Baghdad,
which he founded in 762. The dynasty had its base of power in Persia (IRAN).
Although the caliphate flourished under Harun al-Rashid (ca. 764–809) – one
of the central characters in *The Thousand and One Nights* – it had already
started disintegrating: in 756 MUSLIM SPAIN was brought under the rule of
Abd ar-Rahman, an Umayyad who had survived the massacre of his kinsmen
by the Abbasids; the Maghreb passed to the IDRISIDS in 788; the AGH-
LABID EMIRATE was founded in Afriqiya (modern Tunisia) in 800, with its
capital in Kairouan; the Tulunids established themselves in Egypt and the
TAHIRIDS in Khurasan during the course of the 9th cent. The famous Barme-
cides, one of whose members was called Jafar, were a family of administrators
under the Abbasids. From 836 to 892, the Abbasid capital was established in
Samarra, in central Iraq. In Syria, Abbasid rule gave way during the 10th cent.
to emirates, among which Mosul, Aleppo, and Homs were founded by the
Hamdanid dynasty. The Tahirids were nominally Abbasid vassals. By the late
10th cent., the Abbasid empire was reduced to Baghdad and western Persia.
Under BUYID PERSIA (11th cent.) the caliphate had mainly religious and
dynastic prestige. The last Abbasid caliph of Baghdad, Al Musta'sim, was
murdered by Hulagu, grandson of Genghis Khan in 1258 (ILKHANID
PERSIA). An Abbasid fled to Egypt where he was used by the Mamelukes to
legitimize the caliphate in Cairo. When the Ottoman sultan Selim I conquered
Egypt in 1517, he assumed the caliphate, which was held by his successors
until the deposition of the last Ottoman sultan, Muhammad VI, by Mustafa
Kemal in 1922. The caliphate itself was abolished in 1925.
(*See chronology under* Iran.)

Abu Dhabi (UNITED ARAB EMIRATES)

Abyssinia (ETHIOPIA)

Achaea (LATIN STATES)

Achaean League (4th–2nd cents. BC; Ancient *Greece*)
The Achaean League was constituted in 338 BC in the northern Peloponnesus
against MACEDON, but was defeated the following year by an alliance
between Macedon and Corinth. A second Achaean League was constituted in
280 BC and drove the Macedonians out of Corinth in 247 BC. To thwart

Sparta, the League deferred to Macedon and decayed. Achaea became a Roman ally in 198 BC (ROME), but the distrustful Romans dissolved the League in 146 BC and incorporated Greece into the Roman province of Macedonia (*Rome*).

(*See chronology under* Greece (Ancient).)

Achaemenid Empire (6th–4th cents. BC)

SEE ENTRY IN 'PROVINCES AND REGIONS'

The Achaemenid Empire is often referred to as the Persian Empire. Many trace the roots of Iran to its foundation. The Achaemenids were lords of the region of Persis, centred around the modern city of Shiraz. They were vassals of MEDIA, which they absorbed, led by Cyrus the Great ca. 550 BC creating the core of their future empire. Both Medes and Persians spoke languages, ancestral to modern Iranian, belonging to the Indo-Iranian group of the Indo-European family of languages, which includes Greek, Latin, Hindi, and the German and Slavic languages. The Achaemenids conquered successively Lydia and Ionia (546 BC) in Anatolia, Babylonia (539 BC), and Egypt (525 BC). At its acme ca. 500 BC, the Achaemenid Empire extended, in modern terms, from Turkey across north-western Iran and along the southern coast of the Caspian Sea to north-eastern Iran and Turkmenistan, southern Uzbekistan, western Tajikistan and western Kyrgyzstan, and eastward to Pakistan; then west along the southern coast of Iran, Persis, Susiana (west of Persis, at the head of the Persian Gulf), Arabia (western Iraq to the Sinai), Syria (including Lebanon and Palestine), Egypt, and Putaya (Libya). It had footholds in eastern Mediterranean islands and in Thrace. An inscription from 518 BC also claims GAND-HARA as an Achaemenid satrapy, which could mean that the eastern border of the empire was the Indus River, in Pakistan, but there is no archaeological evidence for this claim.

ANCIENT GREECE

Starting in 500 BC, under Darius I, the Empire, which had already annexed Ionia, tried to conquer European Greece. The Greeks under Miltiades defeated the Persians in Marathon (490 BC). Darius died in 486 BC, but his son Xerxes I carried on the struggle. Led by Themistocles, the Greeks defeated the Persians in the naval battle of Salamis (480 BC). The Persians were again defeated by the Greeks, led by the Spartan Pausanias, in the Battle of Plateae (479 BC). The war dragged on until 449 BC. As a result the Greek cities of Ionia became independent but, in 387 BC, reverted to Persian rule. In 334 BC, the Macedonian king Alexander had conquered most of Persian Anatolia (MACEDON). Under Darius III, the empire fell apart after the Battle of Gaugamela (331 BC) and it was over-run by Alexander's armies. The Achaemenid Empire was divided into satrapies, some of which were semi-autonomous centres of culture in Anatolia. Greek-influenced Caria in 377 BC

was ruled by Maussolos, whose tomb was one of the wonders of the ancient world (Bodrum). Lycia was another Persian satrapy which had greater cultural links with Greece than with the lands of its suzerains. The capitals of the Achaemenid Empire were Susa, the ancient Elamite capital; Ecbatana, the former capital of Media; Persepolis, founded by Darius; and Babylon.
(*See chronologies under* Ancient Near East, Greece (Ancient), Anatolia, *and* Iran.)

Acre (CRUSADER STATES)

Adal (16th cent. AD; eastern Africa)
Adal was a Muslim kingdom in what today is southern Eritrea. It invaded Ethiopia in the 16th cent. Its existence is reported by the Portuguese, who came to the assistance of their fellow Christians in Ethiopia. As a rule, the African coast of the Red Sea was home to small kingdoms, which belong to history to the extent their existence was reported by outsiders.

Aden (SOUTH YEMEN)

Aetolian League (4th–2nd cents. BC; Ancient *Greece*)
The Aetolian League, with its centre at Thermum in the mainland Greek region north of the Gulf of Corinth, was founded in 367 BC. Throughout most of its history, it warred with MACEDON, in alliance with the ACHAEN LEAGUE (239–229 BC), and with ROME. In 192 BC the Aetolian League attempted to do battle with Rome, which was in alliance with the Achaeans, but was defeated, becoming a Roman dependency in 189 BC.

Afghanistan
Afghanistan today comprises partially or wholly the ancient regions of Aria, Bactria, Sogdiana, Arachosia, and Drangiana (*Achaemenid Empire*). Despite its ruggedness, it has been one of the most fought over lands in the history of mankind, with the result that, until its relative unification in the 18th cent., its fortunes can be assigned to three distinct regions: the Iranized west around Herat, the east centred on Kabul and Ghazni, and the north (BACTRIA). Persian influence was predominant during much of its history, but it was also ruled by Greeks, Tokharians, Huns, Arabs, Turks, and Mongols. The KERTS, GHAZNAVIDS, and GHURIDS were native ruling dynasties. During the 17th and early 18th cents. Afghanistan was under Mughal and Persian influences, although Afghans invaded Persia (IRAN) from 1722 to 1736 provoking the downfall of the SAFAVIDS. A new Persian dynasty, the Afshar, then conquered Afghanistan.

Durrani

After the death of its last Persian ruler, Nadir Shah, in 1747, Afghanistan was ruled by the native Durrani dynasty. This was the origin of today's

Afghanistan. The Durrani line was extinguished in 1818 and was followed by a period of unrest until Dost Muhammad took power in 1826. Relations with BRITISH INDIA and the Sikh kingdom of PUNJAB were stormy. The first Afghan war, from 1838 to 1842, resulted in the deposition of Dost Muhammad, but things only got worse and he was restored to power in 1857. After his death in 1863, relations between Afghanistan and British India deteriorated over the frontier lands between them – peopled by Pathans, who speak Pashto, an official language of Afghanistan – until, in 1878, war flared again resulting in the annexation by the British of the Khyber Pass and the occupation of Kabul in 1880. Afghani territorial claims in the west and north varied with the fortunes of war. From the 18th cent. to the 19th cent. Afghanistan and Persia seesawed over Herat in eastern Khurasan, which definitely passed to Afghanistan in 1881 with British backing. The actual border with Iran was established in 1905. In the 1870s the Russians encroached on Afghani claims on the Upper Amu Darya River. Treaties with Russia in 1885 and 1895 finally defined the frontier. The frontier with British India was established in 1905 by a treaty in which Afghanistan ceded the actual North West Frontier province of Pakistan. In 1907, an understanding was reached between Great Britain and Russia which guaranteed the neutrality of Afghanistan but gave the British control of Afghani foreign policy. In 1919, the Afghans once again invaded British India and British influence was curtailed in Afghanistan itself. Afghanistan's claim on territories inhabited by Pashto-speaking Pathans in Pakistan was ignored in the 1947 partition of the Indian subcontinent. In 1978 the USSR, under Brezhnev, invaded Afghanistan, summoned by this country's leftist government. With American and Pakistani aid, Afghan Islamic resistance movements inflicted heavy losses on the Soviets who abandoned the fight in 1988–1989.

Today the capital of Afghanistan, Kabul was the centre of various central Asian states, often the starting point for invasions of the Indus River Valley and northern India.

Many languages are spoken in Afghanistan, but the main ones are Pashto and Dari (Iranian), which belong to the Indo-Iranian branch of the Indo-European family, which includes Latin, German, Russian, and English, among many.

Afghanistan
Predominant political influences

6th–5th cents. BC	3rd cent. BC	Yüeh-chih/
Achaemenid Empire	Seleucid Empire	Tokharians
	Bactria	Saka
	Parthia	
4th cent. BC		1st cent. BC
Achaemenid Empire	2nd cent. BC	Parthia
Alexandrian Empire	Bactria	Tokharians
Seleucid Empire	Parthia	Saka

1st–4th cents.	9th cent.	Chagataite Khanate
Parthia	Tahirids	Timurid Empire
Kushana	Saffarids	
	Samanids	15th cent.
5th cent.		Timurid Empire and
Kushana	10th cent.	Successor States
Sasanid Empire	Samanids	
Ephthalites	Ghaznavids	16th–17th cents.
	Buyid Persia	Mughal Empire
6th cent.		Shaybanids
Sasanid Empire	11th–12th cents.	Safavids (Persia)
Ephthalites	Ghaznavids	
	Ghurids	18th cent.
7th cent.		Persia
Sasanid Empire	13th cent.	Durrani
Islam	Ghurids	(Afghanistan)
	Khwarizm	
8th cent.	Kerts	19th cent.
Islam	Mongol Empire	Afghanistan
Abbasids		British India
Tahirids	14th cent.	Russia
	Kerts	

Aghlabid Emirate (9th–10th cents.; northern Africa)
After the turmoil following the fall of the Umayyads in Damascus in 750 (ISLAM) and a period of political influence from the Umayyad caliphate of CÓRDOBA, the Aghlabids took control of Tunisia in 800 and ruled it from the city of Kairouan. Their power extended to eastern Algeria and western Libya. It was this dynasty that sponsored the conquest of SICILY during the 9th cent. However, they did not exert direct control over the island. The Aghlabids, who were Sunni Muslims, were overthrown by the Shia FATIMIDS from Algeria in 909.
(*See chronology under* Maghreb.)

Ajman (UNITED ARAB EMIRATES)

Akkad (mid-3rd mil. BC; ancient *Near East*)
An important city in SUMER, probably hegemonic ca. 2500 BC, Akkad centralized power in Mesopotamia ca. 2340 BC under Sargon. It conquered EBLA in Syria ca. 2300 BC. Akkad was the first Near Eastern empire. Its sway extended to ELAM, Syria, and PALESTINE. It was destroyed by GUTIANS, mountain tribesmen from Iran, ca. 2250 BC. The fall of Akkad allowed first Lagash, then Ur to dominate Sumer.
(*See chronology under* Ancient Near East.)

Akwamu (17th–18th cents.; *Sub-Saharan Africa*)

Formed by Akan-speaking tribes, the kingdom of Akwamu occupied territory of today's Ghana. It was succeeded by ASHANTI. Akan and Ashanti are related languages, members of the Niger Congo family of languages spoken in western and south-western Africa.

(*See chronology under* Western and Sub-Saharan Africa.)

Alans (3rd–5th cents.; southern *Russia* and *Spain*)

The Alans, Indo-Iranian speakers (Indo-European family of languages), are related to the SARMATIANS, whom they appear to have absorbed in southern Russia by the time the GOTHS reached the Black Sea (3rd cent. AD). It has been argued that the Alans might have descended from a people identified by the Chinese as WU SUN, who occupied the Ili River basin from the 2nd cent. BC to the 2nd cent. AD. However that may be, the Alans joined the German migrations and were in Spain ca. 420, where they mixed with the SUEVES in Galicia and the Goths. Catalonia conceivably could derive from Goth-Alan. There is mention of Alans east of the Black Sea up to the 13th cent. The Ossetians, who speak an Indo-Iranian language, are possibly their descendants.

(*See chronology under* Southern Russia.)

Albania

One of the most contested territories in Europe, Albania was home to Greek colonies and independent Indo-European-speaking mountain peoples in the 3rd cent. BC. Upon the division of the Roman Empire (ROME) into western and eastern sections in AD 395, the territory of Albania became part of the eastern or BYZANTINE EMPIRE. Starting in the 7th cent. Albania was the object of territorial ambitions of Serbs, Bulgars, Franks, Venetians, and Normans, until the arrival of the Ottomans in the mid-14th cent. (OTTOMAN EMPIRE). The Albanians were converted to Islam early into Turkish rule. Skanderbeg, a local leader, liberated the country in the mid-15th cent. The Ottomans returned in 1478, although Albania retained a considerable degree of autonomy, and in the early 19th cent. had its own kings of Egyptian extraction. In 1878, Albania fell to SERBIA, but it gained independence in 1912 during the First Balkan War. In 1913, after the Second Balkan War, its borders were defined, ceding Albanian-inhabited territories to Serbia, MONTENEGRO, and GREECE. Albania was a multiple battleground during World War I but it retained its independence after the war. In 1939 it was occupied by Italy but by 1944 it had liberated itself, with the aid of the Yugoslav resistance movement, and became a hermit Stalinist state, ruled by Hoxha, which broke with the USSR during the anti-Stalinist Khruschev period. The Albanian regime was so paranoid that it also broke with China when this country was recognized by the United States in 1979. It shed communism in 1992, but fell into anarchy in 1997 when its economy was prey to fraudulent and uncontrolled pyramidal schemes. Albania had no sooner begun to recover than Serbia unleashed a systematic armed policy of ethnic cleansing in Kosovo, whose inhabitants, also Albanians, were forced into refugee status in Albania and Macedonia during 1999. Tirana is the capital of Albania.

Aleppo (SELJUK EMIRATES)

Alexandrian Empire (4th cent. BC; *Achaemenid Empire*, Ancient *Greece*, and *Pakistan*)
Alexander became King of MACEDON in 336 BC. After assuring the subjection of GREECE with the complicity of the Corinthian League, he began the conquest of the ACHAEMENID EMPIRE by invading Asia Minor in 334 BC. After the defeat of Darius III in the Battle of Gaugamela (331 BC), the empire of the Persian Achaemenids disintegrated and Alexander and his generals very quickly extended Greek sway over its former satrapies. In 327 BC, Alexander crossed into Pakistan where he defeated the local kingdoms of Taxila and Porus. Except for Greece and Macedon, which the Achaemenids never managed to conquer, and the Indus River Valley and the foothills of the Himalayas, the Achaemenid and the Alexandrian empires are almost identical in extension. After the death of Alexander in 323 BC, the DIADOCHI WARS ensued to parcel out the empire among his principal generals. The Alexandrian empire was a glorious flash in the pan. It had no appreciable influence on the course of history east of the Zagros mountains (border of Persia), except for the influence of Gandhara on later Indian art. Its greatest achievement was closer to home: the Hellenistic period of Greek culture, which was Greece's cultural legacy to Rome. Of Alexander's foundations, only the great city of Alexandria (332 BC) had a lasting impact on world history, although it too became a backwater after ISLAM. BACTRIA was an offshoot of the Alexandrian Empire. PARTHIA was founded with post-Alexandrian Greek territories.
(*See chronologies under* Greece (Ancient), Anatolia, *and* Iran.)

Algeria
The territory of Algeria corresponds to the ancient Berber-populated NUMIDIA. Berber is distantly related to the Semitic Hebrew and Arabic languages. Algeria was under the influence of CARTHAGE but became Roman after the 2nd cent. BC. Numidia had mostly espoused Christianity by the 4th cent. The influential Christian philosopher and saint, Augustine, was born in Numidia and was probably Berber. He died during the siege of his see, Hippo, by the VANDALS in 430. The Vandals destroyed social cohesion which was not restored until the 6th cent. with the Byzantine occupation, led by Belisarius in the reign of Justinian the Great (BYZANTINE EMPIRE).

THE FATIMIDS

ISLAM conquered the country in the 7th cent. After the fall of the Umayyads in Damascus (750), Algeria was briefly governed by the ABBASID CALIPHATE and then fell under the influence of the Umayyad emirate of CÓRDOBA. As a rule the western part of Algeria was under Moroccan influence and the eastern under Tunisian influence. However, during the 8th and 9th cents. Tlemcen was a flourishing native theocracy. Algeria came under the hegemony of the Moroccan IDRISIDS during the 9th cent. In the early 10th cent., eastern Algeria produced a native Shia dynasty, the FATIMID CALIPHATE, who disputed Algeria with the resurgent Umayyads from Muslim Spain and went on to conquer Egypt in 969. During the 11th cent. western Algeria was fragmented into independent ZIRID EMIRATES, successors of the Fatimids who had adopted Sunni Islam and were assailed by Bedouin hordes sent from Egypt. The Bedouins accelerated the process of Arabization of the country. Algeria later came under the influence of the Moroccan ALMORAVIDS. In Morocco, the Almoravids were supplanted by the ALMOHADS (mid-12th cent.), who ruled the Maghreb for a time during the 13th cent. The Tunisian HAFSIDS wrested Algeria from the Almohads towards the end of the cent. but during the 14th cent. they lost control of western Algeria to the Ziyanids, another local dynasty, which was, in turn, succeeded by the Moroccan MARINIDS in the 15th cent. Hafsid rule in eastern Algeria was weak. After the conquest of Granada in 1492, sensing easy prey, Spain occupied parts of the Algerian coast which were retaken for Islam by the OTTOMAN EMPIRE in the 16th cent.

BARBARY STATES AND INDEPENDENCE

From 1671, Algeria was autonomous but very divided. The coast harboured BARBARY STATES, havens for pirates who preyed on commerce for tribute payments. The United States warred on the Barbary States starting in 1800, but did not achieve much until 1815 when it forced Algiers to renounce its raids on American shipping. In 1816, an Anglo-Dutch expedition put an end to the Algerian naval threat. After prolonged campaigns from 1830 to 1847, France conquered Algeria and settled its cities and coast with European emigrants, many from Spain, who became known as *pieds noirs*. The Algerian war of independence began in 1954. It was characterized by terrorism and guerrilla warfare on the side of Algerians and by unscrupulous French military repression and bloody reprisals by European settlers against the Arab-speaking population. With the support of the armed forces, who wanted unequivocal backing for their war in Algeria, General De Gaulle came to power in 1958, in what amounted to a *coup d'état* against the Fourth Republic leading to the creation of the Fifth Republic. After, De Gaulle equivocated and in 1962, having put down an insurrection of the French garrisons in Algeria – led by the

military hero Salan and the bespectacled intellectual Soustelle, one of the all-time great authorities on Aztec civilization – accepted Algerian independence. This resulted in the resettlement in France of the million or so European-descended *pied noirs* who until then had considered Algeria their homeland. Their claim had been strongly and controversially publicized by the leftist intellectual Albert Camus, who was Algerian by birth and refused to endorse the nationalist terrorist campaign against French rule. Algiers is the capital of Algeria.
(*See chronology under* Maghreb.)

Al-Hirah (6th–7th cents.; *Near East*)
An Arab-speaking kingdom in central Iraq, Al-Hirah was a vassal of the Sasanid Empire. It helped the Sasanid Empire contain the Arabs for a time until, with the expansion of Islam, it was in turn conquered by the Arabs.

Almohads (12th–13th cents.; northern Africa and Muslim Spain)
The Almohads were a Moroccan dynasty who replaced the ALMORAVIDS in Morocco and MUSLIM SPAIN (ca. 1150). During the rest of the 12th cent. they over-ran Algeria and Tunisia. Almohad rule in Spain disintegrated after the Battle of Navas de Tolosa won by CASTILE (1212). In Morocco the Almohads were overthrown ca. 1250 by the MARINIDS. They were replaced by the HAFSIDS in Tunisia and Algeria.
(*See chronology under* Maghreb.)

Almoravids (11th–12th cents.; Morocco and Muslim Spain)
The Almoravids were Berber tribesmen from Mauritania and southern Morocco, who took Fez from the CÓRDOBA Umayyads in 1056 and went on to conquer the Taifa emirates in Spain (MUSLIM SPAIN). They also subjugated the Algerian emirates created by Bedouin hordes instigated against the ZIRIDS by the FATIMIDS in Egypt. Almoravid rule lasted until ca. 1150, when it was displaced by the ALMOHADS.
(*See chronology under* Maghreb.)

Amalfi (9th–11th cents.; southern *Italy*)
Originally a Roman foundation, Amalfi was an independent city–state and maritime power in Italy, south of Naples, in the 9th cent. It was taken by French Normans in 1131.

Amorites (2nd mil. BC; Ancient *Near East*)
The Amorites were a Canaanite people that had a powerful influence in Babylon until the rise of Hammurabi, whose legal code has Hebrew influence. EBLA probably fell to Amorites ca. 1800 BC. Amorites living around the Dead Sea were absorbed by ancient ISRAEL.

Amphictyony (GREAT AMPHICTYONY)

Anatolia
Predominant political influences

17th–13th cents. BC
Hittite Kingdom

12th–10th cents. BC
(Dark Ages)

9th cent. BC
Ancient Greece
Urartu
Phrygia

8th cent. BC
Ancient Greece
Urartu

7th cent. BC
Ancient Greece
Urartu
Lydia
Assyria
Babylonia

6th cent. BC
Ancient Greece
Lydia
Achaemenid
  Empire

5th cent. BC
Ancient Greece
Achaemenid Empire

4th cent. BC
Achaemenid Empire
Alexandrian Empire
Diadochi Wars

3rd–2nd cents. BC
Diadochi Wars
Seleucid Empire
Bithynia
Cappadocia
Pergamum
Pontus
Rome

1st cent. BC
Bithynia
Cappadocia
Pontus
Rome

1st–5th cents. AD
Rome

6th–10th cents.
Byzantine Empire

11th–12th cents.
Byzantine Empire
Rum Sultanate
Seljuk Emirates
Armenia Minor

13th cent.
Byzantine Empire
Byzantine successor
  states
Rum Sultanate
Seljuk Emirates
Armenia Minor
Trebizond

14th cent.
Byzantine Empire
Armenia Minor
Trebizond
Mongol Empire
Ilkhanid Persia
Anatolian Emirates
Ottoman Empire
Timurid Empire

15th cent.
Ottoman Empire
Trebizond
Anatolian Emirates
Aq-Qoyunlu

16th–19th cents.
Ottoman Empire

Anatolian Emirates (14th–15th cents.; *Anatolia*)
During the process of dissolution of the Seljuk sultanate of RUM to its final downfall (1302), Anatolia became fragmented into emirates. The emirates in eastern Anatolia became vassals of ILKHANID PERSIA in the 13th cent. One of the emirates was founded by the Ottomans, led by Osman, who had lands in Bithynia and Phrygia ceded to them by the Seljuks. During the last decade of the 14th cent., the Ottomans, under Bajazet, made a clean sweep of the other Anatolian emirates: Karaman, the strongest of all, in eastern Turkey, fell in 1390, followed by Aydin and Saruhan; Mentese and Kermian (1391); and

Kastamonu and Sivas (1392). Tamerlane's defeat of the Ottomans in 1402 was the signal for the rebirth of the Anatolian Emirates, but as soon as the TIMURID EMPIRE AND SUCCESSOR STATES started crumbling (after 1405), the OTTOMAN EMPIRE returned in force and had recovered most of Anatolia by the middle of the 15th cent.
(*See chronology under* Anatolia.)

Andorra

In 1278 Andorra was created in the heart of the Pyrenees as a joint dependency – known as *paréage* – of the Count of Foix and the Bishop of Urgel, in the kingdom of Aragon. The rights of Foix passed to Béarn and thence to Henry IV, King of France. Under republican regimes in France, they were transferred to the presidency. This status is merely nominal today. Andorra adopted a democratic constitution in 1993. Andorrans speak Catalan.

Angkor (CAMBODIA)

Angola

Before the arrival of the Portuguese, Angola was divided into Bantu-speaking tribal kingdoms, the most important of which was KONGO in the north. Angola was under Portuguese influence from the 15th cent. Portuguese rights to the territory were recognized in the BERLIN CONFERENCE (1884–1885). Angola was granted independence in 1975, together with the other Portuguese African colonies. It has been in an almost constant state of civil war since its inception, in which, besides the national factions, South Africa and Cuba have been involved. It is perhaps the longest, large-scale conflict in contemporary history. Portuguese is the official language in Angola. The capital is Luanda.

Annam (VIETNAM)

Antigua and Barbuda

Originally peopled by native Arawak indians and later by black slaves, the Caribbean island of Antigua was part of the BRITISH COLONIAL EMPIRE from 1632. In 1981 it became independent with the sister island of Barbuda and smaller Redonda Island. The capital is St John's.

Antioch (CRUSADER STATES)

Aq-Qoyunlu (15th–16th cents.; *Anatolia* and western *Iran*)

The Aq-Qoyunla or White Sheep Turks (from their banner) benefited from Tamerlane's restoration of the ANATOLIAN EMIRATES. From their base in Diyarbakir (Turkey), they attacked and conquered western Persia from the QARA-QOYUNLU in 1467. They were overthrown by the SAFAVIDS in 1502. Eastern Turkey was conquered by the OTTOMAN EMPIRE in the 16th cent.
(*See chronology under* Anatolia.)

Aquileia (11th–15th cents.; *Italy*)

An important see – although schismatic in the 6th cent. – Aquileia was granted sovereign privileges by the HOLY ROMAN EMPIRE in the 11th cent. It was absorbed by VENICE in 1420.

Aquitaine (7th–15th cents.; *France*)

The name Aquitaine derives from the Roman Aquitania, which was southwestern France (south of the Loire River), and Aquitaine in a very wide sense is just that. It can also refer to a more restricted area, but in all instances it has Bordeaux at its centre, which means that it roughly corresponds to Guienne. The cause of many territorial disputes from the 7th to the 10th cents., Aquitaine was semi-independent and powerful during the 11th and 12th cents. It passed to the English crown through the marriage of Eleanor of Aquitaine to Henry II (1137). In the 15th cent., it was annexed by France in the course of the Hundred Years War.

Arabs and Arabic

Arabs are mentioned in Assyrian inscriptions from the 9th cent. BC. They inhabited the Arab peninsula and were nomads, a condition which they retained in their homeland into the 20th cent. Arabia today comprises Bahrain, Kuwait, Oman, Qatar, Saudi Arabia, the United Arab Emirates, and Yemen. In time, nomadic Arabs came to be known as Bedouins, from the Arabic word for desert-dweller, which is exactly the root cause of nomadism in Arabia. However, there always were Arab city-dwellers, which in Arabic are called 'hadar'. Muhammad, the founder of ISLAM, was a citizen of Mecca. In the 7th cent., inspired by their religion, the Arabs conquered widely. Under the Umayyads their empire stretched from the Atlantic Ocean to Central Asia. Their language (the principal member of the Semitic group, including Hebrew) was adopted by the peoples of Morocco, Algeria, Tunisia, Libya, Egypt, Palestine, Lebanon, Syria, and Iraq. It usually displaced previous languages of the Afro-Asiatic family, which includes Semitic tongues. The Arabization of these lands often involved invasions and migrations of the Arabs themselves. However, Islam spread further afield – among the Turks, to the Indian subcontinent, and as far as Indonesia – and did not necessarily involve the diffusion of Arabic, except for the frequent adoption of Arabic script.

Aragon (11th–15th cents.; *Spain*)

The tide of Islam in Spain reached the foothills of the Pyrenees in the 8th cent. (MUSLIM SPAIN). It was contained by the CAROLINGIAN EMPIRE ca. 800. Christian Northern Spain was reunited by Sancho III the Great, King of NAVARRE, from 1029 to 1035. The kingdom of Aragon, on the southern watershed of the Pyrenees, was established by one of his heirs, Ramiro I, with the capital in Huesca. This was during the height of the *reconquista*, the Christian 're-conquest' of Spain from the Muslims. In 1076 Aragon annexed

NAVARRE, which it held until it was ceded to the French crown in 1305. In 1118, Zaragoza (Saragossa) was conquered and became the capital of Aragon. In 1137, Aragon was united with the county of BARCELONA. In 1032, Valencia, in the Spanish Levant, became an independent Taifa kingdom, which between 1094 and 1099 was taken by the epic hero Ruy Diaz de Bivar, El Cid. Valencia fell to the ALMORAVIDS and later to the ALMOHADS, but in 1238 it was taken by the Aragonese king, James I, who the same year occupied the Balearic Islands, under Islamic rule since the 8th cent. After the Sicilian Vespers that ended French rule in SICILY (1282), its inhabitants accepted Peter III of Aragon as their king. With the annexation of NAPLES in 1442, Aragon formed the kingdom of the TWO SICILIES. In 1479, the marriage of Isabella of Castile and Ferdinand of Aragon created the kingdom of Castile and Aragon, which became Spain after the conquest of GRANADA, the last Muslim kingdom in the Iberian Peninsula (1492). Aragon retained its *cortes* (parliament) and *fueros* (municipal rights) until 1716 when they were curtailed by the new Bourbon monarch Philip V in retribution for Aragonese backing for the Habsburg cause during the War of Spanish Succession (1701–1714).

Arelate (ARLES)

Argentina
SEE ENTRY IN 'PROVINCES AND REGIONS'
Argentina was peopled by Amerindians. The last tribes were wiped out in the second half of the 19th cent. The territory of Argentina was Spanish from the early 16th cent. In 1776, the viceroyalty of La Plata ('plata' meaning silver in Spanish) was created, capital Buenos Aires, with jurisdiction over the Banda Oriental (north of the River Plate, today's Uruguay), Paraguay, and Bolivia. The latter had been dependent on Peru and quickly returned to that status (SPANISH COLONIAL EMPIRE). During 1806 and 1807, Buenos Aires was occupied by British forces which were driven out by local militias.

JOSE DE SAN MARTIN

When ca. 1810 news reached America that Napoleon had deposed the Spanish Bourbons in 1808, in Buenos Aires, as in Caracas (Venezuela), juntas to defend Spanish legitimacy were created, which were not recognized by the Spanish government in Cadiz and became independence movements. In 1812, Belgrano defeated Spanish forces in the Battle of Tucumán and, in 1816, the United Provinces of the River Plate (Provincias Unidas del Rio de la Plata) declared their independence and later were renamed Argentina. There was still a Spanish colonialist threat over the Andes in Chile, which the Argentine general Jose de San Martin dispatched with the Chilean patriot Bernardo O'Higgins. In Paraguay Spanish colonial authorities had been deposed in

1811. In 1814 Uruguay declared itself independent of Buenos Aires. The threat of Brazilian annexation of Uruguay prompted Argentine intervention and the containment of the Brazilian forces in 1827. In the war of the Triple Alliance (1865–1870), in which Argentina, Brazil, and Uruguay fought against Paraguay, Argentina acquired a portion of land between the Uruguay and the Paraná rivers. After 1878, Argentine colonization increased towards the south (Patagonia) but the Chileans were already in control of the Strait of Magellan when the Argentinians got there. Tierra del Fuego was divided between the two, Argentina retaining the eastern half. There were disputes over the Andean border with Chile settled in 1904. Argentina developed very quickly during the first decades of the 20th cent. It was a supplier of the Allies during World War I. But, during World War II, it was conspicuously neutral and from 1946 to 1955 it was ruled by the nationalist and populist government of Perón. Despite losing economic ground, Argentina re-elected Perón in 1973. He died in 1974 and his wife Isabel Perón assumed the presidency. In 1982, the Argentine military under General Galtieri, then military dictator, invaded the Falklands and South Georgia but were ejected by a large British task force. Argentina still claims the Falklands which, in Spanish, are called Malvinas. Argentina also claims a wedge of Antarctica.

Arles (Kingdom of) (5th–14th cents.; *France*)
There was an early kingdom of Burgundy along the Rhône River down to Arles, founded ca. 480, taken by the Franks in 534. Although in 814 there was no doubt about who ruled continental western Europe, after Charlemagne's death (and even before) authority in Europe consisted of linkages of fealties and much of the land was still for the taking. In 879 a kingdom was established in Arles (Cisjurane Burgundy or Provence) and, in 888, another one in Transjurane Burgundy (south of the province of Burgundy). In 933 a lord joined them as Arelate or the kingdom of Arles, which embraced, besides Provence, the future provinces of Lyonnais, Dauphiné, Franche Comté, and Savoy including part of Switzerland. In 1043 it was annexed to the HOLY ROMAN EMPIRE, which mostly neglected it, and in 1378 the kingdom was absorbed entirely by France.

Armenia
It would be possible to trace the origins of Armenia to URARTU a kingdom whose name evokes Ararat, the Armenian name for the mountain in eastern Turkey where, in Biblical myth, Noah's Ark came to rest after the Flood. But Armenian is an Indo-European tongue (related to the languages of Western Europe) whereas the language of Urartu is an isolate with no known relatives. It is difficult to be precise about the ancient extent of Armenia. Armenians have at one time or another inhabited an area from eastern Turkey to Georgia and the western shore of the Caspian Sea. In the time of the ACHAEMENID

and ALEXANDRIAN EMPIRES the name Armenia designated a satrapy in north-eastern Turkey. In the early 2nd cent. BC, it 'seceded' from the SELEUCID EMPIRE, but in AD 114 became a vassal of ROME. At the end of the 3rd cent. Armenia became the first nation as a whole to convert to Christianity. Absorbed by the SASANID EMPIRE it was during Persian rule that Yerevan became its capital. Disputed by Romans and Persians, in the 7th cent. it was part of the BYZANTINE EMPIRE, but from 886 to 1046 it was an autonomous kingdom, which the Byzantines annexed again and then lost to the Seljuks after 1071. Armenia was one of the SELJUK EMIRATES during the 12th cent. until ca. 1210 when it was autonomous once more. It became a vassal of the MONGOL EMPIRE in 1243. Conquered by Tamerlane in the late 14th cent., Armenia afterwards remained in the hands of Turkish rulers (TIMURID EMPIRE AND SUCCESSOR STATES). In 1548, it was annexed by the OTTOMAN EMPIRE, which disputed its territory with the Persians.

GREATER ARMENIA

In 1828, Russia took eastern Armenia from Persia. Within Ottoman eastern Anatolia, Armenians were subjected to strong repressive measures. During World War I, the Armenians in the lake Van region resisted Turkish pressure (1915). In occupied southern Russia (1918), Armenia became an independent republic under German auspices. Greater Armenia, comprising the eastern Russian part and the western Anatolian part, was stipulated in the Treaty of Sèvres (1920) (VERSAILLES), but the Turkish nationalist reaction led by Mustafa Kemal from Ankara resulted in the expulsion of the Armenians from eastern Turkey. At the same time, the Soviet government occupied eastern Armenia, which in 1922 was joined to Azerbaijan and Georgia as the Transcaucasian Soviet Federated Socialist Republic. In 1936, this entity was dissolved and the Armenian Soviet Socialist Republic was created. Armenia has been independent since 1990. After independence, Armenia got into a war with Azerbaijan over the Armenian-inhabited Azerbaijani enclave of Nagorno-Karabakh. The Armenians have retained control, but the territory is still formally in Azerbaijan.

Armenia Minor (11th–14th cents.; *Anatolia*)
Under the auspices of the Crusades (CRUSADER STATES), Armenians established Armenia Minor (Lesser Armenia), a small kingdom in the ancient region of Cilicia, which lasted from 1080 to 1375, when it was destroyed by the Egyptian MAMELUKE SULTANATE.
(*See chronology under* Anatolia.)

Ashanti (18th–19th cents.; *Sub-Saharan Africa*)
Founded by Akan-speakers, Ashanti was an African kingdom at least partly in

the territory of today's Ghana that flourished after AKWAMU. Akan belongs to the Niger–Congo group of languages spoken in western and south-western Africa.
(*See chronology under* Western and Sub-Saharan Africa.)

Asoka's Empire (MAGADHA)

Assyria (2nd mil.–7th cent. BC; ancient *Near East*)
The Semitic city of Assur, capital of Assyria, began its rise to power in northern Mesopotamia ca. 1800 BC. It became a vassal of BABYLONIA (ca. 1700) and later of the MITANNI KINGDOM (after ca. 1450). Assyria came into its own in the 14th cent. It probably controlled Babylon in the late 12th cent. It had a period of eclipse during the 11th and 10th cents. Assyria was restored ca. 880. It flourished – and became famous for its cruel war tactics and reprisals – until its destruction in 612 by an alliance of MEDIA and Babylonia led by the Babylonian king Nabopolassar. Among the most powerful Assyrian monarchs were Ashurnasirpal (865–860), who ruled from the city of Kalhu, better known as Nimrud, and Assurbanipal (645–635), who sponsored the glory of the city of Nineveh. Semiramis was a historical regent in Assyria around the late 9th cent. In the myth she was the Assyrian founder of Babylon. The Assyrian empire reached its greatest extent in the 7th cent. occupying the Near East from the frontiers with Media across southern Anatolia to PHARAONIC EGYPT, which it held briefly.
(*See chronologies under* Ancient Near East, Anatolia, *and* Iran.)

Astrakhan (Khanate of) (15th–16th cents.; *Central Asia*: Kirghiz Steppe)
The khanate of Astrakhan, at the mouth of the Volga River, was created out of the GOLDEN HORDE in 1466. It occupied western Kazakhstan. In 1556, it was conquered by Russia during the eastern drive launched by Ivan the Terrible from Moscow.

Asturias (8th–10th cents.; *Spain*)
When heirs to the VISIGOTHIC KINGDOM in Spain asked for help from Africa, the Islamic Berber Tarik ibn Zayid, later the lord of the region of Gibraltar (Jebel al Tarik, the mountain of Tarik), responded and, in 711, crossed the straits and defeated the usurper Rodrigo in the Battle of Guadalete. Instead of handing power to the claimants, he brought in reinforcements and conquered Iberia. The Islamic onslaught was contained ca. 720 in the Battle of Covadonga, in the Cantabrian mountains, by the legendary king Pelayo, who founded the kingdom of Asturias with its capital in Oviedo. By the mid-8th cent. the Asturian king Alfonso I initiated the *reconquista*, the centuries-long Christian recovery of Iberia, extending his kingdom to northern Castile and Aragon. In the 9th cent., after establishing its centre in the city of Leon, Asturias became the kingdom of Asturias and Leon, later LEON. Sancho III

the Great of NAVARRE reunited northern Spain (1029–1035) and bequeathed CASTILE to his son Ferdinand I, who absorbed Leon in 1037 as the kingdom of Castile and Leon, which lasted until 1157, when the two realms were divided. Castile and Leon were definitely reunited in 1230 under Ferdinand III of Castile.

Asturias and Leon (ASTURIAS)

Athenian Empire (DELIAN LEAGUE)

Athens (DELIAN LEAGUE; DIADOCHI WARS; Ancient GREECE)

Athens (Duchy of) (LATIN STATES)

Au Lac (VIETNAM)

Australia
In 1770, Captain James Cook sailed the coast of eastern Australia, which was inhabited by aborigines – aboriginal languages are all related but different from the languages of the Austronesian family of languages prevalent in Polynesia and Indonesia – and claimed it for Great Britain. Australia was gradually colonized and incorporated as different provinces during the 19th cent. The Commonwealth of Australia – whose head of state is the King or Queen of the United Kingdom of Great Britain – consists of two federal territories, six states, and the Australian external territories. The states are: New South Wales, Queensland, South Australia, Tasmania, Victoria, and Western Australia.

THE STATES

The British claim on what today is known as New South Wales (NSW) included all of Australia and Tasmania save Western Australia. In 1788 a penal colony was established in Port Jackson, which later grew into Sydney, the chief administrative centre of the Commonwealth of Australia until the capital was established in Canberra. NSW obtained self-rule in 1856.

Tasmania was first visited by the Dutch navigator Tasman, in the employ of the Dutch East India Company, in 1642. It was named Van Diemen's Land. It became the separate colony of Tasmania in 1825, capital Hobart, founded in 1804. It was self-governing in 1856.

Victoria was settled after 1834 and became a separate colony in 1851. Its capital, Melbourne, was first settled in 1835. Victoria had self-rule in 1855.

Queensland became a separate, self-governing colony in 1859. Its capital was a penal settlement in 1824, named Brisbane in 1834.

The coast of Western Australia was explored by George Vancouver in 1791. After 1826 it was a penal colony. It was run separately from NSW and was self-ruling by 1893. Perth was founded in 1829.

All the Australian colonies were incorporated into the self-ruling Commonwealth of Australia in 1901. The Australian Capital Territory was created from lands in NSW in 1909. Canberra was inaugurated as the capital in 1927. Formerly part of NSW, the Northern Territory, capital Darwin, devolved to the commonwealth or federal government in 1911. Under the statute of Westminster, Australia was one of the British dominions that formed the Commonwealth of Nations in 1931, at which time they became fully sovereign states.

In 1905, Great Britain transferred British Papua (south-eastern New Guinea) to Australia. After World War I, Australia was given a mandate over former German colonial territory in north-eastern New Guinea, which in 1949 it incorporated into one dependency with British Papua. Papua New Guinea achieved independence in 1975.

In 1933, Australia laid claim to a piece of Antarctica, the Australian Antarctic Territory, south of 60 degrees south latitude, excluding Adelie (FRANCE), and between 160 degrees and 45 degrees east longitude. It is part of the Australian External Territories which also include the following island dependencies: Cocos or Keeling Islands, Christmas Island, and Ashmore and Cartier Islands, in the Indian Ocean; Norfolk Island and the Coral Sea Islands, in the Pacific Ocean; and Heard and McDonald Islands, in the Southern Ocean.

Austria
SEE ENTRY IN 'PROVINCES AND REGIONS'

The HABSBURG EMPIRE is the antecessor of Austria and it was often referred to as Austria until the organization of the Dual Monarchy, also known as Austria–Hungary. Austria proper was created with the borders it has today upon the dissolution of Austria–Hungary after World War I under the terms of the Treaty of Saint-Germain (1919) (VERSAILLES). In 1938 it was annexed by Germany. In 1945, it was partitioned by the Allies into four zones of occupation, but in 1955 it was reunited as a sovereign state on condition of its neutrality between the Western powers and the USSR. Austria joined the EUROPEAN UNION in 1995. Vienna, the capital of Austria, was a celtic settlement named Vindobona by the Romans. It was the centre of a German march. Around 1150 it became the capital of the duchy of Austria. In 1282, Vienna was adopted as the official residence of the Habsburg.

Austria–Hungary or Austro-Hungarian Monarchy (HABSBURG EMPIRE)

Austrian Netherlands (SPANISH NETHERLANDS)

Avars (6th–9th cents.; *Central Asia*: Western Turkestan; *Southern Russia*; eastern Europe)

Of Mongol stock, the Avars were a nomadic people possibly related to the

HUNS. In the early 6th cent. they were ousted from the Ili River basin by the T'U-CHÜEH, which is the name the Chinese gave the Turks in their first historical appearance. In Russia, they assimilated the remnants of Attila's Huns, driven back from the Hungarian plain by the GEPIDS and the Ostrogoths (GOTHS). Allied to the Lombards (LOMBARD ITALY), the Avars dispersed the Gepids and occupied the former Roman province of Pannonia, rampaging as far south as the central Balkans. At the height of its power, Avaria extended from the Volga to Hungary and the Balkans. In the 7th cent. the Avars were repulsed by the BYZANTINE EMPIRE, and in the 8th cent. they were crushed by Charlemagne (CAROLINGIAN EMPIRE). During the 9th cent. the Pannonian Avars were subsumed under Slavic GREAT MORAVIA.
(*See chronologies under* Greater Mongolia *and* Southern Russia.)

Axum (ETHIOPIA)

Ayutthaya (THAILAND)

Ayyubid Sultanate (12th–13th cents.; *Near East*)
During the decline of the FATIMIDS, Shia rulers of Egypt, Damascus became a separate state under Nur ad-Din (1118–1174). Shirkuh, a Kurdish lieutenant of the Damascene ruler, invaded Egypt to forestall the CRUSADER STATES and overthrew the Fatimids. His nephew, Saladin, proclaimed himself sultan and founded the Ayyubid dynasty after Shirkuh's death in 1169. Saladin defeated the Crusaders decisively in the Battle of Hattin (1187). He inherited Syria upon the death of Nur ad-Din and conquered as far as Yemen. The Ayyubids adopted the practice, initiated by the ABBASID CALIPHATE in the 9th cent., of training non-Muslim central Asian slaves as soldiers, who converted to Islam during their military upbringing and formed the caste of the Egyptian Mamelukes. The Mamelukes grew increasingly powerful and, in 1250, their leader became sultan with the extinction of the Ayyubid line (MAMELUKE SULTANATE).

Azerbaijan
Modern Azerbaijan was, in the past, a Persian province. The Romans called it Albania. It was part of ARMENIA in the early 3rd cent. before being annexed in the same century by the SASANID EMPIRE. Its territory began to acquire its historical contours – independent Azerbaijan and north-western Iran – with the expansion of ISLAM (7th–8th cents.). It became a particular bone of contention between two Mongol successor states: ILKHANID PERSIA and the GOLDEN HORDE (13th–14th cents.). After that it was disputed by Tamerlane (TIMURID EMPIRE AND SUCCESSOR STATES) and the Golden Horde. The OTTOMAN EMPIRE (15th cent.) acquired the habit of occasionally occupying the country starting in the 16th cent., but in the 18th cent. Azerbaijan was under Persian influence. In 1813 Russia carved out the northern

part of Azerbaijan from Persia, which the USSR in 1922 integrated into the Transcaucasian Soviet Federated Socialist Republic, from which, in 1936 was detached the Azerbaijan Soviet Socialist Republic. Iran still has a province of Azerbaijan, which includes Tabriz, the traditional Azerbaijani capital. Although Azeris speak a Turkic language, Azerbaijan was culturally Persian during much of its history. Azerbaijan itself became independent in 1991. Shortly after independence, Azerbaijan got into a war with Armenia over the territory of Nagorno-Karabakh, peopled by Armenians. The Armenians have retained control of the area, but officially it is still Azerbaijan. The capital of Azerbaijan is Baku. Nakhichevan is an Azerbaijani enclave separated from Azerbaijan proper by Armenia. It borders on Iran.

Aztec Empire (13th–16th cents.; *Mexico*)
The Aztecs, a lowly tribe from the north, founded a city–state called Tenochtitlán on reclaimed lands of Lake Texcoco (Mexico City) around 1200. They were hegemonic allies of the cities of Texcoco and Tlacopan. Upon this model, they created an informal empire with all the surrounding territories down to Guatemala. Ancient MESOAMERICAN CIVILIZATIONS are known from their Aztec designations. The conquest of the Aztecs was begun by Cortez in 1519 and completed in 1521 with the help of tribal enemies of the Aztecs and the spread of epidemics. Tenochtitlán itself was dismantled stone by stone. Nahuatl, an Aztec language, is still spoken in parts of Mexico.

B

Babylonia (2nd mil.–6th cent. BC; ancient *Near East*)
Babylon was founded by Semites ca. 2000 BC in Mesopotamia, just north of
the territory dominated by the city–states of SUMER. Babylon became
politically significant ca. 1900, when it was under the influence of the
AMORITES. The empire of Babylonia was established by Hammurabi
(1792–1750), who conquered Assur, the future capital of ASSYRIA, and
united Mesopotamia. After him the kingdom divided and Babylon, as well as
the rest of Sumer, had to fight off the HURRIANS and the KASSITES. It was
the latter who finally occupied Babylon ca. 1500. In the durable melée after
the dissolution of Babylonia, the MITANNI KINGDOM, probably non-
Semitic, was formed ca. 1450 BC in northern Mesopotamia. This kingdom fell to an alliance of the Indo-European HITTITE KINGDOM and the
Assyrians ca. 1350 BC. The Hittite kingdom collapsed ca. 1200 BC. The Kassites were overthrown in Babylon ca. 1180 BC. There followed a period of
anarchy until Babylon was restored and prospered ca. 1140 BC. After that
Babylon decayed and probably became a vassal of Assyria. The Semitic
Chaldeans expelled Assyria from Babylon and restored Babylonia under
Nabopolassar (625 BC). MEDIA and Babylonia destroyed Assyria (614–
608 BC). Nebuchadnezzar, son of Nabopolassar, defeated the Egyptians in
the Battle of Carchemish (605 BC). During his reign, JUDAH rebelled and
was put down. Many leading Jews were taken captive to Babylonia, an early
example of ethnic cleansing and the commencement of the Jewish Diaspora.
Nebuchadnezzar was the builder of the famous Hanging Gardens of Babylon.
The New Babylonian Empire lasted to 538 BC and covered a crescent from
Shatt el Arab, the mouth of the Tigris and Euphrates rivers, to the Sinai. It
became a satrapy of the ACHAEMENID EMPIRE and then part of the
ALEXANDRIAN EMPIRE.
(*See chronologies under* Ancient Near East *and* Iran.)

Bactria (3rd–2nd cents. BC; Afghanistan and *Pakistan*)
A satrapy of the ACHAEMENID EMPIRE, Bactria is the ancient name of
north-eastern Afghanistan. It was sheared off by Diodatos, a Greek viceroy,
from the post-Alexandrian SELEUCID EMPIRE in 256 BC. As an independent kingdom, it annexed Gandhara (north-western Pakistan). In 167 BC,
Bactria successfully resisted an attempt by the Seleucids, based in Syria, to
recover the territory. However, Bactria was very disunited, reportedly having
at one time as many as 40 different Greek kings. The most famous of all
Bactrian kings was Menander who, ca. 160 BC, was active in northern India.
In Buddhist tradition, Menander (Milinda in Pali) forms a trilogy of great

Asian rulers with Asoka and Kanishka, king of Kushana. Harsha is sometimes included in that exclusive group. The SAKAS assailed Bactria. The Greeks were reduced to Gandhara. An Indo-European-speaking people called YÜEH-CHIH by the Chinese invaded Bactria ca. 130 BC. These have been identified as the TOKHARIANS. They drove the Sakas into Gandhara, where the latter put an end to the Indo-Greek kingdom. In the 1st cent. AD the Tokharians established KUSHANA. Greek influence on the art of Bactrian Gandhara was transmitted to India. This influence persisted during Kushana. Balkh, a city in northern Afghanistan, was at some time capital of Bactria.

(*See chronologies under* Afghanistan *and* Indian Subcontinent.)

Baghdad (Caliphate of) (ABBASID CALIPHATE)

Bahamas

A Bahamian island was Columbus' American landfall in 1492. The Bahamas were part of the BRITISH COLONIAL EMPIRE from 1629 until their independence in 1973. The country consists of around 700 islands and more than 1,000 cays. The capital of the Bahamas is Nassau on New Providence island.

Bahmani Sultanate (14th–15th cents.; central *India*)

During the decadence of the DELHI SULTANATE, Zafar Khan, a Turk or Afghan leader, founded the Muslim Bahmani Sultanate in Karnataka ca. 1345, almost simultaneously with the formation of Vijayanagar (SOUTHERN INDIA). In 1425 the Sultanate conquered Warangal in Andhra Pradesh and was also at war with Vijayanagar. Eventually it disintegrated through internal quarrels into the Deccan Sultanates of Bijapur (1489), Ahmadnagar and Berar (1491), Bidar (1492), and Golconda (1512) (CENTRAL INDIA). Of all, Bijapur was the most expansive. Allied, the Deccan Sultanates defeated Vijayanagar in 1565. After that they were gradually absorbed by the MUGHAL EMPIRE. The last two, Golconda and Bijapur, fell to Aurangzeb in 1686–1687.

(*See chronology under* Indian Subcontinent.)

Bahrain

The Persian or Arabian Gulf island of Bahrain was the site of an ancient kingdom known as DILMUN. Later, it was an independent emirate which controlled the peninsular territory of QATAR. Later it became a dependency of the OTTOMAN EMPIRE in 1555. During the 17th and 18th cents., it was successively under Portuguese and Persian influence. It maintained its autonomy from the late-18th cent. to 1861, when it was turned into a British protectorate until 1971. The capital of Bahrain is Manama.

Balkans
Predominant political influences and their durations

2nd cent. BC–4th cent. AD	9th–13th cents.	16th cent.
Rome	Byzantine Empire	Ottoman Empire
	Serbia	
	Bulgaria	**17th–18th cents.**
5th cent.		Ottoman Empire
Rome/Constantinople		Habsburg Empire
Goths	**14th cent.**	
	Byzantine Empire	**19th cent.**
	Serbia	Ottoman Empire
6th–7th cents.	Bulgaria	Habsburg Empire
Byzantine Empire	Ottoman Empire	Russia
Goths		Greece
Avars		Serbia
	15th cent.	Romania
8th cent.	Byzantine Empire	Montenegro
Byzantine Empire	Ottoman Empire	Bulgaria

Bambara (17th–18th cents.; western Sahara)
Occupying lands which had formerly been part of ancient MALI and SONGHAI, the Bambara state was taken over by the FULANI. Its capital, Timbuktu, was founded in the 11th cent. by Tuaregs. A member of the west African Niger–Congo group of languages, Fula is today a lingua franca in western Africa.
(*See chronology under* Western and Sub-Saharan Africa.)

Bangladesh
The modern Muslim state of Bangladesh was part of the British Indian province of BENGAL. In 1905, the latter was divided into two halves along religious lines. After the partition of BRITISH INDIA in 1947, eastern Bengal became East Pakistan. In 1971 a bloody civil war resulted in the separation of Bangladesh from Pakistan with the help of India. The capital of Bangladesh is Dakha.

Barbados
Possibly at one time inhabited by Amerindians, Barbados was uninhabited when the British arrived. It was part of the BRITISH COLONIAL EMPIRE from 1627 to 1966. Although it is often mentioned as being in the Caribbean Sea, the island of Barbados is in the Atlantic Ocean. The capital of Barbados is Georgetown.

Barbary States (16th–19th cents.; northern Africa)
After the annexation of Algeria, Tunisia, and Libya by the OTTOMAN EMPIRE during the 16th cent., the Porte named beys in the coastal cities. The

Map 2   Balkans and Eastern Europe

beys acted autonomously and soon began to prey on Mediterranean commerce. The naval Battle of Lepanto (1571) was a blow to Turkish sea power but the pirates of northern Africa were a nuisance and not a threat, explicable in any case by the undeclared state of hostilities that existed between Muslims and Christians in the Mediterranean from the 16th to the early-19th cents. Collectively the privateering cities along the northern coast of Africa were known as the Barbary States and subsisted by exacting ransom and tribute from western shippers. Because of American reluctance to pay tribute, there was a state of war between the Barbary States and the United States which lasted from 1800 to 1815. After failed attempts to take Libyan Tripoli, the Americans finally forced Algiers to agree to cease preying on its ships. In 1816, an Anglo-Dutch force destroyed what pirate ships Algiers still had. Privateering in the Mediterranean was gradually shut down thereafter. Algeria was conquered by France after 1830. Tunisia became a French protectorate in 1883. Libya, mostly in the hands of local emirs, was invaded by Italy in 1914.
(*See chronology under* Maghreb.)

Barcelona (CATALONIA)

Basques
The Basques speak what in linguistics is called an isolate, a language with no known 'relatives'. They have inhabited the same Pyreneean and Cantabric homelands since before Roman times. Around 600 AD they formed the duchy of VASCONIA, which extended far beyond the limits of today's Vasconia or the Vascongadas in Spain. The kingdom of NAVARRE was formed by Basques in their homeland.

Bavaria (6th–19th cents.; *Austria*; *Germany*)
The Roman province of Rhaetia included southern Bavaria. The German duchy of Bavaria was created in 562. It was integrated into the CAROLINGIAN EMPIRE in 788. During the 10th cent. it became part of the HOLY ROMAN EMPIRE. The Duchy's territory extended to Austria and the Rhineland. Through the centuries, Bavaria's core territory, with its capital in Munich, remained unchanged, although it shed its various extensions, last of which to go was the Tyrol in 1778. In 1070, Bavaria was ceded by Emperor Henry IV to Welf IV, of the Ferraran house of Este, who began the Guelph line and the tradition of contesting imperial successions, particularly against the Hohenstaufen. This contentiousness was transplanted into Italy as the political struggles between Guelphs (anti-imperial) and Ghibelline (pro-imperial) factions. The name Ghibelline stems from the castle of Waiblingen, a Hohenstaufen property. The Emperor Frederick Barbarossa, whose partitions left their imprint on the Holy Roman Empire, deposed the ruling Guelph in Bavaria, Henry the Lion, and in 1180 gave the Duchy to Otto of Wittelsbach, in whose family the land remained until 1871, although the Wittelsbach retained their nominal kingship

until 1918. The ruler of Bavaria became an imperial elector. During the 17th cent. wars of religion, Bavaria led the Catholic party. In 1806, allied to Napoleon, Bavaria became a kingdom, part of the Confederation of the Rhine (FRENCH EUROPEAN EMPIRE), but in 1813 it switched sides and retained its autonomy after the fall of Napoleon and the Congress of VIENNA (1815) as part of the GERMAN CONFEDERATION. The most famous 19th-cent. Bavarian king was Louis II, who built an extravagant castle in the Bavarian Alps. Bavaria sided with Austria (HABSBURG EMPIRE) against PRUSSIA in 1866. Prussia defeated Austria and formed the NORTH GERMAN CONFEDERA-TION, which Bavaria joined after Prussia defeated France in 1871 and just before the proclamation that year of the German Reich (GERMANY). Bavaria is today the largest of the states (*Länder*) of Federal Germany.

Bedouins

Bedouins is the general name for nomadic Arabs. During the 11th cent., the Shia FATIMIDS in Egypt sent Bedouin hordes to subdue the ZIRIDS, former subjects who had founded independent Sunni emirates in Tunisia and Algeria.

Belarus

Part of the homeland of the SLAVS, Belarus was annexed by Poland–Lithuania (POLAND) in the 14th cent. In 1795 it went to Russia after the final partition of Poland. In 1919 the Soviets created the Byelorussian Soviet Socialist Republic with the Byelorussian territory they controlled. Soviet Russia fought a war with Poland in 1921 and lost western Belarus. In 1939 the Soviets occupied the Baltic states and eastern Poland and all of Belarus reverted to the USSR. It was declared a sovereign nation in 1991. The capital of Belarus is Minsk. Belarus consists of the provinces of Brest, Homel, Hrodno, Minsk, Mahiyou, and Vitebsk. Western Belarus was part of the Pale of Jewish settlement.

Belgian Colonial Empire (19th–20th cents.)

The Belgian colonial empire mainly comprised the area of today's Democratic Republic of CONGO. It was originally the personal property of Leopold II, King of Belgium, who, from 1878 to 1884, subsidized treaty-making expeditions by the newspaperman and adventurer Henry M. Stanley along the Congo River Basin. In 1885, at the conference of BERLIN, which had begun in 1884 to carry out the formal partition of Africa among European colonial powers, Leopold's claims were recognized as the Congo Free State and he became its king. Despite ruthless exploitation, the colony was not self-sufficient and, in return for loans in 1889 and 1895, Leopold ceded the territory to Belgium (1901), who took over in 1908. Germany had been given rights over the lands of RWANDA and BURUNDI, but never exercised them. In 1916, in the middle of World War I, the Belgians took over these territories, which in 1919 became the Belgian League of Nations mandate, and later UN trust territory, of Ruanda-Urundi. In 1960, the Belgian Congo became the Republic of

Congo-Kinshasa (the hyphenation was used to distinguish it from the ex-French Republic of Congo-Brazzaville) and in 1962 Rwanda and Burundi also became independent states.

Belgium
SEE ENTRY IN 'PROVINCES AND REGIONS'

The territory of Belgium embraces the ancient province of FLANDERS, the French-speaking lands sometimes identified as Walloonia, southern Brabant, and northern LUXEMBOURG. The history of Belgium before independence is that of the SPANISH NETHERLANDS, later Austrian Netherlands. In 1794 Republican France occupied the Austrian Netherlands, which Napoleon annexed to France. After 1815, they were turned over to the kingdom of the NETHERLANDS. Dissatisfied with Dutch rule, Brussels rebelled in 1830 and the Netherlands, under French and British pressure, evacuated Dutch-speaking and Catholic Flanders and the rest of the former Austrian Netherlands, retaining the northern part of Brabant. Luxembourg was also divided between a northern part, to Belgium, and the rest, the actual territory of the state of Luxembourg, to the Netherlands. During World War I, the Germans invaded Belgium to reach Paris quickly. The Belgians resisted and held a part of the northern front during the war. After the atrocious German bombing of Rotterdam in 1940, Belgium surrendered and was occupied during all of World War II. Belgium is a bilingual country with Flemish (same as Dutch) spoken in the north and French in the south. Brussels, the capital, is bilingual officially, but mostly French-speaking. In 1948, Belgium formed the economic union with Luxembourg and Netherlands known as Benelux, which became part of the European Economic Community in 1957 (EUROPEAN UNION).

Belize
Once part of MAYA CIVILIZATION, later neglected by Spain, Belize was under informal British control from 1638 as British Honduras (BRITISH COLONIAL EMPIRE). It became a colony in 1862 until its independence in 1982, when it took the name of its capital city. Guatemalan claims on the territory were rejected by Great Britain.

Benevento (7th–11th cents.; southern *Italy*)
The Lombard duchy of Benevento, including much of southern Italy, was created ca. 600 (LOMBARD ITALY). Though much reduced by the 9th cent., it was nevertheless the dominant state in the region, except for Naples. It became part of NORMAN ITALY in the 11th cent. Subsequently it was transferred to the PAPAL STATES.

Bengal (8th–18th cents.; northern *India*)
Bengal was part of the kingdom of the GUPTAS in the 4th cent. It rose to prominence as a kingdom with the Pala dynasty (8th–11th cents.), which also

ruled Bihar. Chronic disunity and constant warring weakened the kingdoms and dynasties in NORTHERN INDIA, and the Pala were no exception. They were substituted by the Sena dynasty. The GHURIDS conquered as far as Bengal, where the Sena were destroyed ca. 1200. However, Bengal retained a great degree of autonomy and, in 1338, separated from the DELHI SULTANATE. The MUGHAL EMPIRE conquered Bengal in 1576. But even under the Mughals, Bengal tended to go its own way. The British first arrived in 1642. They founded Calcutta in 1691. In 1756, when the Mughal empire was but a shadow of itself, the Nawab of Bengal Siraj ud-Daula captured Calcutta, where he cast the British into the prison known as the 'black hole', in which many perished, but Clive defeated him decisively in the Battle of Plassey in 1759. Bengal served as the springboard for the formation of BRITISH INDIA.

Benin (Ancient) (12th–19th cents.; *Sub-Saharan Africa*)
Benin was a kingdom created by Yoruba-speaking tribesmen in south-western NIGERIA and the coast of BENIN, contiguous to OYO. Its original capital, Ife, from which the Oyo also claimed descent, is famous for its sublimely beautiful heads of terracotta and bronze.
(*See chronology under* Western and Sub-Saharan Africa.)

Benin
From the 17th to the 19th. cent., DAHOMEY, a Yoruba raiding state engaged in the slave trade, controlled the territory of today's Benin. In 1863 France established a protectorate on the coast and after 1890 it subjugated the local rulers in the interior. Dahomey became part of French West Africa in 1899 until its independence in 1960. It changed its name to Benin in 1975. Yoruba is a member of the Niger–Congo group of languages, spoken in western and south-western Africa. The capital of Benin is Porto-Novo, founded by the Portuguese in the 16th cent.

Berbers
The Berbers are the base population of northern Africa between Egypt and the Atlantic Ocean. The nomadic Saharan Berbers are known as Tuaregs. The Berbers of northern Africa were Christianized early on. The greatest Berber figure was St Augustine, Bishop of Hippo, in Algeria. With the Islamization of North Africa, Arabic tended to replace the Berber language, which, like Arabic, belongs to the Afro-Asiatic family of languages. The conquest of Iberia in the 8th cent. was accomplished by Muslim Berbers. The Arabization of Northern Africa was accelerated by the invasion of Bedouin tribes encouraged by the FATIMIDS in Egypt during the 10th and 11th cents.

Berlin (Conference of)
In 1884, Germany sponsored a conference in Berlin, involving the European powers, the United States, and the Ottoman Empire, to deal with the colonialist

rivalries in Africa. Its purpose was to recognize claims and safeguard trade. Its main results were the validation of Leopold II's claim on the Congo River Basin to the exclusion of the French and the Portuguese, the recognition of British ascendancy in Nigeria, and informally the right of Germany to acquire colonies. Most of the other colonialist claims in Africa were tacitly or explicitly recognized. The conference, which lasted to 1885, did not in fact do much to avert confrontations such as that between France and Great Britain over Sudan and between France and Germany over Morocco. However, the Conference of Berlin is considered the paradigm of the European scramble for Africa, the last great land grab in world history.

Berlin (Congress of)
By the Treaty of San Stefano (1878), imposed on the Ottoman Empire by the Russians – victorious in the Russo-Turkish war of 1877–1878 – Russia acquired lands in the Caucasus; Serbia, Romania, and Montenegro were recognized by the Porte as independent states; Romania acquired Dobruja; and Bulgaria was created, comprising Macedonia. Greece was ceded Epirus. Great Britain and Austria–Hungary (HABSBURG EMPIRE) resented the increase of Russian influence in the Balkans and, through mounting pressure, achieved the convocation of the Congress of Berlin in 1878, hosted by Bismarck, in which the terms of San Stefano were modified. In the arrangement that emerged, the recognition of the independence of the Balkan states was kept, as well as the aggrandizement of Greece, but Bulgaria was divided into two autonomous provinces (Bulgaria proper, which retained Dobruja, and eastern Rumelia) over which the Ottomans maintained formal rights. Macedonia was left under Ottoman sovereignty. Russia retained its Caucasian acquisitions and was compensated with southern Bessarabia. Austria–Hungary was given the administration of Bosnia and Herzegovina, much to the annoyance of the Serbs, and Great Britain was allowed to occupy Cyprus. The Russians were aggrieved and this eventually resulted in their alliance with France against Germany and Austria–Hungary, which set the stage for World War I. Serbian nationalist resentments can also be traced, in part, to the Congress of Berlin, which, however, has its fervent admirers, among them the American diplomat and historian George Kennan. Since it is to Bismarck that the order in the Balkans and eastern Europe was mostly attributed, admirers and rejectionists of Berlin can be recognized by their opinions on Bismarck himself.

Bhutan
Bhutan was a small, mainly Buddhist Himalayan kingdom with ties to NORTHERN INDIA in the 16th cent. and subsequently to TIBET. In 1910 it became a British protectorate until 1949, after which it became an Indian dependency. In 1971 it was admitted to the UN. The Bhutanese capital is Thimphu.

Bihar (MUGHAL EMPIRE)

Bijapur (MARATHA KINGDOMS)

Bithynia (3rd–1st cents. BC; *Anatolia*)
Minor kingdom in Anatolia, Bithynia (197–74 BC) was bequeathed to Rome by its last ruler who followed the example of the Attalids in PERGAMUM. The King of PONTUS, Mithridates IV, invaded Bithynia and was defeated by Rome, who proceeded to annex Bithynia and Pontus (65 BC).
(*See chronology under* Anatolia.)

Black Sheep Turks (QARA-QOYUNLU)

Bohemia (9th–20th cents.; eastern Europe)
The first Bohemian state was created by Slavs in the 9th cent. It was absorbed into GREAT MORAVIA but became independent again towards the end of the century. Including Moravia and Silesia, which it had taken from POLAND, Bohemia was incorporated into the HOLY ROMAN EMPIRE in 950. In 1198, it had the status of a kingdom within the Empire. In 1526, it became part of the HABSBURG EMPIRE. In 1742, Silesia was ceded to PRUSSIA. When the Habsburg Empire was organized as the Dual Monarchy of Austria–Hungary, Bohemia was part of the Austrian side. After World War I, Bohemia and Moravia formed the Republic of CZECHOSLOVAKIA with Slovakia.

Bolivia
Bolivia was, like a handful of other countries (Colombia, the Marshall Islands, the Philippines), named after a historical personage, Simon Bolivar. His loyal and competent lieutenant Antonio Jose de Sucre actually did the job of mopping up what remained of Spanish authority in the former judicial province of Charcas (created in 1559), as Bolivia was known under Spanish rule. Originally attached to the viceroyalty of Peru, capital Lima, in 1776 it was made part of the viceroyalty of La Plata, created the same year with Buenos Aires as its capital, but shortly afterwards reverted to Lima (SPANISH COLONIAL EMPIRE). Although the first rebellion against Spain began in Chuquisaca (today Sucre) in 1809, it was not until 1825, after the Battle of Ayacucho (1824), in which Sucre defeated the last Spanish army in PERU, that Bolivia declared its independence and adopted a constitution written by Bolivar himself.

ACRE AND CHACO

Given these jurisdictional antecedents, it is not surprising that Bolivia has had perhaps the most complex and unstable territorial history of any Latin American nation. On its foundation, it claimed lands extending from the port of Antofagasta, today part of Chile, to large expanses of Amazonian jungle and most of what today is the Chaco region of Paraguay, west of the Paraguay River. In 1879, allied to Peru, Bolivia was defeated in a war with Chile, who took Antofagasta from Bolivia and Iquique from Peru. After conflict with Brazil, it ceded for an indemnity in 1903 what today is the western Brazilian state of Acre, although Bolivia retains Amazonian jungle lowlands. Between 1932 and 1935, it engaged in another losing war, this time with Paraguay, to whom it ceded all of its claims to Chaco. Bolivia is a landlocked nation and it is, with the Himalayan states and provinces, one of the highest countries in the world. The capital of Bolivia is La Paz (1548), but the city of Sucre, founded in 1538 as La Plata, and also known as Charcas and Chuquisaca, is considered the constitutional capital and is the seat of the Bolivian supreme court as well as of the national university.

Bophuthatswana (20th cent.; South Africa)
The collective name for the seven Bantustans, or tribal homelands, created by South Africa along or near the border with Botswana and Zimbabwe. In 1971 they were granted nominal self-rule. They were incorporated into South Africa in 1994. The capital of Bophuthatswana is Mmbatho.

Bornu (KANEM-BORNU)

Bosnia-Herzegovina
During the 14th cent., a Bosnian principality conquered a province then named Hum, which during the 15th cent. separated as Herzegovina (southern Bosnia). Bosnia was annexed by the Ottoman Empire in 1463 and Herzegovina in 1482. Bosnia and Herzegovina were peopled by Serbs and Croats. Part of the population converted to Islam during the centuries of Ottoman rule. The two territories were integrated as the province of Bosnia-Herzegovina under Austrian administration in 1878 and in 1908 were annexed outright by Austria–Hungary (HABSBURG EMPIRE). Sarajevo, the capital, was the scene of the assassination of Archduke Francis Ferdinand, heir to the Habsburg throne, which was the immediate cause of World War I. In 1918, Bosnia-Herzegovina became part of the Kingdom of Serbs, Croats and Slovenes (1918), later named YUGOSLAVIA (1929). It was the setting of intense partisan resistance to German conquest during World War II. After the war, it was incorporated in federal Yugoslavia. With the disintegration of Yugoslavia, starting in 1991, a savage ethnic civil war began in the province, which eventually led to the Dayton Agreement of 1995 by which Bosnia-Herzegovina would remain nominally one state divided into two self-administering territories: one a Croat–Muslim federation and the other Serbian.

Bosporan Kingdom (1st–15th cents.; Crimea)
Created in the ancient Greek region of Chersonese (southern Crimea), the Bosporan kingdom was a Roman dependency from the 1st to the 4th cent.,

when it was invaded by the HUNS. The territory was retaken by the BYZAN-
TINE EMPIRE in the 6th cent. In the 12th cent. it was seized by the PETCHE-
NEGS. The GOLDEN HORDE occupied southern Russia from the 13th to the
15th cent. In the early 15th cent., southern Crimea was seized by the Genoese
and called Gothia. It was used as a commercial terminus for trade with Asia.
By 1480, Gothia had fallen to the khanate of CRIMEA, an offshoot of the
Golden Horde.

Botswana

Inhabited by Bantu-speaking tribes, the southern African territory of Bechuanaland was made part of the BRITISH COLONIAL EMPIRE in 1886. It
became independent Botswana in 1966. The capital is Gaborone. Bantu
tongues are spoken all over central and southern Africa.

Brazil

SEE ENTRY IN 'PROVINCES AND REGIONS'

By the Treaty of Tordesillas (1494), Spain and Portugal divided the 'non-
European world' along a north–south axis that supposedly granted the western
hemisphere to Spain. Unwittingly, the line cut off north-eastern Brazil which
was sighted accidentally and claimed for Portugal by Alvares Cabral in 1500.
The Portuguese colonized along the Brazilian coast. In 1539, Salvador was
founded and became the acting capital of the territory. Rio de Janeiro was
founded in 1567. The Dutch began their attacks on the north-eastern hump of
Brazil and in 1633 managed to occupy Salvador and Recife. They were dislodged by an expedition from Rio de Janeiro in 1654. In 1763, the capital of
Brazil was moved to Rio de Janeiro.

SLAVERY AND EMPIRE

Upon Napoleon's occupation of Portugal (1807), the Portuguese court of John
IV moved to Rio de Janeiro and established the Portuguese Empire. The court
moved back to Lisbon in 1821 and, in 1822, the Brazilians declared their
independence under the leadership of Emperor Pedro I, son of the Portuguese
king John VI. In 1831, Pedro I abdicated in favour of his son Pedro II. Legisla-
tion providing for the gradual abolition of slavery was approved in 1871, but
in 1888, during the Emperor's absence in Europe, the government decreed its
complete abolition. This alienated the planters, mainstay of the monarchy, and
Brazil became a republic in 1889. In 1830, Brazil recognized the independence
of Uruguay. During the war of the Triple Alliance against Paraguay
(1865–1870), Brazil made minor acquisitions. The territorial configuration of
Brazil was largely determined – apart from areas of Brazilian colonization led
by pioneers from Sao Paulo called *bandeirantes* – by its claim to the entire
basin of the Amazon River. The Brazilian frontiers were mostly established
through the diplomacy of Rio Branco during the late-19th and early-20th

cents., although the actual delimitation of the frontiers went on for much longer. The largest gain for Brazil was the western Amazonian territory of Acre which it acquired from Bolivia in 1903. In 1960, the capital of Brazil was moved from Rio de Janeiro to Brasilia, surrounded by the state of Goias, largely the work of president Juscelino Kubitschek. Brazil is the fifth most populous nation in the world.

British Colonial Empire (12th–20th cents.)
If there is any truth in that the British Empire was acquired in a fit of absent-mindedness, this would only serve to show that humans, and politicians in particular, do their thinking and planning in the subconscious. Even if unplanned, no empire of this magnitude could have arisen without deliberate-ness. IRELAND could be considered the first colonialist–imperialist acquisi-tion in the Western sense. Its conquest started in 1170 and culminated in the Battle of Boyne (1690). Ireland became independent in 1937.

Newfoundland, the first British landfall in America, discovered by John Cabot in 1497, was certainly no accident, even if it did not become a colony until 1713. By then, the Hudson's Bay company had been established to leap-frog French Quebec and Nova Scotia (FRENCH COLONIAL EMPIRE). England began colonizing Virginia in 1607 and Massachusetts in 1629. Bermuda was settled by shipwrecked travellers to Virginia in 1609. Simultan-eously, the BRITISH EAST INDIA COMPANY was active in India, where it established footholds in Surat (1613), Madras (1639), Bombay (1661), and Calcutta (1691). The name of the company indicates that the intention was to go further east and the British did try to take the East Indies from the Dutch, but gave up in 1623 concentrating instead on the Indian subcontinent. Even though Calcutta was the last of the initial British outposts, it became the plat-form for the conquest of BRITISH INDIA. In the Caribbean Sea and outlying waters, the British arrived in Nevis in 1628, to which was added French St Christopher in 1783 (ST KITTS AND NEVIS). They either occupied or took BARBADOS (1625), ST VINCENT (1627), the BAHAMAS (1629), Antigua and Montserrat (1632), Turks and Caicos Islands (1638), British Honduras (1638; BELIZE), Anguila (1650), JAMAICA (1655–1670), the Cayman Islands (1670), and the British Virgin Islands (1672). In the North American Atlantic seaboard, further colonies were founded during the 17th and 18th cents.: Maryland (1632), Rhode Island (1635), Connecticut (1636), North Carolina (1670), South Carolina (1670), New Hampshire (1680), Pennsylvania (1681), Delaware (1702), and Georgia (1732) (UNITED STATES OF AMERICA). While these large acquisitions were being made, the British also claimed, starting in 1661, the tiny Atlantic Ocean islands of St Helena and Ascension. In Africa, the first British *de facto* acquisition was The GAMBIA (1661). During the War of Spanish Succession, Great Britain took Gibraltar (1704), which it still possesses.

OLD AND NEW EMPIRES?

While French missionaries from Quebec were plying the waters of the Great Lakes and the Mississippi River (1682), the Hudson's Bay Company was exploring western CANADA and laying claims to lands southwards into what would later become territory of the United States. These developments meant that in North America, India, and the Caribbean, Anglo-French rivalry was very strong. In the Caribbean it eventuated in minor cession of islands, but in North America and India a great deal was at stake and it all came to a head during the Seven Years War, called the French and Indian war in American history (1756–1763). In India, the British and French were vying for influence among the southern Indian states, but in 1756 Clive took the route of war and defeated Indian forces under the Nawab of BENGAL at Plassey. Subsequently, the British defeated the French near Pondicherry and reduced the presence of France to a few small enclaves on the western and eastern coasts of India. In North America the decisive encounter was the Battle of the Plains of Abraham (1759), near Quebec City, where Wolfe defeated Montcalm and the French had to give up New France, which included part of Ontario and Prince Edward Island (formerly Île St Jean). In 1762, France transferred the province of Louisiana to Spain, which was ruled by a branch of the French house of Bourbon, but it had to cede all claims east of the Mississippi, which were lands American colonists had been settling since the late 17th cent. In the Caribbean the British gained GRENADA. For a brief time Great Britain also occupied Guadeloupe and Martinique (FRANCE). British naval power was incontestable and it was demonstrated in the occupation of Havana and Manila between 1762 and 1764. Despite these successes, it was the British Colonial Empire that experienced the first major loss of any colonial empire (if we except New France) when the eastern seaboard American colonies obtained their independence (1776–1781) and carried with them all British claims east of the Mississippi. This significant event has given rise to the academic thesis that it is possible to make a distinction between an old and a new empire with 1776 as a pivotal date. Although there developed a more tolerant attitude from Britain towards the political rights of the colonists in its colonies of European settlement – most of Canada, for example, was federated and self-governing by 1867 – the facts of colonialist imperialism – that is, the conquest and annexation of nations of non-Western cultural extraction – do not tally with this interpretation. The loss of the United States did not affect British momentum in Asia or in any other colonial front. And if self-rule was quickly granted to the Dominions, it was largely withheld from INDIA until independence.

THE NAPOLEONIC 'HARVEST'

NEW ZEALAND was visited by Captain Cook in 1769 and became a colony in 1840. The eastern coast of AUSTRALIA was explored by Cook in 1770.

Australia itself was gradually occupied and, in 1901, it was federated as a self-governing dominion. British Malaya (MALAYSIA) was the result of a long process from 1786 (foundation of Penang) to the final territorial integration of the colony (1909), highlighted by the foundation of SINGAPORE (1819) by Raffles. British Malaya was first run by the British East India Company but in 1867 became the Straits Settlements Colony. In 1842, the British occupied Hong Kong island and in 1898 took out a 99-year lease from China on the mainland area known as the New Territories. During the Napoleonic Wars, Great Britain gained a slew of colonies (date of occupation; default date 1814): MALTA (1800), TRINIDAD AND TOBAGO (1802), ST LUCIA, SEYCHELLES, Ionian Islands, MAURITIUS, Ceylon (1795; SRI LANKA), Cape of Good Hope (1806) and British Guiana (GUYANA). The Ionian Islands had been Venetian until 1797, after which they changed hands various times and were a Russian protectorate from 1799 to 1807. Great Britain took them from France. In 1864, they were ceded to Greece. Heligoland, an island on the mouth of the Elbe River in the North Sea, was occupied by Great Britain in 1807 and ceded to Germany in 1890 in exchange for minor territorial adjustments in Africa. BRITISH INDIA passed from the British East India Company to total British government administration after the Sepoy Mutiny in 1857–1858. The territories under British Indian administration eventually included, besides the territories of India and PAKISTAN, Ceylon, Burma (MYANMAR), the small Himalayan kingdoms of BHUTAN and Sikkim, Aden (YEMEN), and the Persian or Arabic gulf emirates (UNITED ARAB EMIRATES). British Burma was put together between 1826 and 1886. Aden was occupied as a naval station to control piracy in the Arabian coast and the Persian Gulf (1839). In the South Atlantic Ocean, Great Britain claimed South Georgia in 1775, Tristan da Cunha in 1816, and the Falklands in 1833. In the Pacific Ocean it annexed Pitcairn, settled by the *Bounty* mutineers, in 1839.

THE SCRAMBLE FOR AFRICA

After The Gambia, the next British African acquisition was the Gold Coast (GHANA) starting in 1821. Whereas in tropical Africa the colonial process was sluggish, in southern Africa it was quick: Great Britain took Natal in 1843 and the Boers founded TRANSVAAL and the ORANGE FREE STATE in the 1850s. In 1868, Great Britain established a protectorate over Basutoland (LESOTHO) and annexed Griquanaland West (next to the Orange Free State). From 1899 to 1902 there was war between Great Britain and the Boer republics, which resulted in their annexation. Federated with the Cape Colony (former Cape of Good Hope) and Natal (1843), they formed self-ruling SOUTH AFRICA in 1910. In the Indian Ocean, Great Britain constituted a protectorate over Zanzibar in 1870. In 1874, it acquired FIJI, its second possession in the Pacific Ocean, after New Zealand. In 1878, it occupied

CYPRUS, the only possession it took directly from the OTTOMAN EMPIRE before World War I. EGYPT was a British protectorate from 1882 to 1923. It had been self-ruling, if nominally a vassal of the Porte, since the early 19th cent. There is a famous thesis that claims that the British hegemony in Egypt was what set off the scramble for Africa which led to the conference of BERLIN (1884–1885). However, Great Britain's largest colony in Africa, after South Africa, was NIGERIA, whose colonization began in 1881. The events in southern Africa – the formation of Bechuanaland (1884; BOTSWANA), Nyasaland (1888; MALAWI), Southern Rhodesia (1888; ZIMBABWE), and Northern Rhodesia (1889; ZAMBIA) – had more to do with Rhodes' wheeling and dealing than with European political rivalries. What Great Britain did annex to its colonial empire during and after Berlin were: British New Guinea (1884), British Somaliland (1884; SOMALIA), KENYA (1887), the MALDIVES (1887), New Hebrides (1887; a condominium with France, later VANUATU), BRUNEI (1888), UGANDA (1890), the Gilbert Islands (1892; KIRIBATI), the Ellice Islands (1892; TUVALU), the SOLOMON ISLANDS (1893), and TONGA (1900), which is a very mixed rather than an African bag. SWAZILAND was formed in 1890 with South African territories. The SUDAN was occupied as an Anglo-Egyptian condominium in 1898, giving rise to the singular situation of a protectorate (Egypt) half-having a colonial dependency. In World War I, Great Britain acquired as League of Nations mandates from Germany: Tanganyika (1919; TANZANIA), NAURU (1919), and Western Samoa (1919; SAMOA); and from the Ottoman Empire, PALESTINE, and IRAQ (1917–1919). Iraq was given its independence in 1932. Transjordan (JORDAN) was separated from Palestine in 1920 as a dependent Hashemite kingdom. German South West Africa (NAMIBIA) was given as a mandate to South Africa. South-eastern New Guinea went to Australia as Papua (PAPUA NEW GUINEA) in 1905.

THE COMMONWEALTH OF NATIONS AND DECOLONIZATION

In 1931 the Statute of Westminster was promulgated in London. It created the COMMONWEALTH OF NATIONS and the sovereignty of the dominions was recognized. This was achieved by the abrogation of laws which imposed colonial limitations. The original members of the Commonwealth were Great Britain, Ireland, Australia, Canada, Newfoundland, New Zealand, and South Africa, but not colonies, protectorates, or other dependencies. It was intended that the strongest bond between them would be allegiance to the British Crown, but in practice many members have opted for republican status. Ireland, known as the Irish Free State, became the Republic of Ireland in 1949 and withdrew from the Commonwealth. So did South Africa in 1961.

The dismantling of the British colonial empire after World War II is best described by regions. In the Near East, Jordan was independent in 1946.

Arab–Jewish conflict delayed the independence of Palestine, which Great Britain handed over to the United Nations and, in 1949, became mostly ISRAEL. Aden was independent SOUTH YEMEN in 1967. British India in 1947 became the independent states of India and Pakistan. Ceylon (later Sri Lanka) and Burma (later Myanmar) achieved independence in 1948. The independence of Malaya (1957) was delayed by a communist insurrection the British suppressed. With the addition of Singapore, Sabah, and Sarawak it became Malaysia in 1963. Singapore separated peaceably from Malaysia in 1965. Brunei was a protectorate until 1979. In Africa, Sudan gained its independence in 1954, Ghana in 1957, Nigeria in 1960, Tanganyika in 1961 (it became Tanzania after union with Zanzibar, which became independent in 1963), Uganda in 1962, Kenya in 1963 (delayed because of the Mau Mau insurrection), Zambia and Malawi in 1964, and The Gambia in 1965. White-dominated RHODESIA seceded in 1964. It became Zimbabwe in 1980, when the previous regime caved in. Swaziland achieved independence in 1968. In the Mediterranean, Cyprus became independent in 1960 (delayed because of attempts to unite with Greece) and Malta in 1964. In the Caribbean, Great Britain consolidated some of its possessions into the Federation of the West Indies, which lasted from 1958 to 1962. Jamaica and Trinidad and Tobago became independent in 1962, Barbados in 1966, The Bahamas in 1973, Grenada in 1974, Dominica in 1978, St Vincent and St Lucia in 1979, ANTIGUA AND BARBUDA in 1981, and Belize in 1982, the last of the colonies to go, delayed because of Guatemalan territorial claims. In the Indian Ocean, Mauritius achieved independence in 1968 and Seychelles and the Maldives in 1976. In the Pacific Ocean, tiny Nauru became independent in 1968, Fiji and Tonga in 1970, Tuvalu and the Solomons in 1978, Kiribati in 1979, and Vanuatu in 1980. Hong Kong reverted to China in 1997. Great Britain still has some dependencies: Pitcairn Island, various small islands in the Indian Ocean (British Indian Ocean Territory), the Falklands and other islands in the South Atlantic Ocean, Bermuda, and the British West Indies (Montserrat, the British Virgin Islands, the Cayman Islands, and Turks and Caicos Islands). Other British possessions are: Ascension Island, the South Orkney Islands, and the South Shetland Islands. The last two are in the South Atlantic Ocean, near Antarctica. Great Britain also claims a wedge of Antarctica south of 60 degrees south latitude between 20 degrees and 80 degrees west longitude.

British East India Company (17th–19th cents.)
Chartered by Queen Elizabeth I in 1600, the British East India Company established a trading outpost in Amboin, one of the Moluccas, which the Dutch eliminated in 1623 (DUTCH COLONIAL EMPIRE). The British then concentrated on India, where they had been established since 1611 in Masulipatam. They were on good terms with the MUGHAL EMPIRE and by the early 18th cent. had established themselves in Bombay (1661), Madras (1639), and

Calcutta, which was founded by the Company in 1691. However, as Mughal power declined, the British came into conflict with local governors and the Company took a more aggressive stance, especially under Clive. In 1756 the Nawab of Bengal Siraj ud-Daula captured Calcutta, where he cast the British into the prison referred to as the 'black hole', in which many perished, but Clive defeated him decisively in the Battle of Plassey in 1759. This was the time of the Seven Years War (1756–1763) and Clive also outmanoeuvred the French. In 1765, the British took over Bengal outright and from then on gradually conquered the entire Indian subcontinent. The East India Company generally had a free hand in India, but this began to change with the appointment of Warren Hastings by the British government as governor general of India. Further reforms in 1813 and 1833 curtailed the Company's power and after the Sepoy Mutiny in 1857–1858, control of India devolved entirely to Great Britain. The East India Company also promoted British establishments in Malaya during the 18th cent. and it administered the Straits Settlement from their consolidation in 1826 until 1867, when Malaya became a British colony. Calcutta was the capital of BRITISH INDIA from 1833 to 1912, when it was moved to Delhi. New Delhi itself was inaugurated in 1931.

British India (17th–20th cents.; *India*, *Myanmar*, *Pakistan*, and Sri Lanka)
The British India Company was founded in 1600 to make profits in Asia by any means available. The Dutch, who had founded their own company in 1602, went in the footsteps of the Portuguese and took control of the Indian Ocean as far as the East Indies (DUTCH COLONIAL EMPIRE). In 1613, the British gained a commercial foothold in Surat, the chief Mughal port in Gujarat. They were expelled by the Dutch from the Moluccas in 1623 and thereafter concentrated on India. Further entrepôts were opened in Madras (1639) and Bombay (1661). In 1691, the British East India Company founded Calcutta on the site of an Indian village.

PLASSEY

After the sack of Delhi by the Persian Nadir Shah in 1739, the MUGHAL EMPIRE literally went to pieces. The 'emperor' was a mere local ruler. The history of India was in the hands of diverse political forces among which the most important were: the British in Calcutta and Bombay; the French in Pondicherry (near Madras, in Tamil Nadu); the nawabs of Oudh (in Uttar Pradesh) and of BENGAL; the MARATHA KINGDOMS in Maharashtra, particularly Pune, founded by the Peshwa; and the nizams of Mysore and Hyderabad (NORTHERN, CENTRAL and SOUTHERN INDIA). The French had their own East India Company, which they had established with little success in 1664 and then relaunched in 1685 (FRENCH COLONIAL EMPIRE). In 1742, under Dupleix, the French had formed European-type Indian regiments. In 1748, they became influential in Hyderabad, but the company directors were appalled at the expense and in 1754 retrenched. In 1756, the British, led by Clive, defeated the Nawab of Bengal at Plassey, where the commander of the Indian forces had been bought. The British East India Company, reinforced with British troops and supported by British naval supremacy, then defeated the French near Pondicherry in 1760. French India was reduced to a few enclaves on both coasts of India and the British had a free hand. By 1785, under Warren Hastings, the British controlled Bengal and Bihar and the coast to the eastern Ghats (a line of hills parallel to the Indian Ocean coast of Orissa and Andhya Pradesh). Of all of India's local rulers, the one who put up the longest and stiffest resistance was Tipu Sultan, ruler of Mysore, and he was finally killed defending his capital Seringapatam by forces under Lord Wellesley and his brother Arthur, future Duke of Wellington. Clive realized that the British East India Company could not by itself take on the task of creating and holding British India. By regulatory acts in 1773 and 1784 a system was devised whereby the Company retained its trading privileges, but ultimate political control resided in London. The British colonial government in the Indian subcontinent was called The Raj.

Burma and Pakistan

If the British Indian Empire later seemed like the result of lack of vigilance (absent-mindedness), it could only have been because the British public was either not concerned by or not interested in what its government was doing overseas. This included in 1796 the annexation of Ceylon, taken from the Dutch. The only remaining independent state in Central India after Mysore fell (1799), was Pune and since it was surrounded by British-dependent Maratha principalities (Gwailor, Indore, and Baroda), it soon entered the imperial ranks. Indore attempted to become independent but was subjected in 1818. In 1826, the British occupied the western (Arakan) and eastern (Tenasserim) coasts of Burma (MYANMAR). By 1833, Great Britain had deprived the East India Company of its trade monopoly. In 1857, a regiment of Sepoys (Indian soldiers in British service) rebelled in Meerut rather than have to bite cartridges smeared with animal grease. The rebellion, known as the Sepoy or Indian mutiny, became generalized. Delhi and Lucknow were taken. It was put down when the British regrouped with crucial help from the Sikhs, whose kingdom in PUNJAB had been suppressed by Sepoys earlier. The scapegoat for the rebellion was the British India Company, which in 1858 was dissolved. Although not much of a leader, the last Mughal emperor, Bahadur Shah II, whom the Indian troops had acclaimed as ruler, was deposed. By 1860, Great Britain had annexed Sind (southern Pakistan) and lower Burma. For those territories it did not control directly, it set up or constituted protectorates over local rulers, notably, besides Mysore and Hyderabad, various Rajput kingdoms, Baluchistan, Kashmir, and Bhutan. It had troubles on the north-western frontiers with AFGHANISTAN, which it tried to eliminate with invasions in 1838–1842 and in 1878–1880. After each period of open hostilities, British India seized extensive portions of Afghan territory until, in 1891 and 1893, the boundaries were definitely established and the north-western frontier was pacified.

SATYAGRAHA

Upper Burma (Mandalay) was annexed in 1886. The British had taken Ladakh (western Tibet) in 1846. Border areas with Tibet were annexed to Assam during 1913–1914, with which the territory of British India was rounded out. The colony of Aden (SOUTH YEMEN) was under British Indian administration from 1839 to 1937. Ceylon (1931) and Burma (1937) were granted separate status. Indian troops, some, like the Nepalese, more than others, participated in both World Wars. But India wanted independence. The Indian National Congress, later the Congress Party, was formed in 1885. After the Amritsar massacre in 1919 – in which troops fired on a crowd of protesters, killing hundreds – nationalist sentiments grew, inspired by Gandhi. His message was *satyagraha* or passive resistance and was not endorsed by the Congress Party, which nevertheless deferred to his disciple Jawaharlal Nehru. In 1935, India was given partial self-rule. There were separate constituencies for Hindus and Muslims. The latter were led by Muhammad Ali Jinna. After World War II, when independence approached, the two Indian sides could not come to an agreement. Riots ensued and an Indian fanatic assassinated Gandhi, who clamoured for peace. In 1947, INDIA and PAKISTAN went their separate ways. Almost immediately they began warring over KASHMIR.
(*See chronology under* Indian Subcontinent.)

Brunei
A Malay sultanate in the 15th cent. that at one time controlled most of Borneo, by the 19th cent. Brunei was a small privateering state. In 1888, Great Britain constituted a protectorate which terminated in 1979. Malay and English are official languages in Brunei. The capital is Bandar Seri Begawan.

Buganda (13th–18th cents.; eastern Africa)
The durable but not very unified kingdom of Buganda partially covered the territory of today's Uganda, a British colony after 1890. Around 40 different native languages, mostly of the Bantu family, are spoken in Uganda.

Bukhara (Khanate of) (17th–19th cents.; *Central Asia*: western Turkestan)
The khanate of Bukhara was founded ca. 1600 by a branch of the ruling Shaybanid dynasty of ASTRAKHAN. It annexed Transoxiana and Ferghana. It lost Ferghana ca. 1710 to the KOKAND KHANATE and Merv in 1826 to Russia. In 1866, it became a Russian protectorate and in 1920 was annexed by the USSR, eventually becoming part of Uzbekistan.
(*See chronology under* Western Turkestan.)

Bulgaria

The Slavs had occupied the territory of Bulgaria by the 6th cent., but the first Bulgarian state was founded by Bulgar Turks (681) who arrived from southern Russia and were assimilated by the Slavs. The kingdom lasted until 1018, when it was conquered by the BYZANTINE EMPIRE. Strife within the empire and attacks from PETCHENEGS loosened the Byzantine hold and a new Bulgarian state was created in 1186, which, by the 13th cent., dominated the southern Balkans except Greece. This brought conflict with the Serbs, who had created a state of their own to the west (SERBIA). In 1396, the incipient OTTOMAN EMPIRE absorbed Bulgaria. Despite centuries of rule, Turkish efforts to stamp out the Bulgarian cultural identity failed. In 1877, strong Ottoman repression of Bulgarian nationalism resulted in a Russian declaration of war on the Porte. The Turks were defeated and by the Treaty of San Stefano (1878) they agreed to the independence of Romania, Serbia, and Montenegro and to an autonomous Bulgaria, which included Macedonia. The other European powers, fearful of Russian domination in the Balkans, modified the treaty in BERLIN (CONGRESS OF) and in particular reduced autonomous Bulgaria to its northern area and left eastern Rumelia (southern Bulgaria) and Macedonia under Ottoman rule. In 1908, Bulgaria took advantage of political unrest in Istanbul to declare its independence. As a result of the Balkan Wars (1912–1913), which first pitted Bulgaria and Serbia against the Ottomans and then Bulgaria against Serbia, Bulgaria first gained, then lost Macedonia, but it annexed Rumelia and an outlet to the Aegean Sea.

WRONG CHOICES

Bulgaria chose the wrong side in both World Wars. In 1915 Bulgaria entered the war on the side of the Central Powers and, reinforced with German and Austrian troops, over-ran Serbia and Montenegro. Greece entered the war in 1917 on the side of the Allies, who landed troops in Salonika. Bulgaria was knocked out of the war on 30 September 1918. After the war, it lost bits of land all around, especially the outlet to the Aegean. It had the basic configuration it has today. During World War II, it tried to recoup its losses. It was invaded by the Soviets in 1945. After the war, despite its alliance with Nazi Germany, the USSR allowed communist Bulgaria to retain the territories it had possessed since 1919. Bulgarian is a south Slavic language closely related to Macedonian. Sofia is the capital of Bulgaria.
(*See chronology under* Balkans.)

Bulgars

The Bulgars were nomadic Turks who, from the 6th cent., occupied Russian lands from the Urals to the Kuban. In the 7th cent., Bulgar territory was split by the Turkish Khazars: to the north, the VOLGA BULGARS, who lasted until the 13th cent.; to the south, Bulgarian tribes that migrated to the eastern

Balkans and founded BULGARIA. They were culturally absorbed by the Slavs, as the Varangians had been in Kievan Rus (RUSSIA).
(*See chronologies under* Southern Russia *and* Balkans.)

Burgundians

The Burgundians were Germanic semi-nomads who occupied the modern province of Burgundy and down to the Rhône river valley ca. 440. They were conquered by the FRANKS ca. 530. They gave their name to a kingdom and a duchy (ARLES; BURGUNDY).

Burgundy (Duchy of) (9th–15th cents.; south central *France, Belgium, Luxembourg*, and *Netherlands*)

The duchy of Burgundy, corresponding roughly to the French province of that name, was created in 879. In 1002 the French crown made it a fief. With Philip VI, the Valois became the ruling dynasty of France after the death of the last Capetian, Charles IV, in 1328. In 1364, John II Valois bestowed on his son Philip the Bold the duchy of Burgundy, which, under the Valois heir, expanded north bringing under its dominion: Lorraine, LUXEMBOURG, Nevers, Charolais, Picardy, Hainaut, FLANDERS, Namur, Brabant, Zeeland, Limburg, Geldern, Holland, practically all of what would become Luxembourg, NETHERLANDS and BELGIUM and a portion of north-eastern France. Franche Comté became part of the duchy in 1369. A nearly independent state, Burgundy was at the height of its political power during the early 15th cent. It had supported ENGLAND in its dynastic claims on much of France, and when Philip the Good switched allegiances in 1435, the English cause was doomed. However, Burgundian ambitions were checked in 1476 by French king Louis IX and, after the death of Burgundian Charles the Bold in battle in 1477, his daughter Mary married Maximilian I Habsburg, Emperor of the Holy Roman Empire, and brought the Low Countries and Franche Comté to the HABSBURG EMPIRE. The Low Countries later became the SPANISH NETHERLANDS. The Habsburg acquisitions gave rise to the celebratory saying that while other nations warred to expand, Austria happily married. Burgundy itself and Picardy were seized by the French crown. The Franche Comté was conquered by Louis XIV in 1674. Dijon is the traditional capital of Burgundy

Burgundy (Kingdom of) (ARLES)

Burkina Fasso

Formerly harbouring states of the Mossi people, who fended off invasion by SONGHAI, Upper Volta (Haute Volta) became a colonial province in French West Africa in 1895. It gained its independence in 1960 and changed its name to Burkina Fasso ('land of the honest') in 1984. The capital of Burkina Fasso, and in the past the centre of the principal Mossi kingdom, is Ouagadougou. French is the official language. An important local language, among around

70, is More, a member of the Niger–Congo group of languages spoken throughout western Africa.

Burma (MYANMAR)

Burundi

Burundi is a state created in 1962, from the former League of Nations mandate of Ruanda-Urundi, under Belgian administration, which after World War II became a United Nations trust territory (BELGIAN COLONIAL EMPIRE). In the 19th cent. Burundi was ruled by Tutsi tribal lords. The majority of the population is Hutu. Both Tutsi and Hutu speak Bantu languages. The capital of Burundi is Bujumbura.

Buyid Persia (10th–11th cents.; *Middle East*)

The Buyids were a Muslim Persian dynasty that, in 932, became overlords of western Persia, Baghdad, and Syria. They did not abolish the ABBASID CALIPHATE in Baghdad, which retained its religious and dynastic prestige, but deprived it of political power outside of Baghdad itself. This was a step towards the relative separation of religion and politics more characteristic of Sunni than of Shia Islam, although these categories must be highly nuanced. With the conquest of Khurasan from the GHAZNAVIDS towards the end of the century, the Buyids briefly reunited IRAN. They succumbed to the Seljuks (1055), Turkish hordes that were on the move from central Asia (SELJUK PERSIA).

(*See chronology under* Iran.)

Byzantine Empire (5th–15th cents.; core area: *Balkans* and *Anatolia*)

The complexity and weakness of the Roman Empire – after it had lost Mesopotamia and Armenia to the Sasanians and chunks of Rhaetia, Germania, and Dacia to the barbarians, who were obviously knocking at the gates – induced Diocletian (284–305) to divide the empire among four co-rulers, two in the east and two in the west. This brought political complications and struggles (ROME). Although Diocletian himself abdicated, the other co-rulers fell to bickering and fighting until Constantine the Great concentrated imperial power in his hands in 324. In 330, Constantine established his capital in the ancient Greek city of Byzantium (renamed Constantinople), at the entrance to the Bosporus, which later determined that the Roman Empire of the East became known as the Greek-speaking and Greek-ruled Byzantine Empire. Jovian, who ruled briefly (363–364), was emperor of west and east. His successor Valentinian I (364–375), who was emperor in the west, appointed Valens emperor in the east (364–378). Valens was defeated and killed by the Goths in Adrianople. Much later, as Edirne, Adrianople became the first European capital of the Ottoman Empire. It has the unfortunate historical distinction of having been the site of 15 battles or sieges, more than any other place in the world. Valens was succeeded in the east by Theodosius the Great. Gratian, emperor in the west, was murdered, after which there were various usurpations, which were put down by Theodosius in 379. He appointed Honorius as emperor in the west (384–423) and he was succeeded in the east by Arcadius (395–408). After that, the eastern and western empires remained permanently divided.

JUSTINIAN THE GREAT

In the east, Arcadius was succeeded by various emperors drawn mostly from the military. Leo I (457–474) was succeeded by Zeno (474–491), who was forced to recognize Odoacer as ruler in Italy. At the time of the fall of the Roman Empire in the west (476), the Roman Empire in the east controlled the Balkans up to Illyria and the Danube River; Anatolia to Georgia; the Levant (Mediterranean coast of the Near East), Egypt, and Libya; Crete and Cyprus. Over the centuries until its last burst of energy in the 14th cent., the Empire expanded and retrenched depending on the force with which it was assailed on its frontiers and on its internal cohesion. Under Justinian I the Great (527–565), adopted nephew of Justin I – a swineherd who rose to emperor from the ranks – Byzantine forces led by Belisarius and Narses against the barbarians conquered the north-western coast of Africa in 535, occupied the southern coast of Spain, and reclaimed Sicily, Italy, and Illyria, so that, by 556, the Byzantine Empire practically made the Mediterranean a Roman sea again. It expanded immensely against strong odds, and by 600 it had been reduced by the Lombards in Italy to Rome and Ravenna, separated by the Lombard duchy of Benevento from Byzantine southern Italy and Sicily. By 650, the Byzantine Empire had lost its Spanish shoreline. During the 7th cent. it gave up the Levant, Egypt, and Tunisia to ISLAM. Armenia was well within its bounds. Ravenna fell in 751.

MANZIKERT

In the course of the early 7th cent., the AVARS struck hard at the empire in the Balkans and, although they were eventually contained, they appreciably reduced Byzantine control in the region. Despite the tide of Islam the Empire managed to recover eastern GEORGIA. However, prior to its own downfall in 637, the SASANID EMPIRE displaced the Byzantines from Georgia as well as from most of Cappadocia. During the 8th cent. the Empire suffered losses all around: besides Africa, it was much reduced in Calabria and Pugliese and it lost territory in the Balkans to the BULGARS. Islam pushed to Cilicia and absorbed Georgia. The islands of Corsica and Sardinia also escaped Byzantine control. Tunisian Muslims had been encroaching on SICILY which was lost by 890, as had been Cyprus earlier. But at the same time, in one of those feats of resourcefulness which the Empire managed to achieve occasionally as if from nowhere, it fully reconquered the territories of Calabria and Pugliese from the divided Lombard lords of southern Italy. Except for the occupation of Sicily by Muslims, the Byzantine Empire, under Constantine VII Porphyrogenitus (913–959), had been stabilized in the early 10th cent., and not only that: it began to grow again. After the mid-10th cent., led by Nikephoros II Phokas (963–969), it regained Crete and Cyprus and took lands from the Armenians, who had previously founded an independent kingdom. From 998 to 1025, under Emperor Basil II, the Byzantines destroyed the Bulgarian Empire and re-established for a time the Balkan frontiers to the Dalmatian coast and the Danube. By 1028 the Empire had absorbed Armenia (surrendered later to the Seljuks) and expanded its beachhead in the Crimea. However, after the mid-11th cent. it lost all of Italy to the French Normans (NORMAN ITALY). The most devastating blow was the loss of Anatolia to the Seljuks after the Battle of Manzikert (1071), in which the Emperor Romanos IV was captured by the Seljuk Sultan Alp Arslan (RUM). The Empire also definitely lost its hold on Cyprus. Disunion among the Turks allowed John II Comnenos, by 1130, to recoup western Anatolia and the southern coast of the Black Sea, which the Byzantines held even as they rode roughshod over the burgeoning Slavic realms to the Dalmatian coast.

THE NICAEAN 'EMPIRE'

Just as its last hold on life, as we shall see, was a gift from the Turks, albeit unwitting, and not from Christians, so the worst damage to the Byzantine Empire was not done by Turks but by French and Flemish crusaders. Instead of attacking the infidels in Egypt, in 1202, with the enthusiastic naval support of VENICE, who pursued commercial advantages, the crusaders attacked Constantinople, took it (1204), sacked it, created the LATIN STATES with shreds of Byzantine lands, and reduced the empire to a strip of territory from the Black Sea to the Aegean Sea. This was the successor state known as Nicaea or the Nicaean Empire (around modern Iznik), to which the Byzantines retreated until, through diplomacy and sheer courage, they got on their feet again and, led by Michael VIII Palaiologos, liberated Constantinople from the Latins in 1261. TREBIZOND, another successor state, on the south-eastern shore of the Black Sea separated physically by Seljuk states from the reconstituted Byzantine Empire, escaped the onslaught of Tamerlane around 1400, but was finally absorbed by the OTTOMAN EMPIRE in 1461. Although not much of an empire, Constantinople in 1270 still managed to control western Anatolia, Thrace, and MACEDONIA to the Adriatic Sea. But this was to be its last imperial fling. The Ottomans, to whom the Seljuks had given the task of facing the Byzantine Empire, had taken western Anatolia, crossed the Hellespont, occupied the southern Balkans, and were at the doors of Constantinople by the late 14th cent. At this moment, the brunt of Tamerlane's hordes fell on them, destroyed the unified state they had been building in Anatolia – they had earlier moved their capital from Bursa in Turkey to Adrianople (Edirne) in Thrace – and gave Constantinople another 50 years of precarious existence (TIMURID EMPIRE AND SUCCESSOR STATES). The Byzantine Empire was reduced to Constantinople, its surrounding lands, and Salonika. The Ottomans recovered from their rout by Tamerlane. During the early 15th cent. they reconquered western Anatolia. They took Salonica in 1430 and, after an unsuccessful siege from 1424 to 1429, they entered Constantinople on 29 May 1453. The last Byzantine Emperor, Constantine XI Palaiologos, went down fighting during the siege.

BYZANTINE EMPERORS

One of the meanings of the adjective Byzantine derives from the complexities involved in following the lines of succession in Constantinople. Justinian the Great was succeeded by his nephew Justin II. The latter was followed by various emperors chosen to rule from the military. The last was Phokas (602–610), a detested tyrant, who was overthrown by Heraclius (610–641), summoned by the people of Constantinople from Carthage. Heraclius established a dynasty which lasted until Justinian II, who was dethroned in 695. His nose was cut off and he was banished to Crimea, from where he managed to gather a Bulgarian army and recover his throne in 705. His vindictive second reign lasted until 711, when he and his entire family were executed. There followed a brief period of rule by military emperors and, in 717, Leo III established the Syrian or Isauran dynasty. It was followed by a brief line of Phrygian emperors (820–867), the last of whom, Michael III, was betrayed by Basil, a co-emperor he himself had appointed. Basil I (867–868) inaugurated the line of the Macedonian emperors, which was extinguished with Empress Theodora in 1056. Under Constantine IX Monomachos, who had married Zoe, Theodora's sister, the schism between Rome and Constantinople became definitive in 1054. After a few brief reigns, Constantine X, chosen by the previous emperor, Isaac I Komnenos (1057–1059), established the Doukas dynasty, who came from the civil aristocracy of Constantinople. A nephew of Isaac, Alexios I Komnenos, founded the dynasty of his name in 1081. It was on his appeal for help against the Seljuks, who in 1071 had defeated and captured Emperor Romanos IV Diogenes at Manzikert, that Pope Urban II called for the First Crusade. But the Latin west soon became a threat to the Greek east. During the reign of Andronikos I Komnenos, who came to the throne on a wave of massacres of westerners in Constantinople, the Byzantine Empire became very fragmented and he himself was murdered by the populace in 1185, the last of his line. It was under the Angelos dynasty, acclaimed to the throne by the mob after it had murdered Andronikos I Komnenos, that the Fourth Crusade was deflected by the Venetian doge Dandolo (Venice) against

Constantinople in 1202. This act was justified as reprisal for the treaty that Issac II Angelos had made in 1189 with Saladin (AYYUBIDS). In 1195 Isaac was overthrown and blinded by his brother Alexios III Angelos, who was, in turn, overthrown by Isaac and his son Alexios IV, ally of the Crusaders and instigator of the conquest of Constantinople in 1204. The city was part of the Latin Empire, one of the Latin States, during the following decades. The Laskaris family ruled the Nicaean Empire until, in 1259, Michael VII Palaiologos assumed the throne and, in 1261, liberated Constantinople. The Palaiologos were to rule the Byzantine Empire until its downfall in 1453.
(*See chronologies under* Anatolia *and* Balkans.)

Byzantine Italy (6th–11th cents.; *Italy*)
After the fall of the Roman Empire in the west (5th cent.), the Byzantine Empire, under Justinian I the Great, began the recapture of Italy in the 6th cent. (BYZANTINE EMPIRE). At the height of its Italian expansion, directed by General Belisarius, the Byzantine Empire held most of Italy, with its administrative and political capital in Ravenna, against the Lombards. Ravenna fell in the 751 to the Lombards (LOMBARD ITALY). During the 10th cent., the Byzantines still held on to Calabria, but during the late-11th cent. their hold on southern Italy was ended by the French Normans (NORMAN ITALY).

C

Calicut (SOUTHERN INDIA)

Cambodia
The territory of Cambodia was known from the 1st to the 6th cents. as the kingdom of Funan, which is a Chinese designation. Funan itself was probably a small kingdom on the coast of what today is southern Vietnam. The first Khmer inscriptions date from the early 7th cent. The Khmer language belongs to the same family as Vietnamese. During the 7th and 8th cents. Cambodia was known to the Chinese as Chenla. The name Cambodia first appears in Khmer in the 9th cent., but there was a kingdom called Kamboja in VEDIC INDIA. Angkor, in north central Cambodia, was the capital of the Indianized Khmer kingdom from 802 to 1431. It was also known as Yasodharapura. Angkor derives from the Sanskrit word *nagara*, meaning city. In the history of Angkor, Sanskrit and Khmer were used side by side. Angkor synchretized Hinduism and Buddhism. Angkor Wat, the most famous of the many splendid temples in the Angkor site, was built from ca. 1112 to ca. 1150. At its height Khmer power extended to LAOS, THAILAND, and southern Vietnam (Mekong Delta). But the fortunes of war were fickle for the Khmers. In the late 12th cent. CHAMPA sacked Angkor. In the late 13th cent., Thais from Yunnan (south-western China) expelled the Khmer from Siam. In the following cents. Cambodia was repeatedly invaded by the Thais, who captured Angkor in the 15th cent. and brought down Khmer power. The capital was moved to Pnom Penh. In the 17th cent. VIETNAM also became a threat. In the 18th cent. Cambodia lost the Mekong Delta to the Vietnamese as well as lands in the west to the Thais. Vietnam kept up its siege of Cambodia during the 19th cent. A Cambodian king asked for French help and the country became a protectorate in 1863 (FRENCH COLONIAL EMPIRE). Under the French, the border with Thailand was rectified in favour of Cambodia. Southern Vietnam became the French colony of Cochin-China. Cambodia regained its independence in 1953. In 1975, the country fell to the communist Khmer Rouge, whose barbarous regime was deposed by the Vietnamese in 1979. The Vietnamese occupation ended in 1989. Fighting went on until a UN-supervised cease-fire in 1992. The UN Transitional Authority in Cambodia steered the country to parliamentary elections in 1993 and the restoration of the constitutional monarchy. The remnants of the recalcitrant Khmer Rouge surrendered in 1999.

Cameroon
Divided into different tribes, the territory of Cameroon was awarded to Germany in 1884. After 1916, during World War I, it was mandated to Great

Britain and France. The western and smaller British part was annexed to Nigeria. The French colony became independent in 1960. The capital of Cameroon is Yaoundé. English and French are both official languages. There are over 250 native tongues, all members of the Bantu group of languages, spoken throughout central and southern Africa.

Canada

The original British colony in Canada was Newfoundland, including the coast of Labrador, reconnoitred for the English crown by John Cabot in 1497. Frenchmen navigated the St Lawrence River in 1534. In 1608, they founded Quebec City and subsequently missionaries explored the Great Lakes and sailed down the Mississippi River, thus establishing claims that resulted in the creation of French Louisiana. French Canadian territories constituted in 1663 the colony of New France (FRENCH COLONIAL EMPIRE).

BRITISH CANADA

In 1670 King Charles II granted a charter to the Hudson's Bay Company with a jurisdiction which eventually extended over Rupert's Land (western and north-western Canada and the Columbia River basin in the United States), northern Quebec, and western Ontario. Nova Scotia was occupied by the British in 1710. French colonists called this region Acadia. Its population was dispersed. Other French colonists moved to Cape Breton Island. In 1759, the British, under Wolfe, surprised the French forces, led by Montcalm, in the decisive Battle of the Plains of Abraham, near Quebec City, and annexed New France. In 1763, the British were awarded the French territories in Canada as well as the territories east of the Mississippi in French Louisiana. Canada was a British military base and a haven for American loyalists during the American War of Independence (1775–1781) (UNITED STATES). The north-eastern border between the United States and British North America was defined after the war of 1812. British Columbia was acquired in 1846 by treaty with the United States, which also set the western American–Canadian border along the 49th parallel. With the federation in 1867 of New Brunswick, Nova Scotia, Ontario, and Quebec, Canada as such came into existence. In 1869 it was ceded Rupert's Land. Prince Edward Island – French as Île St Jean in 1719 and British in 1763 – joined the federation in 1873. The last of Canada's provinces to do so was Newfoundland in 1949. Canada was self-governing since its formation but it became totally sovereign in 1931, with the creation of the British COMMONWEALTH OF NATIONS. Ottawa, founded in 1827 with the curious name of Bytown, was later named after a tribe of Indians and in 1858 was made the capital of the United Provinces of Canada and in 1868 of the Dominion of Canada.

THE PROVINCES AND TERRITORIES OF CANADA

Canada is made up of Alberta, British Columbia, Manitoba, New Brunswick, Newfoundland and Labrador, Nova Scotia, Ontario, Prince Edward Island, Quebec, Saskatchewan, the North West Territories, Yukon Territory, and Nunavut.

Alberta was part of Rupert's Land, under the jurisdiction of the Hudson's Bay Company. In 1882 the southern part was constituted as a district. When joined to Athabasca in the north, it became the province of Alberta, which entered the Canadian federation in 1905. Calgary is the biggest city, but Edmonton is the capital.

Known originally as New Caledonia, British Columbia was part of Rupert's Land, under the jurisdiction of the Hudson's Bay Company. In 1849, Vancouver Island was created as a colony of Great Britain. The mainland of British Columbia became a colony in 1858. The two became the province of British Columbia in 1866, which then joined the Canadian federation. The capital is Vancouver.

Manitoba was separated from the Hudson's Bay Company ca. 1810 as the Red River Settlement. In 1879 it became a province in the Canadian federation. Its territory was enlarged in 1881 and 1912 with lands from the North West Territories. The capital of Manitoba is Winnipeg.

New Brunswick was discovered by Cartier in 1534. Joined to Nova Scotia in the 17th cent. it became French Acadia, which in 1713 passed to Great Britain. In 1784, New Brunswick and Nova Scotia were made two separate colonies. In 1848 New Brunswick enjoyed self-rule and in 1867 became a founding member of the Federation of Canada. St John is its largest city. Fredericton is the capital. English and French are official languages.

Newfoundland and Labrador were sighted by John Cabot in 1497. In 1583 they were claimed by England. In 1855, they were self-ruling, but did not enter the Federation of Canada in 1867. They became a colony in 1934 and in 1949 joined Canada. The proof of the Viking arrival in American shores was found in Anse-au-Meadow in Newfoundland. The capital of the province is St John's.

Nova Scotia was sighted by Cabot in 1497, but in 1605 it became the French Acadia. It was held by the English from 1654 to 1667, when it was returned to France. It became definitely British in 1713. In 1820 the island of Cape Breton was joined to Nova Scotia. The province was self-ruling in 1848 and joined the Canadian federation in 1867. The capital of Nova Scotia is Halifax.

Ontario was explored by Champlain in 1613. In 1627 it became part of New France. In 1763 it was ceded to Great Britain, after the conquest of Quebec. In 1791, the British formed Upper Canada with the territory of Ontario as a home for loyalists from the American colonies, which had successfully rebelled

(1775–1781). As Ontario, it joined the Canadian federation in 1867. Toronto is the capital.

Quebec City was the capital of the French colony of New France. The latter was incorporated into British Canada as Quebec from 1763 to 1790. From 1791 to 1846, it was known as Lower Canada, and Canada East from 1846 to 1867. Upon joining the Canadian confederation in 1867 it became again the province of Quebec.

In 1534, Prince Edward Island was explored by Cartier, who named it Île St Jean. In 1719, it was recognized as French, but in 1758 it passed to Britain. In 1763, it was joined to Nova Scotia, but separated in 1769. Renamed Prince Edward Island in 1799, it joined the Canadian federation in 1873. Its capital is Charlottetown.

Saskatchewan was part of Rupert's Land, under the jurisdiction of the Hudson's Bay Company. It passed to Canada in 1869 and was made a district in 1882. In 1905 it became a province in the Canadian federation. The capital of Saskatchewan is Regina.

Besides the provinces, Canada contains three territories. The Northwest Territory was annexed from the Hudson's Bay Company in 1869. The territory of Nunavut was formally separated as an Inuit or Eskimo homeland in 1992. The Yukon Territory was also created from the Northwest Territory in 1898. Their respective capitals bear the grand names of Yellowknife, Iqaluit (formerly Frobisher Bay), and Whitehorse. Baffin, the fifth largest island in the world, is one of the Arctic islands of Canada.

Cape Verde
Previously uninhabited, the Cape Verde Islands, off the coast of western Africa, came under Portuguese control after the mid-15th cent. The country obtained its independence in 1975. The capital of Cape Verde is Praia.

Cappadocia (3rd–1st cents. BC; *Anatolia*)
An offshoot of the SELEUCID EMPIRE, Cappadocia was a minor kingdom in Anatolia, which was absorbed by ROME (AD 17). In the 11th and 12th cents. Cappadocia was the base for one of the SELJUK EMIRATES.
(*See chronology under* Anatolia.)

Carchemish (HITTITE KINGDOM)

Carolingian Empire (8th–9th cents.; *France, Germany*, and *Italy*)
The Carolingian Empire, the womb of France and Germany, was the creation of Charlemagne (ca. 742–814), grandson of Charles Martel, who stopped the Arabs cold in Tours (France), and son of Pepin the Short, who deposed the last Merovingian monarch in 751, although his family had been running the west Frankish kingdom since the 7th cent. (FRANKS). In 774, Pavia in northern Italy was incorporated into the Empire (LOMBARD ITALY). The Spanish

march was established ca. 800 in BARCELONA. During the early 9th cent., Lower Saxony was created in northern Germany and marches were founded from the Elbe to the Adriatic. There was also a Breton march ca. 790. Upon the emperor's death, his realm comprised, not including the marches: Austrasia, Aquitania, Alamannia, Burgundy, Bavaria, Frisia, Gascony, Lombardy, Neustria, Provence, Saxony, Septimania, Thuringia, and what was later known briefly as Lotharingia, a swath of territory from the Low Countries down to and including northern Italy.

VERDUN

Charlemagne was succeeded by his son Louis I the Pious who ruled until 840. Lothair succeeded Louis and was Emperor from 840 to 855. Due to its size and the primitive means of communication and transport, the Empire was not easy to govern and it soon began to divide through different dynastic claims. By the Treaty of Verdun in 847, imposed on Lothair, it was divided into three parts: northern, western, and southern France, with its centre around Paris, to Charles the Bald, who held the imperial title from 875 to 877; the Low Countries, the Rhineland, and Burgundy down to Italy including Rome, to Lothair II (Lotharingia, from which came the name of Lorraine); and Germany and the eastern marches to Louis the German. Louis II (855–875) succeeded Lothair as Emperor, but he was mainly in Italy defending the imperial claim. When Lothair II died, Lotharingia was divided by the Treaty of Mersen (870) between Charles the Bald and Louis the German. After Charles the Bald, the imperial succession is unclear. Though still theoretically parts of the Empire, France and Germany were separate kingdoms. Charles the Fat, son of Louis the German, was accepted as Emperor, but after failing to relieve Paris, besieged by Norsemen, he was deposed in 887. The final partition in 888 left standing France or the West Frankish Kingdom, under Eudes; Germany or the East Frankish Kingdom, under Arnulf; the kingdom of ARLES; the duchy of BURGUNDY; and a very fragmented entity that is formally designated as the kingdom of Italy (CAROLINGIAN ITALY), which Arnulf had claimed. Charlemagne established his capital in Aachen (Aix-la-Chapelle), which today is in the German state of Rhineland.

Carolingian Italy (8th–9th cents.; northern *Italy*)
Upon Charlemagne's death northern Italy was passed on to his heirs as the kingdom of Italy, which was at best an aggregation of more or less autonomous municipalities, with Pavia as its centre. Louis II (855–875) succeeded Lothair (840–855) as Emperor, but he was mainly in Italy defending the imperial claim (CAROLINGIAN EMPIRE). Carolingian ascendancy in Italy lasted from the taking of Pavia (774) to the reign of Arnulf, King of Germany, crowned Emperor in Rome in 896. By then France had gone its own way under Eudes (888–898), so that the Carolingian claim on Italy even-

tually passed to the predominantly German Holy Roman Empire (IMPERIAL ITALY).

Carthage (9th–2nd cents. BC; ancient northern Africa)
The city of Carthage, in modern Tunisia, was founded ca. 810 BC as a colony of the Phoenician city of Tyre (PHOENICIA). Carthage became the dominant commercial and political power in the western Mediterranean. From the 6th to the 4th cents. BC it occupied Sardinia, Malta, the Balearics, and the coast from Tunisia to Morocco. It tried to take Sicily from the Greeks but only managed a few footholds, from which the Carthaginians were ejected during the First Punic War (264–241 BC) by Rome. Punic comes from Poeni, the Roman name for Phoenician. In the course of the 3rd cent. BC, Carthage seized the coast of Spain, which led to the Second Punic War (218–201 BC), during which Hannibal invaded Italy, repeatedly defeated Roman armies, but was finally crushed in the Battle of Zama. The eventual Roman victory was due in part to the delaying tactics of the Roman general Fabius Cunctator. Carthage recovered economically from defeat, but Roman animosity, kept alive by Cato the Elder (whose proleptic 'Carthago delenda est' became a battle cry), provoked the Third Punic War (149–146 BC), in which Scipio Africanus finally occupied Carthage and razed it to the ground (NUMIDIA).

Castile (11th–15th cents.; *Spain*)
When Sancho, king of NAVARRE, died in 1035, one of his heirs, Ferdinand I, founded Castile, which absorbed LEON in 1037 and formed the kingdom of Castile and Leon, later just Castile (ASTURIAS). From 1126 to 1157, Castile reunited all of Christian Spain except ARAGON. Southern Spain from Estremadura to Valencia formed part of the empire of the ALMOHADS, which included the Maghreb in northern Africa (MUSLIM SPAIN). After 1157 the kingdom divided. In 1212, Castile, under Alfonso VIII, won the Battle of Navas de Tolosa, in which the Muslims were decisively defeated, resulting in the downfall of the Almohads. Castile and Leon were finally and definitely reunited as one kingdom in 1230 by Ferdinand III. By 1252, Castile had conquered the kingdoms of the Moors down to Córdoba (1236). The union with Aragon, through the marriage of Isabella of Castile and Ferdinand of Aragon (the Catholic Kings) in 1479, signalled the formation of modern Spain. In 1492, with the conquest of Granada, Spain ruled over most of the Iberian Peninsula. The principal royal city of Castile was Leon. Madrid, later the capital of Spain, was first known as a Muslim fortress (Magerit) in the 10th cent. It became the residence of the Catholic Kings.

Castile and Leon (CASTILE)

Catalonia (9th–12th cents.; *Spain*)
The area around Barcelona became a march of the CAROLINGIAN EMPIRE against the Muslims in north-eastern Spain ca. 800. It was made a county in

888, which later expanded to create the province of Catalonia. Count Raymond Berangar of Catalonia married Petronilla, daughter of Ramiro II of Aragon, on whose abdication in 1137 the two realms were united. Catalonia retained its laws, its *cortes* (parliament), and its language. The Catalans rebelled against Spain in 1640, which gave PORTUGAL, under Spanish rule since 1580, the opportunity to secede. Catalonia did not become independent but it was not divested of its rights, which showed the internal weakness of the Spanish state. However, during the War of Spanish Succession (1700–1713), Catalonia sided with the Habsburg claimant against the eventual Bourbon winner and it was deprived of its provincial privileges. Catalonia was the last redoubt of the Republic during the Spanish Civil War (1936–1939). It is today a semi-autonomous province of Spain.

Celts (12th–1st cents. BC; western Europe)
The disunited Indo-European-speaking Celtic tribes occupied the lands from central Europe to the Atlantic Ocean and the British islands. They are originally identified with the Hallstatt culture dated back to the 12th cent. BC. The Celtic tribes of France are collectively known as Gauls. The Ligurians are culturally closer to the Italians. In the 5th cent. BC, the Celts were under pressure from the Germanic tribes to the north and north-east. In the early 4th cent. BC, Celtic invaders cut through Liguria and poured into central Italy, but were contained and gradually absorbed by ROME. The Roman Empire in the west was created in mostly Celtic lands. Celtic culture remains alive today in language and tradition in Ireland, Wales, and French Brittany.

Central African Republic
Inhabited by disunited tribes, the territory of Ubangi-Shari was a French colony from 1887 to 1894, integrated with Chad into French Equatorial Africa (1910) (FRENCH COLONIAL EMPIRE). Separated from Chad, it was granted independence in 1960 as the Central African Republic. From 1977 to 1979 it styled itself the Central African Empire. The capital of the Central African Republic is Bangui. The official language is French but there is a lingua franca based on a language of the Niger–Congo group of languages spoken in central and western Africa.

Central American Federation (19th cent.; Central America)
When the countries of Central America gained their independence from Spain, as a result of the ousting of Spanish authority in Mexico and in South America (1810–1824), they first became part of the Mexican Empire (1821–1823) and then tried to form a federal union, known as the Central American Federation, which lasted until 1838. It included Guatemala, El Salvador, Honduras, Nicaragua, and Costa Rica. Panama was then part of the Republic of New Granada, later Colombia. The principal leader of the Central American Federation was the Honduran Morazán, who moved the capital from Guatemala City

to El Salvador in an effort to stem separatism, but could not prevent the federation's eventual voluntary dissolution.

Central India (3rd cent. BC–19th cent. AD)
In recounting the complex history of the Indian subcontinent before British India, a practical approach is to distinguish between NORTHERN INDIA, Central India, and SOUTHERN INDIA. Historically, Central India is usually identified as Deccan, a general and imprecise regional designation which applies to all or large tracts of Karnataka, Maharashtra, Andhra Pradesh, Madhya Pradesh, and Orissa. Even though it is not a political designation, the Deccan over the centuries has been dominated by successive dynasties and states. During the 3rd cent. BC, Kalinga, in Orissa, was an important kingdom. It was as a result of the bloodshed in a war with Kalinga that the great Maurya emperor Asoka converted to Buddhism (MAGADHA). Despite its defeat, Kalinga lasted at least to the 1st cent. BC, when Kharavela became the most powerful king in the region. Kharavela is a solitary figure, but the Satavahana, originally from Maharashtra, did establish a durable kingdom in the Deccan and northern India (1st–2nd cents.). The Satavahana kingdom was attacked by the SAKAS in the north west. Satavahana decayed in the 3rd cent. and the Vakataka dynasty became predominant, at least in the early 5th cent. allied to the GUPTAS. In the 6th cent. it was the turn of the Chalukyas, whose greatest king, Pulakeshin, contained an invasion from HARSHA'S KINGDOM. Pulakeshin was also in constant warfare with the Pallavas of southern India. In the 9th cent. the Rashtrakutas gained the upper hand, but the Chalukyas made a comeback during the 10th cent. These Hindu ruling houses never managed to unify the Deccan, let alone India. The history of Northern and Central India in this period is very complicated, but it is also mostly about ephemeral events and obscure dynasties and kingdoms. Some historians consider it equivalent to the feudal European Middle Ages. During the 13th cent., the Afghan DELHI SULTANATE extended its rule to the Deccan. The sultanate was mortally weakened by Tamerlane in the late 14th cent. (TIMURID EMPIRE AND SUCCESSOR STATES). The vacuum in the Deccan was filled by the BAHMANI SULTANATE, which, ca. 1490, disintegrated into the sultanates of Ahmednagar, Berar, Bidar, Bijapur, Golconda, and Gondwana. The latter name is used in geology to designate the huge landmass from which South America, Africa, India, Australia, and Antarctica started separating 100 million years ago. The whole of Deccan was conquered by the Mughal emperor Aurangzeb during the 17th cent. The MUGHAL EMPIRE soon decayed and was substituted in Central India by the loose control of the Hindu MARATHA KINGDOMS, who were absorbed by BRITISH INDIA in the late 18th–early 19th cents.
(*See chronology under* Indian Subcontinent.)

Ceylon (SRI LANKA)

Chad

Home (with NIGER) to the native kingdoms of KANEM-BORNU and of WADAI, Chad became a French Colony in the late-19th cent., integrated into French Equatorial Africa from 1910 to its independence in 1960 (FRENCH COLONIAL EMPIRE). Official languages are French and Arabic. Hausa, a language distantly related to the Semitic group, is a lingua franca. The capital of Chad is N'Djamena.

Chagataite Khanate (14th–16th cents.; *Central Asia*)

Chagatai or Jagatai, son of Genghis Khan, succeeded to the part of the MONGOL EMPIRE which extended from the Ili River and Kashgaria to Transoxiana. By the early 14th cent. the Chagataite Khanate had separated from the Mongol Empire, which then included all of China (YUAN). By the middle of 14th cent., it had split into a western Muslim part (Transoxiana) and the eastern part known as Mogholistan, but was shortly reunited again under Tughlugh Timur, an obscure descendant of Chagatai who converted to Islam. At their height, Chagataite domains extended from the Irtyish River in Siberia down to Ghazni in Afghanistan and from Transoxiana to the Tarim Basin. It flourished during the 15th cent., when it took Tashkent (1484), but by the early 16th cent. it had lost Tashkent to the SHAYBANIDS (1509) and the dynasty gradually petered out in Kashgaria through internal decomposition and attrition from attacks by the KIRGHIZ-KHAZAKHS, the Oirat or Western Mongols (MONGOLIA), and other hordes that were roaming Central Asia. Around 1600, Kashgaria was ruled by Muslim clerics known as Khojas.
(*See chronology under* Western Turkestan.)

Chaldean Empire (BABYLONIA)

Champa (3rd–17th cents.; Vietnam)

Champa, in central Vietnam, seceded from Chinese-dominated northern VIETNAM and had a separate existence from the 3rd to the 17th cent. The original capital of Champa was established in the vicinity of Hue, but it was later moved south. The Chams, as the people of Champa are known, were of Malay stock. Their culture was indianized, as was that of CAMBODIA. There existed a kingom called Champa in VEDIC INDIA. Much of Champa's history is that of its struggles with its Khmer and Vietnamese neighbours. In the late-12th cent. Champa sacked Angkor, the capital of CAMBODIA, but it later came under Khmer domination, which traditionally extended to the Mekong Delta. During the 15th cent. Champa extended its authority as far as southern Tonkin, but its continuous struggling on two fronts finally led to its division and absorption by Tonkin in the 17th cent.

Champassak (LAOS)

Chenla (CAMBODIA)

Chichimecs (MESOAMERICAN CIVILIZATIONS)

Chieng Mai (THAILAND)

Chile
The coast of Chile was sighted by Magellan in 1520 during the first circumnavigation of the globe. Spain claimed the territory, where, in 1541, Valdivia founded Santiago. During the colonial period Chile was attached to the viceroyalty of Peru until it was made a captaincy general in 1778, dependent directly on Spain (SPANISH COLONIAL EMPIRE). Chilean independence began in 1810, after the French usurpation of the Spanish throne in 1808, under the leadership of Juan Martinez de Rozas, who was joined by Jose Miguel Carrera and Bernardo O'Higgins. In 1814, the patriots were defeated in the Battle of Rancagua by forces sent from Peru. The patriots took refuge in Mendoza, Argentina, where a combined army of Chileans and Argentines, led by O'Higgins and the Argentine general Jose de San Martin, crossed the Andes and defeated the Spanish forces in the Battle of Chacabuco. In 1818, after the victory of Maipú, O'Higgins formally declared Chile independent. With Chilean support, San Martin entered Lima in 1820, where the Spanish forces had fled to the interior. The territory under independent Chile's authority comprised mostly what today is central Chile. In 1847, Chileans founded Punta Arenas, which gave them control of the northern shore of the strait of Magellan. They shared Tierra del Fuego with Argentina, who obtained the eastern part of the island. From 1879 to 1884, Chile fought a war against Bolivia and Peru over the phosphate deposits (avian dung) in the Atacama Desert as a result of which it acquired Antofagasta (from Bolivia), Iquique (from Peru), and their respective hinterlands. The possession of Arica, on the Peruvian border, was not defined until 1929 when Chilean sovereignty was recognized, although Peru obtained the right to use port facilities. In 1902 Chile delimited its Andean frontier with Argentina. The famous Easter Island (Isla de Pascua), geographically and culturally Polynesian, has belonged to Chile since 1888. In 1940 Chile declared a legal claim on a wedge of Antarctica between the 53rd and the 90th west meridians (Chilean Antarctic Territory), overlapping with claims by the British.

Chin (Jin) (JURCHEN)

Ch'in (Qin) (3rd cent. BC; *China*)
The political disunity of the WARRING STATES period ended with the triumph of Ch'in, a state in the north west that had its capital in Xian (Sian) and gave China its name. The ruler of Ch'in called himself Ch'in Shih Huang Ti (Qin Shi Huang Di). Huang Ti means emperor and he is considered the first emperor of China. His rule was materially beneficent but culturally and politically despotic. He centralized the kingdom and expanded its territory to

Zhejiang (Chekiang) and Guangdong (Kwantung). He built walls and defended and expanded the western frontier with the YÜEH-CHIH. He also tried to wipe out the past by burning books, and was accompanied in his incredible underground mausoleum by an army of thousands of realistic, life-size clay figures. Ch'in Shih Huang Ti died in 210 BC. His dynasty succumbed four years later to the HAN.

(*See chronology under* China and Neighbouring Areas.)

China

SEE ENTRY IN 'PROVINCES AND REGIONS'

When the CH'ING (QING) dynasty was forced to abdicate in 1912, China entered a period of prolonged turmoil and uncertainty. Its sovereignty in tatters, the new republic, proclaimed by Sun Yat-sen, founder of the nationalist Kuomintang party, and presided over by Yüan Shih-K'ai, a former imperial official, until 1916, could hardly control its own territory, let alone far away provinces such as Manchuria or Tibet. In 1914, the Japanese occupied Shantung on the pretext of taking over German concessions, although they did later evacuate the province (1922). From 1916, China was prey to separatist warlords and MANCHURIA was effectively out of its sphere until 1929, when the local warlord acceded to fly the flag of the nationalist government in Nanjing (Nanking). After Sun's death in 1925, Chiang Kai-shek became the leader of Kuomintang and tried both to unify China and suppress the communists in their rural bases in Hunan, from where, under the leadership of Mao Zedong, they initiated the Long March which culminated in their occupation of territories near Xian, in Shaanxi (Shensi) province. In 1931 the Japanese occupied Mukden (Shenyang) and the following year set up the puppet kingdom of Manchukuo with the Ch'ing heir Pu Yi as its nominal head.

COMMUNIST CHINA

A virtual state of war existed between China and JAPAN from 1931. At the height of its occupation, Japan controlled the coast of China and territories as far inland as Hubei (Hupeh) and Shanxi (Shansi), which were evacuated in 1945. Manchuria was over-run by the communists who, by 1949, had control of China. The last nationalist forces took refuge in TAIWAN. The new masters of China re-established authority all over its territory, which was basically what the Manchus had accumulated during the rule of their Ch'ing dynasty. In 1951 Chinese troops invaded Tibet. In 1962 China attacked along its frontiers with India to recover territories BRITISH INDIA had annexed in Ladakh in 1846 and in Assam during 1913–1914.

In 1978 China and VIETNAM were briefly at war, possibly over Cambodia. Hong Kong reverted to China in 1997. Macao is the last of the European enclaves to do so. Beijing claims Taiwan and has stated its disposition to go to war if ever the island declared its independence. The capital of the Chinese

republic, Nanjing (Nanking), in Jiangsu (Kiangsu), was taken by the Japanese and brutally ravaged in 1937. The capital had been moved to Chongqing (Chungking), in Sichuan (Szechwan), from where in 1945 it was moved again to Nanjing. The communists established the capital in Beijing (Peking) and captured Nanjing in 1949. China and the United States established full diplomatic relations in 1979. Shortly after, China joined the United Nations and occupied the seat in the Security Council formerly filled by Taiwan as successor state of Nationalist China. China is the most populous country in the world.
(*See chronology under* China and Neighbouring Areas *and* Greater Mongolia.)

China and neighbouring areas

23rd–18th cents. BC	***1st cent. AD***	***5th cent.***
Hsia	Han I	Period of disunity
	Hsin	(after Han)
18th–12th cents. BC	Han II	Juan-juan
Shang	Hsiung-nu	Uigurs
	Korea	Korea
12th–5th cents. BC		Japan
Chou	***2nd cent. AD***	Champa
	Han II	
5th–4th cents. BC	Hsiung-nu	***6th cent.***
Warring States	Hsien-pi	Period of disunity
Hsiung-nu	Korea	(after Han)
Yüeh-chih		Sui
		T'ang
3rd cent. BC	***3rd cent.***	Juan-juan
Warring States	Han II	Tu-chüeh
Ch'in (Qin)	Three Kingdoms	Uigurs
Han I	Hsiung-nu	Korea
Hsiung-nu	Hsien-pi	Japan
Yüeh-chih	Korea	Champa
	Champa	
2nd cent. BC		***7th–8th cents.***
Han I	***4th cent.***	T'ang
Hsiung-nu	Three Kingdoms	Khitan Khanate
Yüeh-chih	Period of disunity	Tu-chüeh
	(after Han)	Hsi-Hsia
1st cent. BC	Juan-juan	Tibet
Han I	Uigurs	Nan Chao
Hsin	Korea	Korea
Hsiung-nu	Champa	Japan
Korea		Champa

Cambodia
Sri Vijaya

9th cent.
T'ang
Khitan Khanate
Hsi-Hsia
Tibet
Nan Chao
Korea
Japan
Champa
Cambodia
Sri Vijaya

10th cent.
T'ang
Period of disunity
   (after T'ang)
Sung (Song)
Khitan Khanate
Hsi-Hsia
Tibet
Nan Chao
Korea
Japan
Vietnam
Champa
Cambodia
Sri Vijaya

11th–12th cents.
Sung
Khitan Khanate
Hsi-Hsia
Jurchen
Tibet
Nan Chao
Korea
Japan
Vietnam
Champa
Cambodia

Sri Vijaya
Myanmar

13th cent.
Sung
Hsi-Hsia
Mongol Empire/Yuan
Tibet
Nan Chao
Korea
Japan
Vietnam
Champa
Cambodia
Sri Vijaya
Majapahit Empire
Thailand
Myanmar

14th cent.
Mongol Empire/
   Yuan
Ming
Mongolia
Chagataite Khanate
Tibet
Korea
Japan
Vietnam
Champa
Cambodia
Majapahit Empire
Thailand
Myanmar
Laos

15th cent.
Ming
Mongolia
Chagataite Khanate
Tibet
Korea
Japan

Vietnam
Champa
Cambodia
Majapahit Empire
Malacca
Laos
Thailand
Myanmar

16th cent.
Ming
Mongolia
Chagataite Khanate
Tibet
Korea
Japan
Vietnam
Cambodia
Laos
Thailand
Myanmar
Iberian colonial
   possessions

17th cent.
Ming
Manchus/Ch'ing
Mongolia
Tibet
Korea
Japan
Vietnam
Cambodia
Thailand
Laos
Myanmar
European colonial
   empires

18th cent.
Ch'ing
Russia
Tibet

Japan	**_19th cent._**	Myanmar
Korea	Ch'ing	British India
Vietnam	Russia	European colonial
Cambodia	Japan	empires
Thailand	Korea	
Myanmar	Vietnam	
European colonial	Cambodia	
empires	Thailand	

Ch'ing (Qing) (17th–20th cents.; _China_)

The Khitai were Mongol nomads in Jehol who, in the 10th cent., destroyed the Tungus-Korean kingdom of PO HAI. The Khitai founded a large empire in northern China called Liao (9th–12th cents.) (KHITAN KHANATE). It was destroyed by the JURCHEN, who were Mongols related to the Khitai. The Jurchen in turn founded their own Chin (Jing) dynasty in northern China (12th–13th cents.), which was destroyed by Kublai Khan (YUAN). The Jurchen or Khitai of Jehol became vassals of the Mongols. After the fall of Yuan China and during the virtual disintegration of MONGOLIA, this people, now called Manchu, created a military kingdom centred on Mukden (today's Shenyang) between 1606 and 1626. Aware of Ming political decadence, they conquered the Ordos and annexed Inner Mongolia in 1635. A Ming general thought he could use them to further his own ambitions but once the Manchus entered Beijing (1644) they set aside the Chinese and proclaimed their own Ch'ing dynasty. They conquered Nanjing (Nanking) in 1645 and Guangzhou (Canton) in 1651.

THE CONQUEST OF TAIWAN

In 1683, the Manchus reconquered Taiwan from a holdout Ming general who had taken it in 1662. Around 1690, all of Mongolia accepted vassalage to Beijing, thus ending the Mongol threat. At the end of the 17th cent., KOREA was a tributary kingdom of China. In 1720, the Manchu occupied Lhasa and made TIBET another vassal state. In 1759, China finally annexed the Tarim Basin, thus putting an end to centuries of dispute. By 1760, Ch'ing China's sovereignty was spread directly or indirectly from eastern Siberia to Lake Balkash down to Tibet and east to Vietnam. In addition, China had political influence on all south-east Asian states on its frontiers. However, the garrisoning and control was uneven and, by the time of the fall of the Ch'ing dynasty (1912), China had lost to Russia its claims to Balkash and to eastern Siberia. In fact, China had been so weak during the 19th cent. that it could not prevent the Western powers from forcing it to open ports, lease territories, and cede sovereignty in different ways. As a result of the Opium wars, in 1839–1842 and 1856–1860 – so-called because British aggression was provoked by Chinese destruction in Guangzhou of opium brought in from British India – Chinese ports were opened willy-nilly to international trade. Foreigners were also given sovereign rights in parts of the 'treaty ports', of which Shanghai was paradigmatic. In 1859 the British and French occupied Beijing and torched the imperial summer residence. With the rise of Western colonialism, Chinese peripheral political influence was totally eclipsed. JAPAN, which had modernized its economy if not its society and politics in a few decades, took Taiwan (1895) and Korea (1910).

Mongolia, which had remained loyal to the Ch'ing since the 17th cent., went its own way with Russia's blessing upon the fall of the dynasty in 1912. Dynastic China was followed by a weak and divided republic (CHINA). The last Ch'ing emperor, Pu Yi, was installed by the Japanese as king in Machukuo. Ch'ing was the last Chinese imperial dynasty. Like the Mongol Yuan dynasty (the Manchus spoke a language of the same family as Mongol), they discriminated against the Chinese – it was the Manchus who made them use the queue – but they brought order and discipline, mixed their customs with those of the Chinese, and had a driving sense of the destiny of China.
(*See chronologies under* China and Neighbouring Areas *and* Greater Mongolia.)

Cholas (SOUTHERN INDIA)

Chou (Zhou) (12th–3rd cents. BC; northern *China*)
More than to a dynasty, Chou, the successor of SHANG, refers to a long age with three periods: Western Chou period (1121–771 BC), Spring and Autumn period (771–484 BC), and the period of the WARRING STATES (484–221 BC). The shared reference for all three periods is the fortunes of Chou – for there was always a Chou king – from 'golden age' (according to Confucius) through the growth of the power of feudal lords (Spring and Autumn) to its demise (Warring States). Archaeology is necessary to gather knowledge of Western Chou, but the following two periods are definitely documented, even though the chronicles of this time survive only in transcriptions from the HAN period. The area of China during the first period of the Chou age was approximately what it was during Shang, but in the Spring and Autumn period it extended south of the Yangtze. There is mention of the Chou capital, near today's Xian (Sian), being sacked by barbarians from the north. It was moved later to Loyang. The Warring States marked a definite territorial expansion, which is one reason they are dealt with separately. Confucius lived in the Spring and Autumn period.
(*See chronology under* China and Neighbouring Areas.)

Cimmerians (13th–8th cents. BC; *Southern Russia*)
The Cimmerians were Indo-European-speakers who dominated the steppes north of the Black Sea from the 13th to the 8th cents. BC. They were displaced

by the SCYTHIANS and, moving south, ravaged PHRYGIA and were absorbed by LYDIA.
(*See chronology under* Southern Russia.)

Ciskei (20th cent.; South Africa)

Ciskei is a Bantustan or tribal homeland created in 1961 within Cape Province by South Africa as part of its former Apartheid policy. Nominally sovereign, it was incorporated, along with the other homelands, into South Africa in 1994. The capital of Ciskei is Bisho.

Colombia

The territory of Colombia was claimed by Spain early in the 16th cent. and named Nueva Granada (New Granada). The capital, Bogotá, was founded by Jimenez de Quesada in 1538. Nueva Granada was made a viceroyalty in 1717. The Colombian independentist movement had its inception in the municipal councils, whose members were called *comuneros*. Antonio Nariño led the *comuneros* of Bogotá in rejecting Spanish rule in 1810. But royalist arms prevailed until general Simon Bolivar entered the country from the plains of Venezuela and defeated them in the Battle of Boyacá in 1819 with the support of the Colombian general Santander. Bolivar then proclaimed the Republic of Gran Colombia, to which Venezuela adhered in 1821 and Ecuador in 1822. Gran Colombia was dissolved in 1830 with the defections of Venezuela and Ecuador. Colombia initially reverted to the name of New Granada, but in 1863 adopted the name of Colombia. After the Colombian congress refused to ratify a treaty with the United States for the construction of a canal across the isthmus of Panama, then a Colombian province, Panama declared its independence under considerable external influence (1903). American warships prevented the intervention of Colombian troops. The much-disputed Colombian frontier with Venezuela was subject to arbitration by the Spanish monarchy and delimited *in situ* in the early 20th cent.

Colonial Empires (15th–20th cents.)

There have been colonies since the beginning of civilization, but colonial empires – possession of far-flung territories and peoples by one metropolitan state – were a European creation. The Portuguese started the first true colonial empire when they began to sail down the western coast of Africa, establishing outposts along the way. Colonial empires were bound to rise in one way or another because they served to fill either total or relative vacuums of power. This could only be done from strength. The Spaniards sailed westward and conquered a huge land empire in the western hemisphere. Although arguably the conquest of Ireland was the first feat of colonialist imperialism, the British began building their empire relatively late, and it was initially more a colonizing than a colonial empire. The Portuguese enterprise was essentially commercial and Lisbon was for a time the richest city in Europe. Portugal's political weakness – it was annexed by Spain from 1580 to 1640 – allowed others to follow the maritime routes it explored. The Dutch went where the Portuguese had been, usually taking over from them. The French, by design or coincidence, competed with the British in the same areas (northern America, the Caribbean, India, Africa) in the same periods.

We know the past of many regions of the world from the reports of European empire builders, just as the Chinese are the primary source of knowledge on the lands surrounding their kingdom. Every remote coastline has harboured enclaves of local sovereignties. We know this to be the case of Africa, the Red Sea, the Persian or Arabian Gulf, Makran, Malabar (western India), Coromandel (eastern India), Myanmar, Malaya, and the East Indies, because Western traders sailed up and down their shores, often assigned them names, and mentioned even the tiniest and most insignificant of statelets, although Arab travellers also made important contributions in this respect. Even when left to their own devices, such places are part of the history of the colonial empires.

The paroxysm of colonialism was the Berlin Conference (1884–1885), where Africa was portioned out, old colonial claims were acknowledged, and the Germans got their modest place under the colonialist sun. The last two colonial empires to be built were those of Italy and Japan.

Germany lost its colonial possessions after World War I, and Japan and Italy after World War II. Spain lost America in the early 19th cent. It lingered as a minor colonial power until it evacuated Western Sahara in 1979. After losing Indonesia (1949) and Surinam (1975), the Dutch retain dependent bits and pieces in the Caribbean, none of which seem too keen on independence. The British and French divested themselves of their empires mostly in the 1950s and 1960s. The last to give in to massive decolonization were the Portuguese (1975).

Commagene (2nd–1st cents. BC; *Anatolia*)

The Kingdom of Commagene was an offshoot of the Seleucid Empire, although its founder was named Ptolemy. The capital was at Samosata. All that remain of it are impressive stone sculptures of the heads of its rulers. An ally of Rome, Commagene was suppressed by Marc Antony in 38 BC for siding with the Parthians.

Commonwealth of Independent States

Founded in Minsk, the capital of Belarus, in 1991, the Commonwealth of Independent States has as its objective the cooperation in all areas between former republics of the USSR. It was founded by Russia, Belarus, and Ukraine and eventually joined by Armenia, Azerbaijan, Kazakhstan, Kyrgyzstan, Moldova, Tajikistan, Turkmenistan, and Uzbekistan.

Commonwealth of Nations

A purely consultative organization constituted by former dependencies of Great Britain, the Commonwealth of Nations was created under the Statute of

Westminster, promulgated in 1931 in London, by which the independence of the dominions was recognized through the abrogation of colonial laws which could infringe on their sovereignty. Its original members were Great Britain, Ireland, Australia, Canada, Newfoundland, New Zealand, and South Africa, but not colonies, protectorates, or other dependencies. It was intended that the strongest bond between all its members would be allegiance to the British Crown, but in practice many of them have opted for republican status. Ireland, known as the Irish Free State, became the Republic of Ireland in 1949 and withdrew from the Commonwealth. So did South Africa in 1961 and Pakistan in 1972.

Comoros

During the 19th cent. the Indian Ocean islands of Comoros were ruled by local sultans. In 1909 they became a French colony. In 1975 Comoros became independent, except for the island of Mayotte, which chose to remain French. The waters off Comoros yielded the *coelacanth*, the only 'living fossil' known. The capital of Comoros is Moroni in Grande Comore. French is the official language. Swahili is a lingua franca used also in east Africa.

Confederate States of America (19th cent.; *United States*)

The issue of slavery divided the United States – legal in the southern American states, illegal in the north, contested west of the Mississippi – and in 1861 caused the secession from the Union of the pro-slavery states of Alabama, Arkansas, Florida, Georgia, Louisiana, Mississippi, North Carolina, South Carolina, Tennessee, Texas, and Virginia, which formed the Confederate States of America, with its capital in Richmond, Virginia. Jefferson Davies was chosen to be President. West Virginia separated from Virginia and was admitted as a State of the Union in 1863. Abraham Lincoln was President of the United States. At first the war favoured the South under the military leadership of General Robert E. Lee, but from the start the North controlled the sea and had more population and industrial capacity. The military fortunes of the Confederacy were set back in the Battle of Gettysburg, in southern Pennsylvania, in July 1863. Earlier the same year, Lincoln had decreed the abolition of slavery. Under the command of General U. S. Grant, the Union forces, which were stalemated in the east, advanced in the west down the Mississippi River, culminating in the siege of Vicksburg, Mississippi, in 1863. Grant was named Chief of the Union Armies in 1864. In a 'war-is-hell' campaign, General Sherman gutted the south in Georgia. Early in 1865, the Confederate situation was desperate – Richmond was evacuated – and Lee surrendered to Grant in April of that year. The Confederate States of America went unrecognized by any other nation during its brief existence.

Confederation of the Rhine (FRENCH EUROPEAN EMPIRE; BAVARIA)

Congo (Democratic Republic of the)

Inhabited by divided Bantu-speaking peoples, many of whom were pygmies, the territory of the Democratic Republic of Congo was claimed by Leopold II, King of Belgium, as his personal fief. It was recognized in the conference of BERLIN (1884–1885) as the Congo Free State. Transferred to Belgium in 1901, the Belgian Congo became independent in 1960, capital Leopoldville, later renamed Kinshasa. From 1960 to 1964, the country nearly came unglued, mainly because of the secessionist mineral-rich south-eastern province of Katanga (now-called Shaba), and its unity was restored through the efforts of the UN and the intervention of foreign mercenaries. In 1971 its name was changed to Zaire but in 1998 changed again to Congo. The subjection of Katanga established the international understanding in Africa that secessions from established nations were not to be encouraged. Ironically, it is Congo again that is being threatened by dismemberment through a civil war in which other African countries are actively participating.

Congo (Republic of the)

Peopled by disunited Bantu-speaking tribes, Congo was a French colony from 1885, part of French Equatorial Africa (FRENCH COLONIAL EMPIRE). It gained its independence in 1960. The capital is Brazzaville, named after one of the principal builders of the French empire in Africa.

Congo Free State (BELGIAN COLONIAL EMPIRE)

Córdoba (Caliphate of) (8th–11th cents.; *Spain*)

A survivor of the massacre of the Umayyads by the Abbasids in Damascus in 750 (ABBASID CALIPHATE) went to MUSLIM SPAIN and established an emirate in Córdoba in 756, which was proclaimed a caliphate – a political title with theocratic implications – in 929. From the start, Córdoba ruled over all of Muslim Iberia, which at the time embraced the entire territory of Spain and Portugal except for pockets of resistance in ASTURIAS and the Pyrenees. In the 10th cent., Córdoba invaded Morocco and western Algeria, which it disputed with the FATIMIDS, an Algerian Shia dynasty. In Spain Córdoba broke up into the myriad Taifa kingdoms in 1031 and the ALMORAVIDS took Fez in 1056. In 1078, Córdoba itself fell to the rival Taifa kingdom of Seville. The most renowned Umayyad ruler of Córdoba was Abd dar-Rahman III, who reigned from 912 to 961, recovered the fortunes of his kingdom at a time when it was beset by its neighbours, and assumed the title of caliph in defiance of the Abbasids.

(See chronology under *Maghreb*.)

Corinth (ACHAEN LEAGUE; MACEDON; PELOPONNESIAN LEAGUE)

Corinthian League (Ancient GREECE; MACEDON)

Costa Rica

After being part of the SPANISH COLONIAL EMPIRE (16th–19th cents.) and of the Mexican Empire (1821–1823), Costa Rica joined the CENTRAL AMERICAN FEDERATION until its dissolution in 1838. Its border with Nicaragua has undergone minor modifications. The capital of Costa Rica is San José, founded ca. 1738.

Côte d'Ivoire

A French colony from 1842, constituted by the territories of many different tribes – 70 languages of the west African Niger–Congo group are spoken there today – Côte d'Ivoire was part of French West Africa until its independence in 1960 (FRENCH COLONIAL EMPIRE). The capital of Côte d'Ivoire is Yamoussoukro. French is the official language.

Cracow (POLAND)

Crete (3rd mil. BC–20th cent. AD; *Greece*)

Crete was the home of the MINOAN CIVILIZATION (3rd mil.–16th BC). The latter was destroyed by MYCENEAN GREECE, which in turn succumbed to invasions of indistinct provenance ca. 1200 BC. The Greek dark ages followed, after which Crete was a politically inactive region of ancient Greece. In 67 BC, it was conquered by ROME. After AD 395 it was part of the Roman Empire in the east (BYZANTINE EMPIRE). It was an Arab emirate from 824 until it was retaken by the Byzantines in 961. In 1204 it was occupied by the Venetians who called it Candia (VENICE). In 1669 Crete was conquered by the OTTOMAN EMPIRE, but its population remained wholly Greek. In 1897, the Cretans rebelled against Turkish rule provoking a war between GREECE and the Ottoman Empire, which the Greeks were losing when the European powers intervened and ended the hostilities. The Turkish garrison in Crete was forced to leave and a European protectorate was established over an autonomous Crete. The Cretan government under Venizelos chose union with Greece, made possible in 1909, when the Western powers terminated their occupation during the Young Turks' military rebellion in Istambul (TURKEY). Iraklion is the modern capital of Crete.

Crimea (Khanate of) (15th–18th cents.; *Southern Russia*)

The Khanate of the Crimea was an offshoot of the GOLDEN HORDE founded ca. 1430. The OTTOMAN EMPIRE occupied its coast towards the end of the 15th cent. In 1783 it was wholly absorbed by Russia.
(*See chronology under* Southern Russia.)

Croatia

The slavs peopled Croatia in the 7th cent. They established a kingdom in the 10th cent. and occupied the Dalmatian coast which led to constant rivalry with

VENICE. In 1091 Croatia was absorbed by HUNGARY. In 1526 the OTTOMAN EMPIRE conquered most of Croatia, but the HABSBURG EMPIRE contested Turkish rule and the Croatians gradually came under Austrian sovereignty, decisively after the last siege of Vienna (1683). After 1867, Croatia was placed under the administration of the Hungarian kingdom in the Austro-Hungarian Dual Monarchy. After World War I, Croatia joined the kingdom of the Serbs, Croats, and Slovenes, later Yugoslavia (1929). In 1941, Croatia became a fascist vassal state of Nazi Germany. In 1945, it joined communist Yugoslavia as a federal republic and in 1991 it declared its independence. Zagreb is the capital of Croatia. Though an independent state, Bosnia-Herzegovina is divided into irregular halves, one of which is administered by a federation of Croats and native Muslims.

Istria is a peninsula in western Croatia, principal city Rijeka (Italian Fiume), which Italy occupied after World War I. After World War II it was awarded to Croatia. Slavonia is the region of eastern Croatia. Croatia occupies most of ancient Illyria, which is the hinterland of the Dalmatian coast. Krajina means borderland and that is exactly what it was inside the frontier of the Habsburg Empire with the Ottoman Empire. Krajina defined the area of Austrian penetration of the Balkans since the mid-18th cent. As Ottoman power gave ground to Serbian nationalism, this border was infringed when Austria annexed Bosnia-Herzegovina in 1908, setting the stage for World War I. Today Krajina is inside the border of Croatia with Serbia.

Crusader States (11th–16th cents.; *Near East*)
When Christian armies invaded the near east in their Crusade to save Jerusalem from the Seljuks (1096), the first states they created were Antioch, today's Antakya, in Turkey, including the coast of Syria, and Edessa (southeastern Turkey), both in 1098. The Crusaders also sponsored the creation of ARMENIA MINOR on the coast of south-eastern Anatolia. The kingdom of Jerusalem, formed after the fall of the city in 1099 and which at its peak extended as far south as the gulf of Aqaba (Red Sea), absorbed Antioch and Edessa. The Christian state of Tripoli was founded in what today is northern Lebanon in 1102. Antioch separated from Jerusalem in 1130 and Edessa was lost to the Muslims in 1146. In 1187, Jerusalem fell to Saladin, the Ayyubid sultan of Egypt and perhaps the greatest Kurd in history, reducing the Crusader States to Antioch and the coastal fortresses of Tripoli, Tyre, and Acre. In 1229, Jerusalem was acquired by treaty but fell definitely in 1244. Antioch fell to the Seljuks in 1268 and Tripoli in 1289. In 1291, Acre was taken, leading to withdrawal from Tyre, Beirut, and Sidon. After the fall of these fortresses, CYPRUS was taken by the Knights of St John (Knights Hospitallers) from the BYZANTINE EMPIRE in 1291. They later removed to RHODES, also snatched from the Byzantines (1310), where they were known as the Knights of Rhodes and stayed until 1522, when the OTTOMAN EMPIRE replaced

them. Armenia Minor, which was not strictly a Crusader State, lasted until 1375. Cyprus remained in Christian hands until 1571.

THE CRUSADES

In all, there were nine Crusades and one 'Children's Crusade'. They were military expeditions to recover Jerusalem for Christianity. The First Crusade (1095–1099) was instigated by Pope Urban II. Its most famous leaders were Godfrey of Bouillon – whose brother Baldwin became King of Jerusalem – and Tancred. The most important Crusader States were founded during the First Crusade. The following Crusades were expeditions to sustain the Crusader States. The Second Crusade (1147–1149) was preached by Bernard of Clairvaux and led by Holy Roman Emperor Conrad III and King Louis VII of France. The Third Crusade (1189–1192) was promoted by Pope Gregory VIII and led by Richard I of England – the famous Lionheart – Philip II of France, and Holy Roman Emperor Frederick I Barbarossa. This was the Crusade that Saladin opposed. Its defeat was decisive for Islam. The Fourth Crusade (1202–1204) became infamous as the sack of Constantinople and the creation of the LATIN STATES. The Children's Crusade was in 1212. The volunteers were either sold as slaves or died from hunger and disease. During the Fifth Crusade (1217–1221) the port of Damietta in Egypt was briefly taken. The Sixth Crusade (1228–1229) ended in a truce with the Muslims obtained by Holy Roman Emperor Frederick II to permit Christian pilgrimages to Jerusalem. The truce was not observed. The Seventh Crusade (1248–1254) was the personal doing of Louis IX the Saint, who also captured Damietta. The subsequent fall of Antioch led to the abortive Eighth Crusade of 1270. The Ninth Crusade was purely English, led by Prince Edward (later Edward I of England), and ended in a truce after which Acre fell in 1291, the last Crusader State in the Levant.

Cuba

Visited by Columbus in 1492, Cuba was quickly colonized and its Amerindian inhabitants mostly died. Havana was founded by Diego de Velasquez in 1515. It was the main staging port for the convoys that plied Spanish–American trade until the 17th cent. Havana was occupied by British forces from 1762 to 1763, when it was returned to Spain by treaty. During the wars for independence in the rest of Latin America (1810–1824), Spain kept a firm hold on Cuba and Puerto Rico, which became refuges for loyalists. Subsequently, Spain refused Cuba any form of self-government and in 1868 a rebellion started which concluded with a truce whose terms the Spaniards ignored. Spain only got around to abolishing slavery, which was a demand of the independentists, in 1886. In 1895, another rebellion began under the leadership of the writer Jose Marti, who was killed in combat. In a state of insurrection, Cuba was taken from Spain by the United States in 1898. American occupation lasted until 1902. The Platt Amendment, approved by Congress in 1901 authorizing American military intervention, was imposed on Cuba and invoked from 1906 to 1909 and in 1912 (to quell black protests against discrimination). It was abrogated in 1934 by the F. D. Roosevelt administration as part of its Good Neighbor policy towards Latin America. In 1903 the United States obtained rights to Guantanamo Bay and surrounding lands, which it still occupies. In 1959, an armed revolution triumphed in Cuba. Its leader, Fidel Castro, established a communist government.

Cumans (POLOVETZY)

Cyprus

Originally occupied by Phoenicia in the 9th cent. BC, Cyprus changed hands many times until it was conquered by ROME in 58 BC. In AD 395 it was part of the Roman Empire in the east. After the fall of the CRUSADER STATES in the Levant in 1291, Cyprus was taken from the BYZANTINE EMPIRE by the KNIGHTS OF ST JOHN and became one of the Crusader States. In 1489 it was occupied by VENICE who surrendered it to the OTTOMAN EMPIRE in 1571. In 1878, the British occupied the mostly Greek island and held it until 1960, when it became independent with a Turkish minority. Turkey invaded the north of Cyprus in 1974. In 1983, the Turks proclaimed the Turkish Republic of Northern Cyprus, which is recognized only by Turkey. Nicosia is the capital of both Cypriot states.

Cyprus (Turkish) (CYPRUS)

Czech and Slovak Federal Republic (CZECHOSLOVAKIA)

Czech Republic

In 1989, CZECHOSLOVAKIA shed its communist government. In 1990 it became the Czech and Slovak Federal Republic, which dissolved amicably in 1992 into the CZECH REPUBLIC and SLOVAKIA. The Czech Republic, whose capital is Prague, is constituted by the ancient realms of BOHEMIA and MORAVIA.

Czechoslovakia (20th cent.; eastern Europe)

Czechoslovakia was formed with BOHEMIA, MORAVIA, and SLOVAKIA. It was created from the dissolved HABSBURG EMPIRE after World War I (1918). In 1938, Hitler threatened war over the Sudetenland – the German-peopled borderlands of Bohemia with Germany and Austria – and as part of the policy of appeasement of the Western powers he was given the go-ahead in Munich to invade Czechoslovakia, which he dismembered into the protectorate of Bohemia and Moravia and the puppet state of Slovakia. After World War II there was some ethnic cleansing in the former Sudetenland, and Czechoslovakia was reconstituted with the loss of a tip of Slovakia in the

Carpathian mountains (Ruthenia), which gave it a border with Soviet Ukraine. In 1948, it became a communist state. It was invaded by its communist neighbours in 1968 to suppress the political reforms known as the Prague Spring. In 1989, protests very quickly resulted in the end of the communist regime. The following year Czechoslovakia became the CZECH AND SLOVAK FEDERAL REPUBLIC, which dissolved amicably in 1992 into the CZECH REPUBLIC and SLOVAKIA.

D

Dahomey (17th–19th cents.; *Sub-Saharan Africa*)
Neighbouring on ancient BENIN, in south-western Nigeria, Dahomey was an inland African kingdom in the territory of today's BENIN. It flourished on the slave trade. The British occupation of Lagos and adjoining coastlines in 1861 cut off Dahomey from the sea. It was annexed to the FRENCH COLONIAL EMPIRE until its independence as Benin.
(*See chronology under* Western and Sub-Saharan Africa.)

Dai Viet (VIETNAM)

Damascus (ISLAM; SELJUK EMIRATES)

Danzig (10th–20th cents.; eastern Europe)
Originally a Slavic settlement first mentioned in the late-10th cent., Danzig became the capital of Pomerelia (Poland). By the 13th cent. it had been settled by German merchants and became a member of the HANSEATIC LEAGUE. In 1466, Danzig became part of Poland, but in 1576 it was granted autonomy, which it defended until, in the second Polish partition, it went to PRUSSIA (1793). In 1807 Napoleon restored its status as free city, but in 1814 it reverted to Prussian rule. After World War I, it was transferred from Germany to Poland to give the latter access to the Baltic Sea. Nazi irredentism over Danzig and its corridor provoked the German invasion of Poland that started World War II. After the war it became Polish Gdansk.

Deccan Sultanates (BAHMANI KINGDOM; CENTRAL INDIA)

Delhi Sultanate (12th–16th cents.; *India*)
In 1173, Afghans from Ghur conquered Ghazni, forcing the GHAZNAVIDS to remove to Lahore, in the PUNJAB, which had been conquered by Mahmoud of Ghazni in the early 11th cent. The Ghaznavids were pursued and defeated by Muhammad of Ghur, who proceeded to annex the rest of northern India in successive victories over Hindu rajahs, in particular a decisive victory over the RAJPUTS. The GHURIDS conquered as far as BENGAL, where the Sena were destroyed. Muhammad had to return to Afghanistan, where he was defeated by his namesake, Muhammad of KHWARIZM, and the Ghurids lost Afghanistan. After Muhammad's death, his general, Qutb-ud-Din, held on to power in India and his successor, Iltutmish, founded the Muslim Delhi Sultanate in 1229. This was the first firm Islamic intrusion into India, which was to become permanent over the centuries, culminating in the conquests of Aurangzeb (MUGHAL EMPIRE). If Muslim rulers predominated politically

in NORTHERN INDIA until the establishment of BRITISH INDIA, culturally there was a stand off. Muslim India produced many artistic riches, but the general population was not converted just as the Muslims were not assimilated by the local Hindu culture.

ALA-UD-DIN

Ala-ud-Din ascended the throne of Delhi in 1296. In 1301 he annexed Gujarat (India) and in the following years inflicted defeats on the Rajputs. Ala-ud-Din had set his sights on the south, where he could capture war elephants. His first foray was against the Deccan (CENTRAL INDIA) where he subjected the Yadava. In 1304 a Delhian army sacked the city of Warangal in Andra Pradesh. In the loot was the famous diamond Koh-i-noor. In 1310 the kingdoms of the Hoysalas and the Pandyas were taken (SOUTHERN INDIA). The Mongols threatened the Sultanate in northern Pakistan and Ala-ud-Din also dealt with them. Genghis Khan had garrisoned Punjab in 1221 (MONGOL EMPIRE) and in 1279 forces from the Mongol CHAGATAITE KHANATE came back and were defeated by then Sultan Balban of Delhi. Under Khan Duwa the Mongols returned in 1297 and thereafter repeatedly invaded northern India. On at least two occasions, in 1299 and in 1303, the Mongols came in strength, but were either frustrated – they took Delhi in 1303 but could not consolidate their hold on the Sultanate – or defeated, repeatedly by Ala-ud-Din. The Chagataite raids continued until 1327 but the Mongols were never able to annex any Indian territory for long. Ala-ud-Din died in 1316. His descendants could not hold on to power and in 1320 the Tughluq dynasty took the Sultanate. Its founder, Ghiyas-ud-Din, was killed in an accident simulated by his son, Muhammad Tughluq. By then the peripheral provinces of Delhi, such as Warangal and Bengal, had been steering their own courses.

THE SULTAN AND THE EXECUTIONER

Muhammad Tughluq was at first a successful conqueror, but he wanted to subjugate his neighbours which, in the Indian tradition, were usually made vassals with a good deal of autonomy. He tried to move the capital from Delhi to a more central position in India, near Aurangabad, but the enterprise proved ruinous and was much resented. After Muhammad abandoned this project and returned to Delhi, the vassal territories started falling away: Bengal in 1338, Vijayanagara in the south in 1346, the BAHMANI SULTANATE in the Deccan in 1347. Towards the end, Muhammad started inventing grandiose campaigns to central Asia that were beyond his resources. He became a paranoid tyrant walking about with his executioner, as the Arab Traveller Ibn Batuta related. In 1351, Muhammad was succeeded by Firoz Shah, a builder of mosques, but after him, in 1388, the Sultanate began to go to pieces. Delhi's immediate downfall, however, was its conquest by Tamerlane, whose troops

caused havoc in 1389. For a while Delhi was practically uninhabited. In 1414 a new dynasty was installed briefly. After 1451, the Sultanate was revitalized by the Lodi sultans from Afghanistan, who again united the lands of the Ganges Basin. Agra was built as a capital by one of the Lodi. Delhi was conquered in 1526 by Babur, founder of the Mughal Empire.
(*See chronology under* Indian Subcontinent.)

Delian League (5th cent. BC; Ancient *Greece*)
The Delian League of Greek city–states was formed in 478 BC by Athens, other mainland allies of Athens, and the Greek cities of Ionia against the ACHAEMENID EMPIRE, which, since 500 BC, had been trying to conquer Greece. After 468 BC, Athens turned it into what many consider an Athenian Empire, for Athenian power could prevent members from leaving the League and imposed policies on them, including coinage. Thebes was inducted forcibly in 456 BC. Athenian power was broken utterly by Sparta and the PELOPONNNESIAN LEAGUE at the end of the Peloponnesian War (431–404 BC). Athens created another League in 378 BC, but Thebes withdrew in 371 BC and in 338 BC Macedon conquered all in Greece.
(*See chronology under* Greece (Ancient).)

Denmark
Denmark was Christianized in the late 10th. cent. It extended south to Schleswig and included Scania, the region of southern Sweden. From 1018 to 1035, it was governed by Canute, the conqueror of ENGLAND, from where for a time he ruled his empire. It was in his reign that Denmark acquired hegemony over a very disunited Norway. Danish England fell to the house of Wessex in 1042. Denmark expanded into Germany and in 1220 it ruled Holstein, Lübeck, Hamburg, Pomerania, and Courland (Latvia), but by 1223 it had lost all its conquests and its influence in Norway was weakened. From 1319 Norway was united to Sweden, but after 1343 it fell again under Danish influence. The Scandinavian thrones were elective and in 1397, by the union of Kalmar, Denmark, Norway, and Sweden were united under the crown of Denmark in the person of Margaret I. The union with Sweden was not dissolved until 1523, but Sweden was self-ruling. Norway became part of Denmark. In 1656, Denmark lost Scania to Sweden.

SCHLESWIG AND HOLSTEIN

The relation of Denmark to Schleswig and Holstein is complex. In 1460, the Danish crown inherited the two provinces, with a preponderantly German population. In 1774, they were declared dynastic 'dependencies' of Denmark. Danish attempts to incorporate them into the kingdom eventually resulted in a process from 1864 to 1866 involving two wars – one between Prussia and Austria against Denmark and the Austro-Prussian War – whereby Prussia separated the two provinces from Denmark and incorporated them into the NORTH GERMAN CONFEDERATION. In 1871, they became part of Germany. In 1920, a plebiscite devolved mostly Danish northern Schleswig to Denmark. Schleswig-Holstein remained German and is today a state of the Federal Republic of Germany. In 1814, Denmark, which had accepted Napoleon's European order, was forced to cede Norway to Sweden. The Norse colonists of Greenland (10th cent.) died out during the 14th and 15th cents. Norwegians recolonized the island in the 18th cent. It is now an autonomous dependency of Denmark. Iceland, which had been Norwegian from the 13th cent., peacefully became independent from Denmark in 1918. Denmark acquired part of the Virgin Islands in the 17th cent., which it sold to the United States in 1917 for $25,000,000, the most the Americans ever paid for a piece of territory. The capital of Denmark is Copenhagen. Denmark became a member of EUROPEAN UNION in 1972.

Diadochi Wars (323–281 BC; Ancient *Greece* and *Near East*)
Upon the death of Alexander (323 BC), his principal generals engaged in a free-for-all over his empire, which was relatively intact but subject to strong disgregative forces (ALEXANDRIAN EMPIRE). After a long and complicated series of campaigns, battles, and sieges, by 301 BC it had been divided roughly into Thrace and Asia Minor to Lysimachus; MACEDON to Cassander; Egypt and southern Syria to Ptolemy; and Persia and the rest of Alexandrian Asia to Seleucus. Another contestant to the imperial succession, Demetrius, then took Athens and Macedon and eliminated Cassander. He, in turn, was defeated by an alliance of the other three, although Macedon later reverted to Demetrius' heirs (the Antigonids) until the Roman conquest (ROME). Seleucus then defeated Lysimachus in 281 BC, putting an end to the Diadochi Wars (SELEUCID EMPIRE; PTOLEMAIC EGYPT).
(*See chronologies under* Greece (Ancient) *and* Anatolia.)

Dilmun (3rd mil. BC; Bahrain)
Dilmun was an independent kingdom on the island of Bahrain ca. 2000 BC, although its foundation goes back some eight cents. before that. It is thought that it was a link in trade between SUMER and the INDUS RIVER VALLEY CIVILIZATION.

Djibouti
In 1862 France created the colony of French Somaliland, which in 1967 was declared the Territory of the Afars and Issas (FRENCH COLONIAL EMPIRE). As Djibouti, also the name of its capital, it became independent in 1977. Somali is a member of the Cushitic group of languages, related to Semitic.

Dominica

Fiercely defended by its Carib aborigines, the Caribbean island of Dominica was mostly in a wild state until it became a British colony from 1805 to 1978 (BRITISH COLONIAL EMPIRE). Dominica was part of the British Windward Islands from 1880 to 1958. The capital is Roseau.

Dominican Republic

Inhabited by Arawak Amerindians, the island of Hispaniola (La Española) was chosen by Columbus as the centre of Spanish power in the Caribbean, which he apparently thought was really the East Indies, although there weren't very many species about (SPANISH COLONIAL EMPIRE). The city of Santo Domingo was founded in 1496. It was the seat of the first Spanish high court (*audiencia*) for its American colonies. The western part of the island drifted out of Spanish control and became a French possession in 1697, known by the Arawak name of Haiti (land of mountains). In 1795, Spain ceded Santo Domingo to France. The native Haitians (mostly slaves) rose up and took the whole country in 1801. After 1802, a French expeditionary force was decimated by sickness and native harassment and in 1804 Haiti became independent. The French retained control of Santo Domingo. The British ejected the French and returned Santo Domingo to the Spaniards in 1809. In 1821, the Spaniards were expelled, but the Haitians invaded in 1822 and retained the entire island until 1844, when they were driven out and the Dominican Republic was created with approximately its present borders. In 1861, the local ruling class opted for Spanish rule which lasted until 1869. The Dominican elite tried unsuccessfully to have the republic annexed by the United States. In 1905, due to incessant disorder, the United States intervened informally but, in 1916, brought in the Marines who stayed in the Dominican Republic until 1924. The Americans intervened again in the 1960s to prevent a leftist takeover.

Dual Monarchy (HABSBURG EMPIRE)

Dubai (UNITED ARAB EMIRATES)

Durrani (AFGHANISTAN)

Dutch Colonial Empire (17th–20th cents.)

The Dutch followed the PORTUGUESE COLONIAL EMPIRE in their pursuit of the spice trade in the East Indies, but they were not distracted by evangelizing concerns. The Dutch East India Company was created in 1602. Its agents occupied Mauritius, founded Cape Colony (1652), and ousted the Portuguese from Ceylon and Malaya. These were basically steps to the East Indies, where the Dutch had ejected the Portuguese by 1610. From the company's headquarters in Batavia, Java, founded in 1619, the Dutch defended their claim in hostilities with Great Britain until 1623. The Dutch also ejected the Portuguese from Taiwan, but they were expelled in 1683 by the CH'ING (QING), who had recently conquered China. In Japan, after the Portuguese had been shut out from commerce because of their Christian proselytizing (1603), the Dutch obtained trade privileges in Kyushu, the only European nation to have access to Japan during the following two-and-a-half cents. In the western hemisphere, the Dutch occupied the coast of Guiana (1597–1616), founded New Amsterdam (1624), and took the island of Curaçao (1634), next door to the Spanish colony of Venezuela. New Amsterdam passed to the British in 1664 and was renamed New York. Peg-leg Peter Stuyvesant was successively mayor of New Amsterdam and governor of Curaçao. From 1624 to 1654, the Dutch intermittently occupied north-eastern Brazil, until their final expulsion by a Portuguese expedition from Rio de Janeiro.

INDONESIA

In 1799, the Dutch East India Company was dissolved and the Dutch East Indies transferred to the government of the Netherlands. By then the British were disputing Dutch possession of the Cape of Good Hope and Guiana. In 1806, the former was ceded to Great Britain and, as Cape Colony, would become the base for the formation of South Africa. In 1815, Dutch Guiana was shared out between Great Britain (the western part) and Dutch Surinam. Dutch claims to the Orinoco Delta would later give grounds for a border dispute between Great Britain and Venezuela. In the West Indies, the Dutch had added nearby Aruba and Bonaire to Curaçao. In 1632, they occupied Saba (the tip of an extinct volcano) and Sint Eustatius. In 1648, they shared out St Martin with France. During the 19th cent., there were outbursts of protest in the Dutch East Indies against harsh economic exploitation. The configuration of the Dutch East Indies was not finally determined until 1914, especially on the island of Timor where the Portuguese had remained since the 16th cent. The Japanese occupied the Dutch East Indies from 1942 to 1945 and gave scope to the movement for independence. In 1949, the Netherlands, who tried to reoccupy the East Indies against strong local resistance, recognized the independence of Indonesia. It retained the western part of New Guinea, which the Indonesians invaded in 1957. Suriname became independent in 1975. The islands in the Caribbean, which form the federated NETHERLANDS ANTILLES, are self-ruling but dependent. Aruba separated from the federation in 1986.

Dutch East India Company (DUTCH COLONIAL EMPIRE)

Dvaravati (7th–11th cents.; Thailand)
Founded by Mon people – linguistically related to the Cambodians – with its capital in Lop Buri, Thailand, Dvaravati was a Buddhist kingdom subjugated by Angkor (CAMBODIA). The Thais seized Lop Buri from the Mon-Khmer in the 13th cent.

Map 3   South east Asia

Dzungaria (17th–18th cents.; *Central Asia*: greater Mongolia)
Dzungaria is the region north of the Tien Shan Range (northern limit of the
Tarim Basin), today in China (Sinkiang) and Kazakhstan. When the Oirats or
western Mongols were driven by the Khalkas or eastern Mongols out of
Kobdo (east of Lake Balkash), a branch of the same people held out in the
Tarbagatai range (south east of Balkash), went south and occupied Lhasa in
Tibet, where they established an independent khanate in 1616 (MONGOLIA).
In 1677, other Oirats had established suzerainty over Kashgaria, then in the
hands of Muslim clerics known as Khojas, and seized the northern Tarim
Basin. It is this branch of the western Mongols which recaptured Kobdo
in 1690 from the divided Kublaids of the east. They proceeded to invade

Mongolia to the Kerulen River (eastern Mongolia), but were quickly ejected by the Khalkas with the help of the Manchus, who at that point made Mongolia their vassal (CH'ING). The territories of these Oirats became the khanate of Dzungaria, which, in 1717, absorbed Lhasa and, in 1718, had taken Tashkent from the KIRGHIZ-KAZAKHS. The vigorous Manchu, who did not want a reborn and threatening Mongol empire, ejected the Dzungars from Lhasa in 1720 and contained them in Dzungaria itself, although they recognized Dzungar sovereignty in Kashgaria (western Tarim). Finally, the persistent Manchu dispossessed the Dzungars of Dzungaria and took the entire Tarim Basin (1757–1759), thus putting an end to the power of the western Mongols.

E

East Germany (20th cent.; *Germany*)

It is as East Germany that the communist German Democratic Republic is usually known. After World War II, a defeated Germany was divided into four zones of occupation: the British, in the north; the American, in Bavaria and the south; the French, in the Rhineland; and the Soviet, comprising the present-day states of Mecklenburg-Pomerania, Brandenburg, Saxony-Anhalt, Thuringia, and Saxony. Within Brandenburg lay Berlin, which was also divided into four zones, one of which became the capital of East Germany. The eastern borders of pre-war Germany were considerably altered by the USSR, which annexed much of pre-war eastern Poland and ceded to it part of eastern Prussia, eastern Pomerania, and all of Silesia. It was with this truncated Germany that the Soviets in 1949 – after Western Germany (the other occupation zones) had been constituted as the Federal Republic of Germany – created the German Democratic Republic. The communist regime was so generally disliked – in 1953 there was a popular uprising against it – that it built a wall in Berlin in 1961 that divided the city and created a no-man's land where East German border guards could shoot to kill those trying to escape. But even border guards themselves risked their lives to flee to West Berlin. In 1991, during the process of the dismantling of communism and the USSR, initiated by Mikhail Gorbachev, the Federal Republic of Germany absorbed East Germany.

East Pakistan (BANGLADESH; PAKISTAN)

East Timor

Half of the East Indies island and former Portuguese colony (from the 16th cent.), East Timor was invaded by Indonesia in 1976 shortly after being given independence by Portugal. This move was greatly resented by the mainly Christian population. In the grip of political turmoil, Indonesia offered self-determination to East Timor and in September 1999, in a UN-sponsored referendum, a vast majority of the population rejected Indonesian rule. The Indonesian military wracked the country before reluctantly evacuating it. Dili is the East Timorese capital. East Timor has an enclave in Indonesian West Timor which is called Oecussi.

Ebla (3rd–2nd mils. BC; ancient *Near East*)

During the 3rd mil. BC Ebla was an important city–state south of Aleppo, Syria. It was destroyed by AKKAD ca. 2300 BC. It flourished again from ca. 2000 to ca. 1800 BC and probably fell to invading Semitic AMORITES. Thousands of cuneiform tablets from Ebla, discovered in 1973, have added

much to the history of the ancient world, including the first mention of Jerusalem.
(*See chronology under* Ancient Near East.)

Ecuador

The territory of Ecuador was the vassal kingdom of Quito in the INCA EMPIRE. The city was conquered for Spain by Benalcazar in 1534. During the SPANISH COLONIAL EMPIRE, Ecuador was a dependency of the vice-royalty of Peru. In 1563 it was constituted as a presidency. There was an unsuccessful independentist movement in 1809 and the country was finally freed of Spanish forces in the Battle of Pichincha by Colombian expeditionary forces led by Sucre in 1822. Bolivar incorporated the country into the newly-formed Republic of GRAN COLOMBIA, from which Ecuador seceded in 1830. In 1832 Ecuador occupied the Galapagos Islands. It claimed territories that extended along the Marañon River to the Amazon River as far as Brazil. These lands were also claimed by Peru, who affirmed its sovereignty over them in a short war in 1941. Eastern Ecuador was reduced to the Amazonian foothills of the Andes, where large oil deposits were later discovered. The port of Guayaquil is the largest city in Ecuador.

Edessa (CRUSADER STATES)

Egypt

Egypt was given to the Greek general Ptolomeus after the death of Alexander in 323 BC (ALEXANDRIAN EMPIRE). PTOLEMAIC EGYPT and the SELEUCID EMPIRE were frequently at war over Palestine. The Roman triumvir Mark Antony, in alliance with Cleopatra, the last of the Ptolemaic rulers, tried to constitute an oriental empire based in Alexandria independent of Rome, but he was defeated by Augustus and Egypt was incorporated as a province of ROME (30 BC). Egypt later became a province of the BYZANTINE EMPIRE. Egypt was conquered by ISLAM and became a part of the Umayyad Empire. Previously Christian, its population mostly became Muslim, although Egypt still has a sizeable community of Coptic Christians. (Copts believe in the exclusively divine nature of Christ.) With the establishment of the ABBASID CALIPHATE in Baghdad, Egypt went its own way under the Tulunids (868–905), whose political influence was felt in eastern Libya.

The Fatimids

After a period of dynastic changes, the Maghrebian FATIMIDS assumed power in 969. Their rule extended from Algeria to Syria and Arabia. Cairo (Al Qahirah) was founded as capital to replace Al Qatai, the Abbasid capital. When the Maghreb began to break away during the late 10th cent., the Fatimids sent Bedouin tribes to subdue it (11th–12th cents.). In Egypt the Fatimids were overthrown by the AYYUBIDS (1171–1250), whose founder and greatest sultan, Saladin, slowed the conquering impetus of the CRU-SADES in the Battle of Hattin, near Tiberias, northern Israel, in 1187. The Mamelukes, a caste of slave-warriors recruited from central Asian non-Muslim boys who converted during military training, dispossessed the Ayyubids and created an Egyptian non-hereditary monarchy in 1250 (MAMELUKE SUL-TANATE). They later legitimized their take over with an Abbasid survivor of the Ilkhanite conquest of Baghdad in 1268 (ILKHANID PERSIA), which gave Cairo a claim on the caliphate.

The caliphs were mere figureheads of the Mameluke rulers. In the reign of the sultan Qutuz, the Mameluke general Baybars defeated the Ilkhanid Mongols in the Battle of Ain Jalut, in Syria, in 1260. It was one of the few set-backs the Mongolian conquerors experienced. Although Egypt was absorbed in 1517 by the OTTOMAN EMPIRE, under Selim I, the Mamelukes retained internal control. They were defeated by the French (1798–1801), but returned to power until their principal leaders were beheaded in 1811 after a dinner invitation by the Turkish pasha, Muhammad Ali, who had been ruling Egypt since 1805 independently of Istambul. An attempt by the Ottomans to take Egypt was rebuffed in 1839. Muhammad Ali established the line of Egyptian kings, which lasted until Farouk was deposed in 1952.

THE UNITED ARAB REPUBLIC

British strategic interest in the French-built Suez Canal (1869), led to the incorporation of Egypt into the BRITISH COLONIAL EMPIRE as a protec-torate. Egypt was granted independence in 1923, although it was effectively under British military occupation during World War II. During the Arab–Israeli War of 1948–1949 (Israeli War of Independence), Egypt managed to retain the Gaza Strip, but lost it to Israel during the Arab–Israeli (Six Day) War of 1967. Israel also occupied Sinai to the eastern shore of the Suez Canal. One of the defenders of Gaza, Gamal Abdel Nasser, became dicta-tor of Egypt and a powerful symbol of Arab nationalism (1952). In 1958, Egypt and Syria agreed to merge as the United Arab Republic (UAR), which YEMEN joined later the same year, forming a federation called the United Arab States. Political rivalries led to the dissolution of the union with Syria in 1961, but Egypt maintained a strong military presence in Yemen after 1962 to defend the republican government against a Saudi-supported internal armed opposition. The Egyptian intervention proved prohibitive and Egypt withdrew from Yemen in 1967. In 1971, Egypt, which was still officially the UAR, became the Arab Republic of Egypt. Then, in 1973, under the rule of general Anwar al-Sadat, and in alliance with Syria, Egypt attacked Israel. Egyptian forces crossed the Suez Canal successfully, but were beaten back by Israeli armies quickly resupplied by the United States. In the truce that followed, Israel returned the eastern bank of Suez to Egypt and ordered its troops, which had been threatening Damascus, back to the Golan Heights. In 1979, President Sadat signed a peace treaty with Prime Minister Menachem Beguin of Israel as a result of which Egypt recovered the Sinai in 1982. Sadat was later assassinated by a dissident soldier. He was succeeded by President Mubarak.

Elam (4th mil.–8th cent. BC; ancient *Near East*)
There were kingdoms in Elam, capital Susa, north of the Persian Gulf and east of the Tigris River, from the late 4th mil. BC. Around 2000 BC Elam conquered SUMER, then under the hegemony of UR. Hammurabi of Babylon broke Elamite power in Sumer ca. 1750 BC. The Elamites retrenched to their own land. They were conquered by ASSYRIA ca. 700 BC. Upon the downfall of Assyria Elam went its own way and later was absorbed by the Persian ACHAEMENID EMPIRE, whose rulers might have been Elamites by origin. Susa became an important centre of the Achaemenid Empire. The code of Hammurabi, the King of BABYLONIA, was found in its ruins. There is a province of modern Iran called Ilam.
(*See chronologies under* Ancient Near East *and* Iran.)

El Salvador
Peopled mostly by Amerindian tribes, the territory of El Salvador was annexed in 1524 by Pedro de Alvarado, Cortez's lieutenant in the conquest of MEXICO, following the annexation of Honduras into the SPANISH COLONIAL EMPIRE. Attached to the captaincy general of GUATEMALA which depended on the viceroyalty of New Spain, El Salvador became part of the Mexican empire of Iturbide until its dissolution in 1823. El Salvador joined with the rest of Central America (except Panama which was a province of GRAN COLOMBIA) in the CENTRAL AMERICAN FEDERATION. In 1838, all of its members went their own respective ways. San Salvador, the Salvadorean capital, was founded in the 16th cent.

England
SEE ENTRY IN 'PROVINCES AND REGIONS'
The island of Britain was conquered by ROME from AD 43 to AD 85. Roman England was abandoned to the Jutes and Anglo Saxons in 410. The country was divided into small kingdoms. As a group they are sometimes referred to as the heptarchy (East Anglia, Essex, Kent, Mercia, Northumbria, Sussex, and Wessex). Northumbria was hegemonic in the north, later superseded by Mercia in the Midlands. During the early 9th cent. Wessex, in southern England, became the dominant kingdom. The Danes began their incursions in the 8th cent. And, in the 9th cent., invaded in earnest. King Alfred the Great of Wessex (871–899) held them to the Danelaw. England was divided by a London-to-Chester diagonal into Wessex and Mercia to the south west and the Danelaw to the north east. During the 10th cent. England was united under Wessex, but it was beset again by Danes, who occupied London in 1013. There was a brief

restoration and Wessex was finally defeated and conquered by the Danish King Canute in 1016. The Danish line was extinguished in 1042 and succeeded by the house of Wessex, whose king, Edward the Confessor, named Harold his successor. Harold had sworn allegiance to William of NORMANDY and upon Edward's death William invaded England. Harold had just previously defeated the Norsemen and he was defeated by the Normans at Hastings in 1066. After Hastings, all of England was conquered by the Normans. The conquest of WALES by England began almost immediately and was accomplished in 1282 by Edward I. The conquest of IRELAND began in 1171 under Henry II, the founder of the Plantagenet line, and lasted until the decisive Battle of Boyne in 1690. It was Henry II who also obtained formal suzerainty over SCOTLAND, which the Scots later repudiated. They repulsed English attempts to annex the country over the following centuries. England and Scotland were joined only when the house of Stuart acceded to the English throne (1603).

Hundred Years War

Henry II, who was Lord of Normandy, inherited Anjou, Maine, and Touraine (*France*), and through his marriage in 1152 to Eleanor of AQUITAINE, this realm and Poitou and Auvergne devolved to the English crown. At his death (1189), English domains in France stretched from Normandy in the north to the Pyrenees (Gascony) and from the Atlantic Ocean to the Auvergne. His fiefs bounded with Languedoc, Burgundy, and Île de France. By 1328, the French monarchy had taken all these lands. The English, under Edward III, reclaimed them by force in 1337, thus starting the Hundred Years War. During its early phase the English defeated the French at Crécy (1346) and took Calais (1347). By 1373, France had taken back most of those conquests. In 1415 England took the offensive once again, defeated the French at Agincourt, and in alliance with BURGUNDY occupied all of northern France including Paris, but the Burgundians switched allegiances in 1435, and by 1453 England had had to relinquish all its French territories except Calais, which fell to the French in 1659. The kingdom of England was the core around which the United Kingdom of Great Britain was built. The English dynastic wars, the Civil War, the subsequent dynastic successions, the Napoleonic Wars, the two World Wars, the post-war period, and the Empire are dealt with under GREAT BRITAIN and BRITISH COLONIAL EMPIRE.

English and British Reigning Dynasties

English dynastic changes have been on occasions radical. The transitions from Lancaster to York and from Tudor to Stuart might have been justified by direct lines of descent from previous kings, but the Tudors were only descendants of a widow of a king and the house of Orange was installed because of Mary, daughter of Charles I and wife of William of Orange, and the last Stuart King,

James II, had heirs. Despite Burke, legitimacy in Great Britain has sometimes derived from the *fait accompli*. Saxon and Danish kings ruled England, more often partially than wholly, from 802. In 1066, William of Normandy defeated Harold, Earl of Wessex and last Saxon king, in the Battle of Hastings and established the house of Normandy. Upon the death of Henry I in 1135, Stephen, Count of Blois and grandson of William, took the throne, but he had to contest the kingdom with Matilda, Queen Maud, daughter of Henry I and wife of Henry V Holy Roman Emperor. Eventually, Matilda's son by her marriage with Geoffrey IV Anjou, Henry of Anjou, became King Henry II of England (1154–1189), founder of the Angevin dynasty, renamed Plantagenet. The Plantagenet dynasty ruled England from 1154 to 1399. Henry of Bolingbroke, grandson of Edward III Plantagenet, forced the last Plantagenet, Richard II (1377–1399), to abdicate and became Henry IV (1399–1413), founder of the Lancaster dynasty. Richard, Duke of York, descended from Edward III Plantagenet (1327–1377), took up arms against Henry VI Lancaster in 1455. The War of the Roses (1455–1485) ensued, during which the throne changed hands various times and was held by the house of York from 1461 until 1485, when Richard III – who himself had usurped the throne against the minor heirs of his brother, King Edward IV York – was killed in the Battle of Bosworth Field won by Henry Tudor, who ascended the throne as Henry VII. His son, Henry VIII, established the Church of England. Elizabeth, daughter of Henry VIII and Anne Boleyn, died childless in 1603. James I Stuart, son of Mary Queen of Scots, daughter of Henry VIII, ascended the throne. In a dispute over funding and legislative rights, his son Charles I got into a quarrel with parliament which became a civil war. After losing the Battle of Naseby in 1645, he surrendered in 1646, attempted to fight again in 1648, was decisively beaten, arrested, tried, and beheaded in January 1649. Great Britain was declared a commonwealth under Oliver Cromwell, who ruled from 1649 to 1653, followed by his son Richard, who ceded power to the restored Charles II Stuart (1660). The Restoration lasted until 1688, when James II was deposed because of his authoritarian and Catholic leanings. In the Glorious Revolution William of Orange and his wife Mary, Protestant daughter of King Charles I, were elevated to the throne. Anne, their daughter, died childless. The Elector of Hanover, great grandson of James I, became George I of England in 1714. The direct line of the house of Hanover became extinct with William IV in 1837 and Victoria of Saxe-Coburg, granddaughter of George III, became queen. The name of the British ruling house was changed to Windsor during World War I.

Ephthalites (5th–7th cents.; *Central Asia*: greater Mongolia; Afghanistan; northern India)
Though not likely related to the HUNS, the Ephthalites, called Hunna by the Indians and White Huns by the Byzantines, were a nomadic central Asian

nation, possibly Turkish. They were minor vassals of the JUAN-JUAN in the area from the north Tarim Basin to Lake Balkash. In the 5th cent. they migrated westwards *en masse* and fought the SASANID EMPIRE, briefly taking Khurasan, Merv, and Herat. The Ephthalites then turned to Kabul. During the 6th cent. they attacked India, where the GUPTAS tried to contain them. They occupied the PUNJAB, but were defeated by HARSHA'S KINGDOM in the early 7th cent. and were eventually assimilated and apparently disappeared from history (RAJPUTS).
(*See chronologies under* Indian Subcontinent *and* Greater Mongolia.)

Epirus (4th–2nd cents. BC; Ancient *Greece*)
Epirus was a Greek kingdom, also known as Molossia, founded under the patronage of MACEDON. The Molossian king, Pyrrhus, invaded Italy on behalf of the southern Greeks (280–275 BC) and fought the Romans, but his costly victories were unavailing and he reputedly acknowledged that if he won another battle like the one at Asculum he would be lost (Pyrrhic victory). Epirus was destroyed by Rome (167 BC) and later annexed.
(*See chronology under* Greece (Ancient).)

Epirus (Despotate of) (13th–14th cents.; Greece)
The Greek despotate of Epirus was created after the Latin conquest of Constantinople in 1204 (BYZANTINE EMPIRE). It held Salonika from 1222 to 1246. It was annexed by the restored Byzantine Empire in 1336. Epirus was annexed by the OTTOMAN EMPIRE in the 14th cent. From 1787 to 1820, Ali Pasha, an Ottoman governor, ruled Epirus and Albania autonomously, after which the Ottomans took them back. Epirus was ceded to Greece in 1878 (BERLIN, CONFERENCE OF).

Equatorial Guinea
Originally mostly peopled by tribal Fangs, who speak a Bantu language, the territories of Equatorial Guinea were claimed by Portugal and ceded to Spain in 1778. Spain's claims to the island of Fernando Po (previously called Bioko) and other nearby islands and the mainland territory were constituted as Spanish Guinea in 1885. In 1968, they became independent as Equatorial Guinea. The capital is Malabo on Fernando Po. Spanish is the official language.

Eritrea
It is thought that Axum (ancient ETHIOPIA) had a loose hold on the southwestern coast of the Red Sea until the 7th cent. Like many coastal regions the Europeans reconnoitred during and after the 15th cent., it was probably divided into statelets. Eritrea fell under the political influence of the OTTOMAN EMPIRE during the 16th cent. In the 1880s the Italians began their own colonization. They named the region Eritrea after the Roman desig-

nation for the Red Sea. A fully-formed colony in 1890, Eritrea was taken by the British in 1941, who administered it as a UN trust territory until, in 1952, it was federated with Ethiopia, of which it became an integral part in 1962. After a prolonged civil war against a leftist military dictatorship which had taken power in 1970, Ethiopia and Eritrea separated in 1993. They were at war over disputed border areas during 1998 and 1999. Asmara is the capital of Eritrea. Eritreans speak Tigrinya, a Semitic language.

Estonia

Estonians speak a Finno-Ugric language. The territory of Estonia was Danish until the 14th cent., when it was conquered by the German LIVONIAN BROTHERS OF THE SWORD and was under the influence of the HANSEATIC LEAGUE. The Livonian Brothers had merged with the TEUTONIC KNIGHTS in 1257 but kept their own theatre of operation. Upon the dissolution of the Knights (1525), the territory of Estonia was shared by Sweden and Poland. It became wholly Swedish in 1629. The Russian Tsar Peter I the Great conquered Livonia (Estonia and Latvia) in 1710. Estonia remained Russian – Estonian revolutionaries were instrumental in the Soviet takeover of Russia in 1917 – until it achieved independence in 1918. It was absorbed by the USSR in 1939 and made a Soviet republic. It was under German occupation during World War II and was recovered by the USSR in 1944. In 1990 it became autonomous in the process of dissolution of the USSR and in 1991 it declared its total independence. Tallinn, the capital of Estonia, was founded as Reval by the Danes in 1219.

Ethiopia

By tradition Ethiopia was founded in the 10th cent. BC. by the legendary Menelik, son of the Queen of SHEBA. The traditional name Abyssinia probably derives from the Egyptian Habashat. Historically, Ethiopia was known as Axum in the 2nd cent. AD. Under King Ezana, Ethiopia was converted to Monophysite Christianity in the 4th cent., when it also invaded and destroyed Meroe (KUSH) Monophysitism is the doctrine, held by Egyptian copts, that Christ was exclusively of divine nature.

In 525, Axum invaded Yemen, but was expelled by the SASANID EMPIRE. In the 7th cent., Ethiopia expanded at the expense of its neighbours, but the kingdom was mostly disunited and unstable. In the 16th cent. it was threatened by Islamic ADAL, which was repulsed with Portuguese aid. During the 17th and 18th cents. Ethiopia was centred in Gondar. The kingdom was reunited in 1855 under Theodore II, but afterwards it fell once again into internal warfare and was subjected in 1868 to a punitive expedition by Great Britain for its high-handed treatment of its envoys. Nevertheless, Ethiopia retained its cohesion and under Menelik II the capital was moved to Addis Ababa. The Italians were defeated in Adowa in 1896. Ras Tafari, a court dignitary, was crowned

King Haile Selasie in 1930. Italy came charging back in 1935 and this time made the country a colony, which, in World War II, British and South African troops conquered in 1941 and returned to Ethiopian rule. In 1952, Ethiopia was federated with Eritrea, which became an integral part of the kingdom in 1962. Haile Selasie was overthrown in a leftist coup in 1974. After a prolonged civil war, the government was defeated in 1991 and the union with Eritrea dissolved in 1993. In 1998 and 1999 Ethiopia and Eritrea warred savagely over the possession of parcels of rocky desert.

Etruria (10th–4th cents. BC; *Italy*)
Etruscan civilization was formed from ca. 900 to ca. 750 BC. The homeland of Etruria extended approximately from Pisa to Arezzo, to the Orvieto region, and to Rome and Ostia. There is evidence of Etruscan influence as far north as Piacenza, south to Campania and across the Tyrrhenean to Corsica. In the late 7th cent. BC, an Etruscan king ruled Rome. The fall of the Etruscan Tarquin dynasty in Rome, in the late 6th cent. BC, marks the beginning of the decadence of Etruria, which culminated with the destruction of Veii by the Romans in 396 BC and was followed by the gradual assimilation of the Etruscans. The Etruscan language remains in many inscriptions, as yet undeciphered, and is considered an isolate.

Etruria (FRENCH EUROPEAN EMPIRE)

European Union
The European Union (EU) is a federation of states in the making. It can be said to have got started with Churchill's call in 1946 in Zurich for a United States of Europe. The Council of Europe was an informal group formed in 1949 to promote European unity. In practical terms, the EU began with an initiative by the French Foreign Minister Robert Schuman. This led to the Treaty of Paris, which created the European Coal and Steel Community, a pooling of resources by Belgium, France, Germany, Italy, Luxembourg, and the Netherlands. The success of this association culminated in 1957 in the Treaty of Rome which created the European Economic Community (EEC), whose goal was the achievement of a common market based on a customs union, and the European Atomic Community. The EEC was expanded between 1970 and 1972 to include Great Britain, Denmark, and Ireland, who by an accession treaty became full members in 1973. Norway was in the negotiations, but later withdrew. Greenland entered with Denmark, but exercising its right of self-rule also withdrew in 1985. Greece joined in 1981, and Portugal and Spain followed in 1986. By this time the structure of the EU, which would be embodied in the Maastricht Treaty of 1992, ratified in 1993 by all member states, was already in place.

The EU consists of six inter-related and complementary institutions. The European Commission (EC) is constituted by 20 members appointed by the governments of the member states. It is considered the executive branch of the EU and, as such, has the right of proposal to the Council of Ministers or, as it is now known, the Council of the European Union, and the power of execution if the Council of the EU accepts its proposals. The EC can take any member state to the Court of Justice of the European Communities – integrated by 13 judges and six advocates general – if it considers that it is not adhering to the constitutive treaties. The President of the EC, which sits in Brussels, is technically the head of the EU.

The Council of the EU is the body which represents the national interests of each state through meetings of its foreign ministers and permanent representations which deliberate on a weekly basis. The Council of the EU is the ultimate decision-making and legislating body of the EU. Proposals from the EC must go to the Council. Its presidency rotates half-yearly and the meetings are held in Brussels and Luxembourg. The President of the EC is a member of the Council of the EU. Notwithstanding these powers, the European Council, which has formally existed since 1974 and refers to the periodic reunions of the heads of states of the members of the EU, is actually where EU policies are sorted out, directions given, and difficult problems considered. In the final instance, what the heads of state agree on fundamentally determines proposals to the Council of the EU or the proposals that the EC will submit to the Council of the EU for approval.

The European Parliament, which sits on a regular basis in Strasbourg, France, has 626 members elected for five years from all the member nations. They represent, in theory, political rather than national interests. The parliament is not legislative but consultative, although in the Single European Act of 1986 it was given the right to reject draft proposals from the Council of the EU and on certain domestic issues it has the right of co-decision with the Council. Even though the President and other members of the EC are chosen by consensus of the governments of the EU, the Parliament can exert influence on the choices.

The EU also has a Court of Auditors of the European Community, which was established in 1975, made a fundamental institution of the EU in the Treaty of Maastricht, and supervises income and expenses.

In 1992, the Maastricht Treaty transformed the EEC into the EU by discretely enhancing the powers of parliament but more significantly by providing for a single currency – the Euro, which came into its own in 1999 – and for a 'social dimension', both of which Great Britain opted out of, with the right to adopt them later.

The EU was further increased with the entry of East Germany, as part of the Federal Republic of Germany after 1990. In view to the further expansion of the EU, the Copenhagen criteria were elaborated in 1993, dealing with fiscal and macroeconomic constraints. In 1995, Austria, Finland, and Sweden joined the EU. Preliminary talks were started with the Czech Republic, Estonia, Hungary, Poland, and Slovenia for possible entry after 2000.

F

Fatimid Caliphate (10th–12th cents.; northern Africa and *Near East*)
Said Ibn Husayn, a religious leader in Syria, upheld the Islamic succession of
Fatima, Muhammad's daughter – which is of the essence in Shia Islam –
against the ABBASIDS in Baghdad, who held the caliphate, a political title
with strong religious significance. One of his followers, Al Shii, went to north-
eastern Algeria, where he rallied the Muslim Berbers against the AGHLABIDS
in the late 9th cent. While trying to rejoin Shii, Husayn had been arrested by the
Aghlabids in Libya. Shii finally overthrew the Aghlabids in Tunisia and, in 909,
was joined by Husayn. The Fatimids by then had taken over Sicily and Libya.
They contested western Algeria and Morocco with the Umayyads of
CÓRDOBA, where Abd dar-Rahman III had proclaimed a caliphate. Husayn,
who had Shii executed (911), assumed the title of caliph, took the name of
Ubaidalla, and proclaimed himself Mahdi, a title which corresponds to the
Jewish concept of Messiah. Fatimid expansion continued in the Mediterranean,
including briefly the occupation of Genoa. Under the caliph Moizz (963–975),
the Shia general Jahr wrested Egypt from the Tulunids in 969 and went on to
invade Palestine, Syria, and western Arabia. In 973, Moizz moved the caliphate
to Cairo, which became the rival of the Baghdad caliphate. Decline set in
during the 11th cent. and most Fatimid conquests gradually fell off. In an effort
to quell the separatism of the Algerian ZIRID EMIRATES, the Fatimids sicced
the Bedouins on the Maghreb, where they caused social instability but also contributed to the Arabization of the region. The Moroccan ALMORAVIDS
subdued the emirates in western Algeria in the 11th cent. The ALMOHADS did
the same thing in Tunisia in the 12th cent. In 1099, the Crusaders took Palestine
(CRUSADER STATES). During the 12th cent., Syrian forces fought their way
to Egypt, where, after the death in 1171 of the last Fatimid, Saladin became
sultan and founder of the AYYUBID SULTANATE.
(*See chronology under* Maghreb.)

Ferrara (13th–16th cents.; northern *Italy*)
In the 13th cent., Ferrara was a principality of the Este family, which had been
deprived by Frederick Barbarossa of the duchy of BAVARIA. MODENA
became part of the Este domains in 1288. In 1598 Ferrara was incorporated
into the PAPAL STATES, but Modena remained in the Este family.

Fiji
The inhabitants of the Fiji islands in the Pacific Ocean speak a language of the
Austronesian family, which includes Malay tongues. Fiji was a British colony
in the Pacific Ocean from 1874 to 1970. Suva is the capital of Fiji.

Finland

Finnish is a member of the Finno-Ugric family of languages, to which Estonian and Hungarian also belong. The Finns had driven the Lapplanders towards the north, where they still live (Lappland). In the 13th cent. Finland was occupied by Sweden and it was made a grand duchy in 1581. Between 1721 and 1743, Russia occupied part of the province of Karelia, in eastern Finland, centred around Vyborg. In 1808–1809, Russia annexed all of Finland from Sweden, but allowed it a great deal of autonomy. During the Russian Revolution in 1917, Finland, including Karelia, declared its independence, which was defended against the Soviets by Marshall Mannerheim. Invaded by the USSR in 1939, Finland fought valiantly but lost most of Karelia. Helsinki, the capital of Finland, has been its principal city since 1828. Previously Turku, which burned down, was the religious and cultural centre. Finland joined the EUROPEAN UNION in 1995.

Flanders (7th–14th cents.; *Belgium*)

Flanders was constituted as a county in 862. It was a fief of the French crown but mostly composed of autonomous municipalities. During the 11th cent. the county of Flanders expanded into lands of the HOLY ROMAN EMPIRE, which were called Imperial Flanders as distinct from French Crown Flanders. The unity of Flanders was represented in the ruling count. In 1191, Flanders was joined with Hainaut, in north-eastern France, by inheritance. The cities of Flanders (Ghent, Bruges, Ypres, *et al*), basically self-governing with flourishing cloth industries, staged the first European industrial revolution starting in the 13th cent. Baldwin, Count of Flanders, participated in the Fourth Crusade and became head of the Latin Empire, with its centre in Constantinople, in 1204 (LATIN STATES). This absence weakened Flanders, which was strongly contested between France and England during the 13th and 14th cents. These dynastic struggles favoured the independence of the cities. In 1384, Philip the Bold annexed the Low Countries, including Flanders, to autonomous BURGUNDY. In 1477, the Low Countries – but not Burgundy, which went to the French crown – passed to the HABSBURG EMPIRE by marriage. When the Habsburg Holy Roman Emperor Charles V (Charles I, King of Spain) divested himself of German Habsburg domains in favour of his brother Ferdinand in 1556, he retained the Low Countries for Spain (SPANISH NETHERLANDS). In 1576, the Flemish rebelled against Philip II of Spain but were suppressed in 1584 by Alessandro Farnese. The Netherlands had detached itself from the Spanish Netherlands in 1581. In 1714, the Spanish Netherlands became an Austrian Habsburg domain, which it remained until it was made part of the NETHERLANDS after the final downfall of Napoleon in 1815.

Florence (13th–19th cents.; northern *Italy*)

Dating back to Etruscan times, the city of Florence became an autonomous commune in the 12th cent. During the 13th cent. it was the stage of political struggles between Guelphs (anti-imperial party) and Ghibellines (pro-imperial party). Dante, who was Ghibelline, took part in these rivalries. During the 14th cent. Florence became hegemonic in Tuscany. It annexed PISA in 1409. The Medici family took power in the 15th cent. Florence was at the heart of the Italian Renaissance during the 15th and 16th cents. Holy Roman Emperor Charles V (King Charles I of Spain) intervened in Florentine affairs in the 1530s, but the city was restored to the Medici. Florence annexed Siena in the mid-16th cent. Tuscany became a grand duchy in 1569, with Florence as its capital. Upon the extinction of the Medici line in 1737, the duchy passed to a branch of the Austrian Habsburg (HABSBURG EMPIRE). France took Tuscany in 1799, but it was restored in 1814. In 1860 it was engulfed by the tide of the *risorgimento*, the complex process by which ITALY was unified.

France

SEE ENTRY IN 'PROVINCES AND REGIONS'

It can be stated with precision that the French *hexagone* – the name the French themselves give to their continental territory from its approximate shape – acquired its final form in 1919, when Alsace and Lorraine returned to the fold. The territory of France was peopled by Celts and called Gaul. In the 1st cent. BC, Julius Caesar conquered it for ROME against strong resistance from its inhabitants led by Vercingetorix, whose final stand was at Alesia. The Romans divided Gaul (AD 14) into three main provinces: Aquitania, Narbonensis, and Lugdunensis, but modern France also includes wholly or partially the Roman provinces of Germania Superior, Alpes Cottiae, Alpes Maritimae, and Italia. The *Roman Empire* lost Gaul to trans-Rhine invaders by degrees but very quickly: by 400, south-western France (Aquitania) to the Visigoths; by 450, the extreme north east to the FRANKS, SAVOY to the Burgundians, and most of central and eastern France to the Franks and VISIGOTHS. By 486, the territory north of the Loire (a pocket of resistance by the Roman general Syagrius) fell to the Franks. At that point, France was divided roughly between Franks in the north east, BURGUNDIANS in the Rhône River valley, and Visigoths in the south and south east. The Franks were united by Clovis (ca. 466–511), who founded the Merovingian dynasty, became Christian, and had his capital in Paris. By 530, the Franks had been forming statelets which extended from the Rhine to the limits of Burgundian lands and the eastern edge of the VISIGOTHIC KINGDOM of Spain stretching along the Mediterranean coast beyond Marseilles. The Visigothic lands were gradually reduced until, by 650, they were a bare foothold around Narbonne. When Islam conquered Spain, it annexed the Visigothic enclave in France. In 732, Charles Martel, founder of the Carolingian dynasty, stopped Muslim penetration at the Battle of Tours. In 759, Narbonne was taken from the Moors, who never again posed a threat to Frankish lands.

CAROLINGIAN FRANCE

The entirety of France became part of the CAROLINGIAN EMPIRE. When Louis I, son of Charlemagne, died, Carolingian lands were divided by the Treaty of Verdun (843) among his three heirs. Charles II the Bald became ruler of France. The imperial succession was more or less maintained until the deposition in 887 of Charles the Fat, who failed to rescue Paris when it was besieged by NORSEMEN. After him the empire was dissolved. France was ruled by Eudes or Odo, Count of Paris. He was replaced by weak Carolingian rulers and France was feudalized. The last Carolingian king of France died childless and was succeeded in 987 by Hugh Capet, Count of Paris and founder of the Capetian line. At this time, the core of what would become France was basically the area of Paris, and the rest of the country would remain fragmented into the 11th cent. In that period the crown domains of France grew to Orléans and there were claims on various small pockets of territory, all in the north east. Given the relative nearness of Paris to German territories, even though its expansion was in all directions, it had more space into which to grow towards the south and west. By the late 12th cent., France included Flanders, Champagne, Nivernais, Burgundy (duchy), Lyonnais, Bourbonnais, and Berry. By the early 13th cent., it had absorbed Normandy, Maine, and Anjou; in 1229, Languedoc (Toulouse); in 1252, Poitou, Touraine, Marche, and Auvergne; in 1314, Saintonge, Angoumois, Perigord, and Limousin; in 1328, Aquitaine and Gascony; in 1349, Dauphiné; and in 1378, the kingdom of Arles. French royal acquisitions during these centuries were the work of the Capetians (987–1328) and the Valois (to 1589). They were made mostly at the expense of English dynastic claims (ENGLAND), but not Dauphiné, Arles, Burgundy, or Languedoc. In 1384, FLANDERS, where French rule was contested, and the rest of the Low Countries, went to the duchy of BURGUNDY, which had become autonomous.

LOUIX XIV

At different times during the Hundred Years War (1337–1453) England reconquered most of its dynastic claims and, for a time, even took northern France, including Paris. Eventually, however, inspired and led by Joan of Arc, who stood in at the crowning of Charles VII in Rheims in 1429, the French recovered all their territories and extinguished all English claims. The last bit of English-occupied France, Calais, held out until 1659. In 1474, the Low Countries passed to the HABSBURG EMPIRE and France put an end to Burgundian autonomy. In 1488, France absorbed Brittany, which had been an autonomous fief. In 1589, with the accession of the first Bourbon king, Henry IV, France annexed French NAVARRE. In 1659, it acquired Bresse, Artois, and Roussillon. Between 1668 and 1678, France obtained from Spain part of Flanders and Franche Comté (SPANISH NETHERLANDS). In 1697, it conquered Alsace and patches of Lorraine from the HOLY ROMAN EMPIRE. Most of the 17th cent. French acquisitions were the result of the wars of Louis XIV. During the 18th cent. France rounded out Lorraine (1766) under Louis XV. In 1791, France recovered Avignon, which had been a self-ruling papal domain since 1348. The only part of non-mainland European France is Corsica, which was acquired in 1768 from GENOA.

REVOLUTIONARY FRANCE

In 1789, a National Assembly gathered in Paris, and virtually overthrew the monarchy. After trying to flee and getting caught in Varennes, Louis XVI was a prisoner of the revolutionaries. Austria invaded in 1792, but the French beat them at Valmy. The king was beheaded in January 1793 and the French Revolution became radicalized through a Committee for Public Safety, controlled by the Jacobins, led by Robespierre. A coalition including Great Britain, Austria, Prussia, Spain, and Holland was formed against France. In 1794, the Jacobin leaders were all guillotined either by their own side or by others, and France undid the coalition forces, occupying Holland and creating the Batavian Republic (FRENCH EUROPEAN EMPIRE). It also annexed the Rhineland. During the period of the Directory, starting in 1795, Napoleon defeated the Austrians in Italy and, in 1797, France closed the war on the continent on a triumphant note. Only Great Britain remained in the fight. In 1798, Napoleon captured Malta and invaded Egypt, but Nelson crippled the French navy in the Battle of Aboukir. France created the Helvetic Republic with Switzerland, which provoked the second coalition involving Great Britain, Austria, Russia, Turkey, Portugal, and Naples. Without anywhere to go in Egypt, Napoleon returned to France, whose armies were losing in the field. In 1800, Napoleon defeated the Austrians decisively at Marengo and by 1801 the coalition had come apart. Great Britain defeated the Danish navy at Copenhagen and recaptured Malta. In 1802, France annexed Piedmont in Italy and was intervening regularly in the affairs of all its neighbours. Great Britain declared war again in 1803.

NAPOLEON

Napoleon crowned himself Emperor in 1804 and King of Italy in 1805. A third coalition was formed with Great Britain, Austria, Russia, and Sweden, which Napoleon roundly defeated at Austerlitz (1806), even as Nelson was mopping up the combined naval forces of France and Spain at the Battle of Trafalgar (1805). In 1806, Napoleon beat the Prussians at Jena and dissolved the Holy Roman Empire. In 1806, he avoided defeat against the Prussians and Russians at Eylau, but in 1807 he defeated the Russians at Friedland, making Prussia a vassal kingdom and creating the Gran Duchy of Warsaw. He placed his brother Joseph on the Spanish throne in 1808. The following year Napoleon defeated Austria again in Wagram and France annexed the Dalmatian coast and the PAPAL STATES. At the height of his power in 1810, Napoleon even married Marie Louise, daughter of Holy Roman Emperor Francis I Habsburg, whose Austrian armies he had variously defeated and whose imperial crown he had abolished. However, after 1810 things began to go awry for Napoleon and the French. There were minor reverses, but the greatest blow was the loss of the Grande Armée during the invasion of Russia in 1812. A fourth coalition comprising Great Britain, Austria, Prussia, Russia, and Sweden defeated Napoleon at the Battle of Leipzig, and in 1814 the allies entered Paris. Napoleon abdicated in favour of his infant son (1811–1832) – called by the French L'Aiglon, King of Parma and Duke of Reichstadt, who died a virtual Austrian prisoner – and he was packed off to the island of Elba (off the coast of Tuscany). He returned in 1814, chased Louis XVIII from the throne, but he could not defeat the allies at the Battle of Waterloo (near Brussels) in 1815, after which Napoleon was finished politically. He died six years later in exile in the tiny island of St Helena, a British dependency. From the start of the Revolution in 1789 to 1815, France temporarily annexed the following territories, which it had to relinquish after Napoleon's first deposition: the Austrian Netherlands, the Rhineland, Savoy, Liguria, Parma, Florence, Rome, and Illyria down to Cattaro.

SECOND EMPIRE AND THIRD REPUBLIC

Louis XVIII returned after Napoleon was deposed. There was an uprising in 1830 and the last French Bourbon was replaced by the scion of Orléans, the citizen-king Louis Philippe, who in turn was washed away by the revolutionary wave that began in France and swept Europe in 1848 (there were nationalistic and liberal outbursts in Hungary, Italy, and Germany) and Louis Philippe was replaced by the second French Republic, which Louis Napoleon Bonaparte, Napoleon's nephew, headed and then overthrew to crown himself Napoleon III in 1852. In the period from 1815 to 1850, France started rebuilding the FRENCH COLONIAL EMPIRE, which the British had badly mauled during the Seven Years War (1756–1763). Some African coast was staked out, but particularly after 1830, under Louis Philippe, the conquest of Algeria was begun. In 1848, Monaco ceded Menton to France. The *risorgimento*, the nationalist, integrationist movement that gave birth to modern ITALY, began with a war between SARDINIA and Austria in which France decisively backed the Italians at the Battle of Solferino in 1859. This resulted in Sardinia's acquisition of much of northern Italy, and in the coronation of Victor Emmanuel as King of Italy in 1861. In 1860, in exchange for Napoleon III's support of Sardinia, France received Savoy and Nice. Napoleon III was a swaggering monarch, who played into Bismarck's provocations and lost the Franco-Prussian War of 1870–1871. Napoleon III was deposed and Germany annexed Alsace and Lorraine. The war was followed by the Paris commune, the first, if short-lived and local, communist government in modern history, which was mercilessly suppressed by Thiers at the head of the Third Republic.

WORLD WAR I

In June 1914, a Serb fanatic assassinated the crown prince of Austria–Hungary, Archduke Francis Ferdinand, in Sarajevo, Bosnia-Herzegovina, a Serb territory which the Austrians occupied in 1908. Austria–Hungary presented Serbia with impossible conditions which Serbia, with Russian backing, did not accept. In July, Austria declared war on Serbia. Germany declared war on Russia on 1 August and on France two days later. Great Britain, ever mindful of the continental balance of power, entered the war as an ally of France (Allied Powers). The Germans had a blueprint for victory in the Schlieffen Plan, which called for a quick traverse of Belgium and on to Paris. The plan almost succeeded but cool Gallieni, a veteran of colonialist wars, and Joffre observed an opening in the German advancing front, which they attacked during the Battle of the Marne and drove the Germans back. France, led by Clemenceau, and Great Britain manned the line of trenches from Switzerland to the English channel. Despite mutinies in the front, French armies under Pétain contained the Germans in the Battle of Verdun (1916). The United States entered the war in 1917. In April 1918 the Allies unified the command structure in the western front under French Marshall Foch, although the national commanders, Pershing in the American sector and Haig in the British, retained direct control of their forces. The Germans attempted a final, failed offensive in 1918. The Allies counter-attacked and the Germans gave up the fight without having been totally defeated. In the Paris Peace Conference of 1919, by the Treaty of VERSAILLES, France recovered Alsace and Lorraine.

DE GAULLE

In September 1939, Hitler invaded Poland and Great Britain and France declared war. After a short period of phoney war, in which the sides just glared at each other, Germany applied the *blitzkrieg* to France in June 1940. Defeated France was divided into the zone of occupation and the puppet Vichy regime in the south, headed by Marshall Pétain, the hero of Verdun. Despite being subservient, the republic of Vichy was invaded by the Germans in 1943. Outside of France, a survivor of the German onslaught, General Charles de Gaulle, organized remnants of French forces and, by assuming the role of France itself, put together a Free French army and practically had to force the Allies to support him. In 1943, after Morocco was invaded – the Vichy authorities there did not oppose the landings on the Atlantic Ocean littoral – De Gaulle was present in Casablanca during the conference between Churchill and Roosevelt. Free French forces entered Paris in 1944 and, after the war, France was given an occupation zone in Germany and power of veto in the Security Council of the UNITED NATIONS.

France had to face a nationalist–communist insurrection in Indochina after the war (VIETNAM). It lost the Battle of Dien Bien Phu in 1954 and Prime Minister Mendès-France got France out of Vietnam in the Geneva conference the same year. A military insurrection in Algeria, in 1958, brought De Gaulle back to power. The *pieds noirs*, Algerians of European descent, thought he would back their cause against Algerian nationalists, but De Gaulle let Algeria go in 1962. The FRENCH COMMUNITY was created in 1958 as the framework for decolonization.

France is a founding member of the EUROPEAN UNION. France also includes the overseas departments of Guadaloupe and Martinique in the Caribbean Sea, French Guiana in northern South America, and Réunion in the Indian Ocean. The French still have numerous small dependencies all over the world: in the Pacific Ocean, French Polynesia (the Marquesas, Society Islands, the Tuamotu archipelago, and the Tubuai or Austral Islands), New Caledonia, and Wallis and Futuna (west of Samoa); the Kerguelen islands in the windy latitudes south of the Indian Ocean; Mayotte, part of the COMOROS archipelago, which chose to remain French; St Pierre et Miquelon, south of Newfoundland; and the French Southern and Antarctic Lands, a collection of tiny islands and a claim on the Adelie coast of Antarctica, between 136 degrees and 142 degrees of east longitude. The capital of French Polynesia is Papeete on the island of Tahiti, in the Society Islands group.

Paris, the capital of France, was known by the Romans in 32 BC as Lutetia, a fishing village of the Celtic Parisii. It was a seat of power in Merovingian times. Hugh Capet, who inherited France from the Carolingians, was Count of Paris (987).

FRENCH RULING DYNASTIES AND REGIMES

Royal inheritance in France was determined by direct-line male descent (Salic Law). The Carolingians ruled from 768 to 987. The last of the line, Louis V, died childless. The successor Capetian dynasty ended in 1328 with Charles IV, who was succeeded by Philip VI Valois, grandson of Philip III Capet. Charles VIII Valois, son of Louis XI, died in 1498 without a male heir and was succeeded by his cousin Louis XII, who in turn was succeeded by his cousin Francis I in 1515. Francis I was succeeded in 1547 by his son Henry II, who died in 1559, and left the crown to his son, the 15-year-old Francis II, who died in 1560, and was succeeded by his brothers Charles IX (1560–1574) and Henry III (1574–1589). France was then torn by religious strife, in which the Valois strenuously opposed the Huguenots, or French Protestants. Henry had no male heirs and the last of his brothers had died, which left Henry Bourbon,

King of French Navarre, a Protestant who had married Margaret of Valois, daughter of Charles IX, as the next in line. Henry III, who had come to resent the power of the Catholic party, was assassinated in 1589 while besieging Paris in alliance with Henry of Navarre. The latter, who is supposed to have said that Paris was 'worth a mass', then ascended the throne as Henry IV, the first of the Bourbon line. By the Edict of Nantes of 1598, Henry granted religious freedom. He was assassinated by a Catholic fanatic, and was succeeded by his son Louis XIII, who died in 1643 leaving a seven-year-old heir, Louis XIV, during whose minority cardinals Mazarin and Richelieu managed to contain religious and civil dissensions. Louis eventually wielded absolute power and, in 1685, revoked the Edict of Nantes. The Bourbons ruled France continuously until the Revolution of 1789. Louis XVI was guillotined in 1793. After the Bourbons came the First Republic (1792–1804), followed by the First Empire of Napoleon I (1804–1814). Louis XVIII, brother of Louis XVI, occupied the throne after Napoleon – with the '100 days' interlude of Napoleon's return in 1815 – and in 1830 Charles X Bourbon was replaced by Louis Philippe Orléans, overthrown in the Revolution of 1848. This was followed by the Second Republic under Louis Napoleon Bonaparte, who in 1852 crowned himself Emperor Napoleon III. Napoleon I's son, who never ruled, was considered by Bonapartists as Napoleon II because of his father's abdication in his favour in 1814. Napoleon III was defeated by the Prussians in 1871. After came the Third Republic (1871–1940), the pro-German Vichy regime (1940–1944), the provisional government under De Gaulle (1944–1946), the Fourth Republic (1946–1958), and the Fifth Republic.

Franks (5th–8th cents.; *France*)

The Franks were a Germanic, semi-nomadic people that founded kingdoms in Western Europe after the German migrations infiltrated and put paid to the Roman Empire in the west (ROME). In the late 5th cent., under the kingship of Clovis, they founded the Merovingian dynasty in France. In the early 6th cent., the Merovingians became masters of Dijon and Autun. They expelled the Visigoths from their French domains except for part of the former Roman province of Septimania in the south east, which became Moorish in the 8th cent. The Franks also conquered Provence and the German lands of Thuringia and Alamannia (*Germany*). Under the Frankish Merovingians France was divided between Austrasia in the north east; Neustria, north of the Loire River; Aquitaine, south of the Loire; and the kingdom of Burgundy. Power under the Merovingian kings gradually passed to their majordomos or household lords, one of whom, Charles Martel, who defeated the Moors at Tours (732), *de facto* substituted the Merovingian line with his own Carolingian dynasty. His son Pepin, father of Charlemagne, deposed the last member of the Merovingian line. Charlemagne subjugated the entire territory of France and founded marches in the frontiers with Muslim Spain (CAROLINGIAN EMPIRE).

Free Imperial Cities (HOLY ROMAN EMPIRE)

Free Italian Communes (HOLY ROMAN EMPIRE)

French Colonial Empire (16th–20th cents.)
Until the 19th cent., France saw its colonialist policies frustrated by Great Britain in the two areas where the two states began to compete: North America and India. They also competed in the Caribbean, but this was not mainly over territory but over booty and commerce. In Africa, France and Great Britain almost clashed over the Sudan in the late 19th cent. Otherwise, they accommodated each others' interests in that continent.

NORTH AMERICA AND INDIA

Great Britain got to North America first – with the discovery of Newfoundland in 1497 – but the French jumped ahead in colonization. In 1534, they sailed the St Lawrence – in 1604 they claimed the tiny island of St Pierre and Miquelon – and in 1608 settled the site of Quebec City. From here French expansion was rapid to the Great Lakes, which permitted the creation of the colony of New France in 1663. Lassalle sailed down the Mississippi to its delta (1682). In 1718 the French founded New Orleans which became the capital of the colony of Louisiana (1722). It extended roughly over the drainage basin of the Mississippi River. French territories neighboured on the SPANISH COLONIAL EMPIRE to the west and south, and on British North America to the west, south, and east. By 1732, the British had colonized the eastern seaboard from Nova Scotia and Cape Breton Island to Georgia (1713) (BRITISH COLONIAL EMPIRE). In India the French were less fleet of foot and French India, with its base in Pondicherry, began in 1673, by which time the British were already established in Surat, Bombay, and Madras. Calcutta, which became the beachhead for British India, was founded in 1691. The French were in Guiana (Cayenne) in 1604. In 1635, in the Caribbean, they were established in Guadeloupe and Martinique, which they have kept, with brief interludes, since. The French were not so successful in other Caribbean ventures. They occupied St Lucia in 1660 but lost it to Britain in 1814. They gradually separated the western part of Spanish Hispaniola and, in 1697, created HAITI, which they later lost to a revolt of their slaves in 1804. The French and Dutch have peaceably co-owned St Martin since 1648. The Indian Ocean island of Réunion has been French since 1665. It is part of the Mascarene archipelago.

THE SEVEN YEARS WAR

The balance of colonial expansion between France and Great Britain was radically altered after the Seven Years War (1756–1763), known in American history as the French and Indian Wars, the first conflict in history with a global dimension. In India, French diplomacy more than arms had gained for them the coast of Coromandel, but the British were strong in BENGAL, and in the Battle of Plassey (1757) Clive broke Indian power in the north and put the French on the defensive. The British ruled the waves of the Indian Ocean and the French were reduced to their enclaves of Pondicherry (near Madras), Karaikal, Yanam, and Mahé, where they had to witness powerlessly the British subjugation of India and surrounding countries.

In one bold stroke, the victory of Wolfe over Montcalm on the plains of Abraham (1759), in front of Quebec, made the British masters of New France. French Louisiana was transferred to Spain in 1762, just before the disastrous settlement of the Seven Years War, but the British retained all its lands east of the Mississippi, which the United States later inherited. Ironically, the British returned to France the tiny island of St Pierre and Miquelon, south of New-foundland, which they had been occupying since 1713. The French got back at the British when they gave the Americans crucial grudge aid in the Battle of Yorktown (1781), which sealed their independence from Great Britain. But their formerly promising colonial empire was in a parlous state. The only French acquisition between 1763 and 1800 were the Kerguelen Islands (1772), closer to the Antarctic than to any other landmass, although their claim was not made good until 1893.

AFRICA AND ASIA

The French colonial empire was rebuilt during the 19th cent. The Seven Years War, which, except to Great Britain and France, was more about European disputes than colonial claims, cannot be said to have been a truly world war because it did not significantly affect Africa or the Far East. France had interests in Senegal dating from the late 18th cent., but the turning point for the French came with the annexation of ALGERIA, which initially obeyed the legitimate grievance of piracy in the BARBARY STATES. The French conquest of Algeria, under the monarchy of Louis Philippe, lasted from 1830 until the defeat of Abd al-Kadir in Oran in 1847. After that, the French occupied CÔTE D'IVOIRE (1842), GUINEA (1849), Somaliland (1862; SOMALIA), and Dahomey (1863; BENIN). In Asia, France constituted protectorates over CAMBODIA (1863), Tonkin and Annam (1884; VIETNAM), and LAOS (1893), which, together with the colony of Cochin China (1867; Vietnam), constituted French Indochina. In the Pacific Ocean, France obtained Polynesia (Tahiti) in 1843 to which was added Tuamotu in 1844. It occupied the island of New Caledonia in 1853. New Hebrides (VANUATU) became a British–French condominium in 1906. Back in northern Africa, France annexed Tunisia as a protectorate in 1883. The French empire grew exponentially in territorial extension in the rest of Africa after the Conference of Berlin (1884–1885). France took TOGO, CONGO, and the island of MADAGAS-

CAR in 1885 and CHAD and Ubangi-Shari (CENTRAL AFRICAN REPUB-LIC) in 1887. In 1895, the French formed French West Africa, a federation of colonies, capital Dakar, which eventually included Dahomey, Guinea, French Sudan (MALI), Côte d'Ivoire, MAURITANIA, NIGER, SENEGAL, and Upper Volta (BURKINA FASSO). Of their African conquests the most recalcitrant was Niger (1900) because of Tuareg resistance. The Italian-born Brazza was instrumental in the creation of the French colonial empire in Africa. French aspirations to cut a path from the Atlantic Ocean to the Red Sea were prevented by Kitchener of Great Britain, with the occupation in 1897 of the Sudanese town of Fashoda, despite a previous French presence there. In 1910, France formed French Equatorial Africa, originally known as French Congo, in 1910, capital Brazzaville, including GABON, Middle Congo (Congo), Chad, and Ubangi-Shari. The COMOROS, between Madagascar and the continent of Africa, were occupied in 1909. France had its eyes set on Morocco since their protectorate over Tunisia, but the Germans acted as defenders of Moroccan sovereignty until, in exchange for some concessions in equatorial Africa, the French were given a free hand. France unevenly shared out Morocco with Spain in 1912: Spain got a mountainous strip along the Mediterranean coast and France retained the rest of the country. The growth of the French colonial empire continued during World War I with the occupation of German CAMEROON (1916) and later with the League of Nations mandate over Syria and Lebanon in 1920.

DECOLONIZATION

French decolonization began with independence for Syria (1944) and Lebanon (1945). The Japanese occupied French Indochina in 1940. The Vietnamese started their war for independence immediately after World War II. The French were hard-pressed and let go of Laos and Cambodia in 1953. They tried to suppress the communists in Vietnam but were painfully defeated in the Battle of Dien Bien Phu in 1954. The French politician Pierre Mendès-France read the signs and became prime minister with the promise that he would get France out of the Indochinese quagmire in a month, which he did at Geneva (1954), where Vietnam was partitioned into a southern pro-western half and a communist north. Independence for Morocco and Tunisia came in 1956. In Algeria, which was home to a million European-descended *pied noirs*, opposition to independence was ferocious. A military insurrection caused the fall of the Fourth Republic, the return of De Gaulle to power, and the creation of the Fifth Republic. After some equivocating, and after having suppressed a rebellion led by the military hero Salan and the intellectual Soustelle, a foremost historian and anthropologist of ancient Mexico, De Gaulle let go of Algeria in 1962. The FRENCH COMMUNITY was created in 1958 as the framework for decolonization. Both French West Africa and French Equatorial Africa were dissolved in 1959. In 1960, France granted independence to its African colonies, which joined the French Community, except Guinea, which voted to go it alone. Guadeloupe and Martinique were made overseas departments in 1946 and French Guiana and Réunion in 1947. The French still have dependencies all over the world: in the Pacific Ocean, the Society Islands, the Marquesas, the Loyalty Islands, Tuamotu, the Tubuai Islands, New Caledonia, and Wallis and Futuna (west of Samoa); the Kerguelen Islands in the windy latitudes south of the Indian Ocean; Mayotte, part of the Comoros archipelago, which chose to remain French; and the French Southern and Antarctic Lands, a collection of tiny islands and a claim on the Adelie coast of Antarctica, between 136 degrees and 142 degrees of east longitude.

French Community

In 1946, France created the French Union which handled affairs related to its dependencies. In 1953–1954, the nations of French Indochina (Cambodia, Laos, and Vietnam) became independent, as did Morocco and Tunisia in 1956. In order to accommodate sovereign entities, France under De Gaulle founded the French Community in 1958. Its original members were France itself, Algeria, all French dependencies, and the soon-to-be independent African states of Central African Republic, Chad, Congo-Brazzaville, Gabon, Madagascar (then called the Malagasy Republic), and Senegal. The French Community was supposed to deal with all matters of common interest to its members, defence and trade in particular, but in practice France's relations with its former dependencies have evolved towards an emphasis on bilateralism.

French European Empire (18th–19th cents.)

While France held the ascendancy over Europe, it made, unmade and remade vassal states, sometimes involving mere name changes.

The Cisalpine Republic, capital Milan, created after Napoleon defeated the Austrians in northern Italy in 1796, existed from 1797 to 1802. After, it became the Republic of Italy, which lasted until 1805 and was then converted into the kingdom of Italy, incorporating Venice, with Napoleon himself as king. It was dissolved in 1814 and its territories were transferred to Austria in 1815.

Genoa was proclaimed the Ligurian Republic, which lasted from 1797 to 1805, when it was annexed by France. Genoa was ceded to Sardinia in 1814.

The kingdom of Etruria (1801–1807), created mostly with Tuscany, capital Florence, after Napoleon's victory over the Austrians in Marengo, was annexed by France. In 1815 it was restored to the Habsburg.

Lucca, declared a Bonapartist principality in 1805, was absorbed by Parma in 1815.

The Kingdom of Naples was separated from Sicily in 1806 and returned to the Bourbons in 1815.

The Low Countries were annexed by France in 1795 and the Netherlands was named the Batavian Republic. It was restored in 1815.

Switzerland was declared the Helvetian Republic from 1798 to 1803. After, it regained its traditional name, but remained subservient to France. The ancient bishopric of Valais was attached to the Helvetian Republic from 1798 to 1802, after which it was 'independent' to 1810, when it was annexed by France. After 1815, it became a Swiss canton.

After the Battle of Jena (1806), the HOLY ROMAN EMPIRE was dissolved and the Confederation of the Rhine created with Germany minus Prussia, Austria, and ironically the western Rhineland itself, which was annexed by France. After 1815, it became the GERMAN CONFEDERATION.

After the Napoleonic victories at Eylau and Friedland over the Russians and Prussians, the Grand Duchy of Warsaw was created in 1807. It was annexed by Russia in 1813.

Denmark received territories between Lübeck and Holstein, which it had to relinquish after 1815.

Joseph Bonaparte, brother of Napoleon, was King of Spain from 1808 to 1813.

Fujairah (UNITED ARAB EMIRATES)

Fulani (18th and 19th cents.; *Sub-Saharan Africa*)
The Fulani were a pious and powerful Muslim people that conquered OYO and went on to annex BAMBARA. They created the last important sub-Saharan kingdom. Starting in 1804, the Fulani, under Usuman dan Fodio, conquered most of HAUSA and established their capital in Sokoto, northern Nigeria. Sokoto was annexed by the BRITISH COLONIAL EMPIRE in 1903. Fula, the Fulani language, belongs to the Niger–Congo family of languages spoken in western Africa.
(*See chronology under* Western and Sub-Saharan Africa.)

Funan (CAMBODIA)

Funj (16th–19th cents.; north-eastern Africa)
An Arabic-speaking Islamic kingdom in NUBIA, in the 18th cent. Funj reached as far as central Sudan. Funj was subjected by the Egyptians in the 1820s. The Sudanese religious and nationalist movement led by the Mahdi in the 1880s originated in Funj lands.

Fur (17th–19th cents.; *Sub-Saharan Africa*)
Fur was a kingdom in western Sudan that, in the 16th cent., conquered Kanem in CHAD. The territory of Fur was taken by Egypt in 1874.

G

Gabon

Mostly peopled by Fang tribes – who speak a language of the Bantu family – Gabon was under French influence from 1839. It was created, like Liberia and Sierra Leone, as a haven for freed slaves. The Berlin Conference (1884–1885) recognized French claims to Gabon, which became part of French West Africa until 1959 and independent in 1960. French is the official language. The capital of Gabon is Libreville.

Galicia (SUEVES)

Gambia (The)

Peopled by tribal speakers of Mandinka, belonging to the Niger–Congo family of languages spoken in western Africa, The Gambia was acquired by Great Britain as its first African colony in 1588. It was granted independence in 1965. From 1981 to 1989 it federated with Senegal as Senegambia. The capital of The Gambia is Banjul.

Gdansk (DANZIG)

Genoa (10th–18th cents.; northern *Italy*)

A Ligurian settlement that prospered under ROME, the port city of Genoa was a free commune in the 10th cent., when it was also briefly occupied by Muslim FATIMIDS. In the 12th cent., allied to PISA, it wrested Corsica and Sardinia from loose Islamic control. Genoa and Pisa fell out over the possession of these islands and in 1284 Genoa broke Pisan naval power. By then Genoa had embarked on commercial empire-building in the eastern Mediterranean, which brought it into conflict with VENICE. It held the island of RHODES from 1248 to 1256. By 1360, Genoa had lost Sardinia to ARAGON, but it had gained islands in the northern Aegean Sea which gave it privileged access to the Black Sea. In 1400 Genoese were established in southern Crimea and used it as a terminus for trade with the east until it fell to the khanate of the CRIMEA ca. 1480 (BOSPORAN KINGDOM). Venice had been edging Genoa out of the eastern Mediterranean since 1381 and Genoese maritime power was much diminished by the end of the 15th cent. On the mainland, Genoa had occupied Liguria during the 14th cent. Caught between French and Habsburg rivalry to dominate it during the 15th and 16th cents., all Genoa could do was retain its relative autonomy. Under Andrea Doria, it had a resurgence in the 16th cent. In the 17th and 18th cents., Genoa was again disputed by different powers, although it managed to loosen a Habsburg hold in 1746. In 1768 it yielded to France its last possession, Corsica, where a year later

Napoleon was born. After 1797 it was part of the FRENCH EUROPEAN EMPIRE and in 1814 it was ceded to the kingdom of SARDINIA.

Georgia

The territory of modern Georgia, which has changed little over time, has had perhaps more different names than any other portion of the planet. From at least the 3rd cent. BC, it had been called successively Sarmatia, Colchis, Abasgia, Iberia, and Lazica. Georgia was Christianized in the 4th cent. It was part of the SASANID EMPIRE, from which it seceded ca. 400. It was self-ruling to the 13th cent. (during the 6th cent. by an Armenian dynasty). Under Queen Thamar, ca. 1200, Georgia reached the peak of its expansion in the Caucasus region. After that, despite attacks and ravagings by Seljuks, Mongols, and Tamerlane's Turks, it managed to survive as a Christian kingdom until a 15th cent. king named Alexander divided the land for his sons into Imeritia, Kaketia, and Karthlia. In the 16th cent., the OTTOMAN EMPIRE took Georgia. Eastern Georgia was under Persian influence in the 18th cent. (IRAN). Western Georgia was subdivided under Ottoman rule into: Abkhazia, Mingrelia, Imeritia, and Guria. The Islamic hold on Georgia was not very stringent and in 1801 a local Georgian prince ceded the Persian half to Russia. In 1829 the Russians obtained the other half from the Ottomans. In 1922 the Soviets integrated Georgia with Azerbaijan and Armenia to form the Transcaucasian Soviet Federated Socialist Republic, from which the Georgian Soviet Socialist Republic was separated in 1936. In 1991 Georgia became independent. The capital is Tbilisi. Georgian is a branch of the Caucasian family of languages, not related to the Indo-European family of languages.

ABKHAZIA, ADJARIA, AND OSSETIA

Abkhazia is the north-western province of Georgia, the ancient Colchis. In 1930 it was made an autonomous republic within Georgia. In 1992, with Russian support, Abkhazia *de facto* separated from Georgia. Georgian forces could not suppress the secession. The capital of Abkhazia is Sukhumi. Georgian and Abkhazian are related tongues.

South Ossetia has also been resistant to Georgian sovereignty and there exists a movement for joining the Russian Republic of North Ossetia (Alania). The capital of South Ossetia is Tskhinvali. Ossetian is an Indo-Iranian language in the Indo-European family of languages.

In 1995 Adjaria was also recognized by Georgia as an autonomous republic under its sovereignty. The capital is Batumi.

Gepids (5th–6th cents.; eastern Europe)

The Gepids were a Germanic semi-nomadic nation which held lands in eastern Europe (borderlands of Hungary and Romania), where, in 454, they defeated the Visigoths in alliance with the Ostrogoths (GOTHS). They were crushed during the 6th cent. by the Avars and Lombards.

German Colonial Empire (19th–20th cents.)
The unification of Germany in 1871 led to its interest in the acquisition of overseas colonies. During the colonialist Berlin Conference, which lasted from 1884 to 1885, Germany – which earlier had ventured into South West Africa – staked claims over various other African territories and in the Pacific Ocean. The German Colonial Empire included: South West Africa (NAMIBIA), Kameron (CAMEROON), Tanganyika (TANZANIA), TOGO, RWANDA, and BURUNDI in Africa; and the island chains of the Marianas and the Caroline Islands (MICRONESIA) in the Pacific Ocean. A revolt of local tribes between 1904 and 1908 in South West Africa resulted in the virtual extermination of the Herero. German control over Rwanda and Burundi was minimal, but the Germans fought the British to a standstill in Tanganyika during World War I. After the war, all of Germany's colonial lands became League of Nations mandates divided among Belgium (Rwanda and Burundi), France (Cameroon and Togo), Great Britain (western Cameroon and eastern Togo), South Africa (Namibia), and Japan (the Pacific Ocean islands).

German Confederation (19th cent.)
The myth of the HOLY ROMAN EMPIRE could be sustained as long as no one challenged the Habsburg 'hereditary–elective' right to the crown. After Napoleon's FRENCH EUROPEAN EMPIRE, Prussia emerged too powerful to accept even the nominal rule of a German Emperor but at that stage not powerful enough to reunite all the German states and statelets. In 1815, the Congress of VIENNA reached the compromise of retaining the Holy Roman Empire's borders and calling it the German Confederation, whose greatest achievement, foreshadowing political union, was the establishment of the Zollverein. This was a customs union initiated by Prussia with North Germany which culminated in 1854, but did not include Austria because of Prussian opposition. The largest political entity wholly within the German Confederation was BAVARIA. The HABSBURG EMPIRE and PRUSSIA were partially in and it was within the German Confederation that Prussian influence superseded that of Habsburg Austria in the rest of Germany. Prussia's victory over Austria in 1866 led to the dissolution of the German Confederation. It was replaced partly by the NORTH GERMAN CONFEDERATION, but Prussia dominated and in 1871 it brought all German lands together with the exclusion of Austria–Hungary.

Germans
The Germans were tribes that came from Scandinavia and Jutland and gradually spread during the history of ancient Rome to occupy all of Europe east of the Rhine, south to the edge of the Balkans, and east to the Black Sea. During the 5th cent. the Germans felt the brunt of invaders from the east, possibly also pressure from the SLAVS, and began their gradual leaching of the Roman Empire

(ROME). However, Germans retained their lands east of the Rhine. Their most famous leader was Arminius, who defeated the Roman legions of Varus (1st cent. AD). BURGUNDIANS, GEPIDS, GOTHS, FRANKS, SUEVES, and VANDALS were all Germanic tribes. The Franks, who occupied the West European heart of the Roman Empire, were strongly Latinized. The Germans within the CAROLINGIAN EMPIRE are often identified as East Franks.

Germany
SEE ENTRY IN 'PROVINCES AND REGIONS'
Modern Germany was created in 1871 from PRUSSIA, the NORTH GERMAN CONFEDERATION, BAVARIA, and the rest of the German principalities of the former HOLY ROMAN EMPIRE. Its core was the kingdom of Prussia. Under Chancellor Bismarck's firm hand, Prussia absorbed Schleswig and Holstein and northern Germany in wars won against Denmark and Austria between 1864 and 1866. After defeating France in 1871, Prussia incorporated Bavaria and southern Germany and the provinces of Alsace and Lorraine, which had been French since the 17th cent. The Prussian Hohenzollern monarch William I proclaimed the unification of Germany, calling itself the German Reich, in occupied Versailles. Germany recklessly pursued policies of overseas colonialist expansion and involvement in the Balkans under William II, after Bismarck's dismissal in 1890.

THE SCHLIEFFEN PLAN

In June 1914, a Serb fanatic assassinated the crown prince of Austria–Hungary Archduke Francis Ferdinand in Sarajevo, Bosnia-Herzegovina, a Serb territory which the Austrians occupied in 1908. Austria–Hungary presented Serbia with conditions which Serbia, with Russian backing, did not accept. In July, Austria declared war on Serbia. Germany, its ally (Central Powers), declared war on Russia on 1 August and on France two days later. Great Britain, mindful of the continental balance of power, entered the war as an ally of France. The Germans had a blueprint for victory in the Schlieffen Plan ('strengthen the right wing'), which called for a quick crossing of Belgium and a swift defeat of outnumbered French armies. Germany quickly over-ran Belgium and Luxembourg and its armies came close to Paris in the first Battle of the Marne but they opened flanks in its advancing line, which the French, with British support, attacked and contained. The Germans next concentrated on the British front in the first Battle of Ypres (Bloody Wipers). The German attack on the British lines was repeated in 1915, this time using gas. The Russians went to war with due enthusiasm but they were woefully unprepared. At first victorious on the Austrian front – the Habsburg Empire was anything but a cohesive fighting machine – they soon got trounced by the Germans in the Masurian Lakes region of East Prussia in 1915. The Russian front held only because the Germans did not want to divert resources from the western front. Italy entered the war that year on the Allies' side. In 1916, a great German onslaught was contained around Verdun and the Allies counter-attacked along the Somme River, where the British were the first to use tanks. In 1916, the Russian armies, under the command of General Brusilov, attempted going on the offensive, but instead they collapsed through defeat, insubordination, and desertion. Negotiations with Germany started very quickly and culminated in the Treaty of Brest-Litovsk in March 1918, whose arrangements were really transitory but which allowed the Germans to move troops to the western front. In 1917 the United States had entered the war on the side of the Allies.

In 1918, the German armies, led by Hindenburg and Ludendorff, attacked once more in the second Battle of the Marne, but by August they had gained little ground and instead were left fighting alone with the defeat of Austria and the loss of Balkan allies. Germany surrendered on 11 November without having been fully defeated. By the Treaty of VERSAILLES, signed at the Paris Peace Conference (1919), Germany was forced to return Alsace and Lorraine to France and to cede to newly-created Poland a corridor to the port of DANZIG on the Baltic Sea, which divided the territory of Prussia into Brandenburg in the west and East Prussia. The period after World War I to the accession of Hitler is known as the Weimar Republic, rich in cultural activity but much-maligned by German ultra-nationalists then.

HITLER

On 30 January 1933, Adolf Hitler, haranguing for revanchism and anti-semitism, manoeuvred himself and his Nazi Party into power. In 1934, Nazi Germany took back the Rhineland, over which the French held but did not exercise the right of occupation. In 1938, it proclaimed its union with Austria, the Anschluss, and German troops marched into Vienna. After the Munich Conference the same year, in which the Western powers tried to appease Hitler, Germany occupied the borderlands of Czechoslovakia, known as the Sudetes, where Germans were a majority, and in effect absorbed Czechoslovakia, which it divided into the subject territories of Bohemia-Moravia and of Slovakia. In August of 1939, Hitler signed a non-aggression pact with the Soviet dictator Stalin, by which Germany and the USSR secretly agreed to share Poland between themselves. The Soviets were given a free hand in the Baltic republics of Lithuania, Latvia, and Estonia. Allied to Italy since 1936 – the Axis, which was extended to Japan in 1940 – Germany started World War II, with the excuse of reclaiming Danzig, by invading Poland on 1 September 1939. In 1940, after what is known as the 'phoney war', during which the allied armies of France and Britain faced the Germans without actually fighting, Germany over-ran Belgium and with astonishing celerity occupied France. They allowed the creation of a puppet French state south of the Loire, headed by Marshal Pétain, hero of Verdun, with Vichy, a spa, as its capital. With the conquest of France, the German Luftwaffe tried to cow Great Britain into neutrality, but the British fended off the German offensive during the air Battle of Britain, which wound down towards the end of 1940. At the same time, to deny Britain bases on the eastern coast of the North Sea, Germany occupied Denmark and Norway. Italy was experiencing military setbacks in northern Greece and Libya, and Hitler went to the aid of the Italian dictator Mussolini by invading the Balkans and taking Crete, Tunisia, and Libya in 1941. In June 1941, Germany launched the invasion of the USSR. Its armies advanced to Leningrad, Moscow, Stalingrad, and the northern Caucasus. After the Japanese attack in December 1941, on the American naval base in Pearl Harbor, Hawaii, the United States declared war on the Axis. At its zenith, the Nazi empire occupied or neutralized all of continental Europe and Scandinavia, save Soviet Russia, and northern Africa from Vichy-held Morocco to the western border of Egypt. This empire crumbled quickly through defeats at El Alamein (1942) and Stalingrad (1943) and after the Normandy invasion (1944). Hitler committed suicide in April 1945 and Germany surrendered one month later.

THE 'MIRACLE'

Germany, shorn of Prussia and Silesia by the Soviets, was divided into four occupation zones to the USSR (eastern Germany), the United States (Bavaria and southern Germany), Great Britain (northern Germany), and France (the Rhineland and the Saar). The Western powers pooled their zones into the Federal Republic of Germany in 1949, capital Bonn, initially led by Adenauer, and the Soviets followed suit by creating in their zone the German Democratic Republic (EAST GERMANY). Berlin, which was engulfed by the Soviet armies, was also divided into four zones, the eastern Soviet part becoming the capital of East Germany. Post-war democratic Germany's economy developed at such a huge pace that its growth was figuratively called miraculous, a qualifier which has become current to apply to countries that individually or as a group grow at exceptional rates, hence the 'Asian miracle'. With the acquiescence of the Soviet leader Mikhail Gorbachev, East Germany collapsed during the process of disintegration of the USSR and the two Germanies were reunified in 1991. Berlin was later chosen to be its capital.

Ghana (Ancient) (7th–13th cents.; *Sub-Saharan Africa*)
A Muslim kingdom, Ghana occupied lands in Mauritania and Mali. It was invaded by the ALMORAVIDS in 1076. Its capital was Kumbi Salih. SONGHAI was a successor kingdom in the region.
(*See chronology under* Western and Sub-Saharan Africa.)

Ghana
Ghana's territory was home to the ASHANTI kingdom. From 1821 to 1906, Great Britain created the colony of the Gold Coast in Ashanti lands, to which British Togoland was added in 1956 (TOGO). In 1960 the Gold Coast gained

its independence, the first British African colony to do so, as Ghana, a name it took from an ancient West African state outside its own territory. English is the official language and the principal native tongue is Kwa, a member of the Niger–Congo family of languages spoken in western Africa. The capital of Ghana is Accra.

Ghaznavids (10th–12th cents.; Afghanistan and northern *India*)
In the first half of the 10th cent., a Turkish clan separated from the kingdom of the Persian SAMANIDS in Transoxiana and established itself in Ghazni (southern Afghanistan) as the Ghaznavids. They over-ran the rest of Afghanistan and seized Khurasan ca. 950. The greatest of the Ghaznavid rulers, Mahmud of Ghazni (998–1030), conquered the PUNJAB. Shortly afterwards the Ghaznavids were ousted from Khurasan by the Seljuks (SELJUK PERSIA). From their base in Afghanistan, under pressure from the GHURIDS ca. 1150, who were northern Afghans, the Ghaznavids retreated to the Punjab in 1173 and installed their capital in Lahore. They perished towards the end of 12th cent. at the hands of the Ghurids, one of whose generals established in 1206 the DELHI SULTANATE.
(*See chronology under* Afghanistan *and* Indian Subcontinent.)

Ghurids (12th–13th cents.; Afghanistan and northern *India*)
The Ghurids were from northern Afghanistan. They ousted the GHAZ-NAVIDS from Ghazni in 1173. Under Muhammad of Ghur (modern Ghowr, between Herat and Kabul), they invaded the Punjab in 1186, defeated the Ghaznavids, and took Delhi in 1192, extending their rule to the Ganges River Basin, which they took ca. 1200 from Hindu rajahs (RAJPUTS). After the death of Muhammad in 1206, Qutb ud-Din Aybar cut free from the Ghurids, who were having a hard time in Afghanistan. His successor, Iltutmish, founded the DELHI SULTANATE. Muhammad was defeated and killed by KHWARIZM, who completed the conquest of Afghanistan by 1215.
(*See chronology under* Afghanistan *and* Indian Subcontinent.)

Ghuzz (11th cent.; *Central Asia*: Kirghiz steppe)
The Ghuzz were a Turkish horde active in the area from Lake Balkash to the north of the Aral and Caspian seas. It is important in history because during the 11th cent. it divided in at least two significant ways. One branch, the Seljuks, destroyed BUYID PERSIA and went on to found the RUM Sultanate in Anatolia. Another branch, following in the footsteps of the Seljuks, but along the western side of the Caspian Sea, established itself in western Anatolia on lands ceded to them by the Seljuks. This horde was ruled by the Osmanlis, also known as the Ottomans. The Ghuzz who remained in central Asia were annihilated by the PETCHENEGS and the BULGARS, Turks like them on the edges of Kievan Rus.
(*See chronology under* Greater Mongolia.)

Golconda (BAHMANI SULTANATE; CENTRAL INDIA)

Golden Horde (13th–15th cents.; *Central Asia*: Kirghiz steppe and western Siberia; *Southern Russia*)
As in the case of all the Central Asian semi-nomadic empires, the borders of the Golden Horde, also known as the Khanate of Kipchak, are impossible to trace with precision. Vaguely, it extended from the middle reaches of the Irtysh River to the northern shores of the Aral and Caspian seas down to the Caucasus across to the Crimea and along the borders of Kievan Rus (RUSSIA) to the margins of the northern Siberian forest and back to the Irtysh. The Golden Horde was formed by the *ulus* (clans) of Jochi, the eldest heir of Genghis, although not likely his son but of a Mongol warlord who held Genghis' wife captive for a time. There was no formal discrimination but there is evidence that Batu, the son of Jochi, and the actual conqueror of the Golden Horde territory from the POLOVETZY (ca. 1230), did not consider his empire to be more than nominally part of the MONGOL EMPIRE. The separation commenced with the Islamization of its rulers ca. 1250, and became unmistakable when ca. 1270 the Golden Horde took the side of the CHAGATAITE KHANATE in its separatist wars against the Mongol Empire. From its establishment ca. 1240 to its dismemberment into successor khanates in the 15th cent., the Golden Horde, from its capital in Sarai near the Volga Delta, made the Russians pay tribute and obey its commands on princely successions. Around 1380, the Golden Horde was conquered by Toqtamish, the leader of the WHITE HORDE, the *ulus* in the eastern part of the Golden Horde. Toqtamish took Azerbaijan, went to war with Tamerlane, and lost. The debilitating effect of this defeat led eventually to the dissolution of the Golden Horde (TIMURID EMPIRE AND SUCCESSOR STATES). The Khanate of CRIMEA separated in 1430, as did the Khanates of KAZAN in 1445 and of ASTRAKHAN in 1466. With the destruction of Sarai by the Mongols of Crimea with the backing of Russia in 1502, the Golden Horde was extinguished.
(*See chronology under* Southern Russia.)

Gondwana (CENTRAL INDIA)

Gothia (BOSPORAN KINGDOM)

Goths
According to a quasi-legendary account, the Swedish island of Gotland is the home of the Goths. Be that as it may, the historical Goths were a Germanic people that, in the 3rd cent. AD, occupied lands from today's Romania to north of the Black Sea. They were divided into the western Goths, or Visigoths, and the eastern Goths, or Ostrogoths. When the famous movements of the peoples (*Volkerwanderung*) began in the 4th cent., with the HUNS migrating towards the west from the Aral Sea, they first pushed the Ostrogoths, who

in turn leaned on the Visigoths and both masses invaded the Roman Empire. This showed the way for all the other Germanic tribes, although Germanic infiltration had begun before that and the Roman emperor Decius had been defeated and killed by the Goths themselves in the northern Balkans in 251. The Goths headed for the Balkans where, in 378, they defeated Emperor Valens in Adrianople (Edirne in European Turkey). The Visigoths separated from the Ostrogoths some time in the late 4th cent. but some Visigoths were with the Ostrogoths when the latter defeated the GEPIDS in 454 and later drove the HUNS out of Hungary. The Ostrogoths were occupying lands east of northern Italy when they fell on Odoacer, the Germanic ruler of Italy who had deposed the last Roman Emperor in 476, and occupied Italy until the BYZAN-TINE EMPIRE displaced them in 535. Later in the 6th cent. the eastern Goths were destroyed by the AVARS, who were in turn crushed by Charlemagne in the 7th cent. The mass of the Visigoths moved into western Europe, where they quickly over-ran France and, by the early 5th cent., were in Spain. It is possible that they were riding with the ALANS, with whom they might have occupied Catalonia ca. 420. In France they were eventually driven out by the FRANKS. But in Spain during the 5th cent. they founded the VISIGOTHIC KINGDOM, which eventually fell to ISLAM in the early 8th cent.

Gran Colombia (19th cent.; Colombia, Ecuador, and Venezuela)
The short-lived Republic of Gran Colombia was first proclaimed by Simon Bolivar upon the final defeat of Spanish forces in New Granada after the Battle of Boyacá in 1819. Venezuela joined Gran Colombia after the Battle of Carabobo in 1821 and Ecuador followed suit after the Battle of Pichincha, won by Sucre, Bolivar's most trusted lieutenant, in 1822. The republic dissolved when Venezuela and Ecuador seceded in 1830. Colombia reverted to its colonial designation as Nueva Granada, but changed to Colombia again in 1863.

Casanare are the plains of eastern Colombia, part of the llanos of the Orinoco River (Venezuela), where resistance to Spanish rule (1814–1821) permitted Bolivar to gather forces, reinforced by British volunteers and arms, for the final independentist campaigns in northern South America.

Granada (13th–15th cents.; Muslim Spain)
The last prize of the *reconquista* – the recovery of Iberia by its Christian kingdoms – Granada, with its famous Alhambra, was ruled by the Nasrids from the fall of the ALMOHADS (ca. 1230) to 1492. Its last ruler, Boabdil, surrendered the city to the Catholic Kings (Isabella of CASTILLE and Ferdinand of ARAGON). The fall of Granada marks the birth of united Spain.

Great Amphictyony (6th–4th cents. BC; Ancient *Greece*)
The originary leagues of the Greek city–states were religious in character (6th cent. BC). The most important was the Great Amphictyony for the upkeep of Delphi. Its council decreed on religious matters, but gradually encroached on

politics. It was powerless during the period of the overtly political leagues during the Persian and Peloponnesian Wars (5th cent.), but it was revived by MACEDON in the 4th cent. BC to justify its annexation of Greece. (*See chronology under* Greece (Ancient).)

Great Britain

The United Kingdom of Great Britain and Northern Ireland is constituted in the main by ENGLAND, WALES, SCOTLAND, and Northern Ireland. The conquest of Wales went on from the start of Norman England, after the Battle of Hastings in 1066, until 1282. Wales was joined to the crown in 1536. The conquest of Ireland was begun by Richard Pembroke in 1170, after which Henry II visited the island. English rule was extended not without hardship during the 13th cent., but during the 14th and 15th cents. there were many rebellions. Harsh English rule led to a general insurrection which Oliver Cromwell put down in 1649–1650 at a high cost in lives. Arbitrary confiscations were carried out which were to inflame Irish repudiation of English rule until independence. In 1690, French-reinforced Catholic forces, led by the deposed British monarch James II, were defeated by a British army in the Battle of Boyne in 1690, which marks the end of effective Irish resistance to British rule. When Ireland became independent in 1937, Northern Ireland (Ulster), which had been peopled by Protestants, especially during the confiscations of the 17th cent., chose to remain part of the United Kingdom. In 1174, Henry II obtained by dubious means the allegiance of Scotland, which was later repudiated, and it was only after centuries of contention that the two countries were united with the accession to the English throne of James I, of the Scot house of Stuart. It was made official by the Act of Union of 1707. Hanover was a dependency of the crown until the accession of Queen Victoria in 1837, who could not keep it because of the Salic Law (only males inherit land).

REASONS TO MAKE WAR

Favoured by natural resources, insularity, and efficient central authority, England's economic development was so rapid that it had a middle class strong enough to question monarchical privileges. Parliament refused to buckle under to King Charles I, and in the Civil War (1642–1648), defeated royalist forces, captured the King, and beheaded him in 1649 (more than 140 years before the French guillotined Louis XVI!). Having tried a policy of territorial expansionism in the continent during the Hundred Years War, England now had two over-riding foreign policy interests – i.e., reasons to make war – and they were: commerce and the balance of power in continental Europe.

For commerce, it needed a powerful navy, which it built up during the 17th cent. against strong Dutch competition. Unlike the Spanish Colonial Empire, British colonialism was oriented towards settlement and was not very impulsive at first. However, this changed through British interest in preventing any continental power from becoming hegemonic, which could have happened had a member of the French ruling house of Bourbon inherited the Spanish crown as bequeathed by the last Habsburg Spanish sovereign Charles II. Great Britain's strong participation in the War of Spanish Succession (1700–1714) was commensurate with its gains overseas. During the following decades, British naval power strengthened apace with its commercial boldness, historical trends which were thoroughly demonstrated in the even more advantageous results of the Seven Years War (1756–1763). In this war, Great Britain's half-hearted participation in the continental campaigns was more than compensated for by its victories against the French in North America and in India. Sustained by a navy of global dimensions, British colonialism now had momentum despite the setback of the independence of its North American Atlantic seaboard colonies. The problem of the European balance of power came to the fore with the ascent of Republican and Napoleonic France. Great Britain not only participated in all the coalitions against France, but in fact, unlike Austria, Prussia, and Russia, it was never defeated on land, so it was virtually in a permanent state of war with France from 1793 to 1815. It bolstered occupied Portugal and Spain and led the Peninsular Campaign to victory in 1813. In the sea it crushed all naval opposition in the Battles of Aboukir (1798), Copenhagen (1801), and Trafalgar (1805). The final defeat of Napoleonic France in the Battle of Waterloo (1815) was a triumph for the British dogged adherence to the principle of the balance of power. Master at sea and unchallengeable in Europe, Great Britain during the 19th cent. concentrated on its empire which it made into the largest ever seen. The Crimean War (1853–1856) was the only European action it engaged in and that was in part to tell the Russians not to even consider approaching British India. If France was the threat to European peace at the beginning of the 19th cent., the spoilsport one hundred years later was the German Reich under the irresponsible Kaiser William II, and it was to prevent the Germans from swamping France and dominating Europe that Great Britain entered World War I.

'BLOODY WIPERS'

In June 1914, a Serb fanatic assassinated the crown prince of Austria–Hungary Archduke Francis Ferdinand in Sarajevo, Bosnia, a Serb territory which the Austrians occupied in 1908. Austria–Hungary presented Serbia with impossible conditions which Serbia, with Russian backing, did not accept. In July, Austria declared war on Serbia. Germany declared war on Russia on 1 August and on France two days later. Germany quickly over-ran Belgium and Luxembourg and Great Britain entered the war and manned the northern front west of Belgium. Germany came close to Paris in the first Battle of the Marne but it opened flanks in its advancing line, which the

French, with British support, attacked. The Germans next concentrated on the British front in the first Battle of Ypres (Bloody Wipers). The German attack on the British lines was repeated in 1915, this time using gas. Italy entered the war that year on the Allies side, but British, Australian, and New Zealand troops suffered a stinging setback when they landed in the Gallipoli peninsula (northern side of the Dardanelles), where, through inaction, they were contained and routed by the Turks. In 1916, a great German onslaught was contained around Verdun and the Allies counter-attacked along the Somme River, where the British were the first to use tanks. In 1917, the United States entered the war, but Russia, after a hopeless offensive, was practically out of it by the end of the year. In April 1918 the Allies unified the command structure under French Marshal Foch, although the national commanders, Haig on the British line, retained direct control of their forces. The Germans attacked one more time in the second Battle of the Marne, but by August they had gained little ground and instead were left fighting alone with the defeat of Austria and the loss of Balkan allies. Germany surrendered in November of 1918. Great Britain gained mandates in Africa and the Near East and the European balance of power seemed re-established in the VERSAILLES conference. But the arrangements were fragile.

WINSTON CHURCHILL

Hitler came to power in Germany in 1933 and inaugurated an aggressive policy of re-armament and annexations. The French did not contain him when he occupied the Rhineland in 1934. Great Britain, under Prime Minister Neville Chamberlain, tried appeasing the German dictator in exchange for promises of peace (CZECHOSLOVAKIA). In 1939, Hitler demanded the DANZIG corridor from Poland and when the Poles refused he invaded on 1 September. World War II had begun. Great Britain chose the combative Winston Churchill as its leader. The greatest threat to the country in all its history came during the air battle for Britain, in which the Royal Air Force held its own, despite nearly crippling losses of ground bases, against incessant attacks by the German Luftwaffe. In 1941, Hitler turned against Russia and the British defeated the German Afrika Korps in the Battle of El Alamein. After being attacked by Japan – allied to Germany and Italy in the Axis – the United States entered the war in December 1941. The USSR proved impossible to subdue and turned the tide of the land war in Stalingrad (1943). With the invasion of Normandy from Great Britain, Germany was doomed. Hitler committed suicide in April 1945 and Germany unconditionally surrendered in May. After the war, Great Britain became the staunchest ally of the United States in its Cold War confrontation with the USSR, beginning with the Soviet blockade of Berlin in 1948–1949. When communist North Korea invaded the south in 1950, Great Britain contributed a significant part of the UN-forces which threw back the invaders and later opposed the Chinese armies that invaded the peninsula to save the defeated Korean communists.

Great Britain gradually divested itself of its colonial empire after the war, though to do so it had to face Jewish terrorism in Palestine and insurgencies in Malaya, Kenya, and other places. It still has some dependencies. In the Caribbean, they are the islands of Anguilla, the British Virgin Islands, the Cayman Islands, Montserrat, and Turks and Caicos Islands. In the Atlantic Ocean, they are the islands of Bermuda, the Falkland Islands, Pitcairn, and the South Georgia and Sandwich Islands. There is a British Indian Ocean Territory, comprising a number of small islands and atolls, including Diego Garcia, a military outpost. Gibraltar, taken by Britain in 1704, is in southern Spain. In 1982, Argentina, under the military regime of Galtieri, invaded the Falklands and South Georgia, from which its forces were evicted by a large British task force with the support of the United States.

NORTHERN IRELAND

In the 17th cent. much of Northern Ireland (*Ulster*) was peopled by Scots Protestants. In the face of nationalist agitation and fighting in Ireland, Great Britain in 1920 granted Northern Ireland a parliament (Stormont). When Ireland became a republic in 1948, Northern Ireland remained attached to the Crown. The Catholic minority in Ulster were discriminated against and in 1969 the 'provisional' wing of the Irish Republican Army (IRA) went underground and initiated an armed struggle using largely terrorist tactics. Protestant loyalists followed suit and Northern Ireland gradually became a divided and warring society. In face of the 'troubles', Great Britain introduced direct rule and dissolved Stormont in 1973. Irish nationalist terrorism spread to southern Ireland and England in the 1970s. The IRA nearly killed Prime Minister Margaret Thatcher in 1984. She remained unbowed but accepted consultations with Ireland in 1986. Negotiations progressed enough for the IRA to announce a unilateral cease-fire in 1994, suspended in 1996, and reinstated in 1997. The settlement arrived at in 1998, provides for an incipient condominium for Northern Ireland between London and Dublin which recognizes local interests. Great Britain has also participated in various UN peace-keeping operations. It has been a member of the EUROPEAN UNION since 1973.

THE CHANNEL ISLANDS AND THE ISLE OF MAN

The United Kingdom also includes the Channel Islands (off the coast of Normandy), which are divided into two bailiwicks with lieutenant governors appointed by the Crown. One is the island of Jersey (with St Helier as its capital). The other is Guernsey (with St Peter as its capital), which also includes Alderney and Sark. The Channel Islands were part of the duchy of NORMANDY in the 9th cent. and were retained by the English Crown when the duchy passed to France in 1204. The official language is French, but English is generally spoken. They were the only part of the United Kingdom that the Germans occupied during World War II. The Isle of Man, in the Irish Sea, was Norwegian to 1266, when it passed to Scotland. It belonged to the Earls of Salisbury and Derby until 1765 when it was purchased for the British Crown by Parliament.

London first came to notice in AD 61 during Boadicea's rebellion against the Romans (Londinium). The city was enveloped in obscurity after the Romans left Britain (410). It was held by King Alfred the Great in 886. William the Conqueror commenced the construction of the Tower of London. In the 14th cent. London was the capital of England and thus later became the capital of Great Britain.

Great Bulgaria (VOLGA BULGARS)

Great Moravia (9th–11th cents.; eastern Europe)
The Slavic kingdom of Great Moravia, founded in the 9th cent., included Bohemia, Silesia, Slovakia, southern Poland, and northern Hungary. It absorbed the AVARS, but early in the 10th cent. it was destroyed by Hungarian raiders. After the Battle of Lechfeld, won by the future Emperor Otto I over the MAGYARS in 955, Moravia became a German march (HOLY ROMAN EMPIRE), and in the 11th cent. it was part of BOHEMIA, to which Moravia has remained linked ever since.

Greece (Ancient) (9th–2nd cents. BC; Greece and *Middle East*)
SEE ENTRY IN PROVINCES AND REGIONS
The fall of MYCENEAN GREECE was followed by a period that is considered the Greek dark ages. When the Greeks emerged from this state, towards the 9th–8th cents. BC, their core territories (mainland Greece and the Peloponnesus, the Anatolian Mediterranean coast, and the islands of the Aegean and the eastern Mediterranean) were divided into regions with characteristics of their own, especially dialectical, containing independent city–states. The regions divided according to dialects are: Ionian, Dorian, North-western, Arcadian, and Aeolic. Colonization went on from the 8th cent. to the 6th cent. The principal areas of colonization were northern Greece, Thrace, the coast of the Black Sea, the coast of Anatolia, Cyprus, Rhodes, Cyrenaica, Sicily, and Magna Graecia. Though generally very disunited and quarrelsome, in the 6th cent. the Greek city–states began to coalesce into leagues, initially for the upkeep of religious sites (GREAT AMPHICTYONY) but later for political reasons, either to defend themselves against foreign attack or to fight among themselves. The ACHAEMENID EMPIRE tried and failed to conquer the Greeks from 500 to 449 BC. However, the main issue, which was the independence of the Greek cities along the Aegean coast of Anatolia, was decided in favour of the Achaemenid Empire when those cities

became Persian vassals in 387 BC. Athens and Sparta and their respective allies fought together against the Achaemenid Empire, but after the Persian Wars they fell out.

THE PELOPONNESIAN WAR

Athens had formed the DELIAN LEAGUE in 478 BC, which virtually became an Athenian empire, and Sparta led a loose federation called the PELOPON-NESIAN LEAGUE. The Peloponnesian War, which lasted from 431 to 404 BC, ended, after the disaster of the Athenian expedition to Sicily (415–413 BC), with the siege and surrender of Athens (404 BC). The Persians were influential in Greece during the early 4th cent. BC, but the real threat to the independence of the city–states began with the unification of the kingdom of MACEDON (358 BC). After the conquest of Thrace by Macedon (342 BC) the Greeks became alarmed and formed the ACHAEAN LEAGUE (338 BC), but the Corinthian League (337 BC), under Macedonian patronage, incorporated all Greek city–states, except Sparta. With the consolidation of his Greek base, Alexander of Macedon set forth to the conquest of the Achaemenid Empire (ALEXANDRIAN EMPIRE). After Alexander's death (323 BC), Macedon, including Greece, was contested by his generals and eventually was obtained by the Antigonids at the end of the DIADOCHI WARS (281 BC). Macedon flourished during the Hellenistic period of Ancient Greek civilization, a time during which politically the Greek tendency towards fragmentation was prevalent in Greek-occupied lands and in Greece itself. The unification of Greece achieved by Alexander was never repeated. Macedon and EPIRUS were two relatively large kingdoms in northern Greece, but the rest of Greece remained as disunited as ever. In 146 BC, ROME defeated Macedon and incorporated all its territories into the Roman Empire. Greek Sicily had become a province of Rome in 241 BC. The rest of the Ancient Greek world, with the exception of some outlying Greek colonies on the shores of the Black Sea, was gradually absorbed by the Romans.
(*See chronologies under* Greece (Ancient) *and* Anatolia.)

Greece
After the fall of the Roman Empire in the west (ROME), Greece remained attached to the BYZANTINE EMPIRE. From the 12th to the 14th cents. it was totally or partially in the power of western Europeans, especially after the conquest of Constantinople by French and Flemish crusader knights supported by Venetian naval power (LATIN STATES). Byzantine authority was re-established in Greece after the mid-14th cent., but towards the end of the cent. northern Greece had fallen to the OTTOMAN EMPIRE. The fall of Constantinople (1453) put an end to whatever power the Greeks still had in the eastern Mediterranean. Athens, which had been a Latin state since the 13th cent., fell to the Ottomans in 1458. Many Greeks, especially those who remained in

---

Greece (Ancient)
Predominant political influences (all dates are BC)

Late 3rd mil.–15th cent.	*6th cent.*	Achaean League
Minoan Civilization	Great Amphictyony	Corinthian League
		Epirus
	5th cent.	
17th–12th cents.	Delian League	*3rd cent.*
Mycenean Greece	(Athenian Empire)	Diadochi Wars
	Peloponnesian	Seleucid Empire
12th–9th cents.	League	Macedon
Ancient Greece (dark	Achaemenid Empire	Achaean League
ages and formation		Epirus
of regions)	*4th cent.*	Rome
	Achaemenid Empire	
8th–6th cents.	Alexandrian Empire	
Ancient Greece	Diadochi Wars	
(colonies)	Macedon	

Constantinople under Ottoman rule – known as Phanariots, from the area of Constantinople where they lived – served the Porte, sometimes even as governors (hospodars) of entire Balkan provinces, where some became infamous for their exactions. But the population of Greece mostly rejected Turkish rule.

NAVARINO

Greece's war of independence from the Ottoman Empire began in 1821 under the leadership of the Ypsilanti brothers and concluded only after the naval Battle of Navarino (1827), where a combined Russian, French, and English force defeated the fleet of Muhammad Ali, the Albanian-born Ottoman pasha of Egypt. Russia declared war and forced the Porte to evacuate Greece in 1829. The war also resulted in the loss by the Ottoman Empire of Black Sea territories, in the opening of the Dardanelles to commercial shipping, and in the autonomy of Serbia. The Porte recognized Greece's independence in 1832. The territory of Greece then barely covered half the mainland peninsula, the Peloponnese, and the Cyclades. In 1864, Great Britain ceded the Ionian Islands to Greece. After losing the war of 1877–1878 against Russia, whose results were determined by the European powers in the Congress of BERLIN (1878), the Ottomans were forced to cede Thessaly and Epirus to Greece. An uprising in Crete in 1896 led to war between Greece and the Ottoman Empire. The Greeks were losing the war but the European powers halted the conflict in 1897. In 1898, they forced the Turks to withdraw from Crete and sponsored an autonomous government in the island. Under Venizelos, Crete opted for union with Greece in 1909, when the European powers put an end to their Cretan

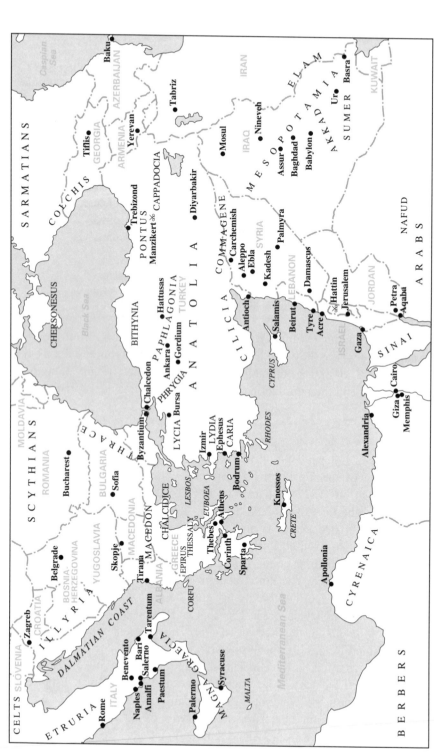

Map 4 Anatolia, Ancient Greece, and Ancient Near East

protectorate during the Young Turks' military rebellion for modernization in Istambul (TURKEY). In 1912, Italy seized Rhodes and the Dodecanese, which it ceded to Greece in 1947. As a consequence of the Balkan Wars (1912–1913), Greece, first allied to Bulgaria, Montenegro, and Serbia against the Turks, obtained southern Macedonia and western Thrace; and in the second round, allied with the other Balkan states against Bulgaria, gained more territory in Macedonia. During World War I, Bulgaria sided with the Central Powers (Austria and Germany) in 1915 and quickly over-ran Serbia. The Western powers prodded Greece, who entered the war in 1917 led by Venizelos. Allied troops landed in Salonika and Bulgaria was knocked out of the fighting on 30 September 1918. In VERSAILLES (1919), Greece obtained the Aegean coast of Bulgaria and most of Turkish Thrace. In 1923, it returned the part of Thrace around Edirne to Turkey. By the Treaty of Sèvres (1920), Turkey was assigned areas of the former Ottoman Empire in Anatolia. The Greeks were given control of Izmir. A Turkish nationalist reaction led by Mustafa Kemal resulted in the expulsion of the Greeks from western Anatolia.

THE TRUMAN DOCTRINE

Italy invaded Albania in 1939, but in 1940 it got bogged down trying to subdue the Greeks. Nazi Germany invaded the Balkans as far as Greece, and German paratroops carried out a daring takeover of Crete. The resistance movement in Greece was strong and leftist and, after the war, it became a communist insurrection with some Yugoslav backing. In 1947, American President Truman declared his country's willingness to help states under communist attack. This became known as the Truman Doctrine and was applied later in Korea. It was an extension of the thinking behind the Truman Doctrine that encouraged the American involvement in Vietnam. In Greece, American aid turned the tide – the country was pacified in 1949 – but it is also likely that, informally at Yalta and Potsdam, the Americans and Russians had reached some degree of agreement on western and eastern spheres of influence in the Balkans.

The Cyclades, Greek islands between mainland Greece and Crete, comprise, among many, Andros, Milos, Naxos, Paros, and Thera. The Dodecanese Islands, Greek islands in the eastern Mediterranean Sea, off south west Turkey, include Rhodes, Kos, and Patmos. Sporades is the general name for all the Greek islands in the Aegean Sea, excluding the Cyclades. They include Lesbos (across from north east Turkey), Chios (west of Smyrna), Samos (off the western coast of Turkey) and Samothrace (south of European Turkey). In the Adriatic Sea, the Greek Ionian islands include Cephalonia, Corfu, Leucas, and Zante. Ithaca is also in the group. Chalcidice is the region of north east Greece formed by peninsulas that jut into the Aegean Sea.

Grenada
Claimed by France and Great Britain during the 17th and 18th cents., Grenada

definitely became a Caribbean British colony in 1784 until its independence in 1974. Grenada was part of the British Windward Islands from 1880 to 1958. To put an end to a Cuban-allied government in Grenada – it began by executing the previous head of state – the United States occupied the island from 1983 to 1985. St George's is the capital of Grenada.

Guatemala

The territory of Guatemala, part of MAYAN CIVILIZATION and possibly later under the influence of the AZTEC EMPIRE, was conquered for Spain (1523–1524) by Pedro de Alvarado, a lieutenant of Cortez in the conquest of MEXICO (1519–1521). During the SPANISH COLONIAL EMPIRE, Guatemala was a captaincy general with jurisdictional authority over all of Central America to the frontier with Panama, which was a province of the viceroyalty of New Granada. The first capital of Guatemala was Ciudad Vieja. From there in 1542 it was moved to Antigua Guatemala and in 1776 to Guatemala City. These changes were due to earthquake damage. With the detachment of New Spain as independent Mexico from the Spanish Colonial Empire in 1821, Guatemala became part of the Mexican empire of Iturbide. When the empire collapsed in 1823, Guatemala and the rest of Central America created the CENTRAL AMERICAN FEDERATION, with its capital in Guatemala City. The Confederation lasted until 1838. In 1954, Guatemala, under Arbenz, had the first genuinely revolutionary government in Latin America. It was toppled by a CIA-backed coup. Starting in the 1980s, Guatemala was engulfed in violence and rural civil war which ended in a truce in 1992, but not before many atrocities were committed by the military, who counted on active American support. Guatemala had an outstanding claim on British Honduras (BELIZE), which Great Britain rejected with military backing in 1982.

Guinea

Peopled by speakers of Fula – of the Niger–Congo family of languages of central and western Africa – Guinea was French from 1849, later part of French West Africa. It did not choose to join the French Community and declared its independence in 1958. The capital is Conakry.

Guinea-Bissau

Mostly divided into tribes speaking different but probably related west African languages, Guinea-Bissau was a Portuguese possession from the mid-15th cent., controlled from the CAPE VERDE Islands until it was made a separate colony in 1879. It became independent in 1974. Bissau is its capital.

Gujarat (SAKA)

Guptas (4th–6th cents.; northern *India*)

The Guptas, who were from Allahabad, west of Varanasi (Benares), established a Hindu kingdom in NORTHERN INDIA ca. 320. The founder was Chandragupta, who ruled until ca. 335. He acquired Bihar by marriage. His son Samudragupta conquered as far as western Pakistan, where he absorbed the remnants of the KUSHANA KINGDOM, and as far east as BENGAL. Later he conquered south to northern Madhya Pradesh. But apparently he was content with making vassals of the kingdoms he attacked. The Gupta kingdom reached its acme under Samandragupta II, who was active in 400. He annexed Gujarat and absorbed Vakataka (CENTRAL INDIA) through a dynastic marriage, although Vakataka was independent during most of the 5th cent. Another ruler, Skandagupta, resisted the EPHTHALITES, also known as White Huns, who nevertheless occupied the PUNJAB ca. 500. There came about a gradual erosion of Gupta power and, by ca. 570, the kingdom was in tatters. Northern India was reunified in HARSHA'S KINGDOM.
(*See chronology under* Indian Subcontinent.)

Gutians (SUMER)

Guyana

Peopled originally by jungle-dwelling Amerindian tribes but later settled by Africans and Indians, the western part of the Dutch colony of Surinam was ceded to Great Britain in 1815. It was granted independence in 1966. Venezuelan claims over British Guiana to the Essequibo River were subjected to arbitration in 1899, which was mostly favourable to Great Britain. Venezuela charged the jury was rigged and revived the reclamation in 1959. After Guyana's independence, the claim was moot. The capital is Georgetown.

H

Habsburg Empire (12th–20th cents.; core area: *Austria*)

The Habsburg Empire is the informal general designation for political entities that, before World War I, went by the names of Austria, Austrian Empire, Austria–Hungary, and Dual Monarchy. The Habsburg Empire was put together by the German house of Habsburg, with roots in the HOLY ROMAN EMPIRE. It established its base in the Duchy of Austria, from where it ruled over many minorities inside and outside the Empire. The strongest of the subject peoples of the Habsburg were the Hungarians who obtained an agreement in 1867 that the Habsburg or Austrian Empire be structured as a Dual Monarchy in which the Habsburg ruled but the crowns of Austria and Hungary were of equal standing.

A COSTLY CONSPIRACY

The Habsburg, who built up their empire from south-eastern Germany, were originally from Aargau in Switzerland and, during the 12th cent., held domains in Alsace and Baden. After making other territorial acquisitions, a Habsburg, Rudolf I (1273–1291), became King of Germany but his claim to the imperial throne was contested. Manoeuvring against much opposition, his son, Albert I, obtained recognition by Pope Boniface VIII of his claim to both the German and the imperial thrones. Albert was assassinated in a conspiracy in 1308 and Habsburg ascent was checked. Before this ignominious end to their first climb to imperial power, the Habsburg wrested from BOHEMIA in 1278 the lands of Carnolia, Styria, and Austria. The latter had been a duchy since the late 12th cent. and they made it their dynastic base, hereditary from 1282. Subsequent Habsburg acquisitions were Carinthia (1335), Tyrol (1363), Istria (1374), and Trieste (1382). Their only setback was in the west, ironically in Switzerland, where they recognized the autonomy of the central cantons in 1386. The legendary adventures of William Tell at the start of the 14th cent. are about Swiss rebelliousness against a Habsburg deputy. By the start of the 15th cent. the Habsburg were the principal power within the HOLY ROMAN EMPIRE and in 1438 a Habsburg, Albert II, was again elevated to the imperial throne, this time through marriage to the daughter of Sigismund, the previous Emperor and King of Bohemia, a realm the Habsburg also acquired, although briefly. Except for a lapse between 1740 and 1762 – during which the Habsburg succession was contested resulting first in the War of Austrian Succession (1740–1748) and then in the Seven Years War (1756–1763) – the dynasty was to hold the throne of the Holy Roman Empire continuously until the empire itself was dissolved in 1815. Austria was raised to the rank of archduchy in

1453. The title was subsequently held by the heirs to the Habsburg throne. In 1477, the Habsburg acquired, by the marriage of Holy Roman Emperor Maximilian I and Mary of Burgundy, the northern possessions of the duchy of BURGUNDY (Low Countries) and Franche Comté. Philip the Handsome, son of Maximilian, married Joanna the Mad, daughter of the Catholic Kings of Spain (Isabella of Castile and Ferdinand of Aragon), from which union the Habsburg heir became Charles I of Spain (1516) with its ballooning colonial empire and Charles V, Holy Roman Emperor (1519). It was in reference to these marriages – and the previous one between Albert II and the daughter of Sigismund – that it was said that while other nations warred to expand, Austria did it by marrying ('tu Felix Austria nube').

TWO HABSBURG EMPIRES

Charles V had to fend off Francis I of France in Italy and confront the Protestant reformation and its effects on the German states. He also undertook various expeditions against Islamic North Africa. This was a heavy load and, in 1556, he divested himself of the eastern Habsburg domains in favour of his brother Ferdinand. Charles retained for Spain the Low Countries and Milan. There were then two Habsburg empires, one with Spain and the other with Austria at their respective centres. The history of the Spanish Habsburg is that of SPAIN. The German Habsburg used the dynastic name for their realms. In 1526, the OTTOMAN EMPIRE had defeated and killed the King of Hungary and Bohemia in the Battle of Mohacs. Ferdinand successfully claimed the crown of BOHEMIA, again through a dynastic alliance. But he had to fight off the first Ottoman siege of Vienna in 1529. After the second siege (1683), when Vienna was saved by the opportune arrival of John II Sobieski of Poland, the Habsburg counter-attacked and, from 1686 to 1697, under Leopold I, conquered Hungary. In 1699, the Habsburg added Transylvania to their Hungarian lands. After that the Habsburg tended to grow, though not exclusively, at the expense of their Ottoman neighbours. In 1718, they acquired the Banat, next door to Belgrade, which they contested indecisively with the Turks until it became the capital of Serbia in 1867. During the course of the 18th cent. the Habsburg continually nibbled at the Ottoman frontiers and acquired territories on the Adriatic and in Moldavia. Austria participated with Prussia and Russia in the partitions of Poland and, in 1795, under Francis II, annexed the province of Galicia (southern Poland).

FROM AUSTERLITZ TO WATERLOO

Some of the empire's darkest hours at the height of its glory occurred during the wars with France from 1793 to 1815. Austria participated in the First and Second Coalitions against republican France (1793 and 1799 respectively) and was twice contained. During the Third Coalition (1805), Austria was crushed at Austerlitz (1806). It was again defeated at Wagram (1809), after which Napoleon asked for and got Marie Louise, daughter of Emperor Francis II, as his wife. However, Napoleon's string of successes was spectacular but brief and, in 1812–1813, the French Grande Armée was decimated in Russia and the Fourth Coalition of which Austria was again a cornerstone invaded France, had Napoleon deposed and exiled to Elba. When he returned in 1815, the Allies decisively defeated him at Waterloo. In VIENNA, the Habsburg Empire lost minor possessions in western Germany, but gained Lombardy and Venetia (1815). In 1859, Austria lost the Battle of Solferino against France and SARDINIA. Lombardy, Tuscany, and most of northern Italy were annexed by Sardinia, which in 1861 became the kingdom of Italy. The year 1866 was also unfortunate for the Habsburg. Austria was defeated by Prussia, who became the dominant power in Germany. Italy sided with Prussia and annexed Venetia. The Hungarians took advantage of Austria's weakness and, in 1867, obtained the conversion of the Habsburg Empire into the Dual Monarchy of Austria and Hungary, although still under the overall rule of the Habsburg dynasty. The frontier with the Ottoman Empire, which had been stable since the 18th cent., began to crumble with the nationalist awakening of the southern Slavs during the 19th cent. (SERBIA). In 1878 Bosnia-Herzegovina had been put under Austrian administration (Congress of BERLIN). Slavic irredentism provoked its annexation in 1908 by Austria–Hungary.

WORLD WAR I AND THE END OF EMPIRE

A Serbian nationalist assassinated the Habsburg heir, Archduke Francis Ferdinand, in 1914 in Sarajevo, at which Vienna declared war on Serbia with the backing of Germany, and World War I began. The Allied powers (France, Great Britain, and Russia) were on one side and the Central Powers (Germany and Austria) were on the other. Austro-Hungarian forces were stalemated in the Russian Front, but advanced during the failed Russian offensive in 1917. German and Austrian forces occupied the Balkans. Italy, which was neutral at the start of the war, entered in 1915 on the side of the Allies with the offer of territorial gains. Fighting was indecisive until the Austrians clearly won the Battle of Caporetto in 1917, but the Italians vanquished them in 1918 at Vittorio Veneto. By 1918, Germany was hanging on with difficulty – especially after the United States entered the war in 1917 – and the Habsburg Empire was exhausted and surrendered on 4 November. In 1919, by the Treaty of Saint Germain (VERSAILLES), Austria–Hungary was dissolved into Austria, Hungary, and Czechoslovakia, with chunks going to Italy, Poland, Romania, and Yugoslavia. (*See chronology under* Balkans.)

Hafsids (13th–16th cents.; northern Africa)
The Hafsids were a local Berber dynasty that replaced the ALMOHADS in TUNISIA ca. 1230. They seized eastern Algeria and western Libya. Their

power lasted to 1574. The Hafsids suffered the brunt of Christian Spain's attacks on Muslim northern Africa during the 16th cent. They were succeeded by the OTTOMAN EMPIRE.
(*See chronology under* Maghreb.)

Haiti

The Spaniards, who occupied the island of Hispaniola in 1492, and founded Santo Domingo in 1496, neglected the western part, which the French obtained in 1697 as a colony known by the Arawak name of Haiti (land of mountains). In 1795, Spain ceded Santo Domingo to France. The native Haitians (mostly slaves) rose up under Toussaint L'Ouverture and took the whole country in 1801. After 1802, beset by tropical diseases, a French expeditionary force led by Leclerc failed to reduce Haiti, which became independent in 1804 with Jean-Jacques Dessalines as Emperor. After his death, the country was divided between the north, controlled by blacks under Jean Christophe, and the mulatto south, whose leader, Alexandre Petion, gave refuge and aid to the South American General Simon Bolivar during 1816–1817. The French retained control of Santo Domingo, but were dispossessed by the British, who returned Santo Domingo to Spain in 1809. The Haitians, united again under Jean-Pierre Boyer, invaded in 1822 (after the Spaniards had withdrawn from Santo Domingo) and retained the entire island until 1844, when they were expelled and the Dominican Republic was created. Due to increasing anarchy, American forces occupied Haiti from 1915 to 1934. In 1937, Dominican troops killed thousands of Haitians who had established themselves in lands across the border between the two countries. With UN support, American military occupied Haiti in 1992 to restore democracy. They withdrew in 1997. The capital of Haiti is Port-au-Prince. The official language is French but most Haitians speak a French-derived creole.

Han (3rd cent. BC–2nd cent. AD; *China*)

The Han dynasty ruled China from 206 BC to AD 221 with an interregnum from AD 9 to AD 25. It built on CH'IN (QIN) conquests and under its rule China proper – China minus Manchuria, Sinkiang, and Tibet – acquired its approximate present configuration. The ethnic designation the Chinese give themselves is Han. Paper was invented around AD 100 and the examination system providing for promotions on merit within the imperial bureaucracy was given its initial form. Han China was founded by Emperor Han Kao Tsu, a soldier of non-aristocratic origin. Han has two periods: Western Han (206 BC– AD 9), capital Sian, and Eastern Han (AD 25–221), capital Loyang. The interregnal period was a usurpation by the general Wang Mang, called the Hsin dynasty. Its founder was reformist and imposed the exchange of gold for bronze, which did not make him popular. He was murdered and the Han resumed, although the relation between the restoration and the last Eastern

Han Emperor is not clear. At its greatest extent (86 BC), reached under Han Wu Ti, reputedly the greatest Han emperor, the empire reached to southern Manchuria and northern Korea, as far west as the Tarim Basin, and as far south as Vietnam. In the south west it incorporated part of Yunnan. Under Han Wu Ti, primogeniture was abolished which diminished the power of the barons. It is from Han times that date extant Chinese chronicles about pre-Han ages, including the writings of Confucius and the doctrines during the period of the Warring States. In accordance with Chinese historiographical patterns, established by the historian Ssu-ma Ch'ien in the Western Han period, the Eastern Han dynasty should have ended with wicked kings, but they were just weaklings.

(*See chronology under* China and Neighbouring Areas.)

Hanseatic League (12th–16th cents.; *Germany* and *Baltic area*)
The Hansa was a commercial network of cities that stretched from central Germany to Estonia taking in adjoining strands and inland areas (including Cracow). It had offices from London to Novgorod. It was founded in 1160 in the town of Visby, on the Swedish island of Gotland. By the middle of the 13th cent. it included scores of cities, including such powerful ones as Lübeck, Hamburg, Dortmund, Bremen, Wismar, and Rostock. Even though the Hansa glue was economic, it needed military power to safeguard trade and, in 1370, it had enough clout to restrain Denmark, which lay athwart the principal navigation routes between the Hanseatic cities and entrepôts west and east. This was probably the acme of its military strength and the Hansa declined gradually and gracefully during the 15th and 16th cents., when British and Dutch naval power were in the ascendancy. The German Hanseatic cities were part of the HOLY ROMAN EMPIRE, which never hampered their profitable operations.

Harappa (INDUS RIVER VALLEY CIVILIZATION)

Harsha's Kingdom (7th cent.; northern *India*)
After the GUPTAS, an able commander, Harsha, unified northern India between 606 and 612. He was defeated by the Chalukya king Pulakeshin when he tried to annex CENTRAL INDIA. After his death in 647, his kingdom, whose capital was established in Kanauj, went to pieces, which was how he had found the lands he conquered. Like his north India predecessor Asoka, Harsha was a Hindu who became a pious Buddhist. According to an interpretation, the end of Harsha's reign marks the beginning of the Indian middle ages, during which fragmented sovereignties were loosely bound by fealties between suzerain and vassal states (samantas). Northern India was not to be unified again until the coming of the Aghan GHURIDS and the foundation of the Islamic DELHI SULTANATE.

(*See chronology under* Indian Subcontinent.)

Hausa (12th–19th cents.; *Sub-Saharan Africa*)
The Hausa formed Islamic states in northern Nigeria. They were vassals successively to KANEM-BORNU, SONGHAI, and the FULANI. Hausa is an Afro-Asiatic language distantly related to Semitic, a family which includes Arab and Hebrew.
(*See chronology under* Western and Sub-Saharan Africa.)

Hawaii (18th–19th cents.; *United States*)
Visited by Captain Cook in 1778, Hawaii was a Polynesian kingdom christianized by American missionaries during the 19th cent. It granted the United States naval rights to Pearl Harbor and was annexed outright in 1898. Hawaii became a state of the Union in 1959. Its capital is Honolulu.

Hephthalites (EPHTHALITES)

Hittite Kingdom (17th–12th cents. BC; ancient *Near East*)
The Hittites were Indo-European speakers who entered Anatolia through Cappadocia and established themselves in what is today central Turkey. They neighboured on the Semitic HURRIANS in the Upper Euphrates River. The history of the Hittites as reconstructed from archaeological and written records is divided into the period of the Old Hittite Kingdom (ca. 1600–ca. 1400 BC) and the period of the Hittite Empire, capital Hattusas (ca. 1400–ca. 1200 BC). There was a third neo-Hittite kingdom from ca. 1050 to ca. 700 BC – its most important centre was Carchemish – but it existed during mainly a time of Assyrian domination. The Hittites took BABYLONIA ca. 1530 BC. Their political influence extended down to Syria, but they were halted by PHARAONIC EGYPT and the MITANNI. They destroyed the latter in alliance with ASSYRIA ca. 1350 BC. Kadesh was a Hittite vassal kingdom in Syria. It was invaded in 1275 BC by the Egyptian Pharaoh Ramses II, who was stopped, near Kadesh itself, by the Hittite king, Muwatallis II. The causes of the downfall of the Hittite Empire are obscure, presumably attacks from neighbouring Thracians, Phrygians, and Assyrians (PELASGIANS). Subsequently, the southernmost Hittite lands fell under Assyrian and Babylonian influence. Anatolia itself was fragmented until the rise of LYDIA. Carchemish was taken by Assyria ca. 700 BC. It was under Egyptian rule ca. 610 and fell to Nebuchadnezzar in 605 BC.
(*See chronologies under* Ancient Near East *and* Anatolia.)

Hohenstaufen Italy (NORMAN ITALY)

Holland (NETHERLANDS)

Holy Roman Empire (9th–19th cents.; Core area: *Germany*)
In 887, the German eastern part of the CAROLINGIAN EMPIRE broke definitely away after the deposition of Emperor Charles III the Fat, also King of Germany. His nephew Arnulf, who had taken Italy in 881, assumed the crown

of Germany, or the east Frankish kingdom, as it is commonly called, and in 896 was also crowned Emperor in Rome. He was the last Carolingian to bear the title. Germany, between the Elbe and the Rhine, and south to the Alps and the frontiers of Hungary, was beset by Norsemen and Magyars. Arnulf was succeeded by Louis the Child, who was the last Carolingian King of Germany. After, there was no single dynastic succession to establish unity and this political handicap resulted in the formation of the duchies of Saxony, Thuringia, Bavaria, Swabia, Lorraine, and Franconia, partly for self-defence. This 'regionalization' of the land was to be determinant in the future history of the Empire, for, despite their disunity, the Germans were agreed on the principle of single rule. The problem was that they seldom agreed on who should rule over them, for even when claims of legitimacy by a dynasty were accepted in principle by the duchies, there was hardly a time when they were not contested in practice, added to which was the necessity of defending the eastern frontiers against the Slavs and German involvement in Italy. The latter stemmed from Arnulf's coronation as Emperor, which made the German kings inheritors of the Carolingian claim on IMPERIAL ITALY.

IMPERIAL DYNASTIES

German emperors from Saxony ruled from 919 to 1024. It was a Saxon emperor, Otto I the Great, who in 962 was crowned Emperor of the Holy Roman Empire in Rome. This harked back to the Carolingian Empire, just as Charlemagne in his time had harked back to the Roman Empire. The Saxons were succeeded by emperors originally from Lorraine (1024–1125), during whose rule the duchies strengthened and the struggle with the papacy over investiture (naming of bishops) began. Opposition to the emperors was especially marked in BAVARIA under the house of Este, whose first ruler, Welf (1070), became the eponym of the Guelph anti-imperial faction in Italy. The imperial party was formed by the Ghibellines, a name that derives from the Saxon imperial castle of Waiblingen. After some manoeuvring and dynastic strife, the Hohenstaufen, who had domains all over the Empire but mainly in Saxony, ruled from 1125 to 1268. In his struggle against dynastic factionalism, the Emperor Frederick I Barbarossa (1155–1190) deposed the ruling house of Bavaria and did much to fragment the Empire politically. The Hohenstaufen hold on Germany became tenuous, having chosen to rule from Sicily and southern Italy, which they tried but failed to incorporate into the Holy Roman Empire. This situation, compounded by papal interference in the process of imperial succession, opened the doors to more dynastic rivalries from which eventually the principle of an elective empire was established in 1356 by the Golden Bull (from 'bulla' or seal) of Emperor Charles IV, of the house of Luxembourg. What had finally been achieved was the essential pattern of German imperial politics until the dissolution of the Empire. The borders of the Holy Roman Empire were effectively congealed through the system of German electors, the German rulers who since the beginning of the Empire had been influential in the determination of the imperial succession. Lands could be separated for dynastic or other reasons, mainly war, but German conquests outside those borders belonged to the dynasties or states that acquired them, which meant that Habsburg interests, for example, did not necessarily coincide with those of the Empire as such. Even though the electors were equal and any one of the principal rulers within the empire could be elected Emperor, it was in fact expansion outside the Empire that carried weight. The Habsburg had tried but failed to impose the idea of a 'hereditary elective' monarchy (1308). They achieved their objective upon the accession to the imperial throne of Albert II (1438) through marriage with the daughter of Sigismund, King of Bohemia and Holy Roman Emperor. Except for a lapse between 1740 and 1762 – during which the Habsburg succession was contested resulting first in the War of Austrian Succession (1740–1748) and then in the Seven Years War (1756–1763) – the dynasty was to hold the throne of the Holy Roman Empire continuously until the Empire itself was dissolved in 1815 (*HABSBURG EMPIRE*).

THE TERRITORIAL PROCESS

Starting from its Carolingian inheritance, Germany at first expanded in all directions, but especially towards the east, where the marches – territories the Germans occupied by various means in the furthest reaches of Slavic settlement – were established from 936. From the shores of the Baltic to the Balkans, the marches were: North, Lusatia or Lausitz, Meissen, Styria, Carinthia, and Carniola. Habsburg power and prestige originated in their activity in the creation of the south-eastern marches (Styria, Carinthia, and Carniola). The spread of Christianity was a principal justification for expansion, and it was by this means that BOHEMIA and MORAVIA were incorporated into the Empire in 950. In the south west, the kingdom of ARLES became part of the Empire in 1043, but it was neglected by the Emperors and in 1378 was ceded to France. The German claim on Italy (northern Italy down to Ancona and Spoleto) was recognized by the papacy with the coronation of Otto the Great (962), but the Empire's hold there never went uncontested by the Italian cities. It suffered a serious setback when the LOMBARD LEAGUE won the Battle of Legnano (1176) and was at its most powerful with the Hohenstaufen (13th cent.) (NORMAN ITALY). But this was climax and denouement, for the Hohenstaufen lost their power in Italy in 1268, when also the imperial claim on Italian territory was restricted by the incorporation of Romagna and Pentapolis into the PAPAL STATES. During the early 14th cent. German activity in Italy was much reduced due to dynastic struggles in Germany. Papal interference in matters of succession tended to grow, from which resulted the Golden Bull of Charles IV, in effect a constitutional arrangement of sorts for the Holy Roman Empire. As it was accepted by the papacy, it also meant in principle that popes and emperors agreed not to invade their respective spheres of influence. Although the imperial claim on Italy was formally intact, the late-14th and 15th cents. were a time of self-assertion for Italian states (MILAN, FLORENCE, VENICE). Within the Holy Roman Empire itself, cities had been acquiring commercial and other privileges which, in many instances, culminated in corporate self-rule. This was not dissimilar to a process, starting in 11th cent., by which the Italian cities became free communes rather than part of the Empire. However, whereas the Italian cities proclaimed their own liberties – often behind the aegis of local rulers – in opposition to German imperial claims, the German free imperial cities were usually sponsored by the Emperors in opposition to local rulers or because of commercial reasons. Thus it was that numerous German cities could remain loyal members of the Empire while, at the same time, participating in the web of local sovereignties – in effect a state within a state – which formed the HANSEATIC LEAGUE. Brilliantly successful instances of free imperial cities were Nuremberg (1219), Dortmund (1220), Lübeck (1226), Cologne (1288), Bremen (early 14th cent.), Frankfurt am Main (1372), and many others. As Vienna, Dresden, Munich, and Berlin demonstrate, being capitals of important states of the Holy Roman Empire was not a lesser road to prestige, growth, and splendour.

WIN SOME, LOSE SOME

In the east, Silesia (1163) and Pomerania (1181) became imperial dependencies. In 1226, the TEUTONIC KNIGHTS were charged with Christianizing the Baltic Lands and, in the 14th cent., the Empire reached out in that direction, but in the 15th cent. then powerful POLAND circumscribed the Germans to Pomerania. Also in the 15th cent., Venice expanded territorially in northeastern Italy at the expense of imperial claims.

From the start, the Holy Roman Empire comprised the Low Countries. The expansion of the French Duchy of BURGUNDY under the Valois during the 14th cent. brought these lands and the Franche Comté under its domain. In 1477, Burgundian territories, except Burgundy itself, passed to the Habsburg. Though extending in principle to Italy at the beginning of the 16th cent., the Holy Roman Empire effectively ended at the Alps. During the 1520s and 1530s, the Italian ambitions of the French king, Francis I, rekindled the imperial concern of Charles V, but this time not so much on behalf of the Empire as on behalf of the Habsburg. Imperial Italy, which had been a political fiction for so long, evaporated under the pressure of *realpolitik*. In 1556, Holy Roman Emperor Charles V (King Charles I of Spain) divested himself of the German Habsburg domains in favour of his brother Ferdinand (1556) and retained the

Netherlands and Franche Comté for the Spanish crown. The Holy Roman Empire had reached the cusp of its expansion long before and, torn by religious conflict during the 16th and 17th cents., it had indeed ceased being Holy, Roman, or an Empire. In 1648, it consisted of around 300 different political entities, foremost among them: Bavaria, Hanover, Saxony, Brandenburg-Prussia, Hesse, Austria, and the aforementioned free imperial cities. In 1697, it lost Alsace and part of Lorraine to France. In 1766, the rest of Lorraine became French. Until its disappearance, the Empire was mostly under the influence of Austria, giving rise to the curious situation of an empire that was weaker than one of its constituent entities. The rise of PRUSSIA during the 18th cent. dented Habsburg pre-eminence but did not over-ride it. After Napoleon's victories at Austerlitz (1805) and Jena (1806), the Holy Roman Empire was dissolved. France annexed the Rhineland. Excluding Austria and Prussia, the rest of Germany was loosely integrated into the FRENCH EUROPEAN EMPIRE as the CONFEDERATION OF THE RHINE (1806–1813). In 1815 (VIENNA), the virtually extinct Holy Roman Empire was reconstituted territorially as the GERMAN CONFEDERATION, which was dissolved by Prussia in 1866.

Italy
Duration of recognizable political entities or historical periods

13th cent. BC–19th cent. AD Sicily	***7th–9th cents.*** Spoleto	***11th–13th cents.*** Pisa Norman and 　Hohenstaufen Italy
10th–4th cents. BC Etruria	***7th–11th cents.*** Byzantine Italy Benevento	***11th–15th cents.*** Aquileia
8th cent. BC–5th cent. AD Rome	***7th–18th cents.*** Venice	***11th–19th cents.*** Savoy/Sardinia 　(Kingdom)
7th cent. BC–19th cent. AD Naples	***8th–9th cents.*** Carolingian Italy	***12th–13th cents.*** Lombard League
5th–6th cents. AD Ostrogothic Italy	***9th–11th cents.*** Amalfi Muslim Sicily	***12th–15th cents.*** Verona
6th–8th cents. Lombard Italy	***10th–14th cents.*** Imperial Italy	***12th–19th cents.*** Milan Lucca
6th–11th cents. Salerno	***10th–18th cents.*** Genoa	Modena Mantua

13th–16th cents.	16th–19th cents.	19th–20th cents.
Ferrara	Parma	Italy
13th–19th cents.	**18th–19th cents.**	
Florence (Tuscany)	Habsburg Italy	
15th–19th cents.	(Lombardy and Venetia)	
Two Sicilies (Kingdom)	French and Napoleonic Italy	

Honduras

The territory of Honduras is home to various sites of MAYAN CIVIL-IZATION, among them spectacular Copán. The coastline of Honduras was sighted by Columbus in 1502. Pedro de Alavarado, Cortez's lieutenant in the conquest of Mexico (1519–1521), claimed Honduras in 1524, but the Spaniards later met resistance from the native inhabitants, who were put down in 1537–1538. The capital, Tegucigalpa, was founded in the late-16th cent. Like all of Central America to the frontier with Panama, which was a province of the viceroyalty of New Granada, Honduras was attached to the captaincy general of Guatemala which depended on the viceroyalty of New Spain (SPANISH COLONIAL EMPIRE). Upon Mexico's detachment from Spain (1821), Honduras became part of the Mexican Empire of Iturbide and after its dissolution (1823) joined the CENTRAL AMERICAN FEDERATION, which lasted until 1838, when Honduras, like the other Federation members, went its own independent way. The eastern coast of Honduras as well as the adjacent coast of Nicaragua are known as Mosquitia.

Hsia (SHANG)

Hsien-pi (2nd–3rd cents.; *Central Asia*: Greater Mongolia)

Hsien-pi is the Chinese name for a Mongol horde that roamed the Khingan mountains (Manchuria). During the 2nd and 3rd cents. it was turned by the Chinese against the northern HSIUNG-NU in Mongolia, whom they defeated. When China, after the fall of the HAN, divided into three kingdoms, the Hsien-pi fell on the southern Hsiung-nu, who went to China, leading to the period in Chinese history called the SIXTEEN KINGDOMS OF THE FIVE BARBARIANS. Under pressure from the JUAN-JUAN to the north, the Hsien-pi themselves moved southward and were gradually absorbed by China. (*See chronology under* China and Neighbouring Areas *and* Greater Mongolia.)

Hsi-Hsia (9th–13th cents.; *Central Asia*: Greater Mongolia)

Tibet emerged from obscure origins in the 7th cent. with its centre in Lhasa. After 842, Tibet broke up into local statelets. Tanguts, as Tibetans are also known in Chinese sources, controlled Gansu (Kansu) and roamed western

China at will. In 887, a Tangut band, the Hsi-Hsia, founded a kingdom in the Ordos, the inner Mongolian lands within the large northern bend of the Yellow River. In 1028, the Hsi-Hsia annexed Gansu, then divided among other Tangut bands. They maintained good relations with SUNG (SONG) China. The Hsi-Hsia kingdom was destroyed by the MONGOL EMPIRE in 1209.
(*See chronologies under* China and Neighbouring Areas *and* Greater Mongolia.)

Hsin (HAN)

Hsiung-nu (5th cent. BC–3rd cent. AD; *Central Asia*: greater Mongolia; *China*)
The Hsiung-nu were nomads who roamed Mongolia during the 5th and 4th cents. BC. They could have been Mongols or Turks, for the languages of these peoples are distantly related. It is believed, for phonetic reasons, that they might have been the ancestors of the HUNS. In the 3rd cent. BC, their base was in the Upper Orkhon River in Mongolia. They drove the Indo-European speaking YÜEH-CHIH out of the Chinese province of Gansu towards the west. In the 2nd cent. BC they were defeated but not destroyed by the Chinese HAN dynasty, with whom they disputed the Tarim Basin (Sinkiang). During the 1st cent. BC, the western HSIUNG-NU were chased out of Mongolia by the core Hsiung-nu. Internecine struggles weakened the Hsiung-nu, who became vassals of the Han. In the 1st cent. AD, the Hsiung-nu divided into northern and southern branches. The latter branch occupied the territory corresponding more or less to today's Chinese province of Inner Mongolia and remained in vassalage to China. Pursuing an arm's-length policy with the dangerous northern Hsiung-nu, the Han got another horde, the Mongolian HSIEN-PI, who roamed Manchuria, to harass and destroy them, which they did, occupying Mongolia in their turn. This policy backfired when, upon the fall of Han in the 3rd cent., the Hsien-pi attacked the southern Hsiung-nu, who fell on China (THREE KINGDOMS). The Hsiung-nu, whose leader was known as the shan yü of the five hordes, provoked the turbulent two centuries known in Chinese history as the SIXTEEN KINGDOMS OF THE FIVE BARBARIANS.
(*See chronologies under* China and Neighbouring Areas *and* Greater Mongolia.)

Hsiung-nu (Western) (1st cent. BC–5th cent. AD; *Central Asia*: western Turkestan; eastern Europe)
In the 1st cent. BC, the western branch of the Hsiung-nu were defeated by the other HSIUNG-NU. The western Hsiung-nu attacked the WU SUN in the Ili River valley but did not dislodge them. They headed westward, probably roaming the Kirghiz Steppe, and in the 5th cent. reappeared as the mighty HUNS who spawned the scourge of God, Attila.

Hungary
The Magyars, of Finno-Ugric linguistic roots, became known as Hungarians from their association in southern Russia with the Onogur Turks. They were

feared raiders in Europe until the Germans after the Battle of Lechfeld (955) literally put them in their place – today's Hungary. They thereafter behaved so well that their first king, Stephen (1001–1038), was canonized. The 13th cent. was a period of anarchy for Hungary with assaults from Bohemian Slavs and Mongols. The kingdom was restored in the 14th cent. under Angevin monarchs who, in 1308, succeeded the native Arpad dynasty. Under Louis the Great (1342–1382) Hungary included TRANSYLVANIA, Dalmatia, the northern Balkans, and POLAND, of which he was also king. Buda, on the right bank of the Danube, became the Hungarian capital. Much of Hungarian history consisted of the struggles between the magnates and the lesser nobility. It was in the midst of these contentions that the Ottoman sultan, Suleyman the Magnificent, struck, defeating the Hungarians in the Battle of Mohacs in 1526 (OTTOMAN EMPIRE). Pest, on the left bank of the Danube, fell into Turkish hands. The Habsburg Emperor Leopold I liberated both Buda and Pest in 1686 and, in 1697, the Austrians retook Hungary (HABSBURG EMPIRE). Transylvania was wrested from the control of the Rakozy, a local dynasty, in 1711. The Hungarian-populated Banat, today divided between Romania, Serbia, and Hungary, was annexed in 1718. Hungary and Hungarian-inhabited lands thus became a part of the Habsburg Empire.

Louis Kossuth

In 1848, Hungary participated in the nationalist–constitutionalist movement spreading in Europe. The Habsburg applied suppressive measures and, in 1849, Louis Kossuth proclaimed the republic, which was put down with Russian aid. After the Austrian defeat at the hands of Prussia in 1866, the Habsburg accepted the conversion of the Empire into the Austro-Hungarian Dual Monarchy. The Hungarian part included Transylvania, Slovakia, Ruthenia, Croatia, and Slovenia. With the end of the Dual Monarchy in 1918, as a consequence of defeat in World War I, Hungary became independent and attempted to retain all its territories. It fell into communist power under Bela Kun, whose regime was overthrown with Romanian participation in 1919. By the Treaty of Trianon, Hungary was much reduced, especially from the loss of Transylvania to Romania. In its efforts to recover lost territory, Hungary became an ally of Nazi Germany in 1941. The Germans took over in 1944 when Hungary tried to leave the war. The USSR occupied the country and installed a communist regime in 1949. Popular discontent exploded in 1956 and a reformist government under Imre Nagy was put down by Soviet tanks. In 1968 Hungary participated, as a member of the communist Warsaw Pact, in the invasion of Czechoslovakia. The communist regime ended in 1989 and, in 1991, the last remaining Russian troops left the country. The capital of Hungary, Budapest, was constituted by the integration of the cities of Buda and Pest in 1873.

Huns (5th–6th cents.; *Central Asia*: Kirghiz steppe; *Southern Russia*; Europe)
The Huns probably stemmed from the western HSIUNG-NU. They could have been Mongols or Turks. It is possible that the entire Hun nation moved westward sometime during the 1st cent. BC. In the 4th cent., the Huns had reached the Aral Sea, from where they invented the 'domino theory' by falling on the Ostrogoths, a Germanic people in the lands north of the Black Sea, who in turn drove the Visigoths (GOTHS) and the ALANS to the Danube, thus setting off the final phase in the decline of ROME (5th cent.). During the middle of the 5th cent., the Huns themselves, under their greatest leader, Attila, ravaged western Europe, spared Rome, and were defeated by the last of the great Romans, Aetius, a general of barbarian extraction, in the battle variously known as the Catalaonian or Maurican Fields, near Châlons-sur-Marne, in eastern France. The lands of the Huns at their Attilan cusp extended from the Aral Sea to Hungary where Attila formed a base. However, the Huns were apparently also the sort of people who lived and died by their ruler, so that when Attila passed away, the GEPIDS and the Ostrogoths massacred them and the AVARS finished them off in the Russian steppes in the 6th cent. The people known as EPHTHALITES or White Huns who were also active during the 5th cent. – in the area south of Lake Balkash and later against the Sasanians and Kushana – were probably not related to the Huns.
(*See chronology under* Southern Russia.)

Hurrians (BABYLONIA; HITTITE KINGDOM)

Hyderabad (MUGHAL EMPIRE)

Hyksos (17th–16th cents. BC; ancient *Near East*)
The Hyksos were a Semitic warrior-people from Canaan, whose chariots overran the Nile Delta ca. 1650 BC. They established their capital in Avaris. Their rule lasted until ca. 1570 BC, when they were defeated in the Battle of Tanis by Amasis I, who thus inaugurated the New Kingdom (PHARAONIC EGYPT).

I

Iceland

Known as Ultima Thule by the Irish, the island of Iceland was peopled by NORSEMEN during the 10th cent. The Icelandic parliament (Althing) was established in 930. It has sat continuously since then with a period of suspension between 1800 and 1843. Iceland was Christianized by the Norwegian King Olaf I ca. 1000. The sagas, Icelandic epic literature written in the same language the Icelanders speak today, were composed during the 13th cent. Norwegian suzerainty was not fully acknowledged in Iceland until 1264. With Norway, the country passed to Denmark in 1397, under whose sovereignty it remained until the 20th cent. In 1874, Iceland had its own constitution. In 1918, it became independent with ties to the Danish Crown. During World War II British troops (1939–1941) and then American (1941–1945) were stationed in the country. Iceland declared its total independence from Denmark in 1944. The capital of Iceland is Reykjavik. Iceland, which sits astride the Mid-Atlantic ridge and could be described as one vast permanent eruption, could be geologically the youngest country in the world. The Icelanders are the only people who have extinguished a volcanic lava flow (partly at least).

Idrisids (8th–10th cents.; northern Africa)

After ISLAM began to dissolve politically with the end of Umayyad imperial rule (750), the Berber Idrisids took over in Morocco and western Algeria from ca. 790 to ca. 950. The kingdom fragmented and Morocco was taken over by the Umayyad Caliphate of CÓRDOBA. The Umayyads fought the Shia FATIMIDS over western Algeria during the 10th cent.
(*See chronology under* Maghreb.)

Ilkhanid Persia (13th–14th cents.; *Middle East*)

The MONGOL EMPIRE conquered Persia and Syria in 1231. Hulagu, grandson of Genghis Khan, was later sent as overlord. After 1240, the Mongols re-established their suzerainty over the SELJUK EMIRATES in Iraq. In 1256, Hulagu conquered Alamut, the fortress of the ISMAILITES (known as Assassins) in north east Persia. In 1258, he took Baghdad and executed the last Abbasid caliph, Al Musta'sim, in the Mongol fashion for the nobility by smothering him in rugs without shedding his blood. In 1260, the Mongols conquered Aleppo and Damascus, but in the same year they suffered defeat in Ain Jalut, Syria, at the hands of the MAMELUKE SULTANATE. With the disintegration of the Mongol Empire, Hulagu (d. 1265) converted to Islam and founded the Ilkhanid dynasty (lesser khans) who ruled Persia from Tabriz in Azerbaijan. Ilkhanid Persia's rule extended to Syria and Anatolia. With the death of the last Ilkhan in 1335, the country went to pieces. The SARBEDAR-IANS were the first to try to pick them up in the east while the AQ-QOYUNLU, the JELAIRS, and the MUZZAFARIDS did the same in the west.

(*See chronologies under* Iran *and* Anatolia.)

Imperial Italy (10th–14th cents.; northern *Italy*)

Upon the deposition in 887 of Charles III the Fat, the last ruler of the CARO-LINGIAN EMPIRE, his nephew Arnulf became ruler of Germany, or the east Frankish kingdom, as it is known. He was crowned King of Italy and Emperor in 896, but his brief did not run as far as France. After him, Italy became prey to various dynastic rivalries, both local and foreign. Although still nominally a part of the German side of the Carolingian imperial inheritance, the claim was in abeyance until Otto I the Great vanquished all rivals and in 962 was crowned in Rome as Emperor, and founder, of the HOLY ROMAN EMPIRE, in which Italy was included. It was a country divided into different fiefs and sovereignties, roughly (not counting effective local rule, which was probably the norm): Milan, the march of Verona and Aquileia (north-eastern Italy), Romagna and Pentapolis (the Po valley), Venice, the Margravate of Tuscany, the Papal States (Lazio), the principalities of Salerno and Capua (Naples), the duchies of Spoleto, Apulia (north of the province of Pugliese), and Benevento. Southern Italy was Byzantine and Sicily Islamic. Imperial rule in northern Italy was intermittent and weak and this permitted every important town there to become a free commune from the 10th to the 12th cents.

GUELPHS AND GHIBELLINES

German claims on northern Italy, and the struggles this caused with the papacy, led to the formation during the 13th cent. of two great Medieval Italian factions, which ironically were what the politics of the different cities had in common. These factions were the Ghibellines (pro-imperial) and Guelphs (anti-imperial), although their origins can be traced to the struggles in the Holy Roman Empire between the Saxon emperors, who possessed the castle of Waiblingen, and their principal rivals, from the 11th cent., the ruling house of BAVARIA, the Este dynasty founded by Welf and deposed in the 12th cent. by the Emperor Frederick I Barbarossa. Italy and the Holy Roman Empire (which claimed Italy down to Rome and Spoleto) were inextricable in politics and war and especially in the constant bickering between emperors and popes, which had principally to do with the cavalier attitude of the emperors to the Patrimonium Petri and the papacy's political interests. The emperors also had to contend with Italian separatism and localism, the rise of Venice, and French interventions – by the house of Anjou, beginning in the 13th cent. against Hohenstaufen southern Italy – so that in 1355–1356 the Emperor Charles IV (1355–1378) virtually extricated the Holy Roman Empire from Italian affairs.

In sum, Rome and the Empire were reconciled on the understanding that each would keep to its own spheres of influence. In practice, this meant the separation of Italy from the Empire. After that, the history of Italy is that of its principal component states: Naples and Sicily in the south and Venice, Milan, Genoa, Florence, and the Papal States in the rest of the country. The German claim to northern Italy was theoretically undiminished and was not finally extinguished until the 16th cent. Holy Roman Emperor Charles V Habsburg fought Francis I of France tooth and nail for Milan, which became Spanish in 1535 until 1713, when it passed to Austria. Northern Italy had become a national rather than an imperial issue.

Inca Empire (13th–16th cents.; South America)

The Inca Empire was created in the 13th cent. It is often assumed that the ruins of Tiahuanaco, Bolivia, of which little is known, are those of a kingdom from which the Inca derived. At its height, the Inca Empire, with its capital at Cuzco, Peru, stretched from Ecuador to northern Chile and was united by a vast system of paved trails. After assassinating the last Inca, Atahualpa, the Spaniards under Pizarro conquered Cuzco in 1533. It is thought that Machu Picchu might have been an Inca redoubt, possibly built after the fall of Cuzco. The languages of the Inca Empire, Quechua and Aymará, are still widely spoken in Peru and Bolivia.

India

See entry in 'Provinces and Regions'

The territorial history of India is that of periodic attempts at imperial unification – Maurya, Gupta, Mughal – separated by long periods of mostly disunion and conflict during which certain regional dynasties are more heard of than others (SOUTHERN, CENTRAL, and NORTHERN INDIA). The British physically unified the country, although there was no integration of its different ethnic components (BRITISH INDIA). The movement for Indian independence gained strength in the late 19th cent. The Indian National Congress, later the Congress Party, was formed in 1885. After the Amritsar massacre in 1919 – in which troops fired on a crowd of unarmed protesters killing hundreds – nationalist sentiments grew inspired by Gandhi. His message was *satyagraha* or passive resistance and was not endorsed by the Congress Party, which nevertheless deferred to his disciple Jawaharlal Nehru. In 1935, India was given partial self-rule. There were separate constituencies for Hindus and Muslims. The latter were led by Muhammad Ali Jinna. After World War II, when independence approached, the two Indian sides could not come to an agreement. A Hindu fanatic assassinated Gandhi. In 1947, India and Pakistan went their separate ways. The bloodshed that ensued was the result of fighting at a very basic community level and between Hindu and Muslim refugee populations moving in different directions. Conflict between the two nations exploded in 1948 in the province of KASHMIR, where a Muslim population had a Hindu nominal ruler who opted for Indian sovereignty. The province was unevenly divided in 1949, with India retaining most of the population and the Srinagar heartland. This open sore in the relations between India and Pakistan has resulted in two additional wars: in 1965, over the Gujarat border; and in 1971–1972, when India intervened in support of Bangladeshi independence. After the partition of Kashmir, the border between the two countries has been *de facto* unchanged according to the principle that you get to keep what you have in your power (*uti ibi uti possidetis*).

DELHI

In 1956, India peaceably acquired Pondicherry and the other French enclaves on its coast. In 1961, it occupied Portuguese-controlled Goa, which became a state in 1987. In 1962, the Chinese launched offensives in Ladakh and in north-eastern India for territories that had been annexed by British India in the 19th and 20th cents. To try to quell guerrilla warfare and terrorism by Tamil separatists, Indian forces intervened unsuccessfully in northern Sri Lanka, with, initially at least, the acquiescence of Colombo, from 1987 to 1990. India is the second most populous country in the world. Its capital, Delhi (also

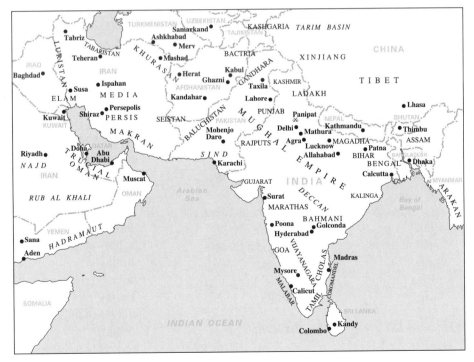

Map 5   Indian Subcontinent and Iran

known as New Delhi), is the consolidation of seven previous foundations from the 13th to the 17th cents., although the date of its original foundation is not clear and the site itself is mentioned in the epic poem the *Mahabharata*, the composition of which possibly dates to ca. 200 BC. Delhi, a Union Territory in 1956, became the National Capital Territory in 1995. India has some island dependencies.

(*See chronology under* Indian Subcontinent.)

Indian Subcontinent
Predominant political influences

3rd–2nd mils. BC
Indus River Valley
Civilization

15th–7th cents. BC
Vedic India
(Indus River
Valley and
northern India)

6th–4th cents. BC
Achaemenid Empire
(Indus River
Valley)
Alexandrian Empire
(Indus River
Valley)
Magadha (northern
India)

3rd–2nd cents. BC
Bactria (Indus River
Valley)
Saka (Indus River
Valley)
Magadha (northern
India)
Kalinga (central
India)

1st cent. BC
Saka (Indus River
Valley)

Magadha (northern
India)
Satavahana (northern
and central India)
Kalinga (central
India)

1st cent. AD
Kushana (Indus River
Valley)
Saka (northern
India)
Satavahana
(northern and
central India)
Cholas I (southern
India)

2nd cent.
Kushana (Indus River
Valley)
Northern India
disunited
Satavahana (central
India)
Vakataka (central
India)
Cholas I (southern
India)

3rd cent.
Kushana (Indus River
Valley)

Northern India
disunited
Vakataka (central
India)
Cholas I (southern
India)

4th–5th cents.
Kushana (Indus River
Valley)
Guptas (northern
India)
Vakataka (central
India)
Cholas I (southern
India)

6th cent.
Ephthalites (Indus
River Valley)
Guptas (northern
India and Indus
River Valley)
Vakataka (central
India)
Chalukyas (central
India)
Cholas I (southern
India)
Pallavas (southern
India)
Pandyas (southern
India)

7th cent.
Ephthalites (Indus River Valley and northern India)
Harsha's Kingdom (northern India)
Bengal (northern India)
Chalukyas (central and southern India)

8th cent.
Indus River Valley and northern India disunited
Bengal (northern India)
Chalukyas (central India)
Pallavas (southern India)

9th–10th cents.
Rajputs (Indus River Valley and northern India)
Bengal (northern India)
Chalukyas (central India)
Rashtrakutas (central India)
Cholas II (southern India)

11th cent.
Afghanistan (Indus River Valley)
Rajputs (Indus River Valley and northern India)
Bengal (northern India)
Chalukyas (central India)
Rashtrakutas (central India)

Cholas II (southern India)

12th cent.
Rajputs (Indus River Valley and northern India)
Ghaznavids (Indus River Valley and northern India)
Delhi Sultanate (Indus River Valley and northern India)
Rashtrakutas (central India)
Cholas II (southern India)
Hoysalas (southern India)

13th cent.
Delhi Sultanate (Indus River Valley to central India)
Rashtrakutas (central India)
Pandyas (southern India)

14th cent.
Delhi Sultanate (Indus River Valley to central India)
Timurid Empire (Indus River Valley and northern India)
Bahmani Kingdom (central India)
Pandyas (southern India)
Vijayanagara (southern India)

15th cent.
Timurid successor states
Delhi Sultanate (northern India)
Bahmani Kingdom (central India)
Deccan Sultanates (central India)
Vijayanagara (southern India)

16th cent.
Mughal Empire (Indus River Valley and northern India)
Deccan Sultanates (central and southern India)
Vijayanagara (southern India)

17th cent.
Mughal Empire (India)
Maratha Kingdoms (central India)
British India (enclaves)
French India (enclaves)

18th cent.
Mughal Empire (Indus River Valley and northern India)
British India (northern India)
Maratha Kingdoms (central India)

19th cent.
British India

Indonesia

SEE ENTRY IN 'PROVINCES AND REGIONS'

Indonesia consists of some 11,000 islands, the largest of which are Irian (western New Guinea), Borneo (shared with Malaysia), Sumatra, Java, Celebes, and Timor. Sumatra was home to the SRI VIJAYA empire (7th–13th cents.). The MAJAPAHIT EMPIRE was established in Java (13th–16th cents.). Islam was brought to the islands of Indonesia by Arab traders during the 14th and 15th cents. By the fall of Majapahit the country was divided into statelets. The Portuguese arrived in Malacca, Malayan Peninsula, in the early 16th cent. From there, they occupied and exploited the Moluccas Islands for spices, especially nutmeg and cloves in tiny Tidore. The Dutch were in the East Indies by the end of the 16th cent. (DUTCH COLONIAL EMPIRE) and, by 1610, had replaced the Portuguese, who retained only EAST TIMOR. From 1610 to 1623, the Dutch and British warred over the mastery of the East Indies, finally retained by the Dutch, who expanded their hold during the following centuries, with a Napoleonic interlude (1811–1814) during which the British under Raffles occupied the territory. There were various rebellions against the Dutch, especially in Java and Bali.

SOEKARNO

It was only early in the 20th cent. that the Netherlands gave the Dutch East Indies its final configuration, basically that of modern Indonesia. The Japanese occupied the Dutch colony from 1942 to 1945, giving some space to Indonesian leaders, notably Soekarno, who proclaimed the independence of Indonesia. There was fighting with the Dutch from 1945 to 1949, when Indonesia obtained full independence. In 1957, Indonesia annexed the western part of New Guinea, still in Dutch hands, which it called Irian. In 1976 it invaded the mostly Christian Portuguese dependency of East Timor, which has been restive since and was offered self-determination in 1999. The capital of Indonesia during the Dutch period was Batavia, originally a fort built in the early 16th cent. near the Malay settlement of Jakarta, today's capital. Indonesia is the fourth most populous nation in the world.

Indus River Valley Civilization (3rd–2nd mils. BC; *Pakistan*)

The remains of the Indus River Valley Civilization were first discovered in the 1920s. At first they were thought to be an offshoot of SUMER, but the discovery of successive layers demonstrated that it was an autochthonous culture whose sedentary roots go back possibly to the 7th mil. BC, but more likely later. The culture had a script which has not yet been deciphered. The Indus River Valley Civilization arose around 2600–2500 BC. It flourished around 2300–2000 BC. It is possible that there might have been some political centralization after 2500 BC. The most important urban sites discovered are Harappa, in the north, and Mohenjo Daro, in the south. If there was

empire building it had the latter site at its core. The consensus at present is that the collapse of the Indus River Valley Civilization antedated the Aryan invasion of northern India (VEDIC INDIA). But there are speculations that it might have overlapped with the first Aryan arrivals ca. 1500 BC, and even that it was Aryanized towards its close. Why it disappeared around 1800–1700 BC is not known, but there is no evidence of destruction and it is presumed that the causes were 'natural', possibly climate change, e.g., centuries of drought.
(*See chronology under* Indian Subcontinent.)

Iran
SEE ENTRY IN 'PROVINCES AND REGIONS'
Even though the Persis of the Achaemenid Empire, today's Fars, capital Shiraz, was the core of Persia, it is the entire territory of modern Iran, plus areas that have been torn from it in the east (eastern Khurasan) and in the north (Azerbaijan), that has been considered immemorially to be Persia. Since the time of MEDIA, this territory has been either the centre of empires (ACHAEMENID EMPIRE, PARTHIA, SASANID EMPIRE) or part of other empires and states (ALEXANDRIAN EMPIRE, SELEUCID EMPIRE, ISLAM, ABBASID CALIPHATE, KHWARIZM, ILKHANID PERSIA, TIMURID EMPIRE AND SUCCESSOR STATES). It did not maintain its integrity through all these changes. Under Parthia (3rd cent. BC–3rd cent. AD) Persis was only partly in its orbit. The real scission came after the initial Islamic conquests and the establishment of the TAHIRIDS in Khurasan (9th cent.) during the Abbasid Caliphate. From that time until the SAFAVIDS, western and eastern Persia had significantly different political fortunes, except during brief reunifications as BUYID PERSIA (10th cent.) and Khwarizm (12th cent.) and under the heels of the MONGOL EMPIRE (13th. cent) and of Tamerlane and the Timurids (14th cent.). Eastern Persia, mainly Khurasan, has been fought over by the SAFFARIDS, SAMANIDS, GHAZNAVIDS, the KARA-KHITAN KHANATE, SARBEDARIANS, and SHAYBANIDS, who have either not wanted or not been able to intervene in western Persia. In turn, western Persia has been contested by Buyids (BUYID PERSIA), Seljuks (SELJUK PERSIA, which did, however, have a foothold in northern Khurasan), JELAIRS, MUZZAFARIDS, QARA-QOYUNLU, and AQ-QOYUNLU, who, likewise, have either not wanted or not been able to intervene in eastern Persia. The dispossession by the Safavids of the Aq-Qoyunlu in western Persia (ca. 1500) and of the Shaybanids in Khurasan (ca. 1590), signalled the reconstitution of Persia. At the time Iran extended from Baghdad in the west to Herat in the east, and from Azerbaijan and the Caucasus in the north to the Gulf of Persia and the coast of Makran in the south.

NADIR SHAH

Persia lost Baghdad to the OTTOMAN EMPIRE in 1638. This conquest with the adjoining lands marked thenceforth the frontier with Iraq. During the 18th cent. Persian influence was strong in AFGHANISTAN, although the Afghans invaded Persia and overthrew the SAFAVIDS (1722). Nadir Shah expelled the Afghans in 1736 and established his own Afshar dynasty. He invaded Afghanistan and northern India (1738). The occupation of Afghanistan ended with the assassination of Nadir Shah in 1747. The Afshar were substituted by

---

Iran

Predominant political influences

2nd mil.–9th cent. BC Elam	***4th–6th cents.*** Sasanid Empire	***13th cent.*** Khwarizm Mongol Empire Ilkhanid Persia Kerts
8th cent. BC Elam Media	***7th cent.*** Sasanid Empire Islam	
7th cent. BC Media Assyria Babylonia	***8th cent.*** Islam Abbasid Caliphate	***14th cent.*** Ilkhanid Persia Kerts Muzzafarids Sarbedarians Timurid Empire

6th cent. BC
Babylonia
Achaemenid Empire
	9th cent.
	Abbasid Caliphate
	Tahirids
	Saffarids
	Samanids
		15th cent.
		Timurid Empire
		  and successor
		  states
		Jelairs
		Qara-Qoyunlu
		Aq-Qoyunlu
		Safavids

5th–4th cents. BC Achaemenid Empire Alexandrian Empire Seleucid Empire	***10th cent.*** Samanids Ghaznavids Buyid Persia	
3rd. cent. BC Seleucid Empire Parthia	***11th cent.*** Buyid Persia Seljuk Persia	***16th cent.*** Safavids Shaybanids Persia

***2nd cent. BC–2nd
  cent. AD***
Parthia
	12th cent.
	Seljuk Persia
	Khwarizm
	Kara-Khitan
	  Khanate
		17th–19th cents.
		Persia
		Ottoman Empire
		Russia

3rd cent. Parthia Sasanid Empire		

---

the Zand (1750–1794), who ruled mostly from Shiraz. The capital was moved to Teheran in 1788. In the past, Rai had been considered the principal city in central Persia. The Qajar dynasty lasted from 1794 to 1925. The border with Afghanistan was the subject of much fighting until Herat definitely passed to Afghanistan in 1863 with British backing. During the 18th cent., Persia was influential, in rivalry with the Ottomans, in the Caucasus, but Iranian claims there were surrendered to Russia in 1828. This resulted in the partition of Azerbaijan, with Iran retaining the ancient capital Tabriz and Russia keeping the north, with Baku as capital. The last Persian dynasty was established by Reza Khan, an army officer who led a coup in 1921 and, in 1925, named himself emperor and founder of the Pahlavi dynasty. The dynasty's second and last member, Muhammad Reza Shah Pahlavi, was overthrown in the Shia Islamic revolution of 1979, led by Ayatollah Khomeini. The ancient name of Persia was changed to Iran *urbi et orbe* in 1934. In 1980 Iraq invaded Iran. The ensuing war, costly in human lives and in economic terms, lasted until 1988 and resulted in a territorial stalemate.
(*See chronology under* Iran.)

Iraq

Mesopotamia, wholly within Iraq, was home to one of history's three earliest civilizations, SUMER. The issue of precedence is still open between Egypt and Sumer, both going back to before the 3rd mil. BC. Sumer itself contained the ancient cities of Ur, Lagash, and others, and was the centre of many ancient kingdoms, notably BABYLONIA and ASSYRIA. Egyptian influence sometimes reached the margins of Mesopotamia. Iraq became part of the ACHAEMENID and later the ALEXANDRIAN EMPIRES. It was part of the post-Alexandrine SELEUCID EMPIRE. It fell to PARTHIA and later was part of the SASANID EMPIRE until its conquest in the early 7th cent. by ISLAM. An Umayyad province, the Abbasids chose Iraq, with the foundation of Baghdad in 762, as the centre of their empire (ABBASID CALIPHATE). In subsequent centuries, Iraq and Iran were closely integrated and shared a common history. They were distinguished as Iraq Arabi (Iraq proper) and Iraq Ajami (Iran). (Ajami in Arabic means non-Arab.) Thus, Baghdad was part of BUYID PERSIA, before becoming a Seljuk protectorate (SELJUK PERSIA). It was taken by KHWARIZM, ravaged by Mongols (MONGOL EMPIRE) and by Tamerlane (TIMURID EMPIRE AND SUCCESSOR STATES), and was alternatively part of the QARA-QOYUNLU and the AQ-QOYUNLU, before becoming part of Persia itself until being absorbed into the OTTOMAN EMPIRE.

USELESS WARS

The definite separation between Iraq and Persia came with the Ottoman conquest of Baghdad in 1638. The Ottomans divided Iraq into the provinces of Basra, Baghdad, and Mosul. After World War I and the dissolution of the

Ottoman Empire, the British obtained Iraq as a mandated territory in which they established in 1921 a kingdom headed by the Hashemite Faisal Ibn Hussain. At the expiration of the mandate in 1932, Iraq became independent but remained under strong British influence. In 1958, Faisal II was overthrown and killed by the military. The country has been ruled by the dictator Sadam Hussein since 1979, under whose rule Iraq invaded Iran in 1980 and fought a bloody war which ended in a stalemate in 1988. In 1990, Hussein annexed Kuwait, but the Iraqis were expelled by international forces led by the United States, with United Nations backing, in a brief but devastating war in 1991. Interdiction zones, where Iraq was enjoined not to fly or engage in military activities, were established in the northern and southern parts of Iraq. Iraq was also forced to comply with inspection programmes to deter the development of nuclear, chemical, or biological weapons. Iraq refused to cooperate in 1999 and has been subjected to sporadic attacks by American planes.

Ireland

SEE ENTRY IN 'PROVINCES AND REGIONS'

Ireland is the Celtic Erin, known to the Romans as Hibernia. According to legend, Ireland was invaded by waves of Celtic Gaels. The last of these invaders were the Tuatha de Danann which have been the subject of much speculation and literary elaboration. Ireland was divided into the kingly realms of Ulster, Munster, Connaught, Leinster, and Meath, all of which supposedly paid allegiance to one central ruler at Tara, in Meath. The reality of Irish history to the 8th cent. is that the country flourished culturally after Christianization but was politically divided and quarrelsome. Ireland had partially accepted Christianity before the arrival of St Patrick in the 5th cent. Irish cultural and religious influence crossed the Irish Sea to Scotland during the 5th and 6th cents. The Vikings were destructive assailants during the 8th cent. although they laid the foundations of cities such as Dublin, Waterford, and Limerick. Brian Boru in 1014 defeated the NORSEMEN, but Ireland remained much fragmented. The English Normans were granted overlordship of Ireland by Pope Adrian IV and, in 1170, Richard Pembroke began the conquest of the country, which Henry II visited the following year. The English chose Dublin as their seat of power, from where they gradually annexed Ireland, but their presence was not strong and the Scottish King Bruce invaded in 1315. Although Scot intervention was not durable, the country again became politically unstable. English rule was circumscribed to the pale of Dublin, until in 1495 Henry VII sent Edward Poynings who organized the country politically but ignored Irish rights to self-government.

IRELAND DEPOPULATED

Henry VIII put down rebellions from 1534 to 1537. Under the English king, James I Stuart, Protestants settled in the north of Ireland. The Irish revolted again in 1641 and Oliver Cromwell put them down in 1649–1650 through exceptionally bloody, repressive means. Confiscations of land and other arbitrary measures ensued which created bitterness between Ireland and Great Britain. The last outburst of organized resistance in Ireland before the 20th cent. was led, with French backing, by the deposed Catholic English king, Charles II. He was defeated in the Battle of Boyne in 1690 by William of Orange, the king who had succeeded Charles in 1688. It is this event that is celebrated by Protestants in Northern Ireland with fife and drums, a patent case of music as *casus belli*. English rule was harsh and so economically damaging that even Irish Protestants led opposition movements during the 18th cent. These resulted in the political union of Ireland and Great Britain in 1800. The potato blight struck Ireland in the 1840s and the country was largely depopulated through famine and emigration. It went from some eight million inhabitants in the first half of the 19th cent. to the two million it had at independence. In 1916, at Easter, Irish nationalists rebelled in Dublin. Their leaders were executed. From 1919 to 1921 the Irish, led by Michael Collins, adopted effective guerrilla tactics and, in 1922, Great Britain accepted the creation of the Irish Free State, still attached to the crown, which brought the wrath of extremists, led by Eamon de Valera, and resulted in Collins' assassination. In 1937, Ireland became totally independent of Great Britain, though still a member of the Commonwealth of Nations, from which Ireland egressed in 1948. Ireland became a member of the EUROPEAN UNION in 1972. English and Gaelic are official languages in Ireland.

Irish Free State (IRELAND)

Iroquois Confederacy (16th–18th cents.; United States)
A very loose confederation of North American Indian tribes founded in the 16th cent., the Iroquois Confederacy lasted until the formation of the United States. It comprised the Mohawk, Oneida, Onondaga, Cayuga, and Seneca, who spoke related languages. Their combined territories extended from northern and western New York to Lake Huron. As a rule, during the 18th cent. they were friendly to the British and hostile to the French.

Islam (7th–8th cents.; core area: *Arabia* and Syria)
Before the prophet Muhammad, the Meccans were idolaters. They resisted his preaching, which led to the *Hegira*, or his flight from Mecca to Medina. This event marks the beginning of the Islamic calendar (AD 622). In 630, Muhammad returned to Mecca, now converted. Muhammad was both ruler and spiritual leader. His governance was theocratic. After his death in 632, he was succeeded by three caliphs (successors) chosen among his principal followers. These were the elected caliphs: Abu Bakr (632–634), Umar (634–644), and Uthman (644–656). All three ruled from Mecca, but Islam spread widely under their military agents. The last two, Umar and Uthman, were assassinated. All

three elective caliphs are recognized by Sunni Islam. Shia Islam believes that Ali (656–661), the fourth caliph, was designated by Muhammad as his successor and thus count him as the first caliph. Be that as it may, Ali's son Hasan inherited the caliphate but was deposed the same year by Muawiya (661–680), who had been close to Muhammad and had the backing of one of the Prophet's widows. Hasan's brother Husein upheld the cause of Ali and he was killed by his opponents in the Battle of Karbala in 680. While Muawiya went on to found the Umayyad Caliphate in Damascus (661–750), Shias took a generally oppositionist attitude to constituted authority that did not accept the Alid claim. The word Shiite itself is an abbreviated form of *shi-at Ali* or Party of Ali. Thus, it is Shiite doctrine which underlay the FATIMIDS in their lunge for power in the 9th cent., and their claim to the caliphate; and in the 20th cent. it is the same set of beliefs that legitimized the rule of the Ayatollahs in Iran.

THE UMAYYAD OR DAMASCUS CALIPHATE

Despite this rift, it would appear that there is a fundamental political and territorial continuity from the foundation of Islam by Muhammad and his successors, the elective caliphs and Ali, to the Umayyad Empire. The period of the elected caliphs saw the consolidation of Islam in Arabia under Abu Bakr and its extension to Syria (636), Egypt (640), and Persia (642). Under the Umayyad Caliphate, Islamic control was extended to Afghanistan (652), Transoxiana (709–712), and Pakistan (712). The Maghreb was conquered between 642 and 708. Iberia was invaded in 711. In 749, the Abbasids, descendants of Abbas, uncle of Muhammad, formed (at least partially in league with Shiites) an opposition to the Umayyads, whose last caliph, Murwan II, was killed with most of his family in 750. Abu al-Abbas, the first Abbasid caliph, was succeeded by Al Mansur, who founded Baghdad in 762 and established the Caliphate there. With the ABBASID CALIPHATE, Islam begins to disintegrate as a relatively unified political entity, starting with the foundation of the independent emirate of Córdoba in 756 by Abd ar-Rahman, a survivor of the massacre of the Umayyads. The Maghreb and Egypt soon followed suit. Abbasid control of Persia foundered in the 9th cent.

THE SPREAD OF ISLAM

As a religion, Islam today is spread in the continent of Africa down to Tanzania and across to Nigeria and west Africa. In Asia, beyond its Arabian and Near Eastern cradle, Islam extends from Turkey to Pakistan across western and northern India to Bangladesh. It embraces most of central Asia down to Afghanistan and east to Sinkiang and southern Mongolia. It is also found in areas of central and southern China. It is the dominant faith in Malaysia and Indonesia and has a strong influence in the island of Mindanao in the Philippines. Islam is also the majority religion in parts of Bosnia-Herzegovina and in

Albania and the Yugoslav province of Kosovo. Since Islam is a universal religion it can be found in all countries of the world. Shia Islam is predominant in Iran, eastern Iraq, and in patches of Pakistan and Afghanistan.
(*See chronologies under* Iran *and* Maghreb.)

Ismailites (12th–13th cents.; *Iran*)
An Ismailite sect – from its allegiance to Ismail, the eldest son of a Shiite Imam in the 8th cent. – captured the fortress of Alamut, in north east Iran, ca. 1090, where it founded a terrorist state. Alamut resisted the Seljuks and was finally destroyed by the Mongol Il-Khan Hulagu in 1256 (ILKHANID PERSIA). The Ismailites of Alamut were also known as Nizaris from their support for Caliph Nizar of Baghdad. More commonly they were referred to as assassins, a name which has entered various languages for the activity the sect practised with great success. An Ismailite branch, known as the Druzes, took hold in the Levant during the 11th cent. They have descendants in Lebanon and Israel. Finally, the modern Ismailites are known today as the sect headed by the Aga Khans, who trace their descent to the original Ismail.

Israel (Ancient) (11th–8th cents. BC; ancient *Near East*)
Geographically in northern Canaan (PALESTINE), the ancient kingdom of Israel existed from the 11th to the 8th cent. BC. It was united to JUDAH by King David in the late 11th cent. BC, but they were divided again in 926 BC, the north led by Rehoboam. The Assyrians conquered Israel and destroyed Samaria, its capital, in 722 BC. The land of Israel fell to the New Babylonian Empire (BABYLONIA). It became a satrapy of the ACHAEMENID EMPIRE in 539 BC and after 332 BC passed to the ALEXANDRIAN EMPIRE and its successor states (SELEUCID EMPIRE and PTOLEMAIC EGYPT). In 63 BC, it became a province of the Roman Empire (ROME).
(*See chronology under* Ancient Near East.)

Israel
Appalled by the anti-semitism surrounding the Dreyfuss trial, the Jewish journalist Theodor Herzl published an appeal for the creation of a Jewish state, which found echo and led to the foundation in 1897 of the Zionist World Congress. Jewish emigration to Israel began slowly, picked up somewhat after the Balfour declaration of 1917 – in which the British Prime Minister favoured the idea of a Jewish homeland – and became intense after World War II and the experience of the Holocaust ordered by Hitler in Nazi Germany and carried out systematically by Himmler. By 1947, Jews represented one third of the total population of Palestine and were a majority in cities such as Tel Aviv and Haifa. Under attack in 1948 from neighbouring Arab states despite a UN-sponsored partition plan, the Jewish population of Palestine, led by Ben Gurion, constituted the state of Israel in 1949

comprising Palestine minus the Gaza Strip (Egypt) and the West Bank (Jordan). In 1956, in connivance with Great Britain and France resentful of the Egyptian nationalization of the Suez Canal, Israeli forces led by Moshe Dayan invaded the Sinai and Gaza, which they evacuated under intense international pressure, especially from the Eisenhower presidency in the United States. In the Arab–Israeli (Six Day) War of 1967, Israel, during the Prime Ministership of Levi Eshkol, occupied Sinai, the Gaza Strip, the West Bank and east Jerusalem, and the Golan Heights. In 1973, Egypt and Syria attacked. After a successful crossing of the Suez Canal, the Egyptians were beaten back by Israel, who received strong material support from the United States. The Syrians were quickly pushed towards Damascus. A truce was negotiated and Israel returned the eastern shore of the Suez Canal to Egypt and ordered its troops back to the Golan Heights. In 1979, Egypt, under President Anwar Sadat (the architect of the initially successful Egyptian offensive), and Israel, under Menachem Begin (who was the leader of the terrorist Irgun organization during the post-war British administration of Palestine), made peace and, in 1982, Israel returned the Sinai.

LEBANON

In 1978 Israel briefly invaded southern Lebanon to destroy Palestine guerrilla bases. It invaded Lebanon again in 1982 as far as Beirut, where civil war raged and militiamen were allowed entry into the Palestinian refugee camps of Sabra and Shatilla. A massacre ensued. The Israeli incursion was ineffectual and was terminated in 1985. Israel created a buffer zone in southern Lebanon, where it claimed the right of intervention for self-defence. It also created and armed in the zone a Christian militia called the South Lebanon Army. During the civil war in Lebanon, the Shiite Hizbollah became, and has remained, the greatest military threat to northern Israel. The official language of Israel is Hebrew, the language of the Bible, which is comparable to a state declaring Latin to be its official language and its inhabitants enthusiastically learning it. Hebrew is a Semitic tongue, like Arabic. In 1993, with strong misgivings in its conservative government, Israel agreed to the creation of the PALESTINIAN AUTHORITY, headed by the tenacious Palestinian leader Yasser Arafat, to govern the Gaza Strip and the West Bank, which are to be ceded in stages except for Jewish settlement areas.

JERUSALEM

The site of Jerusalem was occupied from before the 3rd mil. The city, which had been the centre of JUDAH, was captured by David ca. 1000 BC and made the capital of ISRAEL. David's son, Solomon, built the first Temple in the 10th cent. BC. In 586 BC, Jerusalem was taken by Babylonia and many Jews were settled in Mesopotamia. The founder of the Achaemenid Empire, Cyrus the Great, restored Jerusalem to the Jews and the Temple was rebuilt between 538 and 515 BC by Zerubbabel. Part of the Alexandrian Empire, Jerusalem afterwards fell to the SELEUCID EMPIRE. During the 2nd and 1st cents. BC, Jerusalem was the capital of the MACCABEES. Pompey incorporated Judaea into the Roman Empire in 63 BC. The Herod family ruled Jerusalem as Roman agents. Jewish restiveness resulted in the destruction of the Temple by Titus in AD 70. In the 2nd cent., Hadrian went further and, after the rebellion of Bar Kochba, even renamed the city Aelia Capitolina and tried to make it a centre of pagan worship. He did not succeed. Jerusalem remained in the Byzantine Empire after the fall of the Roman Empire in the west. In 637 it was conquered by Islam. From 1099 to 1187 it was ruled by the Crusaders and was the capital of the kingdom of Jerusalem (CRUSADER STATES). Retaken by Saladin, it was under Egyptian rule (MAMELUKE SULTANATE) and then under the Ottoman Empire (16th cent.). The city was surrendered to the British during World War I (1917). It was the capital of British Palestine until 1948, when Great Britain handed the mandate to the United Nations. Fighting broke out between Arabs and Jews in 1948 and Jerusalem was divided between Israel, who controlled the western, modern part, and Jordan, who retained the eastern, ancient part. Initially, Tel Aviv was the capital of Israel, but Jerusalem was made the capital in 1950. The last conquest of Jerusalem was by Israel in the Six Day War.

Italian Colonial Empire (19th–20th cents.)
If Germany was a late colonialist European power, Italy can only be said to have been very late. In the 1880s it occupied the south-western coast of the Red Sea and, with its hinterland, constituted the colony of Eritrea (Roman name for the Red Sea, which has stuck). In 1896, Italy made a bid for Ethiopia and was overwhelmed by the numerically superior Ethiopians in Adowa. In 1935, with more fire power and planes, it finally annexed the African kingdom. In 1941, Italy surrendered both colonies to Great Britain. In 1912, it occupied the Dodecanese Islands, next to the south-western coast of Turkey, and ceded them to Greece in 1947. By 1914, after war with the Ottoman Empire (1911–1912) and against strong native resistance, Italy had occupied Libya, which it lost to the British after the Battle of El Alamein (1942). It invaded Albania in 1938, but left it to the Germans in 1943. The Albanians, with the support of the Yugoslav partisans, had liberated their territory by 1944.

Italy
See entry in 'Provinces and Regions'
The history of modern Italy begins with the resurgence of the kingdom of SARDINIA which comprised Piedmont, Savoy, Liguria, and the island of Sardinia. Under the dual leadership of its king, Victor Emmanuel II, and Prime Minister Cavour, Sardinia, in alliance with France under Napoleon III,

defeated the Austrians (HABSBURG EMPIRE) in the Battle of Solferino (1859) and annexed Lombardy (MILAN). The carnage there prompted the creation of the Red Cross by the Swiss Jean-Henri Dunant. In exchange for French help, Sardinia ceded Nice and Northern SAVOY to France. In 1860, in the wake of Solferino, Tuscany (FLORENCE), PARMA, MODENA, and the PAPAL STATES – but not Rome itself, which Napoleon protected for the papacy until 1870 – became part of Sardinia. At the same time, Garibaldi did away with the Bourbon kingdom of the TWO SICILIES, so that, in 1861, the King of Sardinia became the King of Italy. In 1866, Italy sided with Prussia against Austria and annexed Venetia. The process of the unification of Italy is called the *risorgimento* and was promoted nationally and internationally by the Republican Mazzini.

VITTORIO VENETO

Italy, which was neutral at the start of World War I, entered it in 1915 on the side of the Allies with the offer of territorial gains. The fight was indecisive until the Austrians clearly won the Battle of Caporetto in 1917, but the Italians vanquished the Austrians in 1918 at Vittorio Veneto. After the war, Italy acquired Trieste, Istria, some Adriatic islands, and the Alto Adige (South Tyrol) from the dissolved Habsburg Empire. The Croatian port of Rijeka (known in Italian as Fiume) was in dispute with Yugoslavia. The romantic writer and adventurer D'Annunzio seized it by assault with a handful of followers. While negotiations about its status were going on, the fascists occupied it in 1922. Italy also held the tiny enclave of Zara further south along the Adriatic coast. In 1936, the Italian dictator Mussolini, who came to power in 1922, joined Hitler in creating the Axis, which Japan joined in 1940. Italy invaded Albania in 1939. It did not enter World War II until 1940. In 1941, Italian forces were contained by the Greeks and Germany invaded the Balkans. The Italians were driven out of Libya, Eritrea, and Ethiopia by the British. Italy sued for peace in 1943 but was invaded by Germany. Albania had fought off its invaders by 1944. When the war in Europe ended, the Allies were still fighting the Germans entrenched in northern Italy. After World War II, Italy lost Istria, Rijeka, and its other Adriatic conquests to Yugoslavia, and barely managed to hang on to Trieste. Italy became a republic in 1946. It is a founding member of the EUROPEAN UNION.

(*See chronology under* Italy.)

J

Jamaica

Claimed by Spain, the Caribbean island of Jamaica was mostly neglected. During the 16th and 17th cents. it often served as a haven for corsairs against Spain. Great Britain occupied Jamaica in 1665. It achieved independence in 1962. Kingston is the Jamaican capital.

Japan

SEE ENTRY IN 'PROVINCES AND REGIONS'

The history of Japan starts around AD 400 in the Kansai Plain of central Honshu. The Japanese tongue probably belongs to the Altaic family, which includes Mongol and Turkic. It uses Chinese characters in its written form. Japanese history is divided into distinctly recognizable periods – some, in turn, classified into subperiods – mostly based on political circumstances but with cultural traits as well. Yamato, named for the plain around Osaka, lasted until the early 8th cent., during which time the clans were strong and the monarchy was weak with no fixed capital. However, it was in the Yamato period that the islands of Honshu, Shikoku, and Kyushu were united under imperial authority. Though the elementary Shinto worship was and remains traditionally Japanese, Bukkyo (Buddhism) was introduced from China and Korea in the 6th cent. and became very influential. The Fujiwara clan, whose ascendancy in Japan lasted for centuries, first became known for their organization of the imperial government along centralizing lines. The Nara period began with the establishment of the imperial capital in the city of Nara in 710 in the Kansai Plain, which also includes Yamato and Kyoto. The transfer of the capital from Nara to Kyoto in 794 inaugurates the Heian period, which was a time of artistic development whose results, such as *Tale of Genji*, by Lady Murasaki (ca. 1000), are considered classic. It was also a time when the nobility grew in strength and Buddhism acquired great influence. The island of Hokkaido, originally populated only by Ainu (who speak an isolate or unique language), was annexed during the early 9th cent. by Sakanoue Tamuramaro, the first to have the title of shogun or military leader. The Minamoto family managed from 1185 to consolidate power in their seat in Kamakura, which has lent its name to the period that followed and lasted until 1333. Kamakura is located near Tokyo, formerly called Edo.

SHOGUNATE

In 1192, the head of the Minamoto clan obtained the heritability of the title of shogun, which marks the consolidation of the system of indirect rule with the emperors as figureheads. This arrangement became known as bakufu (tent government) and was retained through successive period changes. At the start of the 13th cent. power passed to the Hojo family, who transferred the shogunate to imperial princes while they controlled both the shoguns and the emperors (*indirect indirect control*). In 1274 Kublai Khan, the Mongol founder of the YUAN dynasty in China, attempted for the first time to subject Japan, but his forces turned back due to adverse weather, which the Japanese saw as a divine wind or kamikaze. Successive Mongol emissaries were executed by the Japanese until Kublai Khan assembled a huge fleet which managed to land an equally immense army in the bay of Hakata, on the island of Kyushu. The Japanese contained the beachhead and weather once again proved treacherous to the Mongols, who escaped only in small numbers. However, these attacks weakened Kamakura and an uncommonly ambitious emperor, Go-Daigo (Daigo II), tried to grab power from the Hojo, an action which provided the Kamakura general, Ashikaga Takauji, the opportunity to do so, thus inaugurating a new period in Japanese history, the Ashikaga period (1333–1603). During this time, the shogunate functioned in Kyoto, next door to the imperial palace. The bakufu system continued, but central authority crumbled, which benefited the power of the daimyo, or feudal lords, and favoured, towards the end of the period, the rise of the warlords.

TOKUGAWA

The first of the warlords was Oda Nobunaga, of whom it was said that if the cuckoo did not sing he would kill it. Nobunaga came from Nagoya and he was active in the Kansai area and in west Honshu beating down factionalism, including the temporal power of Buddhist sects. He was famous for his cruelty and was killed by one of his lieutenants in 1582. The task of restoring authority in Japan then fell to Toyotomi Hideyoshi, of whom it was said that if the cuckoo did not sing he would make it. His base was in Osaka and he subjugated autonomous chiefdoms in Shikoku, Kyushu, and northern Honshu. Hideyoshi also invaded Korea in 1592 and fought a long war against the MING, who showed that Chinese suzerainty was not just nominal. The hostilities ended upon Hideyoshi's death in 1598. Like Nobunaga, Hideyoshi declined the shogun title but adopted the ancient Fujiwara one of kampaku or regent. Of Tokugawa Ieyasu it was said that if the cuckoo did not sing he would wait. His base was Tokyo and he stood out of Hideyoshi's way, but as soon as he could, he removed Hideyoshi's successors and assumed the title of shogun in 1603, with which he inaugurated the Tokugawa period. It was to last until the so-called Meiji restoration in 1868. On Ieyasu's accession the daimyo still existed, but they had lost the ability to disrupt the kingdom's unity. Japan was stable and mostly prosperous, which meant that *vis à vis* Europe it stagnated. Among the things it did not do was adopt gunpowder as the sine qua non of warfare, although the warlords had availed themselves of its use.

The first Europeans to visit Japan, the Portuguese, arrived there in 1542. They were well received and soon there were Catholic missionaries in the kingdom – the most famous was Francis Xavier – who did considerable prose-lytizing. After 1581, with the annexation of Portugal to Spain, the Spanish also came. Hideyoshi became suspicious of Christian influence and, in 1587, he ordered the expulsion of the missionaries. The decree was not at first applied, but after 1597 it was done so with a vengeance, crucifixion becoming a common way of executing Christians. The Dutch had arrived in 1600 for the sole purpose of trade, to which, in a limited way, the Japanese did not object. The Christian penetration of Kyushu was finally wiped out in 1637–1638 in a shogunal campaign, backed by Dutch naval power, against rebellious Chris-tians in the area of Nagasaki, in Kyushu.

Meiji

The Tozama were daimyo not in particular favour with the Tokugawa shoguns. Among them were the powerful clans of the Choshu (in southern Honshu) and the Satsuma (in Kyushu). Between 1853 and 1864, in a process initiated by the American commodore Perry, who entered the Bay of Tokyo with warships without Japanese authorization, the Japanese bakufu government came under intense western pressure. Gradually the shogun accepted the necessity of coop-eration, but in this he was opposed by the Tozama, whose fortresses were bombarded by western flotillas. In an ironic twist, the Tozama clans then became the supporters of westernization, deposed the shogun, and installed Emperor Meiji in Edo, which was renamed Tokyo. Japan was provided with a constitution in 1889, which did not diminish the power of the feudal lords or the militarization of the country. The Japanese colonization of the Ryuku Islands (including Okinawa) began in the 17th cent. They became part of Japan in 1879. The Kuriles were disputed by Japan and Russia. In 1875 Japan gave up claims to Sakhalin in exchange for the Kuriles, but in 1905, after it won the 1904 war against Russia, it was awarded southern Sakhalin, which it named Karafuto. Japan acquired TAIWAN in war against China in 1894–1895. During World War I, which Japan entered on the side of the western allies, it occupied German colonies (JAPANESE COLONIAL EMPIRE). Japan was in a virtual state of war with CHINA, starting from 1931.

Hirohito

Dissatisfied with Japanese policy in China, the Americans were seen as a threat by the Japanese, who attacked Pearl Harbor, Hawaii, by surprise in December 1941, and entered World War II on the side of the Axis. Very quickly Japanese forces over-ran south east Asia to the Indian Assam frontier, where the Japanese were stopped by the British. In the central Pacific the Japanese navy suffered a crushing defeat in Midway, a few months after Pearl Harbor. Two Aleutian islands were the limit of the Japanese advance in the northern Pacific. The Japanese advance in the South Pacific reached as far as the Solomon Islands, but was halted in Guadalcanal and before it reached Port Moresby in south-eastern New Guinea. The Allies, under the overall command of MacArthur, counter-attacked from Polynesia towards Honshu and from New Guinea towards the Philippines. The Japanese navy was finally crushed in the Battle of the Philippines Sea in 1944. The Philippines fell during 1945. After the bloody battles of Iwo Jima and Okinawa, atomic bombs fell on Hiroshima and Nagasaki and Japan surrendered in August. The USSR had declared war after the atomic bombings and occupied Manchuria and northern Korea. It took southern Sakhalin and the Kuriles. Japan has maintained its right of ownership to the Kuriles. In 1947, occupied Japan, who was allowed to retain its emperor, Hirohito, got a new constitution, and a peace treaty with the United States – but not the USSR – was signed in 1951. MacArthur was the overlord during the period of occupation. Post-war Japan, like post-war Germany, developed economically so quickly and vastly that it left far behind all pre-war references.

Japanese Colonial Empire (19th–20th cents.)
The last bout of colonialist empire-building was that of the Japanese, who were late in industrializing. In 1875, they acquired the Bonin Islands, but since they were made part of Tokyo prefecture and were settled by Japanese, it would be unfair to class them as colonies. They were occupied by the United States from 1945 to 1968. The first truly colonial Japanese acquisition was Taiwan, after Japan defeated China in 1895. Korea, the hermit kingdom, was defenceless and Japan annexed it in 1910. In 1914, upon declaring war against Germany, Japan occupied the Marianas and the Caroline Islands. Japan was virtually at war with China from 1931 to 1945, although the state of war formally existed only in 1937. In 1932, the Japanese annexed Manchuria, renamed it Manchukuo, and set it up as a puppet kingdom. After 1937, Japanese aggression against China was rampant. By 1941, the Japanese controlled the coast and invaded territories as far west as Shanxi (Shansi) and Hubei (Hubeh). These conquests were part of the war empire the Japanese military quickly created, starting in 1940, and just as quickly lost (1945). At its height this empire stretched from the frontier between Burma and Assam in British India to the island of Midway – which the Japanese tried to occupy in 1941 but failed, after losing one of the decisive naval battles of World War II – and south to the Dutch East Indies and western and northern New Guinea. They also failed to take Port Moresby in Papua and this, too, signalled the rollback of their forces. In 1945, after two atomic bombs dropped on Hiroshima and Nagasaki, Japan unconditionally surrendered with all the lands it had taken from its neighbours. It was also forced to hand over to

the USSR the southern half of Sakhalin and the Kuriles. The latter were home territories and Japan still claims them. The American occupation ended in 1952 with the signing of a peace treaty.

Jelairs (14th–15th cents.; *Middle East*)
The Jelairs were a minor Mongol dynasty that, after the dissolution of ILKHANID PERSIA in 1335, occupied Baghdad and, in 1360, conquered Azerbaijan, possessions which shortly afterwards were taken from them by the QARA-QOYUNLU (ca. 1390). The latter were defeated by Tamerlane ca. 1400 (TIMURID EMPIRE AND SUCCESSOR STATES). The Jelairs seized Baghdad briefly after Tamerlane's death (1405), but were dispossessed by the AQ-QOYUNLU.
(*See chronology under* Iran.)

Jerusalem (Kingdom of) (CRUSADER STATES)

Johore (16th–20th cents.; *Malaya*)
The state of Johore was founded in 1511 after MALACCA had been taken by the Portuguese. It had Malay sultans to whom the British gained influential access in the 19th cent. In 1819, it was a ruler of Johore who ceded to the British the island of SINGAPORE. In 1914, Johore became a British protectorate, which in 1948 entered the Federation of Malaya (MALAYSIA).

Jordan
The Hashemites, who held the title of Sharifs of Mecca under the OTTOMAN EMPIRE, became boon companions of T. E. Lawrence. After World War I, they were driven out of Mecca by the Saudis (SAUDI ARABIA). In compensation, the British sheared off the trans-Jordanian Bedouin lands from their Palestinian mandate and handed over a throne in Amman to Abdullah, son of Hussein of Hejaz, the last Hashemite sharif of Mecca, under British tutelage. In 1946, Transjordan became the Hashemite Kingdom of Transjordan, changed in 1949 to Jordan. During the Arab–Israeli War of 1947–1948, which established the state of ISRAEL, the Jordanian Arab Legion held its own against American-equipped Israeli forces and retained the West Bank and East Jerusalem, the ancient part of the city, holy to three religions. Both were lost to Israel in the Arab–Israeli (Six Day) War of 1967. Much of the Arab population of Palestine emigrated to Jordan during the creation of Israel and afterwards. In response to the formation of the United Arab Republic (Egypt and Syria) in 1958, King Hussein of Jordan formed the Arab Federation with Iraq, which was dissolved when the King of Iraq, his Hashemite cousin Feisal, was overthrown and murdered by the military. Amman is the capital of Jordan.

Juan-juan (4th–6th cents.; *Central Asia*: greater Mongolia)
A Chinese pejorative, Juan-juan is the name that has stuck to Mongol nomads

who, in the 4th cent., substituted the HSIEN-PI in the control of Mongolia. Ironically, although Juan-juan means 'the wriggling of insects', they themselves were the first to use the mighty Mongol titles of khan and khagan (khan of khans). Their khanate lasted from 402 to 552 and, at its peak, stretched from Manchuria to far beyond Lake Balkash. In the 6th cent., they attacked the T'U-CHÜEH in the Altai mountains (border of western Mongolia and China), but were driven back to China, where they were eventually assimilated (PERIOD OF DISUNITY (AFTER HAN)). These events are reported in Chinese chronicles and T'u-chüeh is the first historical mention of the Turks. (*See chronology under* China and Neighbouring Areas *and* Greater Mongolia.)

Judaea (JUDAH)

Judah (11th–6th cents. BC; ancient *Near East*)
The Biblical Judah occupied southern PALESTINE after the exodus. The kingdom of Judah, capital Jerusalem, was probably formed in the 11th cent. BC. It was united to ISRAEL (ANCIENT) under David in the late 11th cent. BC until the 10th cent. BC, when Rehoboam, son of Solomon, formed a separate state with the northern tribes. After, there were frequent wars between north and south. ASSYRIA conquered Palestine in 722 BC and took Jews captive. It is from this captivity that the question of the 'lost tribes' of Israel arises (KHAZARS). BABYLONIA, under Nabuchadnezzar, seized Palestine and destroyed the Temple of Solomon in 587 BC. Jews were again taken into captivity. Later, Palestine became first a satrapy of the ACHAEMENID EMPIRE (539 BC) and then a part of the ALEXANDRIAN EMPIRE and its successor states (after 332 BC) (SELEUCID EMPIRE; PTOLEMAIC EGYPT). The Maccabees, also known as Hasmodeans or Asmodeans (from the name of an ancestor), rebelled against Seleucid rule and by 166 BC, under Judas Maccabeus, Judaea had independence, which it defended against repeated Seleucid attacks. The power of Judaea grew after 135 BC, but there was also internal strife and it was annexed by ROME in 63 BC. (*See chronology under* Ancient Near East.)

Jurchen (12th–13th cents.; *Central Asia*: eastern Siberia; northern *China*)
The Jurchen were a semi-nomadic Tungus nation originating in the Ussuri River Basin, who, allied to the SUNG (SONG) dynasty from 1114 to 1125, defeated the sinicized KHITAN KHANATE. That whiff of glory led them to found, at Sung expense, their own Chin (Jin) dynasty in northern China, which lasted from 1126 to 1234, and at its peak extended from the Pacific Ocean coast of Siberia to Shanxi (Shansi). They lost their Manchurian and other northern stomping grounds to roaming Mongol bands and their dynasty was eventually crushed by Kublai Khan (YUAN). Tungus is a language of the Altaic family, to which Turkic, Mongol and Manchu belong. (*See chronologies under* China and Neighbouring Areas *and* Greater Mongolia.)

K

Kairouan (AGHLABID EMIRATE)

Kalinga (CENTRAL INDIA; MAGADHA)

Kama Bulgars (VOLGA BULGARS)

Kandy (SRI LANKA)

Kanem-Bornu (14th–17th cents.; *Sub-Saharan Africa*)
A Hausa-speaking Islamic kingdom, Kanem-Bornu occupied areas of Niger and Chad. It was related to the tribal states of northern Nigeria. Kanem (Niger) and Bornu (Chad) separated after 1500. Both states flourished separately during the 16th and 17th cents. and then dissolved. In the 17th cent. Bornu fell to the Fur kingdom of western Sudan. Southern Niger fell to the FULANI. When the French conquered Niger, it was peopled by nomadic Tuaregs in the north.
(*See chronology under* Western and Sub-Saharan Africa.)

Karakhanids (10th–12th cents.; *Central Asia*: western Turkestan)
The Karakhanids were a Turkish dynasty, originally from Kashgaria, that, in the late 10th cent., took Transoxiana from the SAMANIDS losing it later to the Seljuks (MERV). During the 11th and 12th cents., they were reduced in Transoxiana to the city of Bukhara as vassals of KHWARIZM and the KARA-KHITAN KHANATE. They were eventually wasted by internal rebellion and suppression by their Khwarizmian overlords. The Kara-Khanids were the first Turkish dynasty to rule in Western Turkestan.
(*See chronology under* Western Turkestan.)

Kara-Khitan Khanate (12th–13th cents.; *Central Asia*: western Turkestan)
The Kara-Khitan Khanate was founded by a branch of the Mongol KHITAN KHANATE. In 1128 the Kara-Khitai penetrated and conquered Kashgaria and ruled it as gur-khans. From that base they sallied as far as Khurasan, in eastern Iran, and made KHWARIZM a vassal state. Khwarizm subsequently grew in power and took Transoxiana from the Kara-Khitai. Conflict loomed between the two states, which was resolved when the Mongols of Genghis Khan destroyed the Kara-Khitan Khanate (1218) and captured Urgench, capital of Khwarizm (1221) (MONGOL EMPIRE).
(*See chronologies under* Western Turkestan *and* Iran.)

Karaman (ANATOLIAN EMIRATES)

Karmathians (SAUDI ARABIA)

Kashmir (16th–19th cents.; northern *India*)

A northern Indian region annexed by MUGHAL INDIA in 1586, Kashmir was autonomous but disunited from 1751. In 1846, it was annexed by BRITISH INDIA and provided with a Hindu dynasty (PUNJAB). At the time the British also annexed Chinese territory in Ladakh. Kashmir includes the valley of Srinagar, Ladakh on the Tibetan border, and Jammu in the south. Srinagar and the surrounding country is mainly Muslim. Jammu is majority Hindu. Ladakh, which borders on Tibet, is Buddhist and Tibetan in culture, but it is mountainous and lightly populated. In 1947, during the partition of India and Pakistan, the Kashmiri rajah opted for Indian rule. This brought armed conflict in 1948 between India and Pakistan. In 1949, a cease-fire left India in control of most of Kashmir, including Srinagar. Fighting between the Indian authorities and Muslim forces goes on intermittently. The Kashmir issue is at the heart of the difficult relations between Delhi and Islamabad. Eastern Ladakh was occupied by the Chinese after an offensive against India in 1962.
(*See chronology under* Indian Subcontinent.)

Kassites (BABYLONIA)

Kaya (KOREA)

Kazakhstan

The centre of Kazakhstan is the Kirghiz steppe (*Central Asia*) which has been the corridor for eastern hordes moving towards the west from Mongolia and beyond. By the 17th cent. the steppe was occupied by the KIRGHIZ-KAZAKS, Turks who did not take kindly either to the western Mongols (MONGOLIA) or the Russians. Kazakhstan was formed by Russia from lands loosely attached to the khanates of KOKAND, ASTRAKHAN, and KAZAN. The Soviets incorporated the Kazakh autonomous region into Soviet Russia (USSR). In 1936 they created the Kazakh Soviet Socialist Republic. Kazakhstan became independent in 1991. In 1996, the capital was officially transferred from Alma Ata to Akhmola, renamed Astana. Semipalatinsk is a region of north-eastern Kazakhstan. Semirechye is the infrequently used name for the region south of Lake Balkash.

Kazan Khanate (15th–16th cents.; *Russia*)

Formed in 1445, the Kazan Khanate was the successor of the once feared GOLDEN HORDE. In 1552, it was conquered by Russia in Ivan the Terrible's drive eastward. Kazan is a city in eastern Russia.

Kenya

In 1886 Great Britain and Germany agreed to share east Africa between them. Germany got the mainland territory of today's Tanzania. Great Britain got Kenya, whose interior was mostly peopled by Kikuyu and Masai tribes.

Colonialization began in 1888. The cool highland climate of Kenya attracted British colonists. After the suppression of the Mau Mau insurrection, Kenya became independent in 1963, under the leadership of Jomo Kenyatta. The capital is Nairobi. The official languages in Kenya are English and Swahili. Native languages in the interior are of the Nilotic group, spoken in north east Africa. A lingua franca in east Africa, Swahili is a Bantu language with considerable Arabic influence, also spoken in Tanzania and along the east African coast. The word Swahili itself means 'coast' in Arabic.

Kerts (13th–14th cents.; Afghanistan)
The Kerts were an Afghan dynasty that ruled in Herat (Khurasan) from 1251 to at least the late 14th cent. The Kerts were initially Mongol vassals, but strengthened after the end of ILKHANID PERSIA. They were swamped by Tamerlane in 1381 (TIMURID EMPIRE AND SUCCESSOR STATES).
(*See chronology under* Afghanistan.)

Khazars (7th–11th cents.; *Southern Russia*)
A Turkish people, the Khazars roamed the Volga area, the Kuban, and Dagestan. In the 7th cent. they drove a wedge between the VOLGA BULGARS. The MAGYARS became their clients. During the 10th cent., their power waned under harassment by the PETCHENEGS or Patzinaks, who crossed their lands and drove the Magyars from Azov towards central Europe, where they eventually founded Hungary. In the 11th cent., the BYZANTINE EMPIRE and the Russians destroyed what remained of the Khazars. The Khazars converted to Judaism in the 8th cent. Arthur Koestler believed they were one of the 12 'lost tribes' of Israel (JUDAH), which would explain how the *Pale* of Jewish settlement was peopled.
(*See chronology under* Southern Russia.)

Khitan Khanate (9th–12th cents.; *Central Asia*: eastern Siberia; northern *China*)
The Khitai were Mongols, originally out of Jehol, who in the late 9th cent. defeated the KIRGHIZ and occupied Mongolia. Inside the Chinese walls in 907, they founded the Liao kingdom in northern Hebei (Hopeh) with its capital in Beijing. Europe got from them the name Cathay for all of China. The SUNG (SONG) sought the JURCHEN as allies to defeat the Khitai (1114–1125), which was possibly a wrong move because the Khitai were sinicized and the Jurchen were barbarians who quickly turned on their Sung allies. The remnants of the Khitai took Kashgaria in 1128 and created the KARA-KHITAN KHANATE.
(*See chronology under* China and Neighbouring Areas *and* Greater Mongolia.)

Khiva (Khanate of) (16th–19th cents.; *Central Asia*: western Turkestan)
Khiva was part of KHWARIZM (12th–14th cents.) after which it was alternately in the hands of Mongols and Turks. The Khanate of Khiva, in today's

Uzbekistan and Turkmenistan, was founded in 1510 by a collateral branch of the SHAYBANIDS. It was absorbed by Russia in 1881.
(*See chronology under* Western Turkestan.)

Khojas (CHAGATAITE KHANATE; DZUNGARIA)

Khwarizm (12th–14th cents.; *Central Asia*: western Turkestan; *Iran*)
Chorasmia, the ancient region neighbouring on Sogdiana (eastern part of Transoxiana), later became the core of the Khwarizm of the Turks. It extended from the Syrdarya (Jaxartes) River to the Amudarya (Oxus) River and beyond into Turkmenistan. However, Khwarizm itself tended to move southwards over time so that the name more properly designates northern Turkmenistan. Khwarizm acquired political status around the middle of 12th cent. with the formation of an Iranized Turkish state, which quickly became a vassal of the KHARA-KHITAN KHANATE. Khwarizm incorporated Khurasan (ca. 1180) and later invaded west Persia and destroyed SELJUK PERSIA in 1194. It conquered north Afghanistan from the Afghan GHURIDS (ca. 1200). In 1207, Khwarizm took western Transoxiana from the Khara-Khitai, its former suzerains, and shortly afterwards it rounded out the conquest of Afghanistan by taking Ghazni. Urgench was the capital of Khwarizm. The Kara-Khitai in Kashgaria were threatening Khwarizm when, in 1218, Genghis crushed them and, in 1221, gave short shrift to Khwarizm, whose rulers briefly retained Azerbaijan after the Mongol tide momentarily receded (1227–1231) (MONGOL EMPIRE). After the Mongols returned, Khwarizm was vaguely divided between the GOLDEN HORDE and ILKHANID PERSIA, both of them Mongol successor states. Around 1380, the Turks founded a second, weaker Khwarizm around Khiva, which was annexed by Tamerlane to his Samarkandian base (TIMURID EMPIRE AND SUCCESSOR STATES). After the fall of the Timurids, Khwarizm, by then again just a name for a region, fell to the SHAYBANIDS.
(*See chronologies under* Iran *and* Western Turkestan.)

Kievan Rus (RUSSIA)

Kipchak (Khanate of) (GOLDEN HORDE)

Kipchaks (POLOVETZY)

Kirghiz (9th–17th cents.; *Central Asia*: greater Mongolia and western Turkestan)
The Kirghiz were Turkic nomads of central Asia who, from their original lands around the Yenisei River, defeated the UIGURS and in the 9th cent. briefly occupied Mongolia. They were vanquished by the KHITAN KHANATE ca. 920. They gradually moved to the south west and by the 17th cent. had occupied KYRGYZSTAN. The Kirghiz and the Kirghiz-Kazakhs, who occupied Kazakhstan, are related peoples, probably of the same origin.
(*See chronology under* Greater Mongolia.)

Kirghiz-Kazakhs (15th–19th cents.; *Central Asia*: Kirghiz steppe)
The Kirghiz-Kazaks were Turkish nomads roaming the western reaches of Mogholistan in the late 15th cent. They first joined the Uzbeks (SHAYBAN-IDS) in the Syr Darya River Basin but later went on their own. During the early 16th cent. they raided the CHAGATAITE KHANATE in the Ili River Basin, which they later made the base from which, during the 16th and 17th cents., they peopled the Kirghiz steppe in Kazakhstan. The Oirats or western Mongols (MONGOLIA) invaded the steppe in the 17th cent. but were harassed out by the Kirghiz-Kazakhs, who in the early 18th cent. divided into Little, Middle, and Great Hordes and were active from Lake Balkash to the Ural River. In the early 19th cent., the Great Horde was absorbed by the KOKAND KHANATE. The Kirghiz-Kazakhs probably are of the same origin as the Kirghiz.
(*See chronology under* Greater Mongolia.)

Kiribati
Explored by Byron in 1764, peopled by speakers of Gilbertese – of the Austronesian family of languages which includes Malay tongues – the Pacific Ocean islands of Gilbert and Ellice became British dependencies in 1892. The Japanese occupied some of the islands from 1941 to 1943. Tarawa in particular was the scene of heavy fighting with the invading American Marines. The Ellice Islands became independent in 1978 as TUVALU and the Gilberts in 1979 as Kiribati. The capital of Kiribati is Bairiki, on Tarawa.

Knights of St John (CRUSADER STATES)
The Knights of St John were founded in Jerusalem in the 11th cent. as the Order of the Hospital of St John of Jerusalem. They were also known as Knights Hospitalers. During the time of their rule on the island of Rhodes they were known as the Knights of Rhodes and after they set their headquarters in MALTA they also became known as the Knights of Malta.

Knossos (MINOAN CIVILIZATION)

Koguryo (KOREA)

Kokand Khanate (18th–19th cents.; *Central Asia*: western Turkestan)
The Kokand Khanate branched off into Ferghana from BUKHARA ca. 1710. In the early 19th cent. it annexed Tashkent. After, the Large Horde of the KIGHIZ-KAZAKHS, which was active east of Lake Balkash, became its vassal. In 1876 Kokand was annexed by Russia.
(*See chronology under* Western Turkestan.)

Kongo (15th–17th cents.; Angola)
Kongo was a tribal kingdom in northern Angola controlled by the Portuguese. The language was of the Bantu family.

Korea

Korea was Chinese vassal territory in the 2nd cent. BC. In 57 BC it was divided into four kingdoms: Koguryo, Paekche, Silla, and Kaya. In 562, Silla absorbed Kaya. The three kingdoms lasted until 668, when the Chinese T'ANG (TANG) dynasty destroyed Koguryo and Paekche in northern Korea, which left Silla as the dominant state in the peninsula. In 935 the Koryo dynasty, from Koguryo, took power. The Mongols conquered and occupied Korea in the 13th and 14th cents. (YUAN). The Chinese MING dynasty gave its backing in 1392 to the Yi or Choson dynasty, which established its capital in Seoul. During the 16th cent., Japan, under the warlord Hideyoshi, invaded Korea and warred against Chinese armies, but finally retreated. In the 17th cent., Korea became a CH'ING (QING) or Manchu vassal state. Korean belongs to the Altaic family of languages, which includes Turkic and Mongol.

Two Koreas

The Japanese invaded Korea, deposed the Choson or Yi ruling dynasty and occupied the country, which it named Chosen, from 1910 to 1945. At the end of World War II, Korea was divided along the 38th parallel with Soviet troops north and American troops south of that line. In 1948, two states were created: the communist Democratic People's Republic of Korea, with its capital in Pyongyang, and the Republic of Korea, with its capital in Seoul. In 1949, foreign troops were removed. In 1950, the North Koreans, with the support of Stalin, invaded South Korea, whose defences crumbled. The Security Council of the United Nations took advantage of a Soviet boycott, in protest for the non-admittance of communist China, and voted to intervene.

The 'Tigers'

The Americans held the Pusan perimeter. After a landing in Inchon, UN troops, under the command of the American general MacArthur, outflanked the communist forces and drove the rest to the Yalu River, provoking the intervention of communist China. MacArthur was cashiered for advocating the use of nuclear weapons despite official American policy. The UN forces – from many countries, significantly Great Britain and other members of the Commonwealth of Nations, but mostly American – fought a rearguard action back to approximately where the previous frontier had been, with rectifications to make it more compact. An armistice was signed in 1953 in Panmunjon, but as yet there is no peace agreement. North Korea, heir to the industrial infrastructure left by the Japanese, at first seemed to be the more developed of the two Koreas, but South Korea leaped ahead in the 1970s and, with Singapore, Hong Kong, and Taiwan, constituted the group of the so-called 'Asian Tigers', the first highly developed economies to emerge so far from a condition of economic underdevelopment. Malaysia and Thailand have followed the lead of the Four Tigers. The example of these nations has been influential in the turning of China towards more open economic policies under the continued rule of the Communist Party.

Kush (2nd mil.–4th cent. AD; ancient *Near East* and northern Sudan)
The kingdom of Kush corresponds to the region known as Nubia between the second and the fourth cataracts of the Nile in today's northern Sudan. The region was repeatedly invaded by PHARAONIC EGYPT during the 3rd mil. By ca. 1900 BC, Nubia around the second cataract (today's border between Egypt and Sudan) was under Egyptian control. By ca. 1800 BC Egypt extended its rule to the third cataract. The kingdom of Kush was founded ca. 1560 BC, but later Egyptian dominance was reimposed until ca. 1430, when Kush figures as an independent kingdom. However, Egypt founded Napata ca. 1400 in the area of the fourth cataract. Kush escaped Egyptian control, definitely as far as is known, ca. 1080. The culture of Kush was and remained linked to that of Egypt, although an inverse relation has also been argued. Between ca. 720 and ca. 670 Nubian Kushite monarchs were predominant in the Nile River valley. They struggled with ASSYRIA for control of Egypt, but the fighting was indecisive. The Kushites were dispossessed by Assyria in lower Egypt in 664 BC. There followed in Egypt the 26th dynasty which was overthrown by the Persians.

MEROE

By 430 BC, the capital of Nubia was established in Meroe, north of today's Omdurman in Sudan. Whether Kush and Meroe are continuous can be debated, but the Nubian geography and the Egyptian links are approximately the same for both. Ptolemaic Egypt maintained relations with Meroe, and even though Meroe is not usually included as part of the Roman province of Aegyptus, remains of Roman sculptures have been found there, which probably indicates raiding and unfriendly relations. Meroe virtually disappears during the early centuries AD. It is believed that, in the 4th cent., it was seized by Axum, a kingdom with its base in northern ETHIOPIA, of which country it is considered the historical antecessor. Kushitic, still spoken in Ethiopia and Somalia, is a member of the Afro-Asiatic family of languages, to which ancient Egyptian, Arab, Berber, and Hebrew also belong.

Kushana (1st–5th cents.; Afghanistan and Indus River Valley)
The Kushans were probably the people the Chinese identified as YÜEH-CHIH, otherwise known as TOKHARIANS, Indo-European speakers who settled in the Tarim Basin and reached as far east as Gansu (Kansu) in China. The Yüeh-chih were driven from Gansu by the HSIUNG NU in the 2nd cent. BC. They encountered the SAKA in Ferghana and drove them to Seistan (where they were subjected by Parthia in the 1st cent. BC) and to Bactria.

The Yüeh-chih attacked the Saka in Bactria ca. 130 BC and pushed them to Gandhara. In Bactria, the Yüeh-chih/Tokharians founded Kushana in the 1st cent. AD. The Kushans, under King Kadphises, conquered Gandhara, and the Saka were driven to Gujarat, where they disappear in the 4th cent. Kushana extended its empire further into northern India ca. 230. The greatest Kushana king was Kanishka, under whose rule the empire might have embraced a vast territory from the Oxus (Amudarya) River to Varanasi and Gujarat. Kanishka was a Buddhist and is reputed in Buddhist tradition as one of the three greatest rulers of India with Asoka (MAGADHA) and Menander (BACTRIA). It is likely that Kushana perished in the incursions of the EPHTHALITES against the SASANID EMPIRE during the 5th cent. Under Kushana, a Buddhist-Hellenistic style of carving in Gandhara was influential on later Indian art. (*See chronology under* Indian Subcontinent.)

Kuwait

Part of the OTTOMAN EMPIRE, the port of Kuwait and surrounding lands was ruled by a local dynasty beginning in 1795. In 1899 it became a British dependency until independence in 1961. It was occupied by Iraq in 1990 and liberated in 1991 by an alliance of western and Arab nations led by the United States. The majority of the population of Kuwait is constituted by immigrant workers.

Kyrgyzstan

The Turkic KIRGHIZ started arriving in Kyrgyzstan in the 17th cent., after a centuries-long trek from Mongolia. Today, they form half the population of the country. Kyrgyzstan occupies the territory of the KOKAND KHANATE annexed by Russia from 1855 to 1876. In 1924, the Soviets incorporated the Kara Kirghiz Autonomous Region into the Russian Soviet Federated Socialist Republic, the main body of the USSR. In 1926, Kyrgyzstan was constituted a Soviet republic. It became independent in 1991. The capital is Bishkek.

L

Lagash (SUMER)

Languedoc (TOULOUSE)

Lan Xang (LAOS)

Laos
During the 13th cent., Thais from Yunnan pushed the Khmers from Cambodia out of Laos. From the 14th to the 18th cents. there existed a Laotian kingdom, known as Lan Xang, or Kingdom of the Million Elephants. At its zenith, it overlapped into Thailand and the highlands of Vietnam, but was constantly at war with the Burmese and the Thais. During the 17th cent., it divided into Luang Prabang, Champassak, and Vien Chan (Vientiane). During the 18th and 19th cents. Laos was a Thai dependency, encroaching on the Vietnamese influenced north east. The French, who had established a protectorate in Tonkin in 1884, went on to eliminate Thai suzerainty and create a protectorate in Laos in 1893. Laos was incorporated into French Indochina (FRENCH COLONIAL EMPIRE). It became independent in 1949, but French troops did not leave until 1953. After that it was torn by a civil war from which a mildly communist regime emerged in 1975. Laotian and Thai are related tongues. Vientiane is the capital of Laos.

Latin Empire (LATIN STATES)

Latin States (13th–15th cents.; GREECE)
Before the Ottoman conquest of Constantinople (1453), nothing weakened the BYZANTINE EMPIRE more than the Fourth Crusade, undertaken against Egypt, but in effect turned towards Constantinople. The city was taken (and brutally sacked) by French and Flemish knights in 1204, with the enthusiastic naval support of VENICE seeking commercial advantages in the region. This act was justified as reprisal for the treaty that, in 1189, Isaac II Angelos had made with Saladin (AYYUBID SULTANATE). Allied to knights from NORMAN ITALY and MALTA, the invaders also conquered Thrace and Greece where they established various states. In western Thrace and north-eastern Greece, the Latins created the kingdom of Salonika, which the Byzantines reconquered in 1246. With Constantinople, eastern Thrace, and the territories across the Bosporus, the Sea of Marmara, and the Dardanelles, they created the Latin Empire, which the Byzantines had retaken by 1261. The principality of ACHAEA was formed in the Peloponnesus, where the Latins retained territories until 1278. RHODES was occupied by

the Latins in 1204. It was taken briefly by GENOA in 1248 and returned to Byzantine hands in 1256. The duchy of Athens, founded in 1205, lasted longer than the other Latin states, but had a very spotty history. In 1311 it was taken by Catalans, nominally subject to ARAGON. After 1388 it was controlled by Florentines, with a Venetian interlude, until the Ottomans took the Acropolis in 1458. Venice insisted on claiming Athens, retook it briefly in 1466, and besieged it in 1687–1688, when Venetian cannon bombarded the Parthenon.

Latvia

Latvia, peopled by Indo-European speaking Letts, can be roughly divided into Courland (western Latvia) and Livonia (northern Latvia including Lettland proper and southern Estonia). Latvia was taken and Christianized by the LIVONIAN BROTHERS OF THE SWORD, a German military order, during the 13th cent. At the time the ports in the coast of Courland were incorporated into the HANSEATIC LEAGUE. Germans dominated the economy. In 1561, Livonia was annexed by Poland and Courland became a vassal territory. In 1629 the entire country passed to Sweden. In 1721, it was divided again with Russia taking Livonia and then Courland (1732). Under Russia, Germans remained in economic control but the Letts developed their own culture. In 1918, Latvia acquired its independence. It was occupied by the USSR in 1939 and made a Soviet republic. Occupied by Nazi Germany during World War II, it was reincorporated into the USSR in 1944. It became independent again in 1991. Latvian belongs to the Balto-Slavic branch of the Indo-European family of languages. The capital of Latvia is Riga.

League of Nations (UNITED NATIONS)

Lebanon

The territory of Lebanon was the ancient PHOENICIA, whose principal cities in the Levant were Tyre and Sidon. Carthage was an offshoot of Phoenicia. With SYRIA, LEBANON was annexed by ASSYRIA and BABYLONIA and later became a satrapy of the ACHAEMENID EMPIRE and a province in the ALEXANDRIAN EMPIRE and of ROME. It fell to ISLAM in the 7th cent. Occupied successively by SELJUK EMIRATES (11th) and CRUSADER STATES (11th–12th cents.), it fell under Egyptian influence (AYYUBID and MAMELUKE SULTANATES) and was later annexed by the OTTOMAN EMPIRE in the 16th cent. With the dismemberment of the Ottoman Empire after World War I, Lebanon went to France – who had intervened in the region to protect the Maronite or Arab Christians against the Druzes in the late 19th cent. – as part of its Syrian League of Nations mandate. The French sheared off Lebanon, where half or more of the population was Christian, from Syria in 1925, and after sundry constitutional arrangements to accommodate Muslim and Christian interests, granted independence in 1945, although foreign troops did not leave until the following year.

SABRA AND SHATILLA

A majority of the Arab-speaking population of Palestine left or was forced to leave during the first Arab–Israeli War in 1948–1949. Palestinians emigrated to the Gaza Strip, Jordan, and Lebanon, where the miserable conditions of refugee camps bred strong anti-Israeli activism. Gaza itself is one huge refugee camp that has been turned into the densely packed province of a state in the making (PALESTINIAN AUTHORITY). After 1975 and a brief but intense civil war in which a Palestinian uprising was put down by Syria, Lebanon became fragmented and dangerous to be in. Israel invaded Lebanon in 1978 and (under Ariel Sharon) in greater force in 1982 as far as Beirut, where civil war raged. Christian militiamen were allowed entry into the Palestinian refugee camps of Sabra and Shatilla, where a massacre ensued. The Israeli incursion was ineffectual and was terminated in 1985. Israel created a buffer zone in southern Lebanon, where it claimed the right of intervention for self-defence. It also created and armed a Christian militia in the zone called the South Lebanon Army. During the civil war in Lebanon, the Shiite Hizbollah became the greatest military threat to northern Israel targeting the local militia and Israeli armed forces and civilians. An international contingent, principally French and American, landed in Beirut late in 1983 but was pulled out after a terrorist bomb left hundreds dead. After Lebanon, the United States became wary of foreign interventions. Civil order was restored in Lebanon during 1990–1991 under Syrian supervision.

Leon (9th–13th cents.; *Spain*)
The territory of the kingdom of Leon was taken from MUSLIM SPAIN by ASTURIAS, to which it was joined in the 9th cent. as the kingdom of Asturias and Leon, which became the kingdom of Leon in 923. From 1126 to 1157 CASTILE and Leon were united, then separated. Leon became part of Castile in 1230.

Lesotho
Inhabited by Bantu-speaking peoples, the kingdom of Lesotho, formed with refugees from Zulu expansionism (ZULULAND), was the British protectorate of Basutoland from 1868 to 1966. It is wholly surrounded by South African territory. The capital of Lesotho is Maseru.

Lesser Armenia (ARMENIA MINOR)

Liao (KHITAN KHANATE)

Liberia
Home to many different tribes, Liberia was created on the coast of Western Africa by American abolitionists as a country for freed slaves in 1847. The

capital Monrovia was named after the American President James Monroe. From 1990 to 1997, Liberia was in a state of civil disorder driven by inter-tribal rivalries and disputes.

Libya

Home to colonies of PHOENICIA, Libya was known in Ancient Greece as the thriving region of Cyrenaica (eastern Libya). The territory of Libya was incorporated by ROME. It was part of the BYZANTINE EMPIRE until conquered by ISLAM in 642. Libya did not produce any ruling dynasty of its own and was subject to the rise and fall of political influences from the Maghreb and from Egypt. During the 15th and early 16th cents. it was divided into emirates. In 1551, it became Ottoman Tripoli (OTTOMAN EMPIRE). Western Libya later became known as Tripolitania. Its coast was home to BARBARY STATES. The Italians, who had not been awarded anything in the colonialist Berlin Conference (1884–1885), took the matter into their own hands and seized the country after 1914 against stiff and prolonged native resistance. Libya was occupied by British forces after the Battle of El Alamein in 1942 and became a British trust territory in 1945 until its independence in 1952. Initially a kingdom under Idris, Emir of Cyrenaica, the government of Libya was overthrown in 1969 by the military from whose ranks the actual dictator, Muammar Khadaffi, emerged. Accused of encouraging and practising terrorism in the late 1980s, Libya was the object of international sanctions. It was bombed by the United States during the Reagan administration in 1986. Tripoli is the capital of Libya.
(*See chronology under* Maghreb.)

Liechtenstein

Liechtenstein is modestly wedged between Switzerland and Austria. Vaduz, the capital, was an imperial county in the mid-14th cent. The actual territory of Liechtenstein came into being with the addition to Vaduz of the county of Schellenberg in 1443. In 1719, Holy Roman Emperor Charles VI made the two counties the principality of Liechtenstein, from the name of the ruling house since 1712. The empire was dissolved in 1806 and Liechtenstein became part of the GERMAN CONFEDERATION until 1866. It was under the influence of Austria until 1919 when it established close ties with Switzerland, whose constitutional model it adopted in 1921.

Lithuania

Peopled by Pagan Indo-European speakers, Lithuania, also known in the past as Samogitia, was created ca. 1250 in opposition to German pressure from the TEUTONIC KNIGHTS in the south and the LIVONIAN BROTHERS OF THE SWORD in the north. During the 14th cent. it expanded at the expense of Kievan Rus (RUSSIA) and its domains extended from the Baltic to the Black

Sea. In 1386, Jagiello, son of the Lithuanian ruler, obtained the Polish Crown through marriage. As Ladislaus II, he accepted Christianity and Christianized Lithuania. The kingdom established a loose federation known as Poland–Lithuania and, during the 15th cent., Lithuania had its own foreign interests. In 1569, in order to oppose Russia, the two federated kingdoms were closely merged under Polish dominance. In effect, Lithuania ceased to exist. In the first partition of Poland (1772) its territory went to Russia. Vilnius is the ancient capital of Lithuania.

MEMEL

In 1918, Lithuania declared its independence, which was recognized at the Paris Peace Conference in 1919 (VERSAILLES). Poland annexed Vilnius in 1920. The capital of Lithuania passed to Kaunas. Lithuania occupied Memel, an East Prussian port and its environs, in 1923, but under pressure from the Western powers was forced to recognize its autonomy within its own territory. In 1939, Germany reclaimed and obtained Memel. After the Nazi–Soviet pact of 1939, Lithuania came under the Soviet sphere and was occupied in 1940, when it was incorporated as a Soviet republic in the USSR. Under German occupation during World War II, Lithuania was recovered by the Soviets in 1944 and was restored to the approximate borders it had in 1923, including Memel, now called Klaipeda, and Vilnius. In March 1990, it was the first republic to secede from the crumbling USSR.
(*See chronology under* Southern Russia.)

Livonian Brothers of the Sword (13th cent.; *Baltic region*)
The Livonian Brothers of the Sword were a German military order created in Livonia (northern Latvia) by Bishop Albert of Livonia, who founded Riga in 1201. Christianized LATVIA was integrated in the HANSEATIC LEAGUE. In 1236 the order was defeated by LITHUANIA and in 1237 it merged with the TEUTONIC KNIGHTS, but the Livonian Brothers acted on their own in Latvia. The eastward expansion of the Livonian Brothers was contained by Alexander Nevsky (RUSSIA) in the ice battle of Lake Peipus in 1242. German control of Latvia passed gradually from the Livonian Brothers to the Hanseatic League. With the secularization of PRUSSIA in 1525, the Teutonic Knights lost their political clout.

Lombard Italy (6th–8th cents.; *Italy*)
The Lombards were a Germanic people that, in the early 6th cent., occupied Hungary and eastern Austria. They invaded and dominated Italy from 568 to 774. Lombard Italy began with the conquest of Pavia. During the 7th cent., the Lombards created the principalities of Trent, Friuli, Spoleto, Tuscany, and Benevento. They seized Ravenna from the BYZANTINE EMPIRE in 751. Charlemagne took Pavia in 774 and broke Lombard power in Italy (CAROLINGIAN EMPIRE). Benevento lingered on until annexed to NORMAN ITALY.

Lombard League (12th–13th cents.; northern *Italy*)
After the VERONESE LEAGUE (1164), the Lombard League was formed in 1167 to thwart German imperial pretensions in northern Italy (IMPERIAL ITALY). Among its members were: Milan, Padua, Verona, Cremona, Brescia, Pavia, Genoa, Bologna, and Turin. In the Battle of Legnano in 1176, the League defeated the imperial army, but it dissolved after 1183. It was revived in 1226, but this time around it was defeated and fell into factionalism with some cities favouring the HOLY ROMAN EMPIRE (Ghibellines) and others the papacy (Guelphs), which were the two rivals for power in northern Italy.

Lombardy (MILAN)

Luang Prabang (LAOS)

Lucca (12th–19th cents.; northern *Italy*)
Originally Ligurian, then Roman, Lucca became a Lombard duchy (6th cent.). It was part of CAROLINGIAN, then IMPERIAL ITALY. In the 12th cent. Lucca was a free commune, then a republic. In 1805, it was part of the FRENCH EUROPEAN EMPIRE as a principality. After 1817, it belonged to PARMA.

Lunda (17th cent.; Angola)
A Bantu-speaking tribal kingdom in ANGOLA during the 17th cent., Lunda came under Portuguese influence.

Luristan (12th–17th cents.; *Iran*)
A minor state on the mountainous northern frontier of Iran and Iraq, Luristan lasted from the 12th cent. to the 17th cent., when it was absorbed by the SAFAVIDS. It seemed to have passed unnoticed by history. There was also a Little Luristan north of Luristan. For some reason it was absorbed before its southern big brother.

Luxembourg
From Carolingian times, Luxembourg included today's southern BELGIUM. In 1354, it was constituted a grand duchy in the HOLY ROMAN EMPIRE. After 1364 it was acquired by BURGUNDY and in 1477 it went to the HABSBURG EMPIRE by marriage and later formed part of the SPANISH NETHERLANDS. In 1659 FRANCE annexed part of southern Luxembourg. In 1714 Luxembourg passed again to the Habsburg (AUSTRIAN NETHERLANDS). In 1795 it was annexed by France but in the Congress of VIENNA (1814–1815) Luxembourg was attached to the crown of Netherlands with membership in the GERMAN CONFEDERATION. When Belgium became an independent kingdom in 1830 it claimed Luxembourg and, in 1839, obtained the northern part. The remainder of Luxembourg, its actual territory, remained attached to the Netherlands but under Prussian occupation. Upon the

dissolution of the German Confederation in 1866, the status of Luxembourg was undefined. In 1867, when Netherlands offered to sell it to France, the European powers, to avert war between France and Prussia, declared it neutral territory and the Prussians withdrew. Luxembourg was self-ruling for all intents and purposes and in 1890 it was inherited by a member of the house of Nassau, related to the Dutch house of Orange. Luxembourg was occupied by Germany in both World Wars. The neutrality statute was abrogated in 1944 and Luxembourg joined NATO in 1949. In 1948, it formed the economic union with Belgium and the Netherlands known as Benelux, which became part of European Economic Community in 1957 (EUROPEAN UNION). Luxembourgish is a west German language. French and German are also official languages in Luxembourg.

Lydia (7th–6th cents. BC; ancient *Near East*)
After the fall of the HITTITE KINGDOM (ca. 1200 BC), Anatolia was left in a disorganized state with ASSYRIA and BABYLONIA nibbling at its margins. The first important successor state after the Hittites, the kingdom of Lydia (680–546 BC) at its height ruled all of western Anatolia. It had strong ties to the Greeks. Its last ruler, Croesus, was defeated by Cyrus the Great and Lydia became a satrapy of the ACHAEMENID EMPIRE, later incorporated into the ALEXANDRIAN EMPIRE. Sardis was the Lydian capital.
(*See chronologies under* Ancient Near East *and* Anatolia.)

M

Maccabees (JUDAH)

Macedon (7th–2nd cents. BC; Ancient *Greece*)
Before Greek colonization in the 8th cent. BC, little is known of MACEDO-
NIA, which designates territories in north central and north east Greece and in
the present-day republic of Macedonia. In the 7th cent. BC the kingdom of
Macedon was created in Macedonia, with its capital in Pella. Its rulers were
Greek-speakers. From 358 to 342 BC, under Philip II, Macedon was expanded
by the annexation of Chalcidice and Thrace. It became the most powerful
Greek state and in 337 BC it controlled GREECE through the CORINTHIAN
LEAGUE. On Alexander's accession (336 BC), Macedonian territories
extended from Thessaly to Macedon proper, across Thrace and southern Bul-
garia to the outskirts of Byzantium. In 334 BC Alexander undertook the con-
quest of the ACHAEMENID EMPIRE. Upon Alexander's death, the
ALEXANDRIAN EMPIRE was divided among his Macedonian generals
(DIADOCHI WARS). Macedon became a separate kingdom, under the
Antigonids in 281 BC. Macedon flourished during the Hellenistic period of
Ancient Greek civilization, a time in which politically the Greek tendency
towards fragmentation was prevalent. The unification of Greece achieved by
Alexander was never repeated. Macedon and EPIRUS were two relatively
large kingdoms in northern Greece, but the rest of Greece remained disunited.
This situation would not change until the Roman conquest (ROME). After mili-
tary defeats, Macedon became a Roman province in 146 BC, which was later
part of the BYZANTINE EMPIRE.
(*See chronology under* Greece (Ancient).)

Macedonia
SEE ENTRY IN 'PROVINCES AND REGIONS'
Macedonia was part of the Roman Empire of the east, later the BYZANTINE
EMPIRE. A multi-ethnic province of the OTTOMAN EMPIRE from 1389 to
1912, today the majority of its population speaks a southern Slavic tongue (related
to Bulgarian), but the Albanians are a sizeable minority and there are also Serbs
and Turks. Macedonia was shared out between Serbia, Greece, and Bulgaria after
the Balkan Wars (1912–1913). In 1918, the part of Macedonia that fell to Serbia
entered into the Kingdom of the Serbs, Croats, and Slovenes, which became
YUGOSLAVIA in 1929. In 1946, Macedonia became a federated republic within
communist Yugoslavia. In 1991, it declared itself independent, still very multi-
ethnic. Alleging a sort of copyright infringement on a Greek name, Athens at first
withheld recognition. The capital of the Republic of Macedonia is Skopje.

Madagascar

The fourth largest island in the world, Madagascar was peopled by Indonesians around the 7th–8th cents. Autonomous during most of the 19th cent. under its own Merina rulers, the island became a French protectorate in 1885 (FRENCH COLONIAL EMPIRE). The monarchy was abolished and Madagascar became a French colony in 1886. It was independent as the Malagasy Republic in 1960. The name was changed back to Madagascar in 1975. The capital is Antananarivo.

Magadha (6th–1st cents. BC; northern *India*)

Magadha was probably created some time in the 6th cent. BC (VEDIC INDIA). It emerged from a constellation of Vedic states (mahajanapadas) among which Koshala (north of Varanasi), Vatsa (west of the confluence of the Ganges and Yamuna rivers), and Magadha itself (south of Patna, in northern Bihar) were strategically located. Magadha lasted until ca. 30 BC. It was the first important state in NORTHERN INDIA. Its rise occurred under the kingship of Bimbisara, of the Nanda dynasty, who conquered the ancient Vedic kingdom of Anga. His successor Ajatashatru was defeated by Koshala, but later Magadha became predominant. Magadha had its capital in Pataliputra (Patna). The founder of the Maurya dynasty, Chandragupta, seized the throne of Magadha ca. 320 BC. In 305 BC a Macedonian general, Seleukos, founder of the SELEUCID EMPIRE, forayed as far as the Indus River Valley where Chandragupta interdicted his claim to India. The Greeks ceded whatever rights they had over the Indus River Valley to the Mauryas.

Asoka's Empire

The greatest Maurya king, Asoka, acceded to the throne in 268 BC, at which time Magadha already reached as far as Karnataka. He reigned for three decades and left the testimony of his sovereignty in inscribed pillars which tell the story of his kingdom in snatches. Asoka was converted to Buddhism after a bloody battle he won over the Kalinga kingdom in 261 BC (CENTRAL INDIA). His importance in the spread of Buddhism, beginning ca. 260 BC, makes him the second most important figure in that religion, after Buddha himself. The instrument for Buddhist proselytizing was the community of monks or sangha. Asoka's son taught Buddhism in SRI LANKA. Asoka's pillars and other stone inscriptions have been found as far north as Taxila in northern Pakistan, as far west as Kandahar in Afghanistan, and as far south as Karnataka. In one of his rock edicts Asoka mentions coeval rulers of PTOLEMAIC EGYPT and MACEDON. The decadence of Magadha set in after Asoka. The outlying provinces probably separated. Division was characteristic of the Indian political tradition since Vedic times. BACTRIA conquered the Indus River Valley ca. 200 BC. The last Maurya ruler was murdered in 185 BC by a general of his army, Pushamitrya Shunga, who founded the Shunga dynasty. The last Shunga king was murdered in 73 BC. The last king of the Kanva dynasty, which followed Shunga, was defeated in 28 BC by the Satavahana of Central India.

(*See chronology under* Indian Subcontinent.)

Maghreb

Predominant political influences

7th–8th cents.

Islam
Umayyads
Abbasids
Idrisids (Morocco and
    Algeria)

9th cent.

Idrisids (Morocco and
    western Algeria)
Aghlabids (Tunisia,
    eastern Algeria, and
    western Libya)
Tulunids (eastern
    Libya)

10th cent.

Aghlabids (Tunisia,
    eastern Algeria, and
    western Libya)
Córdoba (Spain and
    Morocco)
Fatimids (Algeria,
    Tunisia, and Libya)
Zirid Emirates (Tunisia
    and Algeria)

11th cent.

Córdoba (Spain and
    Morocco)
Fatinids (Libya)
Zirid Emirates (Algeria
    and Tunisia)
Almoravids (Morocco
    and Spain)
Bedouin Emirates
    (Tunisia and Algeria)

12th cent.

Bedouin Emirates
    (Tunisia and
    Algeria)
Fatimids (Libya)
Almoravids (Morocco
    and Spain)
Almohads (Morocco,
    Spain, Algeria, and
    Tunisia)
Ayyubids (Libya)

13th cent.

Almohads (Spain,
    Morocco, Algeria,
    and Tunisia)
Ayyubids (Libya)
Morocco (Marinids)
Ziyanids (western
    Algeria)
Hafsids (Tunisia and
    eastern Algeria)
Mamelukes (Libya)

14th cent.

Morocco (Marinids)
Hafsids (Tunisia and
    Algeria)
Mamelukes (Libya)

15th cent.

Morocco (Marinids)
Hafsids (Tunisia and
    Algeria)
Mamelukes (Libya)
Portugal (Morocco)

16th cent.

Morocco (Marinids
    followed by Sa'adis)
Hafsids (Tunisia and
    Algeria)
Mamelukes (Libya)
Portugal (Morocco)
Spain (Morocco,
    Algeria, and Tunisia)
Ottoman Empire
    (Algeria, Tunisia,
    and Libya)

17th cent.

Morocco (Sa'adis
    followed by
    Alawites)
Ottoman Empire
    (Algeria, Tunisia,
    and Libya)
Barbary States
    (Algeria, Tunisia,
    and Libya)

18th cent.

Morocco
Barbary States

**19th cent.–early
    20th cent.**

Morocco
Barbary States
France (Algeria,
    Tunisia, and
    Morocco)
Italy (Libya)

Magyars (9th–10th cents.)
The Magyars were nomadic Finno-Ugric speakers from central Asia who eventually peopled HUNGARY. They were tributaries to the KHAZARS in southern Russia. Driven out by the PETCHENEGS, their final trek began during the 9th cent. initially under the leadership of Onogur Turks (hence Hungarians). The Magyars destroyed GREAT MORAVIA and ravaged the territories of BOHEMIA, Austria, and Hungary. They made the latter their base. Otto I the Great, first Holy Roman Emperor, put an end to their raiding in the Battle of Lechfeld in 955.
(*See chronology under* Southern Russia.)

Majapahit Empire (13th–16th cents.; *Indonesia*)
In the second half of the 13th cent. King Kertanagara founded a state in eastern Java which probably subjected Sumatra. Following a usurpation and a vague Mongol intervention, Prince Vijaya established the Majapahit Empire. Its acme was reached in the late-14th cent., during the reign of King Hayam Wuruk, but under the control and guidance of the chief minister, Gaja Mada, when its rule embraced most of Indonesia and as far as Malaya. These lands had become Islamic during the 14th and 15th cents. In 1478, Majapahit was attacked by a coalition of Islamic coastal kingdoms led by the harbour state of Demak. The empire disappeared in the early 16th cent. Its territories were divided into harbour and estuary states. The Portuguese made inroads during the 16th cent., but were eventually ousted by the Dutch. According to a traditional account, the ruling circles of Majapahit took refuge on the island of Bali, where they preserved Indian culture against the Mohammedan tide.

Malacca (15th–19th cents.; *Malaya*)
The Islamic Malay kingdom of Malacca was sliced from the MAJAPAHIT EMPIRE ca. 1400. It expanded in the Malay Peninsula and in Sumatra. Malacca was taken by the Portuguese under Alfonso de Albuquerque in 1511 (PORTUGUESE COLONIAL EMPIRE). As a result, the Sultan of Malacca established his kingdom in JOHORE and the Arab trade moved to the Islamic harbour states in Sumatra, especially Aceh. In 1641 Johore, with Dutch assistance, annexed Malacca. In 1824 Malacca came under British influence (BRITISH COLONIAL EMPIRE) and in 1826 was incorporated into the Straits Settlement administered by the BRITISH EAST INDIA COMPANY.

Malawi
Peopled originally by Bantu-speaking tribes, the territory of Malawi became the British colony of Nyasaland in 1891 (BRITISH COLONIAL EMPIRE). In 1953 Nyasaland was included with Southern Rhodesia and Northern Rhodesia in the white-dominated Federation of Rhodesia and Nyasaland. The Federation was dissolved in 1963 and Nyasaland became independent Malawi in 1964. The capital of Malawi is Lilongwe.

Malaysia

See *MALAYA* in 'Provinces and Regions'

The British presence in Malaya starts with the foundation of Penang in 1786 by the BRITISH EAST INDIA COMPANY. Malacca came under British influence in 1794. It was ceded to the Dutch from 1814 to 1824. In 1819, Sir Stamford Raffles founded Singapore on an island ceded to him by the Sultan of JOHORE. The rest of the Malay Peninsula gradually came under British control. The East India Company consolidated its Malayan possessions as the Straits Settlements (1826). The Company was dissolved in 1858, after the Sepoy Mutiny (1857) in India, and Malaya was administered by BRITISH INDIA until 1867, when the Straits Settlement Colony was created including Penang, Malacca, and Singapore. Labuan was a dependency of Singapore. In 1896, Great Britain divided its Malay dependencies into the Federated Malay States, with Penang as capital – the other states were Negri Sembilan, Perak, and Selangor – and the Unfederated Malay States (Malacca and Singapore). Johore became a protectorate in 1914, part of the Unfederated Malay States. In 1948, all of British Malaya – except Singapore which had been made a separate Crown colony in 1946 – was formed as the Federation of Malaya, which became independent in 1957. In 1963, Malaysia was formed with the addition of Singapore, Sabah (northern Borneo), and Sarawak (south-western Borneo). Sabah had been a colony since 1882. Sarawak actually belonged to a British family! It became a protectorate in 1888 and a full colony in 1947. Singapore seceded from Malaysia in 1965. The capital of Malaysia is Kuala Lumpur.

Malayu (SRI VIJAYA)

Maldives

Populated by Indo-Aryan speakers from India, the Indian Ocean islands of the Maldives were visited by the Portuguese in the 16th cent. After that they were used as way stations by other Europeans. In 1887, they became a British protectorate until 1965. The capital of the Maldives is Malé.

Mali (Ancient) (13th–15th cents.; *Sub-Saharan Africa*)

An Islamic kingdom (1234–1468), ancient Mali covered territories from Senegal to Mali that had been in the past part of ancient GHANA. Musa, a Mali king, was noted for his riches on a pilgrimage to Mecca in the 1330s. Mali was followed by SONGHAI in the 15th cent. Timbuktu was within the Mali kingdom. Today the area is inhabited by speakers of Arabic and of Malinke, Soninke, and other Niger–Congo languages spoken in western Africa. (*See chronology under* Western and Sub-Saharan Africa.)

Mali

Partially or entirely home to various African kingdoms – notably ancient GHANA, ancient MALI, and SONGHAI – Mali, conquered by 1898, was made part of French West Africa as the French Sudan (FRENCH COLONIAL EMPIRE). It became independent in 1960. Arabic and various African tongues – among them Malinke, a member of the Niger–Congo family which is also spoken in the rest of western Africa – are spoken in Mali. The official language, however, is French. The capital of Mali is Bamako.

Malta

Originally peopled by speakers of Maltese, a Semitic tongue, the island of Malta was occupied by Norman knights in the 10th cent. (NORMAN ITALY). Bequeathed to the HOLY ROMAN EMPIRE (12th cent.), in 1530 it was given to the KNIGHTS OF ST JOHN after they were expelled from Rhodes by the OTTOMAN EMPIRE (1522). Napoleon ended their rule in 1798, but Great Britain soon took Malta, which stayed in British hands until 1964. Malta resisted resolutely months of German aerial assaults in 1941–1942. Valetta is the capital.

Mameluke Sultanate (13th–16th cents.; *Near East*)

The practice of using slaves as soldiers under Islam was initiated by the ABBASID CALIPHATE (9th cent.) and followed by the AYYUBID SULTANATE (12th cent.), possibly in part to respect the commandment that the faithful should not fight among each other. (However, the Romans, who were under no injunction about fighting each other, employed barbarians to beef up the Praetorian guards.) Be that as it may, the Mamelukes were slave horse-warriors recruited from non-Muslim boys from central Asia and Circassia who were converted during military training. They formed a caste that took power in Egypt in 1250 and held it until the OTTOMAN EMPIRE defeated them in 1517. The first Mameluke who actually held power was Aybak. He inaugurated the line of Mameluke rulers known as the Bahris, which lasted until 1382. The Mameluke sultans in this period were mostly of Turk and Mongol origins and were selected from the principal Mameluke families. The Bahri line was substituted by that of the Burjis, mostly from Circassia, which lasted until the Ottoman conquest in 1517. Under the Burjis, there was much turbulence as the successions were frequently contested. The average duration of a sultanate was less than ten years. Although Mameluke kingship was not hereditary but elective, Mameluke sultans founded madrasas and other religious institutions, usually attached to their grandiose tombs, for their heirs.

THE CAIRO CALIPHATE

The Mamelukes, under Baybars, successfully defended Syria against the Mongols in 1260. To legitimize Mameluke authority, Baybars installed in Cairo a relative of the last Abbasid, killed by the Mongols in 1268, as caliph. Selim I, the Ottoman conqueror of Egypt, assumed the title of caliph, which his successors held until the deposition of Muhammad VI, the last sultan, by

Mustafa Kemal in 1922. Kemal abolished the caliphate in 1925. At its height, Mameluke power extended to south-eastern Anatolia, where it destroyed ARMENIA MINOR in 1375. When Ottoman power weakened in the 18th cent., the Mamelukes were there to fill the vacuum, although they ruled in the name of the Porte. They were defeated by Napoleon in 1798 in the Battle of the Pyramids, but recovered power after the French left in 1801. Their hold on EGYPT was finally broken by Muhammad Ali, the Albanian-born Turkish pasha since 1805, who had the principal Mamelukes beheaded in 1811.

Manchukuo (MANCHURIA)

Manchuria (17th–20th cents.; northern *China*)
The vast north-eastern region of China, which includes the provinces of Liaoning, Jilin (Kirin), Heilongjiang (Heilunkiang), Manchuria was the home of the Manchus. The JURCHEN founded their own Chin dynasty in northern China (12th–13th cents.), which was destroyed by Kublai Khan (YUAN). The Jurchen or Khitai of Jehol became vassals of the Mongols. After the fall of Yuan China and during the virtual disintegration of MONGOLIA, this people, now called Manchu, created a military kingdom centred on Mukden (today's Shenyang) in 1606. In 1644 the Manchu imposed the CH'ING (QING) dynasty in China. In 1932, the Japanese established the puppet kingdom of Manchukuo in Manchurian territory. The throne was occupied by Henry Pu Yi, the last of the Ch'ing, later a common citizen of communist China. At the end of World War II, Manchuria was in communist hands and served as the platform for the conquest of all of China.
(*See chronology under* China and Neighbouring Areas.)

Mantua (12th–19th cents.; northern *Italy*)
Originally Etruscan and then Roman, Mantua was part of the CAROLINGIAN EMPIRE and of IMPERIAL ITALY. It was a free commune, home of the Gonzaga, from the 12th cent. to its absorption by the HABSBURG EMPIRE in 1708. It was made part of the FRENCH EUROPEAN EMPIRE in 1797. Returned to Austria in 1815, it finally joined the kingdom of ITALY in 1866.

Maratha Kingdoms (17th–18th cents.; central *India*)
Maratha is the name applied to a group of Hindu states founded in Maharashtra which came to prominence during the 18th cent., but were already entrenched in the previous century. In resisting both the MUGHAL EMPIRE and BRITISH INDIA, the Marathas came to symbolize Indian nationalism. CENTRAL INDIA was attacked by the Mughal emperor, Aurangzeb, during the 17th cent. The greatest obstacle to Aurangzeb's ruthless expansionism – which was financed with levies on his Hindu subjects – was Shivaji, the rajah of the Marathas, who had his capital at Pune. The two rulers rivalled in the conquest of the Deccan sultanates. For a while it was touch-and-go, but Shivaji

died first (1680). Even though he did not reduce the Marathas, Aurangzeb did subject most of the Deccan. Aurangzeb's successor in 1707 was Bahadur Shah, who tried to conciliate the Marathas in order to ensure peace. The move backfired because under the capable Peshwa ministers – like the Japanese shoguns, they ruled indirectly through puppet kings – Maratha power was restored in Pune. The Mughal–Maratha rivalry allowed Nadir Shah, ruler of Persia (IRAN), to sack Delhi in 1739. After the sack of Delhi, Mughal rule literally went to pieces. The 'emperor' was a mere local ruler. The history of India was in the hands of diverse political forces among which the Marathas were one of the most powerful. BRITISH INDIA gradually reduced all the recalcitrants in the subcontinent, especially Tipu Sultan in MYSORE, so that by the end of the 18th cent. the only remaining independent state in the subcontinent was Pune and, since it was surrounded by British dependent principalities (Gwailor, Indore, and Baroda), it soon entered the imperial ranks. Indore tried to become independent and was put down in 1818.
(*See chronology under* Indian Subcontinent.)

Marinids (13th–16th cents.; Morocco)
Preceded by the ALMOHADS, the Marinid kingdom was established in Morocco from 1259 to 1550. It was during Marinid rule that the Moors of GRANADA were conquered by Spain (1492). During the 15th–16th cents., Portugal and Spain proceeded to seize most of the Moroccan ports on the Mediterranean coast. Modern MOROCCO occupies roughly the territory which was ruled by the Marinids. They were substituted by the dynasty of the Saadis, who inflicted on the invading Portuguese in 1578 the stinging defeat of Alcazarquivir, in which the Portuguese king Sebastian was killed.
(*See chronology under* Maghreb.)

Marshall Islands
Peopled by speakers of an Austronesian language – a family of languages which includes the Malay tongues – the Marshall Islands (named after a British explorer) were claimed by Germany in 1884. In 1914 they were occupied by Japan, who surrendered them to the United States in 1943. They have been independent since 1991 in 'free association' with the United States. The Marshalls include the islands of Bikini and Eniwetok, sites of nuclear bomb tests. The largest island of the group is Kwaialcin. The capital of the Marshall Islands has the sonorous name of Dalap-Uliga-Darrit.

Mauritania
Partially within the west African kingdoms of ancient MALI and SONGHAI, the territory of Mauritania was peopled by Arabic-speaking Muslim Berbers usually under Moroccan influence. The Berber ALMORAVIDS got their start in Mauritania in the 11th cent. In 1903, Mauritania was annexed to French West Africa (FRENCH COLONIAL EMPIRE). It became independent in

1960. When Spain relinquished the Western Sahara in 1979, Mauritania claimed the southern part but later deferred to Morocco. The capital of Mauritania is Nouakchott.

Mauritius

Dutch in the 17th cent., the Indian Ocean island of Mauritius became French from 1721. It passed to Great Britain in 1810 until its independence in 1968 (BRITISH COLONIAL EMPIRE). Its population is mostly of Indian origin. The capital of Mauritius is Port Louis. It was the Dutch who depicted the dodo, whose extinction is the first noted in history. Mauritius is part of the Mascarene Islands, which includes the French overseas department of Réunion.

Maurya (MAGADHA)

Mayan Civilization (10th cent. BC–16th cent. AD: *Mexico* and Central America)

Mayan civilization is divided into three periods: (1) preclassic from 1000 BC to AD 250, when the first temples were built, notably Copán; (2) classic from ca. AD 250–ca. AD 900, when it was at its height and saw the development of such magnificent sites as Chichen Itzá and Uxmal, although archaeological sites are counted by the dozens; and (3) postclassic from 900 to the arrival of the Spaniards, when most of the cities had dwindled, possibly as a result of environmental exhaustion. Mayan civilization extended from Yucatan and Tehuantepec down to Honduras. Mayan languages, which were written in glyphs, are still spoken in parts of southern Mexico.

Mecca (16th–20th cents.; *Arabia*)

Mecca is the religious centre of ISLAM. It was the birth place ca. 570 of Muhammad, who broke with his idol-worshipping neighbours in 622 and made the *hegira* to Medina. In 630 he returned to a by-then converted Mecca. Mecca was the capital of the first four caliphs, the elected caliphs and Ali. The fifth caliph, according to the orthodox Sunni count, was Muawiya, who founded the Umayyad dynasty and moved the caliphate to Damascus. Mecca was taken by the OTTOMAN EMPIRE in 1517 and made a sharifate or Arab principality. Before World War I, Mecca was ruled by the Hashemites, who were dispossessed by the Saudis (SAUDI ARABIA). The Hashemites were later enthroned by the British in Jordan and Iraq.

Media (8th–6th cents.; ancient *Near East*)

The homeland of the kingdom of Media today surrounds the Iranian city of Ispahan. Although it is difficult to be precise about its borders, Media is usually represented as occupying northern Mesopotamia to its own homeland bordering on the new empire of BABYLONIA. Medes were Indo-Iranian speakers, related to the ancient Persians. Under Sargon ca. 700 BC they

conquered Persia and fought off Assyria. Allied to Babylonia, Media helped bring down the power of Nineveh in 608 BC (ASSYRIA). It absorbed URARTU ca. 590. The Achaemenids, rulers of Persis, were initially vassals of the Medes, but ca. 550, under Cyrus the Great, they overthrew the Medes and, with the combined territories of Media and Persis, created the core of the ACHAEMENID EMPIRE.
(*See chronologies under* Ancient Near East *and* Iran.)

Mercia (ENGLAND)

Meroe (KUSH)

Merovingian France (FRANKS)

Merv (11th–12th cents.: *Central Asia*: western Turkestan)
As the Seljuks descended towards Persia along the eastern side of the Caspian Sea (GHUZZ), they conquered Transoxiana and Khurasan ca. 1040 and established their centre of power in Merv (today Mary, in south-eastern Turkmenistan), which became an emirate of SELJUK PERSIA ca. 1100. It had fallen into anarchy ca. 1150, after which KHWARIZM took over.
(*See chronology under* Western Turkestan.)

Mesoamerican Civilizations (13th cent. BC–16th cent. AD; *Mexico*)
Civilization in Mesoamerica began with the Olmecs (1200 to 400 BC). The Olmecs had cities and carved huge heads of stone. Their culture occupied the southern coast of the Gulf of Mexico and its hinterland. Zapotec culture lasted from 500 BC to AD 1000 in the present-day state of Oaxaca. Zapotecs built Monte Albán. The classic civilization of Teotihuacán, the only urban rival to Aztec Tenochtitlán in size and grandeur, flourished from AD 50 to AD 1050. The Toltecs were active from AD 950 to AD 1150. Their centre was Tula. Both Teotihuacán and Tula are north of Mexico City. The Aztecs considered Toltec culture a classic model. The Mixtecs, also in Oaxaca, left many codices from AD 900 to AD 1521, but their culture is not as well known as that of the AZTEC EMPIRE, who were the main interlocutors of the conquering Spaniards. The Huastecs were possibly related to MAYAN CIVILIZATION and had a culture that thrived from AD 1200 to AD 1521 on the western shore of the Gulf of Mexico. The Aztecs applied the name of Chichimecs to barbarian tribes in the north, from where they themselves had emerged.

Mexico
SEE ENTRY IN 'PROVINCES AND REGIONS'
Mexico was home to various higher cultures and civilizations before the arrival of the Spaniards in 1517 (AZTEC EMPIRE; MAYAN CIVILIZATION; MESOAMERICAN CIVILIZATIONS). The last native kingdom was that of the Aztecs, who had to face the expedition of Hernan Cortez from

Havana in 1519. The Aztec monarch Montezuma procrastinated and tried to buy Cortez off. After entering the Aztec capital, Tenochtitlán, the Spaniards were expelled in 1520, during an Aztec reaction against the brutality of his lieutenant Pedro de Alvarado in which Montezuma was killed. Having made alliances with anti-Aztec nations, Cortez returned and conquered Tenochtitlán, which he proceeded to destroy as thoroughly as possible. The site was renamed Mexico City. In 1528, Mexico acquired its first high court (*audiencia*) under the governorship of Nuño de Guzmán, who annexed western Mexico from 1529 to 1531 as Nueva Galicia, with Guadalajara, founded ca. 1530, as its capital. Antonio de Mendoza (SPANISH COLONIAL EMPIRE). Guadalajara obtained an *audiencia* of its own in 1548 and, in 1563, was made a presidency, in theory dependent on Spain but in practice ruled from Mexico City. By the mid-16th cent. western North America, the future American states of Arizona, California, Colorado, Nevada, New Mexico, Texas, and Utah had been annexed wholly or in part to New Spain. This did not mean large-scale occupation and Texas was only settled by Europeans in the late 18th cent. Although part of the captaincy general of GUATEMALA, all of Central America to the frontier with Panama – a province of New Granada – was also more or less dependent on Mexico.

The Mexican 'empire'

Even if a Spanish dependency, New Spain had its own entrenched Creole ruling class, who feared any threat to the inequitable social order such as was posed by the liberal government installed in Spain in 1820. This development was all the more ominous as it came after the start of a Mexican independentist movement with social-reformist overtones first launched by the priest Miguel Hidalgo in 1810. The movement was carried on by rebels, among whom Morelos and Guerrero were the most conspicuous. Hidalgo's uprising was put down in 1811 and Morelos was defeated in 1815. Only Guerrero still resisted as a guerrilla leader. The royalist general Iturbide was charged with eliminating him, but in 1821 he came to an understanding with Guerrero whereby Mexico would become an independent empire. The last viceroy, O'Donojú, was deposed and in 1822 Iturbide became emperor over the territories of New Spain and Central America. But it was a flimsy construction and Guerrero, allied to General Santa Anna and Guadalupe Victoria, overthrew it in 1823. Central America broke loose as the nearly fictive CENTRAL AMERICAN FEDERATION. There followed various 'revolutions' and much political manoeuvring. The liberal regime in Spain was suppressed with French troops acting for the Holy Alliance (Congress of VIENNA). Ferdinand VII of Spain, a very reactionary and authoritarian monarch, tried as soon as he could to regain Mexico, but the Spanish incursion of 1829 only got as far as Tampico, where Santa Anna forced it to turn back. In 1836, TEXAS revolted and, despite Santa Anna's extermination of the garrison at The Alamo, its American settlers became independent and joined the United States in 1845. The American annexation of Texas led to a full-scale invasion of Mexico by the Americans in 1846. Mexico City was captured and Mexico surrendered all its territories north of the Rio Grande and Gila rivers and a line separating upper from lower California (1848). In 1853, the United States bought from Mexico the lands between the Gila River and the present frontier (Gadsden Purchase).

THE SECOND MEXICAN 'EMPIRE'

In 1857, under the leadership of half-Indian Benito Juarez, a reform movement began. It was cut short by a French invasion which installed Maximilian, brother-in-law of Napoleon III, as emperor (1864) and then abandoned him to the tender mercies of his 'subjects', who stood him in front of a firing squad in 1867. Juarez returned but Mexico was resistant to change. In 1876 Porfirio Diaz became dictator, committed to the welfare of the ruling classes. Diaz ruled on and off until his overthrow by the well-meaning Madero in 1911. This got the Mexican revolution started, in which bandits such as Villa mixed with true popular figures such as Zapata. Madero was murdered by Huerta in 1913, who, in turn, was deposed by Carranza. Carranza promulgated the constitution of 1917. Between 1926 and 1929 there was a peasant revolt in western Mexico which invoked Christ as its inspiration. The Cristeros were viciously repressed. In 1928, President Calles founded the Partido Revolucionario Institucional, which ruled Mexico until 2000. Mexico joined the North American Foreign Trade Agreement with the United States and Canada in 1994.

Micronesia

The Caroline Islands were occupied by Spain in 1886. Germany purchased them in 1898. They were occupied by the Japanese in 1914. They were taken by the United States during World War II after heavy bombardment, especially in Yap and Truk. The Carolines, minus PALAU, became independent Micronesia in 1991, associated to the United States. Micronesians speak a variety of tongues of the Austronesian family, to which the Malay tongues belong. The capital of Micronesia is Kolonia.

Milan (12th–19th cents.; northern *Italy*)

Possibly a Celtic settlement, Milan was the Roman Mediolanum and capital of the empire from 305–402. During the Ostrogothic, Byzantine, Lombard, Carolingian, and Imperial periods of Italian history, Milan deferred in importance to Ravenna and Pavia. In the 12th cent. it joined the LOMBARD LEAGUE against German imperialist pretensions. After the late 14th cent. under the Visconti, who were rulers of Milan since the 13th cent., the city was hegemonic in northern Italy. Its influence was much diminished in the early 16th cent. during the wars between Francis I of France and Holy Roman Emperor Charles V (King Charles I of Spain). After 1535 it definitely went to Spain. From 1713 to 1797 it was a Habsburg domain. In 1797, Napoleon made Milan capital of the Cisalpine Republic and from 1805 to 1814 of the kingdom of Italy (FRENCH EUROPEAN EMPIRE). In 1815, Milan passed, with Lombardy-Venetia, to the HABSBURG EMPIRE. In 1859, it was absorbed by the kingdom of SARDINIA after a war in which France participated against the Austrians.

Ming (14th–17th cents.; *China*)

Even for the Mongol YUAN dynasty, China proved hard to keep in subjection. There were natural disasters combined with insurrections and the Yuan were replaced by the Ming (1368), who were from Nanking and initially ruled from there. Ming was the last native Chinese dynasty. It was replaced by the Manchurian CH'ING (QING) dynasty, which gave way to the republic in 1912. The founder of Ming was a warrior of peasant extraction named Chu Yuan-chang. He assumed the emperorship with the name Hung Wu. Unlike previous emperors, he was against trade with foreigners, yet it was under his reign that Admiral Cheng Ho commanded a large imperial fleet that sailed the Indian Ocean as far as Zanzibar. The feat had never been attempted and was never repeated. Although it brought back 'tribute' most historians read this as traded goods. The Yuan had chosen the emperor from the ruling family. Hung Wu established the principle of primogeniture inheritance, although his own son was deposed by Hung Wu's brother. The Emperor Yung Lo (1403–1424) moved the Ming capital from Nanking to Peiping, which was renamed Beijing (Peking). It was Ming China that European sailors first visited and most early reports about China – Marco Polo was exceptional – are about Ming China.

THE MING WALLS

The Ming dynasty was much influenced by Confucianism. Its emperors in time tended to be ineffectual. One of them was even captured by the Mongols in 1449. However, when in the 1590s the Japanese under Toyotomi Hideyoshi invaded Korea, they were opposed by the Chinese and in the end the invaders retreated. At its greatest extent (ca. 1420), Ming Chinese rule went from eastern Siberia down to northern Vietnam, and from the China Sea to the eastern frontier of the Tarim Basin and Yunnan. The Mongols were divided but posed enough of a threat to have the Ming repair the old Chinese walls and build new ones. These constituted the effective boundary with MONGOLIA and are mostly the walls we know today. Towards the end, the Manchu were aware of the absence of effective governance in China. As had happened before, the Chinese – in this case the warlord Li Tzu-ch'eng in need of allies – asked them for help, which they gladly provided in exchange for an empire in 1644, sinicized as the Ch'ing (Qing) dynasty.
(*See chronology under* China and Neighbouring Areas.)

Minoan Civilization (3rd mil.–15th cent. BC; Ancient *Greece*)
Minoan civilization was born and flourished in CRETE. Its principal site was located at Knossos, although there were many other important Minoan centres. It is not really known what sort of government it had. At the height of its power, Minoan civilization must have dominated much of the eastern Mediterranean Sea. Knossos was destroyed ca. 1500 BC. Rebuilt, it eventually came under attack by MYCENEAN GREECE as attested by the presence in Crete of the Linear B tablets, which date to ca. 1450. Linear B was deciphered by Michael Ventris in 1952. There is also a Linear A which has not been deciphered and is in the pictographic Minoan writing. The language is presumed to be Semitic in origin. Knossos was definitely overthrown ca. 1400. Its Greek rulers afterwards fell ca. 1200.
(*See chronology under* Greece (Ancient).)

Mitanni Kingdom (15th–14th cents. BC; ancient *Near East*)
The Mitanni spoke a Semitic language with an admixture of Indo-Aryan terms. The Mitanni kingdom lasted from ca. 1450 to ca. 1350 BC and occupied a core area where the borders of Syria, Turkey, and Iraq converge. Mitanni was destroyed by an alliance of the HITTITE KINGDOM and ASSYRIA. Its land today is inhabited by Kurds, who speak an Iranian tongue of the Indo-European family.
(*See chronology under* Ancient Middle East.)

Mixtecs (MESOAMERICAN CIVILIZATIONS)

Modena (12th–19th cents.; northern *Italy*)
Originally an Etruscan settlement named Mutina by the Romans, Modena was part of LOMBARD ITALY, the BYZANTINE EMPIRE, the CAROLINGIAN EMPIRE, and IMPERIAL ITALY. It became a free commune in the 12th cent. It was absorbed by FERRARA in 1288. Modena became the seat of the Este family when Ferrara was annexed by the PAPAL STATES in 1598. In 1797, it was incorporated into the FRENCH EUROPEAN EMPIRE until 1814, when it was returned to the Este allied to Austria. It went with Lombardy to SARDINIA after the defeat of Austria in 1859.

Mohenjo-Daro (INDUS RIVER VALLEY CIVILIZATION)

Moldavia (14th–19th cents.; eastern Europe)
SEE *BESSARABIA* IN 'PROVINCES AND REGIONS'
Part of the Roman province of Dacia, Moldavia was a corridor for invaders from southern Russia (GOTHS, HUNS, GEPIDS, AVARS, and SLAVS). From the 9th to the 11th cents. the territory of Moldavia was under the influence of Kievan Rus (RUSSIA). In the following centuries it was raided or controlled by southern Russian semi-nomads, particularly the Turkish

POLOVETZY. It was sideswiped by the Mongols in the 13th cent. Moldavia became an autonomous principality including Bessarabia and Bukovina ca. 1360. It neighboured on the south west with ethnically identical VALACHIA. Moldavia's apex came with Stephen the Great (1457–1504), who briefly held Valachia in 1502. However, his kingdom became a tributary of the OTTOMAN EMPIRE. Early in the 18th cent. Moldavia was ruled by Greek hospodars (governors), who were Phanariots (Istambuli Greeks) appointed by the Porte. This changed with the Greek war of independence and thereafter the hospodars were local. In 1775 Bukovina passed to the HABS-BURG EMPIRE and, in 1812, southern Bessarabia was taken by RUSSIA. In 1828–1829, after the Russo-Turkish War which sealed Greek independence, Moldavia and Valachia became virtual Russian protectorates. ROMANIA was formed by the two provinces in 1856, still nominally vassal to the Porte, but fully independent in 1859 upon the accession of Alexander John Cuza. This was a result of the Congress of Paris convened after the Crimean War (1853–1856), which checked Russian designs on the Ottoman Empire. In 1878, the rest of Bessarabia was ceded to Russia (BERLIN, CONGRESS OF). Both Bukovina and Bessarabia to the Dniester River ended up as part of Romania after World War I.

Moldova

SEE *BESSARABIA* IN 'PROVINCES AND REGIONS'

ROMANIA reached its greatest extension after World War I, when it embraced Valachia, Transylvania, northern Dobruja (which has a coast on the Black Sea), and Moldavia as far as the Dniester River. It sided with Germany in World War II and in 1947 the USSR annexed Moldavia as far as the Prut River and eastern Bukovina. The Moldavian Soviet Socialist Republic was created with Eastern Moldavia (Bessarabia) and eastern Bukovina. Southern Bessarabia was annexed to the UKRAINE. Upon the dissolution of the USSR in 1991, the Moldavian Soviet Socialist Republic declared its independence as Moldova, a move the local Russians resented. With Russian military backing, they created a statelet-within-a-statelet called Trans-Dniestra, formally still part of Moldova. The capital of Moldova is Chisinau. Tiraspol is the principal city in Trans-Dniestra. Moldovans speak Romanian.

Molossia (EPIRUS)

Monaco

The principality of Monaco was founded in the 13th cent. by a member of the noble Grimaldi family of Italian extraction. It was a protectorate of SAR-DINIA after 1815 and of France after 1861. The only change to its territory in its history was the cession of next-door Menton to France in 1848. Monaco is a member of the United Nations.

Mongol Empire (13th–14th cents.; core area: *Mongolia*)

The homeland of the Mongol Empire was the valley of the Orkhon River, near which the Mongol capital, Karakorum, was built by Genghis Khan ca. 1220. Mongol and Turkish (Tatar) hordes roamed the territories of northern Mongolia and adjacent areas. The different hordes were unified and the Tatars assimilated ca. 1205 by Genghis, who organized a *khuriltai* or grand meeting of his subjects in 1206 and began his career as conqueror of lands outside of Mongolia. He headed south and west. He crippled the JURCHEN Chin dynasty in northern China, but he did not advance further south against SUNG (SONG) China. He did utterly destroy the Tangut or Tibetan HSI-HSIA kingdom, the KARA-KHITAN KHANATE, and KHWARIZM. In pursuit of the ruler of Khwarizm, Genghis invaded northern India in 1221. The ruler of the DELHI SULTANATE, Iltutmish, did nothing to obstruct him and Genghis was satisfied with garrisoning the PUNJAB. Genghis died in 1227. His empire at its climax extended basically over Mogholistan, northern China, and Western Turkestan to Persia. Genghis' successors carried on with his conquests. In the direction of the west, the rest of Persia and Baghdad were subjected to Mongol rule in 1231 by Hulagu, a grandson of Genghis (ILKHANID PERSIA). The Russian lands of the POLOVETZY fell ca. 1230 to Batu, son of Jochi, an illegitimate son of Genghis, and became the core of the khanate of the GOLDEN HORDE. The Seljuks of eastern Anatolia (ANATOLIAN EMIRATES) and the RUM SULTANATE were subjected ca. 1240, but not the MAMELUKE SULTANATE, which, under Baybars, contained the Mongol onslaught at Ain Jalut, Syria, in 1260.

A 'NOBLE' EXECUTION

Previously, a secessionist attempt by Baghdad was crushed and the last caliph, Al-Musta'sim, was rolled into rugs and trampled to death by horses in 1258 (ABBASID CALIPHATE). The Mongols reserved a bloodless death for the nobility. Towards the east, the Korean kingdom of PO HAI was destroyed and Korea itself was made a vassal state in 1236. Southwards Kublai Khan, grandson of Genghis, followed a roundabout route to conquer China by first taking Yunnan in 1253 – and, incidentally, destroying the NAN CHAO kingdom, scattering its rulers and followers to LAOS and THAILAND, and annexing its land to China – and in 1279 defeating the Southern SUNG (SONG), thus attaching all of China to his own YUAN dynasty and to the rest of the Mongol Empire. By then it had started to disintegrate. The Golden Horde had been practically autonomous from the start. The vassal CHAGATAITE KHANATE, which occupied the lands west of Mongolia to Transoxiana and to the limits of the Golden Horde, was independent of Karakorum by the early 14th cent., and this in effect meant the separation from Mongolia of Ilkhanid

Persia. In 1368, the Chinese overthrew the Mongols and inaugurated the MING dynasty, after which the Mongols were reduced to their homeland (MONGOLIA).

WERE THE MONGOLS INVINCIBLE?

Despite their fame of invincibility the Mongols were defeated on occasions, but in historically significant ways. They were contained by the Mamelukes in Syria in 1260 and again near Damascus in 1303. In 1279 the Chagataite Mongols invaded the Punjab and were defeated by then-sultan Balban of Delhi. Under Khan Duwa they returned in 1297 and thereafter repeatedly invaded northern India. On at least two occasions, in 1299 and in 1303, they invaded with huge forces, but were either frustrated – they took Delhi in 1303 but could not consolidate their hold on the sultanate – or defeated, repeatedly by Sultan Al ad-Din (1295–1315). The Chagataite raids continued until 1327 but the Mongols were never able to annex any Indian territory. The Mongols in 1274 under Kublai Khan attempted for the first time to subject Japan, but his forces turned back due to adverse weather, which the Japanese saw as a divine wind or 'kamikaze'. Successive Mongol emissaries were executed by the Japanese until Kublai assembled a huge fleet which managed to land an equally immense army in the Bay of Hakata, on the island of Kyushu. The Japanese contained the beachhead and weather once again proved treacherous to the Mongols, who escaped only in small numbers. The Mongols were so truly vincible that they couldn't even subdue Champa, a tiny Malay kingdom in central Vietnam, nor Vietnam itself, a former Chinese province, which the Ming would conquer and hold briefly in the 15th cent. In eastern Java, where they thought they would put the fear of God into its very minor dynastic squabblers, the Mongols were used, out-manoeuvred, and booted out.

TÄNGRI

The Mongols were originally shamanists who revered Tängri (the sky). During the heyday of empire, they were sympathetic to Nestorian Christianity and the Crusaders were distantly sympathetic to them, but when push came to shove they did not seem especially welcoming in their Levant fortresses when the Mongols approached and were contained by the Mamelukes (1260). Nestorians believe that there are distinct divine and human natures in Christ. Outside Mongolia, the Mongols usually converted to Islam. In Mongolia itself they were influenced by Buddhism.

(See chronologies under China and Neighbouring Areas, Greater Mongolia, Anatolia, and Southern Russia.)

Mongolia
SEE ENTRY IN 'PROVINCES AND REGIONS'

The end of the YUAN (1368) in China forced the Mongol descendants of Kublai Khan back to their homeland (Orkhon and Karakorum). The history of Mongolia after that is like a huge puzzle, with some large pieces but mostly tiny ones. Along very general lines, the struggle for Mongolia involved the Kublaids (a patchwork of tribes among which the Khalkas emerged as dominant), who tended to be active in the east and in Inner Mongolia (CHINA), and the Oirats, or western Mongols, known to the Turks as Kalmucks, who for a time held all of Mongolia but then moved west towards Western Turkestan. A branch of the Oirats, the Dzungars, at one time conquered central Mongolia, but mainly they created a khanate of their own (DZUNGARIA). The western Oirats attempted to build an empire but failed and their history can be subsumed under Mongolia, considered as Greater Mongolia or Mogholistan.

OIRATS OR WESTERN MONGOLS

The remnants of Yuan China tried to dominate their ancient Mongolian heritage but they had lost ascendancy over the other Mongol clans. In 1399 they were defeated by the Turkic KIRGHIZ, who came from the Yenisei River Basin but could not hold down the Mongols, among whom the Kublaids again tried to assert their authority during the early 15th cent. The Oirats had been occupying the Lake Baikal area since before the time of Genghis. By 1439, they had extended their domain to Lake Balkash and to the western sections of the Chinese walls, from where they conquered Mongolia. The Kublaids drove them out of eastern Mongolia and kept it united until 1543, when it fragmented again. The Oirats had retained Karakorum (central Mongolia) and were only driven out when the dominant Kublaids, the Khalka, made a comeback ca. 1580. In the early 17th cent. the Khalka managed to oust the Oirats even out of Kobdo, their base east of Lake Balkash. It is at this point that the western Mongols thrust westwards, defeated the KIRGHIZ-KAZAKS, and went as far as the Caspian Sea, where they accepted Russian suzerainty. Another branch of the Oirats occupied Tibet and founded Dzungaria. In Mongolia itself the different Kublaid clans were so chronically divided that the history of their wars is part of the minutiae of history.

East of Mongolia during the early 17th cent. the Manchus, descendants of the JURCHEN, had been building an empire of their own (MANCHURIA). By 1634 the Manchus had conquered down to the Ordos, at which time they exerted influence over the territory of Inner Mongolia, which had been more or less under the control of one of the Kublaid clans. When the Manchus subdued all of China (1644–1651) and founded the CH'ING (QING) dynasty, they added Inner Mongolia to China. The rest of Mongolia was so weak that, in 1691, its Khalka rulers accepted the condition of Ch'ing vassals. The weakness of Mongolia permitted the Oirats of western Turkestan to retake Kobdo

(1690). But the empire of the Western Mongols was inherently fragile and the Oirats were harassed by the Kirghiz-Kazaks until, ca. 1770, they were driven back to Kobdo, where Ch'ing China, by then master of Dzungaria, settled them. Upon the fall of Ch'ing China, Mongolia's independence was recognized by Russia, subject to border rectifications which excluded Mongol claims to Siberia. The country became part of the SOVIET EMPIRE, but never actually lost its status as an independent nation. In Chinese historiography the history of Mongolia after the fall of Yuan is known as Northern Yuan. Ulan Bator is the capital of Mongolia.

(*See chronologies under* China and Neighbouring Areas *and* Greater Mongolia.)

Monomotapa or Mwanamutapa (16th–17th cents.; south-eastern Africa)
Peopled by speakers of a tongue of the Bantu group – which covers southern and central Africa – Monomotapa, in western Mozambique, came under Por-

Greater Mongolia		
Predominant political influences		
4th cent. BC	***7th cent.***	Mongol Empire
Hsiung-nu	Tu-chüeh	Yuan China
Sarmatians	Uigurs	
		14th. cent.
3rd cent. BC–1st	***8th cent.***	Yuan China
cent. AD	Uigurs	Timurid Empire
Hsiung-nu		Kublaids
	9th cent.	
2nd–3rd cents.	Uigurs	***15th cent.***
Hsiung-nu	Kirghiz	Mongolia (Kublaids,
Hsien-pi	Hsi-Hsia	Oirats)
	10th cent.	
4th. cent.	Hsi-Hsia	***16th cent.***
Hsiung-nu	Khitai	Mongolia (Oirats,
Juan-juan		Khalka)
	11th cent.	
5th cent.	Mongol Tribes	***17th cent.***
Juan-juan	Ghuzz	Mongolia (Oirats,
Ephthalites		Khalka)
	12th cent.	Ch'ing (Qing)
6th cent.	Mongol Tribes	
Juan-juan	Jurchen	***18th–19th cents.***
Tu-chüeh		Ch'ing (Qing)
13th cent.		Russia
Avars	Mongol Tribes	

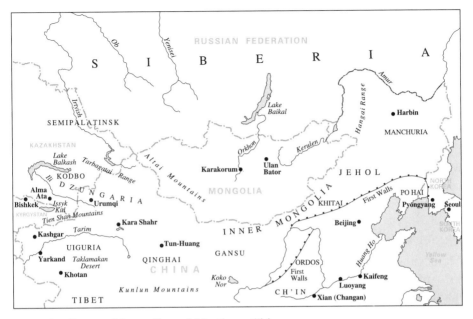

Map 6   Greater Mongolia and Northern China

tuguese influence in the 16th cent. It is from the people of Monomotapa that Europeans first heard of ancient ZIMBABWE and its impressive ruins.

Montenegro (14th–20th cents.; *Balkans*)

Peopled by Serbs – Montenegrin is identical to Serbo-Croat – Montenegro was part of SERBIA during the 13th and 14th cents., although, because of its mountainous topography, it never actually submitted to any strong authority. After the Battle of Kosovo Field in 1389, in which Serbian prince Lazar was defeated by the Ottomans, Montenegro became a refuge for Serbian lords. In 1499 the OTTOMAN EMPIRE conquered most of Montenegro while VENICE occupied the coast. The Montenegrin coast was ceded by Venice to the HABSBURG EMPIRE in 1797. Resistant to Ottoman rule, the interior of Montenegro was governed by the bishops of Cetinje, the ancient capital, whose rule Ottoman sultan Selim III recognized in 1799. Montenegro was secularized in 1852 and its independence was recognized in the Congress of BERLIN in 1878, when it also gained access to the Adriatic Sea. From 1915 to 1918, during World War I, Montenegro was occupied by Austro-German forces. In 1918, the country joined Serbia as part of the Kingdom of the Serbs, Croats and Slovenes (1919), which was renamed YUGOSLAVIA (land of the southern Slavs) in 1929. After World War II, Montenegro's territory was enlarged with an additional portion of Adriatic coast. Separated from Serbia, it joined communist Yugoslavia as a federated republic in 1946. With the disintegration of former Yugoslavia in 1991–1992, Montenegro followed

Serbia in creating the actual rump Yugoslavia. The capital of Montenegro is Podgorica (former Titograd). During 1999, Montenegro proposed transforming its association with Serbia into that of a very loose federation.
(*See chronology under* Balkans.)

Morocco

Morocco was the Mauretania of the Roman Empire (ROME). It is a Berber nation but its inhabitants became better known as Moors after the Arab conquest and their conversion to Islam. Moor is often used synonymously with Muslim. The process of Arabization of Morocco was gradual from the 7th cent., but was accelerated with the Bedouin invasions, encouraged by the FATIMIDS in Egypt, during the 11th cent.

ALCAZARQUIVIR

Morocco was on the margins of the Mediterranean empires but became part of ISLAM and served as the bridge to the invasion of Iberia. After Islamic conquest and Umayyad rule, it separated from the successor ABBASID CALIPHATE under the Idrisids in 788, whose governance ended in tribal division. In the 10th cent. the Umayyads of CÓRDOBA turned the tables on the conquest of MUSLIM SPAIN by invading Morocco and installing themselves in Fez ca. 950. They were Sunni Moslems and contested western Algeria with the Shia Fatimids. In 1056 the southern Moroccan ALMORAVIDS swept over the land and went over to Spain, where the Umayyad Caliphate had disintegrated into the Taifa kingdoms, which they reunited ca. 1060. The Almoravids extended their influence to western Algeria, which had been ravaged by the Bedouins. The Almoravids were succeeded by the ALMOHADS who, during the mid-12th cent., conquered Spain and reunited the Maghreb as far as western Libya. The cause of Islam was more or less lost in Spain after the Battle of Navas de Toledo in 1212. In Morocco itself the Almohads were substituted in 1259 by the MARINIDS, whose rule can be said to inaugurate the history of Morocco proper. Muslim Spain was extinguished in GRANADA in 1492, and during the 16th cent. Portugal and Spain raided and occupied the Moroccan coast. The Saadis took power from the Marinids in 1554. Morocco defeated a Portuguese invasion in 1578 in the Battle of Alcazarquivir, in which Portuguese king Sebastian was killed. Morocco also regained coastal areas it had been losing to the Iberian Christian kingdoms. The Alawites came to power in 1660. The dynasty has been ruling since then.

TETUAN AND RABAT

In 1844, when it intervened in favour of Algeria, Morocco was defeated by France, which thenceforward considered itself to have special rights in Morocco. Continental European rivalries prevented France from annexing

Morocco to its colonial empire. But in 1912, in the aftermath of a cession to Germany of African equatorial territory, France and Spain divided the country. Spain got a strip on the Mediterranean coast, capital Tetuan, and France imposed a protectorate over the rest of the country. The Berber Abd el-Krim resisted Franco-Spanish rule from 1920 to 1924. In 1941, French Morocco adhered to the collaborationist Vichy French regime, but French authorities did not oppose the Allied landing on the Atlantic coast in 1942. After strong nationalist opposition, France relinquished its rights in Morocco in 1956. Tangier was incorporated subsequently and Spain ceded its north Moroccan territory in 1958 except for the enclaves of Ceuta and Melilla. After Spain evacuated its western Saharan colony in 1976, Morocco invaded peacefully, although it has had to contend with the independentist Polisario movement. The principal urban centre of Morocco was Tangier, a Roman city, until the foundation of Fez in 808. Founded by the Almoravids in 1062, Marrakech was the capital of Morocco until 1114, when Fez became the Marinid capital. During the 16th and 17th cents. first Fez again and then Meknes functioned as courts. As a general rule, the capital of Morocco was the place where the sovereign lived. French Morocco established its administration in Rabat, which remains the capital.
(*See chronology under* Maghreb.)

Mozambique
Like the rest of central and southern Africa, Mozambique was peopled by tribes who spoke languages of the Bantu group. It was under Portuguese influence from the 16th cent. The kingdom of MONOMOTAPA was located in western Mozambique. Mozambique became independent in 1975. It underwent a brutal civil war, encouraged by the apartheid regime in South Africa, until a peace treaty in 1992. The capital is Maputo (Lourenço Marques under Portuguese rule).

Mrohaung (15th–18th cents.; *Myanmar*)
A Burmese kingdom in western MYANMAR (Arakan), Mrohaung went independent when the rest of the country was enmeshed in a struggle between Shans, Mons, and Burmese. During the 17th cent. the coast of Mrohaung was occupied by Bengal. In 1785 the Burmese monarchy absorbed the entire kingdom.

Mughal Empire (16th–18th cents.; Afghanistan and *India*)
Babur, the last of the Timurids, was ruler of Ferghana in 1507 (TIMURID EMPIRE AND SUCCESSOR STATES). Failing in his attempt to regain Transoxiana, the Timurid patrimony centred around Samarkand, he turned to NORTHERN INDIA, where in the Battle of Panipat in 1526 he defeated the DELHI SULTANATE. At the time the RAJPUTS had their base in Mewar, today's Udaipur in Rajasthan, which Babur also conquered. Babur was a

contemporary of Sultan Selim I of the Ottoman Empire and of the Safavid Shah Ismail of Persia. The three introduced the systematic use of cannon in Asia. Babur was succeeded by his son Humayun, who was ousted by the Muslim ruler of Bihar, Sher Shah. It was only in 1555, near the end of his life, that, with Persian support, Humayun was able to reconquer his empire. His son Akbar acceded to the throne in 1556. Akbar was illiterate but shrewd and tolerant. He tried to integrate the Hindus through lenient measures rather than forceful methods, such as had been applied disastrously by the Delhi Sultan Muhammad Tughluq. From 1574 to 1576, Akbar invaded Gujarat and BENGAL, which had seceded from the Delhi Sultanate before the Mughal conquest. The process of repeated annexations of the same domains by rulers from Delhi was due to the Indian tradition in which victorious campaigns did not yield annexation but vassalage. This was a consequence of Indian divisiveness which went back to the very inception of states in VEDIC INDIA, but also significantly because, after the GHURIDS conquered Delhi, northern India with its majority Hindu population was continuously in the power of Muslim rulers until the coming of the British. Akbar also managed to take Kandahar (Afghanistan) from the Persians. His Indian empire reached as far north as KASHMIR.

A BUILDER AND A CONQUEROR

Akbar's son, Shah Jahan, who as a prince had conquered Ahmadagar in the Deccan (CENTRAL INDIA), rebelled against his father, which became a sort of Mughal princely rite of passage. He did not succeed but, in the process, he sought Persian support. In compensation, he agreed to the cession of Kandahar after he became emperor in 1627. He later tried to recover the city, but the Persians prevailed and the Mughals, severed from one of their crucial central Asian roots, set aside the dream of an empire outside India. Shah Jahan was a sumptuous builder, whose greatest monument is the Taj Mahal, in Agra, the tomb of his wife Mumtaz. His son, Aurangzeb, rebelled and succeeded in imprisoning his father and taking the throne in 1658. Aurangzeb's Islamic faith was intense and he tried to subjugate India, not just force the other states to recognize his suzerainty. For this purpose, like Muhammad Tughluq, he moved the capital to Aurangabad. The greatest obstacle to Aurangzeb's ruthless expansionism, which was financed with levies on his Hindu subjects, was Shivaji, ruler of the most powerful of the MARATHA KINGDOMS, in Maharashtra. The two rulers rivalled in the conquest of the Deccan sultanates. For a while it was touch-and-go, but Shivaji died first (1680) and, even though he did not reduce the Marathas, Aurangzeb did conquer the Deccan. At its greatest extent, reached under Aurangzeb, the Mughal Empire's frontiers embraced (in modern terms) eastern Pakistan, Kabul and northern Afghanistan, Kashmir, Bangladesh, and all of India except the southern tip of the subcontinent.

THE PEACOCK THRONE

The Mughgal Empire was a giant with clay feet. Aurangzeb's first son Akbar rebelled unsuccessfully allied to Shivaji's son, and died in exile. Aurangzeb's successor in 1707 was another son, Bahadur Shah, who tried to conciliate the Marathas in order to ensure peace. The move was counterproductive because, under the Peshwa – a dynasty of ministers, which, like the Japanese shoguns, ruled indirectly through puppet kings – Maratha power was restored. The Mughal–Maratha rivalry permitted Nadir Shah, ruler of Persia (IRAN), to invade northern India in 1739. Delhi was sacked and the Peacock throne was carted away by the Persians, who used it as their own throne. By then there were centrifugal forces at work in Rajasthan, Punjab, Maharashtra, and Bengal. The visir, Nizzam ul-Mulk, who was the power behind the Mughal throne, founded his own kingdom in Hyderabad, whose rulers (known as Nizams) became British allies. The emperors were reduced to mere local rulers in Delhi. Starting in Bengal, the British gradually encroached on the moribund Mughal Empire. They defeated the Nawab of Bengal in the Battle of Plassey (1757). By the late 18th cent. they were the dominant power in India. The last Mughal emperors were English clients and the dynasty was finally deposed in 1857 (BRITISH INDIA). (*See chronologies under* Afghanistan *and* Indian Subcontinent.)

Muslim Spain (8th–15th cents.; *Spain*)
ISLAM had swept through northern Africa during the 7th cent. In 711, Islamic Berber forces under Tariq Ibn Ziyad crossed from Morocco to Spain – according to a quasi-legendary account, invited by a count Julian to participate in an internecine struggle – and, in the equivalent of an early Medieval *blitzkrieg*, destroyed the VISIGOTHIC KINGDOM and drove its Christian rulers to the ramparts of ASTURIAS and to the foothills of the Pyrenees. Muslim Spain was ruled by representatives of the Umayyad Caliphate in Damascus. The Umayyads were overthrown and mostly killed by the Abbasids in 750. Abd ar-Rahman, a survivor Umayyad, managed to reach CÓRDOBA where he founded an emirate independent of the ABBASID CALIPHATE. Abd ar-Rahman III in 929 proclaimed the caliphate of Córdoba and, ca. 950, he invaded and annexed Morocco. Under Christian pressure from BARCELONA and the kingdom of NAVARRE, which briefly reunited most of northern Spain, the Córdoba caliphate disintegrated in 1031. Its disintegration engendered the Taifa kingdoms, which included Badajoz, Córdoba, Seville, Toledo, Granada, Zaragoza, Valencia, Murcia, Denia, and others. In 1078 Córdoba itself fell to Seville – ruled by the Abbadids (ca. 1020–1091) – which became the most powerful of the Taifa Kingdoms. The Christians also tended to remain divided – in 1035 Navarre broke up into Aragon, Castile, and Navarre – and ca. 1060 the ALMORAVIDS, a Berber dynasty from southern Morocco, invaded Spain at the behest of the Abbadids. The Almoravids defeated a Chris-

tian army in 1086 and deposed the Abbadids in 1091. The Almoravids were overthrown by the ALMOHADS in 1174. By then ARAGON was a flourishing kingdom and CASTILE was an aggressive state at the head of the *reconquista*, the general name for the long war in which the Muslims were expelled from Iberia.

Muslim domains were gradually reduced to the southern part of the Iberian Peninsula from Valencia to Lisbon. In 1212 Alfonso VIII of Castile defeated the Almohads in the decisive Battle of Navas de Tolosa. The Muslims were disunited once again. In 1238, Valencia was seized by Rodrigo Diaz de Vivar, the Cid of epic fame, and Córdoba was lost in 1236. Muslim Spain fell gradually but inexorably to the Christians. With the conquest of GRANADA from Boabdil, the last of the Nasrids, in 1492, Muslim Spain was ended.
(*See chronology under* Maghreb.)

Muzzafarids (14th cent.; western *Iran*)

Out of the struggles that followed the death of the last Mongol ruler of ILKHANID PERSIA (1335), the Muzzafarids entrenched themselves in western IRAN ca. 1350. However, the dynasty did not last very long: Tamerlane conquered and destroyed Ispahan (1387) and Shiraz (1393).
(*See chronology under* Iran.)

Myanmar

SEE ENTRY IN 'PROVINCES AND REGIONS'

Burmese is a member of the Tibeto-Burman group of the Sino-Tibetan family, a wide and disputed linguistic category which includes the languages of China. The early history of Myanmar is that of the struggle between the Burmese and the Mons, a people who spoke an Austro-Asiatic language, related to Cambodian and Vietnamese. In the 11th cent. the Burmese gained control of the Irrawaddy River Delta under King Anawrahta, who adopted Theravada Buddhism and embellished the fabulous Buddhist city of Pagan, which gave its name to his kingdom. Kublai Khan (YUAN) overthrew Pagan in 1287 after which the Mons recovered the Irrawaddy Delta, with their capital at Pegu, and the Tai-speaking Shans in the north strengthened. The Burmese kingdom, with its capital in Ava (near Mandalay), was weak and divided until the 16th cent. when the Toungod dynasty subjugated the Shans and Mons and united the country. The Burmese occupied Siam between 1568 and 1583. The Mons rebelled in the early 18th cent., but in 1758 King Alaungapya, founder of the Konbaung dynasty, defeated them. He also established the capital in Yangon (Rangoon) in 1753. The Burmese again occupied Siam in 1767 and 1777. Myanmar extended to as far north as Assam. In 1826, the British took Arakan (western Myanmar) and Tenasserim (south-eastern Myanmar, bordering on Thailand) and in 1852 annexed Pegu and the Irrawaddy Delta. The Burmese capital was moved to Amarapura and then to Mandalay in 1860. During 1885

and 1886 British rule was extended to Mandalay and the whole of Myanmar was incorporated into BRITISH INDIA, from which it was separated in 1937. Myanmar was occupied by the Japanese from 1942 to 1945. It became independent as Burma in 1948 under the leadership of Aung San. In 1988 the name was changed to Myanmar. The isthmus of Kra shared by Myanmar and Thailand separates the Malay Peninsula from the rest of Asia.
(*See chronology under* China and Neighbouring Areas.)

Mycenean Greece (17th–12th cents. BC; Ancient *Greece*)
It is estimated that the Greek-speaking Myceneans arrived in Greece from the north ca. 2000 BC. Their civilization flourished and Mycenea, among other city–states including Argos, Tiryns, Pylos, and Thebes, emerged as dominant ca. 1600. Since MINOAN CIVILIZATION overlaps with Mycenean Greece, it is to be presumed that they competed for power in the eastern Mediterranean Sea. Knossos, the principal city of the Minoan civilization in Crete, was destroyed by the Myceneans ca. 1400. But Mycenean writing called Linear B on tablets found in Crete and dated to ca. 1450, attests to Greek invasions before the destruction of Knossos. Linear B was deciphered by Michael Ventris in 1952. It is accompanied by Linear A, which has not yet been deciphered. Mycenean civilization lasted until ca. 1200 BC, when its cities, Mycenae itself in particular, were devastated. The causes of its downfall are obscure. A widely remitted thesis is that they fell to invaders from the Balkans, but there is no archaeological evidence for such invasions. The fall of Mycenean civilization coincided with the destruction of other states in the Near East, which fuelled speculations about PELASGIANS. Another thesis is that the Myceneans were conquered by neighbouring tribes, often identified as Dorians, against whom Bronze-age military tactics were at a disadvantage. The end of Mycenean civilization ushered in the dark ages of Ancient GREECE, which lasted until the 9th–8th cents. BC. This was Homer's time (ca. 750–700 BC) whose epics are probably based on collective reminiscences from the times of Mycenae. By then the regionalization of Ancient Greece was well defined.
(*See chronology under* Greece (Ancient).)

Mysore (18th cent.; *India*)
During its history, Hindu SOUTHERN INDIA was mostly beyond the rule of the Muslim empires of NORTHERN INDIA, which began in the 12th cent. Mysore, in Karnataka, did come under the DELHI SULTANATE briefly and was retaken by the Vijayanagar kingdom. Towards the end of the 18th cent. a Muslim ruler, Haider Ali, founded an independent state around Mysore, capital Seringapatam. Advised by French military, he, and especially his son, Tipu Sultan, fought off BRITISH INDIA until 1799.

N

Namibia

Namibia is peopled by speakers of languages of the Niger–Congo family, more usual in western Africa, and of Khoisan, a language family in itself spoken by hunter-gatherers from southern Angola to South Africa. The territory was occupied by Germany from 1883 and officially known as German South West Africa after the Berlin Conference of 1884–1885. The Herero rebelled over land rights starting in 1903 and, by 1908, they had been virtually exterminated. During World War I, German South West Africa was occupied by South African forces. It was mandated to South Africa by the League of Nations as South West Africa and later became a United Nations trust territory under South African administration. There was a resistance movement. Namibia became independent in 1990. The capital of Namibia is Windhoek. Walvis Bay was occupied by Great Britain in 1878 and made part of Cape Colony. In 1922 it came under the administration of South West Africa. It was retained by South Africa and ceded to Namibia in 1994.

Nan Chao (7th–13th cents.; south-western *China*)

Nan Chao was a possibly proto-Burmese kingdom in Yunnan, founded in the 7th cent., vassal to China ca. 1000, which Kublai Khan destroyed in 1253 in the course of his roundabout campaign to subject the Sung (Song) dynasty (YUAN). At its height it extended to Guizhou (Kweichow) and Guangxi (Kwangsi). Thais from Nan Chao went south and founded LAOS and THAILAND.

(*See chronology under* China and Neighbouring Areas.)

Naples (7th cent. BC–19th cent.; southern *Italy*)

The Greek Neapolis, founded ca. 600 BC, was annexed by ROME in 340 BC. With the dissolution of the Roman Empire in the west (476), Italy fell to Odoacer and then to the Ostrogoths (OSTROGOTHIC ITALY). In 556, the Roman Empire in the east (BYZANTINE EMPIRE) recovered Italy from the barbarians (BYZANTINE ITALY). During the 8th cent., Naples was constituted as an independent duchy in LOMBARD ITALY. In the 11th cent. the Normans Robert Guiscard and his brother Roger conquered Sicily and southern Italy (NORMAN ITALY). In 1139 Pope Innocent II, who claimed suzerainty over those territories for the papacy, granted the Normans the right to rule as vassals. Naples was annexed by the Normans in the same year. The last Norman ruler conferred his Italian domains on his aunt Constance, wife of the Holy Roman Emperor Henry VI Hohenstaufen. Their heir, Frederick II Hohenstaufen, established his capital in Palermo, Sicily, thus weakening his hold on the Empire but creating what many historians, Braudel among them, consider the first efficiently centralized European state. The papacy began to perceive the Hohenstaufen as a threat and Pope Honorius III vested southern Italy and Sicily on the French Charles I Anjou, who defeated and executed Conradin, the last Hohenstaufen ruler of southern Italy, in 1268.

ARAGON

The Sicilians, who had been content with their Norman rulers and German successors, rose against the French, ejected them in 1282 – during the massacres of the Sicilian Vespers, which started in Palermo and spread to the rest of the island – and accepted the rule of ARAGON. The French retained Naples but the Angevin claim to Sicily was renounced in 1373. Alfonso V of Aragon annexed Naples in 1442 and the two realms became the Aragonese kingdom of the Two Sicilies. Naples and Sicily became Spanish dependencies when, in 1492, CASTILE and Aragon were united through the marriage of the Catholic Kings, Ferdinand of Aragon and Isabella of Castile. Spain later separated the two realms and ruled through viceroys. In 1707, during the War of Spanish Succession (1701–1714), Naples became a separate Habsburg state, which was reunited with Sicily as the Kingdom of Naples and Sicily under a branch of the Spanish Bourbons in 1738. In 1799, the liberal Parthenopean Republic was proclaimed in Naples, and was quickly and ruthlessly suppressed by Nelson. Naples, though not Sicily, which British naval power in the Mediterranean denied to the French, was part of the Napoleonic European Empire from 1806 to 1815 (FRENCH EUROPEAN EMPIRE). Restored to the Bourbons, it was joined to Italy in 1860 by Garibaldi.

Naples and Sicily (Kingdom of) (NAPLES)

Nauru
Tiny Nauru, whose inhabitants speak a language of the Austronesian family, which includes Malay, was a German Pacific Ocean possession in 1886. It was mandated to Australia after World War I. The Japanese occupied it in 1942. Liberated by the United States in 1943, it has been independent since 1968. Should the oceans rise in the future, Nauru would be one of the first casualties, together with New York City.

Navarre (9th–16th cents.; *Spain* and *France*)
The lands of the Basques originally extended over north-eastern Spain (VASCONIA), Spanish or Upper Navarre, and French or Lower Navarre. Vasconia includes the Spanish provinces of Alava, Guipúzcoa, and Vizcaya. Charlemagne briefly controlled Navarre in 775. In 824 Iñigo Aritza became ruler in Pamplona and expanded his territory to found the kingdom of Navarre, including Vasconia. Navarre reached its apogee with Sancho II the Great, who

married the heiress of Castile and united most of northern Spain from 1029 to
1035. Sancho divided Navarre for his sons, who ruled over separate
ARAGON, CASTILE, and Navarre. Castile acquired Guipuzcoa in 1200.
After 1234, Navarre came under French influence. In 1305, it passed to Philip
IV, King of France. Alava and Vizcaya were annexed by Spain in 1332 and
1370, respectively. Navarre was ruled by different French dynasties until Ferdinand V (the Catholic) of Aragon conquered all of Spanish Navarre in 1515.
Lower Navarre remained French and, in 1589, its ruler became Henry IV, the
founder of the French Bourbon dynasty (FRENCH RULING DYNASTIES
AND REGIMES). Later, Lower Navarre was annexed to Béarn to form a
single province. Over the ages, including the Franco period, Spanish Navarre
retained its *fueros*, special privileges granted by kings.

Near East (Ancient)
Predominant political influences (all dates are BC)

	Egypt	**Rest of Near East**
2900–2000	Old Kingdom	Sumer
		Akkad
		Lagash
		Ur
		Elam
1999–1500	Middle Kingdom	Babylonia
	Hyksos	Hittite Kingdom
1499–1000	New Kingdom	Hittite Kingdom
		Kassites
		Mitanni
		Assyria
		Philistia
		Phoenicia
		Israel
999–500	New Kingdom	Assyria
	Kush	Babylonia
	Assyria	Philistia
	Achaemenid Empire	Urartu
		Media
		Lydia
		Achaemenid Empire

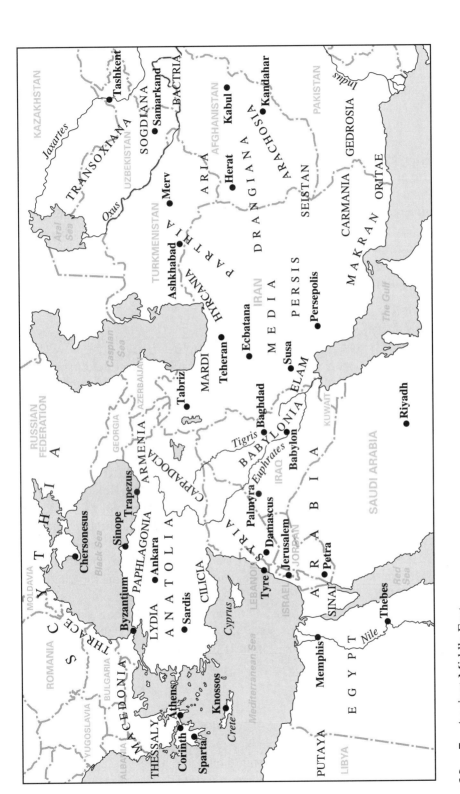

Map 7 Ancient Middle East

Nepal

Nepal's farthest origins are unclear. Buddhism was introduced in 639, but the territory remained divided. Starting in the 12th cent. many Buddhists took refuge in Nepal, fleeing from Muslim conquerors of NORTHERN INDIA. The Hindu RAJPUTS gradually invaded the country, setting up independent states. One of these was Ghurka, in the valley of Katmandu. Various Hindu dynasties ruled, until Prithvi Narayn, a Gurkha king, united the kingdom from 1742 to 1769. He also annexed Sikkim and Simla. Nepal divided again after his death in 1775. In the 19th cent., a Nepalese invasion of northern India led to reprisals and influence by BRITISH INDIA. In 1846, the Rana family united the kingdom as it is today. Its independence was recognized by Great Britain in 1860. The Nepalese speak an Indo-Aryan language, related to northern Indian tongues. The capital is Kathmandu. In a military context, Gurkha means a Nepalese volunteer in the British army.

Netherlands

SEE ENTRY IN 'PROVINCES AND REGIONS'

The Netherlands was, with Belgium and Luxembourg, part of the Low Countries. Its territory occupied the part of the Roman province of Germania Inferior on the left bank of the Rhine River. It was inhabited by Celt Batavii. Beyond the Rhine, the territory of Netherlands was peopled by Frisians, of German stock. The Low Countries belonged to the CAROLINGIAN EMPIRE. When the Empire was shared out among Charlemagne's descendants in the course of the 9th cent. the Low Countries passed to the East Frankish kingdom, which later became the HOLY ROMAN EMPIRE. In 1364, the French king, John II Valois, bestowed on his son Philip the Bold the duchy of BURGUNDY. In 1384, Philip subjected the Low Countries. In 1477, Mary of Burgundy married Holy Roman Emperor Maximilian I and brought the Low Countries to the HABSBURG EMPIRE. Their son Philip the Handsome married Joanna the Mad of Spain, so when Philip died in 1506, their son Charles (future King Charles I of Spain and Holy Roman Emperor Charles V) inherited the Low Countries. In 1556 Charles V divested himself of the imperial crown in favour of his brother Ferdinand I. The following year, he conferred the Low Countries on his son Philip, who, upon his father's retirement to a monastery in 1558, became Philip II of Spain. Thus, the Low Countries became the Spanish Netherlands.

WILLIAM OF ORANGE

The Reformation had made inroads in the Low Countries, especially in Holland and adjoining provinces, inclined to the teachings of John Calvin. In 1567 Philip tried to recover them using the strong, repressive approach of the Duke of Alba. The Low Countries were in a virtual state of insurrection. The future kingdom of the Netherlands drove out the Spanish garrisons in 1572. In 1578, Alessandro Farnase recovered Flanders, but in 1579 the northern provinces of Holland, Friesland, Geldernland, Groningen, Overijsell, Utrecht, and Zeeland subscribed to the Union of Utrecht under the leadership of William of Orange and, in 1581, declared their independence as the United Provinces. The state of war with Spain was constant, although hostilities were intermittent. In 1609 the United Provinces under Maurice of Nassau, son of William of Orange – who was assassinated by a Catholic fanatic in 1584 – won a truce from the Spanish commander Spinola. Fighting resumed again in the Thirty Years War (1618–1648), after which, in the Peace of Westphalia, the Netherlands were recognized by Spain and, in addition, obtained north Brabant and Limburg (Maastricht) as well as control of the Scheldt, the mouth of the Rhine River. When the United Provinces broke away from the Spanish Netherlands, they had already attained a high degree of economic development with the maritime power to go with it. In 1602, the Dutch East India Company was formed, which during the 17th cent. followed the wake of the Portuguese – Portugal was part of Spain then, and fair game – down Africa and across the Indian Ocean. It took Sri Lanka, Malacca, and the East Indies, where it fought off attempts at British penetration (DUTCH COLONIAL EMPIRE). In 1621 the Dutch West India Company was founded, which also had some successes though nothing as spectacular as the control of the East Indies.

JAN DE WITT

Republican tendencies, expressed by the grand pensionary Jan de Witt, resulted in the diminution of power of the house of Orange. Dutch sea power and British mercantilism led to the Dutch Wars in 1652–1654 and in 1664–1667, which were indecisive although, given the disparity in resources, the English had the upper hand by the end of the century. In any event, after 1668 the Dutch were in alliance with the British and the Swedes. In 1672, this turned Louis XIV of France against the Netherlands, where De Witt's popularity also faded and William III Orange was restored. The French Wars – in 1678–1679 and in 1688–1697 – were ruinous but the Netherlands remained intact. The Republican Party made a comeback in the early 18th cent., but the house of Orange regained power in 1747, when the office of stadtholder was made hereditary.

During the latter part of the 18th cent. Dutch military power was much diminished and, in 1783, it lost various colonies. In 1795 the French converted the Netherlands into the Batavian Republic and Napoleon made it the kingdom of Holland with his brother Louis as king. Louis was later deposed by Napoleon and the Netherlands were annexed to France (FRENCH EUROPEAN EMPIRE). In 1815 at VIENNA, the kingdom of the Netherlands was restored and awarded the Austrian Netherlands, i.e., the rest of the Low

Countries and Luxembourg which, in 1714, had passed from Spain to the Habsburg (VIENNA). Brussels rebelled against Dutch rule and, in 1830, Belgium was constituted with most of the Austrian Netherlands. Brabant and Luxembourg were divided. Belgium kept southern Brabant and northern Luxembourg. Southern Luxembourg was physically separated from the Netherlands. After the Dutch offered to sell their province of Luxembourg to France in 1866, a gathering of European powers gave it independence under an oath of neutrality in 1867. The Netherlands was neutral during World War I, unlike Belgium, who suffered the brunt of the German advance against Paris, but in World War II it was shocked into surrender by the savage German bombardment of Rotterdam. After the war, in 1949, the Netherlands lost the Dutch East Indies. In 1948, the Netherlands formed the economic union with Belgium and Luxembourg known as Benelux, which became part of the European Economic Community in 1957 (EUROPEAN UNION). Netherlands has two capitals: Amsterdam, which is the royal capital, and the Hague, which is the seat of government.

The Netherlands Antilles comprise the islands of Curaçao, Bonaire, St Martin, Sint Eustatius, and Saba. Curaçao and Bonaire are off the coast of Venezuela. The other islands are part of the Leeward Islands of the Antilles. Acquired by the Dutch in the 17th cent., the Netherlands Antilles were known as the Dutch West Indies from 1828 to 1845. In 1993, self-ruling Curaçao chose to remain a dependency of the Netherlands. The capital of Curaçao is Willemstadt.

The island of Aruba, off the Venezuelan coast, is a self-ruling dependency of the Netherlands. It was discovered in 1492 by Ojeda. Acquired by the Dutch in 1634, it became part of the Dutch West Indies in 1828 and of the Netherlands Antilles in 1845. In 1981, Aruba separated from the Netherlands Antilles. It has chosen to remain a Dutch dependency. The capital is Oranjestad.

New Zealand

The Maoris, speakers of a language of the Austronesian family, which includes the Malay tongues, arrived in the islands of New Zealand in the 14th cent. They named them Aotearoa. In 1642, the Dutch navigator Tasman was the first European to arrive in New Zealand. Cook visited the islands in 1769. British colonization started in the 19th cent. In 1840 the European settlers signed the Treaty of Waitangi with the Maoris, in which mutual rights were recognized, but in effect it was a British show. New Zealand became a self-governing dominion in 1907, fully independent under the statute of Westminster, promulgated in London in 1931, although Great Britain handled its foreign affairs until 1947. New Zealand consists basically of the large North and South islands. The capital is Wellington, on the North Island. The Kermadec Islands were annexed in 1887. The atolls of Tokelau are a dependency. New Zealand also claims a slice of Antarctica between 160 degrees east and 150 degrees west longitudes, which it calls the Ross Dependency. The Cook Islands, a

British protectorate since 1888, and Nieu, since 1900, became dependencies of New Zealand in 1901. The Cook Islands became self-governing in 1965 and Nieu in 1974. Both are in the Pacific Ocean.

Nicaean Empire (BYZANTINE EMPIRE)

Nicaragua
Upon its sighting by Columbus in 1502, Nicaragua was peopled by native Amerindians. It was conquered for Spain by Gil Gonzalez de Avila in 1522 (SPANISH COLONIAL EMPIRE). The capital, Leon, was founded in 1610. Attached to the captaincy general of GUATEMALA, which depended on the viceroyalty of New Spain (MEXICO), Nicaragua was part of the Mexican empire of Iturbide until its dissolution in 1823. Nicaragua, with the other Central American republics, minus Panama, which was a province of New Granada, joined the CENTRAL AMERICAN FEDERATION, from which all seceded in 1838. During its early history Nicaragua was torn by liberal–conservative struggles with the conservatives strong in Granada and the liberals in Leon. Managua was chosen in 1855 as a compromise capital. Nicaragua was occupied by the United States from 1912 to 1925 and again from 1926 to 1933. During the second occupation, Sandino fought a guerrilla war of resistance until he was assassinated by the American-backed dictator Somoza. The revolutionary Sandinist movement came to power in 1979 but accepted electoral defeat in 1994. The northern coast of Nicaragua and the adjacent coast of Honduras are known as Mosquitia.

Niger
Eastern Niger was part of KANEM-BORNU (14th–17th cents.) and western Niger of SONGHAI (15th–17th cents.). The lingua franca is Hausa, which is also widely spoken in northern Nigeria. In the 19th cent. the FULANI controlled southern Niger. Niger fell under French influence as accorded in the Conference of BERLIN in 1884–1885, but France did not manage to subdue the country until 1904 because of stiff Tuareg resistance. Niger was part of Senegal in French West Africa until, in 1922, it was constituted as a separate colony (FRENCH COLONIAL EMPIRE). Niger has been independent since 1960. The capital is Niamey.

Nigeria
Nigeria is a complex country with a complex history. The north and the south were under different political influences in the pre-colonialist past. And in the south, the east and the west have different cultural backgrounds. The dominant language in the north is Hausa, which belongs to the Chadic family; in the south west, it is Yoruba and in the south east Ibo. Yoruba and Ibo belong to the separate groups within the Niger–Congo language family. Chadic languages are very distantly related to Semitic. During the 11th cent. HAUSA

states were founded in the north, notably Kano and Katsina. In the 15th cent. north-eastern Nigeria was under the influence of KANEM-BORNU. During the 16th cent. Hausaland fell to the SONGHAI empire. In the south the OYO and BENIN kingdoms were neighbours from the 12th cent. Both traced their origins to Ife. The Ibo lived mostly in tribal villages. There are notices of Kanem-Bornu and Songhai until the 17th cent. Oyo disappears in civil wars during the early 19th cent. Starting in 1804, the FULANI, under Usuman dan Fodio, conquered most of Hausaland and established the capital in Sokoto.

THE FORMATION OF MODERN NIGERIA

In the early 16th cent., the Portuguese were the first Europeans to navigate the Nigerian coast, which later thrived chaotically on the slave trade. Great Britain had banned slavery in 1807, and began to actively suppress it in Africa in the 1830s. In 1861 Britain occupied Lagos and its surrounding territories. The commercial efforts of Goldie from 1875 resulted in British control of southern Nigeria by the time of the Conference of BERLIN in 1884–1885. The ancient kingdom of Benin was forcibly annexed in 1897. Lugard conquered Sokoto in 1903. By 1906, the colony of Nigeria had been formed, to which was added the strip of German CAMEROON that went to Great Britain after World War I (GERMAN COLONIAL EMPIRE). In 1954, Nigeria was given a federal structure comprising north, east, west, and Lagos, and in 1960 Nigeria became independent. Biafra, in eastern Nigeria, seceded in 1967, until its subjection in 1970. The capital of Nigeria, originally Lagos, was moved to Abuja in 1991.

Norman Italy (11th–13th cents.; southern *Italy* and Sicily)
During 1040, with the approval of the papacy, French Normans, already established in Malta, began the conquest of southern Italy and Muslim Sicily. Robert Guiscard took Calabria in 1060, Bari in 1071, and Salerno in 1076 from the BYZANTINE EMPIRE. The duchy of Benevento (LOMBARD ITALY) also fell to the Normans, but the city itself became a papal fief. Robert's brother Roger subjected Sicily from 1061 to 1091. He inherited all Norman lands in Italy as Roger I. In 1098, he was named papal legate, although there was later a falling out with the papacy. In 1139 Naples and Capua accepted the sovereignty of the Norman king, Roger II, and Pope Innocent II was forced to recognize the Norman kingdom. By 1154, the Normans had united Sicily and southern Italy to the boundaries with the PAPAL STATES and IMPERIAL ITALY. The last Norman king, William II, named his aunt Constance, wife of the Holy Roman Emperor Henry VI Hohenstaufen, as his heir. After some resistance, Frederick II Hohenstaufen established his capital in Palermo, Sicily, in the 1220s, thus virtually renouncing his claim to the Holy Roman Empire but creating what many historians, Braudel among them, consider the first efficiently centralized European state. The Hohenstaufen were perceived as a threat by the papacy and Pope Honorius III vested

the kingdom of southern Italy and Sicily on the French Charles I Anjou, who defeated and executed Conradin, the last Hohenstaufen ruler, in 1268. The Sicilians rebelled against the French and ejected them in 1282, during the massacres of the Sicilian Vespers. Sicily passed to ARAGON and the Angevins retained NAPLES.

Normandy (10th–15th cents.; *France*)

The duchy of Normandy was founded in 923 from the foothold that marauding NORSEMEN gained in northern France. It was a fief of the French Crown, but Duke William became William the Conqueror by seizing England from its native Saxon lords after defeating Harold, the Earl of Wessex and King of ENGLAND, in the Battle of Hastings in 1066. The succession to the duchy was disputed by the heirs of William. The dispute was not settled until Geoffrey IV of Anjou occupied Normandy in 1144. Geoffrey's son, Henry, inherited Normandy in 1151 and became Henry II of England upon the death of his mother Matilda (Maud), Queen of England and wife of Geoffrey, in 1167 (ENGLAND). Normandy was annexed by France in 1202. It was taken twice by the English during the Hundred Years War (1337–1453), but in the end it passed definitely to France. In 1685, the revocation of the Edict of Nantes, which guaranteed freedom of worship to the Protestants, provoked a large migration of Huguenots from Normandy to England.

Norsemen

Norsemen is the general name given to the marauders and, eventually, conquerors who sailed from Scandinavia and raided the European coast from Russia to France and Ireland from the 9th to the 11th cents. The western Norsemen, called Vikings in Britain and IRELAND, peopled ICELAND and Greenland and, captained by Leif Ericsson, discovered, ca. 1000, a land called Vinland, identified today as Newfoundland, Canada. Humble Norse ruins were found in the site of Anse-au-Meadows in Newfoundland. The Norse invaders of ENGLAND were mostly from DENMARK. The colonizers of Iceland and Greenland, and consequently the discoverers of America, were from NORWAY. In France the Norsemen were known as Normans. The direct Danish conquest of England met with great opposition from the Saxons of Wessex, but the Norsemen founded NORMANDY, northern France, in 923, and from this duchy, vassal of the king of France, they conquered England from the Saxons in 1066. By then the Normans were French-speakers. It is through them that English has deep affinities with Latin. Normans also conquered Naples, southern Italy, and Sicily in the 11th cent. (NORMAN ITALY). These Normans in turn led the Latin attack against the BYZANTINE EMPIRE in Greece (LATIN STATES). The eastern Norsemen or Varangians were from Sweden and their greatest achievement was the creation of the principalities, from Novgorod to Kiev, that later constituted Kievan Rus, the antecessor of RUSSIA. The Varangians were thoroughly Slavicized.

North German Confederation (19th cent.)
A bridging political structure, the North German Confederation was created by PRUSSIA in its drive to unify GERMANY (1866–1871). Although it did not include BAVARIA, Prussian hegemony over southern Germany was indisputable. The constitution of the Northern German Confederation was adopted by the German Reich in 1871.

North Korea (KOREA)

Northern India (4th cent. BC–18th cent. AD)
In recounting the complex history of the Indian subcontinent before British India, a practical approach is to distinguish between Northern India, the Deccan or CENTRAL INDIA, and SOUTHERN INDIA. The heart of northern India is the Ganges River Basin. In modern political terms Northern India embraces the country of Pakistan, the historical kingdoms of KASHMIR and PUNJAB, and the territories of the Indian states of Bihar, Gujarat, northern Madhya Pradesh, Rajasthan, Sikkim, Uttar Pradesh, and Bengal (*India*). The early history of Pakistan is to be found in the perplexing INDUS RIVER VALLEY CIVILIZATION. After that and until the political partition of the subcontinent, its history is inseparable from that of India, except that there were political influences such as BACTRIA, the SAKAS, KUSHANA, and the EPHTHALITES, which originated beyond the subcontinental frontiers. Northern India was the homeland of the Vedic kingdoms (VEDIC INDIA) and saw the formation of the first structured state, MAGADHA, in the 6th cent. BC. Magadha lasted until the 1st cent. BC, when the Satavahana of Central India extended their influence to the north. The SAKAS displaced the Satavahana, but northern India was disunited except briefly under KUSHANA until the GUPTAS, who ruled from the 4th to the 6th cents. AD. After the Guptas, northern India was besieged by the Ephthalites and disunited again until HARSHA'S KINGDOM. However, it would be an error to think of this territory as a politically unified whole. Kingdoms rose and fell amidst the general disunion. During the 7th and 8th cents. northern India was disputed by various warring dynasties, among which the Gurjara Pratiharas of Rajasthan, the Pala and Sena of Bengal, and the Rashtrakutas of Central India figured prominently. They were overwhelmed from the 9th to the 10th cents. by the martial, but also very disunited RAJPUTS from the dry western state of Rajasthan. The history of Northern and Central India in this period is very complicated, but it is also mostly about ephemeral events and obscure dynasties and kingdoms. Some historians consider the history of Northern India from the 9th to the 13th cent. to be the equivalent of the feudalized Middle Ages in Europe. These comparisons are often just incitations to disputes. During the 11th cent. the Rajput

statelets were raided by CHOLAS from southern India and by the Afghans from Ghazni. During the 12th cent., the GHAZNAVIDS exploited the chronic infighting of the Rajputs and conquered Delhi, where they were dispossessed by the GHURIDS, whose generals founded the DELHI SULTANATE in the 13th cent. During the 13th cent. northern India was subjected to Mongol raids and, in the late 14th cent., Tamerlane (TIMURID EMPIRE AND SUCCESSOR STATES) cut the sinews of Delhi. In the 15th cent. Lodi kings from Afghanistan restored the sultanate and warred with the Rajputs. In the 16th cent., northern India was stabilized by the Mughals from Ferghana (MUGHAL EMPIRE), descendants of Tamerlane, who eventually fell to the British in the 18th cent. (BRITISH INDIA).
(*See chronology under* Indian Subcontinent.)

Northumbria (ENGLAND)

Norway

Before the 9th cent. the history of Scandinavia is obscure. The name NORSE-MEN is synonymous with Vikings and applies to Norwegians and Danes, who raided in western Europe. Swedish marauders and traders, who concentrated on the Baltic Sea and Russia, were known as Varangians. The first Norwegian king was Harold I, ca. 900, who united Norway and occupied the Orkneys and the Shetlands. The Norsemen settled ICELAND and Normandy. Norwegians at home resisted political unity. Another king that tried to unify the country was Haakon I, ca. 935. Christianity was introduced in Iceland by the Norwegian king Olaf I, ca. 1000. Norway itself was partly Christianized and it was Olaf II (1015–1028) who completed the process. He was defeated by the Danish king Canute the Great (d. 1035), who also conquered England. Canute's empire was the largest ever known in Northern Europe up to that time. Norway soon fragmented, but it flourished under Haakon IV and Magnus VI from 1217 to 1280. In 1319, it was joined under Magnus VII to Sweden, but in 1343 Norway went its own way. Haakon VI married Margaret of Denmark, who united Norway, Denmark, and Sweden by the Union of Kalmar in 1397. Sweden, though nominally part of the union until 1523, was autonomous, but Norway became part of Denmark.

AN UNPAID DOWRY

The Orkneys passed to Scotland in 1231. Iceland was Norwegian from 1262. The Norse colonists of Greenland (10th cent.) died out during the 14th and 15th cents. Norwegians recolonized it in the 18th cent. The Shetlands were annexed by Scotland in 1472 as an unpaid dowry. After the first deposition of Napoleon (1814), Norway was ceded to Sweden in retribution for Denmark's French leanings. Both Iceland and Greenland remained under the Danish Crown. In 1905 Norway declared its independence from Sweden, who did not take it well but did nothing strenuous to prevent it. Norway was organized as a constitutional monarchy and a prince of Denmark was chosen as king. To deny Great Britain bases on the North Sea, Nazi Germany occupied Norway from 1940 to 1945.

The capital of Norway is Oslo (formerly Christiania). Norwegians speak their own language of the Indo-European family, which includes the Romance languages. Norway possesses overseas territories, beyond or near the Arctic Circle. The Svalbard archipelago, whose main island is Spitsbergen, was discovered by Norsemen in 1194. For most of the time it was unclaimed, but in 1920 Norwegian sovereignty was recognized. Jan Mayen, discovered in the early 17th cent., was incorporated by Norway in 1929. Bouvert Island, discovered in 1739, was occupied by Norway in 1927. Peter I Island was discovered by a Russian in 1821 and claimed by Norway in 1929. In 1939, Norway also claimed a wedge of Antarctica, called Queen Maud Land, between 20 degrees west and 45 degrees east longitudes.

Nubia (KUSH)

Nueva Granada (COLOMBIA)

Numidia (3rd–2nd cents. BC; northern Africa)
Formed by Berbers, ancient Numidia, which territorially corresponds to today's Algeria, was the site of colonies from PHOENICIA, although not under CARTHAGE. It was an independent kingdom in 238 BC. For a time a Roman ally, it became a Roman province in 106 BC. Its most famous ruler, Jugurtha, damned Roman treachery at Rome's very gates. The principal cities of Numidia were Cirtus and Hippo. The latter was the see of Augustine.

O

Oghuz (GHUZZ)

Oirats (MONGOLIA)

Olmecs (MESOAMERICAN CIVILIZATIONS)

Oman
Previously peopled by scattered tribes, the territory of the kingdom of Oman was controlled by the Portuguese in 1508. In 1659, it became part of the OTTOMAN EMPIRE. Ottoman authority was weak and an independent kingdom was established, capital Muscat, in 1741. At its height in the early 19th cent., Oman held a loose sway over all of southern Arabia, Zanzibar, the facing coast of Persia, and the coast of Baluchistan. In 1856, Zanzibar became autonomous under Arab sultans. Other dependent territories gradually fell away, but Oman held an enclave in Pakistan until 1958. Although much influenced by Great Britain, it never became a part of the British Colonial Empire. The capital of Oman is Muscat.

Orange Free State (19th–20th cents.; South Africa)
When the British took Cape Town and created the Colony of the Cape of Good Hope (1806), many of its original settlers, the mostly Dutch Boers with some French, moved in various directions (1835–1845). In Natal, they were pursued and evicted by the British, but in 1854 they achieved recognition for the Orange Free State, capital Bloemfontein. Together with the sister Transvaal Republic, the Orange Free State formed an alliance against British encroachment and fought valiantly but unavailingly the South African or Boer War (1899–1902). In 1910, the Orange Free State, together with Natal, Cape Colony, and Transvaal, constituted the Union of South Africa.

Ostrogothic Italy (5th–6th cents.; *Italy*)
The deposition of Romulus Augustulus by Odoacer (476), a general of Germanic origin in the service of ROME, was not really a transformation of the rump Roman Empire in the west. However, the Ostrogothic invasion and conquest of Italy in 493 under the command of Theodoric, who defeated and later assassinated Odoacer, did mean the definite end of the last vestiges of Imperial Rome. Ostrogothic rule proved ephemeral for, from 535, the BYZANTINE EMPIRE – which was still the Roman Empire in the east – invaded and conquered Ravenna, Rome, Naples, and Sicily (BYZANTINE ITALY). After 568, the Lombards began eroding Byzantine power (LOMBARD ITALY).

Ostrogoths (GOTHS)

Ottoman Empire (14th–20th cents.; core area: *Anatolia* and *Balkans*)
In the second half of the 13th cent., as the Seljuk RUM sultanate in western Anatolia started disintegrating into the ANATOLIAN EMIRATES, the Ottoman Turks occupied a sort of Turkish march across the Bosphorus from Constantinople. The Ottomans became independent of the Seljuks under Osman I in 1290. Led by Orkhan (1326–1362), the Ottomans conquered the Byzantine principalities that still subsisted in western Anatolia (BYZANTINE EMPIRE). In 1326, Bursa fell and became the Ottoman capital. Orkhan crossed the Hellespont and took Edirne (Greek Adrianople) in 1361, where the new Ottoman capital was established. Orkhan was also the first Ottoman ruler to use the title of sultan. Under Murad I, the Ottomans defeated the Serbs in the decisive Battle of Kosovo Fields in 1389 (SERBIA), which made them the most powerful force in the Balkans. They also conquered MACEDONIA. It was Murad who founded the Janissaries, a corps recruited from Christian boys captured by the Turks. Under Bajazet I the Lightning (1389–1402), the empire expanded in eastern Anatolia and in the Balkans. Cappadocia was conquered in 1391. From 1393 to 1396, the Ottomans annexed BULGARIA, and in 1397 they occupied Thessaly. But just as they were closing the circle on Constantinople, Tamerlane fell on their rear (TIMURID EMPIRE AND SUCCESSOR STATES). In 1402 he managed to swing Bajazet's Turkish troops to his side. The Ottoman emperor, left mostly with his Janissaries, was defeated and captured. The Anatolian Emirates, which the Ottomans had suppressed, rose again. Once the fragile Timurid Empire fell apart – even before Tamerlane's death in 1405 – there was a struggle for the succession among Bajazet's sons (1402 to 1413), from which Mehmet I (1413–1421) emerged triumphant and consolidated the core Ottoman territories in western Anatolia. Such rivalries were what led victorious Ottoman heirs to adopt the practice of executing their siblings. By the reign of Murad II (1421–1451) the Ottomans had re-conquered most of Anatolia. Salonika was taken in 1430. The Ottomans then proceeded to their main objective and, in 1453, under Mehmet II (1451–1481), they conquered Constantinople, which is why Mehmet is often considered the real founder of the Ottoman Empire. A successor Byzantine state on the south-eastern shore of the Black Sea, TREBIZOND, which had been founded after the conquest of Constantinople by the Fourth Crusade in 1204, fell to the Ottomans in 1461. Under the Ottomans, Constantinople became known as Istambul and the court itself as the Porte, also the Sublime Porte, because it stood guard on the Bosporus, the door to the Black Sea.

TITLE DEEDS TO EMPIRE

With a new imperial capital, in a sense armed with title deeds to the fallen Byzantine Empire, the Ottomans resumed their triumphant march in Europe.

In 1458, they captured the Acropolis of Athens and in 1461 they invaded Morea (Peloponnesus) and ejected whatever remained there of an occupying Latin presence. Despite desperate resistance, the Serbs were finally subjugated in 1459. VALACHIA (southern Romania), which resisted ferociously under Vlad the Impaler (the historical model for Dracula), was annexed in 1462. Bosnia and adjacent lands were conquered from 1469 to 1482 (BOSNIA-HERZEGOVINA). The Albanians had been subjugated in previous campaigns, but they found an inspired leader, Skander Beg, and they held out until 1478 (ALBANIA). The Montenegrins were not reduced until 1499. Even then the Ottomans did not bother stamping out all pockets of resistance, so that MONTENEGRO was practically autonomous in its more inaccessible redoubts and, in 1799, the Ottomans, without by any means granting independence, simply decided to let them be. Mehmet II's successor, Bajazet II (1481–1513), was challenged by his son, Selim I (1513–1520), and deposed with the support of the Janissaries. Selim was – with his contemporaries Babur, founder of the MUGHAL EMPIRE, and Shah Ismail of the Persian SAFAVIDS – among the first Asian rulers to use cannon. Under his rule, the Ottomans in 1514 rounded out the core territory of future ROMANIA with the annexation of MOLDAVIA to Valachia. It was the policy of the Porte that once it controlled strategic points and garrisoned crucial fortresses, it could save itself toil and trouble. As to the administration of the conquered territories, they left them in the hands either of local lieutenants or of governors (hospodars) sent from Istambul, often Phanariots or Greeks who were willing to collect taxes and do the bidding of their Islamic masters. Under the Ottomans, most of the Balkans, with Sofia as its capital, was known as Rumelia. Eastern Rumelia is southern Bulgaria.

ISLAMIC REUNIFICATION

The Ottomans were motivated not only to reconstitute their predecessor empire. They were Muslims and were also intent on the reunification of Islam. In 1475, they had taken the CRIMEA and part of the Kuban steppe (north east of the Black Sea). Syria, Palestine, and Mameluke Egypt were conquered in 1517 and Selim assumed the title of caliph. Ottoman rule was extended in 1517–1520 as far as Yemen. Under Suleyman I the Magnificent (1520–1566) Cyrenaica or eastern Libya (1521) and Mesopotamia (1534) were annexed by the Ottomans. In 1526, CROATIA and HUNGARY were conquered. The Croatians had a fallback in Habsburg lands, and the Turkish hold on their territory was never secure. The Hungarians were not so fortunate. They were decisively defeated in Mohacs and they became part of the Ottoman Empire for over a century and a half. TRANSYLVANIA was invaded in 1541.

While these land conquests were going on, the Ottomans had built a powerful navy of galleys with which, in 1519, they occupied ALGERIA and took

RHODES in 1522, Tripoli in 1551, and CYPRUS in 1571. They were contained by Spanish and Venetian forces in the Battle of Lepanto in 1571. However, this Christian victory did not do away with Ottoman naval power. Tunis, which had been lost to Charles V in 1535, was recovered by Selim II in 1574. After securing the coast of north Africa, the Ottomans limited themselves to naming beys in the more important ports, who thereafter acted on their own and formed collectively what are known as the BARBARY STATES. Ottoman power reached ARMENIA, GEORGIA, and AZERBAIJAN (1548), but Persia proved a hard nut to crack and Baghdad was only occupied in 1638 under Murad IV (IRAN). Persia itself remained independent and an Ottoman rival. QATAR was annexed in 1555 and the whole of Arabia was encompassed in 1659 with the annexation of OMAN under Mehmet IV (1648–1687). Crete was conquered as late as 1669. The Ottoman Empire had reached the acme of its power. It was also the beginning of its eventual downfall, for under the same ruler the Turks were defeated in the siege of Vienna in 1683, which signalled retreat in the Balkans.

The 'sick man of Europe'

The long and complex phase of the decadence of the Ottoman Empire became manifest with the fall of Hungary to the HABSBURG EMPIRE in 1697. This was immediately followed by the Habsburg annexation of Transylvania and the Banat in 1718. This happened under Ahmed III (1703–1730), who was deposed by the Janissaries, thus indicating the internal weakness of the sultanate. The disintegration of the empire came about in four ways: some islands and territories were or became peripheral to the empire and were left on their own, most of them eventually to be absorbed by other powers; subject nations rebelled and gained their independence; powerful neighbours annexed territory; and World War I came along and gave the empire its quietus. The Greeks won their independence in 1829 with west European help. The Ottomans concerned themselves little with the Barbary States. The Porte presumably was satisfied with their nominal vassalage and could not defend them when Algeria (1830) and Tunisia (1881) fell to France, and Libya was conquered by Italy (1914). In Arabia, Oman (1741) and Yemen (1818) became autonomous and Aden was incorporated into the BRITISH COLONIAL EMPIRE (1839). Without much naval power left, the Ottomans lost Cyprus in 1878 (to Great Britain), Crete in 1889 (to Greece), the Dodecanese in 1912 (to Italy). On their eastern frontiers the Ottomans were replaced by Persia in Armenia and Azerbaijan during the 18th cent. Crimea (1783) and Georgia (1829) fell to Russia. Though not strictly speaking peripheral, Egypt was a difficult land to govern and the Ottomans left that task to Muhammad Ali, a formal vassal who ruled it autonomously, starting in 1805. His descendants were kings of EGYPT until 1952. Serbia achieved its independence in 1867. After a disastrous war against

Russia (1878), the Porte had to recognize the independence of Romania and Montenegro and the autonomy of Bulgaria (Congress of BERLIN). Also in the same year, the Habsburg Empire, which had absorbed Croatia during the 18th cent., took over the administration of Bosnia-Herzegovina. Bulgaria became fully independent in 1908.

Young Turks

In Istambul a reformist and nationalist military movement known as Young Turks became the decisive political influence. Its leader Enver Pasha became dictator in 1913. He refused to accommodate the grievances of the minorities. After the second Balkan War (1913), the Ottoman Empire lost Macedonia, Rumelia, and northern Greece. Enver Pasha lined up his country with the Central Powers (Germany and Austria) in World War I. The Turks inflicted a painful defeat on British, Australian, and New Zealand troops in the Gallipoli campaign, conceived by Churchill to control the Dardanelles and force the entry to the Black Sea (1915). But the Ottoman Empire was beset in the Near East, where its Arabian dependencies rebelled and the British occupied Jerusalem in 1917. Beleaguered in the Balkans by Allied forces, it surrendered on 30 October 1918. In the Paris Peace Conference (1919), by the Treaty of Sèvres, the former vast empire was granted only parts of Anatolia. The Greeks were given control of Smyrna. Mustafa Kemal, who was later called Kemal Ataturk (father of the Turks), rallied Turkish forces, subjected the Armenians, defeated and expelled the Greeks, and in 1922 deposed the last sultan, Muhammad VI (who had accepted the terms of Sèvres). He abolished the caliphate in 1925, by which date he had already launched modern TURKEY. (*See chronologies under* Anatolia, Balkans, Iran, *and* Maghreb.)

Oyo (13th–19th cents.; *Sub-Saharan Africa*)
The kingdom of Oyo was located in northern and western Nigeria and was hegemonic over the Yoruba. The Yoruba were a people of central Nigeria. Yoruba slaves took African animist beliefs to Brazil and Cuba. Oyo dissolved into civil wars during the early 19th cent. It left no successor state. (*See chronology under* Western and Sub-Saharan Africa.)

P

Paekche (KOREA)

Pagan (MYANMAR)

Pakistan
SEE ENTRY IN 'PROVINCES AND REGIONS'
The history of Pakistan is that of the INDUS RIVER VALLEY CIVIL-
IZATION, NORTHERN INDIA, KASHMIR, and PUNJAB. The territorial
formation of modern Pakistan is part of the history of BRITISH INDIA. The
British tried unsuccessfully to pacify the Indian frontier with Afghanistan
starting in 1839. They finally settled the problem by creating the North West
Frontier province in 1901 with the territories they annexed from
AFGHANISTAN. The rest of Pakistan had been occupied between 1843 and
1849. The man-on-the-spot theory of imperialist expansion stems in part from
Napier's *peccavi* ('I have sinned') telegram, which proclaimed the non-offi-
cial-policy occupation of Sind. Pakistan came into being, including the actual
Pakistan and BANGLADESH, as a result of the partition of British India in
1947. The Hindu prince of Kashmir chose Indian sovereignty for his Muslim
subjects. In a war with INDIA in 1948, Pakistan retained part of Himalayan
Kashmir, but lost the heartland around Srinagar. This open sore in the relations
between India and Pakistan has resulted in two additional wars: in 1965, over
the Gujarat border; and in 1971–1972, when India intervened in support of
Bangladeshi independence. After the partition of Kashmir the border between
the two countries, which is illuminated at night from the coast to the
Himalayas, has been *de facto* unchanged according to the principle that 'you
get to keep what you have in your power' (*uti ibi uti possidetis*). East Pakistan
was the Islamic eastern half of Bengal, which had been separated by the
British in 1905. East Pakistan rebelled against the central government in West
Pakistan and with Indian help obtained its independence in 1971. Karachi was
the first capital of Pakistan. After 1960 it was replaced by Islamabad, built for
that purpose. Urdu, closely related to Hindi, is the official language of Pakistan, but nearly half the population speak Panjabi. They are all languages of
the Indo-Aryan group.
(*See chronology under* Indian Subcontinent.)

Palau
Formerly part of the Caroline Islands, successively under Spanish, German,
Japanese, and American control, Palau, whose people speak an Austronesian
language – a family which also includes the Malay languages – became

independent, in free association with the United States, in 1994. The capital of Palau is Koror.

Palestine (16th cent. BC–20th cent.; *Near East*)
The ancient PHILISTIA and Biblical Canaan, Palestine was under Egyptian hegemony during the New Kingdom (PHARAONIC EGYPT). There was a kingdom of Kadesh in the 15th cent. BC, vassal of the HITTITE KINGDOM. Israel and Judah flourished from the 12th to the 8th cents. BC. Palestine was ruled by ASSYRIA and BABYLONIA and later became a province of the ACHAEMENID and ALEXANDRIAN EMPIRES. Under ROME, it was known indistinctly as Palestine or Judae. It became part of the BYZANTINE EMPIRE until conquered by ISLAM in 638. Afterwards it was mostly under the control of Egyptian dynasties (EGYPT). After the Battle of Manzikert (1071), in which the Seljuks trounced the Byzantines, Christianity perceived a menace which was the spark for the Crusades and the eventual establishment of the CRUSADER STATES. Recovered for Islam by Saladin in the Battle of Hattin in 1187, Palestine became part of the OTTOMAN EMPIRE in 1516. The Turks surrendered it to Great Britain in 1917. In Palestine (minus JORDAN), the British held a mandate over territories which today correspond to ISRAEL, the Gaza Strip, and the West Bank (the land west of the Jordan River to the Mediterranean coastal plain) (PALESTINIAN AUTHORITY).

ZIONISM

Since the late 19th cent., harking to the call of Zionism, there was a migratory movement of Jews to Palestine. The Balfour Declaration (1917), offering Jews a homeland in Palestine, was an incentive for more settlement, although Great Britain never actually encouraged it. The movement became a flood after World War II as a consequence of Nazi genocide. By 1947, there were half as many Jews as Arabs in Palestine and they practically colonized entire areas, including cities like Tel Aviv, where they were in the majority, and Jaffa. Conflict between Jews and Arabs was imminent and Great Britain, despairing of finding a solution, handed the problem to the UNITED NATIONS, which elaborated a partition map for Palestine. Upon British departure in 1948, the Arabs attacked and thus began the first Arab–Jewish War, the Israeli War of Independence. It lasted until January 1949, with truces which allowed the Jewish side to supply itself (mainly through purchases of war material in the United States). At the end, ISRAEL had been created with most of Palestine, except for the Gaza Strip, which the Egyptians held successfully, and the West Bank, which the Arab Legion actually carved out for Jordan.

Palestinian Authority
The Palestinian Authority is the result of an internationally-sponsored, American-backed agreement (1993) to give self-rule to the Palestinian people in

Gaza and the West Bank. It is supposed to have control of these territories through their gradual cession by ISRAEL. The head of the Palestinian Authority is Yasser Arafat. The administrative centre is located in Gaza. The territory of Gaza was the land of the Philistines (Philistia). During the Israeli War of Independence (1948–1949), it was held by Egypt, who was forced to give it up, with the Sinai, after the Six Day War (1967). Although Egypt recovered the Sinai (1982), Gaza remained under Israeli control. Modern Gaza evolved from the refugee camps of Palestinians that fled or were driven out during the Israeli War of Independence (first Arab–Israeli War) in 1948–1949.

Palhae (PO HAI)

Pallavas (SOUTHERN INDIA)

Palmyra (3rd cent.; *Near East*)
The Roman general, Septimius Odenathus, held the eastern frontier of ROME against the SASANID EMPIRE, on which he inflicted a defeat in AD 260. He allowed the Roman territories of Syria and eastern Anatolia to become independent of Rome with Palmyra as its capital. He was succeeded by his wife, the ambitious Zenobia, Palmyra was conquered by Emperor Valerian in AD 273. The city itself, which had flourished on trade with the east, fell into ruins.

Panama
Panama was a province of COLOMBIA, inherited from the SPANISH COLONIAL EMPIRE. It was attached to the *audiencia* (higher court) in Bogotá. Under strong foreign prodding, it declared its independence in 1903 when Colombia did not approve a treaty with the United States providing for the construction of a canal across the isthmus of Panama. American warships prevented Colombian troops from intervening. The Panama Canal Zone was created around the canal, which was constructed in a mammoth and costly (in money and lives) engineering feat from 1904 to 1914. The Canal Zone reverted by treaty to Panama in 1977. The handover of the canal was completed in 2000. In late 1989 the United States invaded Panama to overthrow the dictator Noriega, who surrendered and was later tried and convicted on drug charges. Panama City is the capital of Panama.

Papal States (4th–19th cents.; central *Italy*)
The origins of the Papal States were imperial titles of authority granted to the church in Rome and other Italian lands, including Sicily and Sardinia, known collectively as Patrimonium Petri. The Bishop of Rome, primate of the Christian world, was undoubtedly a stabilising influence during the downfall of the Roman Empire in the west (ROME). BYZANTINE ITALY respected the See of Rome, but papal wordly authority was gradually eroded, especially after the Lombard conquest of Italy (LOMBARD ITALY). In 754, Pepin, son of

Charles Martel and father of Charlemagne, granted Rome to the papacy, including the surrounding lands (Lazio), Umbria, the Marche, and Romagna-Pentapolis or the eastern part of Emilia. When Lombard power in northern Italy was definitely broken by Charlemagne, the Emperor made formal recognition of the papal territories in 774, whose legitimacy was further sustained with the forged document called the Donation of Constantine (CAROLINGIAN EMPIRE). Benevento, the former Lombard duchy, was transferred by the Normans to the papacy in the 11th cent. (NORMAN ITALY).

THE BABYLONIAN CAPTIVITY

From the 10th to the 14th cents., the emperors of the HOLY ROMAN EMPIRE tried to validate their claim on CAROLINGIAN ITALY. This gave rise in northern Italy to the Guelph (anti-imperial) and Ghibelline (pro-imperial) parties. By the middle of the 14th cent. the tremendous and complex historical task had ended in failure. Avignon became a papal domain as a consequence of the French sequestration of the popes to that city known as the Babylonian Captivity (1309–1417), during which time the Papal States were deeply divided. The consolidation of the secular power of the papacy was the result of the political labours of two implacable enemies, Cesare Borgia and Pope Julius II (1503–1513). Borgia, son of the sybaritic Spanish Pope Alexander VI (1492–1503), conquered Romagna, Urbino, and other lands. Upon his accession, Pope Julius II evicted him from his possessions, which he annexed to the other papal territories (Lazio and the Marche). Julius later conquered Ravenna, Rimini, and Faenza (1509). The restoration of the Papal States was again tested by the national rivalries that had Italy as a battleground during the 16th cent. (HABSBURG EMPIRE). The secular power of the papacy was much diminished during the 17th and 18th cents. After the French Revolution, Avignon voted to rejoin France (1791). During the Napoleonic era the Papal States as such ceased to exist (FRENCH NAPOLEONIC EMPIRE). They were restored in 1815 but finally had to be surrendered, not gracefully by any means, to the Kingdom of Italy during the *risorgimento*, the unification of Italy by SARDINIA (1858–1870). VATICAN CITY was created in the 20th cent.

Papua New Guinea

Papua New Guinea occupies the eastern part of the island of New Guinea, the second largest in the world. With over 700 languages belonging to the Austronesian and the Papuan families – related Malay tongues are all Austronesian but Papuan is a family of its own – it has the highest density of languages of any country in the world. Papua New Guinea was formed with north-eastern New Guinea, a German colony in 1884 that became an Australian-administered territory after World War I, and south-eastern New Guinea, a British colony (1884), which as Papua was passed to Australia in 1905. They were merged in 1949 and became independent with their actual name in 1975.

The capital of Papua New Guinea is Port Moresby. The Bismarck Archipelago, part of Papua New Guinea, includes New Britain, New Ireland, and the Admiralty Islands.

Paraguay

Peopled by Guaraní Amerindians, the territory of Paraguay, between the Paraná and the Paraguay rivers, was reconnoitred by the Spanish seeking a route to Perú. Asuncion, the capital, was established around 1536. Paraguay was separated from Buenos Aires in 1617 and entrusted to Jesuit missionaries. It became famous as a sort of real-world Utopia. In 1776 it was incorporated into the viceroyalty of La Plata (SPANISH COLONIAL EMPIRE). In 1811 it peacefully replaced colonial authorities and after 1814 was turned by the dictator Rodriguez Francia into a hermit state. In 1865, another dictator, Solano Lopez, tried to intervene in the internal affairs of turbulent URUGUAY and plunged his country into a war with Argentina, Brazil, and Uruguay, the War of the Triple Alliance, which lasted until 1870 and harrowed the land. Brazil, which did most of the fighting on the enemy side, took a chunk out of Paraguay in the north. Argentina also annexed a part for its province of Entre Rios. Between 1932 and 1935, Paraguay fought with Bolivia and won for itself the territory of Chaco, west of the Paraguay River (also known as Gran Chaco in its extension beyond Paraguay to Brazil and Argentina). Guaraní is, with Spanish, an official language of Paraguay, the only Latin American country to have given this status to a native tongue. Guaraní is also spoken in areas of Brazil and Argentina adjacent to Paraguay.

Parma (16th–19th cents.; northern *Italy*)
Originally a Roman colony founded in the 2nd cent. BC, later Byzantine, Ostrogothic, Lombard, Carolingian, and Imperial, Parma became a free commune in the 12th cent., afterwards ruled by MILAN and France. In 1513 it was annexed by Julius II to the PAPAL STATES. In 1545, Pope Paul III created an autonomous duchy with Parma and Piacenza which he conferred on his son Pier Luigi Farnese, in whose family it stayed until 1731. Parma was Spanish Bourbon from 1731 to 1802 and French to 1815, after which it was accorded to Napoleon's Habsburg widow, Marie Louise. Napoleon's son (1811–1832) – called L'Aiglon (eaglet) by the French – was nominally King of Parma from 1811 to 1818. From 1815 he was a virtual prisoner in Austria until his death. In 1847, Parma became a Bourbon domain which passed to Italy in 1860.

Parthenopean Republic (NAPLES)

Parthia (3rd cent. BC–3rd cent. AD; *Middle East*)
The region of Parthia originally extended over eastern Iran and Turkmenistan. The Parthian Empire, constituted by a people that came down the eastern side

of the Caspian Sea (possibly SCYTHIANS), was founded ca. 250 BC by Arsaces as an important and extensive offshoot in the dismemberment of the SELEUCID EMPIRE. It occupied the whole of the northern tier of Persia and had a loose relation of suzerainty to the surrounding more or less autonomous regions: Persis, the homeland of the Persians; Osroeme (Edessa) and Mesene or Characene in Mesopotamia (late 2nd cent. BC); Gordyene and Adiabene east of the Tigris (1st cent. BC); Elymais in Susiana (1st cent. BC). Both Parthia and ARMENIA, which had separated from the Seleucid Empire ca. 190 BC, claimed the territory of Azerbaijan, called Media Atropatene by the Romans. Parthia was besieged by a branch of the SAKA or Asian SCYTHIANS in the late 2nd cent. BC, but they were eventually subjected in the 1st cent. BC. In 53 BC, Parthia defeated a Roman attempt at conquest led by the triumvir Marcus Licinius Crassus, thus virtually setting the limit to Roman expansion towards the east, although Trajan led an expedition against Parthia in 114–116 (ROME). In AD 227, Parthia fell to Artaxerxes, the founder of the Persian SASANID EMPIRE.
(*See chronology under* Iran.)

Patrimonium Petri (PAPAL STATES)

Patzinaks (PETCHENEGS)

Pelasgians or Sea-peoples
It was known in the 19th cent. that the Egyptian New Kingdom had repelled attacks from the west and the east and by sea raiders during the late 13th and early 12th cents. BC (PHARAONIC EGYPT). These invasions were attributed to Libyans and Philistines. A French scholar suggested in 1872 that the invaders were really 'Pelasgians' from the Aegean Sea. The French Egyptologist Maspero turned this suggestion into a grand theory according to which there was a vast migration into the Balkans by Indo-European Illyrians, who pushed other populations down into Greece and against the Aegean coast of Anatolia, where they set off the movement of the Pelasgians. Subsequently, evidence was found for the collapse of some Near Eastern civilizations at the time of the frustrated attacks against Egypt. At around 1200 BC, the dominant cultures and states in the Near East were: MYCENEAN GREECE, the HITTITE KINGDOM in central Anatolia, PHILISTIA in the southern coast of Palestine, ASSYRIA, and Egypt. Mycenean and Hittite civilizations were destroyed at that time, as were Syrian and Philistine cities (Ugarit, Lachish), all of which bolstered the migrations thesis, virtually dogma by the 1920s. The thesis is grievously flawed in various points, particularly the speculations about migrations from the Balkans, for which there is no archaeological evidence. Nevertheless, it was a brilliant coup by Maspero, who wrote before there was any knowledge of the wholesale devastation in the ancient Near East, although there is no basis for talk of a general collapse: Assyria, Egypt, even

231

Philistia survived. It is more likely that the affected regions were overwhelmed by neighbouring peoples, either by land or sea invasion, perhaps employing new methods of combat. The existence of the Pelasgians as a people different from the known or presumed inhabitants of Greece, the Near East, and the Mediterranean islands is doubtful.

Peloponnesian League (5th cent. BC; Ancient *Greece*)
The Peloponnesian League, created by Sparta, existed by 500 BC. Its other principal member was Corinth. Spartans fought with Athenians against the ACHAEMENID EMPIRE during the Persian Wars 500–449 BC. After the Persian threat was over, the Athenian Empire (DELIAN LEAGUE) and the Spartans came to blows because of Corinthian fears of Athenian imperialism. The Peloponnesian War (431–404 BC) resulted in the utter defeat of Athens. It is thought by historians that in the Peloponnesian League Sparta played the hegemon, whereas Athens actually acted as imperial power within the Delian League.
(*See chronology under* Greece (Ancient).)

Pergamum (3rd–2nd cents. BC; *Anatolia*)
A Greek kingdom in western Anatolia, separated from the SELEUCID EMPIRE, Pergamum was ruled by the Greek Attalids from 263 to 133 BC. To fend off MACEDON and Seleucid Syria the rulers of Pergamum followed a pro-Roman policy, which culminated and ended when Attalus III bequeathed the kingdom to the Roman people. Pergamum was a brilliant cultural centre. Its ruins in Turkey are grandiose.
(*See chronology under* Anatolia.)

Period of Disunity (after Han) (4th–6th cents.; *China*)
With the fall of the HAN dynasty in 221, China was divided into three kingdoms. One of these, Wei, absorbed the others and ruled a united China from 266 to 302 as the Western Chin (Jin). At that point, barbarians falling upon each other in the north drove upon China the people known as southern HSIUNG-NU. The lord of the Hsiung-nu was called the shan yü of the five hordes. His onslaught brought about the creation of various sinicized barbarian dynasties. Western Chin was forced south, where it was succeeded by the Eastern Chin dynasty (317–420). China would remain divided between north and south until the SUI reunification in 589.

Toba Wei

In the north, the Toba Turks fought their way through the JUAN-JUAN from their base in western Manchuria, defeated the HSIA (a Hunnic tribe in Shaanxi) and founded a state in northern China which lasted from 386 to 534. Their kingdom was known as Northern Wei or Toba Wei. The Northern Wei

squeezed the kingdoms founded by the Hsiung-nu until they disappeared in 439. Northern Wei stretched from the coast of Hebei (Hopeh) to Gansu (Kansu). Being outside the Confucian tradition, it was the first to patronize Buddhism in China. The Northern Wei divided into Western Wei (534–557) and Eastern Wei (534–550). Northern Ch'i (Qi) (550–577) succeeded Eastern Wei in north-eastern China and Northern Chou (557–581) did the same to Western Wei. In the south, the Eastern Chin were succeeded by Earlier Sung (Song) (420–479), Southern Ch'i (Qi) (479–502), Southern Liang (502–557), and Southern Ch'en (557–589). Around 560, then, there were three main kingdoms in China: Northern Ch'i (Qi), Northern Chou, and Southern Ch'en. Northern Chou conquered Northern Ch'i (Qi). There was a fourth kingdom, centred around Sian and it successively took over Northern Chou (581) and Southern Ch'en (589), thus reuniting China under the Sui dynasty, which only lasted until 618. At the end of the post-Han period of disunity, China was intact but it had retreated from Korea and Manchuria and had given ground in the south west to the Thai kingdom of NAN CHAO. The short-lived Sui dynasty (581–617) was followed by the longer-lasting T'ANG (TANG) dynasty (618–906).
(*See chronology under* China and Neighbouring Areas.)

Period of Disunity (after T'ang/Tang) (10th cent.; *China*)
The weakness of the T'ang dynasty (618–906) had two consequences: one was the creation by barbarians of a sinicized kingdom with northern Chinese lands annexed to Mongolian and Manchurian territories and the other was the division of the rest of China into a part north of the Yangtze ruled successively by Five Dynasties that claimed the T'ang heritage and a southern part known as the Ten Kingdoms, although their number varied from time to time. The barbarian kingdom was first formed by the Khitai, out of Jehol (western Manchuria), who conquered northern Hebei (Hopeh), eventually establishing themselves in Beijing and choosing the dynastic name of Liao. The name Cathay derives from KHITAN KHANATE. South of the Khitan Khanate to Jiangsu (Kiangsu) and Hubei (Hupeh) and later to the Yangtze, were the lands of the Five Dynasties: Later Liang (907–923), Later T'ang (923–936), Later Chin (Jin) (936–947), Later Han (947–951), and Later Chou (Zhou) (951–960). South of the territories of the Five Dynasties were the so-called Ten Kingdoms, the more important of which were: Wu (from Shandong to Jiangxi), Ch'u (Hunan), Later Shu (Shanxi and Sichuan), Wu Yüeh (Zhejiang), Min (Fujian), and South Han (Guangdong). In 960, the Sung (Song) became dominant in the lands of the Five Dynasties and proceeded to conquer the Ten Kingdoms (979), thus putting an end to the post-T'ang period of disunity, although the foreign Liao Kingdom remained in the north.
(*See chronology under* China and Neighbouring Areas.)

Persia (IRAN)

Persian Empire (ACHAEMENID EMPIRE; SASANID EMPIRE)

Peru

The Inca Empire, which had undergone civil war shortly before the arrival of the Spaniards, disintegrated with the conquest of Cuzco in 1533 by Pizarro, who founded Lima in 1535. The brutality of the Spaniards provoked an uprising led by Manco Capac which lasted from 1536 to 1544. In 1542, Peru was constituted as a viceroyalty with its capital in Lima and jurisdiction practically over all of Spanish South America, except Venezuela which had been mortgaged by Charles I to a German banking house. As the SPANISH COLONIAL EMPIRE grew in complexity, other viceroyalties were created: New Granada in what would become COLOMBIA (1717) and La Plata in modern ARGENTINA (1776). Chile depended on Peru until it was constituted as a captaincy-general in 1778. Ecuador was a presidency with its own *audiencia* (high court) from 1563. Only Charcas (Bolivia) remained directly attached to Lima. The habitual harshness of Spanish colonial rule led to the Indian rebellion of Tupac Amaru (1780), who was captured and cruelly executed. His followers held out in La Paz until the following year.

Ayacucho

Peru was not keen on independence as it was practically a self-ruling aristocracy. However, the independence movements in Argentina and GRAN COLOMBIA were loath to allow forces loyal to Spain to subsist at the very centre of South America. An independentist force from Chile, led by the Argentinian general Jose de San Martin, liberated Lima in 1821 and independence was declared. Viceroy La Serna fled to the interior. After a meeting with general Bolivar in Guayaquil, San Martin evacuated Lima, which Bolivar then occupied. In 1824, the Venezuelan general Sucre, Bolivar's principal lieutenant, defeated La Serna in Ayacucho in 1824, thus bringing Spanish rule in South America to a close. Allied to Bolivia (though hardly in military coordination), Peru lost a war against Chile and had to cede the city of Iquique and its hinterland in 1879. The possession of Arica, in Chile, was not defined until 1929 when Chilean sovereignty was recognized, although Peru obtained the right to use port facilities. The frontier with Brazil was defined on the basis of the Brazilian claim to the Amazon River Basin, but Peru had founded the city of Iquitos in 1863 which gave it a huge chunk of Amazonia. In 1941, Peru rejected by force of arms Ecuatorian claims in the Amazonian Basin. This dispute simmered for a long time but has finally been put to rest. Although Spanish is the official language of Peru, Quechua and Aymara, languages of the Inca Empire, are still widely spoken.

Petchenegs (10th–11th cents.; *Southern Russia*)
The Petchenegs, also known as Patzinaks and as Cumans, were Turk nomads active from the 10th to the 11th cents. in southern Russia and eastern Europe. In the 10th cent. they displaced the MAGYARS from north of the Sea of Azov. In 1064, they were defeated by the POLOVETZY. Byzantine Emperor Alexius I finally crushed them after they slashed through VALACHIA and Bulgaria and unsuccessfully attacked Constantinople in 1091.

Petra (4th–1st cents. BC; Jordan)
Petra was a city founded by the Semitic Nabataeans in the 4th cent. BC. It had a shadowy semi-autonomy until the area was annexed by Rome in AD 106. Today it is in Jordan.

Pharaonic Egypt (3rd mil.–4th cent. BC)
Consensus varies on whether civilization was born in SUMER or in Egypt. The earliest Egyptian settlements date from ca. 5000 BC. By ca. 3000 BC, there were cities and kingly burials. The first writings are from ca. 2950 BC. The kingdom of Egypt arose gradually from confederacies and absorptions of towns. The first known ruler of the country, certainly in the south, possibly also in the delta, was Narmer, ca. 2900. His capital was Hierakonpolis, south of today's Luxor. The rulers of Egypt were listed and classified into dynasties by Manetho, a Greek historian who was active in 300 BC in Ptolemaic Egypt. Although his list is not accurate in the detail, it is the general basis for the history of ancient Egypt.

OLD KINGDOM

The first six dynasties ruled the Old Kingdom. Some of the most enduring sites of ancient Egypt were built during the Old Kingdom, including Bubastis, in the delta; Memphis, near Cairo; Asyut; Thinis, Abydos, and Dendera, north of Luxor; and Abu, near Aswan. The Old Kingdom was the time of the pyramids of Giza. The first ones were built at Saqqara, near Cairo. Egypt made Nubia (roughly today's northern Sudan) a vassal territory starting ca. 2900 BC. The capital of the Old Kingdom was at Memphis. With the death of Pharaoh Pepys II, the Old Kingdom divided, ushering in the First Intermediate Period from ca. 2150 to ca. 2080 BC. Nubia was left to its own devices. During the First Intermediate Period, the dynasties of Egypt went on ruling from Memphis, but the kingdom south of Asyut was divided into territories dominated by Thinis, Thebes, and Hierakonpolis. The kingdom was reunified by kings of the 10th and 11th dynasties, based in Thebes.

MIDDLE KINGDOM

The Middle Kingdom was ruled by the 12th dynasty initiated by Pharaoh Amenemhet. Cultivation in the delta was extended and the Fayum depression, irrigated by the Nile, was settled. Fayum is a huge oasis west of the river. Starting ca. 2000 BC the northern Sinai was fortified. Trade with the Levant was intense and Palestine was raided ca. 1830 BC. Nubia, south of the Second Cataract, was annexed and fortified. Egyptian military expansion was the work of Pharaoh Senusret III. After the accession of the 13th dynasty ca. 1700 BC, Nubia separated as a political entity (KUSH) and the kingdom divided, initiating the Second Intermediate period, an obscure era during which the 14th to 17th dynasties ruled from different sites, mainly Memphis and Thebes. It is likely that Thebes controlled Nubia. The Hyksos, a Semitic warrior-people from Canaan, over-ran the eastern Nile Delta on chariots ca. 1650 BC. They established their capital in Avaris. The Hyksos were defeated ca. 1540 BC by a ruler of Thebes, but Avaris was not taken until ca. 1520.

New Kingdom

The New Kingdom was founded by Pharaoh Ahmose, originally from Thebes and listed in the 17th dynasty. It was he who finally subjugated Avaris. The Valley of the Kings, near Luxor – a huge royal cemetery teeming with underground tombs – was started ca. 1500 BC. Pharaonic Egypt ca. 1450 was an empire that briefly extended to the Euphrates River, from where the Egyptians were driven back by the MITANNI KINGDOM and the HURRIANS. Egyptian influence was confined mostly to the eastern Mediterranean coast. Queen Hatshepsut, who built the temple at Deir el-Bahri, the most famous edifice from this time, was active ca. 1470. She carried on from Thutmose I and Thutmose II the conquest of Kush, which ca. 1460 had been consolidated as far as the fourth cataract, far inside northern Sudan. Napata, in Nubia, was founded by Egypt ca. 1400. The great temple at Luxor was built around this time, although it was much modified by following dynasties. From ca. 1460 BC under Thutmose III Egyptian political influence was strong in Palestine.

Pharaoh Akhenaton introduced the heretical monotheistic worship of the sun ca. 1360 BC. During this time, the Near East was divided into diverse kingdoms, but the Levant as a whole was subservient to Egypt. It was contested by the HITTITE KINGDOM ca. 1330 BC. In the indecisive Battle of Kadesh, ca. 1280, Ramses II was checked and subsequently Egyptians and Hittites agreed to share rulership of the Levant. From ca. 1220 to ca. 1180, the Egyptians, especially under Merneptah and Ramses III, successfully fended off invasions from the Libyans, the Philistines, and 'invaders from the sea'. These heroic events became the basis for the thesis about the PELASGIANS. Egypt was weakened and towards the end of the 2nd mil. BC Nubia and Palestine were lost. The period from ca. 1080 is sometimes described as a Third Intermediate Period. Tanis functioned as capital city after ca. 1070. In any event, after ca. 950 there is evidence of division. Political hegemony in the Near East passed to the Mesopotamian empires of ASSYRIA and BABYLONIA. In the

9th and 8th cents. BC, there were overlapping dynasties at Tanis, at Leontopolis, and at Sais in the delta and at Napata in Kush. Between ca. 720 and ca. 670
Nubian Kushite monarchs were predominant in the Nile River valley. Assyria
seized Egypt down to Thebes briefly from the Kushites (ca. 664), but local rule
was later restored in Egypt. In 525 BC, Egypt became a satrapy of the
ACHAEMENID EMPIRE, although it rebelled and had independent existence
from 405 to 349 BC, when it was conquered again by the Persians. It later
became part of the ALEXANDRIAN EMPIRE. A Macedonian general established the post-Alexandrine successor state of PTOLEMAIC EGYPT, which
eventually fell to ROME. Ancient Egyptian is an Afro-Asiatic language, related
to the Semitic group of languages. Its modern form is Greek-influenced Copt.
(*See chronology under* Ancient Near East.)

Philippines

The Chinese colonized the Philippines from the 10th cent. – Luzon, the name
of the largest Filipino island, is Chinese in origin – and the MAJAPAHIT
EMPIRE established a foothold in the Sulu Islands in the 14th cent., but all
the islands which constitute the territory of the Philippines, mostly peopled
by Malays, were only united politically by Spain after 1565. Manila was
founded in 1571 by Lopez de Legaspi. In 1896 the Filipinos rose up against
Spain under the leadership of Aguinaldo, who left the country after a truce.
He returned to the Philippines at the start of the Spanish–American War in
1898 and declared the independence of the Philippines on 12 June 1898. The
Spanish, badly beaten by the Americans in the naval Battle of Manila Bay,
staged a mock-battle before surrendering Manila to the United States. The
Filipinos resisted the American authorities in Luzon until Aguinaldo was
captured in 1901. Although it attained a degree of self-rule during the 1930s,
under President Quezon, the Philippines did not achieve full sovereignty
until 1946. The capital of the Philippines is Manila.

The country has been traditionally divided into three regions: Luzon including the island of this name, Palawan, and others; the Visayas, which are the
islands between Luzon and Mindanao; and the island of Mindanao, including
the Sulu Archipelago. Although the official language is Tagalog, called Filipino, the Philippines has a variety of other languages (Cebuano, Bicol,
Ilocano, *et al.*), all belonging to the Malay group of the Austronesian family.
The compulsory teaching of Spanish was abolished in 1986, but the language
is still valid for certain legal purposes. A dialect of Spanish called Chavacano
is spoken in Samboanga in Mindanao. English is also official today. The
Philippines has an outstanding claim on the Spratly Islands, west of Palawan,
and has strongly objected to the Chinese occupation of tiny Mischief reef. The
Spratly Islands are a chain of small islands covering a large area of the China
Sea west of the Philippines, over which China, Malaysia, Philippines, and
Vietnam have conflicting claims.

Philistia (13th–7th cents. BC; ancient *Near East*)
Philistia was a federation of Semitic cities on the eastern Mediterranean coast (modern Israel) – including Gaza, Ashkelon, Ashdod, Joppa, Gerar, Gath, Lachish – that gave Palestine its name. It was under the hegemony of PHARAONIC EGYPT during the New Kingdom and suffered some devastation around 1200 BC (PELASGIANS), but from Biblical references, it must have flourished from the 12th to the 8th cents. BC. Gaza, the setting of Samson's epic, was its principal centre. Philistia became a province of ASSYRIA and, after that, of BABYLONIA.
(*See chronology under* Ancient Near East.)

Phoenicia (11th–8th cents. BC; ancient *Near East*)
From the 11th to the 8th cents. BC, Phoenicia (mainly in the territory of today's Lebanon) consisted of Semitic city–states, the principal of which was the famously impregnable Tyre. Other cities were Sidon, Byblos, and Aradus. It was conquered by ASSYRIA except Tyre. Phoenicia passed to BABYLONIA in the 6th cent. BC, and then formed part of the ACHAEMENID and ALEXANDRIAN EMPIRES. It became a province of ROME in AD 44. CARTHAGE was founded in the 9th cent. BC as a Tyrian colony. Other Phoenician colonies in NUMIDIA and LIBYA were Hippo Regius, Hadrumetum, Utica, Thapsus, Thenae, and Leptis. Phoenicia also had trading outposts on the coast of Spain. The famous sculpture, the *Dama de Elche* (Valencia), might have been Phoenician. Possibily derived from glyphs via another Semitic writing, the Phoenician alphabet, which has no vowels, was the model for the Greek alphabet, precursor of the Latin letters.
(*See chronology under* Ancient Near East.)

Phrygia (8th–6th cents. BC; ancient *Near East*)
The kingdom of Phrygia in central Anatolia was founded in the 8th cent. BC by Indo-European speakers coming from Thrace ca. 1200 BC. The myth of golden-touch Midas originates in Phrygia, but there was also a real-life King Midas of Phrygia. Phrygia was brought down by the invasions of the CIMMERIANS in the 7th and 6th cents. BC. The capital of Phrygia was Gordium, near modern Ankara, Turkey. The territory of Phrygia was annexed by LYDIA and later partially ruled by PERGAMUM.
(*See chronology under* Ancient Near East *and* Anatolia.)

Piedmont (SARDINIA)

Pisa (11th–13th cents.; northern *Italy*)
Possibly Greek, later an Etruscan site, and a Roman colony in 180 BC, Pisa became a powerful maritime republic in the 9th cent. In the 11th cent., it occupied Corsica and Sardinia in alliance with GENOA, with which it had a falling out resulting in the defeat of Pisa in 1284. It was a Ghibelline (pro-imperial)

city in conflict with FLORENCE, which absorbed it in 1406. Afterwards its political destinies were those of TUSCANY.

Po Hai (7th–9th cents.; northern China)
Po Hai was a kingdom founded by Tungus and Koreans in northern Korea and eastern Manchuria towards the end of the 7th cent. It was wiped out in the 9th cent. by the Khitai (KHITAN KHANATE) before they embarked on their conquering expeditions to northern China.

Poland
SEE ENTRY IN 'PROVINCES AND REGIONS'
From 960 to 1025, Poland was a Slavic principality – founded by Duke Mieszko, with its capital in Gniezmo and an episcopal see in Poznan – that expanded from its homeland west to Pomerania and south to Silesia. Mieszko was also the founder of the Piast dynasty, which ruled until the 14th cent. In 1025 Boleslaus I declared Poland a kingdom. From 1003 to 1029, Poland absorbed Moravia and Lusatia, but lost them both in 1033. After Boleslaus the kingdom was divided. Around 1138, it loosely comprised Little Poland, Silesia, Masovia, Kuyavia, and Greater Poland. The TEUTONIC KNIGHTS annexed north east Poland in the 13th cent. Ladislaus I reunited Poland from 1320 to 1333 and expanded to Pomerelia and Silesia. In 1335 Poland lost Silesia to Bohemia. After the last Piast ruler, Casimir III, Louis of Hungary became King of Poland in 1370, but the union with Poland ended with his daughter Jadwiga. In 1386 she married Ladislaus, Grand Duke of Lithuania, who became Ladislaus II of Poland and founder of the Jagiello dynasty and of the kingdom of Poland–Lithuania. In 1410 the Poles and Lithuanians defeated the Teutonic Knights in the Battle of Tannenberg. Although Ladislaus III was killed by the Turks in the Battle of Varna in 1440, Poland–Lithuania flourished under the Jagiellos. It defeated the Teutonic Knights in 1462 and made PRUSSIA its vassal in 1466. It annexed Ruthenia and Galicia. In the 16th cent. Poland–Lithuania extended from the Baltic to the Black Sea. In 1558 Poland–Lithuania conquered ESTONIA and Courland. Under King Sigismund II, by the union of Lublin in 1569, Poland–Lithuania became one kingdom, which in effect meant Polish ascendancy, but also inaugurated the kingdom's long descent, which is usually attributed to the elective monarchy and the self-serving power of the land-owning nobility. The country was riven by factions and the landed gentry were unruly.

THE 'DELUGE'

In the late 16th cent. Poland was engaged in wars with Russia and, under Sigismund III Vasa, a Swedish prince, it warred with Sweden during the early 17th cent. It also had to contend with the OTTOMAN EMPIRE, to which it lost a war over MOLDAVIA ca. 1610. The reign of John II (1648–1668) was so calamitous it is known as the 'deluge'. From 1660 to 1667, Poland lost

Livonia to Sweden and the Ukraine to Russia. The Vasa dynasty ended in 1668. John III Sobieski restored Polish prestige with the defeat of the Turks in the Siege of Vienna in 1683. But afterwards it was all downhill. During the following decades Poland was ruled by foreign kings, often puppets of the neighbouring powers (Sweden, Prussia, Austria, and Russia). When Russian influence became ascendant, Frederick II the Great of Prussia proposed to Catherine II of Russia in 1772, a partition of Poland in which Habsburg Austria was later included. There were three partitions: in 1772, 1793, and 1795, with Russia getting the largest piece in eastern Poland, Prussia annexing western Poland as far as Warsaw, and Austria acquiring Galicia and Lublin. By the Treaty of Tilsit, Napoleon created the Grand Duchy of Warsaw (1807–1813) under Frederick Augustus I of Saxony (FRENCH EUROPEAN EMPIRE). After the Congress of VIENNA in 1814–1815, Warsaw was awarded to Russia. Prussia retained much of western Poland and the Habsburg Empire, Galicia minus Lublin which went to Russia. Cracow was made an independent state which was annexed by the Habsburg Empire in 1848.

MODERN POLAND

Upon the surrender of Germany in 1918, Poland declared its independence and was generously restored, including a corridor to the port of Danzig, by the Treaty of VERSAILLES in 1919. Poland claimed the 1772 eastern border and under Pilsudsky it warred with Soviet Russia in 1920–1921, and acquired parts of Byelorussia and the Ukraine. It also annexed Lithuanian Vilnius in 1920. Having signed a non-aggression treaty with the Soviet dictator Stalin in 1939, Hitler demanded the Danzig corridor from Poland, who, counting on its alliance with Great Britain and France, refused to cede. Germany invaded on 1 September 1939. In a *blitzkrieg*, Poland was over-run in a matter of weeks. The Soviets invaded from the east. In 1941, Germany attacked the USSR and all of Poland was occupied. Under the Nazis, Poland suffered huge human losses. The Jewish community of more than 3 million members was almost totally exterminated. Poland was at the very heart of the Holocaust and Auch-switz (Oswiecim) remains the greatest symbol of historical evil. The Nazis were driven out of Poland in 1944–1945 by the USSR and the country was made a communist republic, with the borders it has today, part of the informal SOVIET EMPIRE. As a member of the Warsaw Pact, Poland participated in the invasion of Czechoslovakia to suppress the reform movement known as the Prague Spring in 1968. In 1980, the Polish military, under General Jaruzelski, put down labour unrest (led by Lech Walesa), which was making the Soviets nervous. In 1989, in the midst of the *perestroika* process initiated by Mikhail Gorbachev in the USSR, the communists were unable to overcome the opposition in parliament and, in 1991, there were completely free elections.
(*See chronology under* Southern Russia.)

Poland–Lithuania (POLAND)

Polovetzy (11th–13th cents.; *Central Asia*: western Siberia; *Southern Russia*)
The Polovetzy were Turks that, in the 11th cent., roamed the region of the Irtysh and Ob rivers. Moving south they prodded the GHUZZ, setting off the Seljuks. In 1064 they inflicted a defeat on the PETCHENEGS and established themselves north of the Black Sea during the 13th cent. The Polovetzy maintained fairly good relations with KIEVAN RUS. They were vanquished by the Mongols (MONGOL EMPIRE).
(*See chronology under* Southern Russia.)

Pontus (3rd–1st cents. BC; *Anatolia*)
The region of Pontus in Anatolia, occupying the south-eastern coast of the Black Sea, became a kingdom that flourished from 281 to the 1st cent. BC. It was an offshoot of the SELEUCID EMPIRE. Its last king, Mithridates IV, conquered most of Asia Minor during a fit of Roman absent-mindedness, which was soon corrected and the kingdom was incorporated into the Roman Empire in 65 BC (ROME).
(*See chronology under* Anatolia.)

Portugal
SEE ENTRY IN 'PROVINCES AND REGIONS'
Known to the Romans as Lusitania – from its Celtic inhabitants, whose leader in the 3rd cent. BC was Viriatus – the territory of Portugal was part of the VISIGOTHIC KINGDOM, which also included Spain. In the north, the SUEVES were assimilated by the Visigoths in the 6th cent. The Byzantines occupied the Algarve (southern Portugal) during the 6th cent. Like the rest of the Iberian Peninsula, Portugal was conquered by Muslim Berbers after 711 (MUSLIM SPAIN). The *reconquista*, the long Christian war to dislodge the Muslims from Spain, began for Portugal in Galicia, which had been liberated by ASTURIAS in the late 8th cent. By 1064, King Ferdinand I of CASTILE had taken Coimbra in central Portugal. By the late 11th cent. there was a Count of Portucalense, based in Oporto. Alfonso Henriques proclaimed himself king in 1139. Spain recognized the kingdom of Portugal in 1143. The Algarve was annexed by Alfonso III in 1249 and Portugal had the essential continental contour it has today. It is the oldest territorial entity in Europe. Castile tried to annex Portugal but was defeated in the Battle of Aljubarrota in 1385. Under John I, founder of the Aviz dynasty, Portugal began its overseas history with raids on Morocco through which it acquired Ceuta in 1414 and Tangier in 1471 (MARINIDS).

HENRY THE NAVIGATOR

It was through the interest and encouragement of Prince Henry the Navigator (1394–1460), who founded a school of navigation in Sagres, Algarve, that

Portugal was able to take the lead among all nations in the exploration of the world and, in the process, create a colonial empire and for a time dominate the spice trade. In 1420 the Portuguese began colonizing the Madeira Islands and, in 1445, they occupied the Azores. Both groups of Atlantic Ocean islands are an integral part of Portugal. If Portugal did not discover America or send Magellan, a Portuguese by birth, around the world, it was because it wanted to reach the East Indies from the west and it did not want competitors going from east to west. It also did not have the resources to go both ways. In 1488, Bartolomeu Dias rounded the Cape of Good Hope. Vasco da Gama sailed to India in 1497–1498. In 1500, Cabral found the hump of Brazil. It was a part of America which was not supposed to be east of an imaginary line drawn by the Pope in the Treaty of Tordesillas (1494), which assigned the western hemisphere to the Spanish at a time when the Iberian kingdoms thought the world was their oyster. The Portuguese were in their right and colonized the Brazilian coast. Afonso de Albuquerque conquered Goa in 1510, Malacca in 1511, and the island of Hormuz in 1515. The Portuguese established outposts in the East Indies (Indonesia) and especially in Ternate (1522), in the Moluccas Islands, which, though tiny, was a significant producers of cloves and nutmeg. The Portuguese hold was precarious and, in 1607, they were displaced by the developing DUTCH COLONIAL EMPIRE. In sailing to the east the Portuguese built outposts all along the African coast. Those on the west were used later as slaving centres. Some on both coasts became the future cores of small and large Portuguese colonies in Africa. Portugal's resources were stretched thin and, during the 16th cent., the centre of commerce shifted towards the highly developed Low Countries and England. There was also the competition for the eastern trade through the Mediterranean, which by the 15th cent. was dominated by VENICE. In 1578, Portugal suffered a catastrophic defeat in the Battle of Alcazarquivir in which an invasion force led by King Sebastian was annihilated in Morocco and the King himself killed.

THE SPANISH CAPTIVITY

In 1580 the last king of the Aviz line died without heir – he was a chaste cardinal – and Philip II, nephew to King John III of Portugal, successfully claimed the crown. The period from 1580 to 1640 is known as the Spanish Captivity and it finished Portugal's days as a world power. Philip's enmity with England and his attempts to subjugate the NETHERLANDS, which was allied to England against Spanish pretensions, closed the northern markets to Portugal. From the early 17th cent. the Dutch followed the routes pioneered by the Portuguese, picking up the undermanned colonies they had established in Africa and in Asia. When Portugal emerged from Spanish rule – under John IV of Braganza – it was a relative backwater. It had its Brazilian empire and footholds and outposts all over Africa and Asia, but the country had decayed economically. In 1703 it made the famous deal with England – strong wines for English woollens – which sealed their friendship but which Marxist historians have blamed for Portugal's 'underdevelopment'. In 1807 Portugal was invaded by Napoleon, who wanted to close all European ports to England. The court moved to Rio de Janeiro, Brazil, and even though the French were ejected with British help in 1811, it did not return until 1820. Brazil declared its independence in 1822. During the 19th cent. Portugal affirmed its claims to Angola and Mozambique. In 1910 a republic was established. Portugal entered World War I on the Allied side in 1916. In 1932–1933 Salazar became dictator until 1968, when he suffered a stroke. A military coup in 1974, provoked by slow changes at home and wars in the colonies, led to leftist radicalism in 1975. The colonies were let go but the political situation became unstable until 1977, when the country started settling down to democracy.

The capital of Portugal is beautiful Lisbon, devastated by an earthquake in 1755, which made Voltaire sceptical about the mercies of heaven. Portugal joined the EUROPEAN UNION in 1986. The Portuguese language is akin to Galician, spoken in north west Spain.

Portuguese Colonial Empire (15th–20th cents.)
Encouraged by Prince Henry the Navigator, son of King John I, the Portuguese began coasting along western Africa from the early 15th cent. Some attribute this interest in part to the search for the fabulous Christian kingdom of Prester John, but it was more likely a commercial enterprise. In 1488, Bartolomeu Dias rounded the Cape of Good Hope. Vasco da Gama sailed to India in 1497–1498. The first Portuguese (and European) base in India was established in Cochin, which the Dutch captured in 1663 and ceded to the British in 1795. Afonso de Albuquerque conquered Goa in 1510, MALACCA in 1511, and Hormuz in 1515. Many Portuguese outposts were built. Some disappeared but others remained as the nuclei for future colonies. Portuguese explorers and traders visited and established themselves in ANGOLA, the CAPE VERDE Islands, GUINEA-BISSAU, SAO TOME E PRINCIPE Islands, and MOZAMBIQUE. After rounding the Cape of Good Hope, Portugal followed the same policy along the coast of eastern Africa, in the Arabian or Persian Gulf, along the Malabar coast of India, and beyond. Bahrain, Oman, and Zanzibar, under Portuguese influence during the 15th and 16th cents., later reverted to local or regional rulers. The Portuguese were principally interested in the spice trade, for which they required safe coastal havens. During the early 16th cent. they occupied the island of Socotra, at the entrance of the Gulf of Aden, and used the MALDIVES as an anchorage. They also controlled the coast of Ceylon (SRI LANKA). On the western coast of India, they occupied Goa, Diu (1531), and Daman (1534), which gave them control of the pepper trade.

TERNATE AND TIDORE

From Malacca, in the Malay peninsula, the Portuguese went in two directions: towards Japan and China and towards the spice islands in the East Indies (Indonesia). They were active in China, where they founded Macao in 1557 but, especially from 1542, they had trade with Japan to themselves. Christian missionaries, principally Jesuits, made many Japanese converts, until in 1603 the Tokugawa shogunate turned savagely against Christianity and the Portuguese lost their trade privileges. In 1590, Portuguese sailors were the first Europeans to sight Taiwan, which they named 'the beautiful' (Formosa) and tried to occupy, but were ejected by the Dutch in the 17th cent. This pattern of the Dutch treading in the footsteps of the Portuguese would repeat itself over and over. It happened in Ceylon and in Malaya. More significantly, it happened in the spice islands. There was really one large source of nutmeg and clove and that was the Moluccas, between Celebes and New Guinea. Within the Moluccas, the principal producers were the tiny islands of Ternate and Tidore. The Portuguese took over in the early 16th cent. The Dutch first arrived in the late 16th cent. and by 1610 had ejected the Portuguese from Java and the rest of the East Indies. For all their far eastern exertions, the Portuguese were to rescue from Dutch colonialist grasp only the city and territory of Macao, which they founded in 1557, and EAST TIMOR, which was not clearly delimited until 1914. They also kept their Asian enclaves and their African possessions.

AN ACCIDENTAL ACQUISITION

A different branch and history of the Portuguese colonial empire is Brazil. Discovered by chance in 1500 – to round the Cape, Portuguese sailors had to drift west and catch the south-easterlies – north-eastern Brazil was claimed by Portugal under the Treaty of Tordesillas (1494) by which Spain and Portugal agreed to more or less divide the world along a meridian that included land in America the Portuguese had not expected to find. Even here, where no spices were involved, the Dutch followed the Portuguese and occupied Bahia and Pernambuco from 1624 to 1654. Brazil offered refuge and a real throne to the Portuguese royal family when Napoleon extended his empire to Portugal (1807). After the Portuguese monarch returned home, his heir declared the independence of BRAZIL in 1822. By then the Portuguese were well entrenched in their African and Asian domains. At the BERLIN Conference (1884–1885), their African claims were recognized and Angola and Mozambique were delimited. In 1961, India invaded the ancient Portuguese enclaves on its western coast. In 1975, a leftist government in Lisbon gave independence to all Portuguese colonies in Africa. In 1976, the Indonesians invaded East Timor in spite of protests from its Christian population. Macao reverted to China in 1999.

Pre-Columbian Cultures (South America)

Aside from the great Inca Empire, there were minor centres of developing high cultures in South America, most of them along the Peruvian coast: Chavin, Chimú, Moche, Nasca, Paracas, Sipán, and others. The Moche legacy are realistic pottery portraits and figures, an astonishing artistic achievement which is the equal of any from pre-history and an eloquent non-pareil chronicle of their life both public and private. The Nasca left enormous mystifying pattern-drawings that were inscribed on rocky soil by sheer calculation. With the pyramids, they are the stuff that fantasists use to write best-sellers about aliens who made civilization possible on Earth. And the warrior-priest of Sipán is a terrifying apparition from a past of discipline, faith, and cruelty. The gold-working Chibchas of the Colombian *altiplano* are in the same category as these cultures.

Provence (ARLES)

Prussia (12th–19th cents.; *Germany* and *Baltic area*)

The kingdom of Prussia began in 1134 on the Elbe River as the German North March, which, in 1150, absorbed Brandenburg, a region occupied by Slavic Wends. In the east during the 13th cent. the TEUTONIC KNIGHTS had practically exterminated the Prussians, a Baltic people (related linguistically to the Indo-European Lithuanians and Latvians) during the conquest of what became East Prussia, a province separated from Brandenburg physically. In 1323 a Wittelsbach was made Elector of the Margravate of Brandenburg (HOLY ROMAN EMPIRE). In 1417 Brandenburg was given to Frederick Hohenzollern, an imperial Elector, whose family originally came from Swabia in western Germany. Berlin was made the capital of Brandenburg in 1486. In 1525 Albert, Elector of Brandenburg, himself head of the Teutonic Knights, secularized the Order and acquired Prussia for Brandenburg. To achieve this, he accepted vassalage to the Polish king, whose kingdom was the predominant political influence in the region. In 1539 the Elector of Brandenburg accepted the Reformation. In 1614 Brandenburg acquired Cleves, bits of territory in west Germany, on and near the border with Netherlands, and in 1618 Brandenburg was named the Duchy of Prussia. In the course of the Thirty Years War (1618–1648) – which on the whole pitted Catholics against Protestants mainly in Germany – Prussia, under Frederick William the Great Elector, emerged with Pomerania, north of Brandenburg, which it conquered from Poland, and of course fully independent of Polish suzerainty. Poland still had Pomerelia (eastern Pomerania), so that the two parts of the Duchy of Prussia were still not united. As things worked in the Holy Roman Empire, it was the possession of territory outside of its frontiers that brought prestige and the possibility of 'upgrading', so to speak, to the status of kingship.

FREDERICK THE GREAT

In 1701, the Elector Frederick III declared himself King Frederick I of Prussia in Königsberg, which was the capital of East Prussia. Since Prussia also held the Margravate of Brandenburg, the kingdom of Prussia was both within and outside the Holy Roman Empire, as was the case of the Habsburg Empire through the Duchy of Austria. In 1720 Prussia gained Stettin and additional Pomeranian territory from Sweden. King Frederick William I (1713–1740) centralized the state through military and administrative reforms. His son Frederick II the Great (1740–1786) first broached to Catherine II of Russia the partition of Poland. During the War of Austrian Succession, Frederick gained Silesia. In the first partition of Poland in 1772, Prussia further annexed Pomerelia (Polish Pomerania), thus Brandenburg and East Prussia were finally joined physically. Pomerelia was organized as West Prussia and the original Prussia became East Prussia. In the partition of 1793 Prussia gained Pozen (Poznan) and Great Poland and, in the partition of 1795, it extended its rule as far as Warsaw. Prussia joined the first coalition against Republican France but was defeated and withdrew in 1795. In 1806, Napoleon defeated the Prussians at Jena and by the Treaty of Tilsit Prussia lost its lands west of the Elbe. In 1813 Prussia entered the anti-French coalition which, in 1814, resulted in Napoleon's deposition and exile to Elba. Upon Napoleon's return, Prussia again joined the allies against him and, in the Battle of Waterloo in 1815, Blücher's Prussian corps decided the day.

GERMANY

Prussia was a major influence in the Congress of VIENNA (1814–1815). It gained the Rhineland, Westphalia, and northern Saxony and became a crucial supporter of the Holy Alliance, the agreement with Russia and Austria (later joined by France) to put down any threat to the European monarchical order. Austria (HABSBURG EMPIRE) had emerged weaker than before Napoleon, if only because the dissolution of the Holy Roman Empire in 1806 had bereaved the Habsburg Emperor Francis I of the imperial crown. The Holy Roman Empire, which Napoleon had made the Confederation of the Rhine, was turned into the GERMAN CONFEDERATION, in which Berlin and Vienna vied for supremacy. Prussia sponsored the customs union (Zollverein) in 1834. King William I named Otto von Bismarck chancellor of Prussia in 1862. Prussia and Austria were allies against Denmark to obtain Schleswig and Holstein for the German Confederation in 1864. But in 1866 Prussia turned on Austria and defeated it to become the undisputed dominant power among the German states, which were formed into the NORTH GERMAN CONFEDERATION excluding Austria. Prussia gained Hanover, Hesse, Nassau, Schleswig-Holstein, and Frankfurt. In 1870, by playing on French sensitivities, Bismarck engineered the Franco-Prussian War, which France lost in 1871. Alsace and Lorraine were united to Germany and King William I was proclaimed Emperor of GERMANY (German Reich) in Versailles. At the end of World War II, with the partition of East Prussia and the annexation by Poland of much of eastern Germany, Prussia was in effect abolished.

Ptolemaic Egypt (3rd–1st cents. BC)

On the dissolution of the ALEXANDRIAN EMPIRE, one of his Macedonian generals, Ptolomeus, retained Egypt and Palestine and named himself King of Egypt as Ptolemy I. His claim was intact at the end of the DIADOCHI WARS in 281 BC. All his successors were called Ptolemy. Ptolemaic Egypt fought the heirs of Seleucus for possession of Palestine and southern Syria (SELEUCID EMPIRE). Cleopatra and her brother-husband Ptolemy XII – sibling marriages were a royal Ptolemaic custom – ruled together when Pompey, recently defeated by Caesar, took refuge in Egypt in 48 BC (ROME). When Caesar arrived in pursuit, Pompey had been murdered and Cleopatra was feuding with her brother. Caesar took Cleopatra's side. Her brother was accidentally drowned in 47 BC. As his mistress, Cleopatra went with Caesar to Rome. Upon Caesar's assassination in 44 BC, Cleopatra returned to Egypt, where in 42 BC Marc Antony visited her and fell in love. He and Cleopatra attempted to create an independent kingdom, with the capital in Alexandria, but were defeated at the naval battle of Actium (31 BC) by Octavian, Caesar's nephew and future Emperor Augustus. Both Marc Antony and Cleopatra committed suicide in 30 BC and Egypt became a provincial granary of the Roman Empire.

Punjab (18th–19th cents.; northern *India*)

The Punjab today is divided between India and Pakistan. It was invaded by the Aryans (VEDIC INDIA) and became part of MAGADHA. Later it was under the political influence of BACTRIA. In the 1st cent. BC it was invaded by the SAKA. The GUPTAS controlled the Punjab, which was taken by the EPH-THALITES ca. 500. The latter were defeated by HARSHA'S KINGDOM in the early 7th cent. The Punjab is part of the very fragmented history of NORTHERN INDIA. It entered into the formation of the DELHI SUL-TANATE after the arrival of the Afghan GHURIDS in 1186. In pursuit of the ruler of KHWARIZM, Genghis invaded northern India in 1221. The ruler of the Delhi Sultanate, Iltutmish, did nothing to obstruct him and Genghis was satisfied with garrisoning the Punjab. In 1279 the Chagataite Mongols invaded the Punjab and were defeated by then-sultan Balban of Delhi. They repeatedly invaded until 1327, but were not able to consolidate a holding in Northern India. Punjab became part of MUGHAL INDIA. Lahore, the historical capital of Punjab, was founded in 1526. Mughal rivalry with the MARATHA KING-DOMS permitted Nadir Shah, ruler of Persia (IRAN), to conquer Northern India in 1739. Delhi was sacked and the Peacock throne taken to Persia. By then there were centrifugal forces at work in Rajasthan, Punjab, Maharashtra, and Bengal. Sikhism, a monotheistic religion established in Amritsar in the early 17th cent., provided the Punjab with cultural cohesion. Nevertheless, the Punjab remained divided into small kingdoms until Ranjit Singh captured Lahore (1799) and Amritsar (1809), united the country, and ruled as far north as Kashmir. His army was trained by French veterans of the Napoleonic Wars. Ranjit Singh died in 1839 after ruling for 40 years. His successors were not up to the task of containing BRITISH INDIA, which annexed the Punjab in 1849. Gulab Singh, a general under Ranjit Singh, was a British ally and he was rewarded with KASHMIR. In the 1947 partition of British India, Lahore was awarded to Pakistan, close to the frontier with India. The capital of the Indian Punjab is Chandigarh, designed by Le Corbusier.

Q

Qara-Qoyunlu (15th cent.; western *Iran*)

The Qara-Qoyunlu Turks, who ca. 1370 occupied the territory of Armenia, had been defeated by Tamerlane in Azerbaijan ca. 1400 (TIMURID EMPIRE AND SUCCESSOR STATES). But they had not been destroyed and after Tamerlane's death (1405), they began the conquest of west Persia: Tabriz (1406), central Persia around Rai (1452), Ispahan, Persis, and Kerman (1458). In 1467, the Qara-Qoyunlu were dealt a decisive defeat by the AQ-QOYUNLU, who became masters of western IRAN.

(*See chronology under* Iran.)

Qatar

A peninsula in Arabia roamed by Bedouins, Qatar was ruled by the emirate in BAHRAIN until the OTTOMAN EMPIRE took over from 1555 to 1915. After, Qatar was a British protectorate until 1971. The capital of Qatar is Doha.

R

Rajputs (9th–12th cents.; northern *India*)

Rajputs is the name given to military leaders and peoples from Rajasthan who were important in NORTHERN INDIA from the 9th to the 12th cents. more for their disunited hegemony than for any specific state they created. The origin of the Rajputs is not clear. They proudly claimed to belong to the warrior kshatriya caste. Rajasthani is related to the other Indo-European languages of India. It is, however, possible that the Rasputs were descended from the EPHTHALITES, who invaded India in the 6th cent. The Gurjara Pratihara dynasty, which was active in the 9th cent., was probably of Rajput origin, as were the Chandella, whose imposing temples in Khajuraho (Madhya Pradesh), with their incredibly erotic sculptures, reveal a more emollient side to the Rajputs. The Rajputs were decisively defeated by the GHURIDS and later subjected to the DELHI SULTANATE ca. 1200. Rajputs served in MUGHAL INDIA as soldiers and administrators.

(*See chronology under* Indian Subcontinent.)

Ras al-Khalmah (UNITED ARAB EMIRATES)

Rhodes (5th cent. BC–20th cent. AD)

The Greek island of Rhodes was an independent but politically insignificant Greek state from the 5th cent. to the 4th cent. BC when it was occupied by MACEDON. After Alexander's death in 323 BC, Rhodes became independent again and flourished culturally. It was a Roman vassal in the 2nd cent. BC (ROME). Rhodes was part of the BYZANTINE EMPIRE until the fall of Constantinople to Frankish knights in 1204. Ruled by local lords and briefly by GENOA, in 1256 it was occupied by the Nicaean Empire. The Knights Hospitalers seized it ca. 1280. The OTTOMAN EMPIRE captured Rhodes in 1523 and held it until 1912, when Italy took over. The Italians turned it over to Greece in 1947 along with the other Dodecanese Islands.

Rhodes (Despotate of) (LATIN STATES)

Rhodesia (20th cent.; Southern Africa)

In 1953, Great Britain created the Federation of Rhodesia and Nyasaland, also known as the Central African Federation, with white-dominated, self-governing Southern Rhodesia and the protectorates of Northern Rhodesia and Nyasaland. African discontent led to the dissolution of the federation. While Nyasaland and Northern Rhodesia became, respectively, independent MALAWI and ZAMBIA, Southern Rhodesia stuck to its racially-divided structure and declared independence in 1965. Britain refused recognition and called for UNITED NATIONS sanctions, which were applied. Beset by economic shortages and guerrilla attacks, Rhodesia allowed elections which resulted in the formation of ZIMBABWE in 1980.

Rio de la Plata (United Provinces of) (ARGENTINA)

Romania

Romania corresponds to the Roman provinces of Dacia and Moesia. Its inhabitants were strongly latinized, so that Romanian is a branch of the Indo-European Romance languages. A corridor for invaders from the east – GOTHS, AVARS, BULGARS – the territory of today's Romania in the 13th cent. consisted of the principalities of VALACHIA and MOLDAVIA. Valachia (15th cent.) and Moldavia (16th cent.) became vassals of the OTTOMAN EMPIRE. In 1596 a Valachian prince, Michael the Brave, fought off the Ottomans and united Valachia and Moldavia. In 1599 he seized TRANSYLVANIA from the Hungarian Bathory family. His occupation of the land did not go uncontested and, upon his death in 1601, Valachia and Moldavia became Ottoman dependencies again and Transylvania fell to the HABSBURG EMPIRE. Transylvania became a traditional territorial claim of the Romanians, although Hungarians constitute a considerable proportion of the population.

Alexander John Cuza

The Porte-named Greek hospodars (governors) for Romania recruited from Istambuli Greeks, essentially tax-farmers who impoverished the land. When the Greeks rebelled for independence, the Romanians helped the Turks evict them. There was much discontent and, in 1822, the Porte under Russian pressure agreed to name Romanian hospodars. In 1829 Valachia and Moldavia became, in effect, Russian protectorates. The Russians occupied the provinces outright from 1848 to 1854, which was one of the causes of the Crimean War (1853–1856). In 1855 there was a brief period of Austrian occupation, which was a concession of the Russians to keep the Habsburg Empire out of the Crimean War. In 1856, Ottoman suzerainty over Moldavia and Valachia was restored. Southern Bessarabia was awarded to Moldavia by the European powers. In 1859, Alexander John Cuza was chosen as prince of both provinces, which were united as Romania in 1860–1861, although still loosely attached to the Ottoman Empire. In 1877 Romania joined Russia in war against the Ottoman Empire and, in 1878, became totally independent, but had to cede southern Bessarabia to Russia in exchange for northern Dobruja (on the coast of the Black Sea). In 1913, during the second Balkan War, Romania fought against BULGARIA and gained southern Dobruja. Romania entered World War I in 1916 on the side of the Allies. It was occupied by Germany. Under the terms of the treaties of Saint Germain (1919) and Trianon (1920) at the Paris Peace Conference (VERSAILLES), Romania reached its greatest extent when it was awarded Bessarabia from Soviet Russia, Bukovina from Austria, and Transylvania and part of the Banat from Hungary. Romanian forces put down the communist Bela Kun government in Budapest. After World War II, when it fought with Germany against the USSR, Romania lost Bessarabia and northern Bukovina to the USSR and was forced to cede southern Dobruja to Bulgaria, but it kept mostly Hungarian Transylvania. The capital of Romania is Bucharest.

(*See chronology under* Balkans.)

Rome (8th cent. BC–5th cent. AD)

SEE *ROMAN EMPIRE* IN 'PROVINCES AND REGIONS'

The famous rapt of the Sabines, which symbolizes an exogamous fusion of tribes, can be said to mark the foundation of Rome ca. 750 BC. During the 7th cent. Rome was ruled by the Etruscan Tarquin family. A pushy but solitary city–state among the disunited peoples of the Italian peninsula, Rome conquered Veii, in ETRURIA, in 396 BC. It was almost destroyed during the Celtic onslaught ca. 390 BC, but the Celts were repulsed and Rome continued its run of annexations. After Veii, the Etruscans were gradually assimilated. The same fate overtook the Samnites after 290 BC. Pyrrhus, King of EPIRUS, invaded Italy (280–275 BC) on behalf of the southern Greeks, but his costly victories against Rome were unavailing and he reputedly acknowledged that if he won another battle like the one at Asculum he would be lost (Pyrrhic victory). By 240 BC, Rome had annexed all of Etruria and the Adriatic coast of Italy.

THE PUNIC WARS

CARTHAGE had become the dominant commercial and political power in the western Mediterranean. From the 6th to the 4th cents. BC it occupied Sardinia, Malta, the Balearics, and the coast from Tunisia to Morocco. It tried to take Sicily from the Greeks but only managed a few footholds, from which the Carthaginians were ejected during the First Punic War (264–241 BC) with Rome. Sicily was the first Roman conquest outside the Italian mainland, followed by Corsica, Sardinia, and the Balearics. In the course of the 3rd cent. BC, Carthage seized the coast of Spain. This led to the Second Punic War (218–201 BC), during which Hannibal invaded Italy, repeatedly beat Roman armies, but was finally defeated in the Battle of Zama. The eventual Roman victory was due in part to the delaying tactics of the Roman general, Fabius Cunctator. Carthage recovered economically from defeat, but Roman animosity, kept alive by Cato the Elder (whose proleptic 'Carthago delenda est' became a battle cry), provoked the Third Punic War (149–146 BC), in which Scipio Africanus finally occupied Carthage and razed it to the ground. In the course of the Punic Wars, Rome annexed southern Spain and northern Africa and extended its sway to northern Italy, the Alps, and Illyria, absorbing the CELTS who had settled those lands. Numidia, which had been allowed to survive, was annexed in 106 BC by Marius. Rome had set its sights on MACEDON and Greece. Perseus, the last king of Macedon, was defeated in 197 BC. His kingdom and EPIRUS, which had sided with Macedon, were absorbed in 168–167 BC. Asia Minor fell into Roman hands with little resistance. A kingdom in western Anatolia, PERGAMUM was ruled by the Greek Attalids from 263 BC. To fend off Seleucid Syria, the rulers of Pergamum followed a pro-Roman policy, which culminated and ended when Attalus III bequeathed the kingdom to the Roman people in 133 BC. Pamphylia fell in 103 BC and Cilicia in 101 BC. BITHYNIA, following in the footsteps of the Attalids in Pergamum, was bequeathed to the Romans in 74 BC. The King of PONTUS, Mithridates IV, invaded Bithynia and was defeated by Pompey, who proceeded to annex Bithynia and Pontus in 65 BC. With most of Anatolia under its control, Rome in 63 BC proceeded to occupy Syria and Judaea (JUDAH). The latter had been successfully resisting the Seleucids in Syria since the 2nd cent. BC. These conquests brought Rome to the frontiers of PARTHIA and there for the first time the Roman impetus was checked. In 53 BC, Parthia defeated a Roman attempt at conquest led by the triumvir Marcus Licinius Crassus, thus virtually setting the limit to Roman expansion towards the east, although Trajan led an expedition against Parthia in AD 114–116. Cyrenaica in eastern Libya was occupied in 96 BC, as were Crete (67 BC) and Cyprus (58 BC) in the Mediterranean Sea. By 50 BC, Rome had annexed the coast from Spain to Italy. The Mediterranean had indeed become *mare nostrum.*

Julius Caesar

Rome was ready for the conquest of Gaul, which was carried out by Julius Caesar between 58 and 50 BC, extensive to the Rhine River and Portugal. The conquest of Britain was considered but not undertaken. Rome had not expanded without internal stresses. During the 2nd cent. BC the slaves had rebelled twice. In the early 1st. cent. BC the empire was wracked by the social wars which pitted Marius, the popular leader, and Sulla, the aristocracy's defender. Rome ended up in Sulla's hands and when he died his lieutenant Pompey brutally put down Spartacus' rebellion. Pompey also cleansed the eastern Mediterranean Sea of piracy and defeated Mithridates, King of Pontus. Pompey and Julius Caesar became political allies and formed a triumvirate with the wealthy Crassus in 60 BC. Crassus went to war against Parthia and was defeated. Caesar conquered Gaul and returned to Rome without the Senate's permission. His political challenge was expressed by the phrase 'crossing the Rubicon'. Pompey sided with the Senate and he and Caesar had a falling out. Caesar defeated his rival in the Battle of Pharsala in 48 BC.

Pompey was later killed in Egypt, where Caesar went and brought Cleopatra back to Rome as his mistress.

IMPERATOR AUGUSTUS

The assassination of Caesar in 44 BC caused new upheavals in the empire. A new triumvirate was created with Marc Antony, Octavian (Caesar's nephew), and Lepidus. Antony and Octavian vied for Caesar's mantle. Lepidus, who was not a risk-taker, was made governor of Africa but after 36 BC was given honorific titles by Octavian. Antony went to Egypt, where Cleopatra reigned – although Egypt had recognized the suzerainty of Rome since the 2nd cent. BC – and he fell in love with the Queen of the Nile. Antony tried to build an empire of his own in alliance with Cleopatra, its base in Alexandria, but he was defeated by Octavian at the naval Battle of Actium in 31 BC. Egypt was made a Roman province. In 29 BC, Octavian was given by the Senate the title of Imperator – which is a cognate of 'to rule' or 'to command' – and in 27 BC, he was additionally accorded the dignity of Augustus – something like imposing – which became the name by which he was known as the first Roman emperor. Under Augustus, the frontiers of the empire were secured along the Danube (AD 6) and the Rhine (AD 9) rivers. At his death in AD 14, the Roman Empire controlled Europe west of the Rhine and south of the Danube; the entire Mediterranean coast and its north African, Egyptian, Palestinian, and Syrian hinterlands; and Greece and western Anatolia. The position of emperor was not hereditary, as European kingships mostly have been. In fact, heredity and primogeniture are not the universal rule for kingly successions. Augustus was followed by twelve emperors – made infamous by Suetonius – who arrived at their eminence in different ways, mostly collaterally by designation or from military power, although Titus and Domitian were sons of Vespasian. During the 1st cent., Rome annexed the rest of Anatolia, Jordan, Dacia, and Britain. The Bosporan kingdom, though separated physically from the contiguous empire, was also a Roman dependency. Under Claudius, Rome began the conquest of Britain in 43, which culminated with Domitian in 85. Nero was a crapulous tyrant but he laid out Rome after the fire of 64 in the way in which the remnants of the imperial capital can be seen today. During Trajan's reign, Dacia, the province corresponding approximately to Romania, was annexed. Under Hadrian (117–138), with the annexation of Mesopotamia and ARMENIA (eastern and north-eastern Turkey and the southern Caucasus), the empire reached its greatest extension. At the time, if it wasn't the largest empire in history – Alexander might have conquered more territory – it was the best organized. However, as premonitory of times to come, Hadrian later moved the eastern frontier back to the Euphrates and he also built a wall in Britain to contain the Picts and other barbarians in Scotland. After Commodus, who reigned until 192, the Praetorian guards, the personal regiment of the

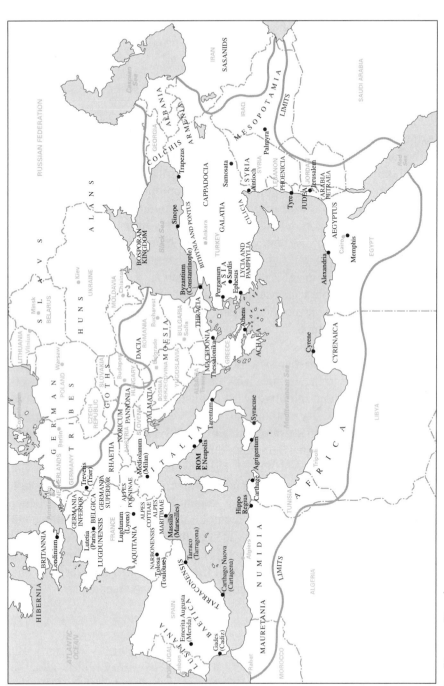

Map 8 Roman Empire

emperor, became so powerful they often decided on the imperial succession. They also tended to be barbarian recruits. They were disbanded by Constantine the Great in 312. Other clear signs of imperial decline were the death of Decius in battle with the Goths in Moesia in 251 and the capture of Valerian by the Sasanids in 260.

DIOCLETIAN AND CONSTANTINE

The complexity and weakness of the empire – after it had lost Mesopotamia and Armenia to the Sasanians and chunks of Rhaetia, Germania, and Dacia to the barbarians – induced Diocletian (284–305) to divide it among four co-rulers, two in the east and two in the west, which might have seemed administratively wise but also brought political complications and struggles. Diocletian relegated the senate to practically the condition of municipal body and tried to counter economic decay with strong measures including the enserfing of the peasantry. Although Diocletian himself abdicated, the other co-rulers fell to bickering and fighting until Constantine the Great in the Battle of the Milvian Bridge in 312 defeated Maxentius, his last serious rival. However, he was not able to concentrate imperial rule until 324. It was in that encounter that Constantine reported having had the vision of the cross and the message 'In hoc signo vinces'. Be that as it may, the following year, in Milan, he dictated an edict establishing religious freedom in the empire, which in effect was a bonus for Christianity although not its officialization. Constantine restored some vigour to the empire, which made marginal recuperations of territory. His most important initiative was to transfer his imperial capital to Constantinople (the Greek Byzantium) in 330, which involved the *de facto* division of the empire into western and eastern halves. This division, roughly along a line from Sirmium (Belgrade) down to the central coast of Libya, became permanent after the death of Theodosius in 395. Honorius in 402 established the capital of the Roman Empire in the west in Ravenna. Although not immune to attacks from invaders, the Roman Empire in the east had better natural defences and it was the western empire that had to take the full weight of the barbarians. The HUNS, who invaded in the 5th cent. under Attila, have taken a disproportionate amount of opprobrium because of their devastations, but their share of spoils were minimal and transitory. It was the Germans and confederates such as the Alans that brought the Empire to an end.

ROMULUS AUGUSTULUS

The Visigoths (GOTHS) began their incursions in 357 and, by the early 5th cent., were well entrenched in western France. They also raided into the Balkans as far as Constantinople itself. Britain was abandoned in 410. The FRANKS moved slowly but ponderously and occupied the territory they invaded from the Elbe to the Atlantic coast of France, pushing the Visigoths to

the Iberian Peninsula, where they established their kingdom. By the end of the 5th cent. the Franks had established Merovingian France. The OSTROGOTHS followed their western cousins and after marauding in eastern Europe, where they were whipped by the Huns, eventually conquered Ravenna (493) and Italy. The ironically named Romulus Augustulus, last emperor in the west, had been deposed in 476 by Odoacer, a German chieftain who tried to defend Italy but succumbed to the Ostrogothic king, Theodoric. Nothing remained of the western empire, but the Roman Empire in the east, the BYZANTINE EMPIRE as it became known, was intact, except for the maulings it received at the height of the Barbarian invasions. It would soon try to fulfil its imperial destiny as repository of the Roman tradition.
(*See chronology under* Balkans.)

Rum Sultanate (11th–13th cents.; *Anatolia*)
After their conquest of Persia (SELJUK PERSIA), Seljuk hordes ranged over Iraq and Syria and formed the SELJUK EMIRATES. In 1071, a force of Seljuks defeated in Manzikert (central Turkey) an army of the BYZANTINE EMPIRE and opened Anatolia to Seljuk conquest. The principal result of this was the creation of the Rum Sultanate, which absorbed the other emirates Seljuk atabegs or chieftains created after Manzikert. It lasted from 1081 to 1302, with its capital successively in Nicaea and in Iconium, and gradually dissolved into the ANATOLIAN EMIRATES, two of which became domin- ant: Karaman, in eastern Turkey, and that of the Ottomans (OTTOMAN EMPIRE) in Phrygia and Bithynia.
(*See chronology under* Anatolia.)

Russia
SEE ENTRY IN 'PROVINCES AND REGIONS'
European Russia is the heartland of the SLAVS. By AD 200 they occupied territories from the Upper Volga to the Vistula River. By 550 they had expanded to the Elbe River and the Black Sea. They seized territories which the GOTHS and other Germanic tribes mostly abandoned, lured by the riches of ROME. By 700, the Slavs were occupying lands from the Baltic to northern Greece and across to the north-western shore of the Black Sea. During the 9th cent. the Magyars opened space for themselves in the midst of the Slavic lands.

KIEVAN RUS

Led by Rurik, Swedish Varangians (NORSEMEN), marauders and traders, were established ca. 860 in Novgorod. According to the Russian medieval *Primary Chronicle*, ca. 880 the heirs of Rurik had their base in Kiev. Vladimir unified the Varangian and Slavic territories along the Dnieper River from Kiev to Novgorod ca. 980, and can thus be said to have founded Kievan Rus. He also converted to Orthodox Christianity, which he made the official religion of his kingdom. After his son Yaroslavl, Kievan Rus was shared out between Rurik princes. It is often assumed that Kievan Rus fragmented into warring principalities and ceased to exist ca. 1050. However, the lands that were united under Kievan Rus were mainly ruled by descendants of Rurik, who recognized the ascendancy first of Kiev and then of Suzdal and Vladimir. It is also possible to discover a generational pattern in Rurik successions which would explain the predominant roles of those principalities. In any event, the Rurik line, which dominated Russia until Ivan the Terrible, became established in Kiev and it is from Kiev that it drew its continuity. In the 11th cent., Kievan Rus comprised the heartland of Russia to the southern Ukraine. During the 12th cent. marginal additions were made to this territory. By the early 13th cent., Kievan Rus extended from the shores of Lake Ladoga to the Lower Dnieper River. At its greatest extent, it comprised the following principalities: Chernigov, Galich, Kiev, Murom, Novgorod, Novgorod-Seversk, Pereyaslavl, Polotsk, Rostov, Ryazan, Smolensk, Suzdalia, Tmutorokan, Turov-Pinsk, Viatka, Vladimir-Suzdal, Vladirmir-Volinsk, and Volhynia. Novgorod was an oligarchic republic dependent on the Ruriks. Viatka refers to northern lands explored and colonized by Novgorodian fur traders. Tmutorokan, the only Rurik principality on the Black Sea, fell to the POLOVETZY in the 12th cent. By the mid-12th cent., Kiev had declined to such an extent that it was sacked ca. 1170 by Andrei Bogolubski, Prince of Suzdal, who established his capital and the chief Rurik political centre in Vladimir. By the end of the 13th cent. it was Tver that held the ascendancy. Kievan Rus was beset on the north west by the Swedes and the German LIVONIAN BROTHERS OF THE SWORD, in the west by LITHUANIA, and in the south by the PETCHENEGS, who were replaced by the Polovetzy. Russian relations with the Polovetzy were not bad as a rule. To the east, Kievan Rus neighboured on the VOLGA BULGARS with whom it was also on good terms. However, the Swedes, the Germans, and the Lithuanians mounted successive assaults against the Russians in the 1240s. Prince Alexander Nevsky, Grand Duke of Vladimir, defeated the Swedes on the Neva River in 1240 – hence the name Nevsky – the Germans on Lake Peipus in 1242, and the Lithuanians west of Pskov in 1245. The battles against Swedes and Germans occurred on ice, which makes Alexander the living prototype of 'general winter'.

THE MONGOL PERIOD

The Mongols, generally known in Russia as Tatars, first started raiding Kievan Rus between 1223 and 1227. They returned in force in 1236, crushed all resistance, went as far as Poland and Hungary, and founded the Khanate of the GOLDEN HORDE on the steppes formerly occupied by the Polovetzy. They did not annex the Kievan Rus principalities but made them vassals, especially Vladimir, where Alexander Nevsky – bowing to the inevitable – became an agent of Mongol overlordship, even forcing his fellow Ruriks to obey Mongolian dictates. Even if the Ruriks did have a complex system for establishing the headship of the dynasty, after the arrival of the Mongols, what counted on issues of succession was what Sarai, the capital of the Golden Horde, decided. Russia's weakness was a benefit for LITHUANIA, which, first by itself and later with POLAND, in the early 15th cent. had taken Galich, Pinsk, Kiev, Polotsk, and Smolensk. Under Mongol overlordship, the principality of Muscovy expanded and grew stronger from the early 14th cent. Although it was not as decisive as it is sometimes said to be, the Battle of Kulikovo, won in 1380 by Prince Dmitry Donskoi of Moscow over Khan Mamai of the Golden Horde, was the first defeat inflicted on the Mongols in Russian lands. Under the rule of Ivan Kalita, Moscow was recognized as the strongest Rurik domain. But what really made its fortunes was the dismemberment of the Golden Horde – from internal causes rather than external aggression – into separate khanates in the early 15th cent. (CRIMEA, KAZAN, ASTRAKHAN).

Ivan IV the Terrible

Under strong rulers, from 1463 to 1533 Moscow annexed Yaroslavl (1463), Rostov (1474), Tver (1485), Pskov (1510), Ryazan (1521), Chernigov (just short of Kiev), Smolensk, and Pskov (1533). Novgorod, who had taken advantage of the Mongol menace to ignore Rurik overlordship, had been returned to the fold in 1478. In the north east, Russian trappers had been extending Moscow's claims to beyond the Urals. When Ivan IV the Terrible acceded to the throne in 1533 – he became Tsar of all the Russias in 1547 – Russia was ready to get its revenge on the Tatars. In 1552, the Khanate of Kazan was conquered with huge cannon. In 1556, it was the turn of Astrakhan and in 1598, of SIBIR. The rise of the OTTOMAN EMPIRE prevented the absorption of the Khanate of the Crimea, the last of the Golden Horde successor states, until 1783. Ivan died in 1582. Boris Godunov, an important courtier, assumed the regency for Ivan's son Fyodor, who died in 1598. Fyodor's younger brother, Dmitry, had died in 1591. Godunov, who himself became tsar in 1598, was suspected in both deaths, and when he died (1605) Russia was torn by factions fuelled by pretenders, one at least claiming to be Dmitry. Russia was finally subjected to invasion by the Poles, who, with the connivance of Russian grandees (boyars), occupied Moscow in 1610. An anti-Polish reaction came about in 1612. Moscow was recovered and in 1613 a national council of boyars and churchmen accepted Michael Romanov – descendant of Ivan IV's first wife – as Tsar Michael I, founder of the Romanov dynasty, which was to last until 1917. Michael was only 14 at the time and it was his father, patriarch Philaret, who manoeuvred his son to the throne.

PETER THE GREAT

Under the Romanovs, Russian expansion continued. In 1634, Kiev was taken from the Poles. In 1667, the Ukraine was enlarged south of Kiev, also at the expense of Poland, to the frontiers of the Ottoman Empire, then at its zenith. Peter I the Great inherited the throne in 1689. He wanted to be a great reformer and it is true that Russian military strength was bolstered, but Russian absolutism was more enforced than weakened during his reign. He tried to create a class of nobility along western European lines, but he made sure that it could not claim any political privileges, and it was Peter who founded the bureaucratic system that was the day-to-day face of Tsarist autocracy. His authority was so thorough that he could abolish the Patriarchate of the Russian Orthodox church, the very marrow of Russia, and substitute it with a Holy Synod wholly subservient to him. In extremely punishing conditions, he forced huge masses of his subjects to build the new and splendid Russian capital, St Petersburg, inaugurated in 1712. On the territorial front, Peter gained parts of Karelia in 1714, and he conquered Ingria (west of St Petersburg), Estonia, and Livonia in 1721, all at the expense of Sweden. But in his drive towards the Black Sea, he made no headway against the Ottomans. Peter was succeeded by a series of weak or unremarkable monarchs until the accession of the overwhelming Catherine II. Nevertheless, Russia practically had its own momentum, in part because, towards the east, it was inexorably filling a vacuum of power that offered itself with each mile gained. By 1762 it had reached the frontiers of eastern Mongolia absorbing along the way northern Kazakhstan and Semipalatinsk (1740). Henceforward, the northern Mongolian frontier would be determined by Russian expansion. In the south, the unruliness of ZAPROZHYE, a Cossack no-man's land north west of the Sea of Azov, permitted the annexation of more territory to Ukraine between 1725 and 1762.

CATHERINE II THE GREAT

Catherine II the Great was a German princess married to Tsar Peter III. With the complicity of her lover Orlov and the Tsar's own guard, she took the throne of Russia from her husband shortly after his accession in 1762. During the Seven Years War and through the partition of Poland, proposed to her by Frederick I the Great of Prussia, she made Russia a paramount power in European politics. Russia benefited little from the first partition of Poland (1772), but in the second (1793) and third and final (1795) partitions, Russia gained Courland, Byelorussia, Volhynia, and Podolia. Catherine gave impetus to Russia's push against the Ottoman Empire. In all, Russians and Turks fought eight wars from 1736 to 1878. Russia did not win them all, but over the long run it was Russia who gained Ottoman territory and who encouraged and even actively supported fissiparous tendencies within the Ottoman Empire. The weakening hold of the Ottomans resulted in the Russian acquisition of Jedisan (north of Odessa), the Crimea, and the Kuban (east of the Sea of Azov) between 1774 and 1786. By Catherine's death in 1796, Russia ruled Siberia to the Sea of Okhotsk and Kamchatka, both of which had actually been claimed by Russia in 1728, before south-eastern Siberia. Between 1763 and 1784, Russia had rounded out Siberia with the annexation of Chuckchi (tip of Eurasia) and settled Alaska. Catherine was succeeded by Paul I, murdered in 1801. Alexander I (1801–1825) became a key figure in the European resistance to Napoleon's ambitions. Russian armies consistently suffered defeats at the hands of the French, culminating in the Peace of Tilsit in 1807, by which Russia lost Poland. But when Napoleon invaded Russia with a huge army (Grande Armée) in 1812, the master strategist Kutuzov, after the indecisive Battle of Borodino, led him on a useless chase all the way to burned-out Moscow, so that the French had to retreat into the unfriendly hold of a Russian winter. In VIENNA, after Napoleon's defeat in Waterloo, Russia obtained all it wanted territorially in Europe, especially Poland, which remained part of the Russian empire until 1918. In 1809 Russia had taken Finland from Sweden and just before the French invasion it acquired Bessarabia from the Turks in a short war in 1811–1812. In 1853, Russia occupied MOLDAVIA and VALACHIA, vassals of the Ottoman Empire. The Porte declared war and Great Britain and France (later joined by Sardinia), distrustful of Russia's influence in the Balkans, joined the Ottomans in the Crimean War which lasted to 1856. Although Russia was not defeated, the Crimea was invaded and Russia's power was curbed. Moldavia and Valachia were restored to the Ottomans as vassal states. Southern Bessarabia was ceded by Russia to Moldavia, but Russia took it back in 1878. Under Nicholas I (1825–1855), Russia became the strongest enforcer of the so-called Holy Alliance, an agreement with the HABSBURG EMPIRE and Prussia to stifle nationalist, liberal, or democratic tendencies. In 1830–1831, Russia stripped Poland of every political right and in 1848–1849 it intervened to quell the Hungarian nationalist uprising against the predominance of Austria within the Habsburg Empire. There was only one tsar who showed a certain measure of liberalism and that was Alexander II, who was killed by an anarchist bomb in 1881.

THE FALL OF THE ROMANOVS

The annexation of the Kuban and a southward advance from Astrakhan at the expense of Persian claims had taken Russia to the Caucasus, where its borders expanded with successive annexations: western Georgia in 1801, from the Ottomans; Dagestan and AZERBAIJAN on the western shore of the Caspian Sea in 1813, from Persia; and eastern GEORGIA and ARMENIA in 1828, also from Persia (IRAN). The Kirghiz Steppe (from Lake Balkash to the Aral Sea) had been occupied by 1855. Russia had extended its political influence to the

KOKAND KHANATE by 1865, when it came into conflict with BUKHARA resulting in the annexation of both territories in 1876. The future TAJIKI-STAN was occupied in 1880 – the Pamirs in 1895 – followed by Khiva (UZBEKISTAN) in 1881 and Merv (TURKMENISTAN) in 1884. The border with AFGHANISTAN was defined by treaty after 1885, under the watchful eye of BRITISH INDIA. In the far east, China was too weak to do anything about Russia's annexation of the maritime province (Vladivostok). Apart from minor exchanges of territory in the west, the only considerable territorial loss that Russia experienced during the 19th cent., and voluntarily at that, was the sale of Alaska to the United States for $7,200,000.

After the assassination of Archduke Francis Ferdinand, the Habsburg heir, by a Serbian fanatic in June 1914, Austria presented SERBIA with impossible conditions which Serbia rejected with Russian backing. In July Austria declared war on Serbia. Russia, who claimed special rights in the Balkans – to some extent justified given its history of opposition to the Porte – came to the side of Serbia and declared war on Austria. Germany declared war on Russia on 1 August and on France on 3 August. Great Britain, who did not want to have the balance of power on the continent tilted, entered the war against Germany and Austria. That was how World War I began. Finishing it was not so easy. The Russians went to war with due enthusiasm but were woefully unprepared because of entrenched incompetence fostered by despotism. Nicholas II, the last of the Romanovs, was despised by his own father, Tsar Alexander III, and as a ruler showed nonpareil fecklessness except on his blind adhesion to the principle of absolute rule. At first victorious on the Austrian front – the Habsburg Empire was anything but a cohesive fighting machine – Russia soon got trounced by the Germans in the Masurian Lakes region of East Prussia in 1915. The Russian front held only because the Germans did not

Map 9   Southern Russia, Caucasus, and Northern Anatolia

want to divert resources from the western front. In 1916, the Russian armies, under the command of General Brusilov, attempted going on the offensive, but instead they collapsed through defeat, insubordination, and desertion. The home front was in an explosive state and in February 1917 the monarchy was overthrown and a provisional government installed. Nicholas abdicated in March. The provisional government, under first the well-intentioned Lvov and then the vain Kerensky, tried to have Russia stay in the fight, but the Russians were not in the mood and, in November, the Bolsheviks led by Lenin took St Petersburg (then Petrograd), and thereafter the rest of Russia under the slogan

---

Southern Russia
Predominant political influences

13th–8th cents. BC
Cimmerians

7th–5th cents. BC
Scythians

4th cent. BC
Scythians
Sarmatians

3rd cent. BC
Sarmatians
Slavs

2nd cent. BC–5th cent. AD
Slavs
Germans (Goths)
Alans
Huns

6th cent.
Slavs
Avars
Bulgars

7th–8th cents.
Slavs
Avars
Bulgars
Khazars

9th cent.
Slavs
Avars
Bulgars
Khazars
Magyars
Varangians
  (Norsemen)

10th cent.
Khazars
Russia (Kievan Rus)
Petchenegs

11th cent.
Khazars
Russia (Kievan Rus)
Petchenegs
Polovetzy

12th cent.
Russia (Kievan Rus)
Petchenegs
Polovetzy

13th cent.
Russia (Kievan Rus)
Polovetzy
Mongol Empire
Golden Horde

14th cent.
Golden Horde
Lithuania
Poland–Lithuania
Zaprozhye

15th cent.
Golden Horde
Poland
Zaprozhye
Crimea (Khanate)
Ottoman Empire

16th–17th cents.
Poland
Zaprozhye
Crimea (Khanate)
Ottoman Empire

18th cent.
Zaprozhye
Crimea (Khanate)
Ottoman Empire
Russia

19th cent.
Russia

of power to the Soviets. Nicholas and his entire family and immediate retainers were assassinated by the communists, on instructions from Lenin himself, in July 1918 in Yekaterinburg (Soviet Sverdlovsk).

After 1917 Russia became the nucleus of the USSR (Union of Soviet Socialist Republics) and did not become Russia again until the USSR dissolved during 1990–1991 into its constituent republics. Thus the Soviet fiction of a federation of sovereign states became a reality to the detriment of what was the largest land empire in history. Considering this huge loss of territory – also the largest in history – Russia has taken it remarkably well. And Russia is still the sixth most populous nation in the world.

(*See chronologies under* Southern Russia, China and Neighbouring Areas, Greater Mongolia, Iran, *and* Western Turkestan.)

Rwanda

Peopled mostly by Hutus but ruled by Tutsi lords in the 19th cent., Rwanda became a mandate (1919) and later a trust territory of Belgium (BELGIAN COLONIAL EMPIRE). It was given independence in 1962. Tutsis and Hutus speak related Bantu languages, spoken all over central and southern Africa. The capital of Rwanda is Kigali.

S

Safavids (16th–18th cents.; *Iran*)
The Iranian dynasty of the Safavids overthrew the AQ-QOYUNLU in 1502 and became master of western IRAN. It fought over Khurasan with the SHAYBANIDS and finally secured it in 1597. The Safavid Shah Ismail was among the first Asian conquerors to introduce the use of cannon. The others were Babur, founder of the Mughal Empire, and Sultan Selim I of the Ottoman Empire. The Safavids restored Persia after centuries of division and Mongol and Turkish domination. They were contained by the OTTOMAN EMPIRE in the west. The Safavid restoration marks the beginning of the modern territorial history of Iran. They were overthrown during the Afghani invasion of Persia (1722–1736) and were succeeded by the Afshar, another Persian dynasty.
(*See chronology under* Iran.)

Saffarids (9th cent.; *Iran*)
The Persian Saffarid dynasty originated in Seistan. After ca. 860 they took Khurasan from the TAHIRIDS and even attempted to take Baghdad. They were displaced from Khurasan by the SAMANIDS (ca. 900) and retreated to their homeland where they ruled until it was absorbed by the SAFAVIDS in the 16th cent. Seistan acquired its name from the SAKA or Asian Scythians.
(*See chronology under* Iran.)

St Kitts and Nevis
Discovered by Columbus in 1493, British after 1623, the north Caribbean islands of St Kitts and Nevis became independent in 1983. The capital is Basseterre.

St Lucia
It is believed that St Lucia was originally peopled by Arawaks, who were later displaced by Caribs. It was probably visited by Columbus in 1502. After 1642, it was settled by the French, who had a hard time subjecting the Caribs. It passed between France and Great Britain various times before British sovereignty was recognized in 1814 (BRITISH COLONIAL EMPIRE). St Lucia was part of the British Windward Islands from 1880 to 1958. It was also part of the British-sponsored Federation of the West Indies from 1958 to 1962. In 1979 St Lucia became independent. The capital is Castries.

St Vincent and the Grenadines
Peopled by Caribs, discovered by Columbus in 1498, the island of St Vincent was occupied by the British in 1762, seized by France in 1779, and restored

definitely to Great Britain in 1783 (BRITISH COLONIAL EMPIRE). The Caribs were deported by the British to small islands in the Gulf of Honduras. St Vincent was part of the British colony of the Windward Islands from 1880 to 1958. From 1958 to 1962 it was part of the British-sponsored Federation of the West Indies. With the smaller Grenadines to the south, St Vincent became independent in 1979. The capital is Kingstown.

Saka (2nd cent. BC–4th cent. AD; *Central Asia*: western Turkestan; Afghanistan; northern *India*)

When the YÜEH-CHIH or TOKHARIANS were expelled from China in the 3rd cent. BC, they moved towards the Ili River Valley, east of Lake Balkash, where its inhabitants, the WU SUN, resisted their advance and sent them towards the Amu Darya River. There they encountered the Saka, or Asian SCYTHIANS. The Saka ca. 130 BC attacked BACTRIA, then divided into many small Greek kingdoms. Under attack by the Yüeh-chih, a branch of the Saka invaded Seistan and Kandahar. Apparently allied to their pursuers, the Saka killed King Phraates of PARTHIA, but eventually they were subjected by the Parthians ca. 100 BC. Another branch of the Saka went to Kabul, where the Yüeh-chih, who were firmly established in Bactria, drove them to Gandhara. The Saka founded a large but short-lived empire in NORTHERN INDIA. In the territory of Bactria, the Yüeh-chih/Tokharians founded KUSHANA in the 1st cent. AD. Kushana invaded Gandhara and drove the Saka to Gujarat, where they eventually disappeared from history in the 4th cent.
(*See chronologies under* Afghanistan *and* Indian Subcontinent.)

Salerno (Duchy of) (5th–11th cents.; southern *Italy*)
A Greek site, Salerno became a Roman colony in 197 BC. Part of the Lombard duchy of Benevento in the 6th cent. (LOMBARD ITALY), it became an independent duchy in the 9th cent. and was incorporated by Robert Guiscard into NORMAN ITALY in 1076. In the 1220s it was part of the Hohenstaufen inheritance and later belonged to the Kingdom of NAPLES.

Salonika (LATIN STATES)

Samanids (9th–10th cents.; eastern *Iran*)
The Samanids were a Persian dynasty that had its base ca. 880 in Transoxiana, where the TAHIRIDS had not reached. Beginning in the 10th cent., they took Khurasan from the SAFFARIDS and reduced TABARISTAN in 902. Their empire extended in the east as far as Ferghana. They were displaced from Khurasan by the GHAZNAVIDS and towards the end of the century Transoxiana and their lands further east fell to the KARAKHANIDS.
(*See chronology under* Iran.)

Samarkand (TIMURID EMPIRE AND SUCCESSOR STATES)

Samoa

Peopled by speakers of a Malayo-Polynesian language, the Pacific Ocean island of Western Samoa, as opposed to American Samoa but part of the same archipelago, was German from 1899 to 1914, when it was occupied by New Zealand, who administered it as a League of Nations mandate from 1920 and as United Nations trust territory after 1945. It has been independent as Samoa since 1962. The capital of Samoa is Apia.

San Marino

San Marino is a tiny, independent republic in central Italy. It was probably founded in mid-5th cent. It was a free commune in the 12th cent. Though surrounded by the Papal States, the papacy recognized its independence in 1631, which the Congress of VIENNA ratified in 1815.

Sao Tome and Principe

Portuguese since the 15th cent. the African equatorial islands of Sao Tome and Principe were a depot for slaves bound for the western hemisphere during various centuries. They became independent in 1975. The capital is Sao Tome.

Sarbedarians (14th cent.; eastern *Iran*)

After the death of the last of the rulers of ILKHANID PERSIA in 1335, the Sarbedarians set up a kingdom in north-western Khurasan (1337) with lands they wrested from the Afghan KERTS. It was destroyed by Tamerlane towards the end of the century (TIMURID EMPIRE AND SUCCESSOR STATES). (*See chronology under* Iran.)

Sardinia (Kingdom of) (14th–19th cents.; *Italy*)

The island of Sardinia has variously been used or occupied by Phoenicians, Romans, Vandals, Byzantines, Popes, Arabs, Pisans, and Genoese. It was a patrimony of the Crown of ARAGON after 1297. In 1713 it was awarded to the HABSBURG EMPIRE, given to Bourbon Spain in 1717, and ceded to the Turinese house of SAVOY in 1720, who named its kingdom after the island. The kingdom of Sardinia served as the platform to unify Italy during the *risorgimento* using the abilities of Victor Emmanuel II, the crafty Cavour, the impulsive Massini, and the daring Garibaldi.

SOLFERINO

Originally Sardinia was the Duchy of SAVOY and Piedmont, created by a nobleman from the kingdom of ARLES as part of the HOLY ROMAN EMPIRE in the 11th cent. After 1356, its affairs, like those of the rest of northern Italy, ceased to be of imperial concern. During the first half of the 16th cent. Savoy was under French and Swiss influences. It was restored in 1559 with Turin as its capital. In 1713, during the War of Spanish Succession, Savoy was awarded Sicily, which it exchanged in 1720 with Bourbon Spain for Sardinia. Sardinia, except the island, was absorbed by the French in 1797 and became part, first, of the Cisalpine Republic and then of the kingdom of Italy (FRENCH EUROPEAN EMPIRE). Sardinia was restored in 1815 and given Liguria (GENOA). Allied to the French Emperor Napoleon III, it defeated the Austrians in 1859 in the Battle of Solferino and annexed most of northern Italy, but ceded northern Savoy and Nice to France in 1860. In 1866, Sardinia sided with Prussia against Austria and annexed Venetia. With the annexation of the kingdom of the TWO SICILIES, which was Garibaldi's epic doing in 1861, the kingdom of Italy was proclaimed under the ancient house of Savoy. Napoleon III stayed the hands of the Italians in regard to Rome until France was engaged in war with Prussia (1870–1871), when Italy took it from the papacy.

Sarmatians (4th cent. BC–3rd cent. AD; *Central Asia*: greater Mongolia; *Southern Russia*)

During the 3rd cent. BC, the Sarmatians gradually replaced the SCYTHIANS in southern Russia. Both Scythians and Sarmatians were Indo-Iranian speakers. The WU SUN were a people – described by the Chinese as red-bearded and blue-eyed – known from Chinese sources to have occupied the Ili River Basin from the 2nd cent. BC to the 2nd cent. AD, when they were conquered by the HSIEN PI. It has been argued that the Sarmatians might have been a branch of the Wu Sun that detached itself in the 4th cent. BC. There are traces of Sarmatian culture in central Siberia (Minusinsk) into the 3rd cent. AD. In southern Russia itself, the Sarmatians were pushed towards the east by the GOTHS and later seem to have been assimilated by the ALANS.

(*See chronologies under* Greater Mongolia *and* Southern Russia.)

Sasanid Empire (3rd–7th cents.; *Middle East*)
SEE ENTRY IN 'PROVINCES AND REGIONS'

Under Ardashid I, the Persian Sasanids overthrew PARTHIA in AD 224 and consolidated its empire and vassal territories. The Sasanids established their capital in Ctesiphon. The Parthians had contained Roman expansion eastwards and it fell to the Sasanids to carry on with this task (ROME). In 260, the Sasanids, under Shapur I, captured Emperor Valerian. In the 4th cent., they annexed ARMENIA, which had been a Roman vassal state. During the 5th and 6th cents. the Sasanians were kept busy in the east fighting off intermittent but vigorous incursions by the EPHTHALITES, and no sooner had these been repelled than they had to face the first onslaughts of the Turks out of their central Asian homelands (T'U CHÜEH). By 628, the Sasanids had conquered as far as Egypt and Arabia, but their hold over their empire was weak and, in 637, it was over-run by ISLAM.

(*See chronology under* Iran.)

Saudi Arabia

SEE *ARABIA* IN 'PROVINCES AND REGIONS'

Saudi Arabia occupies the greater part of the Arabian peninsula, which ca. 1000 BC was home to SHEBA and other small kingdoms. Darius, ruler of the ACHAEMENID EMPIRE, conquered north Arabia, but the rest of the peninsula was mostly occupied by BEDOUINS, who, over the centuries, were the only inhabitants of the Arabian desert. ROME occupied the northern Hejaz. The western coast of Arabia came under the control of the African kingdom of Axum (ETHIOPIA) in the 6th cent. AD. The SASANID EMPIRE replaced Axum as the predominant political influence in the region. In the 7th cent. ISLAM was born in Mecca and Medina, in the Hejaz, from where it spread to the entire peninsula. When the caliphate was moved from Mecca to Damascus, Arabia reverted to its fragmented, tribal state although adhering to Islam. The Karmathians, who were Ismaili Shiites, ruled during the 10th and 11th cents., but their power waned and Arabia again became disunited. In 1508, the Portuguese established themselves in OMAN. By 1520, the OTTOMAN EMPIRE had conquered as far as YEMEN and in 1659 annexed Oman. Great Britain seized Aden in 1839 and in 1853 the Trucial States (UNITED ARAB EMIRATES) came under its influence. Arab nationalism was stimulated during the 19th cent. by the Wahhabi sect, whose leader, Ibn Saud (b. ca. 1888–1953) had his capital in Riyad, in the Najd. Husein Ibn Ali, of the Hashemite family, was the Ottoman sharif of Mecca. By the beginning of World War I, Ibn Saud had established an independent kingdom. To counter the Turks, Great Britain, represented by T. E. Lawrence, approached the Hashemites of Mecca and incited them to rebel against the Ottomans, which they did in 1916 with considerable success. However, after the war, the British did not support Husein's claim to Arabia and in 1924 Ibn Saud took Mecca and joined Nejd and Hejaz. Husein was forced to abandon his claim to the caliphate, which he had assumed after its abolition by Mustafa Kemal (TURKEY). The Hashemites were compensated with Transjordan which became the kingdom of JORDAN after World War II. Ibn Saud went on to found modern Saudi Arabia.

Savoy (15th–18th cents.; *France* and *Italy*)

Savoy today is the part of France south of Lake Geneva. ROME lost Gaul to Germanic invaders during the 5th cent. The territory of Savoy was occupied by the BURGUNDIANS. There was an early kingdom of BURGUNDY along the Rhône River down to Arles founded ca. 480, taken by the Franks in 534. After Charlemagne's death, authority in Europe consisted in linkages of fealties and much of the land was still for the taking. In 879 a kingdom was established in Arles (Cisjurane Burgundy) and in 888 another one in Burgundy (Transjurane Burgundy). In 933 a lord joined them as Arelate or the kingdom of ARLES which embraced, besides Provence, the provinces of Lyonnais, Dauphiné, Franche Comté, and Savoy including part of Switzerland. In 1043 it was annexed to the HOLY ROMAN EMPIRE, which neglected it, and in 1378 the kingdom was absorbed by France. However, Savoy had been mostly autonomous and in 1416 it became a duchy, with its capital in Chambery. It extended south to north west Italy and to Nice. During the first half of the 16th cent. Savoy was under French and Swiss influences. It was restored in 1559 with Turin as its capital. During the War of the Spanish Succession (1700–1713), the ruler of Savoy, Victor Amadeus II, became King of SICILY. Spain recaptured the island in 1718, but in 1720 Savoy was awarded Sardinia, whose name was adopted for the entire kingdom. Sardinia ceded northern Savoy to France in 1860.

Scotland (9th–18th cents.; Great Britain)
SEE ENTRY IN 'PROVINCES AND REGIONS'
The Picts, of whom little is known, and the CELTS were in Scotland when ROME conquered Britain. After the Romans departed, Scotland (anciently known as Caledonia) was divided into various kingdoms. Northumbria, an Anglo-Saxon kingdom (ENGLAND), extended to east Scotland. Irish culture filtered in through the island of Iona. The NORSEMEN intermittently besieged Scotland from the 8th to the 12th cents. They settled the Hebrides, the Shetlands, and the Orkneys. In the mid-9th cent. a Scots king, Kenneth I, ruled Scotland north of the Firth of Forth. Scottish kings, notably David I, ruled the land during the 11th and 12th cents. Strathclyde, an ancient but obscure Celtic kingdom, was absorbed as south west Scotland in the 11th cent. Henry II obtained an oath of fealty from the Scottish king, William the Lion (1174), who later repudiated it and Richard I ambiguously absolved Scotland from fealty. The Danes were defeated in 1263. The Orkneys passed to the Scots in 1231 and the Hebrides in 1266. The Shetlands were taken by the Scots in 1472 as an unpaid dowry owed by the Danish Crown. The English persisted in their claim on Scotland and, in 1299, Edward I made John of Baliol his vassal. Scotland sought support from France at this time, thus establishing the long historical links between the two countries. The English were defeated by Robert the Bruce in the Battle of Bannockburn in 1314 and, in 1328, Edward III recognized Scottish independence. The first Stuart king was Robert II in 1371. Scottish history during the 14th, 15th, and 16th cents. was very turbulent, except for periods of stability such as the reign of James IV (1488–1513), who married Margaret Tudor, daughter of Henry VII. James himself was killed in the English victory at Flodden Field. Mary Queen of Scots, granddaughter of James IV, was beheaded by Elizabeth I Tudor, but when the latter died childless, Mary's son James V, who had brought order to Scotland, ascended the English throne in 1603 as James I. The direct male Stuart line ended with the deposition of James II in 1688. In 1707, by the Act of Union, England and Scotland were joined as one kingdom under Queen Anne, daughter of James II. Edinburgh, which dates from the 11th cent., is the capital of Scotland. (GREAT BRITAIN).

Scythians (8th–3rd cents. BC; *Central Asia* and southern Russia)
Originally from western Turkestan, the Scythians were Indo-Iranian speaking nomads who dominated the steppes north of the Black Sea from the late 8th cent. BC to the mid-3rd cent. BC. From this base they raided all over south west Asia as far as Palestine. They were contained by MEDIA. At the height of their prosperity the Scythians traded with the Greek colonies of the Black Sea. They were gradually replaced in southern Russia by the SARMATIANS, who were also Indo-Iranian speakers. Indo-Iranian is a major branch of the Indo-European family of languages (to which most of the languages of Europe belong as well as Hindi and other Indian languages). It has been argued that the Sarmatians might be descended from the WU SUN, a people who are known from Chinese sources to have occupied the Ili River Basin from the 2nd cent. BC to the 2nd cent. AD, when they were conquered by the HSIEN PI. Not all the Scythian tribes moved to southern Russia. It is believed that a majority of them remained in Ferghana and Kashgaria. These were the Scythians of Asia, known to the Indians as SAKA.
(*See chronology under* Southern Russia.)

Sea-peoples (PELASGIANS)

Seistan (SAFFARIDS)

Seleucid Empire (3rd–1st cents. BC; *Middle East*)
Even before Alexander's death (323) autonomous statelets were being created in the eastern confines of the empire: Omphis and Porus in the Indus Valley and Abhisara in the western reaches of the Himalayas. Little is known of these kingdoms. During the sharing out of the ALEXANDRIAN EMPIRE known as the DIADOCHI WARS, the Macedonian general Seleucus had, by 301 BC, obtained Asia Minor, Syria, Judaea, and Persia as far as the Indus River Valley. His capital was established in Antioch ca. 300. Although he sallied as far as north west India, Seleucus could not control the lands east of Persia. His defeat of Lysimachus in 281 BC signalled the end of the Diadochi Wars. The Seleucid Empire began unravelling even before the death of its founder in 280 BC. Anatolia divided into different kingdoms: PONTUS (4th cent. BC–1st cent. AD), BITHYNIA (297–274 BC), PERGAMUM (263–133 BC), CAPPADOCIA (3rd cent. BC to AD 17), all of which ended as provinces of ROME. By 261 BC, Palestine had been taken by PTOLEMAIC EGYPT. In fact, from the middle of the 3rd cent. BC the history of the empire is mainly that of its recurrent wars with Egypt over Palestine and its efforts to retain territories in Asia Minor. In the east, the Greek kingdom of BACTRIA was founded in 256 BC. PARTHIA came into being in 247 BC. Nearer to home ARMENIA existed in 189 BC. Media Atropatene (Azerbaijan) was a vassal of Armenia and subsequently of Parthia. Antiochus III (223–187 BC) made a valiant effort to rebuild the empire. From 211 to 205 BC he went as far

as India and he recovered part of Asia Minor, but in 190 BC he suffered defeat at the hands of the Romans and all of Asia Minor was permanently lost. For all intents and purposes, starting with the creation of Parthia, the Seleucid Empire was based in northern Syria. In 63 BC, the Syrian remnants of the formerly vast Seleucid Empire were annexed by ROME.
(*See chronologies under* Afghanistan, Anatolia, *and* Iran.)

Seljuk Emirates (11th–12th cents.; *Near East*)

The Seljuk Turks separated from the GHUZZ, a sort of mother horde, and rode down the eastern side of the Caspian Sea. Like most hordes, the Seljuks were not adept at creating centralized states. As they descended on Persia from Central Asia, they founded south of the Amudarya River (Khurasan) the emirate of MERV (1040–1150). With SELJUK PERSIA, they at least shaped a semblance of empire around Hamadan and Ispahan and west to Syria (11th–12th cents.). The Seljuk empire quickly fragmented into emirates in the western Seljuk territories. As distinct geographically from Seljuk Persia and the later ANATOLIAN EMI-RATES, the Seljuk Emirates were created in Iraq, Cappadocia, Syria, and Azerbaijan. The most important of these was founded in Cappadocia by the Danishmandids (1084–1130). Emirates were also established in: Aleppo (1084–1117) and Damascus (1076–1154), which fell to the Zangids; Tabriz (1054 to 1260), which became the capital of ILKHANID PERSIA; Mosul, where the Zangids originated in the early 12th cent.; and in general around any significant urban centre in the area. Most of these statelets were subjugated by the RUM SULTANATE, which in the 13th cent. fragmented into the Anatolian Emirates.
(*See chronology under* Anatolia.)

Seljuk Persia (11th–12th cents.; *Iran*)

The Seljuks were a branch of the Ghuzz, a Turkish central Asian horde from the Balkash Lake region, that took Khurasan from the GHAZNAVIDS around the beginning of the 11th cent. and went on to conquer Persia. They captured Baghdad in 1054 and extended their sway to Syria and Cappadocia. Initially they established their capital in Hamadan from where they proclaimed themselves protectors of the ABBASID CALIPHATE. In Transoxiana ca. 1090, they made the KHARAKANIDS their vassals. The sultanate of the Persian Seljuks started to disintegrate even as it was created. Seljuk chieftains founded independent emirates in Iraq, Azerbaijan, Syria, and Cappadocia (SELJUK EMIRATES). At the beginning of the 12th cent. the sultanate itself was split between Baghdad and Ispahan. A separate emirate was created in Shiraz. The Kharakanids were left to their own devices in Transoxiana. KHWARIZM first took Khurasan in 1181 and then went on to conquer the rest of Seljuk Persia, although not as far as Baghdad.
(*See chronology under* Iran.)

Seljuks (GHUZZ)

Senegal

Peopled by Wolof tribesmen, Senegal was part of the ancient MALI empire. French-controlled since the 17th cent., it was the core of French West Africa, created in 1895, whose administrative centre was the Senegalese capital of Dakar (FRENCH COLONIAL EMPIRE). It became independent in 1960. The official language is French. Native languages belong to the Niger–Congo family of west Africa.

Senegambia (GAMBIA, THE)

Serbia (9th–20th cents.; *Balkans*)

The Serbs, who speak a language of the Slavic branch of the Indo-European family of languages, were in the Balkans in the 6th cent. They were Christian-ized in the 9th cent. The first structured kingdom of Serbs was Raszia, created in Bosnia. Under its own rulers, with Byzantine auspices, the kingdom expanded to the territory of Serbia proper in rivalry with BULGARIA. In 1219, the Serbs formed an autocephalous Orthodox Church with the blessing of the patriarchate in Constantinople. During the 13th cent. Bulgaria was hege-monic in the Balkans, but after 1334, under Stephen Dushan, Serbia briefly controlled the Balkans. In 1371 the Serbs were defeated by the OTTOMAN EMPIRE. The kingdom was reduced to a vassal principality. Prince Lazar tried to overthrow Ottoman suzerainty but he was defeated decisively by the Ottoman sultan, Bajazet I, in the Battle of Kosovo Field in 1389. The much-diminished Serbian state was tributary to the Turks until its final absorption by Sultan Mehmet II. Belgrade was seized from the Hungarians in 1521.

THE BALKAN WARS

The Serbs launched their independence movement in 1804 under Karageorge. The Ottoman Empire was under constant Russian pressure – in a brief war in 1811–1812 Russia annexed Bessarabia – and Serbia by 1817 was mostly autonomous, although the Turks still garrisoned Belgrade. After 1829, Serbia came under Russian protection, and after the Crimean War (1854–1856), when Russia's belligerent anti-Ottoman policy was curbed by the western European powers, Serbia's autonomy was guaranteed. By 1867 all Ottoman troops were out of the country and Belgrade became the Serbian capital. In 1876, Serbia tried to take on the Ottomans and was defeated provoking the intervention of Russia and the routing of the Turks. By the Treaty of San Stefano and the subsequent Congress of BERLIN (1878), Serbia's independ-ence in the approximate territory it has now was recognized internationally. Kosovo, which by then had been settled by Muslim Albanians, was a province of Serbia. Serbs were dissatisfied at not having been awarded more land and, in 1885, went to war with Bulgaria over eastern Rumelia and Mace-donia and lost. Their pro-Slavic agitation led to confrontations with

Austria–Hungary (HABSBURG EMPIRE), which had been awarded the administration of BOSNIA-HERZEGOVINA in 1878, and to the Balkan Wars (1912–1913), first against Turkey in alliance with Bulgaria and Greece and then against Bulgaria, after which Serbia obtained lands all around its frontiers, especially Macedonia.

SERBS, CROATS, AND SLOVENES

Much to Serbian resentment, Austria–Hungary had annexed Bosnia-Herzego-vina in 1908. In June 1914, a Serb assassinated Archduke Francis Ferdinand, the heir to the Habsburg throne, in Sarajevo, capital of Bosnia-Herzegovina. Austria–Hungary presented Serbia with impossible conditions which Serbia, with Russian backing, did not accept. In July, Austria declared war on Serbia. Germany declared war on Russia and on France. Montenegro entered the war on the Serbian side. The Serbs held their lines against Austria, but in 1915 Bulgaria entered the war on the side of the Central Powers and with German aid over-ran Serbia and Montenegro. In 1917, Greece entered the war on the side of the Allies, who landed troops in Salonika. Bulgaria was knocked out of the war in 30 September 1918. The Ottoman Empire surrendered on 30 October and Austria on 4 November. Germany capitulated on 11 November. After the war, with the dissolution of the Austro-Hungarian Empire by the Treaty of Saint-Germain in 1919 (VERSAILLES), Serbia was central to the creation of the Kingdom of the Serbs, Croats, and Slovenes, or YUGOSLAVIA as it became in 1929. In 1991, the Yugoslav federation disin-tegrated, but Serbia and Montenegro (whose inhabitants are Serbs) formed the actual much-reduced Yugoslavia.
(*See chronology under* Balkans.)

Serbs, Croats, and Slovenes (Kingdom of the) (YUGOSLAVIA)

Seychelles
A melting pot of Africans and Europeans, who speak a French-derived Creole, the Indian Ocean islands of Seychelles were French from 1756 and British after 1794. They became independent in 1976. The capital, Victoria, is on Mahé Island.

Shang (3rd mil.–12th cent. BC; northern *China*)
After the quasi-legendary Hsia (Xia) dynasty (traditional dates: 2205–1766 BC) – there is archaeological evidence for its existence, which is reported in a chronicle from the 1st cent. BC – came Shang (1766–1122 BC), later named Yin, during which period characters were invented and the art of bronze-casting was perfected. The capital was Anyang, in Henan (Honan) province. The history of both Hsia and Shang was written by Ssu-ma Ch'ien (145–90 BC), who described the first emperors as paragons and the last as degenerates. This

pattern was to be imposed by Chinese historians on succeeding dynasties. Hsia and Shang were established in northern China around the basin of the lower Huang Ho or Yellow River. At its apex, Shang territories reached the left bank of the Yangtze River. Shang was succeeded by CHOU.
(*See chronology under* China and Neighbouring Areas.)

Sharjah (UNITED ARAB EMIRATES)

Shaybanids (16th cent.; *Central Asia*: western Turkestan; *Iran*)
The Shaybanids were a mixture of Mongols and Turks led by descendants of Shayban, a grandson of Genghis Khan, along the southern reaches of the Ural mountains. In the early 15th cent. they took the name of Uzbeks and under Abu'l Khair founded a brief kingdom along the Syr Darya River, the northern border of Transoxiana. Abu'l Khair was attacked and defeated by the Oirats or western Mongols (MONGOLIA) and he was abandoned by his initial supporters, among which were the KIRGHIZ-KAZAKHS, who made a name for themselves in the Kirghiz Steppe (central Kazakhstan). The real founder of the Shaybanid realm was Muhammad Shaybani, grandson of Abu'l Khair, who ca. 1500, with the backing of the CHAGATAITE KHANATE, then based in Tashkent (Uzbekistan), conquered Samarkand and Transoxiana from the last Timurids (TIMURID EMPIRE AND SUCCESSOR STATES). The founder of the dynasty then turned on his benefactors and took Tashkent and conquered as far as Ferghana (1503). He took KHIVA in 1506 and in 1507 he swooped down on Khurasan and Herat, in today's AFGHANISTAN. Subsequently, the Shaybanids lost their eastern conquests but retained Transoxiana and Tashkent. They contested Khurasan during the 16th cent. with the Persians until, in 1597, the Shaybanids were defeated and Khurasan passed definitely to the Persian SAFAVIDS. The Turkish KIRGHIZ took advantage of the Shaybanid defeat at the hands of the Safavids and plundered and occupied their Transoxonian lands. The Shaybanids were finished as a unified political force by 1598, but the Uzbeks peopled Transoxiana and formed the nucleus of modern UZBEKISTAN.
(*See chronologies under* Afghanistan, Iran, *and* Western Turkestan.)

Sheba (10th cent. BC–6th cent. AD; ancient *Near East*)
According to legend, the Queen of Sheba visited Solomon in the 10th cent. BC. Her Semitic kingdom, also known as Saba and its people as Sabeans, apparently flourished from the 9th to the 5th cents. BC in the territory of today's YEMEN and the Hadramaut (*Arabia*). The remains of its ancient capital, Marib, included the ruins of a huge dam built in the 6th cent. BC. Sheba was invaded by Axum (ETHIOPIA) in AD 525. Ethiopian rule was brief. Yemen was absorbed by ISLAM and, after the caliphate was moved from Mecca to Damascus, it was mostly on its own.

Siam (THAILAND)

Sibir Khanate (16th cent.; *Central Asia*: western Siberia)
A descendant of the SHAYBANIDS, Kuchum defeated and occupied ca. 1570 an obscure khanate, vassal of Russia, along the middle reach of the Irtyish River in western Siberia, near the town of Tobolsk. Ivan the Terrible, who was then wiping out the remnants of the Mongol khanates in Russia, sent the Cossack Ermak against him. Ermak at first defeated Kuchum, for which Ivan rewarded him with a suit of armour, but Kuchum kept up the fight and surprised Ermak near a river. In trying to escape by swimming, Ermak was dragged under by the weight of his war gear and drowned. The Russians had to fight until 1598 to recover the Sibir Khanate which Kuchum had briefly led.

Sicily (13th cent. BC–19th cent.; southern *Italy*)
It is believed that Sicilians were among the peoples who tried to conquer the New Kingdom of Egypt in the late 13th–early 12th cents. BC (PHARAONIC EGYPT). Greek colonization began in the 8th cent. BC. Palermo, the traditional Sicilian capital, is the Greek Panormus. CARTHAGE tried to absorb the island starting in the 6th cent. BC, but failed. After its first victory over Carthage (241 BC), ROME made Sicily a province. With the fall of Ravenna and the end of the Roman Empire in the west, Sicily was occupied by the VANDALS and the GOTHS. It was taken and held by the BYZANTINE EMPIRE from the 6th to the 8th cents. Arabs from Tunisia occupied it from the 9th to the 11th cents. The Norman Roger Guiscard took Sicily from the Arabs from 1061 to 1091. He created the kingdom of Sicily in 1130 including southern Italy, to which NAPLES and Capua were added in 1139. The last Norman king, William II, named his aunt Constance, wife of the Holy Roman Emperor Henry VI Hohenstaufen, as his heir. After some resistance Frederick II Hohenstaufen established his capital in Palermo in the 1220s, thus virtually renouncing his claim to the HOLY ROMAN EMPIRE, but creating the first centralized European state. The Hohenstaufen were perceived as a threat by the papacy who vested the kingdom of Sicily on Charles I Anjou, who defeated and executed Conradin, the last Hohenstaufen ruler, in 1268.

THE SICILIAN VESPERS

The Sicilians rebelled against the French and ejected them during the massacres of the Sicilian Vespers (1282), which started in Palermo and spread to the rest of the island. They accepted the sovereignty of the kingdom of ARAGON. (A highly suspect etymology has it that Mafia stands for *morte ai francesi Italia anela*.) With the annexation of Naples in 1442, Aragon formed the kingdom of the Two Sicilies, which, after the formation of Spain from Castile and Aragon (1492), was ruled separately by Spanish viceroys. In 1713, during the War of Spanish Succession, Sicily went to the house of SAVOY, who in 1720 ceded it to the Habsburg in exchange for Sardinia. In 1735 Sicily was accorded to a branch of the Spanish Bourbons who created with it a new

Kingdom of the Two Sicilies, momentarily disjoined by Napoleon and restored after 1814. In 1860 Garibaldi's *carbonari* overthrew the ruling Bourbons and integrated Sicily with resurgent ITALY.

Sierra Leone
Mostly tribal, Sierra Leone grew out of the foundation of Freetown in 1787, by British anti-slavery groups. The interior was declared a British protectorate in 1896. It became independent in 1961. English is the official language. Native languages belong to the Niger–Congo west African family of languages.

Silla (KOREA)

Singapore
The BRITISH EAST INDIA COMPANY established Penang, MALAYSIA, in 1786. MALACCA came under British influence in 1794. There was a settlement called Sangapura at the tip of the Malay Peninsula. In 1819, Sir Stamford Raffles founded Singapore as part of British Malaya on an island ceded by the Sultan of JOHORE. The rest of the Malay Peninsula gradually came under British control. The East India Company consolidated its Malayan possessions as the Straits Settlements (1826). After the Sepoy Mutiny (1857–1858), the Company was dissolved and BRITISH INDIA administered Malaya until 1867, when the Straits Settlement Colony was created including, basically, Penang, Malacca, and Singapore. Labuan was a dependency of Singapore. In 1896, Great Britain divided its Malayan dependencies into the Federated Malay States, with Penang as capital – the other states were Negri Sembilan, Perak, and Selangor – and the Unfederated Malay States (Malacca and Singapore). Johore became a protectorate in 1914 and an unfederated part of British Malaya. In 1946 Singapore was made a Crown colony. In 1963 it became part of independent Malaysia. It separated in 1965 as an independent state. Singapore has four official languages: Chinese, English, Malay, and Tamil.

Sixteen Kingdoms of the Five Barbarians (4th–5th cents.; northern *China*)
In the 1st cent. AD, the HSIUNG-NU, Mongolian nomads, possibly ancestors of the HUNS, divided into northern and southern branches. Pursuing an arm's-length policy with the dangerous northern Hsiung-nu, the HAN got another horde, the Mongolian HSIEN-PI, who roamed MANCHURIA, to harass and destroy them, which they did occupying Mongolia in their turn. This policy backfired when, upon the fall of Han in the 3rd cent., the Hsien-pi attacked the southern Hsiung-nu, who fell on China. The Hsiung-nu, whose leader was known as the shan yü of the Five Hordes, provoked the downfall of Western Chin (Jin), from which emerged, according to traditional reckoning, sixteen kingdoms. This unquiet period of northern China lasted from 302 to 439. The Sixteen Kingdoms were superseded by Northern Wei (PERIOD OF DISUNITY (AFTER HAN)).

Slavs

The Slavs, speakers of Indo-European tongues, remained more or less in their homelands in Russia, the Ukraine, and Byelorussia from at least the middle of the first mil. BC. They neighboured successively on the SCYTHIANS and SARMATIANS and might have absorbed them. The ALANS, who were related to the Scythians and Sarmatians, remained a distinct group that participated in the Germanic invasions of the Roman Empire (ROME). When the GERMANS began their massive penetration of the Roman frontier (4th cent.), the Slavs expanded westwards to the edges of formerly Germanic lands. They gave a wide berth to HUNS, AVARS, and MAGYARS. During Carolingian times (8th–9th cents.), they began to form states of their own either opposite to or within the German marches (CAROLINGIAN EMPIRE). Thus arose BOHEMIA and GREAT MORAVIA followed by other Slavic states. The Slavs were never displaced from their central Russian homeland, where Kievan Rus (RUSSIA) was structured starting in the 9th cent. by Varangian marauders and traders (NORSEMEN).
(*See chronology under* Southern Russia.)

Slovakia

The Slavs occupied the territory of Slovakia in the 5th cent. The Slavic kingdom of GREAT MORAVIA, founded in the 9th cent., included BOHEMIA, Silesia, Slovakia, southern POLAND, and northern HUNGARY. It absorbed the AVARS, but early in the 10th cent. it was destroyed by Hungarian raiders (MAGYARS). The German emperor, Otto I the Great, defeated the Hungarians in 955, after which they settled down and founded a state, which included Slovakia. During the OTTOMAN EMPIRE's invasion of Hungary (16th cent.) Slovakia was retained by the HABSBURG EMPIRE, who later restored it to their Hungarian province (1697). After the Austrian defeat at the hands of Prussia in 1866, the Habsburg accepted the conversion of the Empire into the Austro-Hungarian Dual Monarchy. The Hungarian part included Croatia, Ruthenia, Slovakia, Slovenia, and Transylvania. Czechoslovakia was created from the dissolved Habsburg Empire after World War I (1918) with the territories of Bohemia, Moravia, and Slovakia. It was dismembered by Germany in 1938 into Bohemia-Moravia and Slovakia. It was reconstituted in 1945 with the loss of a tip of Slovakia in the Carpathian Mountains (Ruthenia). In 1948, Czechoslovakia became a communist state. It was invaded by its communist neighbours in 1968 to suppress the political reforms known as the Prague Spring. In 1989, protests very quickly resulted in the end of the communist regime. The following year Czechoslovakia became the Czech and Slovak Federal Republic. Slovakia separated amicably as an independent state on 1 January 1993. The capital of Slovakia is Bratislava. Slovak and Czech are mutually comprehensible.

Slovenia

Like most of Slavic eastern Europe, Slovenia, whose language is related to Serbo-Croat, was settled in the 5th and 6th cents. The Carolingian march of Carniola was the historical predecessor of Slovenia. In the 14th cent. it became a Habsburg domain. When the HABSBURG EMPIRE became the Dual Monarchy of Austria and Hungary, Slovenia was attached to the Hungarian part. After World War I, Slovenia became part of the Kingdom of the Serbs, Croats and Slovenes (1918), later YUGOSLAVIA (1929), or the kingdom of the southern Slavs. After World War II, Slovenia became a federated republic in communist Yugoslavia. It elected a non-communist government in 1990 and, in 1991, it went its own independent way, setting off the process of dissolution of Yugoslavia. The capital of Slovenia is Ljubljana.

Sogdiana (5th–6th cents.; *Uzbekistan*)

Between the fall of the SASANID EMPIRE and the advent of ISLAM, an autonomous Iranized kingdom of Sogdiana may have existed in what today is Samarkand. The extinct Sogdian language is part of the Indo-European family, including most European languages.

Solomon Islands

Peopled by speakers of a Malayo-Polynesian language, the Solomon Islands, due east of Papua New Guinea, became a British protectorate in the 1890s and acquired their independence in 1978. They were bloody battlefields during World War II. The capital of the Solomon Islands is Honiara, on Guadalcanal.

Somalia

The language of Somalia belongs to the same family of languages as the Semitic tongues, which include Arabic and Hebrew. The inhabitants of Somalia converted to Islam in the 10th cent. Mostly divided into tribal statelets, the territory of Somalia, on both sides of the horn of Africa, was shared out in the late 19th cent. between Great Britain, who took the north, and Italy, who had the south. The British took Italian Somaliland, which, with the original British colony, became independent Somalia in 1960. Somalia was torn by factional strife and scourged by famine in the early 1990s, which resulted in a fruitless UN military intervention from 1992 to 1994. The capital of Somalia is Mogadishu. Northern Somalia, former British Somaliland, capital Hargeisha, is autonomous but has no international recognition.

Songhai (15th–16th cents.; *Sub-Saharan Sahara*)

An Islamic kingdom in the western Sahara (1464–1591) that succeeded the kingdom of MALI, Songhai extended from Senegal in the west to Niger in the east and from Mauritania in the north to Guinea in the south. It was attacked from Morocco in 1591. The capital was Timbuktu. BAMBARA succeeded Songhai. (*See chronology under* Western and Sub-Saharan Africa.)

South Africa

South Africa was settled by Bantu-speakers. The Zulu, of the same language family, arrived in the 17th cent. to north east Natal. Besides the native tongues, of which there are around 30, South Africans speak Afrikaans, a Dutch-derived language, and English. The Dutch East India Company founded Cape Town in 1652. After 1795 British influence in the area grew until in 1814 the territory became part of the BRITISH COLONIAL EMPIRE as the Province of the Cape of Good Hope, later Cape Colony. Dissatisfied with British rule, the descendants of the original Dutch settlers started the Great Trek inland from 1835 to 1845. In 1838 they settled in Natal, where they fought the Zulus (ZULULAND). The British annexed Natal in 1843. The Boers founded the republics of ORANGE FREE STATE (Bloemfontein) in 1854 and TRANS-VAAL (Johannesburg) in 1857. King Moshoshoe of the Sotho, under pressure from both Boers and Zulus, requested British aid and the protectorate of Basutholand was created in 1868. In 1871, Great Britain annexed Griquana-land West, west of the Orange Free State. In 1877 Great Britain annexed Transvaal, but in 1884 it was restored. Wars between the British and the Zulus erupted in 1879 and, in 1887, Great Britain annexed Zululand.

De Klerk and Mandela

The Boer republics made an alliance to resist the pressure from the British territories to the north, orchestrated by the empire builder Cecil Rhodes, and in 1899 they declared war on Great Britain, which they lost in 1902. In 1910, Great Britain organized the self-governing dominion of South Africa with the provinces of the Cape, Natal, Orange, and Transvaal, to which was added the territory of southern Bechuanaland. The functions of a capital were divided among Pretoria (administrative), Cape Town (legislative), and Bloemfontein (judicial). Recognition of its independence was accorded by the Statute of Westminster in 1931. After World War I, German South West Africa was mandated to South Africa, which retained the colony until its independence as Namibia in 1990. Until 1992, South Africa maintained a draconian and repressive racial regime known as Apartheid. It began to be dismantled under the leadership of De Klerk. In free elections, Mandela, a former long-term prisoner of the racialist regime, was elected president. In 1994, the so-called Bantustans or tribal areas (BOPHUTHATSWANA, CISKEI, TRANSKEI, VENDA) were annexed to South Africa, whose territory was divided into nine provinces (capitals in parentheses): Eastern Cape (Bisho), Free State (Bloemfontein), Gauteng (Johannesburg), Kwazulu-Natal (Pietermaritzburg), Mpumalanga (Nelspruit), Northern Cape (Kimberley), Northern Province (Pietersburg), North-West (Mmabtho), and Western Cape (Cape Town).

South Korea (KOREA)

South Vietnam (20th cent.; Vietnam)
South Vietnam, which lasted from 1954 to 1975, occupied the Mekong Delta up to the 17th parallel including Hué. Therefore, it can be said that historically it included ANNAM (southern TONKIN) and CHAMPA. The Mekong Delta was under the direct political influence of CAMBODIA until the 18th cent. To end French involvement in Indo-China (FRENCH COLONIAL EMPIRE), the Geneva Conference of 1954 divided Vietnam along roughly the 17th parallel. The north became the communist Democratic Republic of Vietnam, capital Hanoi, and the south the pro-western Republic of Vietnam, capital Saigon. South Vietnam became the base for American intervention against the communists, who accepted the division of their country only as a provisional arrangement. This situation begat the Vietnam War which began almost immediately after the division of the country and went on until the communists took over the south in 1975, two years after the Americans decided to cut their losses and leave the country.

South Yemen (20th cent.; Yemen)
The city of Aden was part of the OTTOMAN EMPIRE in 1538. In 1839 it was placed by Great Britain under the administration of BRITISH INDIA. In 1937 it became a separate colony and was made part successively of the Federation of the Emirates of the South and of the Federation of South Arabia. In 1967 it became independent as South Yemen, which, in 1990, fused with YEMEN itself.

Southern India (1st–19th cents. AD)
In recounting the complex history of the Indian subcontinent before British India, a practical approach is to distinguish between NORTHERN INDIA (the Indus River Valley to the Ganges Basin), the Deccan or CENTRAL INDIA, and Southern *India*. In Southern India, the first prominent state was created by the Cholas, based in Tamil, in the 1st cent. AD. The greatest Chola king was Karikala, who was active ca. 190 AD and defeated the Pandyas and the Chera of Kerala. The obscure tribe of the Kalabhras gained ascendancy over these dynasties in the 4th cent., but had been defeated by the Pallavas from the Madras area by the 5th cent. During the 6th cent., the Pallavas and the Pandyas fought for dominance. The Pallavas became ascendant and had to fight off the Chalukyas from the Deccan during the 7th cent. The Cholas, who survived by keeping their heads down, came back in the 9th cent. and founded a state, which, at first allied to the Pandyas, destroyed the Pallavas, and then absorbed the Pandyas and warred with Ceylon. The powerful Cholas went overseas to attack the SRI VIJAYA kingdom in Malaya and established a foothold in the Malay Peninsula. The Cholas waned in the 12th cent. giving way to the Hoysalas and finally, in the 13th cent., succumbing to the resurgent Pandyas. In the 14th cent. the kingdom of Vijayanagara dominated southern India until 1564, when it fell under the influence of the Deccan. The

MUGHAL EMPIRE in the 17th cent. conquered the Deccan and as far south as the Tamil coast. The western coast of India was then mostly in the hands of local rulers, such as the zamorin of Calicut (Kerala), and of European commercial enclaves. Southern India comprises what today are the Indian states of Karnataka (the southern part), Kerala, and Tamil Nadu, where Dravidian languages are spoken. The dominant kingdoms and dynasties were often based in Tamil lands. BRITISH INDIA, which conquered the Mughal empire in the 18th cent., vied with the French for southern India (FRENCH COLONIAL EMPIRE), but brought it under its control after the defeat of MYSORE in 1799. Southern India is sometimes referred to as the Carnatic, a name which is also applied in maps to the eastern coast of India. The latter is also referred to as Coromandel.

(*See chronology under* Indian Subcontinent.)

Soviet Empire (20th cent.; core area: *Russia*)

Soviet Empire is an informal designation for the system that Stalin established after World War II with the USSR as the huge metropolis of politically subservient Albania, Bulgaria, Czechoslovakia, East Germany, Hungary, Poland, and Romania. These countries and the USSR were grouped into the Warsaw Pact, a military alliance of communist countries created to counter the North Atlantic Treaty Organization (NATO), formed in the west in 1949. Stalin also wanted to lord it over Yugoslavia but the foxy, able Tito cut loose in 1948, which permitted Albania to also go its own reclusive and retrograde way after it broke with the USSR in 1956. North Korea was sponsored by the USSR, who possibly instigated the Korean War. Mongolia was definitely part of the Soviet Empire, but China was too powerful to be considered a Soviet satellite despite the strong Russian presence there until relations with the USSR soured after 1956. The Soviet Empire was never popular – despite the liberal use of 'popular' and 'democratic' in the official names of communist countries – and there were rebellions in East Germany (1953) and Hungary (1956), put down by Soviet tanks. The Czechs tried to liberalize their regime in 1968 provoking the intervention of the USSR and neighbouring Warsaw Pact countries. In 1981, Poland attempted a reform of its communist system, but the Polish military stopped it, under pressure from Moscow. The Soviet Empire disintegrated even before the dissolution of the USSR in 1991.

Spain

SEE ENTRY IN 'PROVINCES AND REGIONS'

Spain is the larger part of Iberia – its ancient Celtic name – which also includes Portugal. Spain has a riches of cave paintings. Some believe that the Basques could be descendants of the Palaeolithic artists that covered the rock faces at Altamira in northern Spain. It is known that, in the 10th cent. BC., Spain was mostly peopled by CELTS. In the 9th cent. BC, PHOENICIA had footholds in the coast of Andalusia. Greek influence began in the 7th cent. BC. CARTHAGE occupied the southern and eastern coasts during the 3rd cent. BC, which was one of the causes of the Second Punic War (218–201 BC), won by ROME. The Carthaginians founded the city of Cartagena in Murcia. Except for the Basque country, Roman control of Iberia was firm in the 1st cent. BC. Iberia took to Christianity early. In the 5th cent., the SUEVES and the VANDALS over-ran the peninsula. The Vandals were driven to north Africa by the VISI-GOTHS. The BYZANTINE EMPIRE sent forces under Belisarius, which reclaimed the Spanish Mediterranean coast, but by 585 the VISIGOTHIC KINGDOM had ejected them. It also absorbed the Suevian domain in Galicia.

THE 'RECONQUISTA'

In 711, Muslim Berbers invaded and quickly destroyed the Visigothic kingdom. They established themselves in Spain and Portugal as vassals of the Umayyads in Damascus (ISLAM). Before the new ABBASID CALIPHATE could make its authority felt in Iberia, an Umayyad who had survived the extermination of his kinsmen, Abd ar-Rahman, established an emirate in CÓRDOBA in 756. The defeated Christians took refuge in ASTURIAS, where they founded a kingdom. By the mid-8th cent. the Asturian king, Alfonso I, initiated the *reconquista*, the centuries-long Christian recovery of Iberia. In the 9th cent., after establishing its centre in the city of Leon, Asturias became the kingdom of Asturias and Leon. Anti-Muslim activity was also present in the Pyrenees. Carolingian forces had invaded north-western Spain in 775. The area around BARCELONA became a march of the CAROLINGIAN EMPIRE against the Muslims in 801. It was made a county in 888, which later expanded to create the province of Catalonia. In 929, Abd ar-Rahman III proclaimed the Caliphate of Córdoba and ca. 950 invaded and annexed MOROCCO. Sancho III the Great of NAVARRE reunited northern Spain (1029–1035) and bequeathed Castile to his son Ferdinand I, who absorbed Leon in 1037 as the kingdom of Castile and Leon divided again in 1157. The Christian war against the Muslims in Iberia also included PORTUGAL. However, by the 11th cent., Portugal had been constituted separately from the mainly Castilian-speaking rest of the Iberian Peninsular. Under Christian pressure the Córdoba Caliphate disintegrated in 1031 into the Taifa emirates of Badajoz, Córdoba, Seville, Toledo, Granada, Zaragoza, Valencia, Murcia, Denia, and others. Córdoba itself fell to Seville in 1078. The ALMORAVIDS were Berber tribesmen from Mauritania and southern Morocco, who took Fez from the Córdoba Umayyads in 1056 and went on to conquer the Taifa emirates. In 1076 ARAGON annexed Navarre. In 1118, Zaragoza was conquered and became the capital of Aragon. In 1137, Aragon was united with the county of Barcelona. Almoravid rule lasted until ca. 1150, when it was displaced by the ALMOHADS, a Moroccan dynasty. During the rest of the 12th cent. the Almohads over-ran ALGERIA and TUNISIA.

CASTILE AND ARAGON

From 1126 to 1157, Castile reunited all of Christian Spain except Aragon. Southern Spain from Estremadura to Valencia formed part of the empire of the Almohads. In 1212, Castile, under Alfonso VIII, won the Battle of Navas de Tolosa, in which the Muslims were decisively defeated resulting in the downfall of the Almohads. Castile and Leon were definitely reunited in 1230 under Ferdinand III of Castile. Disunited once again, the Muslims lost Córdoba in 1236. In 1238, Aragon seized Valencia and the Balearic Islands. After 1234, Navarre, which included Basque French lands known as Lower Navarre, came under French influence. In 1305, all of Navarre passed to Philip IV, King of France. The Basque provinces of Alava and Vizcaya were annexed by Spain in 1332 and 1370 respectively. Spanish Navarre was annexed by Ferdinand V of Aragon (Ferdinand the Catholic) in 1515. Lower Navarre remained French. After the Sicilian Vespers that ended French rule in SICILY in 1282, its inhabitants accepted Peter III of Aragon as their king. With the annexation of NAPLES in 1442, Aragon formed the kingdom of the TWO SICILIES. The union of Castile and Aragon, through the marriage of Isabella of Castile and Ferdinand of Aragon (the Catholic Kings) in 1479, signalled the formation of modern Spain. In 1492, with the conquest of GRANADA, Spain ruled over most of the Iberian Peninsula. The principal royal city of Castile was Leon. Originally a Muslim fortress named Magerit (10th cent.), Madrid became the residence of the Catholic Kings. Also in 1492, Spain financed Columbus' discovery of America, which in the following decades resulted in an immense empire with two political centres: Mexico, conquered by Cortez in 1521 from the Aztecs, and Lima, founded by Pizarro in 1535. During the 16th cent. Spain occupied or claimed lands in the western hemisphere from northern California to the Tierra del Fuego, including Florida and the larger Antillean Islands. In Asia it had also taken the Philippines, named after the Spanish king, Philip II (SPANISH COLONIAL EMPIRE).

THE REVOLT OF THE CATALANS

Joanna the Mad, daughter to the Catholic Kings, married Philip the Handsome, the heir to the Habsburg Low Countries, and the two begat the Spanish king, Charles I (1516), grandson of the Holy Roman Emperor Maximilian I Habsburg, to whose crown Charles acceded in 1519 as Holy Roman Emperor Charles V. Thus, Spain, who had the largest colonial empire of its time and also possessed Sicily and Naples, acquired the Low Countries then extending from north-eastern France to the Dutch province of Groningen including Luxembourg. Charles had to fight off Francis I of France in Italy and confront the Protestant reformation and its effects on the HOLY ROMAN EMPIRE. He also undertook various expeditions against Islamic North Africa. These were demanding tasks and, in 1556, he divested himself of the Habsburg dominions in the east in favour of his brother Ferdinand (HABSBURG EMPIRE). The Spanish Habsburg retained the Low Countries and northern Italy (MILAN). In 1580, through dynastic politics, Spain under Philip II absorbed Portugal and its considerable overseas possessions. At that point Spain appeared to have more power than any state ever had. But things were not entirely what they seemed. The Low Countries included Luxembourg and the provinces of today's *Belgium* and the *Netherlands*. Roughly half those provinces were Catholic and the other half was strongly Calvinist. The Catholic provinces formed in 1578 the Union of Arras and the mainly Protestant provinces created the United Provinces of the NETHERLANDS in 1584. Under the leadership of the *statdthouder* of Amsterdam, William of Orange, the United Provinces became independent. The remaining provinces constituted the SPANISH NETHERLANDS. The defeat of the Spanish Armada (1588), harassed by English warships in the English Channel but mainly the victim of the elements, did not in itself signal the decline of Spain but it did ominously point to the future. Many historians believe that Spain's fortunes took a downward turn during the Thirty Years War (1618–1648), a conflict initially pitting Protestants against Catholics in the Holy Roman Empire which ensnared Spain into having to fight the Dutch allied to GREAT BRITAIN. This situation permitted the Portuguese to secede from Spain and the Catalans to revolt against Spanish rule (1640). The Catalans did not achieve independence but retained their self-governing privileges. In 1648, Spain was forced to recognize the independence of the Netherlands.

THE BEWITCHED

After Philip II, who was dutiful though not particularly successful, the Habsburg kings of Spain did not stand out. The last one, Charles II (1665–1700), who was called 'the bewitched' because he was apparently retarded, died without heir, although he had designated a Bourbon to succeed him. The Austrian Habsburg and the French Bourbon claimed the throne. The French claim, which was advanced by Louis XIV, an aggressive, expansionist monarch, alarmed Great Britain and a generalized state of war took hold of Europe. During the War of Spanish Succession (1701–1714) there was talk of a partition of Spain, so weak had the country become. In the end Louis' claim stood and the Bourbon Philip V was recognized as king, but Spain lost all its Italian vassal territories: Lombardy, Naples, and Sardinia to Austria, and Sicily to SAVOY. The Habsburg also gained the Spanish Netherlands. In 1704, Great Britain took Gibraltar, which it still holds with the support of its inhabitants. After 1714, the Spanish Bourbons made it a point to recover some of their Italian possessions. In 1720, they recovered Sicily and in 1734 they regained Naples, which, together, became the Bourbon kingdom of the TWO SICILIES – except during the period of the FRENCH EUROPEAN EMPIRE – until it passed to Sardinia in 1860 and became part of the reunified kingdom of

ITALY in 1861. In 1807 Napoleon persuaded the Spanish king, Charles IV, to allow French forces to cross Spain and occupy Portugal in order to shut down its ports to British commerce. The following year a palace coup forced Charles to abdicate in favour of his son, Ferdinand VII.

THE FARCE IN BAYONNE

Napoleon set up a confrontation in Bayonne between Charles and Ferdinand, during which Ferdinand returned the crown to Charles who, in turn, gave it to Napoleon, who put his brother Joseph Bonaparte on the Spanish throne. This farce pleased neither the Spanish nor the British and almost immediately the country was up in arms. In Portugal, Wellington checked the French but by 1811 Spain was under French occupation. The Spaniards fought back wherever they could in their own territory. Thus was begotten the word 'guerrilla' ('small war', in Spanish). Under Wellington's military leadership, Spanish forces consolidated and the occupiers were pushed back into France in 1813. Ferdinand was restored in 1814 and promptly set about undoing the liberal institutions created in his absence. His contempt for democracy and progress was so great that he once named a bullfighter as minister of education. Ironically, this Spanish war of independence overlapped with the Latin American wars of independence, which were set off by the same causes as in Spain, but for different ends. When news of Napoleon's usurpation arrived in the colonial capitals in America, the municipal councils, alleging loyalty to Ferdinand, formed juntas which dispossessed the Spanish authorities. This happened in Caracas and Buenos Aires in 1810. These independence movements – some were bloodless separations, occasionally with social undercurrents as in Mexico – resulted in the dismemberment of the Spanish Colonial Empire in America, which by 1824 was reduced to Cuba and Puerto Rico.

CIVIL WARS

The 19th cent. in Spain was characterized by civil war, instability, and occasional military rule. There was a liberal movement in 1820 which was put down in 1823 by French troops summoned by Ferdinand VII. Spanish weakness was demonstrated when the United States declared war in 1898 – over the sinking of the battleship *Maine*, docked in Havana, which probably exploded from a careless handling of gunpowder – and very quickly destroyed the Spanish navy in Santiago de Cuba and in Cavite, Philippines. King Alfonso XIII was deposed in 1931 and a republic was created. There was a military uprising in Morocco and Seville in 1936 and in the civil war that followed the nationalist forces defeated the republican loyalists. Their *caudillo* (leader), Franco, became dictator. Franco had been helped by Nazi Germany and Fascist Italy, but he kept Spain out of World War II. When he died in 1975, he was succeeded by Juan Carlos Bourbon, who had been carefully groomed for the throne and successfully led Spain to democracy. Of its former colonial empire, Spain retains only Ceuta and Melilla, known as *plazas de soberanía*, and as loyal to Madrid as Gibraltar is to London.

The medieval dynasties of Spain mostly went by the name of their kingdom or region, hence Isabella of Castile and Ferdinand of Aragon. Their daughter Joanna the Mad married Philip the Handsome, son of Emperor Maximilian I Habsburg and ruler of the Low Countries. When Isabella died, Philip became King of Castile (1506). The son of Philip and Joanna became King Charles I of Spain (1515–1556) after Ferdinand's death, and Holy Roman Emperor Charles V (1519–1556) after Maximilian's death. The succeeding Habsburg kings were Philip II, III, and IV and Charles II, who died barren but not intestate. However validly, he designated a nephew of Louis XIV Bourbon as his heir, whose accession set off the War of Spanish Succession. The Bourbon claimant was finally accepted but at the expense of most of Spain's possessions in Europe. The first Bourbon was King Philip V and he was followed by Ferdinand VI, Charles III, Charles IV, Ferdinand VII, and Isabella II who was deposed in 1868. She abdicated in favour of her son, Alfonso XII, who reigned from 1874 to 1885 after a provisional monarchy and a republic. Alfonso XIII reigned from 1886 to 1931. The republic (1931–1939) was followed by the Franco regime, which lasted until 1975. Juan Carlos of Bourbon became king the same year.

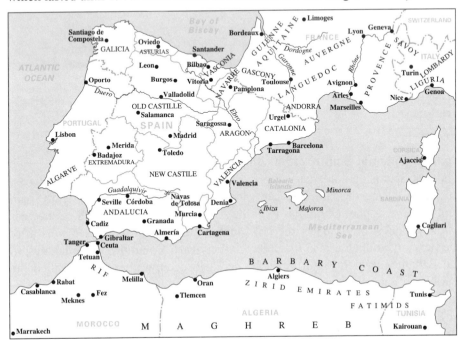

Map 10   Iberia, Southern France, and Maghreb

Spain

Predominant political influences

3rd cent. BC	9th cent.	Leon
Carthage	Córdoba	Castile
Rome	Asturias	Aragon
	Navarre	Navarre
2nd cent. BC–3rd cent. AD	Catalonia	
Rome	**10th cent.**	**13th cent.**
	Córdoba	Almohads
4th cent.–5th cent.	Asturias and Leon	Muslim Spain disunited
Rome	Leon	Castile
Sueves	Navarre	Aragon
Visigothic Kingdom	Catalonia	
		14th cent.
6th cent.	**11th cent.**	Castile
Visigothic Kingdom	Córdoba	Aragon
Byzantine Empire	Taifa Kingdoms	Granada
	Seville	
7th cent.	Almoravids	**15th cent.**
Visigothic Kingdom	Leon	Granada (to 1492)
	Navarre	Spain
8th cent.	Castile	
Visigothic Kingdom	Aragon	
Islam	Catalonia	
Córdoba		
Asturias	**12th cent.**	
Basques	Almoravids	
	Almohads	

Spanish Colonial Empire (15th–20th cents.)

The first Spanish colonialist ventures were raids on the northern Muslim coast of Africa during the late 15th cent. following a Portuguese precedent. Spain sent out Christopher Columbus over the Atlantic Ocean in 1492, the same year as the conquest of Granada, the last Muslim kingdom in Iberia. He went after the riches of India but also to subject and convert. Columbus made landfall in the Bahamas (which Spain never bothered to occupy afterwards), sailed the Caribbean Sea, discovering islands right and left, went back to Spain, and in successive expeditions in 1493, 1498, and 1502, finished exploring the shores of the Caribbean Sea to near the delta of the Orinoco River. These voyages created the base of Spanish colonial power in the Americas. At the same time, Spain began its piecemeal invasion of Muslim northern Africa, which was to go on during the 16th cent. until the OTTOMAN EMPIRE interdicted further expeditions. The first capital of the Spanish Colonial Empire in the western hemisphere was Santo Domingo, founded in 1496 by Batholomew Columbus, brother of Christopher. It was from Havana, founded in 1515 by Diego de Velasquez, that Hernan Cortez sailed to Mexico and, between 1519 and 1521, conquered the AZTEC EMPIRE and created New Spain, capital Mexico, the first Spanish viceroyalty in America. Francisco Pizarro arrived in PERU in 1531 and by 1534 had subjugated the INCA EMPIRE and gained for Spain its second viceroyalty, capital Lima. Though less spectacularly, the Spaniards at the same time were spreading all over South America: Buenos Aires (1536), Bogota (1538), Santiago (1541), Caracas (1567). Florida was visited by Ponce de Leon in 1515 and Narvaez explored it in 1528. De Soto penetrated southeastern North America from Florida in 1539. He died in 1541 after sighting and crossing the Mississippi River. From 1540 to 1542 Coronado explored and claimed much of the land west of the Mississippi, which later was part of independent MEXICO. Spain did not have resources to establish a permanent presence in such a vast area. If it managed to retain so much of western North America for so long it was probably only because its sovereignty was not challenged. By the end of the 16th cent., Spain either occupied or claimed territories between the two oceans which extended from northern California to Patagonia. It did not occupy the rest of South America because Portugal discovered BRAZIL in 1500 and very quickly sailed and colonized its coast. During much of the 18th cent., Spain's North American possessions bounded on British (Ruperts Land and Georgia) and French (the basin of the Mississippi) territories. Across the Pacific Ocean, Spain had occupied the Philippine Islands by 1571. It also claimed Guam (1521), the Caroline Islands (1526), and the Marianas Islands, which it only occupied in 1668. Spain was not active in Africa or India, which it had agreed by the Treaty of Tordesillas (1494) to leave in the Portuguese sphere of influence. Besides, Spain was decidedly over-extended. Its maintenance of so huge an empire depended more on the loyalty of its transplanted subjects than on its own military might.

IBERO-AMERICA

In America, Spain's colonies were becoming restless late in the 18th cent., more the local elites than the masses, and after Napoleon deposed the Spanish Bourbons in 1808, Caracas and Buenos Aires set up autonomous *juntas* (1810). These were not recognized by Cadiz, which was the seat of the Spanish government during the Napoleonic occupation, and the long struggle began which, by 1824, had produced the string of independent states, that, with Brazil, constitute Ibero-America, usually if inaccurately referred to as Latin America. Brazil itself peacefully proclaimed its independence from Portugal in 1822. Spain retained Cuba and Puerto Rico. After changing hands various times during the 18th cent., Florida was recognized as Spanish in 1783, but much wrangling over this territory finally resulted in Spain reluctantly transferring it to the United States in 1819. Spain, who, apart from its abortive attacks on northern Africa in the 16th cent., had never showed much interest in Africa, reclaimed the island of Fernando Po and the territory of Rio Muni in 1844. They had been Portuguese cessions in 1778, abandoned as insalubrious in 1781. These claims, as well as a Spanish protectorate over the Western Sahara, were recognized in the Berlin Conference of 1884–1885. In the Spanish–American War of 1898, Spain lost Cuba, Puerto Rico, the Philippines, and Guam to the United States. The following year it ceded the Carolines and the Marianas to Germany. Under Spanish influence (1884), the Western Sahara was divided into the provinces of Saguia el Hamra and Rio de Oro (Golden River). After a process which had begun in the early 20th cent., France and Spain agreed to share out the territory of Morocco, Spain retaining the hinterland of Ceuta, Melilla, and Tangier, with the capital in Tetuan. Tangier, conquered by the Portuguese in 1471 and transferred to Great Britain as the dowry of Catherine of Braganza, the Portuguese wife of Charles II, was abandoned in 1648. It was internationalized in the 1920s, controlled by Spain during World War II, internationalized again, and, together with the rest of Spanish Morocco, integrated with Morocco in 1956. Spain retains Ceuta, seized by the Portuguese in 1415 and transferred to Spain in 1580, and Melilla, occupied by Spain in 1496. Its African equatorial lands were constituted as Spanish Guinea in 1885. In 1968, they became independent as EQUATORIAL GUINEA. The Saharan provinces formed the colony of Spanish Sahara, which Spain relinquished in 1979. Mauritania had claims to it but deferred to Morocco, who occupied it in 1979. The Polisario is a resistance movement that wants independence for Western Sahara.

Spanish Netherlands (16th–19th cents.; *Belgium*, Luxembourg, and *Netherlands*)

The Low Countries (modern Netherlands, Belgium, and Luxembourg) were part of the HOLY ROMAN EMPIRE from the 9th cent. During the 12th cent. France annexed much of FLANDERS (western Low Countries), but during the 13th cent. French rule was resisted. In 1364 the French king, John II Valois, conferred on his son Philip the Bold the Duchy of BURGUNDY. Philip acquired the Low Countries. Through the marriage of Holy Roman Emperor Maximilian I and Mary of Burgundy in 1477, the Low Countries passed to the Habsburg. Philip the Handsome, son of Maximilian I, married Joanna, the daughter of Isabella and Ferdinand of Spain, and upon Philip's death in 1506, the Low Countries passed to their son Charles I of Spain (1516–1556) and Holy Roman Emperor Charles V (1519–1556). Charles annexed Friesland (1523), Overijssel and Utrecht (1527), and Gelderland (1543), previously autonomous. In 1555, Charles (who died in

1558) transferred the Low Countries to his son Philip, who in 1556 became Philip II of Spain. Thus, the Low Countries became the Spanish Netherlands. They included Luxembourg, Artois, Hainaut, Brabant, Flanders, Namur, Limburg, Geldern, Zeeland, Holland, Utrecht, Overijssel, Maastricht, Drenthe, Groningen, and Friesland. Territorially, roughly half these provinces were Catholic and the other half mostly Calvinist. The Catholic provinces formed in 1578 the Union of Arras and the mainly Protestant provinces created in 1584 the United Provinces of the Netherlands. The latter fought ably against Spanish rule under the leadership of the *statdthouder* of Amsterdam, William of Orange, and became independent in 1572. The rest of the Low Countries remained under the Spanish Crown until the War of Spanish Succession which ended in 1714, when they passed, with minor territorial losses, to the Austrian Habsburg. During 1668–1678, France, under Louis XIV, took part of Flanders (Lille). After the revolution of 1789, France annexed the whole of the Low Countries (1795) and converted the Netherlands into the subservient Batavian Republic. In 1815, after the final fall of Napoleon, the Netherlands was restored and obtained the rest of the Low Countries. In 1830, most of the former Spanish and Austrian Netherlands became BELGIUM. LUXEMBOURG was divided between Belgium and the Netherlands.

Spoleto (Duchy of) (7th–9th cents.; central *Italy*)
A Lombard duchy founded ca. 600, Spoleto, in Umbria, was annexed to the CAROLINGIAN EMPIRE in 774. During the 9th cent. it was part of the mostly nominal kingdom of Italy (IMPERIAL ITALY). In the 13th cent. it became a papal domain (PAPAL STATES).

Sri Lanka
Ceylon, as Sri Lanka was known before independence, is a corrupt pronunciation of Sri Lanka. Some historians, arguing that, e.g., Spain is not pronounced 'España' in English, prefer to retain the name Ceylon, Others apply the same logic to Burma and Myanmar. Be that as it may, Sri Lanka was peopled by Sinhalese from India in the 6th cent. BC. The Tamils, who occupied the north, arrived in the 11th cent. Sinhalese is an Indo-Aryan tongue, related to the languages spoken in central and northern India. Tamil belongs to the Dravidian family of languages, spoken in southern India.

BUDDHISM

The spread of Buddhism, the religion of the Sinhalese, who are a majority in Sri Lanka, had some influence on the political culture of the nations of southern and south east Asia. Buddhism was founded by Siddharta Gautama, an Indian prince, ca. 400 BC. Historically, it must be understood in relation to Vedic writings and the social practices of the Indo-Aryans who gradually occupied the Indus River Valley and northern India (VEDIC INDIA). The diffusion of Buddhism was due, in great part, to Asoka, King of MAGADHA in the 3rd cent. BC. From northern India, Buddhism first caught on in Sri Lanka, where Mahinda, Asoka's son, preached. After AD 200, it reached central Asia and China. It is known in Korea after AD 400, from where, in the 6th cent., it spread to Japan, which also received Chinese Buddhist influence. Tibet was converted after 600. The essence of Buddhism is the *sangha*, or monastic life. No matter how otherworldly, monasteries tend to accumulate land and to have political influence. The monasteries were suppressed in T'ANG (TANG) China in the 9th cent. and in Japan in the 16th cent. But Buddhism flourished in Tibet, Sri Lanka, and south east Asia. The first Sinhalese king of Sri Lanka was Vijaya in 483 BC. The Sinhalese capital was established in Anuradhapuri, in the north of the island. During most of its early history, Sri Lanka was divided into small kingdoms. There is mention in the time of the Indian GUPTAS of a King Meghavanna of Sri Lanka (5th cent.). The Cholas of southern India annexed the island in the 11th cent. and ruled until the 12th cent. The Chola capital was Polonnaruwa. The Hindu Tamils settled in the north and drove the Sinhalese to the south. After, the island was mostly divided again. The Portuguese occupied the coast in the early 16th cent. and built a fort in Colombo.

KANDY

In 1592, the Sinhalese founded a kingdom whose capital was established in Kandy, in central Sri Lanka. The Dutch arrived in 1636 and dispossessed the Portuguese, but could not capture Kandy. The BRITISH EAST INDIA COMPANY intervened in 1796 and annexed the coast of Ceylon to the presidency of Madras. Ceylon was made a colony in 1802 and Kandy was occupied in 1815. Ceylon was ruled by BRITISH INDIA but in 1931 it was given separate status. It became independent in 1948 within the British Commonwealth of Nations. In 1972 it was declared a republic and renamed Sri Lanka. In 1983 the Tamils launched a separatist movement. To try to quell guerrilla warfare and terrorism by Tamil separatists, Indian forces intervened unsuccessfully in northern Sri Lanka with, initially at least, the acquiescence of Colombo, from 1987 to 1990. Internecine fighting has continued.

Sri Vijaya (7th–13th cents.; *Indonesia*)
Indian influence in Malaya and Indonesia led in the 7th cent. to the creation of the Indo-Sumatran kingdom of Sri Vijaya, capital Palembang, probably by the Sailendra, who also ruled in Java. The Sailendra constructed the Buddhist temples at Borobudur in central Java (8th–9th cents.). Sailendra rule was curtailed in Java by the Hindu Mataram kingdom, which constructed the rival temple complex of Prambanan (9th–10th cents.) near Borobudur. The Hindu rulers moved to east Java where they were crushed by Sri Vijaya in the 11th

cent. It has been speculated that Sri Vijaya might have been influential in the establishment of the Cambodian capital at Angkor in the 8th cent. In the 11th cent. the Cholas from SOUTHERN INDIA attacked Sri Vijaya, which gradually declined until it disappeared during the 13th cent. During the decline of Sri Vijaya, a kingdom known as Malayu, capital Jambi, became predominant in central Sumatra. In Java there followed a dark period during which only some minor history is known until, in eastern Java, King Kertanagara founded a state which conquered Malayu (1278). Shortly after that, the MAJAPAHIT EMPIRE was created as successor to Kertanagara and heir to the Sri Vijaya domains.

Sudan

The northern part of Sudan was known as Nubia, home to the KUSH kingdom. Egypt was under Kushite rule from ca. 720 to ca. 670 (PHARAONIC EGYPT). The Kushites were displaced by Assyria in lower Egypt in 663 BC, but shortly afterwards both Assyrians and Kushites were pushed out by the Egyptians. The Kushite capital was moved from Napata to Meroe. The kingdom was destroyed by Axum (ETHIOPIA) in the 4th cent. AD. Sudan was divided into statelets. Islamic influence became predominant in the north during the 13th cent., but the south remained and still is unconverted and animist. During the 16th cent., a vague state known as Funj, was established in the north, but the Sudan remained mostly disunited until it was conquered by Muhammad Ali, the Ottoman pasha of EGYPT in 1821. Khartoum, Sudan's capital, was founded by the Egyptians in 1823. In 1881, a local leader calling himself the Mahdi (Messiah) united the Islamic Sudanese tribes and took over northern Sudan. From 1896 to 1898 Lord Kitchener subjected the Sudan and, in 1899, an Anglo-Egyptian condominium was established. In practice it was the British who ruled. After World War II, Cairo tried to stimulate a movement in the Sudan for union with Egypt, but the Sudan, still ethnically divided between an Islamic north and a non-Islamic south, became independent in 1956. The country's division has resulted in continuous guerrilla activity in the south. Arabic is spoken in the north and Hausa (vaguely related to Semitic tongues) is common as a lingua franca in the south, where related Nilotic languages, widely used in central and east Africa, are also spoken. Kordofan is a region of central Sudan, sometimes mentioned as a kingdom.

Sueves (5th–6th cents.; *Spain*)

The Sueves were Germanic semi-nomads who, in 411, founded a kingdom in Galicia that lasted to ca. 580. It was conquered by the VISIGOTH KINGDOM.

Sui (PERIOD OF DISUNITY (AFTER HAN))

Sumer (4th mil.–17th cent. BC; ancient *Near East*)

Sumer is the area of southern Mesopotamia, south of Babylon, where the first cuneiform-using city–states emerged during the late-4th mil. BC. The first dynasty of Ur dates from ca. 2750 BC. There were also kingdoms in Umma and Uruk ca. 2340. The legendary Gilgamesh ruled Uruk. Under Sargon (2334–2279), AKKAD became dominant and united Mesopotamia. Akkad was destroyed by GUTIANS, mountain tribesmen from Iran, ca. 2250 BC. After the fall of Akkad, Lagash became predominant under Gudea, who ruled from 2141 to 2122. Lagash fell to the AMORITES and to ELAM, and Ur rose again ca. 2100 until ca. 2000. The last period of Ur is known as the 3rd Dynasty, when Lagash was absorbed. Elamite attacks ended the hegemony of Ur in Sumer, after which the cities of Larsa and Isin were rivals until the 18th cent. BC. BABYLONIA became politically significant ca. 1900. It unified Mesopotamia under Hammurabi (1792–1750). There was a late resurgence of Sumerian political influence in Samsuditana from ca. 1630 to ca. 1600, but Mesopotamian history was mostly determined after Hammurabi by Babylon and Assur (ASSYRIA). Other Sumerian sites are Uruk, Mari, Eshnunna, Kish, Der, Larsa, Adab, and Shuruppak. The Sumerian language is an isolate with no known relatives.

(*See chronology under* Ancient Near East.)

Sung (Song) (10th–13th cents.; *China*)

During the PERIOD OF DISUNITY (AFTER T'ANG/TANG), the Sung, under Emperor Sung T'ai Tsu, founder of the dynasty, became dominant in the territories of the Five Dynasties (from Hebei to the Yangzi). The northern Sung capital was Kaifeng. In 979, Emperor Sung T'ai Tsung conquered the land of the Ten Kingdoms (south of the Yangzi), thus reunifying most of China. Simultaneously, the Mongol Khitai had created a kingdom called Liao with its capital in Beijing (KHITAN KHANATE). In trying to be rid of their northern neighbours, the Sung over-reached themselves when they encouraged the nomadic JURCHEN to attack Liao, which they did successfully in 1125. Once the Jurchen had camped in Beijing, they not only refused to budge – and founded their own Chin (Jin) dynasty – but they went on to occupy Kaifeng and attack the Sung in their dynastic territories. In 1127 Chin reduced the Sung to the lands south of a frontier between southern Shandong (Shantung) and southern Gansu (Kansu). The southern Sung capital was Hangzhou (Hang-chow). The Sung period was one of prosperity in part traceable to the invention and successful use of paper money. It was also a time of artistic creativity, which to some makes the Sung emperors seem effete.

The Sung empire at its height extended from Tianjin (Tientsin) to Gansu and south to Guangxi. The Tibetans on its western frontiers were at the height of their power. Around 1207, Genghis Khan got the Mongols started on their conquering rampage through Eurasia. Although he did crush Tibetan power, he attacked but did not destroy the Jurchen Chin kingdom. His grandson Kublai Khan returned and finished that job in 1234. A frontal assault against the Sung was not advisable, so Kublai went around, conquered NAN CHAO (Yunnan province) in 1253, and attacked the Sung on their western flank, ending their rule and annexing China to the Mongol Empire in 1279. The new Mongol dynasty took the name of YUAN. It was followed by MING. (*See chronology under* China and Neighbouring Areas.)

Suriname

Peopled by Amerindians, Surinam was occupied by the Dutch in the early 17th cent. The British also had claims to Guiana. In 1664, the Dutch lost New Amsterdam to the British, who renamed it New York. In compensation, the Dutch obtained all British claims to Guiana in 1674. They ceded the western half of Suriname to Great Britain in 1815. Dutch Guiana became independent in 1975 as Suriname. The capital of Suriname is Paramaribo.

Susa (ELAM)

Swaziland

Peopled by Bantu-speaking tribes, Swaziland became a dependency first of Transvaal (1894), then of Great Britain (1906). It became independent in 1968. The capital is Mbabane.

Sweden

According to an unlikely account, the Swedish island of Gotland is the home of the GOTHS. Sweden, historical home of the Varangians (NORSEMEN) – the eastern equivalent of the Vikings and founders of Kievan Rus – took shape during the 10th cent. In the 12th cent. Sweden was Christianized by Eric IX. In the 13th cent. it annexed FINLAND. Swedish cities, especially Visby, were part of the HANSEATIC LEAGUE. In 1319 Sweden and NORWAY were united under the Norwegian king, Magnus VII, until 1343 when Norway came under Danish influence. By the dynastic Union of Kalmar, DENMARK, Norway, and Sweden were joined under Margaret of Denmark. Denmark and Norway remained united but Sweden, mostly under the rule of local nobles, went its own way. From 1521 to 1559, the Swedes occupied ESTONIA. In 1523, the Danish king, Christian II, tried to make valid the Danish claim on Sweden and was defeated. Denmark retained Scania (southern Sweden). Gustavus I Vasa became King of Sweden in 1523. He massacred the nobility and eliminated the German influence of the by then not-so-powerful Hansa. From 1592 to 1599 the Polish king, Sigismund III, was nominal ruler of Sweden. Gustavus II (1611–1632) launched Swedish military and political ascendancy in the north. He annexed Ingria, Karelia, and Livonia in 1617. In 1648, the Swedes obtained Bremen and western Pomerania, including Stettin. Under King Charles X (1654–1660), the Swedes recovered Scania from the Danes. The diminution of Swedish power followed the crushing defeat of Charles XII by RUSSIA in Poltava (1709). In 1720–1721, Sweden had to cede most of its

German and Baltic possessions to PRUSSIA and Russia, respectively. A remaining part of Swedish Pomerania was lost when the HOLY ROMAN EMPIRE was dissolved by Napoleon in 1806. In 1809 Sweden was forced to relinquish Finland to Russia. But in 1815, at the VIENNA Congress, Sweden, which had joined the anti-Napoleonic coalition in 1813, was awarded Norway, whose independence it grudgingly accepted in 1905.

In 1810, the Swedish king, Charles XIII, was childless. The Swedes turned to the French marshal Charles Baptiste Jules Bernadotte, who had risen from the ranks and whose fairness had impressed the Swedes, and offered him the succession to the Swedish Crown. After getting the nod from Napoleon, Bernadotte was adopted by Charles, converted to Lutheranism and, in 1818, became King Charles XIV of Sweden, founder of the still reigning dynasty. Stockholm is the capital of Sweden, which joined the EUROPEAN UNION in 1995.

Switzerland

Peopled by the Celtic Helvetians, the territory of Switzerland was part of the Roman provinces of Italia, Alpes Poeninae, and Germania Superior (*Roman Empire*). In the 6th cent. the FRANKS were occupying the territory of Switzerland. In the 9th cent. it was divided between Swabia and the Kingdom of ARLES. In 1033 it was incorporated into the HOLY ROMAN EMPIRE. The origin of Swiss sovereignty was the pact joining the cantons of Schwyz, Uri, and Unterwalden in 1291 against Habsburg encroachment (HABSBURG EMPIRE). In the 14th cent., the original cantons were joined by Lucerne, Glarus, Zug, Zurich, and Berne (1351–1353). In 1386, the Swiss forced the Habsburg to recognize their autonomy. They were formidable fighters, often as mercenaries, and went from victory to victory during the 15th cent. Their separation from the Holy Roman Empire was accepted in 1499. In 1513, Fribourg, Solothurn, Basel, Appenzell, and Schaffhausen joined the federation. As a result of the French victory in Marignano (1515), the Swiss adopted a strict policy of neutrality, although for a time Swiss soldiers served under the French Crown. The country was split by religious differences during the 16th cent., but it did not deviate from its neutrality during the European wars of religion, especially the Thirty Years War, and in 1648 their independence was recognized by the rest of Europe. By then, Berne had annexed Vaud, and Grisons, Geneva, and St Gall were associated with the Swiss federation. From 1798 to 1815, as the Helvetian Republic, Switzerland was part of the FRENCH EUROPEAN EMPIRE. In VIENNA, its independence and neutrality were recognized and the other cantons that constitute Switzerland were incorporated (Valais, Vaud, Aargau, Thurgau, Ticino, Neuchâtel, and Jura). Most had been dependent territories of other cantons. VALAIS was an independent bishopric until the French made it part of the Helvetian Republic in 1798. Berne is the capital of Switzerland. Switzerland has four official languages (spoken in different areas): German Swiss (the majority language), French (in the west), Italian (in the south), and Romansh, also known as Rhaetian and more spoken in parts of northern Italy than in Switzerland.

Syria

The coast of Syria was the ancient PHOENICIA. Syria was part of the Persian ACHAEMENID and the Greek ALEXANDRIAN EMPIRES. The SELEUCID EMPIRE had its base in Syria. It was a province of ROME and later of the BYZANTINE EMPIRE. Syria was among the first acquisitions of ISLAM (644) and Damascus was the capital of the Umayyad caliphs (661–750). In 1516, Syria – designating most of the lands from the eastern Mediterranean to the Euphrates – became part of the OTTOMAN EMPIRE, which held it until its own dissolution in 1918. Syria was handed over to France as a mandate of the League of Nations (UNITED NATIONS). Under French administration, LEBANON was separated from Syria in 1925. Syria itself became independent in 1944, although foreign troops did not leave until 1946. In 1958, EGYPT and Syria agreed to merge as the United Arab Republic, which YEMEN joined later the same year, forming a federation called the United Arab States. Political problems led to Syria's separation in 1961. In the Six Day War of 1967, Israel invaded Syria and occupied the Golan Heights on Syria's south-western border. Syria intervened in Lebanon to quell a Palestinian uprising in 1978. After years of fighting, civil order was restored in Lebanon during 1990–1991 under Syrian supervision.

T

Tabaristan (7th cent.; *Iran*)

After the invasion of Persia by ISLAM in 637, the remnants of the SASANID EMPIRE took refuge in Tabaristan, in the Elburz Mountains of northern IRAN and along the southern coast of the Caspian Sea. They were dislodged in 902 by the SAMANIDS.

Tahirids (9th cent; eastern *Iran*)

The Tahirids were a Persian dynasty that, even though it ruled Khurasan in the 9th cent. as vassal of the ABBASID CALIPHATE, begat the historical tendency to separate eastern from western IRAN. They were displaced from Khurasan by the SAFFARIDS.

(*See chronology under* Iran.)

Taifa Kingdoms (MUSLIM SPAIN)

Taiwan

Taiwan was originally peopled by Austronesian-speakers. Chinese colonialization began in the 7th cent. In 1590 the Portuguese called the island Formosa (beautiful). The Dutch occupied it in the 17th cent., but a MING general, escaping from the Manchu conquerors of China, expelled them in 1662. The Manchu CH'ING (QING) dynasty reclaimed Taiwan in 1683. The Japanese took the island after defeating CHINA in 1895. They returned it in 1945. In a curious historical replay of the Ming–Manchu events in the 17th cent., after the communist victory in the mainland, Chiang Kai-shek and the remnants of his armies took refuge in Taiwan in 1949, but he, like the Beijing government, never accepted that Taiwan could be anything but part of China. The United States, under President Nixon, recognized the People's Republic of China in 1979. Even though the Americans withdrew official recognition of Taiwan, the country, which still calls itself the Republic of China, is sovereign for all intents and purposes. China has said it would be willing to go to war if Taiwan ever attempted to declare itself independent. The capital of Taiwan is Taipei. Tiny islands off the coast of Fujian (*China*), Quemoy and Matsu, manned by the Chinese nationalists of Chiang Kai-shek (TAIWAN), were the object of intense bombardment by China in the late 1950s.

Tajikistan

The Tajiks speak an Indo-Iranian language. Their presence in western Turkestan is probably ancient. They occupied Sogdiana, which corresponds partially to modern Tajikistan. In the 16th cent. this land was part of the Khanate of BUKHARA. In the 19th cent. it was fragmented. RUSSIA, which annexed Bukhara in 1856, occupied Tajikistan in 1880. The Tajiks rebelled against the Soviet state in 1917, but were brought to heel by the Bolsheviks in 1921 and incorporated into the Turkistan Autonomous Soviet Socialist Republic, created in 1918, also including TURKMENISTAN and UZBEKISTAN. The Uzbek Soviet Socialist Republic, including Tajikistan, was separated from it in 1924. In 1929, the Tadzhik Soviet Socialist Republic was formed. Tajikistan declared itself independent in 1991. The capital is Dushanbe.

T'ang (Tang) (7th–10th cents.; *China*)
Sui China was succeeded by the T'ang dynasty in 618 (PERIOD OF DISUNITY (AFTER HAN)). The T'ang, founded by T'ang Kao Tsu and his son T'ang T'ai Tsung, of an aristocratic family, inherited approximately the territories of Sui China. The T'ang capital was Changan, another name for Xian (Sian), in Shaanxi (Shensi) province. T'ang rule was extended to Quangdong (Kwantung), where people identify themselves as 'men of T'ang' rather than the customary Han for ethnic Chinese. The T'ang adopted an imperialistic policy towards the west. In 630 and 657, the T'ang defeated the T'U-CHÜEH. In 670 they were being threatened by the Tanguts (Tibetans), who had conquered Gansu (Kansu) and the Tarim Basin, from which the T'ang ejected them in 692. The T'u-chüeh were saved by the Tangut diversion and intermittently fought off the Chinese until they made peace in 722. The Tanguts hung on to western Gansu during the entire T'ang period, which constrained the Chinese to a corridor through which their armies marched westwards. In 736, China controlled the Balkash Lake area. The Tanguts had conquered Kashgaria in the early 8th cent., but the T'ang displaced them from that region from 737 to 750. In 744, China extended its rule to the Issyk Kul Basin and made its power felt as far as Samarkand. But in the Battle of Talas (751), in Ferghana, the Chinese were decisively defeated by the Arabs allied to Islamicized Turks. This battle determined that the region west of Kashgaria would eventually constitute Islamic Western Turkestan. After Talas, T'ang gradually abandoned its conquests west of Gansu (Kansu). The T'ang, who at first favoured Buddhism but later turned against it, lasted until 906. China then entered the PERIOD OF DISUNITY (AFTER T'ANG/TANG). Chinese historians consider the Five Dynasties of that period as the legitimate successor of T'ang.
(*See chronologies under* China and Neighbouring Areas *and* Western Turkestan.)

Tanguts (TIBET)

Tanzania
Peopled by disunited Bantu-speaking tribes, the mainland-Africa territory of Tanzania became German in 1885 as Tanganyika. The Germans fought off British attempts to take over during World War I, but after the war Tanganyika was mandated to Great Britain. It became independent in 1961 and was named

Tanzania when it federated with the island of Zanzibar in 1964. In 1978 Tanzania invaded Uganda and overthrew the dictator Idi Amin. Tanzanian troops left in 1981. The Bantu-related Swahili, a lingua franca in east Africa, is an official language in Tanzania. The capital, previously Dar es Salaam, is Dodoma since 1990.

Teutonic Knights (13th–16th cents.; *Baltic region*)

The German military-religious order of the Teutonic Knights was founded in Acre in 1190–1191 (CRUSADER STATES). In the early 13th cent., it was charged with Christianizing the Baltic lands. Its greatest feat, under the leadership of Hermann von Salza, was the conquest of the Prussians, a people of Baltic stock, whose territory (later East Prussia) passed into their hands in 1226 and was constituted as an autonomous state separated physically from the Holy Roman Empire with its capital in Marienburg (today Polish Malbork). Peopled by Pagan Indo-European speakers, LITHUANIA was created in the early 13th cent. in opposition to German pressure from the Teutonic Knights in the south and the LIVONIAN BROTHERS OF THE SWORD in the north (Latvia). Threatened by the Lithuanians, the order of the Livonian Brothers merged with the Teutonic Knights in 1236. The advance eastward of the Livonian Brothers was contained by the Russian Alexander Nevsky in the ice battle of Lake Peipus in 1242. The Teutonic Knights were also active in TRANSYLVANIA during the 13th cent. In the early 14th cent., the order annexed Pomerelia (Polish Pomerania) and warred with POLAND over its possession. In 1346 it occupied ESTONIA and, between 1402 and 1404, seized portions of Lithuania and Poland. In 1410 the Poles and Lithuanians defeated the Teutonic Knights in the Battle of Tannenberg. In 1466, the western part of East Prussia and Pomerelia passed to Poland and the rest of East Prussia was constituted under the knights as a Polish dependency with its centre in Königsberg. In 1525, Albert, Elector of Brandenburg and head of the order, secularized and annexed Prussia, thus eliminating the political role of the Teutonic Knights.

Texas (19th cent.; *United States*)

Under Mexican sovereignty, the territory of Texas was part of the state of Coahuila. In 1835, American settlers, who outnumbered the Mexicans, rebelled. At the head of a Mexican army, General Santa Anna over-ran the Texan defenders of the Alamo, San Antonio, but in 1836, Texan forces ably led by Sam Houston defeated the Mexicans in the Battle of San Jacinto. Texas asked to join the Union but was held at arm's length – because of the slavery issue – until 1845, when it was annexed by the United States, which led to the Mexican–American War of 1846–1848.

Thailand

During the 7th cent., Thais, who are linguistically related to the Laotians, created small states along the southern borders of the Chinese province of

Yunnan, then the NAN CHAO kingdom, and probably had already started migrating to LAOS and northern Thailand. The foundations of Siam, as Thailand was known until 1939 (from the Chinese designation of its territory), was the result of the destruction of Nan Chao by Kublai Khan in 1253 (YUAN). The Thais migrated south and ca. 1280 took northern Thailand from the Mon-Khmers (CAMBODIA), establishing their capital in Sukhotai. Another Thai kingdom was established in Chieng Mai, in north-western Siam, which came under the influence of Myanmar in the 16th cent. It was also known as Lan Na. During the 14th and 15th cents. Thais and Khmers were frequently at war, until the Thais crushed the power of Angkor. During the 14th cent. the Thais moved the capital of the kingdom to Ayutthaya and extended their rule to northern Malaya. Between 1568 and 1583, the country was occupied by the Burmese (MYANMAR), who returned in 1767 and destroyed the Thai capital. The Burmese were driven out in 1777 and the capital was moved to Thon Buri, on the Menam-Chao Phraya River. In the early 19th cent. it was definitely fixed in Bangkok, across the river. During that time the kingdom consolidated its rule in northern Thailand – it finally succeeded in recovering Chieng Mai – and attempted to annex Laos until the French constituted a Laotian protectorate in 1893 (FRENCH COLONIAL EMPIRE). The French, who had established a protectorate in Cambodia in 1863, delimited Siam's border with Cambodia in their favour. In 1909, Siam also lost lands to British Malaya (BRITISH COLONIAL EMPIRE). Siam served as a buffer state between British and French colonialist encroachments and thus managed to retain its independence, which it used to adopt some Western ways, not however to the degree the Japanese did in their secure island kingdom. In 1941, under a militarist government sympathetic to JAPAN, Thailand allowed Japanese troops in their territory and, under Japanese pressure, declared war on the Allies in 1942. The Japanese recognized Thai claims to neighbouring countries, all of which were returned after the war. The isthmus of Kra shared by Myanmar and Thailand separates the Malay Peninsula from the rest of Asia.

Thebes (DELIAN LEAGUE; MYCENEAN GREECE)

Three Kingdoms (3rd–4th cents.; *China*)
Upon the fall of HAN, China divided into three kingdoms: Wei (220–266), Wu (222–280), and Shu Han (221–263). Wei, who had overthrown Han, occupied northern China and a strip of territory in Gansu (Kansu). The lands of Wu were south of the Yangtze as far as northern Vietnam. Shu was the southern limit of Wei and the western limit of Wu. Shu extended west as far as Qinghai (Chinghai) and the western borders of Sichuan (Szechwan). Wei absorbed Shu in 263. In 266, a palace coup changed the name of Wei to Chin (Jin), also known in Chinese historiography as Western Chin to distinguish this period from the Jurchen kingdom known also as Chin (Jin). Chin absorbed Wu in

280, reuniting China until 316. Pushed from the north, the southern HSIUNG-NU fell on Chin ushering in the time Chinese historians call the SIXTEEN KINGDOMS OF THE FIVE BARBARIANS, which is part of the PERIOD OF DISUNITY (AFTER HAN).
(*See chronology under* China and Neighbouring Areas.)

Tibet (7th–20th cents.; *China*)
The foundation of Lhasa dates to the 7th cent. It was known to T'ANG (TANG) China as Tufan and the Tibetans themselves as Tanguts. The Tibetans, who outside Tibet were feared warriors, adopted the Lamaist form of Buddhism in the 7th–8th cents. In the late 7th cent. the Tanguts occupied Gansu (Kansu). From 700 to 750 they occupied Kashgaria, which comprises the western Tarim Basin and adjoining lands to the west. The T'ang, who had tried to extend Chinese power beyond Kashgaria but gave up after the Battle of Talas, evacuated the Tarim Basin and left the Tanguts in possession of Gansu. Tarim fell to the UIGURS. After 840, Tibet broke up into statelets. A Tangut band established in 887 a kingdom in the Ordos, which in 1028 absorbed Gansu (HSI-HSIA). Tibet itself had no political power and came under the influence of MONGOLIA from the 13th to the 17th cents., although this was a reciprocal relation, for the Mongols adopted Buddhism of the Lamaist type practised in Tibet. A branch of the Oirats or Western Mongols invaded and controlled Tibet from 1616 to 1720, when they were ejected by the Manchus (CH'ING/QING), who imposed their suzerainty over Tibet, later converted into outright claims of sovereignty. Tibet lost most of Ladakh to BRITISH INDIA in 1846, which is why the Chinese attacked INDIA in 1962. In 1890, the British sheared off Sikkim. After the fall of the Ch'ing dynasty in 1912, Tibet tried to go independent, the way Mongolia did, but unlike the latter, over which powerful Russia hovered, Tibet was on its own and reverted to Chinese suzerainty in 1914. It was incorporated outright by China in 1933, even then retaining some autonomy, which was definitely abolished by the communists after 1949.
(*See chronology under* China and Neighbouring Areas.)

Timbuktu (14th–17th cents.; *Western Africa*)
Although usually figuring as the capital of African kingdoms, Timbuktu, in today's MALI, was an important caravaneering and commercial centre for Saharan north–south trade routes and, as such, formed the political nucleus of the kingdoms of Mali, SONGHAI, and BAMBARA.

Timurid Empire and Successor States (14th–15th cents.; *Central Asia*: western Turkestan; *Iran*; Afghanistan)
Tamerlane or Timur the Lame was a Turk from Samarkand who drove his Mongol suzerains (CHAGATAITE KHANATE) from Transoxiana, to which mostly, in his time, the name Samarkand itself was applied. In 1370, Tamerlane

started his multiple destructive forays and expeditions ranging from Lake Balkash in the east, where he went to force the Chagataites to renounce their claim to Transoxiana; to Delhi, in the south, where he shattered the DELHI SULTANATE; to Anatolia in the west, where he nearly destroyed the incipient OTTOMAN EMPIRE and restored the ANATOLIAN EMIRATES (and, according to many historians, gave the BYZANTINE EMPIRE over half a century more of life, until the fall of Constantinople); and to the south, Russia, where he went to settle the ownership of AZERBAIJAN, which was being contested by Toqtamish, lord of the GOLDEN HORDE and a former protégé of his. However, there was little cohesion in his conquests, so that the actual extent of his empire was much less than the territories he devastated and, after his death, it rapidly disintegrated, much more so than the successor states of the Mongol Empire. His actual imperial conquests were: the restored KHWARIZM (ca. 1380), to the west of Samarkand in Transoxiana; after 1380, Herat and the rest of AFGHANISTAN, which had belonged to the KERTS; Khurasan (1384), which he took from the SARBEDARIANS; and from 1386 to 1403, the rest of Persia (IRAN), including Baghdad, and the Caucasus, which were in the hands of the MUZZAFARIDS and the QARA-QOYUNLU, respectively.

SHAH RUKH

On Tamerlane's death in 1405, his empire was divided into five parts among his heirs, roughly: (1) Azerbaijan; (2) north-central Persia to Baghdad; (3) eastern Afghanistan and as far north as Ferghana; (4) Khurasan and western Afghanistan; and (5) his Samarkandian homeland as far south as Kandahar. The JELAIRS quickly tore off Baghdad. The Qara-Qoyunlu, which apparently laid low, over-ran all of Western Persia during the first half of 15th cent. The kingdom of Samarkand did rather well under Shah Rukh, a sensible and refined son of Tamerlane, who by the middle of the century had reunited Transoxiana and Khurasan. Ulugh Beg, son of Shah Rukh, ruled in Samarkand itself during his father's lifetime, he is considered one of the greatest cultural figures of Uzbekistan. From 1469, Transoxiana was prey to internecine struggles and by ca. 1500 it fell to the Uzbek SHAYBANIDS, who went on to conquer Khurasan. Though probably much fragmented, Afghanistan was the only Timurid realm to survive the general downfall of the founder's heirs. Babur, a descendant of Tamerlane from a Chingisid bride, became monarch in Ferghana (1494). Failing in the early 16th cent. to recover Transoxiana, he went to Kabul and, in 1519, descended on Indian pastures to found the MUGHAL EMPIRE. (*See chronologies under* Western Turkestan, Indian Subcontinent, Greater Mongolia, Anatolia, *and* Iran.)

Tlemcen (ALGERIA)

Toba Wei (PERIOD OF DISUNITY AFTER HAN)

Togo
Peopled by Kwa tribesmen – Kwa belongs to the Niger–Congo family of languages, predominant in western Africa and spread as far east as Somalia – Togo was a German colony on the Gulf of Guinea in 1885. It was mandated to Great Britain and France after World War I as Togoland. British Togoland was annexed to Ghana and the French part became independent Togo in 1960. Its capital is Lomé.

Tokharians (3rd cent. BC–1st cent. AD; *Central Asia*; Afghanistan)
Before the Turks and Mongols (whose tongues belong to the Altaic family of languages) started a counterflow westwards, Indo-Iranian speakers had actually penetrated central Asia as far as the Tarim Basin and the Chinese province of Gansu (Kansu). These peoples are known collectively as Tokharians by the Greeks and as Yüeh-chih by the Chinese. Tokharian languages were deciphered in the early 20th cent. The Yüeh-chih/Tokharians were chased out of China by the Hsiung Nu in the 3rd cent. BC. They pursued the Saka or Asian Scythians, also Indo-Iranian speakers, across western Turkestan and finally expelled them from Bactria in the late 2nd cent. BC. The Tokharians founded KUSHANA in the 1st cent. AD. Descendants of the Tokharians are known to have existed in the Tarim Basin until the 8th cent., when the UIGURS occupied the region. Indo-Iranian is a major branch of the Indo-European family of languages, which include the major European languages and the Indo-Aryan languages of India. The designation Tokharistan is vague. It refers to lands that were occupied by Tokharians and this can mean anywhere from Gansu to Bactria.

Toltecs (MESOAMERICAN CIVILIZATIONS)

Tonga
Peopled by speakers of a language of the Austronesian family, which includes Malay, the southern Pacific Ocean island of Tonga became a British protectorate in 1900 and in 1970 obtained its independence. The capital is Nuku'alofa.

Tonkin (VIETNAM)

Toulouse (9th–13th cents.; southern *France*)
The Frankish county of Toulouse, known also as Languedoc, was founded in 843. Manicheism in its European form of Cathar doctrine became widespread in Languedoc, where its followers were known as Albigensians. They held a council in 1167 in Toulouse. The papacy wanted the heresy exterminated and France coveted Toulouse. The Albigensian Crusade was launched in 1208 by Pope Innocent III, with Simon de Montfort leading the French forces opposed by Raymond VI, Count of Toulouse, who had the support of Aragon. Arms

favoured the French in 1213 and, in 1229, Raymond VII capitulated and Languedoc was incorporated into France. The heresy was not eliminated and, in 1233, Pope Gregory IX established the Inquisition, later made famous in Spain, which, after a century, finally extirpated Catharism. Toulouse was renowned for its patronage of the Troubadours. Even though Toulouse was its capital, most of Languedoc is on the right bank of the Rhône, across from Provence.

Transkei, The (20th cent.; South Africa)
A so-called tribal homeland or Bantustan, The Transkei was created south of Natal in South Africa in 1963 and given nominal independence in 1976. With the end of apartheid, it was incorporated into South Africa in 1994. The capital of The Transkei is Umtata.

Transvaal (19th–20th cents.; South Africa)
Following the annexation of Cape Province by the British, many of its Boer inhabitants trekked to the interior of South Africa (1835–1845) where they created states of their own. Recognized by Great Britain in 1852, Transvaal was annexed by the British from 1877 to 1884. With its sister Boer republic, the ORANGE FREE STATE (1854), it formed an alliance against the British, who defeated them in the South African or Boer War (1899–1902). With Natal and Cape Colony, Transvaal and Orange Free State became part of the British-sponsored Union of South Africa. Pretoria was the capital of Transvaal.

Transylvania (16th–20th cents.; Hungary and Romania)
Transylvania is north west Romania. It is paradigmatically a borderland and has one of the stormiest histories in Europe. It was annexed by ROME in 107 and abandoned in 271. Invaded by GOTHS, HUNS, GEPIDS, AVARS, and SLAVS, it was eventually occupied by MAGYARS in the 9th cent. Stephen I of Hungary annexed Transylvania in the early 11th cent. There were German settlements in the 12th and 13th cents. (The German name for Transylvania is Siebenbürgen, which refers to seven fortresses the Germans built.) In the 13th cent. it was besieged by the PETCHENEGS and the Hungarian king, Andrew II, called in the TEUTONIC KNIGHTS. Settlers from VALACHIA – better known by their modern name of Romanians – started arriving in the early 13th cent. In 1241, the Mongols briefly passed through. When the OTTOMAN EMPIRE defeated the Hungarians in the Battle of Mohacs in 1562, a local governor, John Zapolya, took advantage to bring Transylvania under his rule, which was opposed by the Austrians (HABSBURG EMPIRE). In 1540, however, the Ottoman sultan, Suleyman I the Magnificent, over-ran Hungary and in effect checked the Austrians. Transylvania was contested between Ottomans and its Hungarian local rulers. In 1571, the Hungarian Bathory family accepted being vassals of the Ottomans. Incursions by Valachians and

Austrians weakened their hand and in 1606 Stephen Bocskay became Prince of Transylvania with the approval of the Habsburg Emperor. Transylvania flourished, but after the defeat of the Ottomans at the gates of Vienna in 1683, Austrian influence grew and Transylvania became part of the Habsburg Empire in 1711. When the Hungarians rose against the Habsburg Empire (1848), the Romanians in Transylvania sided with the Austrians to suppress them. However, when the Dual Monarchy of Austria–Hungary was created in 1867, Transylvania became part of the Hungarian kingdom. After World War I, Romania seized Transylvania (1918), which was ceded to it by the Treaty of Trianon (1920) (VERSAILLES). Hungary, allied to Nazi Germany in World War II, took it back but returned it to Romania in 1945.

Trebizond (13th–15th cents.; *Anatolia*)
Trebizond, on the south-eastern coast of the Black Sea, was a successor state of the BYZANTINE EMPIRE, founded by members of the imperial Comnenus family after the conquest of Constantinople by the Latins in 1204. While the Mongols were hegemonic in the Near East during the early 14th cent., Trebizond prospered, but later, when the Turks became predominant, it decayed. In 1461 it was occupied by the OTTOMAN EMPIRE.
(*See chronology under* Anatolia.)

Trinidad and Tobago
Sighted by Columbus in 1498 but sparsely colonized by Spain, the Caribbean islands of Trinidad and Tobago, later peopled by Africans and Indians, became British in 1802 and independent in 1962. The capital is Port of Spain.

Tripoli (BARBARY STATES)

Tripoli (CRUSADER STATES)

Troy (late-2nd mil. BC; *Anatolia*)
Homer's *Iliad* is the source of Troy's fame. Archaeology reveals that there was an ancient city of Troy in the region of Troas on the Dardanelles. Of its various layers it is believed that the one dated to ca. 1200 corresponds to the Homeric site, which is basically why it is also speculated that Homer's epics are based on collective reminiscences of Mycenean times. The Trojan War could then have been fought over commercial rivalries, possibly access to the Black Sea. Troy might have fallen for the same reasons as MYCENEAN GREECE.

T'u-chüeh (6th–8th cents.; *Central Asia*: greater Mongolia)
T'u-chüeh is the Chinese name by which the Turks were first identified as a people of Central Asia. In the 6th cent., they overpowered the Mongol JUAN-JUAN and were occupying Mongolia and lands as far east as Jehol (western Manchuria) and as far west as the Aral Sea. The T'u-chüeh evicted the AVARS

from the Ili River Basin. After 580, they divided into a western and an eastern branch, which weakened their power and permitted the aggressive T'ANG (TANG) Chinese to defeat the eastern T'u-chüeh in 630 and practically destroy their western branch in 657. In 670, the Tanguts (Tibetans) over-ran the Chinese garrisons in the Tarim Basin, which gave the T'u-chüeh breathing space. Although the T'ang had retaken the Tarim Basin by 692, the reunited T'u-chüeh had previously reconquered their lands north of the Tien Shan range (northern limit of the Tarim Basin) and began rebuilding their empire. In 697, allied with the Chinese, they contained the Khitai in Jehol, from which the latter emerged only in the 9th cent. In 716, the T'u-chüeh suffered another setback from the Chinese, but by 730 had conquered as far as the Orkhon (central Mongolia). T'u-chüeh power was broken by the UIGURS, who decisively defeated and dispersed them in 741. The T'u-chüeh migrated to the west and roamed western Turkestan. The GHUZZ are probably their descendants. A group in the Altaic family of languages, which includes Mongol and probably Korean and Japanese.
(*See chronologies under* China and Neighbouring Areas *and* Greater Mongolia.)

Tufan (TIBET)

Tulunids (EGYPT)

Tungus (JURCHEN)

Tunisia
From the 10th cent. BC, the coast of Tunisia – the interior was and remained Berber – was occupied by Phoenicians, who created the Carthaginian Empire (6th to 2nd cents. BC), destroyed by ROME. Tunisia was the core of the Roman province of Africa. In the 429, the VANDALS crossed to Africa and founded a kingdom in Tunisia, which lasted until the Byzantine conquest (533). Called Ifriqiya by the Arabs, Tunisia was annexed by ISLAM in 698. It was then known by the name of its capital, Kairouan. When the Umayyad caliphate fell (750), Islam lost its unifying centre and it disintegrated into different kingdoms. An Umayyad who survived the Abbasid coup, constituted a caliphate in CÓRDOBA, which exerted influence on northern Africa. However, by ca. 800, Tunisia was being ruled by the Berber AGHLABIDS, who sponsored the Muslim invasion of Sicily starting in 827. The Aghlabids were influential in eastern Algeria and western Libya. They were dispossessed in 909 by the FATIMIDS, from eastern Algeria, who went on to fix their seat of power in EGYPT. When the Maghreb showed signs of separatism the Bedouins were let loose by the Fatimids. These semi-savage tribes created independent emirates during the 11th and 12th cents. and contributed significantly to the Arabization of the Maghreb. In MOROCCO and ALGERIA

they were brought to heel by the ALMORAVIDS. In Tunisia it was the ALMOHADS who, in 1159, fresh from triumphant campaigns against the Almoravids in Morocco and Spain, took over and ruled to ca. 1230.

THE HUSSEIN BEYS

Following a period of disunity, the local HAFSIDS came to power in 1278. Until the 16th cent., they extended their influence over Algeria and western LIBYA. The Tunisian coast had been besieged in the 12th cent. by Normans from Sicily and again in the 16th cent. by Spain. After 1574, the Ottomans expelled the Christians and appointed ruling beys in the coastal cities of Tunisia, Libya, and Algeria. These beys, who acted autonomously and engaged in piracy, constituted what are called the BARBARY STATES, which subsisted until the 19th cent., when they were gradually put down and absorbed by European powers, principally France. Tunisia itself was ruled from 1705 by the Hussein beys. After France conquered Algeria (1847), Tunisia came under French influence. It became a protectorate between 1881 and 1883. Tunisian nationalism actively opposed French rule after World War II and, in 1956, Tunisia became independent. The last French outpost, Bizerte, was handed over in 1963 after a massacre of Tunisian protesters in 1961. Tunis, established by the Hafsids, is the capital of Tunisia.
(*See chronology under* Maghreb.)

Turkey
In 1908 a reformist and nationalist military movement known as Young Turks became the decisive political influence within the OTTOMAN EMPIRE. Its leader Enver Pasha was the power behind the sultanate in 1913. He refused to accommodate the grievances of the minorities within the empire and, in 1914, lined up with Germany in World War I. The empire was beleaguered by the insurrection of the Arabs in the south, where the Hashemite Sharif of MECCA, Hussein of Hejaz, was a British ally. Ibn Saud had already established his own autonomous kingdom in Riyadh. The Turks contained an offensive of British, Australian, and New Zealand troops against the Gallipoli peninsula in 1915, but in 1917 they surrendered Jerusalem to the British. With the Allies in control of the Balkans, the Ottomans surrendered in 1918. Authority promptly dissolved within Anatolia itself (Asian Turkey). The VERSAILLES Conference, which met in different sites around Paris during 1918–1919 to sort out the consequences of the war, dealt with the Ottoman remnants in the Treaty of Sèvres. By its terms, accepted by the Sultan Mehmet VI, the former Ottoman Empire was divided between the victorious Allies, and Turkey was reduced to areas in Anatolia and barely the city limits of Istanbul. Smyrna was placed under Greek administration, the Kurds were offered a state in eastern Turkey, and north-eastern Turkey was to become Armenia.

KEMAL ATATURK

It was at this point that Mustafa Kemal came in. He was a distinguished soldier who had opposed the pro-German policy of his friend and colleague Enver Pasha and participated in the repulse of the Allied Gallipoli campaign. In central Anatolia Kemal organized an army of Turks with which by 1920 he had secured the approximate present borders of Turkey. One inevitable consequence, lamentably carried out, was the expulsion of the Armenians. Greek military had landed in Smyrna (Izmir) in 1920 but in 1921 and 1922 Mustafa Kemal routed them and expelled both military and civilians. The area surrounding Istambul was expanded, but the capital was moved to Ankara, which was Kemal's base. At Lausanne – where Sèvres was modified (1922–1923) – Turkey was recognized by the other European powers as Kemal had shaped it. Mehmet was deposed and the sultanate abolished in 1922. In 1924, in his drive to modernize and secularize Turkey, Kemal also abolished the caliphate. He became the first president of republican Turkey, a hard but necessary leader, and his influence, through the secularism of the Turkish armed forces, is still predominant in Turkey today. In 1934, Kemal ordered all Turks to adopt a surname and he himself opted for Ataturk, father

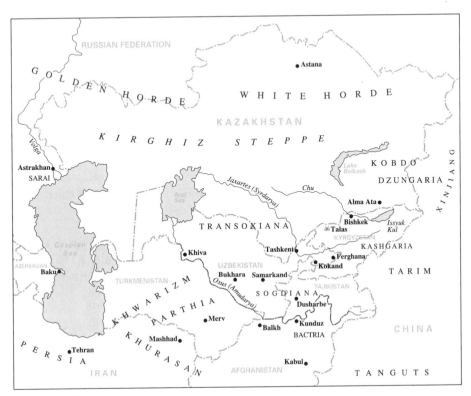

Map 11 Western Turkestan

of the Turks. Thus it is that he is known to history as Kemal Ataturk. Antakya (the ancient Antioch), which had been awarded to France as part of its Syrian mandate, was turned over to the Turks in 1939. In 1974, Turkey invaded northern Cyprus, the independence of which, declared in 1983, is recognized only by Ankara.

Western Turkestan
Predominant political influences and their durations

6th–5th cents. BC
Achaemenid Empire

4th cent. BC
Achaemenid Empire
Alexandrian Empire
Seleucid Empire
Sarmatians

3rd.cent.–1st cent. BC
Seleucid Empire
Parthia

1st–3rd cents.
Parthia

4th–5th cents.
Kushana
Turkic nomads
Sasanid Empire
Avars

6th cent.
Sasanid Empire
Turkic nomads

7th cent.
Sasanid Empire
Turkic statelets
Islam
T'ang China

8th cent.
Turkic statelets
Islam
T'ang China
Abbasids
Tahirids

9th cent.
Turkic statelets
Tahirids
Samanids

10th cent.
Samanids
Karakhanids

11th cent.
Karakhanids
Merv (Seljuks)

12th cent.
Karakhanids
Merv (Seljuks)
Khwarizm
Kara-Khitan

13th cent.
Khwarizm
Kara-Khitan
Mongol Empire
Chagataite Khanate

14th cent.
Chagataite Khanate
Timurid Empire

15th cent.
Chagataite Khanate
Timurid Empire and
    successor states
Shaybanids

16th cent.
Chagataite Khanate
Shaybanids
Khiva (Khanate)
Kirghiz
Bukhara (Khanate)

17th cent.
Khiva (Khanate)
Bukhara (Khanate)

18th cent.
Khiva (Khanate)
Bukhara (Khanate)
Kokand (Khanate)

19th cent.
Khiva (Khanate)
Bukhara (Khanate)
Kokand (Khanate)
Russia

Turkmenistan
Historically, Turkmenistan can be identified with KHWARIZM. It was peopled by Turks of the GHUZZ horde in the 11th cent. In the 15th cent. the territory was taken over by Uzbeks (SHAYBANIDS). In the early 16th cent. a collateral branch of the Shaybanids created the Khanate of KHIVA, the predecessor of independent Turkmenistan. It lasted until its conquest by Russia in 1881. In 1918, the Soviets created the Turkistan Autonomous Soviet Socialist Republic, which included the present territories of TAJIK-ISTAN, Turkmenistan, and UZBEKISTAN. The Uzbek Soviet Socialist Republic, including Tajikistan, was separated from it in 1924. The follow-ing year the Turkmen Soviet Socialist Republic was formed, which became Turkmenistan upon independence in 1991. The capital is Ashgabat.

Turks (T'U-CHÜEH; GHUZZ)

Tuscany (Duchy) (FLORENCE)

Tuvalu
The southern Pacific Ocean islands of Ellice separated from the British Gilbert and Ellice Islands in 1975 and became independent in 1978 as Tuvalu. The inhabitants speak a language of the Austronesian family, to which Malay also belongs. The capital of Tuvalu is Fongafale, on Funafuti Island.

Two Sicilies (Kingdom of) (15th–19th cents.; Naples and Sicily)
Two Sicilies refers to SICILY and NAPLES. In 1442, ARAGON first used the title of Kingdom of the Two Sicilies, which was dropped shortly after. In 1735 the title was revived by a branch of the Spanish Bourbon, who retained the kingdom, barring the Napoleonic interregnum, until Garibaldi made it part of ITALY in 1860.

Tyre (CARTHAGE; CRUSADER STATES; PHOENICIA)

U

Uganda

In 1894 Great Britain established a protectorate on the kingdom of BUGANDA, which the British expanded as the colony of Uganda, including many mostly Bantu-speaking tribes. It became independent in 1962. From 1978 to 1981, Tanzanian troops occupied Uganda after overthrowing the dictator Idi Amin (a former non-com in the British army). Swahili is used as lingua franca. The capital of Uganda is Kampala.

Uigurs (8th–9th cents.; *Central Asia*: greater Mongolia and *Tarim Basin*)

With the encouragement of T'ANG (TANG) China, the Turkic Uigurs dispossessed the T'U-CHÜEH in Mongolia (741). They were displaced by the KIRGHIZ Turks from the Yenisei River ca. 780 and went on to conquer and populate the Tarim Basin, which they ruled from 744 to 840. They found there cities peopled by Manicheans, who after disappear from history (TOKHARIANS). In the 13th cent. the Mongols conquered Tarim but did not stay, another reason why Central Asia is more Turkish than Mongol outside of Mongolia itself. The Tarim Basin is sometimes referred to as Uiguria. It was finally annexed by the Manchu CH'ING (QING) dynasty of China.

(*See chronologies under* China and Neighbouring Areas *and* Greater Mongolia.)

Ukraine

SEE ENTRY IN 'PROVINCES AND REGIONS'

The Ukraine was part of Kievan Rus (RUSSIA), but later was occupied by POLAND. In 1634, Kiev was recovered by Russia. In 1667, the Ukraine was enlarged south of Kiev, also at the expense of Poland, to the frontiers of the OTTOMAN EMPIRE, then at its zenith. The unruliness of ZAPROZHYE, a Cossack no-man's land north west of the Sea of Azov, permitted the annexation of more territory to Ukraine between 1725 and 1762. The successive partitions of POLAND (the last one was in 1795), left all of Ukraine in Russia. Upon the surrender of Germany in 1918, Ukraine was chaotically independent, but soon became a battlefield in the Russian civil war and then in the war between Poland and Russia. It lost some territory to Poland in 1920. Ukraine became a republic of the USSR in 1922. After World War II, it absorbed eastern Galicia from Poland and Bukovina and southern Bessarabia from ROMANIA. It also gained the tip of Slovakia in the Carpathian Mountains (Ruthenia). In 1954, the Crimea was ceded to Ukraine, an act which became a bone of contention with Russia after Ukraine became independent in 1991. The capital of Ukraine is Kiev.

Umayyad Caliphates (ISLAM; CÓRDOBA)

Umm al Qaiwain (UNITED ARAB EMIRATES)

United Arab Emirates
The United Arab Emirates is a federation of seven small kingdoms on the Persian or Arabian Gulf. The federation is integrated by Abu Dhabi (also the capital), Ajman, Dubai, Fujairah, Ras al Khalmah, Sharjah, and Umm al Qaiwain. Another emirate, Kalba, was merged with Sharjah in 1952. The territory of the United Arab Emirates was known after 1820 as Trucial Oman, from treaties BRITISH INDIA negotiated against piracy in the Gulf. The seven sheikhdoms became a British protectorate in 1892, when they renounced all foreign relations except with Great Britain. They federated shortly before independence in 1971. BAHRAIN and QATAR, which were part of the federation talks, chose to go their own way.

United Arab Republic (EGYPT; SYRIA)

United Arab States (EGYPT; SYRIA; YEMEN)

United Kingdom (GREAT BRITAIN)

United Nations (UN)
The treaties signed in Paris after World War I (VERSAILLES) contemplated the formation of a League of Nations, which was founded in 1919 and functioned in Geneva. It had, among other bodies, a council and an assembly. But it was hamstrung by the need for unanimity in its decisions. The Senate of the United States rejected American membership in the League of Nations, which could do nothing to prevent the re-armament of Germany after 1933. Considerable blows to its prestige and authority were dealt when Japan withdrew in 1933 after criticism for its invasion of Manchuria in 1931 and when Italy ignored the threat of sanctions after its occupation of Ethiopia in 1935. Some of the League of Nations institutions, such as the International Labour Organization, the International Court, and the Trusteeship Council, were absorbed by the United Nations.

The name United Nations was first used by American President F. D. Roosevelt on 1 January 1942 in reference to the nations opposed to the Axis in World War II. In 1944, China, Great Britain, United States, and the USSR elaborated in Dumbarton Oaks, near Washington, proposals for an organization of all states, which were debated and adopted by 50 sovereign nations meeting in San Francisco from 15 April to 26 June 1945. The Charter of the UN was ratified on 25 October 1945. The first General Assembly of the UN convened in London in 1946. It was agreed to move the seat to the eastern United States and from 1946 to 1950 the UN functioned in Lake Success, near New York City, after which it moved to New York City itself, where its headquarters were finished in 1952.

The UN consists of a General Assembly, which can debate all issues of interest to its members in the context of its international character; a Security Council, which can decide on measures, including armed intervention, for the maintenance of peace; an Economic and Social Council, created to deal with issues relative to the amelioration of social conditions in all nations as independent entities and as members of the UN; the Trusteeship Council, assumed from the League of Nations to supervise mandated territories and their administration by trustee powers; the International Court of Justice, which sits at The Hague, Netherlands, and has to listen to legitimate grievances raised by nations in their international relations; and the Secretariat, which attends to administration and the needs of the other five basic bodies of the UN.

The UN was first integrated by 50 founding members, to which Poland was added immediately after the San Francisco conference. It expanded slowly from 1947 to 1955 with the entry of Burma (Myanmar), Indonesia, Israel, Pakistan (India was a founding member), and Yemen. But after 1955 the entry of members increased very rapidly over the years and in 1999 there were 185 members.

The Security Council is formed by 15 members from different countries, five of which are permanent members – China, France, Great Britain, United States, and Russia (formerly the USSR) – and have the right of veto. The others are rotated in two-year terms. During the Cold War between the USSR and the Western powers – roughly from 1948 (Berlin Blockade) to 1991 (dissolution of the USSR) – the power of the veto was much used by the Soviets. The UN also has 18 agencies, many of them specialized in economic development, and a number of commissions and programmes for social problems of international concern, among which the problem of refugees was much highlighted during the 1990s.

The UN has been involved in some notable military and peace-keeping operations. In 1947 it devised a partition plan for Palestine after the British handed over the problem of Arab–Israeli relations in that trust territory. The UN plan was not accepted by the Arab side and the first Arab–Israeli War ensued, which resulted in the formation of Israel and the voluntary and forced exodus of Palestinian refugees to the Gaza Strip, the West Bank, Jordan, and Lebanon. In 1950, during a Soviet boycott against the non-admittance of communist China to the UN, the Security Council approved a military intervention in the Korean peninsula to halt the communist invasion of South Korea by the North Korean regime. It was initially a mostly American holding action in the Pusan perimeter, but it was later reinforced with the participation of many other UN members, notably Great Britain. The Korean War ended in stalemate and a cease-fire in 1953. In 1956, the General Assembly condemned the Anglo-Israeli occupation of the Suez Canal, and the occupying forces were withdrawn. From 1960 to 1963, the UN intervened in

Congo-Leopoldville to reunite the separatist Katanga province (Shaba today) with the newly independent republic. In 1963, the UN intervened in Cyprus to separate warring Greeks and Turks. In 1965, the UN called for sanctions against breakaway Rhodesia, whose white-minority government ceded in 1980. In 1991, it was under UN auspices that a large multinational force, headed by the United States, assembled in the Persian or Arabian Gulf area to dislodge the Iraqi forces that had annexed Kuwait. In 1991, the UN called for democracy in Haiti and in 1995 American forces landed with UN backing to stabilize that troubled country. In 1992, the UN supervised a cease-fire in Cambodia and ran the country until a parliamentary election in 1993. In 1994–1995, the UN unsuccessfully intervened to halt internecine conflict in Somalia. American and other forces were withdrawn without having accomplished much. In general, the UN has been very antagonistic to colonialism – the vast majority of its members were still colonies or dependencies at the end of World War II – and today the Trusteeship Council is one of its least active agencies. The number of UN humanitarian missions all over the world is too numerous for listing.

United States of America
SEE ENTRY IN 'PROVINCES AND REGIONS'
The territory of the United States of America (USA) was explored by Englishmen, Spaniards, and Frenchmen. John Cabot sailed the coast of eastern North America for the English in 1498. The Spaniards explored Florida and the south-eastern and western USA during the 16th cent. The French started exploring the north-eastern USA and the Great Lakes in the early 17th cent. The north west USA was chiefly explored in the second half of the 18th cent. by Spaniards and Britons. The only significant pre-Columbian culture in the USA is known as Pueblos. It flourished during the 14th–15th cents. in the south west.

THE BRITISH ATLANTIC SEABOARD COLONIES

The first settlement in the USA was St Augustine, Florida, founded in 1565 by the Spaniard Pedro Menendez de Avilés. Spanish claims embraced the coast of Georgia. The first permanent English settlement in North America was Jamestown, which became the nucleus of the colony of Virginia formed in 1624. The English Puritans, who were non-conformist Protestants, though hardly inclined to religious tolerance, landed in Plymouth in 1620 and the Massachusetts Bay colony was created in 1630. Connecticut (1662) and Rhode Island (1663) were offshoots of Massachusetts. The harbour of New York was discovered by Verrazano exploring for France. In 1609, James Hudson sailed the river that bears his name for the Dutch and northern New York was explored by the Frenchman Champlain. In 1624 the Dutch West India Company founded New Amsterdam on the site of today's New York City. The

Dutch also claimed the eastern coast of Chesapeake Bay. In 1637, Sweden established a colony in today's state of Delaware, which the Dutch, under Peter Stuyvesant, seized in 1655. The Dutch colonies were taken by the British in 1664. Stuyvesant became the governor of Dutch Curaçao. In 1632, Maryland was granted to Lord Calvert as a refuge for English Catholics and was settled in 1634, although later its government fell into the hands of Puritans from Massachusetts. South Carolina was a royal grant of 1663, first settled in 1670. Charleston was founded in 1680. The territory of the state of New Hampshire was separated from Massachusetts in 1679. Chesapeake Bay, with the mouth of the Delaware River at its apex, was the access to Pennsylvania and New Jersey. In 1681, the Quaker William Penn was granted the territory of the state of Pennsylvania with jurisdiction over Delaware, which had separated by 1704. Georgia was a grant by the King in 1733. It was disputed by Spain until the British settlers beat back Spanish forces from Florida in 1742. Jurisdiction over New Jersey was mostly in New York until, in 1738, it became a separate colony. North Carolina was an offshoot of Virginia formed in 1771.

INDEPENDENCE

The American colonists were dissatisfied with the way they were governed from Great Britain without consultation, which restricted trade and imposed levies. This colonial rejection coalesced in the Continental Congress, which deliberated from 1774 to 1789. Though somewhat hyperbolic, the designation 'continental' was not entirely innaccurate – at the time, all of North America, except for the Spanish south west, was in British hands. Nevertheless, there were no delegates from Canada. Independence was declared on 4 July 1776 and the Articles of Confederation were adopted in 1781. Even before the Declaration of Independence, British troops and armed colonists had begun skirmishing in Lexington and Concord, Massachusetts, in April 1775. Boston was in a state of rebellion, which the British reduced in the Battle of Bunker Hill. In June 1775, George Washington, a Virginian planter with military experience in the British Army in America, was made Commander-in-Chief of the Continental Army, which he formed. From 1775 to 1780 the fighting in New York, New Jersey, and Pennsylvania first favoured the British then became a stalemate. The British evacuated Boston in 1776 and set up headquarters in New York City under Howe. Philadelphia fell in 1777 and Washington was driven to Valley Forge, Pennsylvania. However, a British invasion from Canada in October 1777 was foiled by Gates at Saratoga, New York, where the British general, Burgoyne, capitulated. In 1778, command of the British forces passed to General Clinton. France declared war on Great Britain and French aid began arriving. Spain also declared war on Great Britain in 1779, despite having its own colonies in America. As a rule, the British controlled the sea and in 1778 occupied Savannah, Georgia, and Charleston, South

Carolina, in 1780. British forces under Burgoyne had the run of the south, but the Americans gathered their forces in the interior and drove the British into Virginia. Leaving the northern theatre, where the British still occupied New York City, Washington marched to Virginia, where the British were cornered in the Yorktown peninsula. When the French navy outmanoeuvred the British and blockaded Chesapeake bay, cutting the British rear, Burgoyne surrendered (once again) on 19 October 1781. By the Treaty of Paris (1783), American independence was recognized by Great Britain.

CONSTITUTION

Under the Articles of Confederation there was no central authority and, in 1787, a Constitutional Convention was convened in which a more centralist, though still federalist, constitution was adopted. The new constitution was ratified between 1778 and 1790 by the thirteen original states (Delaware, New Jersey, Pennsylvania, Connecticut, Georgia, Maryland, Massachusetts, New Hampshire, New York, South Carolina, Virginia, North Carolina, and Rhode Island). George Washington was elected President and served two four-year terms, setting a precedent which held until F. D. Roosevelt was elected consecutively four times starting in 1932. (As a consequence of the long Roosevelt presidency, a two-term limit was incorporated into the Constitution.)

Vermont had been occupied by settlers from New Hampshire starting in 1741. New York claimed jurisdiction and Vermont was not recognized as a state by the Continental Congress. After Yorktown, Vermont acted as a sovereign state until 1791, when, in exchange for a compensatory payment to New York, it was admitted as a state of the Union. Kentucky was admitted to the Union in 1792 and Tennessee in 1796.

At the end of the war, British territories east of the Mississippi and north of the Ohio River, which Great Britain had taken from the French province of Louisiana in 1763, were organized as the North West Territory in 1787. From this vast expanse were formed the states of Ohio (1803), Indiana (1816), Illinois (1818), Michigan (1837), and Minnesota (1858). The French colonial province of Louisiana, extending like a funnel from New Orleans and along the west side of the Mississippi River up to Minnesota, had been ceded by France to Spain in 1762. Spain secretly retroceded Louisiana and its territories to France in 1800, which alarmed the American government when the transfer became known in 1802. Given British naval supremacy, Napoleon knew that New Orleans was indefensible. He surprised the American government with an offer of sale for $15,000,000, which the USA promptly took up with a discount of $3,750,000 as compensation for claims against Spain by American citizens (Louisiana Purchase). Louisiana as such entered the Union in 1812.

From the halls of Montezuma to the shores of Tripoli

Washington had established a policy of no foreign entanglements for the nascent USA. However, there was a state of war between the USA and the BARBARY STATES which lasted from 1800 to 1815. After failed attempts to take Libyan Tripoli, the USA finally forced Algiers to agree to cease preying on its ships. The Napoleonic Wars in Europe resulted in British actions at sea which damaged American shipping. American expansionism into Ruperts Land, British claims which extended south of Canada in the west, bolstered war hawks in the USA, leading to a declaration of war against Great Britain in 1812. American plans to annex Canada were frustrated and there was indecisive fighting in New York State. The Americans won a naval engagement on Lake Erie in 1813. The following year the British captured and sacked Washington, but were repulsed in Baltimore. The war was ended late in 1814, although its greatest battle took place in New Orleans, where, in January 1815, Andrew Jackson, a renowned Indian fighter and future American president, defeated the British. A boundary commission was set up, which defined the border between New Brunswick and Maine, an offshoot of Massachusetts which entered the Union in 1820. In 1823, fearing the possibility of European intervention in the newly-created Latin American states, whose independence had been recognized by the USA, President James Monroe stated the policy which bears his name and which rejected European interference in the western hemisphere. Upon independence, slavery – euphemistically described by slavers as the 'peculiar institution' – was entrenched in the southern American states, but was illegal in the north. This set off a race for territories by pro- and anti-slavery settlers which resulted in the rapid incorporation of new states into the Union. The states formed from the Northwest Territory did not accept slavery, but Mississippi (1819), Alabama (1819), and Arkansas (1836) were pro-slavery. Florida had been Spanish from the early 16th cent., but it had been at various times either besieged or occupied by the British or by American colonists. Nevertheless, it was reluctantly that Spain transferred Florida to the USA in 1819 in exchange for $5,000,000 in claims by American citizens. It too became a pro-slavery state in 1845, along with TEXAS, which had been Mexican until American settlers rebelled and won their independence in 1836. The annexation of Texas and American designs on California led to a full-scale invasion of MEXICO by the USA in 1846. Mexico City was captured and, in 1848, Mexico surrendered all its territories north of the Rio Grande and Gila rivers – which had been approximately demarcated with Spain in 1819 – and a line separating upper from lower California. In 1853, the USA bought from Mexico for $10,000,000 the lands between the Gila River and the present frontier (Gadsden Purchase). The border between the USA and British territorial claims in the west was set in 1846 along the 49th parallel (the actual boundary) running from north-western Montana to Puget Sound. Further additions to the non-slavery ranks were Iowa in 1846, Wisconsin in 1848, California in 1850, Oregon in 1859, and Kansas in 1861.

CIVIL WAR

The issue of slavery finally led to the secession from the Union in 1861 of Alabama, Arkansas, Florida, Georgia, Louisiana, Mississippi, North Carolina, South Carolina, Tennessee, Texas, and Virginia, which formed the Confederate States of America, with its capital in Richmond, Virginia. Jefferson Davies was chosen as president. West Virginia separated from Virginia and was admitted as a state of the Union in 1863. Abraham Lincoln was President of the United States. At first the war favoured the southern forces competently led by General Robert E. Lee, but the north had the run of the coastline and more resources. The military hopes of the Confederacy were set back at the Battle of Gettysburg (1863), in southern Pennsylvania, which checked the Confederate invasion of the north. Earlier the same year Lincoln had decreed the abolition of slavery. Under the command of General U. S. Grant, future American President, the Union forces, which were bogged down by indecisive but costly fighting in the east, advanced in the west down the Mississippi River and seized the strategic fortified site of Vicksburg, Mississippi, in July 1863. Grant was named chief of the Union armies in 1864. In a 'war-is-hell' campaign, General Sherman harrowed the south, crucially in Georgia. Early in 1865, the Confederate situation was desperate – Richmond was evacuated – and Lee surrendered to Grant in April of that year.

MANIFEST DESTINY

From territories gained in the Louisiana Purchase and the Mexican–American War and delimited by the north-western frontier, the following states were also formed: Nevada in 1863; Nebraska in 1867; Colorado in 1876; Montana, North Dakota, South Dakota, and Washington in 1889; Idaho and Wyoming in 1890; Utah in 1896; and Arizona and New Mexico in 1912. In the demarcation of the frontier between Spain and the USA in 1819, Oklahoma had been left on the American side, which was set aside as Indian territory. In 1889 it was opened to a wholesale landgrab by settlers, leading to the incorporation of Oklahoma into the Union in 1907. American westward expansion, known as Manifest Destiny, was at the cost of the destruction and massacre (Wounded Knee) of Amerindian tribes, whose most famous act of resistance was the Battle of Little Big Horn in 1876, in which General Custer and about 200 soldiers were killed. Relations between the USA and Spain had been deteriorating in the 1890s because of Cuba, where successive insurrections had been brutally suppressed by Spain. In 1898, Cuba was up in arms again and the American battleship *Maine* exploded – probably from careless packing in the ship's arsenal – while docked in Havana. In 1898, during the McKinley administration, the USA declared war on Spain and very quickly destroyed the Spanish navy in Santiago de Cuba and in Manila Bay, in the PHILIPPINES. The USA annexed Puerto Rico and the Philippines. CUBA became independent in 1902 but saddled with the Platt Amendment, approved by Congress in 1901 authorizing American military intervention. It was abrogated in 1934 by the F. D. Roosevelt administration as part of its Good Neighbor policy towards Latin America. In 1903 the USA obtained rights to Guantanamo Bay and surrounding lands, which it still occupies.

WILSON AND ROOSEVELT

During World War I, the USA, under the administration of President Woodrow Wilson, at first adhered to a policy of neutrality, tinged with sympathy for the Allies. Reckless German submarine tactics enforcing the blockade of Great Britain, led to the American declaration of war on Germany in 1917. American troops, under General Pershing, were assigned a section of the western front in the Argonne (Champagne and Lorraine), where in 1918 they helped contain a German offensive (second Battle of the Marne) and participated in the counter-offensive which led to the capitulation of Germany. President Wilson was influential in steering the post-war Paris Peace Conference (VERSAILLES) towards the principles of self-determination and democracy, but his efforts were only partially successful and, in America, there was outright rejection to European wranglings. The USA did not join the League of Nations created in 1919.

After 1929, the USA fell into the Great Depression, which President F. D. Roosevelt tried to ease with only limited success. In 1939 World War II started in Europe. In the Far East, Japan was at war with China. The USA was again neutral, but this time openly sympathetic to Great Britain, who had to face Nazi Germany alone after the collapse of France in 1940. On 7 December 1941, the Japanese attacked Pearl Harbor, the American naval base on the island of Hawaii. The USA declared war on the Axis. American efforts were at first concentrated on the Pacific Theatre against Japan, but soon its huge economic resources were feeding all the Allied fronts. In the Pacific Ocean, the Japanese suffered a catastrophic defeat in the naval Battle of Midway (June 1942), crucially due to the Americans' ability to decipher the enemy's military codes. From their base in Australia, American and allied forces, principally Anzac (Australia and New Zealand), contained the Japanese in the Solomon Islands and in New Guinea in 1942 and began a dual advance along the archipelagos of the Pacific Ocean towards Japan and along the coast of New Guinea towards the Philippines, which fell in 1945. The Japanese imperial navy was annihilated in the Battle of the Philippines Sea (late 1944). In Europe, Soviet forces defeated the Germans at Stalingrad in 1943 and in 1944 the Allies, led by General Eisenhower, future US president, landed in Normandy and fought their way to Germany, which collapsed in May 1945. In April 1945, President Roosevelt died and the task of ending the war was left to his successor, Harry S. Truman. In the Far East, after the liberation of the Philippines, the Allied forces under General MacArthur thrust north, conquered Okinawa, and finally bent Japan's will to resist after the cities of Hiroshima and Nagasaki were wiped out by atomic bombs. Japan surrendered unconditionally in August 1945. The UNITED NATIONS had been founded in San Francisco in June 1945.

THE COLD WAR

Allies in the war – at the Yalta Conference, in February 1945, they more or less decided the territorial shape of the post-war world – the USA and the USSR became enemies in the Cold War, which can be said to have started with the Soviet blockade of Berlin in 1948. It was suspended when the USA and its allies showed they could supply the city by air. To counter Soviet power in Europe, the USA and its western European allies formed the North Atlantic Treaty Organization (NATO) in 1949 – followed by other regional alliances sponsored by Dulles, the secretary of state under Eisenhower – to which the USSR riposted with the Warsaw Pact.

After the war, Greece had an armed communist insurrection on its hands. In 1947, President Truman declared his country's willingness to help states under communist attack. This became known as the Truman Doctrine and was applied later in Korea. It was an extension of the thinking behind the Truman Doctrine that encouraged the American involvement in Vietnam. In Greece, American aid turned the tide and the country was pacified in 1949. In 1950, North Korea, probably with Soviet backing, invaded South Korea and the USA took advantage of a Soviet boycott of the Security Council to get UN support for its intervention in the peninsula. Under MacArthur, UN forces, mainly American, outflanked the communists at Inchon and drove them to the Yalu River frontier with China. The communist Chinese intervened and fought the UN armies until 1953, when a cease-fire was agreed at Panmunjon.

Alaska – which had been occupied by Russia since 1784 and was sold to the USA in 1867 for $7,200,000 – became a state in 1959, at the same time as HAWAII, which had been an American possession since 1898.

In 1979 the USA officially recognized the People's Republic of China, which entailed withdrawal of recognition from Taiwan and China's membership in the UN, including a place in the Security Council with the right of veto. When the French tried to reoccupy Indochina, Vietnamese nationalists, with Chinese and Soviet backing, took up arms. In 1961, the USA, under President John F. Kennedy, signed treaties committing itself to aid the pro-western regime in SOUTH VIETNAM, which had been established after the partition of VIETNAM in 1954. Intervention escalated during the presidency of Lyndon Johnson until, by 1969, there were 550,000 American servicemen in Vietnam. Yet it proved impossible to defeat the combined Vietnamese forces of southern guerrillas and northern regular troops. In 1973, the USA evacuated South Vietnam, which was over-run by North Vietnam in 1975.

An international contingent, principally American and French, landed in Beirut late in 1983 but was pulled out after a terrorist bomb left hundreds of dead. After Lebanon, the United States became wary of foreign military interventions. In 1990–1991, at the head of a large multinational force, the USA, during the Bush administration, participated in the Gulf War to dislodge Iraqi forces which had annexed Kuwait. American troops disembarked in famine-stricken Somalia in 1992, but became entangled in internal factional strife and were pulled out. American forces have intervened in the Dominican Republic (1962), Grenada (1983–1984), and Panama (1989–1990). Libya was bombed by USA planes in 1986 in retaliation for its presumed responsibility for terrorist actions. The USA has also participated in other UN operations.

PEAK OF EMPIRE

At its peak (1916–1924), the American colonial empire included: the Philippines, Puerto Rico, the Virgin Islands (purchased from Denmark for $25,000,000 in 1917), American Samoa (capital Pago Pago) and Guam (1899). During those years the USA was simultaneously occupying Haiti, the Dominican Republic, and Nicaragua, and the Platt Amendment to the Cuban constitution, which allowed American intervention (and had been invoked twice), had not been abrogated. Alaska and Hawaii were still territories. The Panama Canal Zone was formed by strips of land on both sides of the canal (built 1904–1914), ceded by the newly-created republic of PANAMA (1903). In 1978, a treaty provided for its return to Panama. Puerto Rico, the only sizeable dependency the USA still has, had been a Spanish colony until occupied by the USA in 1898. The Northern Marianas (German in 1899; Japanese from 1914; occupied by the USA in 1944) became a commonwealth in the western Pacific Ocean in 1975. There are no southern Marianas. Incredible though it may sound, roughly one third of the territory of the American Union was acquired for less than $30,000,000, not considering, however, that much of this land could probably have been taken by the USA without paying a penny.

WASHINGTON, D.C.

Philadelphia, the seat of the Continental Congress, was mostly the capital of the USA until 1800, when Congress moved to Washington, whose site, on lands ceded by Maryland and Virginia (District of Columbia), was chosen by Washington. The French architect L'Enfant designed the city. The lands ceded by Virginia were returned in 1846. The USA is the third most populous nation in the world.

Ur (SUMER)

Urartu (10th–6th cents. BC; ancient *Near East*)
Urartu, a non-Indo-European speaking kingdom around Lake Van in eastern

Anatolia, existed ca. 1000 BC. It flourished between 640 and 590 BC. Attacked by SCYTHIANS, it was eventually absorbed by MEDIA. Urartu occupied territories that later became Armenian.
(*See chronologies under* Ancient Near East *and* Anatolia.)

Uruguay

Uruguay was part of the Spanish viceroyalty of La Plata (ARGENTINA). At various times during the 17th and 18th cents., the Portuguese tried to occupy the territory but were conclusively chased out by Spaniards from Buenos Aires in 1724. Uruguay accepted the 1810 declaration of independence in Buenos Aires, presumably as part of Argentina. However, the Uruguayan Artigas declared the Banda Oriental – as Uruguay was known and is still often referred to – independent in 1814. Brazil invaded in 1820 but was finally defeated in 1827. Under prodding from Britain, Argentina and Brazil agreed on an independent constitution for Uruguay in 1830. After this the early history of Uruguay is mostly one of civil strife in which it is hard to disentangle who was for whom and for what. The most confusing of all these events came about when, in 1864, the Brazilians invaded Uruguay, with the connivance of a Uruguayan political faction, which provoked the almost gratuitous intervention of PARAGUAY on the side of the government in Montevideo, which by then had been toppled. An alliance was formed between Argentina, Brazil, and Uruguay itself against Paraguay. That is part of the history of Paraguay. The end result is that Uruguay became independent of Spain in the wake of Buenos Aires in 1810 and after it proclaimed its separation from Argentina in 1814 the consensus of all parties involved was that, whatever the political or military circumstances, its independence should be maintained. Uruguay was a very prosperous democracy between the two World Wars. Its capital, Montevideo, developed from a fort built by the Portuguese in 1717.

USSR (Union of Soviet Socialist Republics) (20th cent.; *Russia*)

In February 1917, in the midst of World War I, RUSSIA was under such stresses – Tsarist incompetence and absolutism, defeat and indiscipline in the army, lack of food in the cities, unrest and violence in the countryside – that almost without deliberation the monarchist government was overthrown and a provisional government installed in St Petersburg (or Petrograd as the city had been named at the start of the war in repudiation of its Germanic etymology). (Something similar happened in Great Britain with the dynastic transformation of Hanover into Windsor.) Tsar Nicholas II abdicated the following month. Lvov and Kerensky attempted the impossible task of reforming Russia and keeping it in the war.

LENIN AND TROTSKY

In November the Bolsheviks, an authoritarian extreme leftist wing of the Marxist Russian Social Democrats, took power under the leadership of Lenin and used the Soviet – a parallel parliament created during the provisional government as a popular rival of the Duma – to justify their revolution. Various events of consequence happened: Russia left the war in which it had sided with the western Allies, a civil war on at least three fronts was fought, Poland invaded Russia, and the USSR was created. One of the reasons the Bolsheviks could seize power was that they were against the war without buts or ifs, and the masses knew it. (The masses, despite historical debunkings, were instrumental in everything that happened in Russia after the overthrow of Tsarism up until the consolidation of the Soviet regime, when everything devolved to the Communist Party.) Negotiations with Germany started very quickly and culminated in the Treaty of Brest-Litovsk in March 1918, whose arrangements were really transitory but which allowed the Germans to move troops to the western front. Russia was diminished to the territory behind a line that ran from St Petersburg to Kiev across to the Caspian Sea and from there to the Arctic west of the Urals. Finland became independent in 1917. To the south and east were 'white', anti-Bolshevik armies, led in the south initially by Kornilov (then by Denikin and at the very end by Wrangel) and in the east by Kolchak. Though initially promising, the whites' successes were reversed by their own incompetence but also through the tenacity and ruthlessness of Soviet commissars. Kolchak's offensive in the east was the first to be routed by the Bolsheviks (1919). Yudenich had opened a third front in 1919, but he was repulsed within sight of the spires of Petrograd. The southern offensive lasted longer but it was contained in Tula. A crucial figure in all these events was Trotsky, a Menshevik (moderate) Social Democrat who turned into a rabid Bolshevik and Lenin's right-hand man.

War with Poland

Upon the surrender of Germany in 1918, Poland went independent and was generously restored, including a corridor to the port of Danzig, by the Treaty of Versailles in 1919. Poland claimed the 1772 eastern border and, under Pilsudsky, it warred with Soviet Russia in 1920–1921. Though at one point the communists were at the gates of Warsaw, Poland finally acquired parts of Byelorussia and the Ukraine. After the war with Poland and the civil war, Russia was intact save for the Baltic States (Lithuania, Latvia, and Estonia), which had seceded under German tutelage but were later recognized by the Western powers, and the portions of Ukraine and Byelorussia which Poland had annexed. The Soviets moved the capital to Moscow and later changed the name of Petrograd to Leningrad. (It is now St Petersburg again.) In 1918 Russia had been named the Russian Soviet Federated Republic and on 30 December 1922 the Union of Soviet Socialist Republics was formed. Joining with Russia were the Ukranian Soviet Socialist Republic – Ukraine had a brief moment of independence in 1918 – the Byelorussian Soviet Socialist Republic

(Belarus), and the Transcaucasian Soviet Federated Socialist Republic. The rest of former Russia was under Soviet direct or indirect control. The Tajiks rebelled against the Soviet state in 1917, but were brought to heel by the Bolsheviks in 1921 and incorporated into the Turkistan Autonomous Soviet Socialist Republic, created in 1922, also including Turkmenistan and Uzbekistan. In 1924, the Uzbek Soviet Socialist Republic was formed (including Tajikistan) from Turkistan, which in 1925 became the Turkmen Soviet Socialist Republic (Turkmenistan). In 1929, the Tadzhik Soviet Socialist Republic was separated from the Uzbek Republic. The Soviets incorporated the Kazakh autonomous region, including Kyrgyzstan into Soviet Russia. In 1936 they created the Kazakh Soviet Socialist Republic and the Kirghiz Soviet Socialist Republic. The same year Transcaucasia dissolved into the Soviet republics of Armenia, Azerbaijan, and Georgia.

STALIN

Looking as if he were already a cadaver, Lenin died in 1924, felled by strokes. While Trotsky conquered, another prominent Bolshevik, Stalin, had nurtured the Communist Party apparatus. After Lenin's death a collective leadership of sorts was formed, but in 1925 Stalin undercut Trotsky and his other rivals and gradually became absolute dictator. In the 1930s, Stalin's totalitarianism turned murderous through periodic purges and sham trials. The Gulag 'archipelago' – concentration camps dispersed over the geography of Russia, especially in bleak areas – was formed and eventually held millions of prisoners. It has not yet been adequately explained how the USSR managed to survive World War II with a second-rate economy, a deadening party bureaucracy, and armed forces which had been bereft of its high command. However it may be, in 1939 Hitler and Stalin signed a non-aggression pact which was, in effect, a secret alliance. On 1 September 1939 Nazi Germany invaded Poland with the pretext of recovering DANZIG and its corridor. The Allies entered the war against Germany but the USSR remained on the sidelines. The Soviets took the Baltic States and Hitler and Stalin divided Poland. In 1940, the USSR fought a bullyboy war with Finland and annexed most of Karelia to Russia. The same year the USSR forced Romania to cede Bessarabia and created the Moldavian Soviet Socialist Republic. The latter's territory was seized by Romania from 1941 to 1944, when the USSR retrieved it. In 1940, France was defeated and occupied and, in 1941, Hitler was set to invade the USSR – astonishingly, to Stalin's later surprise – but Mussolini had made a hash of the invasion of Greece and Hitler held off while his armies invaded the Balkans. The German offensive against the USSR got under way in June 1941. (In the Far East, Japan had tried to invade Siberia in 1938 and got a bloody nose.) The Germans drove quickly to Leningrad, Moscow, and the northern Caucasus. Both of Russia's major cities held against a terrific battering – Leningrad was encircled and survived with supplies transported over frozen Lake Ladoga –

and in 1942–1943 the USSR, beefed up with Allied materiel, began counter-attacking. In Stalingrad (the former Tsaritsyn, now Volgograd) the Soviets annihilated a huge German army. Russia had momentum and, in 1944, it invaded Poland and the Balkans. Hitler committed suicide in April 1945. Berlin fell in May and GERMANY surrendered.

KHRUSHCHEV AND GORBACHEV

The shape of the post-war world was determined principally by the Americans and the Soviets in the conferences of Yalta (1944) and Potsdam (1945). The USSR sovietized the Baltic republics and enlarged its territory at the expense of post-World War I eastern European frontiers, gaining lands which gave it borders with Hungary and Czechoslovakia. It annexed eastern Poland and compensated with a large slice of German territory. In the Far East it took southern Sakhalin and the Kuriles from Japan. Germany was divided into four occupation zones. The Soviet zone was eastern Germany (Brandenburg, Pomerania, and Saxony), enveloping Berlin. Antagonism between the United States and the USSR was strong and in 1948–1949 the Soviets blockaded Berlin and the Cold War was on. Stalin created an informal SOVIET EMPIRE. No sooner had the Berlin blockade been frustrated through a western airlift when communist North Korea, very possibly with Stalin's backing, invaded the pro-western south of the peninsula. It was contained and KOREA divided along approximately the same border it had before the war.

Stalin died in 1953. He was succeeded by Khrushchev, who in 1956 – though he was of peasant origin and died a communist – denounced Stalin's crimes in a Communist Party congress. Castro came to power in Cuba in 1959. He established a revolutionary regime and, in 1962, was letting the USSR install bases in Cuban territory when the American President Kennedy challenged the Soviets and, in an incident which is as close as the world came to nuclear holocaust (as far as is known), forced them to turn back ships carrying missiles. Brezhnev came to the fore in the USSR in 1963. His regime was internally 'conservative' (in the sense that communism was entrenched as the legitimate system of the USSR) but externally it recklessly occupied Afghanistan in 1979 and suffered as humiliating a defeat as the Americans had in Vietnam. Soviet forces evacuated Afghanistan in 1989. The United States, which had learned lessons from the Vietnam War, had indirectly armed Afghani resistance to frustrate Soviet ambitions. The USSR was also beleaguered by periodic uprisings in its communist satellites. Whether the confrontational and swaggering policies of American President Reagan (1981–1989) were decisive or not, the USSR, under the reformist leader Mikhail Gorbachev (1983–1991), entered a process first of *glasnost* (openness) and then *perestroika* (reorganization) which ended in the dissolution of the

USSR into its constituent republics (COMMONWEALTH OF INDEPEND-ENT STATES) and in the gradual toppling of the communist system after 1991. China, which is also transforming itself into a capitalist country, did not, as did the Russians, forego the use of the communist political apparatus in the process.

Uzbekistan

Uzbekistan, homeland of Tamerlane (TIMURID EMPIRE AND SUCCES-SOR STATES) occupies the southern half of the historic regions of Transoxiana and Sogdiana. It was ruled by the SHAYBANIDS, an Uzbek dynasty, from the middle of the 15th cent. to the end of the 16th cent., when its territory was divided into the khanates of KOKAND and BUKHARA. The Shaybanid lands along the valley of the Amudarya had separated at the beginning of the 16th cent. to form the khanate of KHIVA, future TURKMENISTAN (although Khiva itself is today part of Uzbekistan). The Russians annexed the territory of Uzbekistan between 1865 and 1868. In 1918, the Soviets created the Turkistan Autonomous Soviet Socialist Republic, including the present territories of TAJIKISTAN, Turkmenistan, and Uzbekistan. In 1924, the Uzbek Soviet Socialist Republic was formed, including Tajikistan until 1929. It became Uzbekistan upon independence in 1990. There were minor border changes with Kazakhstan in 1956, 1963, and 1971. The capital of Uzbekistan is Tashkent. Ferghana is a valley in the part of Uzbekistan that juts into west Kyrgyzstan. It is a historical neighbour of Kashgaria to the east and south. It is traditionally part of Western Turkestan.

Uzbeks (SHAYBANIDS)

V

Valachia or Walachia (13th–19th cents.; *Balkans*)
The Valachians, who speak Romanian, might have been descendants of the inhabitants of the Romanized province of Dacia (*Roman Empire*). Valachia was crossed by LOMBARDS, AVARS, and BULGARS from the 6th to the 11th cents. In the 12th cent. it was under the PETCHENEGS who were defeated by a Mongol incursion in 1240. Valachia was a Christian principality ca. 1290, at about the same time as MOLDAVIA. In the 14th cent. it was tributary to the OTTOMAN EMPIRE, whom Vlad the Impaler made the object of his fury in the 15th cent. This was to be to no avail for the territory passed as vassal to the Ottomans in 1462. Stephen of Moldavia conquered Valachia briefly in 1502. Michael the Brave initiated an attempt to liberate Valachia, but in 1601 Ottoman rule was reinforced. During the late 18th cent., until 1822, Valachia was ruled by Greeks sent as hospodars by the Porte. In 1829, Valachia became relatively autonomous under Russian protection but still vassal to the Ottoman Empire. In 1854 it was annexed by Russia but ceded to Austria as a bribe for its neutrality in the Crimean War. The Western powers in 1856 guaranteed Valachian independence still subject to recognition of Turkish suzerainty, but in 1859, on the accession of Alexander John Cuza as king of both Moldavia and Valachia, the two principalities constituted what was in effect ROMANIA.

Valais (15th–18th cents.; Switzerland)
An independent bishopric from 1475 to its incorporation into the Helvetian Republic (FRENCH EUROPEAN EMPIRE) in 1798, Valais after 1815 became a canton of SWITZERLAND.

Valencia (ARAGON)

Vandals (5th–6th cents.; Tunisia)
The Vandals were German semi-nomads who made a lightning-fast crossing of the European continent and finally settled in Tunisia in 429. There they founded a kingdom which the Byzantine general Belisarius destroyed in 535. The Vandals share with the Brigantes of England, the Assassins of north east Persia and Lebanon, and the thugees of India, the dubious honour of having made lasting but sombre contributions to the English language.
(*See chronology under* Southern Russia.)

Vanuatu
The New Hebrides islands in the western Pacific Ocean became an Anglo-French condominium in 1906. They achieved independence in 1980 as

Vanuatu. Its inhabitants speak a Polynesian language of the same family as Malay. The capital of Vanuatu is Vila.

Vasconia (7th–9th cents.; *Spain* and *France*)
A province created by BASQUES ca. 600, Vasconia was associated to AQUITAINE. In 778 the Basques ambushed the rearguard of a Carolingian expeditionary force into northern Spain. This was the epic hero Roland's downfall and fame. In 824 Basques founded the kingdom of NAVARRE. Historically, Vasconia embraces Upper Navarre (Spanish), Lower Navarre (French), and the Spanish provinces of Alava, Guipuzcoa, and Vizcaya. Strictly speaking, however, there is no Vasconia. It is a general designation for an ethnic area. Otherwise, we would have to say French and Spanish Vasconadas or the Basque provinces of Spain and France, and so on. But there are Basques and they form the majority of the population of the provinces of north-eastern Spain including Navarre. Bilbao is the traditional capital of Vasconia. Pamplona is the capital of Navarre.

Vatican City
The papacy lost its Italian domains (PAPAL STATES) to the kingdom of SARDINIA in 1860, but it retained Rome under French auspices until 1870, when the newly-formed kingdom of ITALY occupied the city. In 1929, Mussolini signed the Lateran Treaty which created Vatican City, the tiny but sovereign Papal see.

Vedic India (15th–7th cents. BC; northern *India*)
The Aryans, who came down into Pakistan and India from the north ca. 1500, might have influenced the INDUS RIVER VALLEY CIVILIZATION during its decadence (after ca. 2000). It is more likely that they came after its extinction. The Aryans left a unique, vast body of written works, which, although not history as such, contain abundant allusions to events and places. These, in combination with archaeology, permit sophisticated inferences about early Indian political development. Vedic literature comprises four types of texts in order of precedence: the *Mantras*, which are the *Vedas* in the strict sense of the earliest compositions and contain incantations and other ritual expressions; the *Bhramanas*, which describe the rituals themselves; the *Upanishads*, which are philosophical treatises of some obscurity; and the *Sutras*, which are instructions for rituals. Assuming the arrival of the Aryans ca. 1500 BC, the *Vedas* and the *Bhramanas* were composed between 1300 and 800 BC. The *Upanishads*, whose contents influenced the Buddha, were composed ca. 700 BC. These compositions were being created even as the Aryans after ca. 1000 BC were making the transition from semi-nomadism to sedentarization and had occupied lands in the Indian subcontinent from the mountain passes in the north to the Ganges River Basin. This transition is reflected in the epic *Mahabharata*, possibly composed sometime during the 8th and 7th cents. BC.

THE ORIGINS OF CASTES AND STATES

The Aryans occupied lands belonging to a dark-skinned people, known as Dravidians, whom they subjected. Dravidian languages are spoken in central and southern India. The premise is that the inhabitants of southern India are descended from the pre-Aryan inhabitants of India some of whom, but not all, were subjected by the Aryans. Apparently, within Aryan society there were no castes, but the Aryans discriminated the Dravidians on the basis of colour. Later caste discriminations based on social roles remained even as the skin-colour distinction was somewhat blurred. The roles were, roughly, priests or Bhramins, warriors or Kshatriyas, farmers, and sudras, who did menial work including pottery. However, caste interdictions were not so severe that there was no racial mixing or even that a sudra could not reach the summit of power. The greatest Aryan deities were Varouna, Mitra, Indra, and Agni. Krishna, prominent in Hindu mythology, was a dark-skinned god adopted from the Dravidians. The doctrine of Buddha, who probably died after 400 BC and is the first Indian historical personage, goes counter to Aryan social and ritual practices. By the time of Buddha, originally Siddharta Gautama, a prince of Sakya, a marginal Vedic state, northern India had been divided into many small kingdoms (mahajanapadas) the most prominent of which were (important cities in parentheses): Kamboja and Ghandara, in northern Pakistan; Kuru, Surasena (Mathura), and Panchala, in the western part of the doab or the mesopotomia formed by the Ganges and the Yamuna rivers; Vatsa (Kausambi), in the eastern doab; Kasi (Varanasi) with Koshala (Sravasti and Saketa) to the north; Magadha (Rajagriha), south of Patna; to the east Anga (Champa), on the actual border between Bihar and Bengal; and Avanti (Ujjain), in north central India. It is from this general state of affairs – in which tribes first acquired territory and then states were founded – that sometime during the 6th cent. BC MAGADHA, one of the mahajapandas, became the first important Indian kingdom.

(*See chronology under* Indian Subcontinent.)

Venda (20th cent.; South Africa)
Venda was a Bantustan or tribal homeland created by South Africa (1963) in the Transvaal. With the end of apartheid, it was incorporated into South Africa in 1994. The capital of Venda is Thohoyandou.

Venezuela
Venezuela was part of the SPANISH COLONIAL EMPIRE from 1498 (when Columbus first sighted the mainland of South America) to the 19th cent. Early in the 16th cent. Venezuela was mortgaged to the Welsers, German bankers, by Charles I of Spain. The country was partially explored by Germans until the concession expired in the mid-16th cent. Juridically Venezuela depended first on the high court (*audiencia*) at Santo Domingo (DOMINICAN REPUBLIC)

and then on the one at Bogotá (COLOMBIA). The actual territory of Venezuela was put together in 1777 as part of the Captaincy General of Venezuela, after which it obtained all the tokens of government. In 1808 Napoleon deposed the Bourbons and received the Spanish Crown, which he gave to his brother Joseph Bonaparte. When news of these events reached America, oligarchic juntas were formed in Caracas (19 April 1810) and Buenos Aires. Under the leadership of General Miranda, a distinguished Venezuelan soldier of fortune, the province of Caracas, followed by other Venezuelan provinces (but not all), declared independence on 5 July 1811. The independentist movement was frustrated by popular resistance headed by loyalist *caudillos* (popular leaders), until Boves, the foremost among them, was killed in battle in 1815.

SIMON BOLIVAR

In 1817, General Simon Bolivar, with the able support of General Paez and with reinforcements and material help from Great Britain, held out in the interior of Venezuela against Spanish line troops, brought in after Napoleon's defeat (1815). In 1819, Bolivar crossed the Andes and with the support of General Santander defeated loyalist troops at the Battle of Boyacá in Colombia. After Spanish troops partially evacuated Venezuelan territory in 1820, Bolivar faced the remaining loyalist forces and defeated them in the Battle of Carabobo in 1821. Afterwards, Bolivar, seconded by General Sucre, headed Colombian expeditionary forces that defeated the vestiges of the Spanish Colonial Empire in South America in successive battles in Ecuador and Peru. Venezuela joined the republic of Gran Colombia, formed additionally by Nueva Granada and Ecuador under Bolivar's guidance, but under Paez Venezuela seceded in 1830. Venezuela's 19th cent. was a period of political instability and civil war. It led to the long dictatorship of Juan Vicente Gomez (1909–1935). In 1958, after overthrowing a military dictatorship entrenched since 1948, Venezuela became a democracy, the longest in Latin America. Venezuela claimed borders on the east to the Essequibo River, which include most of today's Guyana. Great Britain, then possessor of British Guiana, traced a line closer to the delta of the Orinoco. Venezuela broke relations in 1887 and sought American help. The United States at first responded, but a commission in 1899 set the boundary where it is today, mostly according to British claims. In 1960 Venezuela revived its reclamation, but it did not prosper. Venezuela's border with Colombia, the subject of much dispute, was determined on paper by the King of Spain and delimited on the ground in the early 20th cent.

Venezuela became a significant oil-exporting country in the 1930s, mainly at first from fields in the region of Maracaibo, the second largest city. Its oil wealth reached a peak in the 1970s, but after the early 1980s it went into an economic tailspin (purely from political mismanagement) from which it has still to recover. In 1999, under President Chavez, a would-be-coupster elected overwhelmingly in 1998, it embarked on a course of radical institutional and political changes.

Venice (7th–19th cents.; northern *Italy*)

Venice was founded by refugees fleeing the Lombards (LOMBARD ITALY). In 697 they elected a *doge*. The city grew on maritime commerce as a middleman between Asia and Europe. It gradually built a respectable empire for control of the eastern Mediterranean, which for a time it contested with GENOA. From the base of its maritime power, Venice later expanded territoriality in its Italian hinterland, which came to be known as Venetia.

The Venetian Empire

Given its situation at the head of the Adriatic Sea, Venetian expansion started in the 11th cent. with strings of enclaves along the Dalmatian coast, then gradually extended southwards against resistance from the BYZANTINE EMPIRE, which briefly, ca. 1070, had pushed the Venetians back. When Byzantine power in the Balkans waned, it was replaced by CROATIA and HUNGARY along the Dalmatian coast (11th–13th cents.). Despite the initially indecisive situation in Dalmatia, Venice built up its naval power. Under Doge Enrico Dandolo, as a result of its crucial contribution to the conquest of Constantinople in 1204 by French and Flemish crusaders, Venice gained footholds in Epirus and Achaea (the Peloponnesus), the Ionian Islands, Euboea (Negroponte), and Crete (Candia). It was only by the early 15th cent. that Venice was able to hold on firmly to the eastern Adriatic coast down to Epirus in northwestern Greece. In 1381, Venice won a resounding naval victory against Genoa, but did not entirely eliminate its competitor. Venice's presence in Greece had its apogee ca. 1400, when it briefly controlled the southern Peloponnesus and Athens. By 1430, Venice had lost the Ionian Islands and the Peloponnesus, but still occupied Crete and Euboea and had gained an enclave in the tip of the heel of Italy. At this point, its greatest rival was becoming the OTTOMAN EMPIRE, which was adding a powerful navy to its overwhelming territorial impetus.

The bombardment of the Parthenon

Venetian mainland thrust began with the acquisition of lands to the north and south of the Venetian lagoon (1360). By 1435, its domains, taken at the expense of MILAN and Imperial German claims (HOLY ROMAN EMPIRE), extended from Padua to Bergamo and into Friuli (north-eastern Italy), which gave it borders on the HABSBURG EMPIRE. By 1478, Venice had regained the Ionian Islands and was still an imperial presence in Greece, where it maintained its claim on Athens until the 17th cent. However, Venetian economic power had been much diminished by the Ottoman conquest of Constantinople in 1453 and the opening up of the routes of commerce to the east on the Atlantic and Indian oceans during the 15th and 16th cents. (PORTUGUESE COLONIAL EMPIRE). In its last siege of Athens (1687–1688), Venetian cannon, commanded by Francesco Morosini, future doge, blew up an Ottoman arsenal in the Parthenon and left the glorious building in the ruined state we know. In 1489 Venice took CYPRUS from the Knights of St John. The greatest Venetian naval exploit was the defeat of the Turks in the Battle of Lepanto (1571), which it won allied to Spain. Nevertheless, with the loss of trade because of Ottoman control of the Near East, Venetian power declined. In the same year as Lepanto, the Ottoman Empire had absorbed Cyprus. Crete was taken in 1669. By 1715 the Ottomans had absorbed all of Venice's enclaves in Greece. Venice still retained the Dalmatian coast and the Ionian Islands. In 1797, the French made Venice part of the FRENCH EUROPEAN EMPIRE, thus ending the long and glorious history of the *Serenissima*. After 1815, Venice was a sullen Austrian possession and it gladly joined the *risorgimento* in 1866. Less than a genuine major European power, Venice was often a barometer of the political conditions on the Italian mainland. Precisely because of its precarious balancing act, Venice is credited with establishing the first permanent diplomatic service ca. 1500.

Verona (12th–15th cents.; *Italy*)
The city of Romeo and Juliet was a free commune and a centre of anti-imperial (Guelf) resistance. It organized the VERONESE LEAGUE, which later was part of the LOMBARD LEAGUE. In 1387 it was taken by MILAN which gave it up to VENICE in 1405. When independent, it was ruled by the della Scala or Scaliger family.

Veronese League (IMPERIAL ITALY)

Versailles (Treaties of)
After World War I, the participants gathered in the Paris Peace Conference of 1919. The collective name for the treaties that emerged is the Treaty of Versailles, which actually refers to the specific treaty signed concerning GERMANY and POLAND. The Treaties of Saint-Germain (AUSTRIA) and Trianon (HUNGARY) disposed of the Austro-Hungarian Dual Monarchy. The Treaty of Sèvres dealt with the OTTOMAN EMPIRE. The Treaty of Neuilly applied to BULGARIA. The KINGDOM OF THE SERBS, CROATS, AND SLOVENES was recognized at Versailles.

Vichy France (FRANCE)

Vien Chan (LAOS)

Vienna (Congress of)

After the exile of Napoleon to Elba in 1814, the victorious powers met in Vienna where, steered by the Austrian Metternich, with the significant participation later of the Frenchman Talleyrand, they disposed of the map of Europe. The Congress was interrupted by Napoleon's return from Elba. After his final defeat at Waterloo (1815), it was reconvened. In Vienna, the HOLY ROMAN EMPIRE was dissolved and the GERMAN CONFEDERATION constituted. The FRENCH EUROPEAN EMPIRE was dismantled. POLAND was left divided, mostly in Russia. SARDINIA and SWITZERLAND were restored. RUSSIA and PRUSSIA emerged aggrandized. The Balkan frontiers of the OTTOMAN EMPIRE were recognized, although they mostly disintegrated during the 19th cent., as did other borders determined at the Congress. The Holy Alliance was a vague understanding between Russia, Austria, and Prussia, which however resulted in reactionary interventions in Spain – by France, which acted in its name in 1823 – and in Hungary and Germany in 1848.

Vietnam

Vietnamese and Cambodian are related tongues. Historically, Vietnam was home to kingdoms based in Hanoi (Tonkin) and Hué. The delta of the Mekong, in southern Vietnam, was under the influence of Cambodia in the past. Between northern and southern Vietnam was the Indianized kingdom of Champa, centred in Danang (Tourane). The Chinese gave northern Vietnam the designation of Annam (peace of the south) in the 7th cent. Tonkin derives from Dong Kinh, an ancient name for Hanoi. The latter name came into use only in 1831. Vietnam was also known as Dai Viet.

A legendary kingdom called Van Lang was succeeded by Au Lac ca. 258 BC. In 207 BC, Tonkin came under Chinese influence and became a Chinese province from 111 BC to AD 939, when it gained its independence following the fall of the T'ANG (TANG) dynasty. During the 14th cent., Tonkin annexed northern Champa. During the early 15th cent., China harshly occupied northern Vietnam and Champa expanded north. The Chinese were expelled in 1428. In 1620, Vietnam was *de facto* divided between Tonkin and Hué. Champa was annexed to the southern part of divided Vietnam (17th cent.), which was reunited after a long period of civil war and instability (1772–1802) characterized by the popular Tay Son rebellion and by the first significant French intervention in Vietnamese politics in favour of the Vietnamese dynasty overthrown by the Tay Son. The Vietnamese capital was established in Hué. Saigon became definitely Vietnamese in the late 18th cent. The rest of southern Vietnam was taken from Cambodia in 1840. Conflicts between Vietnam and Cambodia led to the French protectorate over the latter country in 1863. In 1867, France created the colony of Cochin China in southern Vietnam. In 1883, the French established a protectorate over Hué, which they called Annam, and the following year the protectorate was extended to the north as Tonkin and Annam (FRENCH COLONIAL EMPIRE).

Ho Chi Minh and Vo Nguyen Giap

The Japanese occupied French Indochina in 1940–1941. After Japan surrendered in 1945, the French returned, but the Vietnamese nationalists, led by Ho Chi Minh, demanded independence. France refused, thus setting off, in 1946, the Vietnamese War of Independence, which was to last until 1975. The Vietnamese guerrillas, who counted on Chinese and Soviet backing, soon had infiltrated most of northern Vietnam. The French thought they could defeat them once and for all if they could be made, literally, to come out and fight. In 1954, French forces occupied and fortified the valley of Dien Bien Phu, in northwestern Vietnam, near the Laotian border, where they hoped to draw out the enemy. The Vietnamese did better than that: they surrounded Dien Bien Phu with troops and cannon, carried piece by piece over the mountainous jungle, and gradually closed the circle on the French forces, which capitulated in May. The French politician Piere Mendès-France became Prime Minister in 1954 with the solemn undertaking that he would end the French involvement in Vietnam in one month. Amazingly he kept his word in the Geneva Conference – convened even as French forces were being besieged in Dien Bien Phu – in which Vietnam was divided along roughly the 17th parallel.

The north became the communist Democratic Republic of Vietnam, capital Hanoi, and the south the pro-western Republic of Vietnam, capital Saigon (SOUTH VIETNAM). Elections in the south, which had been set for 1956, were suspended. This was the signal for the re-start of hostilities, which were carried forward by the so-called Vietcong (Vietnamese communist guerrillas) directed by General Vo Nguyen Giap, the military genius of the war. The United States had taken up the anti-communist task in Vietnam, which was formalized by treaties signed in 1961, during the administration of President John F. Kennedy. The American intervention was at first restricted to mere technical support, but then escalated exponentially after the administration of President Lyndon Johnson fabricated the Tonkin Gulf Incident – Vietnamese torpedo boats repeatedly attacking American warships – and obtained congressional backing in 1964. Intensive bombing of North Vietnam began in 1965, yet American claims of imminent victory were belied when the communists launched the Tet offensive (1968) in Hué and other cities, combining regular troops and guerrillas. American intervention peaked in 1969 with 550,000 servicemen in Vietnam. Negotiations between the United States and Vietnam began in 1968 and were continued under the Nixon administration. Somewhat purposelessly – the justification was the destruction of Vietnamese north–south supply lines – Cambodia's border with Vietnam was energetically bombed (1972–1973). The negotiations culminated in 1973 and the Americans pulled out of Vietnam. In 1975, in a brief but thorough military dash, northern forces overwhelmed the south and Vietnam was reunited. For an as yet obscure reason, involving perhaps national pride, China attacked Vietnam in 1978 and there was a short, vicious war in which the Vietnamese apparently fought the Chinese off. In 1975, Cambodia fell to the communist Khmer Rouge, whose barbarous regime was deposed by a Vietnamese invasion in 1978–1979. The Vietnamese occupation of Cambodia ended in 1989. Fighting went on until a UN-supervised cease-fire in 1992. Hanoi is the Vietnamese capital. The former capital of the south, Saigon, is today Ho Chi Minh City.

Vijayanagara (SOUTHERN INDIA)

Visigothic Kingdom (6th–8th cents.; *Spain* and *France*)
The Visigoths (GOTHS), the second domino in the tumbling game started by the HUNS in the steppes of southern Russia, conquered TOULOUSE and Iberia from the Roman Empire (ROME). They lost most of their French lands in 507, but made Spain their home. In 575 they annexed the kingdom of the SUEVES in Galicia. The Arabs after 711 did away with Visigothic Spain except for ASTURIAS and VASCONIA. Spaniards can trace many names and surnames to the Visigoths.

Volga Bulgars (8th–13th cents.; *Russia*)
The Bulgars had much of eastern RUSSIA to themselves in the 8th cent. The KHAZARS elbowed their way through, driving some Bulgars south to found the ancestor of modern BULGARIA. Those that remained in Russia occupied lands around the Volga River, somewhat hyperbolically known as Great Bulgaria. The Volga Bulgars traded with the principalities of Kievan Rus and, like them, were vanquished by the Mongols in the 13th cent. (MONGOL EMPIRE). Their presence in the Kazan region is attested to as recently as the late 14th cent.

W

Wadai (18th–19th cents.; *Sub-Saharan Africa*)
Wadai was a state that controlled caravan routes in the Sahara (CHAD and NIGER) until it was annexed by the FRENCH COLONIAL EMPIRE. It was loosely related to the Sudanese region of Darfur, which was annexed to the Anglo-Egyptian Sudan in Egypt in 1874.

Wales (9th–13th cents.; Great Britain)
SEE ENTRY IN 'PROVINCES AND REGIONS'
The Roman occupation of Britain left few imprints in Wales. After the Romans left, Welsh clans spread over western England and north to Scotland. Strathclyde was a vague Welsh realm annexed by Scotland in the 11th cent. But Wales proper was mostly divided into clans. These assembled into a kingdom in the mid-10th cent. under Hywel Dda. The kingdom was maintained until the death of Gruffydd Ap Llewelyn in 1063. William the Conqueror set up earldoms on the borders of Wales to control the clans. In 1093 the vale of Glamorgan in south Wales fell to the Normans. Edward I accomplished the final conquest of Wales in 1282. By the 1536 Act of Union Wales became subject to the English Crown, eventually part of GREAT BRITAIN.

Warangal (BAHMANI SULTANATE; DELHI SULTANATE)

Warring States (5th–3rd cents. BC; northern *China*)
The ancient CHOU (ZHOU) dynasty (1122–221 BC) decayed in slow motion. It disappeared during the long but creative period of the Warring States (484–221 BC). Though comparisons between Chinese and Western history are odious, the intellectual achievements of this period measure up in some ways to Ancient Greece. Unlike Europe, however, doctrines such as Tao, Legalism, and Confucianism, all of which can be traced to this time (although Confucius himself lived in the Spring and Autumn period of Chou), remained as if cast in iron for the rest of China's dynastic history. Despite the constant warfare, this period saw northern China grow to the Gansu (Kansu) frontier in the west, north to Mongolia, and east to southern Manchuria. The first walls were built in the 4th cent. BC west and north. It was during this time that the HSIUNG-NU first appear as masters of Mongolia and a hovering threat to China. The period ended with the victory of CH'IN (QIN), a warring state in the north west.
(*See chronology under* China and Neighbouring Areas.)

Wessex (ENGLAND)

West Germany (GERMANY)

Western and sub-Saharan Africa
Predominant political influences

7th–11th cents.
Ancient Ghana
  (western Africa)

12th cent.
Ancient Ghana
Benin (Sub-Saharan
  Africa)
Oyo (Sub-Saharan
  Africa)
Hausa (Sub-Saharan
  Africa)

13th cent.
Ancient Ghana
Benin
Oyo
Hausa
Ancient Mali
  (western Africa)

14th cent.
Benin
Oyo
Hausa
Ancient Mali
Kanem-Bornu (Sub-
  Saharan Africa)

15th cent.
Benin
Oyo
Hausa
Ancient Mali
Kanem-Bornu
Songhai (western
  Africa)

16th cent.
Benin
Oyo
Hausa
Kanem
Bornu
Songhai

17th cent.
Benin
Oyo
Hausa
Kanem
Bornu
Bambara (western
  Africa)
Akwamu (Sub-
  Saharan Africa)

Dahomey (Sub-
  Saharan Africa)

18th cent.
Benin
Oyo
Hausa
Akwamu
Dahomey
Ashanti (Sub-Saharan
  Africa)
Fulani (Sub-
  Saharan and
  western Africa)
Fur (Sub-Saharan
  Africa)

19th cent.
Benin
Hausa
Dahomey
Fulani
Fur
European colonial
  empires

Western Mongols (MONGOLIA)

White Horde (14th–15th cents.; *Central Asia*: Kirghiz Steppe)
The White Horde, part of the *ulus* (clans) of Jochi, the eldest son of Genghis
Khan, occupied the eastern part of the territories of the GOLDEN HORDE.
Although nominally part of the Golden Horde, it was in practice autonomous.
At the time when the Mongols were under pressure from RUSSIA in the west
(ca. 1380), the leader of the White Horde, Toqtamish, a protégé of Tamerlane,
conquered the Golden Horde. He later grabbed Azerbaijan and came into con-

flict with his former protector, who defeated him. This weakening of the Golden Horde eventually led to its dissolution.

White Huns (EPHTHALITES)

White Sheep Turks (AQ-QOYUNLU)

Wu Sun
The Wu Sun were a people who occupied the Ili River Basin from the 2nd cent. BC to the 2nd cent. AD. They are described by the Chinese as red-bearded and blue-eyed. This has led some historians to argue that the Indo-Iranian speaking Sarmatians might have branched off from the Wu Sun in the 4th cent. BC. It has also been said that the Wu Sun might have been the ancestors of the ALANS. It is a great deal of supposing to build on a very ancient physical description, which does not and has never fit the Iranians. It might not even have fit the generality of the Wu Sun themselves.

Y

Yemen

In ancient times, Yemen was known as SHEBA. From the 8th cent. AD the land was ruled by local dynasties. From the 11th to the 13th. cents. it fell first to the FATIMIDS and then to the AYYUBID SULTANATE. Its rulers from the 13th to the 15th cents. were the Rasulids. The OTTOMAN EMPIRE incorporated Yemen in 1520. The local Zaida imams were the local rulers from 1592 to 1962. Acting for the Ottomans, EGYPT occupied Yemen from 1818 to 1840. In 1838 most of southern Yemen was administered by BRITISH INDIA. After World War I, the former Ottoman Yemen was on its own. The boundaries of Yemen proper (excluding the British colony of ADEN) were defined by treaties in 1934. From 1958 to 1961, Yemen was part of a paper federation with Egypt and Syria. In 1962 the ruling Zaida dynasty was overthrown and a republic inaugurated. From 1962 to 1967, Egyptian troops were in Yemen to fight off royalist subversion coming from Saudi Arabia. In 1972 Yemen and southern Yemen agreed to merge, but the merger only became effective in 1990. The capital of Yemen is Sanaia.

Yoruba (OYO)

Yuan (13th–14th cents.; *China*)

Yuan is the dynastic name adopted by the Mongol Kublai Khan (MONGOL EMPIRE) when he subjugated all of China (Sung). Yuan China was in many ways a time of great creativity because the Mongols, though terribly discriminatory with the Chinese, did not interfere with their cultural activities, especially literature. The antecessor of the Beijing opera dates from Yuan times. It was Yuan China that Marco Polo knew and Kublai Khan was the emperor he served and told Europeans about in his controversial memoirs. The Mongol conquest of China, which began in northern China in 1206, including the capture of the JURCHEN capital Beijing, was continued ca. 1260 by Kublai Khan, grandson of Genghis Khan and heir to his Mongolian heartland. It was completed in 1279. Northern VIETNAM and CHAMPA resisted the Mongols. KOREA and TIBET were annexed by Kublai, who also advanced as far as MYANMAR, where he destroyed Pagan. The Mongols tried twice to subdue JAPAN, even getting a foothold on Kyushu, but they were ultimately unsuccessful (1274–1282). The Yuan empire contested the Tarim Basin with the Chagataites, also heirs of Genghis. It controlled the eastern terminus of the Silk Road and thus, before the wars with the CHAGATAITE KHANATE, facilitated trade with the west (incidentally, permitting the arrival of foreigners, among which the Venetian Polo family). At its height, then, the empire of

Kublai Khan covered a vast territory from, roughly, a north–south line from north-western Mongolia to the eastern Himalayas, south to Yunnan and Guangdong (Kwantung), along the Chinese coast to Korea and Manchuria, and along the northern frontier of greater Mongolia. Kublai Khan died in 1294. His empire lasted until 1368, after which the Kublaids were reduced to MONGO-LIA. Although a formal distinction could be made between Mongolia and China during the Yuan dynasty, they were, in fact, part of the same empire. The designation Yuan, however, usually applies to the Chinese territories of the Gingisids. Yuan was succeeded by MING. Chinese historians designate as Northern Yuan the history of Mongolia after 1368 and until 1634, when it was absorbed by the Manchus just prior to their conquest of China (CH'ING/QING).
(*See chronologies under* China and Neighbouring Areas *and* Greater Mongolia.)

Yüeh-chih (3rd cent. BC–1st cent. AD; *Central Asia*: greater Mongolia and western Turkestan; *Tarim Basin*)
Before the expansion of the west that began by sea in the 15th cent., the usual historical pattern had been that of peoples from the east moving by land westwards. However, Indo-European speakers from a homeland somewhere in Russia or the Middle East migrated eastwards before the 3rd cent. BC occupying the Tarim Basin and driving as far as the Chinese province of Gansu (Kansu). These people were called Yüeh-chih by the Chinese. They were known in the west as TOKHARIANS. Their languages were deciphered in the early 20th cent. In the 2nd cent. BC, the Yüeh-chih were driven from China by the HSIUNG-NU (although Indo-Europeans remained in the Tarim Basin until the 8th cent. AD). The Yüeh-chih encountered the SAKA or Asian SCYTHI-ANS in Ferghana and dispersed them to Seistan and BACTRIA (ca. 140 BC). The Saka of Seistan were subjected by PARTHIA in the 1st cent. BC. The Yüeh-chih conquered Bactria from the Saka ca. 120 BC and drove them to Gandhara, where the Saka wiped out what remnants there still were of the Greek Bactrians. In the 1st cent. AD, the Yüeh-chih/Tokharians founded KUSHANA, which subsequently conquered Gandhara and drove the Saka to Gujarat, where they disappear in the 4th cent.
(*See chronology under* China and Neighbouring Areas.)

Yugoslavia
Before World War I, the history of Yugoslavia is that of SERBIA, CROATIA, SLOVENIA, MONTENEGRO, MACEDONIA, and BOSNIA-HERZEGOV-INA. Yugoslavia (the land of the southern Slavs) was formed in 1918, as the Kingdom of the Serbs, Croats, and Slovenes, under King Peter I. As such it was recognized at VERSAILLES (1919). In 1929, to quell Croat separatism, the country under King Alexander was centralized as Yugoslavia. In 1941

Yugoslavia was invaded by Nazi Germany. A fascist state was formed in Croatia, which applied a ruthless anti-Serbian policy. Led by Tito (himself a Croat) and his partisans, Yugoslavia bred the most successful resistance movement in Europe during World War II. The communists under Tito took over in 1945 and divided Yugoslavia into six federated republics corresponding to the ancient realms from which they had originally emerged.

VOJVODINA

In 1989 and in 1990, Serbia, under Milosevic, deprived the provinces of Kosovo and Vojvodina, respectively, of all autonomous powers. In Kosovo, Albanians, who are Muslims, constitute a vast majority of the population. Kosovo is considered by the Serbs as their original homeland. There is a substantial Hungarian minority in Vojvodina. An attempt by the Serbs to control the Yugoslav rotative federal presidency in 1991 led to the secession of Slovenia and Croatia. Macedonia seceded in 1992. When Bosnia-Herzegovina attempted to secede from the federation in 1992, Serbia intervened and civil war and 'ethnic cleansing' followed, which lasted until 1995, when the country, by the terms of the Dayton Accord, was divided into Serb and Croat–Muslim zones. Serbia and Montenegro formed a new Yugoslav federation in 1992. In 1999, despite warnings by the North Atlantic Treaty Organization (NATO) to abstain from applying ethnic cleansing in Kosovo, Milosevic proceeded to do so. For the first time since it was created in 1949 to counter Soviet-Stalinist military pressure in Europe, NATO acted as a unitary force. Led by the United States, after nearly two months of bombing, it forced the Serbian troops to leave Kosovo. Milosevic was charged before the war crimes tribunal, an offshoot of the international court at The Hague. During 1999, Montenegro proposed that Yugoslavia be converted into a very loose confederation between Serbia and Montenegro.

Z

Zaire (CONGO, DEMOCRATIC REPUBLIC OF)

Zambia
Peopled by tribes who speak languages of the Bantu family, Zambia was constituted as Northern Rhodesia in 1889, part of the privately owned South Africa Company. In 1900 it became a British colony and in 1964 it seceded as independent Zambia from the white-dominated Federation of Rhodesia and Nyasaland. The capital of Zambia is Lusaka. Barotseland is a region in west Zambia where various Bantu-speaking native kingdoms were founded in the 19th cent.

Zanzibar (17th–20th cents.; Tanzania)
In the early 16th cent. Zanzibar was under Portuguese influence, but later was ruled by Arab sultans. In 1890 it became a British protectorate, which achieved independence in 1963 and formed Tanzania with Tanganyika in 1964.

Zapotecs (MESOAMERICAN CIVILIZATIONS)

Zaprozhye (14th–18th cents.; *Southern Russia*)
The Cossack region in southern Ukraine, Zaprozhye is reported from the time of the formation of POLAND-LITHUANIA (14th cent.), when Cossacks served indistinctly under Poles or Russians. Given that Russia had not yet acquired the rigidities that were to characterize its society, the Cossacks probably came from different classes, especially free-roaming serfs. Zaprozhye was annexed by RUSSIA in the 18th cent. The term Cossack was retained to refer to certain particularly brutal regiments in the Tsarist armies. The brutality of the Cossacks was reported by Clausewitz, who observed them, from the Russian side, in action against the vestiges of Napoleon's Grande Armée. Merciless against a weak enemy, they ran when faced down even by lesser numbers. However, there is another Cossack ethnic tradition and that refers to the peasants in the Don River Basin – the ancient Zaprozhye – and in the Kuban. The Cossacks of the Don are the subject of the novels of the Russian writer Sholokhov.
(*See chronology under* Southern Russia.)

Zimbabwe (Ancient) (10th–15th cents.; southern Africa)
Ancient Zimbabwe was a kingdom which left impressive ruins and presumably flourished in south central Africa from the 10th to the 15th cents. Zimbabwe is known from reports gathered by the Portuguese in the African kingdom of MONOMOTAPA, in Mozambique.

Zimbabwe

As the decolonization movement gained force in Africa, the white-minority administrations of Northern Rhodesia, Southern Rhodesia, and Nyasaland formed the Federation of Rhodesia and Nyasaland in 1953. In 1963 it broke up. Northern Rhodesia became independent ZAMBIA and Nyasaland independent MALAWI in 1964. The whites of Southern Rhodesia, who were proportionately more numerous than in the other two members of the dissolved federation, chose to go it alone. In 1965 they declared for an independent RHODESIA. Mounting internal and external opposition led to an agreement for elections which, in 1980, resulted in the establishment of Zimbabwe. The official language of Zimbabwe is English, but a majority speak Shona, a Bantu tongue. The capital of Zimbabwe is Harare, formerly Salisbury.

Zirid Emirates (10th–12th cents.; *Maghreb*)

After the FATIMIDS established their political centre in Egypt in 973, their lands in the Maghreb were fragmented into the Zirid Emirates during the 11th cent. The Fatimids were in the tradition of Shia ISLAM, but the Zirids adopted orthodox Sunni doctrine. This provoked the Fatimids, who sent Bedouins to subjugate them. The Bedouins not only displaced the Zirids where they could, but also disrupted social stability in the region (a Moorish historian compared them to a swarm of locusts). They contributed strongly to the Arabization of the Maghreb. The Bedouin emirates were absorbed by the ALMORAVIDS in the late 11th cent. There existed Zirid emirates until the mid-12th cent.

Zululand (19th cent.; South Africa)

The territories occupied by the Zulus in Natal (SOUTH AFRICA) during the 19th cent., Zululand was never more than a loose tribal confederacy, which happened to have a strong leader named Shaka (d. 1828). During the 1840s the Zulus and the Boers were at odds (ORANGE FREE STATE; TRANSVAAL). The Zulus inflicted some defeats on British forces in the 1870s. Zululand was annexed into Natal by Great Britain in 1887. In 1959, it was created as a Bantustan, or tribal homeland, named KwaZulu, reabsorbed by South Africa in 1994. Its capital is Ulundi.

PROVINCES AND
REGIONS

A

Acadia

French Canadian region in the 17th and 18th cents., corresponding today to New Brunswick, Nova Scotia, and Prince Edward Island. The British, who acquired Nova Scotia in 1713 and occupied Cape Breton and the Île de St Jean (later Prince Edward Island) in 1756, expelled the French settlers from 1753 to 1758. French lands were confiscated and the inhabitants dispersed to the Atlantic seaboard, France, and Louisiana. Acadia was the original North American home of the Cajuns.

Aceh

The northernmost province of the Indonesian island of Sumatra became important when Muslim traders abandoned Malacca after the Portuguese conquest in 1511. Aceh was part of the Dutch East Indies and as such remained within independent Indonesia. There is a strong movement for separation in Aceh, which gained strength with the independence of East Timor. Indonesia at first tried to suppress it but is now handling it with kidskin gloves.

Achaemenid Empire

The Achaemenid Empire covered the following satrapies and regions (contemporary geographical references in parentheses): Arabia (western Iraq to the Sinai); Arachosia (southern Afghanistan to south-western Afghanistan, around Kandahar); Aria (northern Afghanistan and southern Turkmenistan); Bactria (north-eastern Afghanistan); Carmania (west of Gedrosia); Cilicia (Anatolia); Drangiana (western Afghanistan between Herat and Kandahar); Gedrosia (western Pakistan); Hyrcania (south-eastern coast of the Caspian Sea); Makran (coast of Iran east of the Persian Gulf); Mardi (south-western coast of the Caspian Sea); Oritae (western coast of Pakistan and eastern coast of Iran); Persis (south central Iran); Putaya (Libya); Seistan (area approximately where the borders of Iran, Afghanistan, and Pakistan meet); Sogdiana (south-eastern Uzbekistan, western Tajikistan, and western Kyrgyzstan); Susiana (area around the head of the Persian Gulf, west of Persis); Syria (Syria and Palestine). All of these provinces later became part of the Alexandrian Empire. Some were the core around which later kingdoms and provinces were formed. Seistan is a later designation from the occupation of that land by the Sakas or Asian Scythians

Afghanistan

See entry in 'Dictionary' for the historical regions of Afghanistan.

Amazonia

The Amazon River drainage basin embraces northern Brazil and large chunks of Venezuela, Colombia, Ecuador, Peru, and Bolivia.

Amerindians

When Columbus sailed the ocean he expected to find Indians, and that's what the peoples he found in America were named, and are still called in the United States, although the name Amerindians is coming into justified use.

Anatolia

Anatolia means east in Greek. It is basically the territory of Asian Turkey. Western Anatolia is also known as Asia Minor. Anatolia comprises the following areas, some of them constituted as kingdoms: Bithynia (east coast of the Bosporus); Cappadocia (eastern Anatolia); Caria (south-western Anatolia); Chalcedonia (western Bithynia); Cilicia (strip of Mediterranean coast in south-eastern Anatolia); Lycia (east of Caria); Lydia (coast of the Sea of Marmara); Mysia (within Phrygia); Pamphylia (east of Lycia); Paphlagonia (north central Anatolia towards the coast of the Black Sea); Phrygia (north central Anatolia towards Lydia); Pisidia (south central Anatolia); Pontus (south-eastern coast of Black Sea).

Antarctica

Unlike the Arctic, which is a sea, Antarctica is a landmass almost entirely covered by huge layers of ice and snow. Antarctica has the form of a pie on which Argentina, Australia, Chile, France, Great Britain, New Zealand, and Norway have made wedge-shaped claims. By a treaty of 1959, it was agreed not to militarize Antarctica. The United States does not recognize Antarctic claims.

Antilles

General name for the islands in the Caribbean Sea, including the Major Antilles (Cuba, Hispaniola, Puerto Rico, and Jamaica) and the rest of the islands known as Minor or Lesser Antilles. Hispaniola contains the Dominican Republic and Haiti. The name derives from the Spanish, La Española (The Spanish). The Lesser Antilles are the small islands fringing the Caribbean Sea. To the north they are the Leeward Islands and to the east they are the Windward Islands. Windward means towards the wind. The principal Windward Islands are St Vincent, St Lucia, and Grenada. Margarita is an island in the Caribbean, part of Venezuela as the state of New Sparta.

Arabia

The so-called peninsula of Arabia includes the following historical regions: Hejaz (Mecca), Nejd (Riyad), Nafud (north), and Hadramaut (coast of eastern Yemen). Today Arabia mainly refers to Saudi Arabia, although geographically it includes Yemen, Oman, the United Arab Emirates, Qatar, Bahrain, and Kuwait. Uninhabited areas of Saudi Arabia are An Nafud, Ad Dahna, and Rub al Khali. The latter region is known as the Empty Quarter.

Argentina

Argentina is divided into 23 provinces and a Federal District. They all fall into the following regions: Pampas (central Argentina, including Buenos Aires), the Andean Piedmont, the Chaco (northern Argentina), Patagonia (a flat semi-arid region from Bahia Blanca to the border with Chile in the south), and *Tierra del Fuego*.

Australia

See entry in the 'Dictionary' for the political divisions of Australia.

Austria

The states of modern Austria are (capital in parentheses): Burgenland (Eisenstadt), Carinthia (Klagenfurt), Lower Austria (St Pölten), Salzburg, Styria (Graz), Tyrol (Innsbruck), Upper Austria (Linz), Vienna, and Vorarlberg (Bregenz). Carinthia and Styria were marches of the Holy Roman Empire.

B

Balkans

The so-called Balkan peninsula extends at the north from Slovenia to Romania. It also includes Albania, Bosnia-Herzegovina, Bulgaria, Croatia, Greece, Macedonia, Montenegro, and Serbia.

Baltic region

The Baltic Sea washes the shores of Sweden, Finland, Estonia, Latvia, Lithuania, Poland, and Denmark. The Gulf of Finland reaches to Russia.

Banat

Banat is the name given to predominantly Hungarian-speaking territories that today include areas of western Romania, southern Hungary, and northern Serbia. The northern Serbian province of Vojvodina occupies part of the Banat.

Belarus

See entry in 'Dictionary' for the provinces of Belarus.

Belgium

Belgium is roughly divided into the Flemish-speaking north and the French-speaking south, with the capital Brussels in the middle. The north corresponds to historical FLANDERS. The south is Walloonia, or the Walloon region. The northern provinces are: Antwerp, Flemish Brabant (Louvain), East Flanders (Ghent), West Flanders (Brugge), and Limbourg. The southern provinces are: Walloon Brabant, Hainaut (Mons), Liège, Luxembourg, and Namur. Walloonia is a general linguistic designation for southern Belgium, where French is spoken. As a designation, Walloonia is akin to Vasconia, a general name to cover an ethnic or linguistic entity. Politically, there never was a Walloonia or a Vasconia.

Bessarabia

Moldavia embraces north-eastern Romania, but historically it extended beyond the Prut River. Bessarabia is the region between the Dniester and the Prut rivers. References to Moldavia and Bessarabia sometimes overlap. The name Bessarabia does not denote ethnicity. Bessarabia is mostly peopled by Moldavians. It is, therefore, eastern Moldavia. The actual republic of Moldova includes a strip of land on the left bank of the Dniester which is mainly peopled by Russians. Southern Bessarabia, which borders on the Black Sea, south west of Odessa, is today part of the Ukraine.

Brazil

Brazil is divided into 26 states and a Federal District. It can also be divided regionally into: *Amazonia*, the Nordeste, the Matto Grosso (central Brazil, including Belo Horizonte and Brasilia), Chaco (north of Paraguay), the south central coastal area (which includes Rio de Janeiro and Sao Paulo), and the south (north of Uruguay). Nordeste refers to the hump of Brazil, adjoining coastlines and their hinterlands. It was infamous for its periodic droughts and famines. The poverty-stricken interior is called the *sertao*, where the *cangaçeiros* or bandits often had the run of the territory. The Pantanal, in south central Brazil, is one of the largest marshes in the world.

C

Canada
See entry in the 'Dictionary' for the provinces and territories of Canada.

Central Asia
Because of the imprecision of political frontiers in Central Asia before the Russians took over (16th–19th cents.), the only reliable references for vaguely defining historical sovereignties over that huge land mass are salient physico-geographical features. However, it is also possible to demarcate extensive disparate areas where specific military and political forces have been at work through the centuries. A combination of both approaches can permit us to classify Central Asia into six more or less discrete regions: (1) eastern Siberia, including the Mongol-Manchurian province of Jehol (*China*), where the more important natural features are the Amur and Ussuri rivers and the Khingan range; (2) greater Mongolia, which comprises lands beyond Mongolia proper and includes the Kerulen, Orkhon, and Selenga rivers, the Gobi Desert, Baikal and Balkash lakes (and the Ili River Basin in today's Kazakhstan), and the Tien Shan, Hangai, Sayan, and Tarbagatai ranges; (3) the basin of the Tarim River, delimited in the north by the Tien Shan range, with the river-swallowing Takla Makan Desert at its centre; (4) western Turkestan, from the Pamir range, the Issyk Kul Lake, and the Valley of Ferghana in the east, across the lands between the Syr Darya (Jaxartes) and Amu Darya (Oxus) rivers to the Aral Sea and on to the eastern shores of the Caspian Sea down to Turkmenistan; (5) the Kirghiz Steppe, which extends from the eastern limits of greater Mongolia to southern Russia north of the Caspian Sea (Kazakhstan, which can be considered part of western Turkestan); and (6) western Siberia, defined by the middle reaches of the Yenisei, Ob, and Irtyish rivers. At their fringes, Central Asia and Siberia are indistinguishable.

Turk–Mongol rivalry
One look at a map of this vast zone will reveal that west of Mongolia there are numerous wrinkles, which would suggest mountainous barriers between the homeland of the Mongols and the rest of Eurasia. In fact, those mountains – Hangai, Altai, and Sayans – contain spacious valleys whose sides slope softly down from rounded low summits. The highest elevation in the Altai reaches 4,506 metres, but this is exceptional. Crossing these ranges was easy to manage by hordes and populations on the move. Beyond them spread steppes without significant obstacles across Kazakhstan and all the way to Hungary and down through Uzbekistan and Turkmenistan to Khurasan. In this immensity, Turks and Mongols came and went and mixed so that, if Mongolia itself

is indisputably the land of the Mongols, everything beyond it to where Russia begins north of the Caucasus could be termed equally well Turkestan or Mogholistan. The Mongols were more apt to move further north than the Turks into Siberian lands, but in the long run central Asia became more Turkic than Mongol. Politically one of the reasons for this is that Chinese ambitions in Central Asia were set back decisively by an alliance of Arabs and Islamicized Turks in the Battle of Talas. Talas is a town in northern Kyzgyzstan, near the border with Kazakhstan. The Tarim only suffered the overflow of the hordes in their movements and struggles north of the Tien Shan, which probably explains why it was the crux of the Silk Road. And east of Mongolia were the lands of the Tungus and the Manchus, who burst out from them but were sucked in by the powerful force of China instead of going west in the footsteps of the Mongols and the Turks.

Chechnya

A republic in southern Russia, in 1994–1995 Chechnya fought the Russian army to a standstill. In 1999, the Chechens, flush with the build up they got in the West ('one Chechen fighter is worth ten Russians'), attempted attacking Dagestan and were suspected of terrorism in Russia itself. It was a grievous miscalculation, because the Russians had been spoiling for a rematch and in early 2000 had conquered most of Chechnya. Grozny, the capital of Chechnya, was devastated during these wars.

China

The regions of China have had different names in the past. Some individual regions have had many names. It is possible to speak of southern, northern, western, etc., China, but the only way to make these categories as precise and illustrative as possible is to relate them to the provinces and metropolitan areas that can be seen in any map of China today. For location purposes, China has been divided into geographical areas with some basis in history. The names are given in Pinyin transliteration with Wade-Giles in brackets. The names of provinces are followed by their capitals. The provinces of Manchuria are: Heilongjiang (Heilunkiang), Harbin; Jilin (Kirin), Changchun; Liaoning, Shenyang. The provinces and regions of northern China are: Anhui (Anhwei), Hefei; Henan (Honan), Zhengzhou; Hebei (Hopei), Shijiazhuang; Hubei (Hupeh), Wuhan; Jiangsu (Kiangsu), Nanjing (Nanking); Nei Monggo (Inner Mongolia), Hohhot; Shaanxi (Shensi), Xian (Sian); Shandong (Shantung), Jinan; Shanxi (Shansi), Taiyuan. The provinces of southern China (below the Yangzi (Yangtze) River) are: Fujian (Fukien), Fuzhou; Guangxi Zhuangzu (Kwangsi), Nanning; Guangdong (Kwantung), Guangzhou (Canton); Hunan, Changsha; Jiangxi (Kiangsi), Nanchang; Zhejiang (Chekiang), Hangzhou (Hangchow). The provinces of south-western China are: Ghizhou (Kweichow), Guiyang; Sichuan (Szechwan), Chengdu; Yunnan, Kunming. The provinces and regions of western China are: Gansu (Kansu), Lanzhou; Qinghai (Tsinghai), Xining; Ningxia Huizu (Ningsia), Yinchuan; Xinjiang Uygur (Sinkiang), Urumqi; Xizang (Tibet), Lhasa. Guangx Zhuangzhu, Ningxia Hui, Xinjiang Uygur, and Xizang are autonomous regions. The municipalities of Beijing (Peking), Tianjin (Tientsin), and Shanghai are centrally administered.

Chinese Turkestan is the name given to a region including Xinjiang Uygur and western Qinghai. Jehol was a Chinese province formed after the fall of the Manchu Ch'ing dynasty. It was shared out among Inner Mongolia, Hebei, and Liaoning in 1949. Jehol was the womb of hordes that usually ended up carving kingdoms in northern China, notably the Jurchen, who founded the Chin dynasty, and the Manchus, who established the Ch'in dynasty. Ordos, the arid region in the northern part of the huge curve of the Huang Ho River, today divided between Inner Mongolia and Shensi, was home to various kingdoms. Tiny islands in the South China Sea, the Paracels were occupied by Vietnam, from where the Chinese expelled them in 1974.

Nanyang is the name the Chinese used to refer to the peoples and states around the South China Sea.

LANGUAGES OF CHINA

The peoples of China speak over 130 different tongues, but all the languages known collectively as Chinese can be placed in the same Sinic branch of the Sino-Tibetan family of languages. Mandarin Chinese is the official language spoken by some 70 per cent of the total population of the People's Republic of China. Other important Chinese tongues – traditionally called dialects but mutually incomprehensible – are Wu, spoken in Zhejiang (Chekiang), and Yue or Cantonese. In Taiwan most of the population speak Southern Min. Tibetan and Burmese are also branches of the same family as Chinese. Other language groups represented in China are Turkic (Sinkiang) and Tungusic (Manchuria).

Croatia
See entry in 'Dictionary' for the historical regions of Croatia.

D

Dardanelles

Dardanelles is the Greek name for the straits between the Aegean Sea and the Sea of Marmara in Turkey. The peninsula to the north, Gallipoli, was the object of a failed campaign by British, Australian, and New Zealand troops to take the German-allied Ottoman Empire out of World War I. Another Greek name for the Dardanelles was Hellespont.

Darien

A jungle region overlapping the border of Colombia and Panama, Darien is famous as the 'missing link' of the Pan-American highway because of the marshy, difficult terrain. The name was occasionally applied to the whole of the Panamanian isthmus.

E

Eastern Europe

The denomination Eastern Europe was generally adopted to refer to communist Bulgaria, Czechoslovakia, East Germany, Hungary, Poland, and Romania. Bulgaria and Romania are also in the Balkans. Since Albania and Yugoslavia broke away from the informal Soviet Empire, they were not usually referred to as Eastern Europe.

England

In a strict geographic sense, England can be divided into the Home Counties (Bedfordshire, Berkshire, Buckinghamshire, Cambridgeshire, Hertfordshire, Oxfordshire, and Surrey), south England (East Sussex, Hampshire, Isle of Wight, Kent, West Sussex, and Wiltshire), south west England (Avon, Cornwall and Isles of Scilly, Devon, Dorset, and Somerset), west England (Cheshire, Gloucestershire, Hereford and Worcester, and Shropshire), north west England (Cumbria and Lancashire), north east England (Cleveland, Lincolnshire, Northumberland, and North Yorkshire), east England (Essex, Norfolk, and Suffolk), and the Midlands (Derbyshire, Leicestershire, Northamptonshire, Nottinghamshire, Staffordshire, and Warwickshire). Besides London, England has five conurbations called metropolitan counties: Manchester, Merseyside (Liverpool), South Yorkshire (Sheffield), Tyne and Wear (Newcastle and Sunderland), West Midlands (Birmingham and Wolverhampton), and West Yorkshire (Leeds).

F

Far East

Far east is the general designation for eastern Asia, especially Japan, China, and Korea. Far East also included countries such as the Philippines, Indonesia, and Vietnam, which are now considered part of south east Asia. Indonesia was also often included in Oceania.

Faroe Islands

The Faroes are self-governing north Atlantic Ocean islands, dependent on Denmark. They were peopled by Norsemen in the 8th cent. and annexed by the kingdom of Norway in the 11th cent. Norway came under the Danish Crown in 1397. When Norway passed to Sweden in 1814, the Faroe remained under Danish sovereignty. The capital is Thorshavn on Stremoy Island.

France

For the sake of convenience, France has been divided here into large regions determined partly by geographical features and partly by historical circumstances. Only the principal provinces are listed. The main city of each province is indicated in parentheses. The following regions are in *north-eastern France*: Artois (Arras); French Flanders (Lille); Hainaut (Valenciennes). The following regions are in *northern France* (mainly north of the Loire River and of Burgundy): Anjou (Angers); Britanny (Rennes); Champagne (Reims); Île de France (Paris); Maine (Le Mans); Normandy (Rouen); Orléanais (Orléans); Picardy (Amiens); Touraine (Tours). The regions of *south-western France* (south of the Loire, west of Languedoc and Auvergne) are: Angoumois (Angouleme); Armagnac (part of Gascony); Berry (Bourges); Bourbonnais (Vichy); Gascony (Auch; includes Béarn and Bigorre); Guienne or Guyenne (Bordeaux); Limousin (Limoges); Marche (Guéret); Périgord (part of Guienne); Poitou (Poitiers); Saintonge (La Rochelle). The regions of *south-eastern France* (east of the Rhône) are: Provence (Marseilles); Savoy (Chambéry); Dauphiné (Grenoble). The regions of *south central France* are: Auvergne (Clermont-Ferrand); Foix; Languedoc (Toulouse and Nîmes); Lyonnais (Lyon); Roussillon (Perpignan). The regions of *east central France* are: Burgundy (Dijon); Charolais (part of Burgundy); Franche-Comté (Besançon); Nivernais (Nevers). The regions of *eastern France* are: Alsace (Strasbourg); Lorraine (Nancy).

Austrasia was the name of north-eastern France in Merovingian and Carolingian times (6th to 9th cents.). Neustria was the name of France south of the River Seine in Merovingian and Carolingian times (6th to 9th cents.).

The historical region of Aquitaine comprises south-western France (south of the Loire River). It can also refer to a more restricted area, but in all instances it has Bordeaux at its centre, which means that it roughly corresponds to Guienne. Septimania is the Latin-derived name of the region that roughly corresponds to Languedoc.

Alsace (eastern France) was part of the Holy Roman Empire until France annexed it in the 18th cent. After the Franco-Prussian War (1870–1871), Germany claimed it back, but had to return it to France after World War I.

In a wide sense, Provence is southern France east of the Rhône River. Languedoc is southern France west of the Rhône River. Marseilles is the historic capital of Provence.

Ancient Burgundy was divided into three regions: Cisjurane Burgundy, to the south side of the Jura Mountains (north of Switzerland), roughly Provence; Transjurane Burgundy, the northern side of the Jura Mountains; and the province of BURGUNDY proper, north of Transjurane Burgundy.

Carthaginian and Roman, later under the influence of the Byzantine Empire, Corsica was loosely held by Islam. Genoa and Pisa jointly seized Corsica in the 12th cent. After falling out with the Pisans, the Genoese kept the island, which they transferred to France in 1768, one year before Napoleon was born there. It is the only part of European France not on the continent.

The province of Franche Comté was one of the most contested areas of France. It was originally part of the first kingdom of Burgundy and in 1034 was nominally part of the Holy Roman Empire. It was annexed by the Duchy of Burgundy in 1390 and in 1477 passed to the Habsburg. In 1556, it became Spanish until, in 1674, it was ceded to France. Charolais has been part of Burgundy since the latter's annexation to France.

G

Germany

Germania was the name of two Roman provinces on the left bank of the Rhine, but also the general Roman designation for the lands east of the Rhine. The following are ancient provinces and regions – some have left the German sphere – and modern states of Germany (*Länder*): Alamannia, ancient German region, today part of Baden-Württemberg; Baden-Württemberg, *Länd* in south-western Germany, capital Stuttgart; Bavaria, modern state and former kingdom in south-eastern Germany, capital Munich; Berlin, a *Länd* in itself, it was designated federal capital in 1997; Billungen, ancient imperial march, today in western Pomerania and southern Schleswig-Holstein; Brandenburg, eastern Germany, formerly western Prussia, capital Potsdam; Bremen, this port in north-western Germany is a *Länd* in itself; Franconia, former duchy, mostly in Hesse; Hamburg, the north German port is a *Länd* in itself; Hessen, a *Länd* in central Germany east of the Rhine, capital Wiesbaden; Lorraine, former duchy corresponding to today's Rhineland (French Lorraine is the western part of ancient Lorraine); Lower Saxony, today a *Länd*, was the Duchy of Saxony in northern Germany; Lusatia, an imperial march, today in southern Brandenburg and eastern Saxony-Anhalt; Mecklenburg-Pomerania, a *Länd* in north-eastern Germany, formerly north-western Prussia, capital Schwerin; Meissen, imperial march, today in Brandenburg; Neumark, imperial march, today in western Poland; North Rhine Westphalia, a *Länd* in west central Germany, capital Düsseldorf; Palatinate, general designation for the southern Rhineland; Pomerania, region of Prussia, today mostly in north-western Poland and in Mecklenburg-Pomerania; Prussia; Rhineland, middle course of the Rhine River; Rhineland-Palatinate, a *Länd* in western Germany, capital Mainz; Saarland, *Länd* in western Germany, capital Saarbrücken; Saxony, *Länd* in south-eastern Germany, capital Dresden; Saxony-Anhalt, *Länd* in central Germany, north of Thuringia, capital Magdeburg; Schleswig-Holstein, *Länd* in northern Germany, south of Denmark, capital Kiel; Swabia, former duchy, now part of Baden-Württemberg; Thuringia, *Länd* in central Germany, south of Saxony-Anhalt, capital Erfurt; Westphalia, region east of northern Rhineland.

The Duchy of Hanover, founded in the 13th cent. in Lower Saxony, provided Great Britain with a ruling house in 1714 – after the death of Queen Anne of the House of Orange – which lasted until the death of William IV in 1837. From 1805 to 1813, Napoleon annexed Hanover to the French European Empire. William's Saxe-Coburg niece, Victoria, could not retain it on her accession to the British throne in 1837 because of the Salic Law, by which land and thrones can pass only to male heirs.

Brandenburg was originally a mark or marche of the Holy Roman Empire. East Prussia was the original Prussia, first conquered by the Teutonic Knights. The Prussians were Balts. When the elector of Brandenburg crowned himself King of Prussia in Königsberg (East Prussia) in 1701, Brandenburg technically became part of Prussia. The lands between Brandenburg and East Prussia were Polish Pomerania or Pomerelia. The core of Prussia was formed with East Prussia, Pomerelia, Pomerania, and Brandenburg. Prussia became East Prussia when Polish Pomerelia was organized as West Prussia. East Prussia is today mostly in Poland and in the Russian enclave of Kaliningrad. Pomerelia and Pomerania are almost totally in Poland. Prussia as an official designation was abolished by the Soviets after World War II. However, Brandenburg is still a German state. Kaliningrad is the Soviet name for Königsberg, the capital of East Prussia, birthplace of Kant.

Pomerania is the region from west of the Oder River to the Vistula River. It was divided between Poland and the eastern marches of the HOLY ROMAN EMPIRE. The Polish part is known as Pomerelia. With the partition of Poland, all of Pomerania went to Prussia. Polish Pomerelia became West Prussia. After World War II, most of Pomerania passed to Poland and East Germany retained a small part west of the Oder which was integrated into the state of Mecklenburg-Pomerania. Stettin was the principal city of German Pomerania. It is today Szczecin in Poland.

Greece (Ancient) (regions)

The regions of Ancient Greece are often divided according to their dialects (parenthetical references are to location and principal cities): (1) *Aeolic*, comprising Aeolis (northern Aegean coastline in western Anatolia; Mytilene); Boeotia (north of Athens; Thebes); Thessaly (north-eastern Greece; Larissa); (2) *Arcadian*, comprising Arcadia (central Peloponnesus; Megalopolis); (3) *Dorian*, comprising Argolis (eastern Peloponnesus; Argos); Corinth (city on north-eastern Peloponnesus); Crete; Laconia (southern Pelopponesus; Sparta); Megara (west of Athens); Messenia (south-western Peloponnesus); (4) *Ionian*, comprising Attica (Athens), the Cyclades, Euboea (off the eastern coast of the Greek mainland; Eretria); Ionia (coast of western Anatolia and islands; Miletus, Ephesus, Samos, Clazomene, Phocaea); (5) *North-western*, comprising Acarniana (western mainland Greece; Stratos); Achaea (northern Peloponnesus); Aetolia (mainland Greece; Calydon); Elis (western Peloponnesus; Elis, Olympia); Phocis (northern coast of Gulf of Corinth; Delphi). Messenia was in a middle ground between Dorian and Arcadian. Northern Thessaly had north-western influence. Attic or Athenian is often a category in itself.

Greece (Ancient) (areas of colonization and principal cities)

The Greeks began founding colonies from the 8th cent. BC. Their colonies extended from the eastern shore of the Black Sea to Sicily and southern Italy.

Colonies were offshoots of parent city–states in the homelands of the Greeks. The Black Sea shoreline – including the Crimea, the northern coast of Turkey, and eastern Thrace – was colonized mainly by Ionian city–states. Their principal colonies were Lesbos, Phocaea, Samos, Miletus, Rhodes, and Thera. Other Ionian colonies were in Phrygia (Dascylum, Cyzicus, and Lampsacus); in western Thrace (Apollonia and Thasos); on the western Black Sea coast often referred to as Scythia (Olbia, Ophiusa, Callatis, and Odessus); in the Crimea also known as Chersonese from the Greek word for peninsula (Chersonesus, Phangoria, and Panticapaeum); in Colchis (Dioscurias and Phasis); in Pontus (Trapezus, Cotyora, and Amisus); on the coast of Paphlagonia (Sinope, Cytorus, and Sesamus). Ionian colonies were also dominant around the rest of the coast of Anatolia, especially in Cilicia (Mallus, Soli, and Nagidus), Pamphylia (Side and Phaselis), and Lycia (Xanthus and Patara). There were also important Ionian colonies in Macedonia (Mende and Apollonia), southern Italy (Elea, Neapolis, Cumae, and Pithecuse), and in Egypt (Naucratis). In the regions of Chalcidice, Anatolian Phrygia, and Bithynia, there were Aeolian (Sestus and Assus), Dorian (Astacus, Mesembria, Byzantium, and Chalcedon), and Corinthian (Potidae) colonies. The Dorian parent cities were Corinth, Megara, and Sparta, which also founded colonies in Sicily (Selinus) and southern Italy (Tarentum). Corinth principally founded colonies in Epirus (Dodona, Corcyra, Leukas, Aulon, Apollonia, and Epidamnus), but it also founded colonies in Sicily (Camarina and Syracuse). Sicily and southern Italy (Magna Graecia) were areas of intense Greek colonization. Besides Ionian, Dorian, and Corinthian foundations, there were also Achaean colonies (Sybaris, Croton, Scylacium, Hipponium, and Locri) and offshoots of Thera and Rhodes (Acragas, Gela, and Lipara). Thera and Rhodes were also the main colonizers of Cyrenaica or eastern Libya (Euhesperides, Tauchira, Baarca, Cyrene, and Apollonia). Other Greek colonies were in Cyprus (Salamis and Paphos) and Rhodes.

Greenland
The island of Greenland, the largest in the world, has been a self-governing dependency of Denmark since 1979. It withdrew from the European Union in 1985 to avoid its fishing quotas. Godthab is the capital of Greenland.

Guiana
Guiana, variously known also as Guyana and Guayana, embraces territories from eastern Venezuela, including the Orinoco River Delta, to the French overseas department of French Guiana (capital Cayenne).

Guinea
Guinea applies to the coast of the so-called Gulf of Guinea. It is sometimes extended as far as Senegal in west Africa.

H

Hong Kong

The island of Hong Kong was ceded to Great Britain in 1842 as a consequence of the Opium Wars (CHINA). In 1860, Great Britain acquired a piece of mainland Chinese territory called Kowloon (peninsula). In 1898, Great Britain leased from China for 99 years additional land in continental China, known as the New Territories. In 1982 talks started for the devolution of Hong Kong. In 1985 it was agreed that it would become a special administrative region of the People's Republic of China. It was handed over in 1997. The part of the city of Hong Kong on the island of that name, called Victoria, was the capital of the British colony. Hong Kong never enjoyed self-rule, although it developed as one of the so-called 'Asian Tigers' (KOREA).

Hudson's Bay Company

In 1670, Charles II of Great Britain granted to his cousin Rupert a charter for a company with jurisdictional rights over the drainage basin of Hudson's Bay. The company was named 'Company of gentlemen adventurers trading in Hudsons's Bay'. Its claim was recognized by international treaty in 1713. It eventually claimed all of western and north-western Canada, the Columbia River Basin in the United States (Oregon and Washington states), and portions of northern Ontario and northern Quebec, a vast area which is known as Rupert's Land, although this name applies mainly to the western lands. The company was not very active, though not unprofitable, until the North West Company started trading in its territories from 1763. The two companies amalgamated in 1821. The company encouraged the settlement of Manitoba after 1808 as the Red River Settlement. However, it did not give up its land rights to Canada until 1869, after compensatory payment.

I

India

The states of India are (capital in parentheses): Arunachal Pradesh (Itanagar); Assam (Dispur); Bihar (Ranchi); Goa (Panjim); Gujarat (Ahmadabad); Haryana (Chandigarh); Himachal Pradesh (Simla); Jammu and Kashmir (Srinagar); Karnataka (Bangalore); Kerala (Trivandrum); Madhya Pradesh (Bhopal); Maharashtra (Bombay); Manipur (Imphal); Meghalaya (Shillong); Mizoran (Aizawl); Nagaland (Kohima); Orissa (Bhubaneswar); Punjab (Amritsar); Rajasthan (Jaipur); Sikkim (Gangtok); Tamil Nadu (Madras); Uttar Pradesh (Lucknow); West Bengal (Calcutta). Modern Indian states do not correspond strictly to the historical division between northern, central, and southern India, itself often disregarded by dynasties and kingdoms. Each historical division comprises the following contemporary states, partially or wholly: *Northern India* (Bengal, Bihar, Gujarat, Kashmir, Punjab, northern Madhya Pradesh, Rajasthan, Sikkim, Uttar Pradesh); *Central India* (Maharashtra, northern Andhra Pradesh, northern Karnataka, Orissa, southern Madhya Pradesh); *Southern India* (Kerala, Tamil Nadu, southern Karnataka, southern Andrha Pradesh, Tamil Nadu); *Northeastern India* (Assam, Arunachal Pradesh, Manipur, Mizoran, Nagaland).

Today a state of India, Goa was occupied by the Portuguese in 1510. It was incorporated into India, together with Daman and Diu, in 1961. Now Union Territories of India, the island of Diu and mainland Daman, both in Gujarat, were seized by the Portuguese in 1531 and 1534, respectively.

Pondicherry or Pondichéry was founded by the French in 1673 near Madras. It was occupied by the Dutch and the British at various times during the 18th cent. In 1816, it was finally restored to France, which ceded it to India in 1956, with the other French enclaves of Karaikal, Mahé, and Yanam. Pondicherry is on the Tamil Nadu coast, Mahé on the Kerala coast, and Yanam on the Andhra Pradesh coast.

The Andaman Islands and the Nicobar Islands are in the Indian Ocean, south of Bengal. The archipelago of Lakshadweep is off the coast of Kerala.

Ladakh, a region of eastern Kashmir and western Tibet, was taken by British India in the 19th cent. In a successful war against India, China recovered most of it in 1962.

Carnatic is a name for the south-eastern coast, and sometimes all, of southern India. It comes from Karnataka, a state of India which today has no coast on the eastern side of the subcontinent.

Coromandel was the name applied to the coast of south-eastern India. It derives from Cholamandalam, a site of the Cholas dynasty of Southern India. It is also referred to as Carnatic.

The south-western coast of India used to be known as Malabar

India has many languages but, roughly, northern and central Indian languages are Indo-Aryan (a group of the Indo-European family) and the languages spoken in the south are Dravidian (a family of languages in itself).

Indochina

The French gave the name Indochina to the region comprised by the countries of Cambodia, Laos, and Vietnam when they were part of the FRENCH COLONIAL EMPIRE. The name sometimes applies to the entire area of continental south east Asia (Myanmar, Thailand, Cambodia, Laos, Vietnam) as opposed to maritime or island South East Asia (Malaysia, Indonesia, Philippines).

Indonesia

The principal islands of Indonesia are: Bali (east of Java), south Borneo or Kalimantan, Celebes or Sulawesi, Flores, Irian (western New Guinea), Java, the Moluccas or Maluku Sumatra, and Timor. The archipelago east of Bali, formerly known as Lesser Sunda islands, is known in Indonesian as Nusa Tenggara, or South Eastern Islands. Western Java is known as Sunda.

New Guinea, the second largest island in the world, is divided between Indonesia and PAPUA NEW GUINEA.

Small but dense in tradition and varied in topography, the Indonesian island of Bali came under Javan influence in the 11th cent. It offered refuge to the rulers of the culturally Indian MAJAPAHIT EMPIRE during its downfall (late 15th cent.), which explains why it remains an Indian cultural enclave in a predominantly Islamic nation. It was divided into various kingdoms in the early 19th cent., which the Dutch subjected to colonial authority.

Kalimantan, the Indonesian and larger part of the island of Borneo, was home in the 16th cent. to the Banjarmasin sultanate, an Islamic harbour or estuary state that competed for a time with Brunei.

The Moluccas, known as Maluku in Indonesian, and better known in the history of European exploration and commerce as the Spice Islands, include many large islands and archipelagos, but the most famous are the islands of Ambon, Buru, Halmahera, Ternate, Tidore, Seram, and the Bandas. Ternate and Tindore were producers of cloves. Ambon and Seram produced nutmeg and mace (a part of the nutmeg seed). The Portuguese occupied the Moluccas in the 16th cent. against strong local resistance. From their base in Batavia, in Java, the Dutch displaced them starting in 1599.

Iran

The provinces of modern Iran are: Ardabil; Azerbaijan East, capital Tabriz, and Azerbaijan West, capital Orumiyeh, both in the north west; Burshehr; Chahar Mahal and Bakhtyari, capital Sharh-e-Kord; Ispahan; Fars, ancient Persis in southern Iran, capital Shiraz; Gilan, capital Rasht; Hamadan; Hormozgan, capital Bandar-e-Abbas; Ilam, ancient ELAM in south west Iran; Kerman; Kermanshah; Khurasan; Khuzestan, capital Ahvaz; Koghiluyeh and Boyer Ahmad, capital Yasuj; Kurdistan, in western Iran, next to Turkey, capital Sanandaj; LURISTAN, ancient realm in the Zagros Mountains, capital Khorramabad; Markazi, capital Arak; Mazandaram, former land of the ISMAILITES until the 13th cent., capital Sari; Semnan; Seistan and Baluchistan, ancient province on the border with Pakistan, capital Zahedan; Tehran; Yazd; Zanjan; Qom. In Arabic Ajami means non-Arab. Iraq Ajami is sometimes used to refer to north central Iran. By contrast, Iraq itself was called Iraq Arabi.

Khurasan included today's Turkmenistan and western Afghanistan. The ancient capital was Herat, now in Afghanistan. The present capital is Mashhad. Historically, Khurasan comprised partially or totally the ancient regions of Parthia, Aria, Hyrcania, and Drangiana (*Achaemenid Empire*). After the Islamic conquest of Persia, Khurasan tended to have a political life different from western Persia until its incorporation into Persia by the SAFAVIDS.

Ireland
The historical provinces of Ireland are (counties): Leinster (Carlow, Dublin county borough, Fingal, South Dublin, Kildare, Kilkenny, Laoighis, Longford, Louth, Meath, Offaly, Westmeath, Wexford, Wicklow); Munster (Clare, Cork county borough, Cork, Kerry, Limerick county borough, Tipperary, Waterford county borough, Waterford); Connaught (Galway county borough, Galway, Leitrim, Mayo, Roscommon, Sligo); Irish republican Ulster (Cavan, Donegal, Monagham). For Northern Ireland, see *Ulster*.

Italy
The historical provinces and regions of Italy are (geographical references in parentheses): Abruzzi (central Italy on the Adriatic coast); Alto Adigio (also known as Trentino and Italian Tyrol, south of western Austria); Basilicata (between the heel and the tip of the Italian boot); Calabria (the front of the Italian boot); Campania (Naples region); Capitanata (east of Campania); Emilia (Bologna area); Friuli (north-eastern Italy); Lazio (Rome area); Liguria (Genoese coast); Lombardy (north central Italy); Marches (central Italy on Adriatic coast, north of Abruzzi); Molise (central Italy on the Adriatic coast, south of Abruzzi); Piedmont (north-western Italy, also known as Savoy); Pugliese (the heel of Italy); Romagna (plain of the Po River); Sardinia; Sicily; Tuscany (central Italy on the coast of the Tyrrhenean Sea, north of Lazio); Valle d'Aosta; Venetia (hinterland of Venice). The Tuscan Archipelago, off the coast of Tuscany, includes the island of Elba.

Pentapolis refers to five cities on the coast of Romagna and the Marches which were part of the Byzantine exarchate or province of Ravenna. Those cities are Rimini, Pesaro, Fano, Senigallia, and Ancona. A region of Italy with Turin as its centre, Piedmont is roughly Italian Savoy in so far as it was part of the kingdom of Sardinia, ruled by the house of Savoy. It also borders on French Savoy to the north.

J

Japan

The territory of Japan consists of the four large home islands of Honshu, Kyushu, Shikoku, and Hokkaido. The Kuriles, a chain of islands north of Hokkaido, though taken by the USSR in 1945, are considered Japanese territory. The Ryuku Islands, south of Kyushu, are also part of Japan. They include Okinawa. The Bonin Islands, part of Tokyo prefecture, are in the Pacific Ocean, south east of Honshu. The Volcano Islands, including Iwo Jima, are south of the Bonins. In all, the country has some 4,000 islands. Within Honshu there are geographically distinct regions, particularly the plain of Kanto, which is the Tokyo hinterland, and the Kansai plain, which contains the cities of Osaka, Kyoto, and Nara. The low country around Osaka is known as Yamato. Administratively Japan is divided into the following regions: Hokkaido, Honshu/Tohoku, Honshu/Kanto, Honshu/Kinki, Honshu/Chugoku, Shikoku, Kyushu, and Okinawa.

Iwo-Jima was taken by the Americans in 1945 against last-ditch Japanese resistance as it was a foothold on the way to the Bonins and Honshu. The flag-raising on Mt Suribachi was the occasion of one of the most famous (rehearsed) photographs in history.

Until the 19th cent., the Ryuku Islands had a court of their own, centred in Okinawa, but it was closely associated with Japan. There remain strong regional cultural traditions.

Java

The large and densely populated island of Java, Indonesia, was home to various states. The Buddhist Sailendra dynasty ruled in central Java and in SRI VIJAYA (7th–13th cents.). In the 8th cent. there was a minor Hindu kingdom known as Mataram in central Java. The Kediri dynasty ruled in eastern Java from the 11th to the 13th cent., when the Singosari dynasty rose to power. Java came under the control of the MAJAPAHIT EMPIRE (13th–16th cents.). Islam first reached Java in the 11th cent. and by the 16th cent. had mostly replaced Indian religions in Indonesia.

K

Kosovo

The formally Serbian province of Kosovo (YUGOSLAVIA), capital Pristina, is very mountainous. It was settled by Serbians (SERBIA), who also occupied the more fertile and smoother lands around Belgrade. By the 19th cent. Muslim Albanians had settled in Kosovo and constituted a majority of the population. Kosovo was recognized as part of Serbia is 1878. As an autonomous province within the Federal Republic of Serbia it entered into the Federation of Yugoslavia and, as such, it remained until the Serb Prime Minister Milosevic, for no other reason than hypernationalism, deprived it of autonomy in 1989 and imposed anti-Albanian restrictions. During the war in Bosnia-Herzegovina the participants – Croats, Muslims, and Serbs – applied measures of ethnic cleansing. Ethnic cleansing is the removal of peoples from their homes by force. Possibly its earliest historical precedent is the so-called Babylonian captivity of the Jews (BABYLONIA), the ordinary Diaspora (7th cent. BC). The Serbs went about it with particular brutality – although the Croats were not far behind and the Muslims themselves engaged in it to a lesser degree – and after the Dayton Accord, which more or less settled things in Bosnia-Herzegovina, the Serbs turned on the Albanian Kosovars. Milosevic was warned off by NATO but persisted and in the first purely airborne war in history (1999), the Serbians were forced to back off. Kosovo was occupied by NATO forces. The Russians, who had not agreed with the Kosovo War, nevertheless claimed a sector for themselves around Pristina. Kosovo is still formally part of Serbia.

Kurdistan

Kurdistan is the name given to the region where the Kurds live today, straddling eastern Turkey and adjacent areas of Syria, Iraq, and Iran. There is a province of Kurdistan in Iran.

L

Lapland

The Lapps, speakers of a Finno-Ugric language, occupy the lands of northern Norway, Sweden, and Finland and the Russian Kola Peninsula. In Norway the Lapp region is called Finnmark. The Lapps were possibly pushed north by the Goths and Finns during the first millennium AD.

Latin America

Latin America includes all the states south of the Rio Grande, the border between the USA and Mexico, including those in the Antilles except former British dependencies. Ibero-America is the same as Latin America minus Haiti. Spanish America is Latin America minus Brazil.

Levant

There are two Levants: the coast of the eastern Mediterranean from Egypt to Turkey and the coast of the Spanish province of Valencia.

Lorraine

When the CAROLINGIAN EMPIRE was first divided, an area from the Netherlands to Alsace including much of the Rhineland went to Lothair II (840–855), son of Emperor Lothair I. His inheritance also included Burgundy and Italy. This territory became known as Lotharingia, the ancient name of Lorraine. When Lothair II died, his lands were divided by the Treaty of Mersen (870) between the West and the East Frankish kingdoms. Emperor Otto I the Great, founder of the Holy Roman Empire, reunited all of Lotharingia. In the late 10th cent. Lorraine was divided into the Duchies of Upper and Lower Lorraine. Upper Lorraine was roughly Rhineland, including Alsace. Gradually Lower Lorraine became part of the Low Countries. The Rhineland was divided among different German states. Upper Lorraine, shorn of Alsace and of territories today in Germany, had been attached to France by 1766. This Lorraine, much reduced from the original Lotharingia, was seized by Germany in 1871 and returned to France in 1918.

Low Countries

The Low Countries, which are not all low, comprised mainly the territories of today's Belgium, Luxembourg, and Netherlands. Netherlands means Low Countries. When the kingdom of Netherlands separated from the rest of the Low Countries in 1581 (officially in 1648), what remained became known as the SPANISH NETHERLANDS.

M

Macedonia
The ancient region of Macedonia embraces the present state of MACEDONIA and north central and north east Greece. Salonika is in Macedonia. Northern Macedonia, peopled by Slavs, was a bone of contention between Bulgaria and Serbia.

Maghreb
Maghreb in Arabic means west and refers to the land from western Libya to Morocco. Ifriqiya is the Arab name for Roman Africa, which corresponds roughly to Tunisia and the contiguous parts of Algeria and Libya.

Malaya
The Malay Peninsula, the core of today's MALAYSIA, has been subjected historically to various sovereignties and political influences. In Kedah, the north-western province of Malaya, there is evidence of Indian cultural influence starting in the 2nd cent. From the 8th to the 13th cent., it was part of the Hindu-Sumatran SRI VIJAYA kingdom. In the 12th cent., it was invaded by Cholas from SOUTHERN INDIA. In 1293 the Hindu-Javanese MAJAPAHIT EMPIRE eliminated whatever power Sri Vijaya still had and took over both Sumatra and Malaya. In the 14th cent. the Thais occupied northern Malaya. The native kingdom of MALACCA was founded in former Majapahit territories during the 15th cent. In 1511, after the Portuguese took over Malacca, the sultans of the latter kingdom moved their base to JOHORE in southern Malaya. Dutch influence superseded that of Portugal, but with the foundation of Penang (1786) and Singapore (1819) British influence became dominant (BRITISH COLONIAL EMPIRE).

Malaysia
See entry in 'Dictionary' for the main provinces of Malaysia.

Maritime provinces
The maritime provinces of Canada are: Newfoundland (including Labrador), Prince Edward Island, Nova Scotia, and New Brunswick.

Memel
Formerly a port in East Prussia, Memel was a member of the HANSEATIC LEAGUE. Lithuania occupied Memel in 1923. Under pressure from the Western powers, Lithuania was forced to recognize its autonomy within its own territory. In 1939, Germany reclaimed and obtained Memel. After World War II Memel, renamed Klaipeda, became part of LITHUANIA. It is the

former territory of Memel which gives Lithuania a coastline on the Baltic Sea.

Mesopotamia

Mesopotamia is the region between the Tigris and the Euphrates rivers ('potamos' means river in Greek). The territory between the Yamuna and Ganges rivers in northern India, called Doab, is also a typical mesopotamia. Since there have been phases in the history of Near Eastern Mesopotamia, it is possible to make a distinction between upper and lower or northern and southern Mesopotamia. Lower or southern Mesopotamia is the land of Sumer, where the first Mesopotamian city–states arose. To the north lies Assur where ca. 1800 the first Assyrian Empire was founded. Babylonia is in the middle. All of Mesopotamia is today in Iraq. Jazira is the Arabic name for northern Mesopotamia.

Mexico

Mexico has 31 states and a capital district. Pre-Columbian civilizations arose in the east and south. Olmec culture (1200–400 BC) flourished in the lands of the states of Veracruz and Tabasco. Maya civilization (1000 BC–AD 1521) extended over the Mexican states of Tabasco, Chiapas, Campeche, Yucatan, and Quintana Roo. The most famous of the earlier discoveries of Mayan sites was Chichen Itzá, in Yucatán. Zapotec (200 BC–AD 1521) and Mixtec (400–1521) cultures had their bases in the state of Oaxaca. The most famous archaeological site there is Monte Albán. The isthmus of Tehuantepec, the borderland of Maya, lies between the Gulf of Mexico and the Pacific Ocean. The ancient site of Teotihuacan (1–650) is north of Mexico City. The heart of the Aztec Empire (1250–1521) was in and around the lands surrounding Mexico City. The actual territory along the border with the USA is known as 'frontera'. Texas was formerly a part of the state of Coahuila. California was formerly a Mexican state. Mexico has a state of Baja California south of the American California. The rest of western North America were dependencies of the states of Chihuahua and Durango. The state of Jalisco, capital Guadalajara, was a captaincy general in the Spanish colonial empire.

Middle East

In the past, Middle East has referred to the Arab provinces of the former Ottoman Empire excluding Libya and the Maghreb, hence Egypt, Palestine, Syria, Iraq, and Arabia. Authoritative maps include Turkey and as far east as Pakistan.

Mongolia

Mogholistan is a vague designation which can be applied either to greater Mongolia (*Central Asia*) or to the eastern part of the CHAGATAITE KHANATE as far as Kashgaria. Inner Mongolia is a Chinese province; Mongolia proper is also known as Outer Mongolia.

Myanmar

Historically, Myanmar has four well-delineated regions: Mandalay in the north, Pegu and the Irrawaddy Delta in the south, coastal Tenasserim in the south east, and coastal Arakan in the west. The Shans, a Tai-speaking people that for a time, starting in the late-13th cent., dominated central Myanmar, today occupy the north east of the country. Arakan was home to a minor Burmese kingdom, capital Mrohaung, from the 15th to the 18th cent.

N

Near East

Near East is the same as Middle East, except that formerly it also included the Balkans. Here it is used to refer to the Middle East up to the Zagros Mountains (western frontier of Iran).

Netherlands

Netherlands is the Dutch part of the former Low Countries. The provinces of today's Netherlands are (geographical references in parentheses): North Brabant (southern Netherlands); Drenthe (north-eastern Netherlands); Friesland (northern Netherlands, known also as Frisia); Gelderland (central Netherlands); Groningen (north east of Friesland); North Holland (Haarlem); South Holland (The Hague and Rotterdam); Limburg (south-eastern Netherlands); Overijssel (eastern Netherlands); Utrecht (central Netherlands); Zeeland (northern Netherlands). Flevoland is made up of polders or reclaimed land in the Zuider Zee. Maastricht is in Limburg. Amsterdam is in Holland.

New Zealand

See entry in 'Dictionary' for the regions and dependencies of New Zealand.

Nigeria

See entry in 'Dictionary' for the regions of Nigeria.

O

Oceania

The islands of the Pacific Ocean are more or less arbitrarily divided into Melanesia, Micronesia, and Polynesia. Melanesia includes New Guinea and the larger islands to the east as far as Fiji. Micronesia comprises the smaller archipelagos in the western and southern Pacific. It is also the name of a state. Polynesia is usually said to include the Hawaiian Islands and the archipelagos of the south central Pacific, especially French Polynesia. Easter Island is part of Polynesia. Oceania refers to these three groupings but traditionally also included Australia and New Zealand. Indonesia is in a continental border zone and can be considered either Oceanian or Asian (which it usually is today).

Oran

Oran is a city in north-western Algeria that was seized and held by Spain from 1509 to 1708, taken by the Ottomans, retaken by the Spaniards in 1732, and finally conquered by the Ottoman ruler of Mascara in 1791. It was annexed by the French in 1841.

Ottoman Empire

See entry in the 'Dictionary' for the territories of the Ottoman Empire.

P

Pakistan

The provinces of Pakistan are: Baluchistan (west), North West Frontier, Punjab (east) and Sind (south). Their respective capitals are Quetta, Peshawar, Lahore, and Karachi. The national capital, Islamabad, is a federal territory. In Pakistan there are also federally administered tribal areas. Gandhara is the ancient name of an area of northern Pakistan. It was part of BACTRIA and KUSHANA, annexed by the GUPTAS in the 4th cent.

Pale, the

Pale means fence. There are at least three geographical pales. One is the territory the British held around Dublin during the 14th and 15th cents. The land around Calais under English occupation from the early 15th cent. until 1659 was also called the Pale. The more famous pale is the Pale of Jewish settlement in eastern Poland and western Ukraine. It was established by Russia after the second partition of Poland in 1793. However, it was not an untrammelled allowance. There were many restrictions and pogroms were frequent in the late 19th and early 20th cents. Most of the Jewish immigration to the USA came from the Pale. The origins of the Jews of the Pale is obscure.

Pentapolis

Pentapolis means 'five cities' in Greek. The most famous Pentapolis are on the Italian Adriatic coast, but analogous quintets are also used in reference to Philistia, Cyrenaica, and Algeria. More than a true geographical designation, Pentapolis is probably a mnemonic device.

Poland

The historical regions of Poland are (political and geographical references in parentheses): Greater Poland (Poznan); Little Poland (Cracow); Masovia (Warsaw); Masuria (north-eastern Poland, formerly in East Prussia); Pomerelia (Polish Pomerania in northern Poland); Sandomir (south-eastern Poland); Silesia.

Pomerelia or Polish Pomerania occupied most of Pomerania, which extended from west of the Oder River to the Vistula River. When Poland was partitioned in 1793, all of Pomerania went to Prussia. After World War II, most of Pomerania, save a bit of East German territory, became part of Poland. Gdansk, formerly Danzig, is the main city in Pomerelia.

The territory of Silesia, today in Poland, was incorporated into the nascent Polish kingdom, passed to Bohemia, and back to Poland from the 10th to the 11th cents. During the Polish decadence starting in the late 17th cent. it passed to the HOLY ROMAN EMPIRE as a Habsburg patrimony. It was conquered by Frederick the Great of PRUSSIA in the 18th cent. and remained in German hands until after World War II, when the Soviets awarded it to Poland. Breslau, the principal Silesian city, became Wroclaw, just as Danzig became and remains Gdansk.

Portugal

Officially divided into 18 districts and two autonomous regions (the Azores and Madeira Islands), the territory of Portugal has also traditional regions: the north, which is centred on the city of Oporto; the centre around the university city of Coimbra; the west, known as Estremadura, which contains Lisbon; and the south, better known as the Algarve. It was here that Prince Henry the Navigator established the famed nautical school of Sagres, which was the foundation for Portuguese world exploration.

R

Roman Empire

The provinces of the Roman Empire ca. AD 280 were (contemporary references in parentheses): Achaea (Greece); Aegyptus (Egypt and the western Sinai); Africa (Tunisia and western Lybia); Alpes Maritimae (south-eastern France); Alpes Cottiae (French Alps); Alpes Poeninae (roughly southern Switzerland); Aquitania (south-western France, roughly medieval Aquitaine); Arabia Petraea (Sinai and Jordan); Asia (western Turkey, same as Oriens); Baetica (roughly Andalusia and Murcia); Belgica (Belgium to Switzerland); Bithynia and Pontus (Black Sea coast of Turkey); Bosporan Kingdom (Crimea); Britannia (England, Wales, and southern Scotland); Cappadocia (east central Turkey to south-eastern Black Sea coast); Cilicia (south-eastern coast of Turkey); Coele (same as Syria); Cyrenaica (eastern Lybia); Dacia (western Romania); Dalmatia (western Croatia, Bosnia, Montenegro, northern Albania, western Serbia, and the Adriatic coast); Galatia (west central Turkey); Germania Inferior (lower Rhine); Germania Superior (upper Rhine); Illyricum (Dalmatia); Italia (roughly Italy including parts of Switzerland, southern France, and Austria); Judaea (present-day Israel, the West Bank, and west Jordan); Lugdunensis (Britanny and Normandy to the Auvergne); Lusitania (Portugal and Estremadura); Lycia and Pamphylia (south-western coast of Turkey); Macedonia (Albania, Macedonia, and northern Greece); Mauretania (northern Morocco and north-eastern Algeria); Moesia (eastern Serbia, Romania, northern Bulgaria); Narbonensis (south-eastern France to Lyon and Savoy); Noricum (eastern Austria and western Hungary); Numidia (eastern Algeria); Oriens; Pannonia (eastern Hungary, Slovenia, Croatia); Phoenicia (Lebanon and southern Syria); Rhaetia (Austria and southern Germany); Septem Provinciae (south-eastern France, same as Septimania); Septimania (same as Septem Provinciae); Syria (south-eastern Turkey and northern Syria); Tarraconensis (north of Baetica to the Pyrenees); Thracia (Thrace and southern Bulgaria).

Romania

See entry in the 'Dictionary' for the regions of Romania.

Russia (formerly USSR)

Russia consists of oblasts (provinces), republics, and autonomous regions. The cities of Moscow and St Petersburg have the status of provinces. The republics are, followed by their capitals: Adygeya (north of Caucasus), Maikop; Altai (south central Siberia), Gorno-Altaisk; Bashkortostan (south of Urals), Ufa; Buryatia (east of Lake Baikal), Ulan Ude; *Chechnya*; Chuvashia (central European Russia), Cheboksary; Dagestan (western coast of Caspian Sea), Makhachkala; Ingushetia (north of Caucasus), Nazran; Kabardino-Balkaria (north of Caucasus), Nalchik; Kalmykia (north of the Caspian Sea), Elista; Karakai-Cherkessia (north of Caucasus), Cherkessk; Karelia; Khakasia (south central Siberia), Abakan; Komi (northern European Russia), Syvtyvkar; Mari (central European Russia), Yoshkar-Ola; Mordovia (central European Russia), Saransk; North Ossetia, also known as Alania (north of Caucasus), Vladiravkaz; Sakha (eastern Siberia), Yakutsk; Tatarstan (eastern European Russia), Kazan; Tuva; Usmurtia (eastern European Russia), Izhevsk; Jewish Autonomous Region (eastern Siberia), capital Birobidzan. The following are historical provinces and regions of Russia, Ukraine, and Belarus: Chernigov; Circassia; Galich (Galicia); Ingria; Kiev; Kuban; Nizhni Novgorod; Novgorod; Pereslavl; Ryazan; Pinsk; Polotsk; Rostov; Ruthenia; Siberia; Smolensk; Suzdalia; Tmutorokan (east of the Sea of Azov); Vladimir; Volhynia; Yaroslavl.

The Maritime Province of Russia is on the Sea of Japan. The territory was disputed with China until final Russian occupation in the 19th cent. Its capital Vladivostok was founded as a military outpost in 1860.

After Germany's collapse in World War II, the USSR dismembered Prussia. Most of it went to Poland. The port of Memel became Lithuanian Klaipeda. And the capital of East Prussia, Königsberg, was renamed Kaliningrad and annexed with its hinterland to Russia. Today it is an enclave wedged between Poland and Lithuania.

Karelia is peopled by Finns and was part of independent Finland until, in 1940, the USSR detached the eastern part including the old capital Vyborg. The autonomous republic of Karelia in Russia extends north of St Petersburg as far as the Kola Peninsula. The capital of Karelia is Ptrozavodsk.

The large island of Sakhalin was divided by Russia and Japan in 1855. The Japanese ceded southern Sakhalin in exchange for the Kuriles in 1875, but recovered it in 1905 after defeating Russia in war. In 1945 the USSR took southern Sakhalin.

Circassia, famous for its white slaves, is a region north east of the Black Sea, north of the Caucasus. The Burjis sultans of Mameluke Egypt were from Circassia.

Tuva is a region of Siberia. Incorporated by the Qing dynasty in 1757. It was briefly independent from 1911 to 1914, becoming a Russian protectorate that passed to the USSR. The capital of Tuva is Kyzyl.

Levedia is the name given by Arab geographers in the 10th cent. to the region north of the Sea of Azov.

Russian is the language of 80 per cent of the population of Russia but over 80 other languages are spoken in the country, representing various diverse linguistic families, prominently the Altaic which includes Turkic and Mongol.

S

Sasanid Empire

The provinces of the Sasanid Empire were: Persis or Fars; Parthia; Susiana or Khuzestan; Maishan or Mesena; Asuristan or Iraq; Adiabene; Arabistan or northern Mesopotamia; Atropatene or Azerbaijan; Armenia; Iberia or Georgia; Machelonia; Albania or eastern Caucasus; Balasagan or Caucasus; Patishkhwagar or the Elburz Mountains; Media; Hyrcania or Gorgan; Margiana or Merv; Aria; Abarshahr; Carmania or Kerman; Sakastan or Seistan; Turan; Mokran or Makran; Paratan or Paradene; India; Kushanshahr or lands comprising Sogdiana down to Peshawar, bounded on the east by Kashgaria; Mazun or Oman.

Scandinavia

Strictly, Scandinavia comprises Denmark, Norway, and Sweden, but Finland, whose language is not Germanic, is usually included, as is Iceland. Visby, the capital of the Swedish island of Gotland in the Baltic Sea, was one of the founders of the HANSEATIC LEAGUE. From the name Gotland some have wildly speculated that it was the homeland of the Goths. Scania is the region of southern Sweden. Jutland, peninsular Denmark, is the only part of Scandinavia in the European mainland proper. Peninsular Scandinavia was anciently known as Thule.

Scotland

The Regions of Scotland are: Borders; Central (Stirling); Dumfries and Galloway; Fife (St Andrews); Grampian (Aberdeen); Highland (Inverness); Lothian (Edinburgh); Strathclyde (Glasgow); Tayside (Dundee); Orkney Islands; Shetland Islands; and Western Islands. The Hebrides are in Highland, Strathclyde, and Western Islands.

Silk Road

Although the Silk Road is not a state or a province, the name does allude to a fairly well-delimited geographical entity which had, in the past considerable influence on political and cultural processes in the areas which it crossed and connected. As such we include it here. As the name implies, the Silk Road was the conduit for the export of silk from China to countries to the west and particularly to Europe. It was originally (3rd cent. BC) a route to Khotan (Hot'ien), in modern Xinjiang (Sinkiang), where the Chinese obtained jade, but it became an important intercontinental trade link at the beginning of the 1st mil. AD through which China exchanged silk with Rome for woollens and precious metals. During its early heyday, which lasted to the 3rd cent., it was also a passage for Nestorian Christian and Buddhist ideas, especially the latter, which became very influential in the countries of the Far East. The Silk Road lost importance as Rome decayed and the central steppes became pastures to lawless hordes. It was also interdicted to Europe by the Islamic advance to Central Asia. The Silk Road was opened again to trade with the West by the Mongols, who at the height of their power virtually controlled it along all of its length. Roughly, the Silk Road began in Xian (Sian), known to Ptolemy, the 2nd cent. AD Greek geographer, as Sera (silk); it followed part of the Great Wall, which it crossed at its western reaches, and went on to Tunghwang, on the eastern edge of the Tarim Basin. There it bifurcated into routes north (Kucha) and south (Khotan) of the Taklamakan Desert. The routes joined in Kashgaria, crossed the passes of the Pamirs between the Tien Shan and the Kunlun ranges and went on to Samarkand and Bactria. There the road went either south through Pakistan to ports on the Arabian Sea or west to Merv, through Persia, and on to Antioch, on the eastern Mediterranean. A related trade route, not usually associated to the ancient Silk Road, crossed the Kirghiz Steppes from Kashgar to the Crimea, where in the 15th cent. the Genoese had trading posts. The Silk Road mainly consisted of caravan routes and was divided into stages where goods were transhipped. To do the entire course, as the Venetian Polos did, was not usual.

South Africa
See entry in 'Dictionary' for the successive political divisions of South Africa.

South East Asia
South East Asia comprises Brunei, Cambodia, Indonesia, Laos, Malaysia, Myanmar, Philippines, Singapore, Thailand, and Vietnam. South East Asia was known to the 2nd cent. AD Greek geographer Ptolemy as the Golden Chersonese, from the Greek word for peninsula.

Southern Russia
Southern Russia is the region north of the Black Sea, half of which is today in Ukraine. In Russia itself it comprises Kuban. From the 13th to the 18th cents., southern Russia was politically separated from Russia itself and dominated mainly by Mongols, Turks, and Cossacks. Tauride is the Ancient Greek name for the area north of the Black Sea.

Spain
The historic regions of Spain are (geographical references in parentheses): Andalusia (southern Spain); Aragon (north-eastern Spain); Asturias (northern Spain; coast of the Cantabric Sea); Balearic Islands; Canary Islands; New Castile (central Spain); Old Castile (north Spain); Catalonia (north-eastern Spain; Mediterranean coast); Estremadura (western Spain); Galicia (north-western Spain); Leon (northern Spain); Levante (Valencia); Murcia (southern

Spain; east of Andalusia); Navarre (north east Spain); Valencia (eastern Spain); Vasconia (north-eastern Spain). Vasconia, the land of the Basques, is also known as País Vasco and Vascongadas. Navarre is Basque.

Sub-Saharan Africa

Sub-Saharan Africa comprises Burkina Fasso, Chad, Mali, Mauretania, Niger and northern Nigeria.

Sudetenland

The Sudetenland or Sudetes were the borderlands of CZECHOSLOVAKIA next to Germany. Peopled by Germans, they were the pretext with which Hitler got the go-ahead from FRANCE and GREAT BRITAIN to dismember Czechoslovakia in 1938. The Germans were expelled after World War II.

Sumatra

The huge Indonesian island of Sumatra (sixth largest in the world) was the home to the SRI VIJAYA empire (7th–13th cents.). Malayu, in east Sumatra, capital Jambi, had a moment of glory in the 13th cent. The island became part of the MAJAPAHIT EMPIRE (13th–14th cents.), after which it divided into Islamic 'harbour or estuary states', among which Samudra and Perlak, in northern Sumatra, were already important in the late 13th cent. Aceh was the most important Islamic state founded in Sumatra before Dutch rule (17th cent.).

Switzerland

See the entry in the 'Dictionary' for the cantons of Switzerland.

T

Tarim Basin

The basin of the Tarim River, which includes the river-swallowing Desert of Taklamakan, is today the southern part of the Chinese province of Xinjiang (Sinkiang). The Tarim Basin was the crux of the *Silk Road* from its beginnings before the Christian era. It was a vassal territory of the Chinese Han dynasty. From the 2nd cent. BC, it contained flourishing Indo-European-speaking communities such as Aksu, Kara Shahr, Kashgar, Khotan, Kucha, Turfan, and Yarkand. They disappeared in the 8th cent. During the 7th cent., Tarim was under T'ang suzerainty, which briefly gave ground to the Tanguts. In the 8th cent. it was invaded by the Turkish Uigurs, who are still a large part of its inhabitants – through emigration the ethnic Chinese or Han have become the majority – for which reason the Tarim Basin is also known as Uiguria or Chinese Turkestan. During the 13th and 14th cents. it was under Mongol influence. Its history after that is mostly of Chinese encroachment until the 18th cent. when the Ch'ing definitely established Chinese authority over the region. Turfan is the region east of the Tien Shan range, in the Xinjiang autonomous region of China. The city of Turfan was the capital of Uiguria. Although Kashgar (today's Kashi) is in the western extreme of the Tarim Basin, Kashgaria often refers to a region that includes the Pamir range as far as Ferghana and even the Issyk Kul Basin.

Thrace

A historical region of the south east Balkans, Thrace comprises southern Bulgaria, European Turkey, and north east Greece.

Tierra del Fuego

Literally land of fire in Spanish, Tierra del Fuego is a large island separated from the South American continent by the Strait of Magellan, named for its discoverer in 1520. Chile founded the city of Punta Arenas in 1847 on the north side of the strait. The city of Ushuaia was originally settled by missionaries in the 1870s in Tierra del Fuego proper. It was annexed by Argentina in 1884. Chile and Argentina delimited the island, with Chile taking the larger western part and Argentina the eastern part.

Transcaucasia

Transcaucasia is the region between the northern Russian watershed of the Caucasus mountains and the borders of Turkey and Iran. It includes Armenia, Georgia, and Azerbaijan.

Transoxiana

Transoxiana is a conventional, as opposed to native or telluric, designation for a territory which extends from the Aral Sea to Sogdiana. It is divided today between Kazakhstan, Uzbekistan and Turkmenistan. Since it lies between the Syrdarya (ancient Jaxartes) and the Amudarya rivers (ancient Oxus), it is literally the land beyond the Oxus. It contains the cities of Bukhara and Samarkand, which have sometimes given their names to states in Transoxiana.

Turan

Turan is a region east of the Aral Sea, divided by the Amudarya into Kizyl-Kum in the north and Kara-Kum in the south. Kizyl-Kum is in Uzbekistan and Kara-kum is in Turkmenistan.

Turkestan

Turkestan is the general designation for Turkic lands in central Asia. Informally, west Turkestan comprises the republics of Kazakhstan, Kyrgyzstan, Tajikistan, Turkmenistan, and Uzbekistan. Eastern or Chinese Turkestan is Xinjiang (Sinkiang), peopled by Uigurs (though not now a majority of the population). In the general area of western Turkestan, Tajiks speak an Indo-European language related to Iranian.

U

Ukraine

The main cities and provinces of Ukraine are: Crimea, Dnipropetrovsk, Donetsk, Kiev, Kharkov, Lviv (Lvov), Odessa. Historically, Ruthenia means Russia. The name was applied to Ukraine, but later to western Ukraine, including Galicia, Bukovina, and the tip of the Carpathians in Czechoslovakia joined to Ukraine after World War II. Bukovina is a region which comprises parts of south-western Ukraine, north-eastern Romania, and northern Moldova. Its historical capital is Chernotzy. Originally part of Kievan Rus (principality of Galich), Galicia became Polish in the 14th cent. After the first partition of Poland in 1772, the Habsburgs created Galicia with its capital in Lemberg (today's Lviv) out of southern Poland. After World War I, Poland acquired Galicia but had to cede eastern Galicia to the Ukraine after World War II. Podolia is a region of south-western Ukraine, north of Romania. Southern *Bessarabia*, which borders on the Black Sea south west of Odessa, today is part of the Ukraine. The huge Pripet marshes, partly in Belarus, are the summer counterpart of the great obstacle to invaders that is the Russian winter. They accounted in part for the slowing down of the invading Germans towards Moscow during World War II.

Ulster

Ulster is the traditional name of Northern Ireland (GREAT BRITAIN). It was settled by Scots Protestants during the 17th cent. Both Scots and English settlers benefited from the confiscations of land carried out under English rule as reprisals for Irish rebelliousness. The traditional counties of Northern Ireland are: Antrim, Armagh, Down, Fermanagh, and Londonderry. The capital is Belfast.

United States

The states of the American Union can be divided by regions (capitals in parentheses): *New England* includes Connecticut (Hartford), Maine (Augusta), Massachusetts (Boston), New Hampshire (Concord), Rhode Island (Providence), and Vermont (Montpelier); the *Mid-Atlantic states* are New Jersey (Trenton), New York (Albany), and Pennsylvania (Harrisburg); the *southern states* are by tradition: Alabama (Montgomery), Arkansas (Little Rock), Delaware (Dover), Florida (Tallahassee), Georgia (Atlanta), Louisiana (Baton Rouge), Maryland (Annapolis), Mississippi (Jackson), North Carolina (Raleigh), South Carolina (Columbia), Tennessee (Nashville), Texas (Austin), Virginia (Richmond), and West Virginia (Charleston); the *Midwest* includes the following states: Illinois (Springfield), Indiana (Indianapolis), Kentucky

(Frankfort), Michigan (Lansing), Ohio (Columbus), and Wisconsin (Madison); the *Plains* states are: Iowa (Des Moines), Kansas (Topeka), Minnesota (St Paul), Missouri (Jefferson City), Nebraska (Lincoln), North Dakota (Bismarck), Oklahoma (Oklahoma City), and South Dakota (Pierre); the *Rocky Mountain states* are: Arizona (Phoenix), Colorado (Denver), Idaho (Boise), Montana (Helena), New Mexico (Santa Fe), Nevada (Carson City), Utah (Salt Lake City), and Wyoming (Cheyenne); the *North-western states* are: Oregon (Salem) and Washington (Olympia); California (Sacramento); Alaska (Juneau); Hawaii (Honolulu). The capital of Puerto Rico, an American dependency in the Caribbean, is San Juan. The American capital is Washington, District of Columbia.

Today a state of the United States, Alaska was annexed by Russia in 1784. The Russian claim extended as far as the state of Washington, but in 1824 the southern borders of Alaska were established where they are today. Alaska was sold to the United States in 1867. Alaska includes the Aleutians Islands, south west of the mainland. Agattu, Attu, and Kiska, in the Aleutians, were occupied by the Japanese during World War II. Juneau is the capital of Alaska although Anchorage is its biggest city.

The largest American cities are New York (New York), Los Angeles (California), Chicago (Illinois), Houston (Texas), Philadelphia (Pennsylvania), San Diego (California), Phoenix (Arizona), and San Antonio (Texas). Except for Phoenix none is a capital of a state, although New York and Philadelphia served briefly as capitals of the Union.

W

Wales

Wales comprises Glamorgan and Gwent in the south, Dyfed and Powys in central Wales, and Clwyd and Gwynedd in the north.

Western Europe

Western Europe historically embraces all of Europe to the limits with Slavic lands. In a certain context it could mean strictly the west of Europe to the line separating the east and the west Franks. In the post-World War II context, Western Europe included all the European countries to the borders with communist countries, but it would include Greece though not Turkey.

BASIC GLOSSARY
OF POLITICAL TERMS

Appanage
A territorial holding usually in Russia and specifically the principalities in Kievan Rus.

Archbishop
A churchly title which can have territorial implications, usually in the Holy Roman Empire.

Archduke
A nobiliary title in the Habsburg Empire, the equivalent of princes, with little or no territorial implications.

Aristocracy
Informal term for government by the 'best', same as oligarchy.

Assembly
Same as Parliament.

Atabeg
A leader of a Turkish horde.

Atheling
English prince in Saxon times.

Autocrat
Greek term for dictator or sole ruler. Same as despot.

Autonomy
Self-rule though not necessarily independence.

Bakufu
'Tent government' in Japanese referring to the peculiar system by which emperors were 'governed' by dynastic warlords. It is the paradigmatic institutionalized form of indirect rule.

Baron
Formerly a holder of a fief, but usually now the lowest member of the nobiliary pecking order; a baronet is even lower.

Basileus
Title of Byzantine emperors.

Bey
Turkish term for governors in the Ottoman Empire, who sometimes became outright kings.

Bishop
A churchly title which in Europe can have political and territorial implications.

Bishopric
The territorial or religious jurisdiction of a bishop; same as See.

Boyar
Russian noble, intermittently powerful.

Buffer
A country that just missed being a dependency because it lay between two colonialist rivals.

Cacique
Chieftain among Amerindians; often now in Spanish, political boss.

Caliph
Strictly speaking, successor of Muhammad in Arabic, but denoted theocratic Arab kingship. The title decayed under the Abbasids but was held by the Ottoman emperors.

Caliphate
The area over which a Caliph ruled, city, country, or empire.

Canton
The basic political subdivision in Switzerland, but can connote region.

Captaincy general
Usually in Spanish, a province in the Spanish Colonial Empire.

Caudillo
Title assumed by Franco in Spain (like Duce and Führer), but in general in Spanish any leader.

Chairman
In China, the equivalent of secretary general of the central committee of a communist party, especially in China, as in chairman Mao; Deng Xiaoping ruled as chairman of the central military committee of the central committee of the Chinese communist party.

Chieftain
Any head of any group.

City–state
A small state comprising a city usually with its surrounding territory.

Colony
A dependency.

Commandery
A military district in Chinese history.

Commonwealth
A country or state, often implying federation or confederation. The French term *mancommunité* leans more to federation. It can also mean an association of independent states.

Comte
A French count, possessor of a *comté* (county).

Confederation
Same as federation, but with greater voluntary implication.

Count
Usually a French nobiliary title with territorial implications, the equivalent of an English earl.

County
The land ruled by a count, usually small. In Great Britain it is the principal political subdivision. In the United States it refers to the subdivisions of states, but there are no American counts.

Daimyo
Japanese feudal lord; very powerful until Meiji restoration.

Dependency
A colony or a dependent state. In Marxist parlance any 'developing country'.

Despot
Same as autocrat, but more formal. It can mean a king without a dynasty. But see despotate.

Despotate
Usually a kingdom, though not necessarily without dynastic implications.

District
In England it can mean a region. Usually a political subdivision of a political subdivision. In Portugal it is the basic political subdivision.

Dictator
Same as autocrat, especially if as a result of *coup d'état*.

Domain
The territory of a ruler. Fiefs were domains.

Dominion
In the British Colonial Empire, dominion denoted self-rule with allegiance to the British Crown. The dominions were Australia, Canada, New Zealand, and South Africa. Ireland was the Irish Free State, although this status was conditioned to allegiance to the Crown, which it shed when it became the Republic of Ireland. South Africa also chose to be a republic. Both countries withdrew from the Commonwealth of Nations. Technically, Australia, Canada, and New Zealand are still dominions. India never achieved the status of dominion, but went straight from colony to independence.

Duce

Leader in Italian, the title assumed by Mussolini. Copy-cat Hitler used Führer.

Duchy

Territory of a duke, frequent in France during the *ancien régime.*

Duke

A nobiliary title with definite territorial implications below kingdom. Comes from Latin *dux* or leader. In German a duke (*Herzog*) is a higher rank than prince.

Dux

In the late Roman empire, leader of troops, whence duke.

Dynast

A king belonging to a dynasty, usually connotes much solemnity.

Dynasty

A succession of rulers tied by blood relationships, though not necessarily father to son. Usually connotes legitimacy.

Earl

English nobiliary title with territorial implications, the equivalent of the French *comte.*

Earldom

The territory of an earl.

Emir

A viceroy in Arabic or the king of a small state. Same as bey.

Emirate

The territory of an emir.

Emperor

The ruler of a kingdom comprising peoples and countries different from the core land and population of the emperor. It can also be an exhalted form of king.

Empire

A state usually large comprising many different populations and dependent states.

Federation

An association, usually voluntary, of states or provinces to form a state. It can also mean an association of dependencies, in this sense much used under the British Colonial Empire.

Fief

The territory of a feudal lord, with obligations to a king, mostly in Europe.

Theoretically a fief lord was sovereign in his domain. Sometimes it just means a parcel of power.

Fiefdom
Same as fief.

Governance
Same as government, with orderly and rational implications.

Government
Any constituted authority but it doesn't entail independence.

Governor
The head of a political subdivision as of the states of the United States.

Grandee
Comes from 'grande' or 'great' in Spanish, and means a super-lord, as opposed to say, hidalgo, a lowly squire, like Don Quixote.

Herzog
Duke in German.

Hospodar
Governor of a province of the Ottoman Empire.

Independent and independence
Same as sovereignty, theoretically untrammelled.

Kaiser
King or emperor in German, from a surmised pronunciation of Caesar in Latin.

Khagan
A Mongol king with the honorific implication of greater than a khan, hence a khan of khans, like the Persian Shahanshah.

Khan
A Mongol king of land or hordes; also Gur-Khan.

Khanate
The land or peoples of a khan.

King
The ruler of an independent state usually belonging to a dynasty. Constitutional kings or monarchs today have mostly purely formal or ceremonial functions.

Kingdom
A state ruled by a king, formerly in fact but today mostly ceremonially, at least in Europe. As there are kings without kingdoms, so there have been kingdoms without kings, such as Arles. Lesser realms in the Holy Roman Empire

upgraded to kingship of emperorship (e.g., Austria or Prussia) by conquering outside its frontiers.

Landgrave
Count in German.

Legislature
Same as Parliament.

Legitimacy
Either dynastic succession or elective government. In any event, a *coup d'état* is a break in legitimacy and tends to breed unbridled ambitions, the enemy of legitimacy.

Lord
Any member of any nobility; in Great Britain, anybody who can be addressed as 'sir' (or 'lady'); frequently, a ruler as in the 'lord of us all'; the Lord of Hosts is Christ.

Lordship
English nobiliary form of address (sometimes ironical), but also rulership.

Mahdi
Muslim Messiah, with strong political implications, especially in the Sudan.

Mandate
Under the League of Nations, any territory or country handed over to another for administrative purposes.

March, Marche, or Mark
A borderland, especially if created for conquest or in opposition to its previous settlers or conquerors. The term is common in early western European history.

Margrave
A German nobiliary title with territorial implications, common in the Holy Roman Empire. It is the equivalent of marquis.

Margravate
The territory ruled by a margrave.

Marquis
Usually a French nobiliary title with territorial implications. In the hierarchy of nobility, it is below duke but above *comte* or earl. In English the equivalent is marquess.

Mirza
Iranian prince, sometimes combined with proper name to designate specific rulers, as Mirza Abdallah.

Monarch
One ruler, meaning pompously king.

Monarchy
Same as kingdom.

Nabob or nawab
A Mughal local ruler in India, originally perhaps a viceroy, but given the peculiarities of Indian history usually sovereign.

Nation
A sovereign state or country, but it can also mean a people whether independent or not.

Nizam
Same as Nawab.

Oblast
Province in Russian, basic subdivision.

Oligarchy
Government by a few; under capitalism, a plutocracy.

Overlord
A ruler in general but also a ruler over other rulers or a people that rules a dependency.

Parliament
The English proto-typical name for legislative bodies, usually under or conjoint with executive authority, but sometimes, as in the Long Parliament of the French *Assemblée Nationale*, virtually sovereign. Parliaments have many names: Congress in America; Duma in Russia; Cortes in Spain; Reichstag in Germany; Diet in Japan (but also in Europe especially in the Holy Roman Empire); Sejm in Poland; Majles in Iran; Folketing in Denmark; Knesset in Israel; and so on. Reputedly, the oldest Parliament is the Icelandic Althing. Parliaments often have an upper and a lower house or chamber: in Great Britain the upper chamber is called the House of Lords and in America the Senate (a Roman term). The lower chambers are, respectively, the House of Commons and the House of Representatives; in France, the Chamber of Deputies. A Soviet is a Russian popular assembly, usually radical and irregularly elected.

Pasha
An Ottoman term connoting merit or distinction, but the Pashas of Egypt were viceroys who effectively became kings.

Patriarch and Patriarchate
The equivalents in the Orhodox Church of Bishop and Bishopric or See;

Although influential, Patriarchs did not attain the political power that some of their Western counterparts did.

Plutocracy
Usually connotes indirect rule of the rich for their own benefit.

Polity
Same as state.

Pope
The head of the Roman Catholic Church, formerly a powerful king in his own right; today, the head of state of Vatican City.

Prefect
The executive of a French prefecture, appointed in Paris.

Prefecture
The basic political subdivision in France.

Premier
Same as prime minister in France.

Presidency
The office of the president but in Spanish history a governor, usually in the Spanish Colonial Empire.

President
The head of state of a republic. It is often a ceremonial post akin to a constitutional king.

Prime minister
The head of state in a parliamentary system, usually where presidents have formal or ceremonial functions.

Primogeniture
The right by which the eldest son of a king inherits the kingdom, or the sons of nobles inherit their titles. This principle is carried to extremes in Spain where grandees have lists of titles as long as those of kings.

Prince
The son of a king, and if with a proper name like Asturias or Wales, the heir to the throne. Princes were rulers of states in the Holy Roman Empire. Princes in Russia were a dime a dozen, because primogeniture did not exist.

Principality
Principally, states in the Holy Roman Empire.

Protector or Lord Protector
The title given to Cromwell, meaning virtual dictator.

Rajah
King in India and ancient South East Asia.

Realm
Same as domain, but connoting kingship.

Regent
Ruler during the minority of a king.

Republic
Government by election, although elections in communist Democratic and People's republics were not, and still aren't, impartial. Under the Soviet system, Russia was a federated republic because it included many autonomous republics; autonomous republic meant non-Russian. The system is still in place.

Satrap
Viceroy or governor in the Achaemenid Empire.

Satrapy
The subdivisions of the Achaemenid Empire.

Satellite
Member of Soviet Empire, often called Democratic Republic or People's Republic.

Secretary General
Strictly speaking, the virtual chief of the political bureau, or standing committee, of the central committee or ruling body of a communist party; in practice, chief holder of power under a communist system. The secretary general of the United Nations has very little power.

Seigneur
A French form of nobiliary address, but also a lord of lands, usually fiefs.

Seigneurie
Same as fief.

Seneschal
In Medieval Europe, chief household lord, through which position the Carolingians took over Merovingian France.

Shah
In Iranian, a king.

Shahanshah
In Iranian, king of kings, like khagan among Mongols. Muhammad Rehza Pallavi styled himself shahanshah.

Sharif

The governor of the sharifate of Mecca in the Ottoman Empire. American sheriffs are usually heads of police in counties.

Shiek

Islamic and specifically Arabic local ruler.

Shogun

In Japan a warlord, usually the virtual king under the Bakufu system.

Signoria

Italian nobiliary form of address, but also government in the Middle Ages, although not fief as in French *seigneurie*.

Sovereign

King in the sense of effective supreme rulership.

Sovereignty

Rule in the full sense or self-rule without restrictions.

Stadholder

Formerly, the political leader of Amsterdam and by extension of the Netherlands.

State

A sovereign entity, but also semi-sovereign entities, as in the Holy Roman Empire. In an abstract very Latin sense, state (invariably capitalized) is the abstract notion of government as the ultimate, 'just' arbiter.

Statelet

A slightly pejorative term implying smallness, impermanency, or lack of history.

Statesman

A distinguished ruler; often, a politician.

Sultan

Ottoman emperor.

Sultanate

The government of the sultan, not, however, synonymous with empire.

Suzerain

In Feudal terms, an overlord, the king being the uppermost suzerain.

Suzerainty

Feudal overlordship.

Theme

The basic subdivisions of the Byzantine Empire, with military connotations.

Theocracy
An informal term designating direct or indirect government by priests of a religion. In Iran today the theocrats are called mullahs.

Trustee and Trusteeship
Same as mandate but under the United Nations.

Tsar
Russian emperor, from Caesar.

Tyrant
Same as autocrat or dictator, emphasizing arbitrary rule, but in Ancient Greece it just meant despot.

Ulus
Mongol clans and, given their nomadic character, basically subdivisions of hordes.

Vassal
The subject of a suzerain, but also anyone in a subservient or dependent condition.

Vassalage
The condition of a vassal.

Zamorin
Obscure title for local king in India.

INDEX OF
CHRONOLOGIES
AND MAPS

CHRONOLOGIES

MAPS

GENERAL INDEX

All names in bold are entries in the 'Dictionary';
references in italics are to 'Provinces and Regions'.

Algeria
Allied Powers (**France**)
Alma Ata (**Kazakhstan**)
Almohads
Almoravids
Alpes Cottiae (*Roman Empire*)
Alpes Maritimae (*Roman Empire*)
Alpes Poeninae (*Roman Empire*)
Alsace (**France**)
Altamira (**Spain**)
Alto Adigio (*Italy*)
Amalfi
Amarapura (**Myanmar**)
Amazonia (*Amazonia*)
Ambon (*Indonesia*)
American Samoa (**United States**)
Amerindians (*Amerindians*)
Amiens (*France*)
Amisus (colonies of *Greece (Ancient)*)
Amman (**Jordan**)
Amorites
Amphictyony (**Great Amphictyony**)
Amritsar (**British India**)
Amsterdam (**Netherlands**)
Amudarya (*Transoxiana*)
Amur (*Central Asia*)
An Nafud (*Arabia*)
Anatolia (*Anatolia*)
Anatolian Emirates
Ancient Lorraine (*Lorraine*)
Ancona (*Italy*)
Andalusia (*Spain*)
Andaman Islands (*India*)
Andhra Pradesh (*India*)
Andorra
Andros (**Greece**)
Anga (**Magadha**)
Angers (*France*)
Angkor
Anglo-Egyptian Sudan (**British Colonial Empire**)

Anglo Saxons (**England**)
Angola
Angouleme (*France*)
Angoumois (*France*)
Anguila (**British Colonial Empire**)
Anhui (Anhwei) (*China*)
Anjou (*France*)
Ankara (**Turkey**)
Annam
Annapolis (*United States*)
Anschluss (**Austria**)
Anse-au-Meadows (**Canada; Norsemen**)
Antakya (**Turkey**)
Antananarivo (**Madagascar**)
Antarctica (*Antarctica*)
Antigonids (**Ancient Greece**)
Antigua and Barbuda
Antigua and Montserrat (**British Colonial Empire**)
Antigua Guatemala (**Guatemala**)
Antilles (*Antilles*)
Antioch
Antioch (**Seleucid Empire**)
Antofagasta (**Chile**)
Antrim (*Ulster*)
Antwerp (*Belgium*)
Anuradhapuri (**Sri Lanka**)
Anyang (**Shang**)
Apia (**Samoa**)
Apollonia (colonies of *Greece (Ancient)*)
Appenzell (**Switzerland**)
Apulia (**Imperial Italy**)
Aq-Qoyunlu
Aquileia
Aquitaine
Aquitania (*Roman Empire*)
Arab Federation (**Jordan**)
Arabia (*Arabia*)
Arabia Petraea (*Roman Empire*)
Arabistan (*Sasanid Empire*)
Arabs and Arabic

Autun (**Franks**)
Auvergne (*France*)
Ava (**Myanmar**)
Avanti (**Vedic India**)
Avaria (**Avars**)
Avaris (**Hyksos**)
Avars
Avignon (**France**)
Avon (*England*)
Axis (*Germany*)
Axum
Ayacucho (**Peru**)
Aydin (**Anatolian Emirates**)
Ayutthaya
Ayyubid Sultanate
Azerbaijan
Azerbaijan East (*Iran*)
Azerbaijan Soviet Socialist Republic
  (**Azerbaijan**)
Azerbaijan West (*Iran*)
Azores (**Portugal**)
Aztec Empire

Babylon (**Babylonia**)
Babylonia
Babylonian captivity (**Papal States**)
Bactria
Badajoz (**Muslim Spain**)
Baden (**Habsburg Empire**)
Baden-Württemberg (*Germany*)
Baetica (*Roman Empire*)
Baffin Island (**Canada**)
Baghdad (**Abbasid Caliphate**)
Bahamas
Bahia or Baia (**Portuguese Colonial
  Empire**)
Bahia Blanco (**Argentina**)
Bahmani Sultanate
Bahrain
Bahris (**Mameluke Sultanate**)
Baikal (*Central Asia*)
Bairiki (**Kiribati**)
Baja California (*Mexico*)

Bakhtyari (*Iran*)
Baku (**Azerbaijan**)
Balasagan (*Sasanid Empire*)
Balearic Islands (**Aragon**; *Spain*)
Bali (*Indonesia*)
Balkans (*Balkans*)
Balkash (*Central Asia*)
Balkh (**Bactria**)
Baltic Region (*Baltic Region*)
Baluchistan (*Pakistan*)
Bamako (**Mali**)
Bambara
Banat (**Habsburg Empire**; *Banat*)
Banda Oriental (**Uruguay**)
Bandar-e-Abbas (*Iran*)
Bandar Seri Begawan (**Brunei**)
Bandas (*Indonesia*)
Bangalore (*India*)
Bangladesh
Bangui (**Central African Republic**)
Banjarmasin Sultanate (*Indonesia*)
Banjul (**Gambia**)
Bannockburn (**Scotland**)
Bantustans (**Bophuthatswana**)
Barbados
Barbary States
Barca (**Carthage**)
Barcelona
Bari (**Norman Italy**)
Baroda (**Maratha Kingdoms**)
Barotseland (**Zambia**)
Basel (**Switzerland**)
Bashkortostan (*Russia*)
Basilicata (*Italy*)
Basques
Basra (**Iraq**)
Basseterre (**St Kitts and Nevis**)
Basutholand (**Lesotho; South
  Africa**)
Batavia (**Dutch Colonial Empire**)
Batavian Republic (**French
  European Empire**)
Batavii (**Netherlands**)

Bouvert (**Norway**)
Boyacá (**Colombia**)
Boyne (**Ireland**)
Brabant (**Belgium**; **Netherlands**)
Brandenburg (*Germany*)
Brasilia (**Brazil**)
Bratislava (**Slovakia**)
Brazil
Brazzaville (**Congo (Republic of the)**)
Bregenz (*Austria*)
Bremen (**Holy Roman Empire**)
Brescia (**Lombard League**)
Breslau (*Silesia*)
Brest (**Belarus**)
Brigantes (**Vandals**)
Brisbane (**Australia**)
Britannia (*Roman Empire*)
Britanny (*France*)
British Antarctica (**Great Britain**)
British Colonial Empire
British Columbia (**Canada**)
British East India Company
British Guiana (**Guyana**)
British Honduras (**Belize**)
British India
British Indian Ocean Territory (**Great Britain**)
British New Guinea (**British Colonial Empire**; **Papua New Guinea**)
British Papua (**British Colonial Empire**)
British Somaliland (**Somalia**)
British Virgin Islands (**Great Britain**)
British Windward Islands (*Antilles*)
Bruges (**Flanders**)
Brunei
Brussels (**Belgium**; **European Union**)
Bubastis (**Pharaonic Egypt**)
Buckinghamshire (*England*)

Buda (**Hungary**)
Budapest (**Hungary**)
Buenos Aires (**Argentina**)
Buganda
Bujumbura (**Burundi**)
Bukhara (Khanate of)
Bukovina (*Ukraine*)
Bulgaria
Bulgars
Burgenland (*Austria*)
Burgundians
Burgundy (Duchy of)
Burgundy (*France*)
Burgundy (Kingdom of)
Burkina Fasso
Burma
Bursa (**Ottoman Empire**)
Burshehr (*Iran*)
Buru (*Indonesia*)
Burundi
Buryatia (*Russia*)
Buyid Persia
Byblos (**Phoenicia**)
Byelorussia or Belorussia (**Belarus**)
Byelorussian Soviet Socialist Republic (**USSR**)
Bytown (**Canada**)
Byzantine Empire
Byzantine Italy
Byzantium (**Rome**)

Cadiz (**Spanish Colonial Empire**)
Cairo (**Egypt**)
Cajuns (*Acadia*)
Calabria (**Norman Italy**; *Italy*)
Calais (**England**)
Calcutta (**British India**)
Caledonia (**Scotland**)
Calgary (**Canada**)
Calicut
California (*United States*)

Chalcidice (**Greece**)
Chaldean Empire
Châlons-sur-Marne (**Huns**)
Chalukyas (**Central India**)
Chambéry (**Savoy**; *France*)
Champa
Champa (**Vedic India**)
Champagne (*France*)
Champassak
Chandella (**Rajputs**)
Chandigarh (**Punjab**)
Changan (**T'ang/Tang**)
Changchun (*China*)
Changsha (*China*)
Channel Islands (**Great Britain**)
Characene (**Parthia**)
Charcas (**Bolivia**)
Charleston (**United States**)
Charlottetown (**Canada**)
Charolais (**Burgundy (Duchy of)**;
  Franche Comté)
Chavin (**Pre-Columbian Cultures
  (South America)**)
Cheboksary (*Russia*)
Chechnya (*Chechnya*)
Chengdu (*China*)
Chenla
Chera (**Southern India**)
Cherkessk (*Russia*)
Chernigov (**Russia**)
Chernotzy (*Ukraine*)
Chersonese (**Bosporan Kingdom**)
Chersonesus (colonies of *Greece
  (Ancient)*)
Cheshire (*England*)
Chester (**England**)
Cheyenne (*United States*)
Chiapas (*Mexico*)
Chichen Itzá (**Mayan Civilization**)
Chichimecs
Chieng Mai
Chihuahua (*Mexico*)
Chile

Chimú (**Pre-Columbian Cultures
  (South America)**)
Chin (Jin)
China
Chinese Turkestan (*Tarim Basin*)
Chios (**Greece**)
Chisinau (**Moldova**)
Cholamandalam (*India*)
Cholas
Chongqing (Chunking) (**China**)
Chorasmia (**Khwarizm**)
Chosen (**Japanese Colonial
  Empire**)
Choshu (**Japan**)
Choson (**Korea**)
Chou (Zhou)
Christiania (**Norway**)
Christmas Island (**Australia**)
Chuckchi (**Russia**)
Chuquisaca (**Bolivia**)
Chuvashia (*Russia*)
Cilicia (**Rome**; *Achaemenid Empire*;
  Anatolia)   ,
Cimmerians
Circassia (*Russia*)
Cirtus (**Numidia**)
Cisalpine Republic (**French
  European Empire**)
Cisjurane Burgundy (*France*)
Ciskei
Ciudad Vieja (**Guatemala**)
Clare (*Ireland*)
Clazomene (regions of *Greece
  (Ancient)*)
Clermont-Ferrand (*France*)
Cleveland (*England*)
Cleves (**Prussia**)
Clwyd (*Wales*)
Coahuila (**Texas**; *Mexico*)
Cochin (**Portuguese Colonial
  Empire**)
Cochin China (**French Colonial
  Empire**)

Cyzicus (colonies of *Greece (Ancient)*)
Czech and Slovak Federal Republic
Czech Republic
Czechoslovakia

Dacca or Dhaka (**Bangladesh**)
Dacia (**Romania**)
Dagestan (*Russia*)
Dahomey
Dai Viet
Dakar (**Senegal**)
Dalap-Uliga-Darrit (**Marshall Islands**)
Dalmatia (**Croatia**)
Daman (**Portuguese Colonial Empire**; *India*)
Damascus
Damascus (**Syria**)
Danang (**Vietnam**)
Danelaw (**England**)
Danishmandids (**Seljuk Emirates**)
Danzig
Dar es Salaam (**Tanzania**)
Darfur (**Wadai**)
Darien (*Darien*)
Darwin (**Australia**)
Dascylum (colonies of *Greece (Ancient)*)
Dauphiné (**France**; **Savoy**)
Dayton (**Bosnia-Herzegovina**)
Deccan
Deccan Sultanates
Deir el-Bahri (**Pharaonic Egypt**)
Delaware (*United States*)
Delhi (**India**)
Delhi Sultanate
Delian League
Delphi (**Great Amphictyony**)
Demak (**Majapahit Empire**)
Dendera (**Pharaonic Egypt**)
Denia (**Muslim Spain**)

Denmark
Denver (*United States*)
Derbyshire (*England*)
Des Moines (*United States*)
Devon (*England*)
Diadochi Wars
Diaspora (**Babylonia**)
Diego Garcia (**Great Britain**)
Dien Bien Phu (**Vietnam**)
Dijon (**Burgundy (Duchy of)**)
Dili (**East Timor**)
Dilmun
Dioscurias (colonies of *Greece (Ancient)*)
Dispur (*India*)
Diu (**Portuguese Colonial Empire**; *India*)
Diyarbakir (**Aq-Qoyunlu**)
Djibouti
Dniester (**Moldavia**)
Doab (*Mesopotamia*)
Dobruja (**Romania**)
Dodecanese Islands (**Greece**; **Italian Colonial Empire**)
Dodoma (**Tanzania**)
Dodona (colonies of *Greece (Ancient)*)
Doha (**Qatar**)
Dominica
Dominican Republic
Donegal (*Ireland*)
Donetsk (*Ukraine*)
Dong Kinh (**Vietnam**)
Dorians (**Mycenean Greece**)
Dorset (*England*)
Dortmund (**Holy Roman Empire**)
Dover (*United States*)
Down (*Ireland*)
Drangiana (**Afghanistan**; *Achaemenid Empire*)
Dravidians (**Vedic India**)
Drenthe (*Netherlands*)
Dresden (**Holy Roman Empire**)

Estremadura (*Portugal*)
Estremadura (*Spain*)
Ethiopia
Etruria
Etruria (**French European Empire**)
Euboea (**Venice**; *Greece (Ancient)*)
Euhesperides (colonies of *Greece (Ancient)*)
European Coal and Steel Community (**European Union**)
European Economic Community (**European Union**)
European Union
Eylau (**France**)

Faenza (**Papal States**; *Pentapolis*)
Falkland Islands (**Great Britain**)
Fano (*Italy*)
Far East (*Far East*)
Faroe Islands (*Faroe Islands*)
Fars (**Iran**)
Fashoda (**French Colonial Empire**)
Fatimid Caliphate
Fayum (**Pharaonic Egypt**)
Federated Malay States (**Malaysia**)
Federation of Malaya (**Malaysia**)
Federation of Rhodesia and Nyasaland (**Rhodesia**)
Federation of South Arabia (**South Yemen**)
Federation of the Emirates of the South (**South Yemen**)
Federation of the West Indies (**British Colonial Empire**)
Ferghana (**Uzbekistan**)
Fermanagh (*Ulster*)
Fernando Po (**Equatorial Guinea**)
Ferrara
Fez (**Morocco**)
Fife (*Scotland*)
Fiji
Fingal (*Ireland*)
Finland

Finnmark (*Lapland*)
First Intermediate Period (**Pharaonic Egypt**)
Firth of Forth (**Scotland**)
Fiume (**Italy**)
Five Dynasties
Flanders
Flemish Brabant (*Belgium*)
Flevoland (*Netherlands*)
Flodden Field (**Scotland**)
Florence
Flores (*Indonesia*)
Florida (**Spanish Colonial Empire**; *United States*)
Foix (**Andorra**; *France*)
Fongafale (**Tuvalu**)
Formosa (**Taiwan**)
France
Franche Comté (**Burgundy**; **France**)
Franconia (**Holy Roman Empire**)
Frankfort (*United States*)
Frankfurt am Main (**Holy Roman Empire**)
Franks
Fredericton (**Canada**)
Free Imperial Cities
Free Italian Communes
Freetown (**Sierra Leone**)
French Colonial Empire
French Community
French Congo (**French Colonial Empire**)
French Crown Flanders (**Flanders**)
French Equatorial Africa (**French Colonial Empire**)
French European Empire
French Flanders (**Flanders**)
French Guiana (**French Colonial Empire**)
French Lorraine (*Lorraine*)
French Louisiana (**French Colonial Empire**)

French Navarre (**Navarre**)
French Polynesia (**France**)
French Ruling Dynasties and Regimes
French Southern and Antarctic Lands (**France**)
French Sudan (**French Colonial Empire**)
French West Africa (**French Colonial Empire**)
Fribourg (**Switzerland**)
Friesland (*Netherlands*)
Frisia (*Netherlands*)
Friuli (**Lombard Italy**; **Venice**; *Italy*)   ,
Frobisher Bay (**Canada**)
Frontera (*Mexico*)
Fujairah
Fujian (Fukien) (*China*)
Fulani
Funafuti (**Tuvalu**)
Funan
Funj
Fur
Fuzhou (*China*)

Gabon
Gadsden Purchase (**United States**)
Galápagos Islands (**Ecuador**)
Galatia (*Roman Empire*)
Galich (**Russia**)
Galicia (**Habsburg Empire**; *Ukraine*)
Galicia (**Sueves**; *Spain*)
Gallipoli (**Ottoman Empire**; *Dardanelles*)
Galway (*Ireland*)
Gambia (The)
Gandhara (*Pakistan*)
Gangtok (*India*)
Gansu (Kansu) (*China*)
Gascony (*France*)
Gath (**Philistia**)

Gauteng (**South Africa**)
Gaza (**Philistia**; **Palestine Authority**)
Gdansk
Gedrosia (*Achaemenid Empire*)
Gela (colonies of *Greece (Ancient)*)
Gelderland (*Netherlands*)
Geldern (*Netherlands*)
Geneva (**Switzerland**; **United Nations**)
Genoa
Georgetown (**Barbados**)
Georgetown (**Guyana**)
Georgia
Georgia (*United States*)
Gepids
Gerar (**Philistia**)
German Colonial Empire
German Confederation
German South West Africa (**Namibia**)
Germania Superior (*Roman Empire*)
Germania Inferior (*Roman Empire*)
Germania (*Germany*)
Germans
Germany
Gettysburg (**Confederate States of America**; **United States**)
Ghana (ancient)
Ghana
Ghaznavids
Ghazni (**Afghanistan**; **Delhi Sultanate**; **Ghaznavids**)
Ghent (**Flanders**)
Ghibellines (**Holy Roman Empire**; **Imperial Italy**)
Ghizhou (Kweichow) (*China*)
Ghur (**Ghurids**)
Ghurids
Ghurkas (**Nepal**)
Ghuzz
Gibraltar (**Great Britain**)
Gila (**United States**)

Gilan (*Iran*)
Gilbert and Ellice Islands (**Kiribati**; **Tuvalu**)
Gilbert Islands (**Kiribati**)
Gingisids (**Yuan**)
Giza (**Pharaonic Egypt**)
Glamorgan (*Wales*)
Glarus (**Switzerland**)
Glasgow (*Scotland*)
Gloucestershire (*England*)
Gniezmo (**Poland**)
Goa (**Portuguese Colonial Empire**; *India*)
Gobi (**Central Asia**)
Godthab (*Greenland*)
Golan Heights (**Israel**; **Syria**)
Golconda
Gold Coast (**Ghana**)
Golden Chersonese (*South East Asia*)
Golden Horde
Gondar (**Ethiopia**)
Gondwana
Gordium (**Phrygia**)
Gordyene (**Parthia**)
Gorgan (*Sasanid Empire*)
Gorno-Altaisk (*Russia*)
Gothia
Goths
Gotland (*Scandinavia*)
Grampian (*Scotland*)
Gran Chaco (**Paraguay**)
Gran Colombia
Granada (**Nicaragua**)
Granada
Grande Comore (**Comoros**)
Graz (*Austria*)
Great Amphictyony
Great Britain
Great Bulgaria
Great Horde (**Kirghiz-Kazakhs**)
Great Moravia
Greater Antilles (*Antilles*)

Greater Armenia (**Armenia**)
Greater Mongolia (*Mongolia*)
Greater Poland (**Poland**; *Poland*)
Greece (Ancient)
Greece
Greenland (*Greenland*)
Grenada
Grenadines (**St Vincent**)
Grenoble (*France*)
Griquanaland West (**South Africa**)
Grisons (**Switzerland**)
Groningen (*Netherlands*)
Grozny (*Chechnya*)
Guadalajara (**Mexico**)
Guadalcanal (**Solomon Islands**)
Guadalete (**Asturias**)
Guadeloupe (**France**)
Guam (**United States**)
Guangdong (Kwantung) (*China*)
Guangxi Zhuangzu (Kwangsi) (*China*)
Guangzhou (Canton) (*China*)
Guantanamo Bay (**Cuba**; **United States**)
Guaraní (**Paraguay**)
Guatemala
Guatemala City (**Guatemala**)
Guayana (*Guiana*)
Guayaquil (**Ecuador**)
Guelphs (**Holy Roman Empire**; **Imperial Italy**)
Guéret (*France*)
Guernsey (**Great Britain**)
Guiana (*Guiana*)
Guienne or Guyenne (*France*)
Guinea
Guinea (*Guinea*)
Guinea-Bissau
Guipúzcoa (**Vasconia**)
Guiyang (*China*)
Gujarat
Guptas
Guria (**Georgia**)

Gurjara Pratiharas (**Rajputs**)
Gutians
Guyana
Gwailor (**Maratha Kingdoms**)
Gwent (*Wales*)
Gwynedd (*Wales*)

Haarlem (*Netherlands*)
Habsburg Empire
Hadar (**Arabs and Arabic**)
Hadramaut (*Arabia*)
Hadrumetum (**Phoenicia**)
Hafsids
Haifa (**Israel**)
Hainaut (**Flanders**)
Haiti
Hakata (**Mongol Empire**)
Halifax (**Canada**)
Halmahera (*Indonesia*)
Hamadan (**Iran; Seljuk Persia**)
Hamburg (**Hanseatic League;**
    Germany)
Hamdanids (**Abbasid Caliphate**)
Hampshire (*England*)
Han (**T'ang/Tang**)
Han
Hangai (*Central Asia*)
Hangzhou (Hangchow) (*China*)
Hanoi (**Vietnam**)
Hanover (*Germany*)
Hanseatic League
Harappa
Harare (**Zimbabwe**)
Harbin (*China*)
Hargeisha (**Somalia**)
Harrisburg (*United States*)
Harsha's Kingdom
Hartford (*United States*)
Haryana (*India*)
Hasmodeans (**Judah**)
Hastings (**England**)
Hattin (**Ayyubid Sultanate**)
Hattusas (**Hittite Kingdom**)

Hausa
Hausaland (**Nigeria**)
Haute Volta
Havana (**Cuba**)
Hawaii
Heard and McDonald Islands
    (**Australia**)
Hebei (Hopei) (*China*)
Hebrides (*Scotland*)
Hefei (*China*)
Heilongjiang (Heilunkiang) (*China*)
Hejaz (**Mecca**)
Helena (*United States*)
Heligoland (**British Colonial**
    Empire)
Hellespont (*Dardanelles*)
Helsinki (**Finland**)
Helvetian Republic (**French**
    European Empire)
Henan (Honan) (*China*)
Hephthalites
Heptarchy (**England**)
Herat (**Iran**; *Khurasan*)
Hereford and Worcester (*England*)
Herero (**Namibia**)
Hertfordshire (*England*)
Hesse (**Holy Roman Empire**;
    Germany)
Hibernia (**Ireland**)
Hierakonpolis (**Pharaonic Egypt**)
Highlands (*Scotland*)
Himachal Pradesh (*India*)
Hippo (**Numidia**)
Hippo Regius (**Phoenicia**)
Hipponium (colonies of *Greece
    (Ancient)*)
Hiroshima (**Japan**)
Hispaniola (*Antilles*)
Hittite Kingdom
Hobart (**Australia**)
Hohenstaufen Italy
Hohhot (*China*)
Hokkaido (**Japan**)

Holland
Holy Alliance (**Vienna, Congress of**)
Holy Roman Empire
Home Counties (*England*)
Homel (**Belarus**)
Homs (**Abbasid Caliphate**)
Honduras
Hong Kong (*Hong Kong*)
Honiara (**Solomon Islands**)
Honolulu (*United States*)
Honshu (**Japan**) , ,
Honshu/Chugoku (*Japan*)
Honshu/Kanto (*Japan*)
Honshu/Kinki (*Japan*)
Honshu/Tohoku (*Japan*)
Hormozgan (*Iran*)
Hormuz (**Portuguese Colonial Empire**)
Ho-t'ien (*Silk Road*)
Hoysalas (**Southern India**)
Hrodno (**Belarus**)
Hsia
Hsien-Pi
Hsi-Hsia
Hsin
Hsiung-nu
Hsiung-nu (western)
Huang Ho (**Shang**)
Huastecs (**Mesoamerican Civilizations**)
Hubei (Hupeh) (*China*)
Hudson's Bay Company (*Hudson's Bay Company*)
Hué (**Vietnam**)
Huesca (**Aragon**)
Hunan (*China*)
Hungary
Huns
Hurrians
Husseins (**Tunisia**)
Hyderabad
Hyksos

Hyrcania (*Sasanid Empire*)

Iberia (**Georgia**)
Iberia (**Spain**)
Ibero-America (*Latin America*)
Ibos (**Nigeria**)
Iceland
Iconium (**Rum Sultanate**)
Idaho (*United States*)
Idrisids
Ife (**Benin (Ancient)**; **Nigeria**)
Ifriqiya (**Tunisia**)
Ilam (*Iran*)
Île de France (*France*)
Île St Jean (**French Colonial Empire**)
Ili River Basin (*Central Asia*)
Ilkhanid Persia
Illinois (*United States*)
Illyria (**Croatia**)
Illyricum (*Roman Empire*)
Imeritia (**Georgia**)
Imperial Flanders (**Flanders**)
Imperial Italy
Imphal (*India*)
Inca Empire
Inchon (**Korea**)
India
Indiana (*United States*)
Indianapolis (*United States*)
Indochina (**French Colonial Empire**; *Indochina*) ,
Indonesia
Indore (**Maratha Kingdoms**)
Indus River Valley Civilization
Ingria (**Russia**)
Ingushetia (*Russia*)
Inner Mongolia (*Mongolia*)
Innsbruck (*Austria*)
Inverness (*Scotland*)
Iona (**Scotland**)
Ionia (regions of *Greece (Ancient)*)
Ionian Islands (**Greece**)

Kairouan
Kaketia (**Georgia**)
Kalabhras (**Southern India**)
Kalba (**United Arab Emirates**)
Kalhu (**Assyria**)
Kalimantan (*Indonesia*)
Kalinga
Kaliningrad (*Russia*)
Kalmucks (**Mongolia**)
Kalmykia (*Russia*)
Kama Bulgars
Kamakura (**Japan**)
Kamboja (**Vedic India**)
Kamchatka (**Russia**)
Kameron (**German Colonial Empire**)
Kampala (**Uganda**)
Kanauj (**Harsha's Kingdom**)
Kandahar (**Mughal Empire**)
Kandy
Kanem-Bornu
Kano (**Nigeria**)
Kansai (*Japan*)
Kansas (*United States*)
Kanto (*Japan*)
Kanvas (**Magadha**)
Kara Shahr (*Tarim Basin*)
Kara Kirghiz Autonomous Region (**Kyrgyzstan**)
Kara-Khitan Khanate
Kara-Kum (*Turan*)
Karachi (**Pakistan**)
Karafuto (**Japan**)
Karaikal (**French Colonial Empire**; *India*)
Karakai-Cherkessia (*Russia*)
Karakhanids
Karakorum (**Mongol Empire**)
Karaman
Karbala (**Islam**)
Karelia (*Russia*)
Karmathians
Karnataka (*India*)

Karthlia (**Georgia**)
Kashgar (*Tarim Basin*)
Kashgaria (*Tarim Basin*)
Kashi (*Tarim Basin*)
Kashmir
Kasi (**Vedic India**)
Kassites
Kastamonu (**Anatolian Emirates**)
Katanga (**Congo (Democratic Republic of the)**)
Kathmandu (**Nepal**)
Katsina (**Nigeria**)
Kaunas (**Lithuania**)
Kausambi (**Vedic India**)
Kaya
Kazakh Autonomous Region (**Kazakhstan**)
Kazakh Soviet Socialist Republic (**Kazakhstan**)
Kazakhstan
Kazan Khanate
Kazan (**Russia**)
Kedah (*Malaya*)
Kediri (*Java*)
Keeling Islands (**Australia**)
Kent (**England**)
Kentucky (*United States*)
Kenya
Kerala (*India*)
Kerguelen Islands (**France**)
Kermadec Islands (**New Zealand**)
Kerman (**Qara-Qoyunlu**)
Kermanshah (*Iran*)
Kermian (**Anatolian Emirates**)
Kerry (*Ireland*)
Kertanagara (**Majaparit Empire**)
Kerts
Kerulen (**Mongol Empire**)
Khajurahq (**Rasputs**)
Khakasia (*Russia*)
Khalkas (**Mongolia**)
Kharkov (*Ukraine*)
Khartoum (**Sudan**)

Labuan (**Malaysia**)
Lachish (**Philistia**)
Laconia (Regions of *Greece (Ancient)*)
Ladakh (*India*)
Lagash
Lagos (**Nigeria**)
Lahore (**Pakistan**; **Punjab**)   ,
Lake Success (**United Nations**)
Lakshadweep (*India*)
Lampsacus (colonies of *Greece (Ancient)*)
Lan Na (**Thailand**)
Lan Xiang
Lancashire (*England*)
Languedoc (*France*)
Lansing (*United States*)
Lanzhou (*China*)
Laoighis (*Ireland*)
Laos
Lapland (*Lapland*)
Larissa (Regions of *Greece (Ancient)*)
Larsa (**Sumer**)
Later Chin (Jin) (**Period of disunity (after T'ang/Tang)**)
Later Chou (Zhou) (**Period of disunity (after T'ang/Tang)**)
Later Han (**Period of disunity (after T'ang/Tang)**)
Later Liang (**Period of disunity (after T'ang/Tang)**)
Later Shu (**Period of disunity (after T'ang/Tang)**)
Later T'ang (Tang) (**Period of disunity (after T'ang/Tang)**)
Latin America (*Latin America*)
Latin Empire
Latin States
Latvia
Lausitz (**Holy Roman Empire**)
Lazica (**Georgia**)
Lazio (**Papal States**)

Le Mans (*France*)
League of Nations
Lebanon
Lechfeld (**Greater Moravia; Hungary**)
Leeds (*England*)
Leeward Islands (*Antilles*)
Legnano (**Lombard League**)
Leicestershire (*England*)
Leinster (**Ireland**)
Leipzig (**France**)
Leitrim (*Ireland*)
Lemberg (*Ukraine*)
Leningrad (**Russia**)
León
León (**Asturias**)
Leontopolis (**Pharaonic Egypt**)
Leopoldville (**Congo (Democratic Republic of the)**)
Lepanto (**Venice**)
Leptis (**Phoenicia**)
Lesbos (colonies of *Greece (Ancient)*)
Lesbos (**Greece**)
Lesotho
Lesser Antilles (*Antilles*)
Lesser Armenia
Lesser Sunda Islands (*Indonesia*)
Letts (**Latvia**)
Levkas (colonies of *Greece (Ancient)*)
Leucas (**Greece**)
Levant (*Levant*)
Levedia (*Russia*)
Lexington (**United States**)
Lhasa (**Tibet**)
Liao
Liaoning (*China*)
Liberia
Libreville (**Gabon**)
Libya
Liechtenstein
Liège (*Belgium*)

Maastricht (*Netherlands*)

Maastricht Treaty (**European Union**)

Macao (**Portuguese Colonial Empire**)

Maccabees

Macedon

Macedonia (*Macedonia*)

Machelonia (*Sasanid Empire*)

Machu Picchu (**Inca Empire**)

Madagascar

Madeira (**Portugal**)

Madhya Pradesh (*India*)

Madison (*United States*)

Madras (**British India**; *India*)

Madrid (**Spain**)

Magadha

Magdeburg (*Germany*)

Magerit (**Spain**)

Maghreb (*Maghreb*)

Magna Graecia (colonies of *Greece (Ancient)*)

Magyars

Mahajanapadas (**Vedic India**)

Maharashtra (*India*)

Mahé (**French Colonial Empire**)

Mahé (**Seychelles**)

Mahiyou (**Belarus**)

Maikop (*Russia*)

Maine (*France*)

Maine (*United States*)

Mainz (*Germany*)

Maipú (**Chile**)

Maishan (*Sasanid Empire*)

Majapahit Empire

Major Antilles (*Antilles*)

Makhachkala (*Russia*)

Makran (*Myanmar*)

Malabar (**Colonial Empires**; *India*)

Malabo (**Equatorial Guinea**)

Malacca

Malagasy Republic (**Madagascar**)

Malawi

Malaya (*Malaya*)

Malaysia

Malayu

Malbork (**Teutonic Knights**)

Maldives

Malé (**Maldives**)

Mali

Mali (Ancient)

Mallus (colonies of *Greece (Ancient)*)

Malta

Maluku (*Indonesia*)

Mameluke Sultanate

Man (Isle of) (**Great Britain**)

Managua (**Nicaragua**)

Manama (**Bahrain**)

Manchester (*England*)

Manchukuo

Manchuria

Manchus (**Manchuria**; **Yuan**)

Mandalay (**Myanmar**)

Manifest Destiny (**United States**)

Manila (**Philippines**)

Manipur (*India*)

Manitoba (**Canada**)

Mantua

Manzikert (**Byzantine Empire**)

Maoris (**New Zealand**)

Maputo (**Mozambique**)

Maracaibo (**Venezuela**)

Maratha Kingdoms

Mardi (*Achaemenid Empire*)

Marengo (**France**)

Margarita (*Antilles*)

Margiana (*Sasanid Empire*)

Mari (*Russia*)

Marianas Islands (**United States**)

Marib (**Sheba**)

Marienburg (**Teutonic Knights**)

Marinids

Maritime or Island South East Asia (*Indochina*)

Maritime Province (*Russia*)

Maritime Provinces (*Maritime Provinces*)
Markazi (*Iran*)
Marne (**France**)
Marquesas Islands (**France**)
Marrakech (**Morocco**)
Marseilles (*France*)
Marshall Islands
Martinique (**France**)
Mary (**Merv**)
Maryland (*United States*)
Masai (**Kenya**)
Mascara (*Oran*)
Mascarene Islands (**Mauritius**)
Maseru (**Lesotho**)
Mashhad (*Khurasan*)
Masovia (**Poland**)
Massachusetts (*United States*)
Masulipatam (**British East India Company**)
Masuria (*Poland*)
Mataram (**Sri Vijaya**)
Mathura (**Vedic India**)
Matsu (**Taiwan**)
Matto Grosso (*Brazil*)
Mauretania (*Roman Empire*)
Maurican Fields (**Huns**)
Mauritania
Mauritius
Maurya
Mayan Civilization
Mayo (*Ireland*)
Mayotte (**France**)
Mazandaram (*Iran*)
Mazun (*Sasanid Empire*)
Mbabane (**Swaziland**)
Meath (**Ireland**)
Mecca
Mecklenburg-Pomerania (*Germany*)
Medak (**Majapahit Empire**)
Medes (**Achaemenid Empire**)
Media
Medina (**Islam**)

Mediolanum (**Milan**)
Meerut (**Burma and Pakistan**)
Megalopolis (regions of *Greece (Ancient)*)
Megara (regions of *Greece (Ancient)*)
Meghalaya (*India*)
Meiji (**Japan**)
Meissen (**Holy Roman Empire**)
Meknes (**Morocco**)
Melanesia (*Oceania*)
Melbourne (**Australia**)
Melilla (**Spain**)
Memel (*Memel*)
Memphis (**Pharaonic Egypt**)
Mende (colonies of *Greece (Ancient)*)
Mentese (**Anatolian Emirates**)
Menton (**Monaco**)
Mercia
Merina (**Madagascar**)
Meroe
Merovingian France
Mersen (**Carolingian Empire**)
Merseyside (*England*)
Merv
Mesembria (colonies of *Greece (Ancient)*)
Mesena (*Sasanid Empire*)
Mesene (**Parthia**)
Mesoamerican Civilizations
Mesopotamia (**Sumer**)
Messenia (regions of *Greece (Ancient)*)
Mewar (**Mughal Empire**)
Mexico
Mexico City (**Mexico**)
Michigan (*United States*)
Micronesia
Micronesia (*Oceania*)
Mid-Atlantic states (*United States*)
Middle Congo (**French Colonial Empire**)

Middle East (*Middle East*)
Middle Horde (**Kazakhstan**)
Middle Kingdom (**Pharaonic Egypt**)
Midlands (*England*)
Midway (**United States**)
Midwest (*United States*)
Milan
Miletus (colonies of *Greece (Ancient)*)
Milos (*Cyclades*)
Milvian Bridge (**Rome**)
Min (**Period of disunity of T'ang/Tang**)
Minas Geraes (**Brazil**)
Mindanao (**Philippines**)
Ming
Mingrelia (**Georgia**)
Minnesota (*United States*)
Minoan Civilization
Minor Antilles (*Antilles*)
Minsk (**Belarus**)
Minusinsk (**Sarmatians**)
Mischief reef (**Philippines**)
Mississippi (*United States*)
Missouri (*United States*)
Mitanni Kingdom
Mixtecs
Mizoran (*India*)
Mmabtho (**Bophuthatswana**)
Moche (**Pre-Columbian Cultures (South America)**)
Modena
Moesia (*Roman Empire*)
Mogadishu (**Somalia**)
Mogholistan (*Mongolia*)
Mohacs (**Hungary**)
Mohawk (**Iroquois Confederacy**)
Mohenjo-Daro
Mokran (*Sasanid Empire*)
Moldavia
Moldavia (*Bessarabia*)

Moldavian Soviet Socialist Republic (**Moldova**)
Moldova
Molise (*Italy*)
Molossia
Moluccas (*Indonesia*)
Monaco
Monagham (*Ireland*)
Mongol Empire
Mongolia
Monomotapa
Monrovia (**Liberia**)
Mons (**Myanmar**; **Dvaravati**)
Mons (*Belgium*)
Montana (*United States*)
Monte Albán (**Mesoamerican Civilizations**)
Montenegro
Montevideo (**Uruguay**)
Montgomery (*United States*)
Montpelier (*United States*)
Montserrat (**Great Britain**)
Moravia
Mordovia (*Russia*)
Morea (**Ottoman Empire**)
Morocco
Moroni (**Comoros**)
Moscow (**Russia**)
Mosquitia (**Honduras**; **Nicaragua**)
Mosul (**Iraq**)
Mozambique
Mpumalanga (**South Africa**)
Mrohaung
Mughal Empire
Mukden (**Manchuria**)
Munich (**Bavaria**)
Munster (**Ireland**)
Murcia (**Muslim Spain**; *Spain*)
Murom (**Russia**)
Muscat (**Oman**)
Muscovy (**Russia**)
Muslim Spain
Mutina (**Modena**)

Muzzafarids
Myanmar
Mycenea (**Mycenean Greece**)
Mycenean Greece
Mysia (*Anatolia*)
Mysore
Mytilene (regions of *Greece*
(*Ancient*))

Nabateans (**Petra**)
Nafud (*Arabia*)
Nagaland (*India*)
Nagasaki (**Japan**)
Nagidus (colonies of *Greece*
(*Ancient*))
Nagorno-Karabakh (**Armenia**)
Nairobi (**Kenya**)
Najd (**Saudi Arabia**)
Nakhichevan (**Azerbaijan**)
Nalchik (*Russia*)
Namibia
Namur (*Belgium*)
Nan Chao
Nanchang (*China*)
Nancy (*France*)
Nanda (**Magadha**)
Nanjing (Nanking) (*China*)
Nanning (*China*)
Nantes (**French ruling dynasties
and regimes**)
Nanyang (*China*)
Napata (**Pharaonic Egypt**)
Naples
Naples and Sicily (Kingdom of)
Nara (**Japan**)
Narbonensis (*Roman Empire*)
Narbonne (**France**)
Nasca (**Pre-Columbian Cultures
(South America)**)
Naseby (**English and British
Reigning Dynasties**)
Nashville (*United States*)
Nassau (**Bahamas**)

Natal (**South Africa**)
NATO (North Atlantic Treaty
Organization) (**United States**)
Naucratis (colonies of *Greece
(Ancient)*)
Nauru
Navarino (**Greece**)
Navarre
Navas de Tolosa (**Castile**)
Naxos (**Greece**)
Nazran (*Russia*)
N'Djamena (**Chad**)
Neapolis (**Naples**)
Near East (*Near East*)
Nebraska (*United States*)
Negri Sembilan (**Malaysia**)
Negroponte (**Venice**)
Nei Monggo (Inner Mongolia)
(*China*)
Nejd (*Arabia*)
Nelspruit (**South Africa**)
Neo-Hittite Kingdom (**Hittite
Kingdom**)
Nepal
Netherlands
Netherlands Antilles (**Netherlands**)
Neuchâtel (**Switzerland**)
Neuilly (**Versailles (Treaties of)**)
Neumark (*Germany*)
Neustria (*France*)
Neva (**Russia**)
Nevada (*United States*)
Nevers (**Burgundy (Duchy of)**;
France)
Nevis (**St Kitts and Nevis**)
New Amsterdam (**Dutch Colonial
Empire**)
New Britain (**Papua New Guinea**)
New Brunswick (**Canada**)
New Caledonia (**Canada**)
New Caledonia (**France**)
New Castile (*Spain*)
New Delhi (**India**)

New England (*United States*)
New France (**French Colonial Empire**)
New Granada
New Guinea (*New Guinea*)
New Hampshire (*United States*)
New Hebrides (**Vanuatu**)
New Ireland (**Papua New Guinea**)
New Jersey (*United States*)
New Kingdom (**Pharaonic Egypt**)
New Mexico (*United States*)
New South Wales (**Australia**)
New Spain (**Spanish Colonial Empire**)
New Sparta (*Antilles*)
New Territories (*Hong Kong*)
New York (*United States*)
New York (**United Nations**; **United States**)
New Zealand
Newcastle (*England*)
Newfoundland (**Canada**)
Niamey (**Niger**)
Nicaea (**Byzantine Empire**)
Nicaean Empire
Nicaragua
Nice (**France**)
Nicobar Islands (*India*)
Nicosia (**Cyprus**)
Nieu (**New Zealand**)
Niger
Nigeria
Nîmes (*France*)
Nimrud (**Assyria**)
Nineveh (**Assyria**)
Ningxia Huizu (Ningsia) (*China*)
Nivernais (*France*)
Nizaris (**Ismailites**)
Nordeste (*Brazil*)
Norfolk Island (**Australia**)
Noricum (*Roman Empire*)
Norman Italy
Normandy

Normans (**Norsemen**)
Norsemen
North Brabant (*Netherlands*)
North Carolina (*United States*)
North Dakota (*United States*)
North German Confederation
North Holland (*Netherlands*)
North Island (**New Zealand**)
North Korea
North Ossetia (*Russia*)
North Rhine Westphalia (*Germany*)
North West Company (*Hudson's Bay Company*)
North West Frontier (**Pakistan**)
North West Territories (**Canada**)
North West Territory (**United States**)
North Yorkshire (*England*)
Northamptonshire (*England*)
Northern Cape (**South Africa**)
Northern Ch'i (**Period of disunity (after Han)**)
Northern Chou (**Period of disunity (after Han)**)
Northern India
Northern Ireland (**Great Britain**)
Northern Marianas (**United States**)
Northern Province (**South Africa**)
Northern Rhodesia (**Zambia**)
Northern Wei (**Period of disunity (after Han)**)
Northern Yuan (**Mongolia**)
Northumberland (*England*)
Northumbria
North West Company (**Hudson's Bay Company**)
North-western states (*United States*)
Norway
Nottinghamshire (*England*)
Nouakchott (**Mauritania**)
Nova Scotia (**Canada**)
Novgorod (**Russia**)
Novgorod-Seversk (**Russia**)

Palestinian Authority
Palhae
Pallavas
Palmyra
Pamirs
Pampas (**Argentina**)
Pamphylia (*Anatolia;* colonies of
   Greece (Ancient))
Pamplona (**Navarre**)
Panama
Panama Canal Zone (**United States**)
Panama City (**Panama**)
Panchala (**Vedic India**)
Pandyas (**Southern India**)
Panipat (**Mughal Empire**)
Panmunjon (**Korea**)
Pannonia (*Roman Empire*)
Pannonian Avars (**Avars**)
Panormus (**Sicily**)
Pantanal (*Brazil*)
Panticapaeum (colonies of *Greece*
   (Ancient))
Papal States
Papeete (**France**)
Paphlagonia (*Anatolia*)
Paphos (colonies of *Greece*
   (Ancient))
Papua New Guinea
Paracas (**Pre-Columbian Cultures**
   (South America))
Paracel Islands (*China*)
Paradene (*Sasanid Empire*)
Paraguay
Paramaribo (**Suriname**)
Paratan (*Sasanid Empire*)
Paris (**France**)
Paris (Congress of) (**Moldavia**)
Paris Peace Conference (**Versailles**)
Parisii (**France**)
Parma
Paros (**Greece**)
Parthenopean Republic
Parthia

Pascua (Isla de) (**Chile**)
Patagonia (*Argentina*)
Pataliputra (**Magadha**)
Patara (colonies of *Greece*
   (Ancient))
Pathans (**Afghanistan**)
Patishkhwagar (*Sasanid Empire*)
Patmos (**Greece**)
Patna (**Magadha**)
Patrimonium Petri
Patzinaks
Pau (*France*)
Pavia (**Carolingian Empire**;
   Lombard League)   ,
Pegu (**Myanmar**)
Peiping (**Ming**)
Peipus (**Russia**)
Peking (**China**)
Pelasgians or Sea-peoples
Pella (**Macedon**)
Peloponnesian League
Penang (**Malaysia**)
Pennsylvania (*United States*)
Pentapolis (*Italy*; *Pentapolis*)
Perak (**Malaysia**)
Pereyaslavl (**Russia**)
Pergamum
Périgord (*France*)
Period of disunity (after Han)
Period of disunity (after
   T'ang/Tang)
Perlak (*Sumatra*)
Pernambuco (**Brazil**)
Perpignan (*France*)
Persepolis (**Achaemenid Empire**)
Persia
Persian Empire
Persis (**Achaemenid Empire**)
Perth (**Australia**)
Peru
Pesaro (*Italy*)
Peshawar (*Pakistan*)
Peshwa (**Mughal Empire**)

Ptrozavodsk (*Karelia*)
Pueblos (**United States**)
Puerto Rico (**United States**)
Pugliese (*Italy*)
Pune (**Maratha Kingdoms**)
Punjab
Punta Arenas (**Chile**)
Putaya (*Achaemenid Empire*)
Pylos (**Mycenean Greece**)
Pyongyang (**Korea**)

Qara-Qoyunlu
Qatar
Qinghai (Tsinghai) (*China*)
Qom (*Iran*)
Quebec (**Canada; French Colonial Empire**)
Queen Maud Land (**Norway**)
Queensland (**Australia**)
Quemoy (**Taiwan**)
Quetta (*Pakistan*)
Quintana Roo (*Mexico*)
Quito (**Ecuador**)

Rabat (**Morocco**)
Rai (**Iran**)
Raj, The (**British India**)
Rajagriha (**Vedic India**)
Rajasthan (*India*)
Rajputs
Raleigh (*United States*)
Ranchi (*India*)
Rangoon (**Myanmar**)
Ras al-Khalmah
Rasht (*Iran*)
Rashtrakutas (**Central India**)
Rasulids (**Yemen**)
Raszia (**Serbia**)
Ravenna (**Rome**)
Recife (**Brazil**)
Reconquista (**Spain**)
Red River Settlement (**Canada**)
Regina (**Canada**)

Reims (*France*)
Rennes (*France*)
Réunion (**France**)
Reyjavik (**Iceland**)
Rhaetia (*Roman Empire*)
Rhineland (*Germany*)
Rhineland-Palatinate (*Germany*)
Rhode Island (*United States*)
Rhodes (Despotate of)
Rhodes
Rhodesia
Richmond (**Confederate States of America**; *United States*)
Riga (**Latvia**)
Rijeka (**Croatia**)
Rimini (*Italy*)
Rio de Janeiro (**Brazil**)
Rio de la Plata (**United Provinces of**)
Rio de Oro (**Spanish Colonial Empire**)
Rio Grande (**United States**)
Rio Muni (**Equatorial Guinea**)
Risorgimento (**Italy**)
River Plate (**Argentina**)
Riyad (**Saudi Arabia**)
Rocky Mountain states (*United States*)
Romagna (**Papal States**; *Italy*)
Roman Empire (**Rome**; *Roman Empire*)
Romania -
Rome
Roscommon (*Ireland*)
Roseau (**Dominica**)
Ross Dependency (**New Zealand**)
Rostock (**Hanseatic League**)
Rostov (**Russia**)
Rotterdam (**Netherlands**)
Rouen (*France*)
Roussillon (*France*)
Ruanda-Urundi (**Belgian Colonial Empire**)

San Antonio (**Texas**)
San Francisco (**United Nations**)
San Jacinto (**Texas**)
San Jose (**Costa Rica**)
San Juan (*United States*)
San Marino
San Salvador (**El Salvador**)
San Stefano (**Berlin (Congress of)**)
Sanaia (**Yemen**)
Sanandaj (*Iran*)
Sandomir (*Poland*)
Sandwich Islands (**Great Britain**)
Sangapura (**Singapore**)
Santa Fe (*United States*)
Santiago de Chile (**Chile**)
Santiago de Cuba (**Cuba**)
Santo Domingo (**Dominican Republic**)
Sao Tome and Principe
Sao Paulo (*Brazil*)
Sao Tome (**Sao Tome and Principe**)
Saqqara (**Pharaonic Egypt**)
Saragossa (**Aragon**)
Sarai (**Golden Horde**)
Sarajevo (**Bosnia-Herzegovina**)
Saransk (*Russia*)
Saratoga (**United States**)
Sarawak (**Malaysia**)
Sarbedarians
Sardinia (*Italy*)
Sardinia (Kingdom of)
Sardis (**Lydia**)
Sari (*Iran*)
Sark (**Great Britain**)
Sarmatia (**Georgia**)
Sarmatians
Saruhan (**Anatolian Emirates**)
Sasanid Empire
Saskatchewan (**Canada**)
Satavahana (**Central India**)
Satsuma (**Japan**)
Saudi Arabia
Savannah (**United States**)

Savoy
Saxe-Coburg (**England**)
Saxony (**Holy Roman Empire**)
Saxony-Anhalt (*Germany*)
Sayan (*Central Asia*)
Scandinavia (*Scandinavia*)
Scania (*Scandinavia*)
Schaffhausen (**Switzerland**)
Scheldt (**Netherlands**)
Schellenberg (**Liechtenstein**)
Schleswig and Holstein (**Prussia**; *Germany*)
Schwerin (*Germany*)
Schwyz (**Switzerland**)
Scilly (*England*)
Scotland
Scylacium (colonies of *Greece (Ancient)*)
Scythia (colonies of *Greece (Ancient)*)
Scythians
Sea-peoples
Second Intermediate period (**Pharaonic Egypt**)
Seistan
Selangor (**Malaysia**)
Selenga (*Central Asia*)
Seleucid Empire
Selinus (colonies of *Greece (Ancient)*)
Seljuk Emirates
Seljuk Persia
Seljuks
Semipalatinsk (**Kazakhstan**)
Semirechye (**Kazakhstan**)
Semnan (*Iran*)
Sena (**Bengal**)
Seneca (**Iroquois Confederacy**)
Senegal
Senegambia
Senigallia (*Italy*)
Seoul (**Korea**)
Septem Provinciae (*Roman Empire*)

Somerset (*England*)
Somme (**Great Britain**)
Songhai
Sotho (**South Africa**)
South Africa
South Africa Company (**Zambia**)
South Australia (**Australia**)
South Carolina (*United States*)
South Dakota (*United States*)
South Dublin (*Ireland*)
South East Asia (*Indochina*)
South Eastern Islands (*Indonesia*)
South Georgia (**British Colonial Empire**)
South Han (**Period of disunity (after T'ang/Tang)**)
South Holland (*Netherlands*)
South Korea
South Orkney Islands (**British Colonial Empire**)
South Ossetia (*Russia*)
South Shetland Islands (**British Colonial Empire**)
South Vietnam
South Yemen
South Yorkshire (*England*)
Southern Bessarabia (**Moldavia**)
Southern Ch'en (**Period of disunity (after Han)**)
Southern Ch'i (**Period of disunity (after Han)**)
Southern India
Southern Liang (**Period of disunity (after Han)**)
Southern Rhodesia (**Zimbabwe**)
Southern Russia (*Southern Russia*)
Southern states (*United States*)
Soviet Empire
Spain
Spanish America (*Latin America*)
Spanish Captivity (**Portugal**)
Spanish Colonial Empire
Spanish Navarre (**Navarre**)

Spanish Netherlands
Spanish Sahara (**Spanish Colonial Empire**)
Sparta (regions of *Greece (Ancient)*)
Spice Islands (*Indonesia*)
Spitsbergen (**Norway**)
Spoleto (Duchy of)
Sporades (**Greece**)
Spratly Islands (**Philippines**)
Spring and Autumn period (**Chou (Zhou)**)
Springfield (*United States*)
Sravasti (**Vedic India**)
Sri Lanka
Sri Vijaya
Srinagar (**Kashmir**)
Staffordshire (*England*)
Stalingrad (**USSR**)
Stettin (**Prussia**)
Stirling (*Scotland*)
Stockholm (**Sweden**)
Straits Settlement
Strasbourg (**European Union**; *France*)
Strathclyde (*Scotland*)
Stratos (regions of *Greece (Ancient)*)
Stremoy (*Faroe Islands*)
Styria (**Habsburg Empire**)
Sub-Saharan Africa (*Sub-Saharan Africa*)
Sucre (**Bolivia**)
Sudan
Sudetenland (*Sudetenland*)
Sueves
Suffolk (*England*)
Sui
Sukhotai (**Thailand**)
Sukhumi (**Georgia**)
Sulawesi (*Indonesia*)
Sulu Islands (**Philippines**)
Sumatra (*Sumatra*)
Sumer

Texas
Texcoco (**Aztec Empire**)
Thailand
Thapsus (**Phoenicia**)
Thasos (colonies of *Greece (Ancient)*)
The Hague (**Netherlands**; **United Nations**)
Thebes
Thebes (**Pharaonic Egypt**)
Thenae (**Phoenicia**)
Thera (colonies of *Greece (Ancient)*)
Thermum (**Aetolian League**)
Thessalonike (**Salonica**)
Thessaly (**Macedon**; *Greece (Ancient)*)
Thimphu (**Bhutan**)
Thinis (**Pharaonic Egypt**)
Third Intermediate Period (**Pharaonic Egypt**)
Thohoyandou (**Venda**)
Thon Duri (**Thailand**)
Thorshavn (*Faroe Islands*)
Thrace
Thracia (*Roman Empire*)
Three Kingdoms
Thule (*Scandinavia*)
Thurgau (**Switzerland**)
Thuringia (**Holy Roman Empire**; *Germany*)
Tiahuanaco (**Inca Empire**)
Tianjin (Tientsin) (*China*)
Tibet
Ticino (**Switzerland**)
Tidore (*Indonesia*)
Tien Shan (*Central Asia*)
Tierra del Fuego (*Tierra del Fuego*)
Tilsit (**Prussia**)
Timbuktu
Timor (*Indonesia*)
Timurid Empire and Successor States
Timurids (**Shaybanids**)
Tipperary (*Ireland*)

Tirana (**Albania**)
Tiraspol (**Moldova**)
Tiryns (**Mycenean Greece**)
Titograd (**Montenegro**)
Tlacopán (**Aztec Empire**)
Tlemcen
Tmutorokan (**Russia**)
Toba Turks (**Period of disunity (after Han)**)
Toba Wei
Togo
Togoland (**Ghana**)
Tokelau Islands (**New Zealand**)
Tokharians
Tokugawa (**Japan**)
Tokyo (**Japan**)
Toledo (**Muslim Spain**)
Toltecs
Tonga
Tonkin
Tonkin and Annam (**French Colonial Empire**)
Topeka (*United States*)
Toronto (**Canada**)
Toulouse
Toungod (**Myanmar**)
Tourane (**Vietnam**)
Touraine (*France*)
Tours (**Franks**)
Transcaucasia (*Transcaucasia*)
Transcaucasian Soviet Federated Socialist Republic (**USSR**)
Transjordan (**Jordan**)
Transjurane Burgundy (*France*)
Transkei, The
Transoxiana (*Transoxiana*)
Transvaal
Transylvania
Trapezus (colonies of *Greece (Ancient)*)
Trebizond
Trent (**Lombard Italy**)
Trentino (*Italy*)

United Arab Emirates
United Arab Republic
United Arab States
United Kingdom
United Nations (UN)
United Provinces of Canada
  (Canada)
United Provinces of the Netherlands
  (Spanish Netherlands)
United Provinces of the River Plate
  (Argentina)
United States of America (USA)
Unterwalden (Switzerland)
Upper Austria (*Austria*)
Upper Canada (Canada)
Upper Lorraine (*Lorraine*)
Upper Mesopotamia (*Mesopotamia*)
Upper Navarre (Navarre)
Upper Volta (Burkina Fasso)
Ur
Urartu
Urbino (Papal States)
Urgel (Andorra)
Uri (Switzerland)
Uruguay
Uruk (Sumer)
Urumqi (*China*)
Ushuaia (Argentina)
Usmurtia (Russia)
USSR (Union of Soviet Socialist
  Republics)
Ussuri (*Central Asia*)
Utah (*United States*)
Utica (Phoenicia)
Utrecht (*Netherlands*)
Uttar Pradesh (*India*)
Uxmal (Mayan Civilization)
Uzbek Soviet Socialist Republic
  (Uzbekistan)
Uzbekistan
Uzbeks

Vaduz (Liechtenstein)

Vakataka (Central India)
Valachia
Valais
Valencia
Valenciennes (*France*)
Valetta (Malta)
Valle d'Aosta (*Italy*)
Valley Forge (United States)
Valmy (France)
Van Diemen's Land (Australia)
Van Lang (Vietnam)
Vancouver (Canada)
Vancouver Island (Canada)
Vandals
Vanuatu
Varanasi (Vedic India)
Varangians (Norsemen)
Varennes (France)
Vascongadas (Vasconia)
Vasconia
Vatican City
Vatsa (Magadha)
Vaud (Switzerland)
Vedic India
Veii (Etruria)
Venda
Venetia (Venice)
Venezuela
Venice
Veracruz (Mexico)
Verdun (Carolingian Empire;
  France)   ,
Vermont (*United States*)
Verona
Veronese League
Versailles (Treaties of)
Viatka (Russia)
Vichy France
Vicksburg (Confederate States of
  America; United States of
  America)
Victoria (Australia)
Victoria (*Hong Kong*)

Victoria (**Seychelles**)
Vien Chan
Vienna (**Austria**)
Vienna (Congress of)
Vietnam
Vijayanagara
Vikings (**Norsemen**)
Vila (**Vanuatu**)
Vilnius (**Lithuania**)
Vindobona (**Austria**)
Vinland (**Norsemen**)
Virgin Islands (**Denmark; United States**)
Virginia (*United States*)
Visayas (**Philippines**)
Visby (**Hanseatic League**)
Visigothic Kingdom
Visigoths (**Goths**)
Vitebsk (**Belarus**)
Vittorio Veneto (**Italy**)
Vizcaya (**Vasconia**)
Vladimir (**Russia**)
Vladimir-Suzdal (**Russia**)
Vladimir-Volinsk (**Russia**)
Vladiravkaz (*Russia*)
Vladivostok (*Russia*)
Vojvodina (**Yugoslavia**)
Volcano Islands (*Japan*)
Volga (**Russia**)
Volga Bulgars
Volgograd (**Russia**)
Volhynia (**Russia**)
Vorarlberg (*Austria*)
Vyborg (*Karelia*)

Wadai
Wagram (**France**)
Wahhabi (**Saudi Arabia**)
Waiblingen (**Holy Roman Empire**)
Wales
Wallis and Futuna (**France**)
Walloon Brabant (*Belgium*)
Walloonia (*Belgium*)

Walvis Bay (**Namibia**)
Warangal
Warring States
Warsaw (**Poland**)
Warsaw Pact (**Soviet Empire**)
Warwickshire (*England*)
Washington (*United States*)
Washington, D.C. (**United States**)
Waterford (**Ireland**)
Waterloo (**France**)
Wei (**Three Kingdoms**)
Weimar (**Germany**)
Wellington (**New Zealand**)
Wends (**Prussia**)
Wessex
West Bank (**Israel; Palestinian Authority**)
West Bengal (*India*)
West Flanders (*Belgium*)
West Franks (**Carolingian Empire**)
West Germany
West Midlands (*England*)
West Prussia (*Germany*)
West Sussex (*England*)
West Virginia (*United States*)
West Yorkshire (*England*)
Western Australia (**Australia**)
Western Cape (**South Africa**)
Western Chin (Jin) (**Period of disunity (after Han)**)
Western Chou (Zhou) (**Chou (Zhou)**)
Western Europe (*Western Europe*)
Western Han (**Han**)
Western Islands (*Scotland*)
Western Mongols
Western Sahara (**Spanish Colonial Empire**)
Western Samoa (**Samoa**)
Western Siberia (*Central Asia*)
Western Turkestan (*Central Asia*)
Western Wei (**Period of disunity (after Han)**)

445

Westmeath (*Ireland*)
Westphalia (*Germany*)
Wexford (*Ireland*)
White Horde
White Huns
White Sheep Turks
Whitehorse (**Canada**)
Wicklow (*Ireland*)
Wiesbaden (*Germany*)
Wight (*England*)
Willemstadt (**Netherlands**)
Wiltshire (*England*)
Windhoek (**Namibia**)
Windward Islands (*Antilles*)
Winnipeg (**Canada**)
Wisconsin (*United States*)
Wismar (**Hanseatic League**)
Wolverhampton (*England*)
Wounded Knee (**United States**)
Wroclaw (**Poland**)
Wu (**Three Kingdoms**)
Wu Sun
Wuhan (*China*)
Wyoming (*United States*)

Xanthus (colonies of *Greece (Ancient)*)
Xian (Sian) (**Ch'in (Qin)**)
Xining (*China*)
Xinjiang Uygur (Sinkiang) (*China*)
Xi Xia (**Hsi-Hsia**)
Xia (**Hsia**)
Xien-Pi (**Hsien-Pi**)
Xin (**Hsin**)
Xiung-Nu (**Hsiung-Nu**)
Xizang (Tibet) (*China*)

Yadava (**Delhi Sultanate**)
Yakutsk (*Russia*)
Yalta (**USSR**)
Yalu (**Korea**)
Yamato (**Japan**)
Yamoussoukro (**Côte d'Ivoire**)

Yanam (**French Colonial Empire;** *India*)
Yangon (**Myanmar**)
Yangzi (*China*)
Yaoundé (**Cameroon**)
Yap (**Micronesia**)
Yarkand (*Tarim Basin*)
Yaroslavl (**Russia**)
Yasodharapura (**Cambodia**)
Yasuj (*Iran*)
Yazd (*Iran*)
Yekaterinburg (**Russia**)
Yellowknife (**Canada**)
Yemen
Yemsei (*Central Asia*)
Yerevan (**Armenia**)
Yi (**Korea**)
Yin (**Shang**)
Yinchuan (*China*)
Yorktown (**United States**)
Yoruba
Yoshkar-Ola (*Russia*)
Ypres (**Flanders; Great Britain**)
Yuan
Yucatán (*Mexico*)
Yüeh-chih
Yugoslavia
Yukon Territory (**Canada**)
Yunnan (*China*)

Zagreb (**Croatia**)
Zagros (**Alexandrian Empire**)
Zahedan (*Iran*)
Zaidas (**Yemen**)
Zaire
Zama (**Carthage**)
Zambia
Zangids (**Seljuk Emirates**)
Zanjan (*Iran*)
Zante (**Greece**)
Zanzibar
Zapotecs
Zaprozhye